Plain English
A Wealth of Words

Bryan R Evans

First Published 2012 by

Anglo-Saxon Books
Hereward, Black Bank Business Centre
Little Downham, Ely, Cambridgeshire CB6 2UA England

Printed and bound by
Lightning Source
Australia, England, USA

Content © Bryan Evans
Design/layout © Anglo-Saxon Books

ISBN 9781898281658

Within

A Wealth of Words

Bring to your mind, if you will, the thought of a great old house, some way out of town, in a still and sheltered valley. The key thing about this house is that it has been lived in by the same family for some hundreds of years. In the last century or two the younger generations have wanted to keep up to date, and they have filled the ground floor with 'the latest': new furnishings and decor, and now all the wizardry of the computer age. But their elders have not been ready to throw out the old, and things have simply been hidden away upstairs. There, on landings and in back rooms, are old oak tables and settles and, in chests, cupboards and drawers, there are all sorts of things loved and treasured by their forebears. These lovely old things are waiting to be brought out again, to be wondered at and to enrich once more the life of the family.

English speech is a bit like this. In the last few centuries new-fangled words have been adopted from all over the world. From French we have taken high society words and words from military engineering. From Italian have come music words. Dutch has given us ship and seafaring words, and mining terms have been taken from German. In the hey-day of the British Empire, words were brought in from the east (from Hindi, Tamil, Malay and such). Above all, we have gone back to Greek and Latin again and again and taken words for the fields of learning and discovery. But even after all this borrowing many words from Old English are still around, in everyday use or 'upstairs' in those half-forgotten chests. If we only will, we may once again draw on this wealth of words to enrich our daily life together.

Old English (the form of the language spoken and written between about AD 450-1100) was a rich language of some 30,000 words. We are told that in the poem *Beowulf* there are thirty-six words for 'hero', twelve for 'battle', eleven for 'ship'.[1] And Old English had about twenty words for different kinds of woodland.[2] Shakespeare's word-stock is reckoned at 'only' 25,000 words. (The man in the street uses 4,000-5,000 words, though he knows many more.[3]) So there ought to be enough English words to meet all our needs, and to make us wonder why we must be for ever taking other folk's words.

To those who know her, English speech that is truly English is a thing of great loveliness. Her words may gladden, warm, woo, stir, rouse our wrath, even floor us. They are heart words, and not cold, dry or bloodless words. Men of feeling among the Anglo-Saxons saw words as truly worthful, things to be carefully locked away in the treasury of their minds, then 'to be brought out when they were needed and to be put back under lock and key against the time when they might be needed again.'[4]

---

[1] Bill Bryson, *Mother Tongue: The English Language*, 1990, p.51.
[2] CM Matthews, *Words, Words, Words*, 1979, p.5.
[3] M Bragg, *The Adventure of English*, 2003, p.144.
[4] PH Blair, *Northumbria in the days of Bede*, 1976, p.150.

Here are some lines from William Barnes's *Sonnet: To a garden, on leaving it* –

> I shall not hear again from yonder bow'r
> The song of birds, or humming of the bee,
> Nor listen to the waterfall, nor see
> The clouds float on behind the lofty tow'r ...

> ... My eyes no more may see, this peaceful scene.
> But still, sweet spot, wherever I may be,
> My love-led soul will wander back to thee.[1]

And then, what of Our Lord's 'love-song', a song from the fourteenth century, put into the mouth of Christ?

> Love brought me,
> and love wrought me,
> man, to be your mate.
> Love fed me,
> and love led me,
> and love forsook me here.

> Love slew me,
> and love drew me,
> and love laid me on the bier.
> Love is my peace;
> for love I chose
> to buy man dearly.

> Dread not at all;
> I have you sought
> both day and night.
> To have you
> I am glad
> I have won you in fight.[2]

Here the only word from a Latin root is 'peace'.

Language and the image of God in man

In his book *Words Words Words* David Crystal notes that the naming of things is there in the beginning of the tale of mankind. So, at least, the Genesis story in the Bible tells us. And other cultures have a like story, where words are seen as special, magical, sacred. 'In the beginning, it seems everywhere, was the word.'[3] It is a striking fact that peoples may lack technology and be seen as 'primitive', yet they will have a richly woven spoken language.

---

[1] ed. G Grigson, *Selected Poems of William Barnes*, 1950, pp.129-30.
[2] ed. Carleton Brown, *Religious Lyrics of the XIVth Century* (Oxford, 1924; revised by GV Smithers, 1957), no.66, quoted in B Cottle, *The Triumph of English 1350-1400*, 1969, p.173.
[3] David Crystal, *Words Words Words*, 2006, p.4.

Another Genesis story that has played a part in the lore of language is the tale of the Tower of Babel. There, we are told, God mixed up the one language of mankind, to break up their confederacy, and to stop them chasing after fame and empire. From this tale sprang the belief that Hebrew was the first language, and the forebear of all others (though this is not what Genesis 10 says). This understanding of the tale was, for long, not to be gainsaid, but when European language scholars came upon Sanskrit some began to wonder if this, rather than Hebrew, might be the true source language. Then those who were not to be shifted from the belief in Hebrew roots said that Sanskrit must be a priestly fraud, made up by Brahmins from words with Greek or Latin roots.[1]

Our business here is with English. So, where does English speech (and those who wield it) come from, and what is its story? We will begin our answer by going back to British India, some 200 and more years ago.

From Indo-European to English

Sir William Jones was a language wonder. It is said that by the end of his life he knew thirteen languages thoroughly and another twenty-eight reasonably well. He studied law, and as Chief Justice at Fort William in Bengal, he set himself to understand the law codes of the land where he worked. Some of these codes were written down in Sanskrit, a language long 'dead', but still held to be of high worth. As he learned this tongue he began to find striking likenesses between it and the Latin and Greek he had been taught in his schooldays. Thus Sanskrit 'pitar' (father) was not so far from Latin 'pater', and Sanskrit 'matar' (mother) was close to Latin 'mater'. He told a meeting of the Asiatic Society, in Calcutta, on 2nd February, 1786, that the many likenesses could not be merely chance. He also noted that Gothic, Celtic and Persian might well be members of the same language kindred.

Sir William Jones was not the first European to alight on Sanskrit. The Italian Filippo Sassetti (1540-88) learned it and found it 'a pleasant musical language'. He noted some likenesses between Sanskrit and Italian – deva/dio (God), sapta/sette (seven), nava/nove (nine), sarpa/serpe (snake). Among early missionaries to India who learned Sanskrit were the Italian Jesuit, Robertus de Nobilibus (1577-1656), and the German Heinrich Roth (1620-68), also a Jesuit. Roth was the first European to put together a Sanskrit grammar (though the Superior General of his order would not allow him to publish it). Another German Jesuit, Johann Ernst Hanxleden (1681-1732) also wrote a Sanskrit grammar (which came to light in an Italian monastery only in 2010). The first European to point out the links between Sanskrit and the European languages in general was the German missionary, Benjamin Schultze (1689-1760). In 1725 he drew attention to the likenesses between the numerals of Sanskrit, German and Latin. He was followed by the French Jesuit, Coeurdoux, in 1767. At this time it was mistakenly thought that Sanskrit was the mother tongue, and that the Europeans were sprung from westward-migrating Hindus, worshippers of the Hindu god Aryas (hence the name 'Aryan'[2]).

---

[1] Bodmer, *The Loom of Language*, 1944, p.181.
[2] O Barfield, *History in English Words*, 1954, p.18.

And then, links between some European languages had been noted before. Joseph Justus Scaliger (1540-1609) found eleven main groups, four greater and seven lesser (though he did not see any links between the groups). His main groups were the Romance, Germanic, Greek, and Slavic tongues, and the lesser groups Epirotic or Albanian, Tartar, Hungarian, Finnic, Gaelic, Old British, and Cantabrian or Basque.

In 1767 the Englishman James Parsons had brought out his *The Remains of Japhet, being historical enquiries into the affinity and origins of the European languages*. He noted, first, the close kinship between Irish Gaelic and Welsh. He went on to look at other languages of Eurasia, taking (wisely) number words, as being basic and a good point of comparison. He came to believe that the languages of Europe, Iran and India were all drawn from one source, the speech of Japhet (son of Noah) and his offspring as they spread out from the resting place of the Ark in Armenia, after the great Flood. Parsons undermined belief somewhat by putting forward the thought that Irish was *the* Japhet language, from which all the others had come.[1] In 1808, the German, Freidrich Schlegel, brought out *Über die Sprache und Weisheit der Inder* ('On the Language and Philosophy of the Indians'). He was one of those who mistakenly made Sanskrit the mother of all tongues. His work was nonetheless a turning-point in the scientific study of language, and the framing of a genealogical tree of language. In 1817, Rasmus Kristian Rask, a brilliant young Dane who had been delving into the roots of Old Norse in Iceland, first drew attention to sound-correspondence between Greek and Latin on the one hand, and the Germanic languages on the other.

So Sir William Jones was not the first to note language likenesses, but he was the first to study them in a thorough, clear-headed way. As others took up wordlore, in the 19th and 20th centuries, and carried these studies further, the word 'Indo-European' was framed for those long-ago forefathers of most of the folk-kindreds of Europe and northern Asia, and for the language they spoke.

How much is known about the Indo-Europeans and their language? Some things can be learned by looking at the oldest remains we have. Among these are inscriptions in Hittite (once spoken in what is now Turkey) dating from about 1,700 BC. Then there are inscriptions in Mycenean Greek from around 1,400 BC, writings in Old Latin (around 600 BC), Gothic (the oldest Germanic tongue of which we have knowledge – around AD 350), and others. By looking at these remains side by side, a good many old Indo-European words can be re-made, and in seeing the sort of words these folk needed we get some idea of where their homeland may have been.

The view most widely believed today is that the Indo-European homeland was in South Russia, some way north of the Black Sea. It is thought that, sometime around 4,000 BC, groups of Indo-Europeans began to spread out through Eurasia. In the 'natural history' of languages there is continual 'differentiation', that is, as time goes on one language becomes two or more, and they in turn divide again. Migration makes the changes happen faster, as speakers of the same mother-tongue become separated from one another and, in new lands, see new things and find themselves in touch with other languages.[2] As they spread further and further afield, and lived lives

---

[1] For James Parsons, see JP Mallory *In Search of the Indo-Europeans* (London: Thames and Hudson, 1996), pp.9-11.

[2] See WF Bolton in Bolton and Crystal, editors, *The English Language*, 1993, p.226).

sundered from each other, Proto-Indo-European split up into a number of language groups. Thus while some moved northwards and westwards into Europe, others moved eastwards and southwards, going to Iran and India, and some as far as north China, where they spoke the Tocharian language.

Delving into old wordstocks gives us clues as to where the folk-groups were, and which ways they were moving. Thus there is evidence from words common to most of those folk-groups who were moving north and west, suggesting that they reached a new country of forests before dispersing. There were common words for trees (alder, ash, beech, birch, elm, hazel, oak), birds (finch, starling, swallow, throstle (song thrush)), and wild animals (wolf, bear, beaver, otter). There were also common words for snow, bee, oxen, sheep, weaving and ploughing. On the other hand it seems that although these north- and west-moving folk-groups had words for stretches of water, and for boats, they did not yet have the words 'sea' or 'ship', or words for sea animals and birds. (The words 'sea' and 'ship' are common to all the Germanic languages, but because they not found throughout the Indo-European family of languages the *Oxford English Dictionary* lists them as 'of unknown origin'.) All this points to a northerly, inland home for these folk-groups, where there was open woodland.

Then there came a time when some folk went westwards and southwards to the lands along the northern shores of the Mediterranean (the Celtic, Italic, Greek and other groups). Others went westwards and northwards, first into central and southern Poland, then on to northern Germany, Denmark, and South Scandinavia. Their branch of Indo-European speech is called 'Common Germanic'. As time went on these language groups split up more and more. Within Common Germanic three old branches are found: North Germanic (from which come the Scandinavian languages), East Germanic (Gepidic, Rugian, Burgundian, Vandalic, Visigothic and Ostrogothic – all of which died out long ago), and the West Germanic of the North Sea coast, the middle Rhine/Weser, and the Elbe. North Sea Germanic divided into English and Frisian (and Old Saxon) after the migrations of the fifth/sixth centuries put the sea between them. Frisian remains the closest living kindred to English speech. It is still spoken in coastland areas and islands of north Holland and Germany. It is said that Frisian has altered so little that many Frisians can read the Anglo-Saxon poem *Beowulf* almost at sight.[1] Among Frisian words of today which still show their close kinship to English are: laam (lamb), goes (goose), buter (butter), brea (bread), tsiis (cheese), see (sea), stoarm (storm), boat (boat), rein (rain), snie (snow), miel (meal), sliepe (sleep).[2]

---

[1] Charlton Laird, cited in Bryson, *Mother Tongue: The English Language*, 1990, p.38.
[2] See M Bragg, *The Adventure of English*, 2003, p.3.

The West Germanic languages

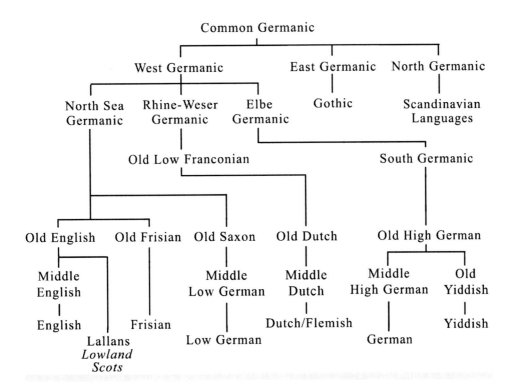

The first borrowings

So Indo-European split up as folk-groups spread out, and moved away from each other. But no folk-group can be an island to itself. There are always to-ings and fro-ings as trade and wars and further folk-migrations happen. And when folk meet in these ways, they must talk with each other, and so they pick up each other's speech and perhaps borrow some of it. (It is perhaps slightly odd that we should talk of 'borrowing' words, because the speech from which they have come still has them, and there is no thought of there being something that must be given back one day. Perhaps 'adoption' would be nearer the mark. However, 'borrowing' is the word long used of taking up other people's words, so we will hold to it.)

The first borrowings happened even before the West Germanic group of languages (of which English is one) evolved from Common Germanic. We have seen that the Indo-Europeans were an inland folk. When they came upon, first, the Baltic, then the North Sea, they borrowed words from other (unknown) folk-groups for such things as sail, sea, ship, and creatures such as the seal.

Borrowings from Old Celtic

There were some borrowings from Old Celtic, when Celtic-speakers and the Germani were neighbours in mainland Europe. 'Ass' is one (though further back Celtic-speakers had borrowed this from Latin speech, and Latin may have learned it from Sumerian).

The roots of Old English 'iron' go back to Old Germanic *'isarno^m' which is very close to Old Celtic *'isarnom'. We cannot now be wholly sure who borrowed the word from the other. The Celtic-speakers had ready access to supplies of iron, and they were well ahead of the Germani in iron-making, so it is likely that Old Germanic borrowed it from Old Celtic.[1]

Old Germanic also borrowed the word 'rich' from Celtic. The Celtic word meant 'king', as in the 'rix' found in Gaulish personal names such as Vercingetorix. (Gaulish was the language spoken by the 'Celtic' folk of Gaul.) This Celtic word is akin to Latin 'rex'. The sense of kingship and rulership is seen in the modern German 'reich' and in the '-ric' of English 'bishopric' (the area ruled by a bishop). Old Germanic used the word as an adjective (meaning 'powerful') and as a noun (meaning 'authority'). It seems that to the English mind power, authority and wealth belonged together, so in time 'rich' came to mean 'wealthy'.

Old English 'dún' ('down' or 'hill') goes back to a Germanic word thought to have come from Old Celtic 'dûn'. The root meaning of the Celtic word seems to have been 'hedged, fenced, fortified', and because a stronghold would often be set on a hill, the meaning 'hill-fort' arose. This sense is seen in the Welsh place-name element 'din' (as in Denbigh, Dinas Emrys and such). Old English used 'dun' as a word for 'hill', and also put it to work as an adverb and a preposition.

The word 'coomb', found in many English place-names, may have been borrowed from the Welsh 'cwm', meaning a bowl- or trough-shaped valley with three fairly steeply rising sides.[2] However, the Anglo-Saxons had their own home-grown word 'coomb', meaning a bowl or basin. It may be that the early Anglo-Saxon settlers, hearing from their British neighbours that the local bowl-shaped valley was a 'cwm' were very ready to accept the name because it was so like their own word for a bowl.

Other early borrowings were 'beet' and possibly 'puck' (meaning a mischievous spirit). Somewhat later on, Old English borrowed bannock, bin, brock (badger), tan, ton/tun and tor. And in the Middle Ages and later, English borrowed from Welsh, or from the kindred Celtic language Gaelic, such words as bard, beak, coracle, crag, flannel, gravel, lance, mine, piece and truant.

Altogether this is a small tally of borrowings from our nearest neighbours. Why should it be so? Was it that Anglo-Saxons looked on Britons as the defeated, folk they had driven out or thrust down into slavery? Or was it that the Anglo-Saxon newcomers found Welsh a hard language to learn (for it is very unlike English) or had they no need to learn or speak Welsh? The *Oxford Companion to the English Language* suggests that there were at least three reasons. First, the lowland areas of England where the Anglo-Saxons settled in the early days of the conquest were not so

---

[1] DH Green, *Language and History in the Early Germanic World*, 1998, pp.153-5.
[2] See Ann Cole, 1982, quoted in M Gelling, *Place-Names in the Landscape*, 1984, p.89.

very different from the old Continental homeland. Here were winding inlets, fens and reed-beds, marsh and mere, otters, waders, meadows, heathland, woodland. Thus the newcomers already had almost all the words they needed. Second, there was little or no 'pidginization', no mis-said, half-understood words of Celtic and Anglo-Saxon through which infiltration could come about (as happened later with Norse and Norman-French). Third, many Celtic-speakers and English-speakers were drawn to Latin culture and religion and, later, they went straight to Latin, and not to each other, for the new cultural and religious words they needed.[1]

Borrowings from Latin

Going on from Celtic to Latin, there were borrowings before ever the Anglo-Saxons left their continental home. Among these were: butter, camp, chalk, cheese, cheap, chest, church, copper, devil, dish, inch, kettle, kitchen, mile, mill, monger, mule, pepper, pile, pillow, pound, sack, street, table, tile, toll, wall, wine. A few Latin words (such as port, -chester) may have been learned from the Britons after the settlement in the British Isles, but Angles and Saxons had direct contact with Latin speakers (Romans) long before their settlement in Britain.

More Latin words came in with Christianity. The North Sea Germanic tribes whose main period of settlement in Britain was about AD 450-550 (Angles, Saxons, Jutes, with likely some Frisians) at first followed the heathen ways of their forebears. Christian outreach to the Anglo-Saxons began in the south-east, in AD 597, with the Augustine mission sent by Pope Gregory the Great. Then in the 630s AD, Irish missionaries from Iona came to evangelise the north of England. From AD 600 to 1100 some 400 words were borrowed from Church Latin, words such as abbot, alb, altar, angel, bishop, candle, clerk, creed, deacon, disciple, hymn, martyr, mass, minster, monk, noon, nun, pope, priest, psalm, saint, shrine, stole, temple, verse. From the Bible came words for Eastern beasts, trees and plants – camel, lion, cedar, myrrh, myrtle. And because monks and nuns cared for the sick and taught the young, in came words such as fever, sponge, plaster, school, master, paper, grammar. Yet there was no wholesale borrowing of Latin words. It was not that the Anglo-Saxons set out to keep borrowings at bay. They chose Anglo-Saxon words simply because they had no need to use the words of outsiders. Their own words came readily to mind and when needed could be given a new slant, words such as God (from which godhead and godly could be made), flock, sheep, shepherd, heaven, hell, evil, sin, the flesh, the world, unclean, fiend. When the English-speaking Christian priest thought of Israel going out of Egypt he did not overlook the word 'exodus', but chose 'outfaring', because for him that was the word for going out. And when Jesus called to him 'disciples' the Anglo-Saxon priest called them 'learning-knights (youths)' because to him that is what they were. 'Pardon' became 'forgive', the 'evangel' (good news) became the 'good-spell/gospel' (the good story), 'judgment day' became 'Doomsday', the 'Spirit' became the 'Holy Ghost'. And Old English made a new word, 'atonement', for one of the core teachings of Christian belief. Man's sin brought a sundering between God and man, but through Christ's death on the cross God and the repentant sinner were again 'at one', hence 'at one-ment'.

---

[1] See Tom McArthur, editor, *The Oxford Companion to the English Language* (Oxford: Oxford University Press, 1996), pp.184-5.

Borrowings from Old Norse

The next wave of borrowing followed the Danish and Norwegian viking settlements in northern England, East Anglia and the East Midlands. Likenesses between Old English and Old Norse make it hard to weigh these borrowings. Wordlore scholars are sure of some 900 words borrowed from Old Norse, which are still around today. There are hundreds more that are likely, but the scholars are not wholly sure of them. (And there are thousands of Old Norse words in the Northern English and Scottish dialects.) Among the borrowings were: leg, law, want, beck, garth, riding, and the 'sk' words (the sk- sound is a characteristic of Old Norse) such as skill, skin, skirt, sky, skein, and so on. Each borrowed words from the other and this was made easier by the people and their language being much alike.

Our English forebears, then, drew words from the first dwellers in northern Europe, from Old Celtic, from Latin, and from Old Norse. These words are 'at home' here now, and to try to turn them out again would be like seeking to unpick the weave of our history. What happened after 1066 is another matter, but before we come to that let us look at some of the things to be learned from the stories of words.

Words with a story

> Philologists who chase
> A panting syllable through time and space,
> Start it at home, and hunt it in the dark
> To Gaul, to Greece, and into Noah's Ark
> (Cowper, *Retirement* lines 691-94)

William Cowper may poke a little fun at the seeking of word roots, but every word has its own tale, and some of these stories can give us insights into our past.

First, there are words which tell us something of the religious outlook of our forebears. The word 'bless' first meant 'to hallow with blood'. 'Giddy' meant 'gripped by a god'. We think of a 'nightmare' as being a bad dream, but the root word tells of an evil spirit believed to fall upon one who is asleep. The word 'oaf' comes from 'elf', and refers to a changeling, that is, an elf's child left behind when one's own child was taken. The verbs 'offer' and 'sell' once meant 'to offer sacrifice'. Then there are names which speak of the awe in which some beasts and birds were once held. It has been suggested that the name 'bear' means simply '*the* wild beast', and 'erne' (eagle) means '*the* bird'. (As an aside, some bird names are of a truly great age. 'Stork' is one such, and 'goose' seems to have been in use by 3,000 BC at the latest, so that it is probably the oldest bird name in the English language.[1])

Some words tell us of old ways of measuring. The word 'fathom' is a measure of six feet. At root it speaks of arms outstretched (to measure and also to embrace). The 'furlong' is the length of a ploughed furrow.

Then there are words from kindred and household life. 'Bridelope' is the oldest Germanic word for a wedding. It is from 'bride' and 'leap', and so means 'bridal run', the taking of the bride to her new home after the wedding. Then there is 'gossip' from 'god' and 'sib'. It meant a godfather or godmother. From this it came to be used of a near friend, and at last was given the meanings 'idle talker' or 'newsmonger'. The first meaning of 'guest' was 'stranger', even 'outsider' or 'foe', but it came to mean a farcomer who was welcomed to one's house and table. 'Heckle' is thought to come from the word for the comb used for combing out flax or hemp. Then it was used figuratively, of hard asking, of seeking to find weak points. From this we get today's meaning of going to a meeting (often a political meeting) and gainsaying the speaker's words. 'Lurch' was the name of a game, thought to be something like backgammon. The word is akin in some way to Old English 'belirt' meaning 'to hoodwink' or 'to cheat'. So 'to leave someone in the lurch' perhaps referred to putting another player in a losing position.

A 'lady' was a 'loaf-kneader' (bread-maker), while a 'lord' was a 'loaf-ward' (loaf-guardian). The lord's men lived in hall with him. They bound themselves to keep troth with him, to fight for him if need be. He in turn undertook to meet their needs (for bread and anything else) and to reward their service.

---

[1] WB Lockwood, *The Oxford Dictionary of British Bird Names*, 1993, p.71.

'Gun' is believed to come from a Scandinavian women's name, 'Gunilda' (Old Norse 'Gunnhildr'). It seems that the name may have been given to such engines of war as the ballista, and in an account of munitions stowed at Windsor Castle in 1330-1 there is a 'great ballista' known as 'the lady Gunilda'. (There are other cases of women's names being bestowed on engines of war.) Then when gunpowder was invented it would seem that the name was given to cannon.

It is thought that the word 'gossamer' (goose-summer) at first referred to a warm fall-time (autumn) when geese were believed to be in season. Then the word was transferred to the filmy, cobwebby stuff found floating in the air or spread over the grass, and seen in calm weather at that time of year. Another country word, 'aftermath', meant 'after-mowing', but its meaning was shifted to refer to outcomes, to things that follow after some happening.

The many seafaring terms used in a forlikening (figurative) sense are witness to our seafaring past. These are words such as headway, leeway, under way, steer clear of, clear the decks, weather the storm, founder, taken aback. And the use of body parts in speaking of the landscape also tells us something of English word-making. So we have a headland, the foot (of a cliff), the mouth (of a river), the brow (of a hill), an arm of the sea, and a neck of land.

Another part of the tale of words is the way in which words can go up or down in the world. 'Stockings' began as something worn by the working man or woman, but then rose to become leg-wear fit for the finest lady. 'Stool' once meant any kind of seat, but at some time it was 'hustled into the kitchen by the smart French *chair*'.[1] 'Villain' has gone from 'farm worker' to 'rogue'. 'Churl' and 'boor' have gone the same way. 'Knave' and 'knight' both meant 'boy' or 'servant' to begin with. But 'knave' went down in the world to mean 'one of low station', then 'rogue'. 'Knight' went up in the world to mean one who followed his lord to war. From this it rose yet further to become the horse-warrior of high worth – bold, wise, and fair of speech (as witness Chaucer's knight among the Canterbury pilgrims). 'Marshal' began life even lower than 'knave' and 'knight', but ended up much higher. At first it meant 'horse-boy' or 'groom', but a marshal in kingly service was a greater marshal, and in time his work of caring for horses was widened to involve the buying and caring for the king's war-gear in general. The word at length reached the great heights of 'field marshal' and 'Earl marshal'. 'Henchman' is from 'hengst' (a stallion) and 'man'. Once it meant 'groom', but it could rise in the world according to the standing of the one served. The henchman or groom in the service of a king would likely be a young man of rank.

Another rising word is 'pretty', which has gone from 'crafty' to 'comely'. 'Quean/queen' has both risen and fallen. Its Indo-European root *gwen* simply meant 'woman' (Greek *gynē*, from whence 'gynæcology', is a far distant cousin). By one path the word rose to become 'queen', meaning the wife of a king (or one who is queen in her own right). By another path it fell to become 'quean', a bold or badly behaved woman, and at last 'whore'.

---

[1] O Barfield, *History in English Words*, 1954, p.50.

Then we may note words that are known only in Old English, and are not found even in kindred speech within the West Germanic group. 'Lady' and 'lord' are two such, and here are some others: adze, bird, bill (of a bird), bless, brier, chide, child, chill, cod, croft, cudgel, distaff, dog, food, fulfil, furze, gorse, hassock, heifer, hemlock, keep, lewd, mattock, oats, reap, reel (for thread), shun, slough, smell, strawberry, swill, tire, wan, woman, worship, yes. 'Glee' is found in Old English and Old Norse only. 'Key' and 'tusk' are found only in Old English and Old Frisian.

One other feature of English speech we may touch on here. This is its abiding love of sound-likeness or alliteration. Sound-likeness, not rhyme, was the very marrow of Old English poetry. Still, today, an English-speaker will readily take up sound-likened words that fit in with what he wishes to say. Here are some examples: bring-and-buy, chalk and cheese, chop and change, faithful few, first and foremost, hale and hearty, hearth and home, last but not least, meek and mild, now or never, pillar to post, rhyme or reason, wrack and ruin.

1066 and afterwards

The coming of the Normans in 1066 was a shattering blow, bringing death and destruction, and leaving a great scar across English history.

We can only guess how many men died at Hastings. CH Lemmon suggests that the English army may have numbered about 8,800, and the Norman host about 8,000. He further suggests that the casualty rate may have been about 30 per cent, which would mean that some 5,000 men from the two sides died in the battle.[1] On the English side it may be that members of the fierd (the citizen army) fled towards the end of the day, and thus saved their lives. But their escape was perhaps balanced out by deaths among Harold's housecarls (probably the finest troops in the field at that time), who like enough fought to the bitter end and died where they stood.

The route of William's encircling march from Hastings to the north of London has been traced through the falls in the value of manors between the time of Edward the Confessor and the making of the Domesday survey in 1086. In other words the Normans so harried the settlements in their path, that the damage still showed a generation later. In research carried out in 1900 FH Baring plotted 217 such places.[2] In many cases the drop in value was more than 20 per cent.

No more can we guess how many died in the later uprisings. The North of England was provoked into rebellion in 1069-70 by unbridled harshness. William answered by setting his men to destroy the means of life. The wasting of the North brought on famine and disease, and wide areas were still derelict at the time of the Domesday survey. It was the most terrible visitation that had fallen on any large part of England since the Danish wars of king Alfred's time[3]. It is sometimes suggested that the rebels caused as much damage, perhaps more. Again it is said that this kind of destruction

---

[1] Lt Col Charles H Lemmon, in *The Norman Conquest*, 1966, pp.102, 115.

[2] CH Lemmon, in *The Norman Conquest*, 1966, pp.116-22.

[3] FM Stenton, *Anglo-Saxon England* (Oxford: Oxford University Press, 1943), pp.596-7.

was typical of the period.[1] But this is no excuse for such inhumanity. Standards of right and wrong do not change. The monk-historian Orderic Vitalis (of French father and English mother) who chronicled Norman achievements, was moved to condemn the brutal slaughter as an evil that could not escape God's judgement.[2] Orderic also told the tale of a Norman monk, Guitmund, who refused William's offer of an English bishopric, saying that the Conquest was robbery, with no authority in Scripture.[3]

David Bates thinks it reasonable to guess that the Normans numbered fewer than 25,000 in a total population of around 2,000,000.[4] Yet this handful gained a near stranglehold on power, and on the nation's wealth. The English nobility was destroyed as a class, for their lands were taken from them to reward William's followers. (William chose to write Harold out of the line of true kings, so that anyone who had fought for him could be called a rebel, and dispossessed.) Those English lords who could not abide the Norman yoke fled abroad. Some went to the other end of Europe and enlisted in the Varangian guard of the emperor in Constantinople.

Many English church leaders were deposed. There were Norman churchmen who had backed William's invasion, and who now sought their reward. For his part, William wanted men in post who he could trust. He and his sons steadfastly refused to raise Englishmen to high office in the church. Its higher ranks thus became wholly foreign, though not wholly Norman. The English church had a long history, and a rich home-grown culture. Yet the Normans despised its 'archaic' Roman liturgy and its 'old-fangled' buildings. There was much church rebuilding, though it is not at all clear that the Normans had an edge on those Anglo-Saxon builders who had gone before them. It has been noted that there was nothing in Normandy that could match the Confessor's Westminster Abbey. Amidst the rebuilding the remains of English saints were often treated roughly.[5]

After the deaths and destruction there was the wresting of wealth from the land. The Domesday Book shows many a royal manor paying a rent considerably greater than its recognised value, suggesting harsh exploitation.[6] And William diverted English resources to help pay for his wars on the borders of Normandy, and for building projects in his dukedom.[7] Meanwhile further resources were poured into building castles the length and breadth of England, to serve as military bases and to overawe the people. William I and his sons also extended the forests, both for their sport and to add to their revenues (from timber, and from the fines for breaches of the forest laws).

There were other ways in which history was turned backwards. In Anglo-Saxon society women had been held in some respect, but Norman society showed the manners of the war-camp. Few women could make their mark in this rough world,

---

[1] F Barlow in *The Norman Conquest*, 1966, p.129.
[2] David Bates, *William the Conqueror* (Stroud: Tempus, 2004), p.128.
[3] Bates, *William the Conqueror*, 2004, pp.215-6.
[4] Bates, *William the Conqueror*, 2004, p.181.
[5] F Barlow in *The Norman Conquest*, 1966, p.157.
[6] Bates, *William the Conqueror*, 2004, p.187.
[7] Bates, *William the Conqueror*, 2004, p.202.

and then only by showing masculine forcefulness.[1]   Again, the illuminated manuscripts of the years 900-1066 are nearly ten times as many as those of the period 1066-1140, and none of the latter can, in the opinion of the art-wise, compare in beauty with the Anglo-Saxon. And a telling comparison can be made between the neat silver pennies of Edward the Confessor and Harold Godwineson and the 'shapeless ill-struck issues' of the Norman kings. Not until the time of Henry II did the coinage again reach pre-1066 standards.[2]

The Norman conquest ensured that England stayed part of the Roman/Mediterranean world, rather than an Anglo-Scandinavian world. But it also entangled England in the business, and the wars, of France, to the lasting cost of both. Under the Angevins England became almost a French province.[3]   It was also warlords of Norman stock who first entangled mainland Britain in Irish affairs, and from that, too, much sorrow has come.

Thoughtful Englishmen believed the nation was being punished for its sins. The tale was told of how Edward the Confessor had a death-bed vision in which heavenly visitors spoke to him of the sign that would show the punishment was at an end. A green tree must be cut down the middle, and half of it carried three furlongs away. Then that half must be joined to the stock again, and leaves and fruit spring forth once more, all this without the hand of man.[4] On the matter of the spiritual reality behind the conquest, an American historian, David Bernstein has made some intriguing suggestions about subversion woven into the Bayeux Tapestry by English needlewomen. Bernstein draws attention to a pair of winged lions in the upper border of the Tapestry, which seem to be associated with the appearances of Duke William. In the Old Testament, in the awesome vision seen by Daniel, the first of the four beasts (symbolising ancient pagan empires) was a lion having eagles' wings. From the first century AD onwards commentators have understood this to be the Babylonian empire. Was it being hinted, then, that Duke William was another Nebuchadnezzar of Babylon? That fearsome tyrant had been the instrument of God's wrath, against sinful Israel and against Israel's king Zedekiah. This Zedekiah had sworn fealty to Nebuchadnezzar, but then broke faith and rebelled. He was punished by first witnessing the execution of his sons, and then having his eyes put out. Further on in the Tapestry Harold at Hastings is shown wounded by an arrow in the eye. He had allegedly sworn to be William's man, and to help him to the throne of England, but had then accepted the throne himself. Was his death seen as punishment from God for the breaking of his oath? And was there the further hint that, as Israel was delivered by the mercy of God, after seventy years of exile in Babylon, the English, too, would be freed of the Norman yoke after their own 'seventy years'?[5] Bernstein thought that the mastermind behind the tapestry was an English monk of Canterbury (either from St Augustine's Abbey or from the cathedral monastery of Christ Church).

---

[1] F Barlow in *The Norman Conquest*, 1966, p.141.

[2] GO Sayles, *The Medieval Foundations of England* (London: Methuen, 1966), p.268, and C Oman, *England before the Norman Conquest* London: Methuen, 1924, pp.649-50.

[3] F Barlow in *The Norman Conquest*, 1966, p.160.

[4] F Barlow in *The Norman Conquest*, 1966, pp.131-2.

[5] See David J Bernstein, *The Mystery of the Bayeux Tapestry* (London: Weidenfeld and Nicolson, 1986), pp.166ff.

Andrew Bridgeford, however, refers to research into the written text of the Tapestry carried out by Professor Ian Short of the University of London, a specialist in medieval French. His study led him to the conclusion that the embroidery was conceived by someone whose first language was French. That someone would seem not to have been well disposed towards the Normans, but rather to sympathise with the English. Bridgeford suggests that this man was a gifted writer-artist from the lands of Count Eustace II of Boulogne, that is, from Boulogne itself, or from neighbouring Picardy or Flanders. Count Eustace had fought for William at Hastings, but the following year he fell out with Bishop Odo of Bayeux, William's half-brother. [1]

So, after 1066 there was death and exile and grief and, in a number of key ways, a turning back of the clock. And it seems that the language, too, was to be conquered.

Norman French influence on English

The newcomers spoke Norman French, and to them the English language sounded barbarous. Although William the Conqueror at first had thoughts of learning English, he soon gave this up. So it was in Norman French that the daily running of the government, the making and upholding of law, and the business of 'upper-class' living were now carried on. English poetry was lost to the sight of the Norman rulers but it lived on, as did English speech among English folk who were mostly deemed to be unlearned and uncouth serfs. Yet the new rulers must still talk with those they ruled, and the English under them needed to hear what they were being told. So there must have been some language-learning on both sides. And as racial tensions eased in the twelfth century, Englishmen who sought to get on in the world began to give their children Norman names, and to learn French.

Thus did French words begin to find their way into English. They are found in the field of what we might call 'modern' warfare. So, whereas bow, sword, shield, spear and such are English, from the French we have the likes of archer, armour, arms, army, assault, battle, fortress, guard, mace, mangonel, portcullis, siege and soldier. Matters of authority were another fertile area for borrowings, words such as crown and throne, govern and governor, nobility, obedience, peasant, servant and vassal. Likewise the realm of law and order is rich in borrowings – arrest and warrant, accuse, acquit, attorney, bailiff, condemn, court, felony, judge and justice, perjury, sentence, gaol. The Normans brought in their own craftsmen, and with them names for tools such as the mallet, chisel, pulley, bucket and trowel. Likewise the newcomers controlled the market, and so we now had the words bargain, contract, embezzle, merchant, money, partner and price. And, as has often been pointed out, words to do with good living, such as beef, pork and venison, were borrowed, while the English words for cow, pig and deer lived on, because the English serfs tended the livestock, but without seeing the meat very often.

After Henry II (king, 1154-89) built his Angevin empire as far as the Pyrennes, words from Central French (Francien) were also borrowed. The upper class and their hold on

---

[1] Andrew Bridgeford, *1066 The hidden history of the Bayeux Tapestry* (New York: Walker, 2005) pp.170-2.

government were again to the fore, as jury, traitor, prison, sovereign, parliament, prince, duke, duchess, countess, viscount and baron were now brought in. Some of the new words had already been borrowed once, from Norman French, and so English came to have both canal and channel, leal and loyal, real/royal, reward/regard. Perhaps oddly, it was only about 1300, as tensions between English and Normans eased (and there was less need to dig in the heels) that wholesale borrowing from French began. By this time Parisian French was the recognised standard on the continent. Hence the number of words borrowed from Norman French is not so great after all.[1]

Out of the darkness

There had been four chief dialects of Old English: Kentish, West Saxon, Mercian and Northumbrian. By 1066 West Saxon was well on the way to becoming standard English, though for wholly non-linguistic reasons. (It was the speech of those who welded the old folkdoms into one.[2]) The Norman conquest interrupted this trend. Any Englishmen still writing in English now wrote in his own dialect. In other words West Saxon was put back on a level with Mercian and Northumbrian.[3]

We have noted borrowings in the fields of 'modern' warfare, authority, law and order, the market, and 'the good life'. But English speech long remained stubbornly deaf to the new ways, so that things changed only slowly. The Middle English of about 1250 was remarkably like the Old English of 1066, so that we could speak of late Old English in the twelfth, or even thirteenth, centuries. (On the other hand some of the characteristics that distinguish Middle English can be traced in texts before 1066.[4]) In the end, after a long 'hibernation', English elbowed aside the inthrusting Norman French. How did this come about?

Weight of numbers is one answer, for English was still the speech of most folk. And there were English men of learning who still spoke it before the world. There was Samson (1135-1211), Abbot of Bury St Edmund's, who could speak freely in both Latin and French, but preached to the people of Bury in the dialect of Norfolk.[5]

Wedlock between Norman and English, and children growing up speaking both tongues, may have been another part of the answer. English wives and English wet nurses were likely to pass on some English to their children. Yet Ranulf Higden (c.1280-1364) an English Benedictine monk at the monastery of St Werburgh in Chester, and a historian and theologian, has a sorry tale to tell. In his *Polychronicon* (a work of universal history from Creation to 1357) he says that the children of the lordly were taught French from the cradle, that at school they were forced to leave their English, and anyone hoping to climb the social ladder learned French.

---

[1] Greenough and Kittredge, *Words and Their Ways in English Speech*, 1901, p.86.
[2] Bolton and Crystal, *The English Language*, 1993, p.230.
[3] Greenough and Kittredge, *Words and Their Ways in English Speech*, 1901, pp.84-5.
[4] Bolton and Crystal, *The English Language*, 1993, p.239.
[5] S Potter, *Our Language*, 1966, p.34.

Another point is that Englishmen did not stop writing English. It was only in 1154 that the writing up of the *Anglo-Saxon Chronicle* came to an end (and with it the writing of 'pure' Old English). Then there was the *Ormulum*, the work of a monk named Orm or Ormin, written some time between about 1150 and 1180. It is thought that Orm lived and worked at Bourne Abbey in Lincolnshire, in the Danelaw. (The Danish areas of England were particularly resistant to Norman French.[1]) The *Ormulum* was written for the lower clergy, who knew neither Latin nor French, to help them teach the Christian faith to their congregations. The method followed was to go through the texts set for the liturgical year, giving a paraphrase of the reading, followed by explanation of the passage. Orm wrote in the East Midlands dialect, and because he believed that folk were not speaking English aright, he set himself to spell words just as they were said, and to show vowel lengths – by doubling consonants after a short vowel, or by using accents when a vowel came at the end of a word. His almost 19,000 lines of verse are not thought to be of great worth either as verse or as theology. But as a record of exactly how East Midlands English was spoken in the twelfth century, and how Old English became Middle English, it is of high worth.

Another English work from the late twelfth/early thirteenth century is the 'The Owl and the Nightingale', written largely in a South-East dialect. It may be the work of one Master Nicholas of Guildford, who features in the text. The poem is about a debate between an Owl who is perched on a bough overgrown with ivy, and a Nightingale sitting on another bough that is in blossom. Master Nicholas is called in to judge in the debate. The poem may be about religion (asceticism against a more joyful religion), but marriage, manners and song have also been suggested as the themes of this ambiguous work.

From the 13th century comes a song (to be sung as a round) with musical notation to go with it. It begins 'Sumer is icumen in, Lhude sing cuccu!' ('Summer has come in, Loudly sing cuckoo!') The song is written in the Wessex dialect of Middle English. It was found in Reading Abbey, though this need not mean that it was written there.

The Hundred Years War with France (1337-1454) fostered Englishness. Then the Black Death carried off many Latin- and French-speaking clergy (and some ran away). Many of those who came in their stead were laymen, who spoke only English. Moreover farm-hands were now scarce and therefore of worth, so uplifting both the working man and his English speech. In 1362 the Statute of Pleading laid down that henceforth the work of the courts was to go on in English (though the written records were to be kept in Latin). In 1399, when Henry IV took the crown, he spoke in the Great Hall at Westminster in English.

We have seen how the Norman conquest 'put the West Saxon dialect in its place'. Now the Midland dialects began to come to the fore. The differences between the speech of the East and West Midlands were marked enough to be reckoned as two dialects. Simeon Potter writes: 'West Midland speech, notably that of the cathedral cities of Hereford and Worcester, was the more direct descendant of Old Mercian and it was in the west country that the continuity of English prose and poetry was most apparent ... By the thirteenth century, however, the East Midland dialect had risen into greater prominence than the

---

[1] Wikipedia article on Orm.

West. It was, after all, the dialect of the Court, of the City of London, and of both universities, Oxford and Cambridge. Later, it became the dialect of Chaucer, whose English was essentially East Midland with Southern and Kentish peculiarities; of the trilingual Gower; and of Wyclif, too, although he was a Yorkshireman born.'[1]

Geoffrey Chaucer (c.1340-1400) played a leading part in the uplifting of the English tongue. He came from the well-to-do burgher class, and held various official posts – Collector of Customs, Superintendent of Buildings, even a Member of Parliament for a short time. He visited France and Italy several times on business of state. Thus he met with 'every sort of person worth knowing, from king to apprentice'.[2] Chaucer's East Midland dialect would probably have become standard English even if Chaucer had never been, but the process might have taken longer and been less sure. It was in the period 1340-1400 (the span of Chaucer's life) that this dialect gained the rank of English literary language. After Chaucer 'nobody doubted that the language as he had written it was the best English'.[3] Since 1400 there has been a very slight shift, so that Modern English is slightly more northerly than Chaucer's dialect.[4] About twenty to twenty-five per cent of Chaucer's words are taken from French, but he did not bring in many new words himself. Almost every borrowed word that he used can be found somewhere else at an earlier date.[5]

The Wycliffe Bible

We may note here the great service wrought by Christianity in upholding the worth of all peoples, and the oneness in Christ of all who believe. From this followed the translation work inspired by the longing to take the gospel to all folkdoms. The Syriac, Coptic and Armenian translations of the Scriptures were made early. The fourth century bishop and missionary to the Goths, Ulfilas or Wulfila ('little wolf'), translated the Bible from Greek into Gothic. (It is not known how much of the Bible he translated, as only fragments of his work have come down to us.) For this task Ulfilas had to make an alphabet, which he did using both Greek and runic letters. This Bible is the oldest written Germanic work. (The Slavonic Bible is also the beginning of Slavonic literature.)

In 14th century England John Wycliffe and his followers brought out the first English translation of the whole Bible. (Some parts of the Scriptures had been put into English in Anglo-Saxon times.) The work was in truth in a very Latinate English. Melvyn Bragg notes of the translators (of whom the chief was Nicholas Hereford of Queen's College, Oxford): 'So in awe were they of the authority of the Latin version that they translated word for word, even keeping the Latin word order', as in 'I forsoothe am the Lord thy God full jealous.' And there are over a thousand Latin words in English that are first recorded in Wycliffe's Bible.[6]

---

[1] Simeon Potter, *Our Language*, 1966, p.17-18.
[2] Greenough and Kittredge, *Words and Their Ways in English Speech*, 1901, p.90.
[3] Greenough and Kittredge, *Words and Their Ways in English Speech*, 1901, p.91.
[4] Greenough and Kittredge, *Words and Their Ways in English Speech*, 1901, p.92.
[5] Greenough and Kittredge, *Words and Their Ways in English Speech*, 1901, p.91.
[6] M Bragg, *The Adventure of English*, 2003, p.87.

William Caxton

Another key figure was William Caxton, who was born around 1415-24, and died 1491/92. He was a merchant and diplomat, who lived for much of his life in Bruges and Cologne. He took up publishing and bookselling as a further business venture, and returned to England in 1475 or 1476, so that he could pick up English material more readily and personally oversee the selling of books. He brought out books of chivalry and romance, classical works, and Roman and English histories. He did much of the translating himself, and he must needs ask himself where to pitch his wording. Being a businessman, he knew that he must write in a way acceptable to his buyers. This was not straightforward, for although English had won its rightful place as the first language of the land, there were yet many who saw it as a poor relation, needing to be enriched from French and Latin. In his *Eneydos* of 1490 (based on Virgil's *Aeneid*) Caxton tells how he sat in his study one day and took up a new work, a French paraphrase of the Virgil. There and then he began an English translation, but after writing a page or two he looked over what he had done and saw that he had used many 'strange terms'. Would common folk be able to understand it? He then looked for help in some old book, but found the English 'rude and broad'. On top of this there was the matter that what was spoken in one shire of England might not be understood in the next. To make the point Caxton tells how a London ship was held up for lack of wind, off the coast of Kent, and the merchants went ashore to buy meat and 'eggys' (eggs). With blank looks the housewife told them she 'coude speke no frenshe'. 'Eggys' is in fact Old Norse, and when another man spoke the Old English 'eyren' the woman understood. 'And thus bytwene playn, rude, and curious', wrote Caxton, 'I stande abasshed. But in my judgemente the comyn termes that be dayli used ben lyghter to be understonde than the olde and auncyent englysshe.' He at length settled on the English of London and the South-East, and sought a mean between the speech of the common folk and that of the gentry, an English that was neither 'over rude nor curious'. [1]

William Tyndale

William Tyndale (c.1494-1536) was one of the foremost figures of the English Reformation. He graduated with a BA as a member of Magdalen Hall, Oxford, then went on to take his MA. It was probably soon after his return home to Gloucestershire that he began to translate the Greek New Testament into English. It was about this time that he met a so-called 'learned man' who told Tyndale that 'we were better without God's law than the pope's'. Tyndale answered, 'I defy the Pope and all his laws', and went on, 'If God spares my life, ere many years I will take care that a ploughboy shall know more of the Scriptures than you do.' He had become wholly convinced of the truth asserted by Luther and others, that salvation from sin and death is gained by faith in Christ's death for mankind, and not through good works of man's own. At the time this was dangerous thinking, and Tyndale went to Germany, so that he might be free to translate without interference by the English authorities. His New Testament translation was published in Worms in 1526. He straightway went on to study Hebrew, and by the spring of 1535 he had translated the Old Testament from

---

[1] Robert McCrum, William Cran and Robert MacNeil, *The Story of English* (London: Faber and Faber/BBC Books, 1986), pp.86-7.

Genesis as far as 2 Chronicles. He was by then living in Antwerp, and it was there that he was betrayed into the hands of the Spanish authorities. After a long examination of his writings, and hearing his answers to gruelling questions, he was condemned for 'heresy' and put to death in October 1536.

The following year 'Matthew's Bible' was published in England. Tyndale's name did not appear, but this was his translation. (The second half of the Old Testament, which he not been allowed time to translate, was the work of Miles Coveradale.) This work was then revised as the 'Great Bible' of 1539, and was placed in every church in the land. The King James Bible of 1611 took over between sixty and eighty per cent of Tyndale's wording. (Among his words and phrases are such as: scapegoat, my brother's keeper, a land flowing with milk and honey, the apple of his eye, a man after his own heart, signs of the times, the spirit is willing, fight the good fight.)

It would be hard to praise too much the high worth of Tyndale's English writing. He sought to be true to the original Greek and Hebrew, and to put these into English that the common man could readily grasp. (He wrote simply because he was in earnest, and his wording is mostly Anglo-Saxon.) One writer sums up, 'It is not fanciful to see a chief agent of the energizing of the language in the sixteenth century in the constant reading of the Bible in English, of which Tyndale was the great maker.'[1] Through its 'second life' in the King James Version Tyndale's writing found its way into all parts of the world. For hundreds of years the English Bible was heard week in week out, by almost all English-speaking Christians wherever they were. Its teachings, its proverbs and parables, its word-pictures, its heroes and heroines, its wretches and wrong-doers, its great sweep of history (from the garden of Eden to the garden-like heavenly city) took deep root in the minds of English men and women. 'It went to the heart of the way we spoke, the way we described the world and ourselves. Its English bound the English together'.[2]

As an example of Tyndale's wording, here is his English version of Matthew 5:1-12, the 'Beatitudes' or blessings spoken by Jesus at the beginning of the Sermon on the Mount:

5:1 When he saw the people, he went up into a mountain, and when he was set, his disciples came unto him, 2 and he opened his mouth, and taught them saying:
3 "Blessed are the poor in spirit, for theirs is the kingdom of heaven.
4 "Blessed are they that mourn, for they shall be comforted.
5 "Blessed are the meek, for they shall inherit the earth.
6 "Blessed are they which hunger and thirst for righteousness, for they shall be filled.
7 "Blessed are the merciful, for they shall obtain mercy.
8 "Blessed are the pure in heart, for they shall see God.
9 "Blessed are the maintainers of peace, for they shall be called the children of God.
10 "Blessed are they which suffer persecution for righteousness' sake, for theirs is the kingdom of heaven.
11 "Blessed are ye when men shall revile you, and persecute you, and shall falsely say all manner of evil sayings against you for my sake. 12 Rejoice and be glad, for great is your reward in heaven. For so persecuted they the prophets which were before your days."

---

[1] David Daniell, article on Tyndale in the *Dictionary of National Biography*, Volume 55, p.787.
[2] M Bragg, *The Adventure of English*, 2003, p.113.

An aside: phrases drawn from the Bible

The Bible has been a rich source of English wording. We have: the blind leading the blind, casting the first stone, the eleventh hour, feet of clay, forbidden fruit, fig-leaf, the flesh-pots of Egypt, gospel truth, going the second mile, heaping coals of fire, a hidden talent, hiding one's light under a bushel, killing the fatted calf, the law of the Medes and Persians, the left hand not knowing what the right is doing, the leopard which cannot change its spots, pearls before swine, taking up someone else's mantle, being a millstone round the neck, reaping what one has sown, salt of the earth, scapegoat, sour grapes, sowing the wind and reaping the whirlwind, a thorn in the flesh, turning the other cheek, washing one's hands of something, wheels within wheels, writing on the wall. We can give 'chapter and verse', and we can urge someone to 'do as you would be done by' or to 'practice what you preach'. Proper names from the Bible are put to use: Armageddon, a Damascus road experience, a good Samaritan, a Jeremiad, a Job's comforter, a Judas kiss, a painted Jezebel, a Philistine. Someone might out-Herod Herod, or he might 'raise Cain', or he might not 'know someone from Adam'. The word 'apocalyptic' is used of a scene of utter devastation, and a really serious famine is 'a famine of biblical proportions'. Other words that have come in from the biblical world are: apocryphal, olive-branch, pharisaism, a prodigal, shibboleth.

Renaissance and Reformation

So did English win through. By the 16th century the time of wholesale borrowing from French was passed, but the next fight was already at hand.

That great rebirth of scholarship that is known by the French word 'Renaissance' was under way and, hard on its heels came the Reformation, and the great era of European seafaring and discovery. At the heart of this new flowering of European endeavour was a deep interest in, and a looking-up to, all things Roman and Greek. In truth, even from Saxon times, there had been some feeling of awe before the remains of Roman civilisation, that is, its buildings, its stone roads, and its writings. Now, with the 'Renaissance', and the pushing back of the bounds of learning and knowledge, many new words were needed. To scholars steeped in the classics the well-springs from which to draw were Greek and Latin. Latin had long been the professional dialect of churchmen and the medium for a shared, Europe-wide scholarship. It was thought that English was hardly up to the task of bringing forth truly 'learned' words for hard subject-matter. Latin was seen as greater, more correct, than English, and so a 'role model' from which the latter ought to learn. Fashion, the liking for novelty, and the wish to seem wise before one's neighbours also played a part. (By the twentieth century it was reckoned that as many as one-fourth of the words to be found in a full-sized Latin dictionary have made their way into English.[1]) And it was in the sixteenth/seventeenth centuries that 'well-meaning meddlers' took to making words conform with their real or supposed Latin roots. A 'b' was put into 'dette' and

---

[1] O Barfield, *History in English Words*, 1954, p.54; Greenough and Kittredge, *Words and Their Ways in English Speech*, 1901, p.106.

'doute', a 'p' into 'receipt', 'island' gained its 's', 'scissors'' its 'c', 'anchor;' its 'h'. 'Rime' became 'rhyme'. Old English 'sinder' became 'cinder' in the mistaken belief that it had come from Latin 'cinis' (ashes).

This was also the time of Shakespeare. It is said that he coined some 2,000 words and that as a phrasemaker there has never been anyone to match him. He has given us: all our yesterdays, as good luck would have it, backing a horse, bag and baggage, to beggar all description, breathing one's last, budge an inch, cold comfort, give him his due, the glass of fashion, go down the primrose path, in my mind's eye, method in one's madness, the milk of human kindness, more honoured in the breach than the observance, more in sorrow than in anger, one fell swoop, pitched battle, play fast and loose, play on words, thin air, to be in a pickle, salad days, snapper-up of unconsidered trifles, the sound and the fury, to be cruel to be kind, to thine own self be true, too much of a good thing, to the manner born, tower of strength, vanish into thin air, well on your way.

The 'inkhorn plot'

An inkhorn is an inkwell made from horn. Because it was such a basic 'tool of the trade' it came to be linked to the business of writing. Then in the sixteenth century 'inkhorn term' became a byword for over-learned, bookish words.

Among keen Latin borrowers there was Sir Thomas Elyot (c.1490-1546), scholar in philosophy and medicine and unwilling diplomat. Elyot wrote *The Book Named the Governour*, perhaps the first book on education printed in English. He did say he was sorry that he should bring in words that were 'strange and dark', but in truth he saw his borrowings as most needful for building the store of words that we have. And so in came the likes of: anachronism, atmosphere, autograph, catastrophe, criterion, enthusiasm, idiosyncrasy, parenthesis, temperature, thermometer, transcribe, and so on.

Sir Thomas More (1478-1535) was another borrower. He wrote his *Utopia* in Latin, and it was not put into English until some years after his death. It is said that we owe him words such as absurdity, contradictory, exaggerate, indifference, monopoly, and paradox. Francis Bacon (1561-1626) was one who wrote in Latin on subjects in which he thought that English would 'play the bankrupt with books'.[1] He used Latin for his *De dignitate et augmentis scientiarum* ('On the dignity and advancement of learning'). Again, when William Harvey wrote what he had learned of the circulation of the blood, he used Latin for his *De Motu Cordis et Sanguinis in Animalibus* ('On the Motion of the Heart and Blood in Animals'), 1628. Sir Isaac Newton wrote his *Principia* (1687) in Latin, but his later work, *Opticks* (1704), in English.

The borrowing went so far that words which had already come into English by way of French were now borrowed again, straight from Latin. So we have both benison and benediction, blame and blaspheme, frail and fragile, poor and pauper, purvey and provide, and others. Some of the inkhorners even took words from Latin that had been borrowed twice before, first from Norman French and then from Central French. So

---

[1] Quoted in M Bragg, *The Adventure of English*, 2003, p.123.

English then had real/royal/regal, and leal/loyal/legal. Altogether some 10,000 to 12,000 words were brought in in the Renaissance/Reformation period. [1]

The love of outlandish words almost asked for some poking of fun. There is Holofernes the schoolmaster in Shakespeare's *Love's Labour's Lost*. He speaks of his skill with words thus: 'This is a gift that I have, simple, simple; a foolish extravagant spirit, full of forms, figures, shapes, objects, ideas, apprehensions, motions, revolutions. These are begot in the ventricle of memory, nourish'd in the womb of pia mater, and delivered upon the mellowing of occasion' (*LLL*, Act 4, scene II).

Thomas Wilson (about 1525-1581) was at one time Secretary of State to Elizabeth I. In his *The Arte of Rhetorique*, 1553, he wrote of 'these fine English clerkes' whose own mothers would hardly know what they were saying. Owen Barfield quotes from Wilson's parody: 'Pondering, expending, and revoluting with myself, your ingent affability, and ingenious capacity for mundane affairs: I cannot but celebrate and extoll your magnifical dexterity above all other. For how could you have adepted such illustrate prerogative, and domestical superiority, if the fecundity of your ingeny had not been so fertile and wonderful pregnant?' [2]

This was also the time of threats from Rome and from Catholic Spain, and English folk had a strong sense of being set apart, of living on an island, close to over-mighty neighbours. There were men ready to stand out against this onslaught of other folk's words, this snobbery of 'outlandish English', and they were upheld by a strong Puritan strain.

Sir John Cheke (1514-57), Regius Professor of Greek at Cambridge, and one-time tutor to prince Edward (afterwards Edward VI), believed that English had to uncover and build on its Anglo-Saxon roots. He translated the Gospel of Matthew using English lexical resources for new words – 'gainrising' for 'resurrection', 'ground-wrought' for 'founded', 'hundreder' for 'centurion', 'crossed' for 'crucified'. He wanted English 'unmixt and unmangeled' lest through always borrowing and never paying we become bankrupt. Roger Ascham (1515-68), who had been tutor to the Princess Elizabeth (afterwards Elizabeth I), likewise spoke against these 'inkhorn terms'. Among others who were aware of the richness of true English were the Elizabethan poet, Edmund Spenser (c.1552-99), writer of *The Faery Queene*, and William Camden (1551-1623) whose great work *Britannia* surveyed the landscape and history of the island.

The Inkhorn Controversy was probably the greatest formal dispute about the English language that we have known, yet still the borrowing went on.

---

[1] McCrum and others, p.93.
[2] Quoted in O Barfield, *History in English Words*, 1954, p.61.

The 'hunter-gatherer' language

In the 18th century there arose deep worries about the language. Writers could see the greatness of Chaucer, but they also saw that his words were now hard to read. Might there come a time when men and women could no longer understand his writing, and his work thus be lost? And if Chaucer was in danger what hope was there for others? Jonathan Swift feared that even written history might slip beyond understanding within a hundred years or so. The language must be defended against change. Swift wanted an academy to 'ascertain' (fix) the language. He wrote: 'I see no absolute Necessity why any Language should be perpetually changing'.[1]

In making his dictionary Johnson came out against foreign words brought in (he believed) through ignorance, vanity or wantonness, 'by compliance with fashion or lust of innovation'. Wordsworth made up his mind to use plain words to put over the weight of strong feelings. Yet the borrowing went on. It seemed that the condition of the patient was incurable. As Melvyn Bragg puts it, 'English was a hunter-gatherer of vocabulary, a scavenger on land and sea'.[2]

English had long been borrowing from Dutch words to do with the sea and ships – bowsprit, shore, skipper in the 14th century, deck, freight, hoy, keel, lighter, pink, pump, scout, marline, sheet-anchor and buoy in the 15th century, aloof, belay, dock, mesh, reef, rover, studding-sail, flyboat, yacht in the 16th century, avast, bow, boom, cruise, cruiser, gybe, sloop, and keelhaul in the 17th century. Other Dutch borrowings were: boor, brackish, landscape, loiter, slender, stove.

From the 1660 Restoration onwards French was the language of diplomacy and polite society, and so society phrases were still borrowed, and also military terms. From Greek English borrowed not only academic words (such as academy), but words from drama (chorus, comedy, theatre and so on), and scientific and technical terms such as automatic, dynamo, metronome, and thermometer. There were Arabic borrowings (alchemy, algebra, nadir, zenith). Music words were taken from Italian (allegro, andante, diminuendo, staccato). From the Spanish of the seafaring age came words such as cigar, flotilla, galleon, grandee, guerrilla, junta, mosquito, renegade, siesta, tornado.

There has been very little borrowing from German. 'Cobalt' and 'nickel' are from the names given by German miners to demoniac spirits. English has borrowed other mining words from German, such as 'quartz' (which German had borrowed from Slavic), and 'shale'. From the hey-day of the British Empire there were borrowings from Hindi (nabob, guru, pundit, juggernaut, thug), from Tamil (pariah, curry), from Malay (ketchup, sago, bamboo, amuck), and many more. Industrial and scientific advances in the 19th/20th centuries brought the need for many new words for the things being studied and made. Again, scholars reared on Latin and Greek went to those languages for omnibus, perambulator (pram), telegraph, telephone, camera, computer, television, video, mobile, and so on.

---

[1] Quoted in M Bragg, *The Adventure of English*, 2003, p.209.
[2] M Bragg, *The Adventure of English*, 2003, p.267.

Some areas are now almost 'no-go' areas for English, among them grammar, law, medicine, money, music. In the nineteenth century William Barnes sought manfully to craft English grammatical terms: end-eking (suffix), fore-eking (prefix), foreputting (preposition), namesame (synonym) – though 'same' is Old Norse – name-token (pronoun), name-word (noun), outreaching (transitive verb), not-outreaching (intransitive verb), thing mark-word (adjective), time word (verb), under mark-word (adverb), wordling (particle), word-strain (accent). But none of these have caught on.

Words which should never have seen the light of day

For the most part the Oxford English Dictionary keeps very much to the business in hand: words and their roots, their meanings, and examples of how they have been used over the years. However, there is a little aside under the entry for one word (and perhaps there are others also). The word is 'behither' and the writer adds in brackets, 'A word worth reviving'. It is a word with good English roots, and it is surely true that it does deserve to live again. But then words (like men and women) do not always get what they deserve in life. Many good English words have been pushed to the borders of the language and now seem 'olde worlde'. (More of this later.)

On the other hand there are some needless borrowings that have died out, and we are surely better off without them. Owen Barfield notes the following from the writings of Francis Bacon: contentation, contristation, digladiation, morigeration, redargution, ventosity.[1] Other amazing coinings are: deruncinate, fatigate, illecebrous, obtestate. These may be gone, but there are many others still around which should surely never have seen the light of day: abreption, aniconic, auspicate, consentience, constringe, diverb, dysphemism, immiscible, ingannation, intempestivity, interclusion, intercommunication, intercurrence, introception, jactitate, obduction, obmutescence, oleaginous, pervicacious, ratiocinate, revendication, sedentarization, tergiversate. One must wonder how many words there are in the Oxford English Dictionary which are, in truth, of no use whatsoever.

Some specimens of outlandish English
(to dazzle or mislead)

One gem from an accountancy textbook refers to a figure that is 'not susceptible of precise calculation'. This simply means that it cannot be worked out to the last penny. Even when the words used are not so 'way out' they can yet be put together in a haze of learning. What about this (from a textbook on economics): "the 'independence of irrelevant alternatives' condition requires that the social ranking of any pair of social states must be the same as long as the individual utility information about the pair of states remains the same."[2] In fact there are no very strange words here, but what does it all mean? I suppose we must take this as economists' dialect, and acknowledge that we are strangers in that land. (The 'insider' wording of different fields of learning and activity – economics, sociology, development work or whatever – are really the dialects of today.)

---

[1] O Barfield, *History in English Words*, 1954, p.60.
[2] D Hay, *Economics Today: A Christian critique*, (Leicester: Apollos, 1989), p.128.

Another example of modern dialect is brought out by David Crystal in *Words Words Words*. He takes the word 'lisp' and puts it into the dialect of speech therapists and such. It becomes 'Lucy's voiceless sibilant articulations are being replaced by voiceless interdental fricatives in syllable-initial positions'.[1]

Among other words and phrases which put one's back up are: 'authorial intentionality' (what the author meant), 'solid-hoofed perissodactyl quadruped' (the Oxford Dictionary's definition of 'horse' – perhaps we should take this as zoologists' dialect), 'umbrageous' (shady) – this in Thomas Hardy, who surely ought to have known better. And what a mouthful is the word 'incomprehensibility', with its root 'hen' and its eight affixes and infixes.[2]

Then there is the use of words for evasion: the following expressions for cutting back on the workforce have been noted: chemistry change, dehiring, deselection, destaffing, downsizing, executive culling, involuntary separation, negotiated departure, personnel surplus reduction, reducing headcount, rightsizing, skill-mix adjustment. Another example is the turning of 'failure' into 'deferred success'.

The Plain English Campaign have found many examples of such use of words (after all, that is their business). They cite the case of an internet business which was asked by a would-be customer if they still sold blank CDs. They answered: 'We are currently in the process of consolidating our product range to ensure that the products that we stock are indicative of our brand aspirations. As part of our range consolidation we have also decided to revisit our supplier list and employ a more intelligent system for stock acquisition. As a result of the above certain product lines are now unavailable through jungle.com, whilst potentially remaining available from more mainstream suppliers.' But all they needed to say in answer was 'No'.

CM Matthews says that it is the lower ranks of officialdom who are the worst offenders in preferring borrowed words.[3] Here is one of their offerings (courtesy of the Plain English Campaign): 'In these Regulations, unless the context otherwise requires, any reference to a numbered regulation is a reference to the regulation bearing that number in these regulations and any reference in a regulation to a numbered paragraph is a reference to the paragraph of that regulation bearing that number.'

A few sums

So what do we have left? Is English really still English at all? By one study, about 85 percent of the 30,000 words of Old English have died out. This would mean that only some 4,500 words live on, or about 1 percent of the words in the *Oxford English Dictionary*.[4] Simeon Potter, however, notes that many of those 30,000 Old English words were peculiar to the wording of alliterative poetry, and not part of everyday life. He says that perhaps some four-fifths of the words from Old English prose still

---

[1] D Crystal, *Words Words Words*, 2006, p.119.
[2] S Potter, *Our Language*, 1966, p.88.
[3] CM Matthews, *Words, Words, Words*, 1979, p.97.
[4] Lincoln Barnett, *The Treasure of Our Tongue* (New York: Alfred A Knopf, 1964), p.97, cited in Bryson, *Mother Tongue: The English Language*, 1990, p.50.

live. He takes one of the best known examples of Old English prose, the tale of the fight at Merton in the *Anglo-Saxon Chronicle* entry for AD 755. He says that fourteen of the one hundred words of this passage have gone from English, three (atheling, mickle, yare) are archaic or dialectal, but eighty-three are still in daily use (though sometimes modified in form and meaning).[1]

Robert Claiborne tells how, some years ago, scholars at Brown University in Rhode Island, USA used a computer to work through over a million words of English prose from our day. Their sources were widespread, from scientific papers to sports writing in the daily press. The computer counted over 50,000 different words, and more than half of these were words borrowed from other tongues. He then goes on to tell how the computer was afterwards set up to pick out the words used most often. It was found that every one of the one hundred most common words had English roots. And of the next one hundred, eighty-three were 'home-born'. Furthermore, the English-rooted words that are still with us are words that must be the true 'flesh and bones' of any tongue: personal pronouns (I, you, him, her), verbs of basic doings or states (begin and end, come and go, eat and drink, live and die, love and hate), adjectives which tell of basic qualities (young, old, great, small, high, deep), names of widely found things (earth, dog, stone, water, fire), names of parts of the body (head, ear, eye, nose, mouth), words for blood kinship (father, mother, brother).[2] Besides this Claiborne notes that the syntax of today's English is closer to that of Old English than to any other speech, even those tongues from which we have borrowed most heavily. Claiborne goes on to note that if one works at it hard enough, one can talk and write about many everyday things with only English words. But the opposite cannot be done. No one can talk or write in English, on any matter at all, without drawing on at least some everyday English. '(A)t least half the words in almost any sample of modern English writing will be of Anglo-Saxon origin'.[3]

The English-rooted words are 'heart' words. The borrowed ones are often high-sounding, yet pompous. What, in truth, is the worth of a 'cordial reception'. Would we not much rather have a warm or kindly welcome? And Claiborne reminds us of Winston Churchill's 1940 speech: 'We shall fight on the beaches, we shall fight on the landing grounds, we shall fight in the fields and in the streets, we shall fight in the hills; we shall never surrender' – nearly all English, true and simple. Claiborne also points out how we turn to English in the gravest times of our life on earth. How telling are the solemn, heart-searching words of the old 1662 marriage service ('With this ring I thee wed … to have and to hold from this day forward, for better for worse …'), and how awe-ful the words of the burial service ('Earth to earth, ashes to ashes, dust to dust').

And the inkhorners have not had it all their own way. Although they have named so many of the new things that have become part of life, there are a good many new words around that have been made from Old English roots. Among them are: back-cloth, back-drop, driveway, highlight, input, landfill, lay-by, light-fingered, light-house, overdraft, overdrive, overeat (though this goes back to 1599!), overfly, roadstead, runway, throughput, wavelength and (of all things) the worldwide web.

---

[1] S Potter, *Our Language*, 1966, p.57.

[2] F Bodmer, *The Loom of Language*, 1944, p.182.

[3] Bryson, *Mother Tongue: The English Language*, 1990, pp.50-51.

The game of cricket and its dialect makes a worthwhile case study. Its roots may go back to the Middle Ages, but it did not truly take shape until the eighteenth/nineteenth centuries. At this time there were great lords among its backers – men such as John Sackville, third Duke of Dorset, Sir Horace Mann, and others – who fielded teams, and gambled on the outcome of matches. Yet there are so many English words in cricket's dialect that one must think that the game arose among the common folk. We have innings, follow on, maiden over, mid-off, mid-on, mistime, off-spinner, outfield, overpitch, overthrow, third man, wide, and many more. (The roots of the name 'cricket' itself are not known for sure, though it likely has something to do with the 'crooked' early cricket bat.)

Some Old English words that seem to have died out still live on, embedded in others. The word 'garlic' includes Old English 'gar' meaning 'spear', for garlic is the 'spear-shaped leek. 'Gar' is also found the name of the tool, 'auger'. The Old English word 'moot' (a gathering or meeting), is no longer heard in its own right, but we speak of a 'moot' point, and of something being 'mooted abroad'. The words 'bliss' and 'blithe' are perhaps a little 'olde worlde', yet we still speak of someone being 'blissfully unaware', and of another going 'blithely ahead'. Many words with the 'be-' prefix can seem quaint, but we still say 'Woe betide you, if ... ' The world of theology has taken up the Latin Last 'Judgement' instead of English Doomsday yet, oddly, the non-theological world today speaks of a 'doomsday' scenario. Old English 'couth' is no longer heard, but 'uncouth' is. The early Middle English word 'ruth' (from Old English 'rue'), meaning 'pity', or 'sorrow', is no longer found. But 'ruthless' is. 'Troth', meaning 'faithfulness, keeping one's word', is no longer heard, but we still sometimes speak of a betrothal, and it is not so long ago that a man and a woman 'plighted their troth' at their wedding. 'Hallow' lives on in 'hallowe'en', 'rice' (meaning 'realm', 'province') in bishopric, 'lac' (offering) in wedlock, while 'ræden' (a word connected with 'rædan', meaning 'to counsel') is still around as the abstract ending in hatred and kindred. The word 'reeve' is used in parts of Canada, to mean 'mayor'.[1]

William Barnes (1801-86)

William Barnes, a poet and word-smith who did much of his writing in the Dorset speech, wrote, sorrowfully, that 'we have not a language of our own; but that when we happen to conceive a thought above that of a plough-boy, or produce anything beyond a pitch-fork, we are obliged to borrow a word from others before we can utter it, or give it a name'.[2]

Barnes was a gentle, humble believer in God, the God who was Creator of heaven and earth, of men and beasts. For Barnes it was words that set mankind above the beasts. Words were a sign of the undying soul breathed into man by God's Spirit. And as the purity of a people's speech was a sign of closeness to the Creator, so 'mongrelisation' stemmed from man's sins.[3] He called this mongrelised English

---

[1] Bryson, *Mother Tongue: The English Language*, 1990, p.104.

[2] *Gentlemen's Magazine*, Supp. Vol. CII, 1832, 'On Compounds in the English Language'.

[3] Andrew Phillips, *The Rebirth of England and English: The Vision of William Barnes* (Hockwold-cum-Wilton: Anglo-Saxon Books, 1996), p.107.

'Englandish' – perhaps a play on the word 'outlandish'. Barnes was not against the use of foreign words for foreign things. What he sought to stem was the taking of foreign words for English things.

But Barnes wished to go further, and shape new words from old roots. How did he do this? His way was to seek the make-up of a thing, and then see if he could find English words for it. Thus he would take a Greek word like 'anachronism' (meaning something that does not fit time-wise), and break it down into prefix, stem, suffix. The Greek has the negative prefix 'an-', the stem 'chronos' (time) and the suffix '-ism'. By looking to the English for these parts the word 'mistiming' can be made. 'Untimely' or 'wrong timing' might also take the place of anachronism. By the same approach we can make 'forestall' instead of 'anticipate', 'two-sided' rather than 'bilateral', and 'upshot' rather than 'conclusion'. Barnes found that much could be done with suffixes, and here he called upon German for help. He was much taken with the suffix '-some' (German 'sam'). And as we have words such as awesome, fearsome, handsome, meddlesome, he put forward others of his own making, such as halesome, heedsome, longsome, sparesome (for salubrious, attentive, tedious, frugal).

Next, Barnes would bring back old words that were dying out, words such as maiden (for 'girl'), chapman (for 'merchant'), gleeman (for 'musician') and winsome (for 'pleasant'). He drew on Old English roots for words such as rimecraft ('mathematics'), leechcraft ('medicine'), shamefast ('modest') and soothfast ('veracious'). His own Dorset speech was to him another well from which to draw words such as forewit ('caution'), sprack ('energetic'), beholden ('obliged'), whiver ('vibrate'). Barnes would also extend the meanings of words that were already around. So 'befoul' could have the meaning 'contaminate', 'befriend' could mean 'acquaint', and 'wrangle' could mean 'argue'. And there was almost endless scope for putting together new compound words (a rich source of words in other Germanic tongues). So we have like-minded, quick-witted, whole-hearted, wrong-headed and so on. Those who would can follow Barnes's way and shape new words today.

Barnes did not go 'over the top' in his search for old words and roots. If he truly could not find a fitting English word to hand, then he would take the borrowed one. Among such were 'civilisation', 'river', 'superstition'. He accepted the half-Latin, half-English 'commonwealth'. His 'English' word for the French 'coup de grâce' was 'masterstroke', from Latin 'magister' and English 'stroke'.

Barnes has been taken to task on the ground that in seeking to take the Latin out of English, he simply brought in the German instead. So with phrasal verbs Barnes would often add a particle before the verb, instead of putting it afterwards. It has to be acknowledged that there was some needless word-making. Why 'outbreathe' (for exhale) when we already have 'breathe out', or 'outleave' (for omit) when we have 'leave out', or 'upgather' (for accumulate) when we have 'gather up'? Again, Barnes came up with many English-rooted words, while other English words were still very much alive. Was there truly any need for 'onquicken' (for accelerate) when 'speed up' was there to hand? Or 'fairhood' (for beauty) when we still have 'loveliness', or 'worksome' (for industrious) when we have 'hard-working'? Overall it was said of Barnes's work that dead root words cannot be made to live again, and seeking to bring them back to life only makes one seem quaint.

Yet since Barnes' time one of his key ways of 'word-shapening' – the use of phrasal verbs and nouns – has become widespread. So we have: back up, look down on, put out, run down, and many such others. Also, many true English words have now won a place again, so that they can be readily used instead of Latinisms. So 'highlight' can be used rather than 'emphasise', 'forerunner' can hold its own against 'precursor', 'ins and outs' against 'ramifications', and 'neighbourhood' against 'vicinity'. Others are 'deed' ('action'), 'handbook' ('manual'), 'slanting' ('oblique'), and 'yearly' ('annual').

In 1884 William Barnes set his hand to putting the Queen's Speech (in 'Englandish') into English. The speech began: 'My Lords and Gentlemen, the satisfaction with which I ordinarily release you from discharging the duties of the Session is on the present occasion qualified by a sincere regret that an important part of your labours should have failed to result in a legislative enactment.' William Barnes put it this way: 'The lightheartedness I do mwostly veel when I do let ye off vrom the business upon your hands in the Sessions, is thease time a little bit damped, owen to a ranklen in my mind, that a goodish lot o' your work vell short o' coming into anything lik laws.' This is very winning, yet, much as we may love William Barnes, it has to be said that it will not do. The London government will not thus be turned from their long-windedness. The Whitehall dialect of the first might put the Members to sleep, but the Dorset speech would, like enough, only make them smile. Perhaps this might make them shift a little guiltily on their benches: 'The gladness I mostly feel when I send you away at the end of your Sitting is somewhat lessened this time, as I see that from much business there has come so little law-making.'

Whither now?

Let us not spend a lot of time grieving over might-have-beens, and striving to think of English-rooted words for all the inventions and discoveries of the scientific/industrial age. To hope that folk will readily take up coined Old English names for today's technical wonders, would be unrealistic. No youngster is going to give up his or her mobile and call their friends on a 'hand far-speaker'. Nor are they going to sit down of an evening to watch a film on a 'seespellbox'. And as for scientific and medical wording in English, nearly all of it has been drawn from Latin and Greek, and there is no way that the worlds of science and medicine are going to sit down and re-write their textbooks in English-rooted words. The same would be true of lawyers, accountants and others. It might even be said that the speech of today's common man is 'Englandish', and that the inkhorners have won the day. Those who would put together English-rooted names for new things will, like as not, be mocked as 'linguistic Canutes'. Anyway, who knows how long these new-made things and their new-made words may last? The gramophone is gone, the telegram nearly so, and cassette tapes and videos. So let us not spend overmuch time seeking out English names for things which may be gone, and forgotten, tomorrow.

So what, if anything, can be done? Should we perhaps be glad that 'Englandish', 'mixt and mangeled' though it is, has been so 'successful', has been taken up as a second language by half the world? (Yet one wonders whether that may be a mixed blessing. It seems the time is fast coming when there will be more folk speaking English as their second language than as their first. Will the native speakers then lose control?)

Surely something needs to be done. Through language, men and women touch and share each other's lives. When some men and women, through pride, choose to take up words that others will not know, then the business of language, as a means of human fellowship, is undone. In today's world we surely have more than enough of jargon and 'insider' language. And worse still is the use of words for evasion. The use of hard words to show off one's learning hinders human fellowship. Using them for evasion harms it.

What we might hope for is that if folk are shown how many English words are still around in everyday life, and they can see that they are good words, and do not make the user sound quaint or 'olde worlde', then they will begin to choose English.

Towards an English Wordbook

The words are there. The key asking is, are we willing to stop and think of them? But the stopping and thinking will only happen if we are already alive to which words are Englandish (or 'Anglo-Latin') and which are English. We will have to work at this, but there are some rule-of-thumb helps around. Here are a few:

1) Nearly all words beginning with 'th' will be English – nearly all, but not utterly all. 'Throne' comes from Latin/Greek, and a number of 'th' words are from Old Norse: them, their, they, though, thrift and thrust.

2) Words beginning with 'wh' are English.

3) As already noted words with the 'sk' sound in them are likely to be Old Norse.

4) There are hardly any English words beginning with 'j', and 'v'. 'Jowl' seems to be the only 'j' word, and it goes back to an Old English word that began with a 'c' (ceafl). Vane, vat, and vixen go back to Old English. There are no 'x' or 'z' words (unless one reckons the old oath 'zounds', from the English words 'God's wounds').

5) A prefix (or 'word-heading' as Barnes called it) may at once show us where a word has come from. Words beginning anti-, con-, dis-, ex-, extra-, para-, per-, pre-, pro-, sub-, super-, trans- are going to be Latin. And words beginning be-, for-, fore-, mis-, out-, over-, un-, under- may well be English. We cannot make hard and fast rules here, as a Latin prefix may be added to an English word (to give us such words as 'dishearten'), or an English prefix may be added to a Latin word (to give us 'misplace', 'misuse' and so on). Likewise suffixes may be mismatched in words such as 'laughable' with its Latin ending on an English stem.

In weighing words we may bear a number of things in mind.

First, the Anglo-Saxons themselves borrowed a few hundred Latin and other words, for things they had not met before. There is no shame in borrowing the words for 'camel' and 'lion', for example. These were unknown in the continental homelands of the English. There would be no sense in making up English terms for these beasts, such as the 'woolly cow' or the 'great maned cat'.

Next, many words have been borrowed from Middle Dutch and Middle Low German. There has always been a lot of to-ing and fro-ing across the North Sea to the Low Countries, and there were Dutch merchants settled in East Anglia from the 12th century. Middle Dutch and Middle Low German are close kin to English and some of the borrowings only took the place of English words that were very like them. It would surely be small-minded, and unworkable, to close the door on them. As noted already a lot of these words have to do with the sea and ships.

Third, there are likewise words borrowed from Old Norse, for which there were kindred Old English words. If there is another English word still around, we may use that, but otherwise the Old Norse will do well enough. There are some everyday words of Old Norse root, which we can now hardly get by without. Among them are: ball, birth, call, get, happen, law, lift, loose, low, take, want, weak, wrong.

Fourth, there are words that have been borrowed from Old French, or Old Norman French, but which, further back in time, came from Germanic roots with Old English words akin to them. Among such are: blue, list, shop, stallion, strive and war.

Fifth, there are so-called 'imitative' or 'echoic' words, which seek to get across those sounds not made by man, but which are so much part of man's life – the cries of birds and beasts, the wind in the trees, the upheaval of a storm, the rasping sound of some tool. These words may not be known Old English words (or Latin, Old Norman French, or Old Norse, for that matter), but we may fairly take it that our forebears did have some such words in their speech. Among the imitative words are: cluck, mew, wistful.

Sixth, there are words that have 'clothed themselves in English dress' so to speak. Here again not everyone will say the same. What looks English to one may seem like an 'outsider' to another. Here are some that might be held to be 'English-like': clear, close, delight, dire, dither, farm, fell, fling, glean, hitch, ill, kindle, meddle, midden, prowl, render, rid, rift, round, search, seem, sign, sling, soar, spiteful, sprightly, store, sum, tangle, tend, tender, thrift, thrive, thrust, tight.

Lastly, William Barnes saw that we cannot always find an English word that meets our need. So when we are stuck, let us not fret. Among borrowed words that we can hardly get by without are: date (time), same, sound, story, use, and the suffixes -able and -ment.

In seeking to make words from English roots we have a good stock of what William Barnes called 'fore-ekings' and 'end-ekings' (prefixes and suffixes). Here are examples of such at work:

Fore-eking,	**as in:**
a	abide, ablaze, aglow, alight, aright
be	befriend, benighted, bereave, bewitch
by	bypath, by-way, by-word
even	even-handed
for	forbear, forgive, forgo
fore	foreboding, forefather, foresee, foreshadow
gain	gainsay
half	half-baked, half-brother, half-hearted, half-truth
high	high-flyer, high-handed, high-hearted, high-minded
in	inborn, inbuilt, indwell, input
long	long-hand, long-headed, long-sighted, long-winded
mis	misdeed, mishandle, mislay, mismatch
off	offcut, off-handed, offload, offspring
on	ongoing, onlooker, onset
out	outburst, outdo, outgrow, outlast, outlook
over	overbearing, overcome, overflow, overhead
self	self-forgetful, selfhood, selfless, self-seeking
un	unbidden, unbridled, unearth, unfeeling, unforgiving
under	undergo, underground, undergrowth, underhanded
up	upbringing, upkeep, upright, upstart
well	well-bred, well-known, well-meant, well-read
with	withdraw, withhold, withstand

For end-ekings we have:

End-eking,	**as in:**
-dom	earldom, kingdom, wisdom
-en	awaken, bedridden, beholden, blacken, brazen
-er	breaker, brewer, runner, spinner, walker, winner
-fast	shamefast, steadfast,
-ful	armful, dreadful, fearful, fistful, forgetful
-head	bridge-head, forehead, hot-head, overhead, spearhead
-hood	brotherhood, childhood, fatherhood, knighthood, livelihood
-ing	abiding, amazing, backing, bearing, becoming
-ish	bookish, childish, churlish, hawkish, sheepish
-less	heedless, helpless, homeless, hopeless, lifeless
-like	lifelike, seamanlike, snail-like, summerlike
-ling	darling, duckling, fledgling, nestling
-lock	wedlock
-ly	bitterly, blithely, queenly, smoothly, wildly
-most	bottommost, innermost, outermost, westernmost
-ness	awareness, backwardness, quickness, readiness, rightness
-red	hatred, kindred

-right	downright, forthright, outright
-ship	craftsmanship, dealership, friendship, hardship, kingship
-some	burdensome, fearsome, foursome, loathsome
-ster	harvester, songster, spinster
-teen	thirteen, fourteen, fifteen, sixteen
-ward	backward, homeward, landward, outward, wayward
-way	back-way, bridle-way, doorway, driveway, through-way
-wise	lengthwise, no-wise, otherwise, rightwise
-worthy	newsworthy, roadworthy, seaworthy
-y	blowy, broomy, cheeky, hairy

In seeking to make your own speech and writing more truly English here are ...

A hundred words to start you off

abbreviate	shorten	impetuous	headstrong
abolish	do away with	indolent	idle
abundant	overflowing	inexorable	unforgiving
accelerate	speed up	innocuous	harmless
accomplish	bring about	interpolate	put in
acquire	come by	intolerable	not to be borne
adhere	abide by	irrational	mindless
adjacent	beside	jubilant	gleeful
adroit	deft	laborious	uphill
advantageous	worthwhile	lethargic	listless
afraid	fearful	loquacious	long-winded
agreement	understanding	macabre	grisly
allow	let	magnificent	great
annual	yearly	malevolent	baleful
anticipate	foresee	marvellous	wonderful
appellation	name	meretricious	showy
approximately	about, roughly	meticulous	thoroughgoing
assist	help	miscellaneous	sundry
astonishment	wonder	monotonous	dreary
captivating	bewitching	nefarious	wicked
castigate	lay into	obdurate	pig-headed
cautious	wary	omit	leave out
cease	stop	opulent	rich
commence	begin	ordinary	everyday
commiserate	sorrow with	pacify	soothe
commodious	roomy	paramount	overriding
compile	draw up	parsimonious	mean
comprehend	understand	patronising	talking down

conceal	hide	peculiar	weird
conclude	end	perception	insight
confusing	bewildering	peremptory	overbearing
conscientious	thorough	perpetrate	do
construct	build	postpone	put off
contemplate	think on	precipitate	rash
continuous	ongoing	predict	foretell
contradict	gainsay	preposterous	far-fetched
crucial	key	prescient	far-sighted
deceased	dead	profound	deep
demolish	pull down	prognosis	outlook
despondent	forlorn	querulous	shrewish
deteriorate	worsen	rapacious	greedy
difficult	hard	recalcitrant	wilful
emphasize	drive home	reduce	lessen
erudite	learned	reiterate	dwell on
expressive	well-worded	relinquish	give up
fabulous	wonderful	subside	die down
flourish	do well	temporary	short-lived
frequently	often	terminate	end
habitual	wonted	uncompromising	unyielding
immediately	forthwith	veracious	truthful

And here are some English words to foster:

abide, asunder, behest, beholden, beseech, bethink, bewitching, blithe, chide, cleave, dearth, deft, delve, dwell, forbear, forlorn, forstraught, forthwith, full-nigh, heedful, hitherward, hopelorn, listful, listless, lithe, maiden, mightless, right-hearted, seethe, slither, straightforth, troth, unbeknown, unbethought, unbidden, unfathomed, unhand, unpathed, unquenched, unready, unriddle, unsay, unshifting, unsought, unsped, unwisdom, unwitful, way-lorn, wend, wilsome, windle, winsome, winter-tide, wit-fast, witling, with-yonder, wonder-deed, wonder-wise, word-craft, word-fast, word-winsome, wrest.

At the beginning of this study we noted the English-speaker's abiding love for sound-likeness (alliteration). There is surely room for putting together more phrases of this kind. For 'the whole of something' what about 'beam and bough', using the picture of the tree? Another tree picture which comes to mind is 'root and rind (bark)', instead of 'root and branch' ('branch' being a borrowing from late Latin). And then, drawing on 'sithe', an old word for 'sigh' we might make 'sithing and sorrowing'. Instead of 'a bee in one's bonnet (which is from Old French/Latin) what about 'a bee in one's breeches'? And other lively phrases of mixed roots can be 'Englished'. For 'the lion's share', we might speak of 'the bear's share'. We could speak of a 'loan wolf' instead of a 'shark', note that he had 'a finger in every bowl' (rather than 'pie'), while his doings might 'make the blood seethe' (rather than 'boil').

Booklist

Owen Barfield, *History in English Words* (London: Faber and Faber, 1954)

David J Bernstein, *The Mystery of the Bayeux Tapestry* (London: Weidenfeld and Nicolson, 1986)

PH Blair, *Northumbria in the days of Bede* (London: Book Club Associates, 1976)

Frederick Bodmer, *The Loom of Language* (London: George Allen & Unwin, 1944)

WF Bolton, David Crystal, editors, *The English Language* (London: Penguin Books, 1993)

James Bradstreet Greenough and George Lyman Kittredge, *Words and Their Ways in English Speech* (London: Macmillan, 1901)

Melvyn Bragg, *The Adventure of English* (London: Hodder and Stoughton, 2003)

ed. Carleton Brown, *Religious Lyrics of the XIVth Century* (Oxford, 1924; revised by GV Smithers, 1957)

Andrew Bridgeford, *1066 The hidden history in the Bayeux Tapestry* (NewYork: Walker, 2005)

Bill Bryson, *Mother Tongue: The English Language* (London: Penguin Books, 1990)

Robert Claiborne, *English: Its life and times* (London: Bloomsbury, 1994)

Basil Cottle, *The Triumph of English 1350-1400* (London: Blandford Press, 1969)

David Crystal, *Words Words Words* (Oxford: Oxford University Press, 2006)

ed. Geoffrey Grigson, *Selected Poems of William Barnes* (London: Routledge and Kegan Paul, 1950)

W Funk, *Word Origins and Their Romantic Stories* (New York: Bell Publishing, 1978)

DH Green, *Language and History in the Early Germanic World* (Cambridge: Cambridge University Press, 1998)

L Heller, A Humez, M Dror, *The Private Lives of English Words* (London: Routledge & Kegan Paul, 1984)

WB Lockwood, *The Oxford Dictionary of British Bird Names* (Oxford: Oxford University Press, 1993)

CM Matthews, *Words, Words, Words* (Guildford and London: Lutterworth Press, 1979)

Simeon Potter, *Our Language* (Harmondsworth: Penguin Books, 1966)

A lead-in to the Wordbook

The English wordbook which follows is in two halves, like a foreign language dictionary. The first part holds the English words. The other half lists some 3,600 'Anglo-Latin' words, and puts forward those English words which might be taken in their stead. (I have used 'Anglo-Latin' for all the un-English words, though some of them are from Greek, Norse and elsewhere.)

A few things need to be made plain. First, there are some words in the English Wordhoard which are not wholly 'home-born', but neither are they wholly 'outsiders'. These are borrowed words which have taken the place of English words of close kinship. They number some 140 words in a hoard of some 11,000, and they are marked with a number which tells where they have come from. The numbering works as follows:

1. Middle Low German/Middle Dutch word akin to Old English
2. Old Norse word akin to Old English
3. Old French word of Germanic root, and akin to Old English
4. Germanic borrowing from Latin
5. Old English borrowing from Latin
6. Old English borrowing from Old Celtic, Old British or Gaulish
7. 'Imitative', 'echoic', 'instinctive' or 'symbolic' words

Next, there are a very few cases where a Latin word has been used in a definition, and these have been put in italics (such as, *oil*, *part*).

Third, so as not to put the same words in again and again, a system of key words has been used. These are underlined, and this means that the word underlined will be found in the English half of the wordbook, with more words to choose from.

Fourth, in places a forward slash has been used, to save a little space. Thus the entry 'put right/straight' is short for 'put right, put straight'. A forward slash has also been used when setting out two spellings of the one word, as in 'dean/dene'. Again it has been used when a new word of Old English roots has been used, with the better known Anglo-Latin term beside it, as in earthlore/*geology*.

The following shortenings/abbreviations have been used:

adj.	adjective
adv.	adverb
adv. phr.	adverbial phrase
conj.	conjunction
intj.	interjection
n.	noun
prep.	preposition
v.	verb

An English Wordhoard

aback, abackward *adv.* backwards, behind, hindward. to be taken **aback** *v.* to be brought to a stand, floored, <u>shaken</u>, speechless.

abide *v.* 1) to bide, dwell, have/make one's home in, live, go on being, put up at, settle at, still be, 2) to bear with, brook, fall in with, forbear, go along with, go/swim with the stream, not mind, put up with, see no harm in, stand, swallow, 3) to fight on, go on, hold fast, hold/keep/stand one's ground or footing, hold on/out, keep at, keep going, keep on, not give up, not yield, outlast, see it through, stand fast, stand shoulder to shoulder, steel oneself, stick at, <u>withstand</u>.

abide by *v.* to be true to, hold to/stand by one's word.

abiding *adj.* 1) deathless, endless, everlasting, lasting, long-lasting, outlasting, longstanding, never-ending, <u>steadfast</u>, timeless, undying, unending, without end, 2) holding, <u>unyielding</u>.

abidingly *adv.* forebearingly, lastingly, steadfastly, trothfully.

ablaze *adj.* 1) afire, alight, blazing, <u>bright</u>, burning, on fire, 2) hot, wild.

aboard *adv. prep.* on board ship.

abode *n.* dwelling, home, homestead, <u>house</u>, household, steading.

about 1) *prep.* beside, near, nearby, on, 2) *adv.* more or less, roughly, everywhere, 3) *adj.* astir, stirring.

above 1) *prep.* higher than, more than, over, better than, beyond, before, 2) *adv.* overhead, upward, foregoing.

above all *adv.* above all things, before/beyond everything, beyond telling/weighing, first and foremost, first of all, the more so, most of all, over and above, fully, overly, truly, utterly, wholly.

above board 1) *adj.* <u>forthright</u>, <u>open</u>, upright, 2) *adv.* <u>forthrightly</u>, openly, truly.

above-written *adj.* ere-written, fore-written.

abreast *adv.* alongside, beside, side by side, neck and neck, shoulder to shoulder.

abroad *adv.* beyond the sea, outside, overseas, about, everywhere, here and there.

accurse *v.* to lay a curse upon someone, beshrew, blast, pitch into, thunder against.

accursed *adj.* baleful, baneful, dreadful, <u>evil</u>, foul, hateful, hellish, <u>loathsome</u>.

achare *adj.* ajar, open a little.

ache *n.* 1) aching, belly/ear/head/tooth-ache, 2) heartache, heartbreak, <u>sorrow</u>.

ache, ake *v.* to be sore, gnaw at one, harrow, tear at one, wring.

ache for *v.* to <u>long for</u>, burn/hunger/thirst for, list, <u>sorrow</u>, yearn after.

aching *n.* gnawing ache, heartache, <u>longing</u>, harrowing, <u>sorrow</u>, <u>worry</u>.

acknowledge *v.* 1) to own, own up, come out with the truth, come out into the open, come clean, tell all, speak the truth, make a clean breast of, put down to, set down to, unbosom, unburden, 2) to believe, fall in with, go along with, see, know, 3) to answer, come back to, write back, 4) to bring to the fore, give thanks, hold up, thank, show one's thanks, mark, put in a good word for, speak highly/warmly/well of.

acorn *n.* the mast or seed of the oak-tree.

acorn meal *n.* oak meal.

acre *n.* the land which a yoke of oxen could plough in a day, later set at 'a *plot* of land 40 poles long by four broad' (220 yards by 22 yards, or 4,840 *square* yards).

adder *n.* snake.

addle *v.* to addle the wits, <u>bewilder</u>, unman.

addled *adj.* awry, <u>bewildered</u>, dizzy, empty-headed, flighty, giddy, wandering.

addle-head *n.* clod, feather-head, half-wit, lackwit, witling, soft-head, know-nothing.

ado *n.* much ado, a to-do, a stir.

adze *n.* axe-like tool with the blade 'at elbows' to the handle.

afar *adv.* far, from far.

afeard *adj.* <u>fearful</u>, frightened, dreading, numbed with fear, in a cold sweat.

afford *v.* 1) to further, 2) to let, give.

affright *n.* fright, dread, cold feet, fear.

affrighten *v.* to frighten, fill with <u>fear</u>, shake, chill with fear.

afield *adv.* on the field, in the field, to the field, away from home.

afire *adj.* 1) ablaze, alight, on fire, blazing, burning, 2) aglow, fiery, hot, quick, wild.

afloat *adv. adj.* 1) at sea, 2) having one's head above water, still in business.

aflutter *adv.* in a flutter.

afoot *adv.* 1) on foot, 2) astir, going forward.

aforehand *adj.* ready beforehand.

aforesaid *adj.* abovesaid, beforesaid, earlier, foregoing, fore-spoken, fore-written.

aforetime *adv.* before in time, formerly.

after 1) *adj.* next, later, 2) *adv.* behind, later in time, next following.

afterclap *n.* thunderclap, the unforeseen, the unlooked-for.

aftercomers *n.* <u>afterkin</u>, after-folk, afterspring.

after-days *n.* the time to come.

after-folk *n.* aftercomers, <u>afterkin</u>, afterspring.

afterglow *n.* the glow left in the west for a while after sunset, after-shine.

after-grass *n.* grass which grows after the first crop has been gathered.

after-growth *n.* aftermath.

afterhand *adv.* afterwards, at a later time.

afterkin (*descendant/s*) *n.* aftercomer/s, afterfolk, afterspring, child, children, son, daughter, young, house, household, kindred, kinsfolk, kinsman, kinswoman, kith and kin, next of kin, offshoot, shoot/s, offspring, one's flesh and blood, seed, the unborn.

after-knowledge *n.* afterthought, hindsight, later thought.

after-life *n.* 1) life after death, the next life, 2) a later time in one's earthly life.

After-litha (*July*) *n.* Meadow-month.

afterly (*second*) *adj.* other.

aftermath *n.* 1) grass-crop after the first mowing in early summer, 2) outcome.

aftermost *adj.* hindmost, last in time.

after-shine *n.* afterglow.

afterspring *n.* 1) aftercomers, afterfolk, <u>afterkin</u>, 2) another spring-time.

afterthought *n.* later thought, hindsight.

aftertime *n.* the time to come.

afterward/s *adv.* after, afterhand, after that, at a later time, following that, thereafter.

after-wise *adj.* wise only afterwards (when what is done is done).

after-wit *n.* knowledge/thoughts/wisdom that come to one only after a deed is done.

afterword (*postscript*) *n.* afterwriting, aftersaying, end-saying.

after-world *n.* the world to come (after the end of time).

after-writing (*postscript*) *n.* afterword.

After-yule (*January*) *n.* Wolf-month.

again *adv.* 1) anew, another time, once more, 2) besides, <u>furthermore</u>, moreover.

against *prep.* 1) over against, near, 2) set against, gainstanding.

againward *adv.* back again, once more, on the other hand.

aghast *adj.* 1) <u>fearful</u>, frightened, 2) <u>shaken</u>, utterly amazed, taken aback.

aglow *adv.* ablaze, afire, <u>bright</u>, gleaming, glowing, shining.

ago, agone 1) *adj.* gone by, 2) *adv.* long ago, in time long gone, long since.

aground *adv.* (of a ship) beached, grounded, high and dry, stranded, stuck.

ahead *adv.* forwards, onwards, in the lead, leading, winning, henceforth, hereafter.

aheap *adv.* all of a heap.

ahind *adv.* behind.

ahungered *adj.* hungry.

ail *v.* 1) to be unwell, 2) to harrow, worry.

ailing *adj.* laid up, on one's back, sick, sickening, under the weather, unwell.

ait, eyot *n.* small *river* island.

ajar *adv.* (of a door) open a little.

akin *adv. adj.* of the same kindred, alike.

alack *intj.* woe!

alack *adv.* lacking.

albeit *conj.* although, even if, even though, though, notwithstanding.

alder *n.* tree.

alderman *n.* a lord, reeve, elder.

ale *n.* beer (of the lighter-hued kind).

ale-bench *n.* beer-settle, meadbench, meadsettle.

ale-house *n.* house where ale is sold.

alight *v.* 1) to climb down, step down, leave, 2) to come to rest, land, light, settle.

alight *v.* to lighten.

alight *v.* to light up.

alight *adj.* ablaze, afire, on fire, lighted, lit up.

alighting (*allusion*) *n.* aside, half-word, hint, sideways word, word-play.

alike *adj.* like one another.

alike *adv.* in the like way.

alikewise *adj.* truly alike.

alive *adj.* 1) alive and well, in life, living, fully awake, 2) afire, aglow, quick.

alive with *adj.* coming thick and fast, ever so many, swarming, teeming.

all 1) *adj.* every, (also as a strengthener, as in 'all-bright' meaning truly bright, 'all-good' meaning truly good), 2) *n.* the whole, 3) *adv.* all through, even, wholly.

allay *v.* 1) to lay down, set aside, 2) to quell, overthrow, 3) to <u>lighten</u>, <u>soothe</u>, smooth, soften, spare, take the sting out, quench.

all-crafty *adj.* almighty.

All-Father *n.* God.

all-fathoming *adj.* full, full-length, hearty, wholehearted.

all-golden *adj.* all of gold.

All-Hallows Day *n.* All *Saints* Day.

allheal (*panacea*) *n.* heal-all.

all-holding (*universal*) *adj.* far-stretching, for all, widespread, worldwide, wholesale.

All-holy *n.* God the utterly holy

allness *n.* oneness, the whole.

all-new *adj.* utterly new.

all out *adv.* wholly, whole-heartedly.

all over *adv.* over the whole of.

all right *adj.* fair, good enough, middling, pretty good, up to the mark, worthy.

all-time *adj.* unmatched.

all-whither *adv.* every way.

all-whole *adj.* outright, out-and-out, sheer, thorough, thorough-going, utter.

All-wielder, the Almighty *n.* God.

almighty *adj.* all-crafty, great.

almost *adv.* full-nigh, more or less, nearing, nearly, not far off, roughly, well-nigh.

alone *adj. adv.* bereft, by oneself, friendless, lonely, lonesome, out on a limb.

along 1) *adv.* ahead, forwards, onwards, 2) *prep.* beside, near, down, up, through, from end to end of.

alongside *prep.* along, along with, beside, near, next to.

aloud *adv.* in loud speech, loudly.

already 1) *adj.* fully ready, 2) *adv.* before now, by now, even now, by this time, heretofore.

also *adv.* as well as, besides, moreover, furthermore, likewise.

although[2] *conj.* acknowledging that, even if, even though, though, notwithstanding.

altogether *adj. adv.* all told, in all, all in all, on the whole.

alway *adv.* throughout all time.

always *adv.* 1) all the time, every time, evermore, everlastingly, endlessly, forever, for all time, till the end of time, 2) anyway, however, nevertheless, now, still.

amain *adv.* in/with full strength, at full speed, much.

amaze *v.* to bewilder, make speechless, overcome, shake, startle, smite/strike dumb, burst upon, come like a thunderclap, take aback, take one's breath away.

amazed *adj.* bewildered, floored, overcome, shaken, speechless, struck dumb.

amazing *adj.* beyond belief, breathtaking, overwhelming, startling, wonderful. **amazingly** *adv.* bewilderingly, overwhelmingly, wonderfully.

amid, amidst *adv.* in the middle, among.

amid, amidst *prep.* in the middle of, in the thick of, amongst, at a time of.

aminded *adj.* minded, in the mind for.

amiss *adj.* all anyhow, awry, at sixes and sevens.

amissing *adj.* missing.

ammer (*bunting*) *n.* yellowhammer.

among, amongst *prep.* amidst, in the midst of, with, between, to, with one another.

among *adv.* betweenwhiles, together.

anchor[4] *n.* 1) ship's hook or claw, 2) backbone, mainstay, strong ground.

anchor[4] *v.* 1) to let go the ship's hook or claw, 2) to bind, bolt, fasten, tie.

and *conj.* also, as well as, along/together with, besides, furthermore, moreover.

anent *prep.* 1) over against, 2) about, as to.

anew *adv.* once more, in a new way, newly.

angel[4] *n.* 1) (heavenly) word-bearer, word-bringer, 2) apple of one's eye, beloved, darling, dear, dear heart, dear one, dearest, lamb.

angle *n.* fish-hook.

angle *v.* 1) to fish, 2) to be after, hunt, run after, seek to take, stalk, woo.

angler *n.* fisherman.

angling *n.* fishing.

anigh *adv.* nigh, near to.

anon ('on one') *adv.* at once, forthwith, now, shortly, soon, straightaway.

another *adj.* 1) a further, one more, 2) *pron.* other, another of like worth/weight.

answer *n.* the why and wherefore, shift, makeshift.

answer *v.* 1) to give answer, say in answer, acknowledge, write back, 2) to have an answer, cut the ground from under, floor, give the lie to, override, overthrow, show up, stop the mouth, sweep aside, 3) to meet (a need), match, fulfil.

ant *n.* emmet.

ant-heap, ant-hill, ant-hillock *n.* emmet-hill.

anvil *n.* the iron stand on which a blacksmith hammers and shapes his work.

anvil *v.* to shape on an anvil, to work at an anvil.

any *adj.* a bit of, crumb of, speck of, every, whichever, anybody, anyone.

anybody *n.* anyone, a soul.

anyhow *adv.* 1) anyway, in any way, for all that, nonetheless, still, 2) carelessly.

anyone *n.* anybody, a soul.

anything *n.* a thing of any kind.

anyway *adv.* anyhow, in any way, for all that.

anywhence *adv.* from anywhere.

anywhere *adv.* in any steading.

anywhither *adv.* to or towards any steading.

anywise *adv.* in any way, at all.

ape *n.* wild *beast* of the *monkey* kind.

ape *v.* to behave like, do likewise, follow, make oneself like, put on.

apple *n.* the yield of the apple-tree.

apple-ale (*cider*) *n.* apple-drink.

apple-blight *n.* a *cotton*-like growth found on trees.

apple-fallow *adj.* yellowish-red, reddish-brown.

apple-grey *adj.* streaky, alike to the apple in hue.

apple-thorn (*crab* apple) *n.* sour appletree, wilding, wood-apple.

apple-tree *n.* tree yielding apples.

apple-yard *n.* paddock with apple-trees.

aquerne/acwern (*squirrel*) *n.* tree-rat.

a-quiver *adj.* all of a flutter, overwrought, restless, wild, worked up.

areach *v.* to reach, get at (with a weapon), get hold of, come by.

aread, arede, areed *v.* 1) to make known, 2) to foresee, warn, 3) to deem.

aready *adv.* in readiness.

arear *v.* to set up, to stir someone against. sea.

armful *n.* as much as one or both arms can hold, a heap, a lot.

arm-hole *n.* the hole in clothing for the arm to go through.

arrow *n.* the tipped shaft shot from a bow, a bolt.

arrow-head *n.* the sharp flint or iron head of an arrow.

arrow-slit *n.* narrow window through which arrows may be shot.

arrow-smith *n.* arrow-maker.

arse *n.* backside, behind, bottom, buttocks.

as *conj.* at the time that, when, while.

as *prep.* because, in the way that, like, seeing that, under the name of.

ash *n.* a broadleaved hedgerow and woodland tree. Spear-shafts were made from it. In northern lore it was the great 'tree of life' whose head reached to heaven and its roots to hell.

ash, ashes *n.* the 'dust' left after a fire has burned itself out, cinders, embers.

ashamed *adj.* 1) forshamed, put to shame, shown up, 2) shamefast, sheepish, shrinking, shrinking back, overshy, loath.

to be **ashamed** *v.* to be sorry about, feel shame, rue, wish undone.

ashen *adj.* of the ash-tree, made from its wood.

ashen *adj.* ashy, grey, hueless, leaden, wan, white, 'like death warmed up'.

ash-holt *n.* spear.

ashling *n.* ash sapling.

ash-play (*battle*) *n.* spear-play, spear-storm.

ash-rind *n.* the rind (*bark*) of the ash tree.

ash-stead *n.* field of fighting.

Ash-Wednesday *n.* the Wednesday marking the beginning of Lent (so known because ashes are sprinkled on the brows of worshippers on that day).

ashy *adj.* ashen, grey, leaden, wan, white.

aside *n.* alighting, half-word, hint, word-play, sideways word (*allusion*).

aside *adv.* to one side, a little way off.

ask *v.* 1) to ask earnestly, beg, beset, bid for, crave, knock at the door, make bold to ask, go down on one's knees, seek, sigh at one's feet, 2) to delve/go deep into, look into, seek an answer.

aright *adv.* rightly, in a right way.

arise *v.* 1) to rise up, stand up, spring up, 2) to grow higher, swell up, 3) to begin, befall, come about, come to light, follow from, start, spring forth, go upward.

arm *n.* 1) upper limb, 2) might (as 'might of the law'), strength, tool (as 'tool of *central government*'), 3) sleeve, 4) offshoot, arm of the

asking *n.* asking about, begging, beseeching, craving, delving, seeking, sifting.

asleep *adv. pred. adj.* sleeping, fast asleep, in a deep sleep, slumbering.

asp *n.* earlier name of the aspen tree.

aspen *n.* asp, firwood tree, quick-beam, quick-tree.

asp-rind *n.* rind (*bark*) of the aspen.

assent *adj.* sent for, sent forth.

as soon *adv.* at once, betimes, forthwith, now, shortly, soon, straightway.

astir *v.* to stir up, awaken, quicken, spur, hearten.

astir *adv.* stirring, a-doing, awakened, restless, up and doing.

astraddle, astride *adv. prep.* bestriding, in the saddle.

asunder *adj.* rent in two, torn in two, sundered, lonely.

asunder *v.* to sunder, put asunder.

as well as also, besides, moreover, furthermore, likewise, along with, together with.

at *prep.* by, in, near, through, as far as, towards, against.

atheldom (*aristocracy*) *n.* high kindred.

atheling (*prince*) *n. adj.* son of the kingly house, lord, high lord, lordly.

athelness (*nobility*) *n.* high standing/worth, knightliness, lordliness, uprightness.

at home *adv.* at one's home, in one's own land, 'thoroughly understanding what one is about'.

at once *adv.* anon, betimes, forthwith, quickly, soon, straightaway.

at one *adv.* in friendship, oneness of feeling, of one mind.

atone for *v.* to answer for, buy back, free from guilt, set free, settle, unbind.

at-oneness *n.* goodwill, understanding, wholeness.

atop *adv. prep.* above, on/at the top of, over, upon.

atter (*poison*) *n.* bane, bitterness, blight, curse, evil, wormwood.

attercop *n.* spider.

auger *n.* a woodcraftman's tool for making holes in wood.

aught *adj. adv.* 1) anything, anything whatever, 2) anything worth, worthy, 3) at all.

aurochs[1] *n.* the great ox of old, the weosand.

awake *adj.* awake to, wide awake, wakeful, all ears, all eyes, alive to, aware, having one's wits about one, <u>heedful</u>, keeping a look-out, mindful, missing nothing, on one's toes, on the look-out, on the stretch, on the watch, open-eyed, prick-eared, <u>ready</u>, restless, <u>sharp</u>, sharp-eyed, sleepless, unsleeping, watchful, watching.

awaken *v.* to waken, wake up, quicken, spark, spur, stir up, <u>hearten</u>.

aware *adj.* 1) knowing full well, 2) <u>wise</u>, understanding, quick, <u>sharp</u>, shrewd.

be/become **aware** of *v.* to come to <u>know</u>, <u>heed</u>, pick up, see it all, <u>understand.</u>

awareness *n.* <u>wisdom</u>, forethought, insight, understanding, wit.

awash *adj.* drowned, flooded, knee-deep in, overwhelmed.

away *adv.* gone away, not at home, nowhere to be seen, out.

awaywards *adj.* wayward.

aweary *adj.* dead-beat, fordone, full weary, limb-weary, <u>weary</u>.

awhile *adv.* for a while, for a little while, for a short time.

awl *n.* a small tool for making holes in leather (or sometimes wood).

awry *adj.* all anyhow, at sixes and sevens, cluttered, tousled, <u>untidy</u>, upside down.

axe *n.* wood-bill.

axe *v.* to cut back, end, <u>stop</u>, throw out, wind up.

axe, ax-tree *n. axle.*

back *n.* 1) back (of a living body), 2) back end, end, other side, 3) ridge.

back *adj.* at the back, backmost, hindmost, behind, earlier, end.

back *v.* 1) to help, side with, stand behind, 2) to gamble by laying *money* on such as a horse or dog.

back *adv.* backwards, again, away, ago, before, earlier.

backache *n.* aching of the back (through hard work, or through a wrench).

back away *v.* to back off, draw back, give ground, pull back, withdraw, <u>yield</u>.

back-bencher *n.* one who sits in *parliament*, but not on the fore-bench with the leaders.

backbite *v.* to blacken, <u>smear</u>, speak evil of, speak foully of.

backbiter *n.* gossip, shrew.

backbiting *n.* evil-speaking, gossiping, hard words, smearing, whispering.

back-board 1) the side of a ship which is to the left hand of the steersman, 2) a board set at the back of anything (such as a wain), 3) a board set on the rim of a water-wheel to stop water running off the floats into the inside of the wheel.

back-board side *n. larboard* side of a ship.

backbone *n.* 1) ridge-bone, 2) heart, mainstay, 3) doughtiness, <u>steadfastness</u>.

back-breaking *adj.* crippling, draining, hard going, tiring, wearing, wearying.

back-door *n.* 1) door at the back of a building, 2) an unworthy hidden way.

back down[6] *v.* to give in, withdraw, <u>yield</u>.

backdrop *n.* backcloth, background.

backed *adj.* having a back, backing, background.

back-end *n.* 1) hinder of two ends, 2) late summer or winter, last days of the year.

backer *n.* <u>friend</u>, helper, henchman, right-hand man, upholder.

backfire *v.* 1) (of an *engine* or *firearm*) to start or go off too soon, 2) (of things one sought to do) to come to naught/nothing, do no good, go awry, misfire.

backflow *n.* the flowing back of water from a *river* into a side-arm or backwater.

backfriend *n.* truthless friend, a foe who does not come out into the open.

backgate *n.* gate at the back of a yard.

background *n.* 1) ground lying behind/beyond, 2) backcloth, backdrop, grounding, upbringing.

backhanded *adj.* not straight or wholly true, deep, <u>knotted</u>, two-edged, two-horned.

backing *n.* 1) blessing, help, helping hand, upholding, willing help, 2) underlay.

back-made *adj.* of a *seeming* root-word made from one which looks to have come from it (though in truth it has not).

backmost *adj.* hindmost.

back off *v.* to back away, draw back, pull back, withdraw, <u>yield</u>.

back out *v.* to back off from, draw back, drop out, give up, pull out, withdraw, <u>yield</u>.

back-rest *n.* backing, bolster.

back room *n.* 1) room at the back of a building, 2) room where key work is done.

backside *n.* behind, bottom, buttocks.

backslide *v.* to fall away, slide back to old ways.

backstairs 1) *n.* stairs at the back of a house, 2) *adj.* of underhand dealings.

back-time (back-*date*) *v.* to put an earlier *date* on a *letter* or other writing, to set an earlier *date* for the beginning of something (such as a *pay* rise) now brought in.

back-to-back *adj.* following hard on one another, truly nearby.

back-stroke *n.* giving back stroke for stroke, a backhanded stroke.

back up *v.* to back, <u>help</u>, side with, stand behind, stand up for, underwrite, uphold.

back-up *n.* backing, friendship, help, stand-by, stand-in, stay.

back-ward *n.* after-watch.

backward *adv.* abackward, behind one, hindward, towards one's back.

backward *adj.* 1) headed towards the back of (or behind) something, headed the other way, set at the back of something, 2) downward, for the worse, 3) half-witted, slow, slow-witted, thick-headed, 4) holding back, shamefast, sheepish, shrinking, shy, overshy, 5) lacking, late, slow-growing, unfledged, ungrown.

backwardness *n.* slowness, thick-headedness, unsharpness.

backwards *adv.* abackward, hindward, towards one's back.

backwash *n.* the outgoing of a wave (after breaking on the strand).

backwater *n.* 1) stretch of still water by a *river* and fed from it at the further end by a backflow, 2) the backwoods, back of beyond, a sleepy town, 'the sticks'.

back-way *n.* a way at/to the back, a bypath.

back-word *n.* 1) going back from what one has said, breaking one's word, 2) a rough answer.

back-wording (back *formation*) *n.* back-made word.

bad *adj.* evil, black-hearted, evil-minded, foul, loathsome, wicked, worthless.

badly *adv.* dreadfully, fearfully, foully, frightfully, shamefully, wickedly, woefully.

badness *n.* evil, misdoing, sinfulness, ungodliness, unrightness, wickedness.

bairn *n.* young child.

bairn-less *adj.* childless.

bake *v.* to ready food (most often bread) by dry heat.

bakemeat (*pastry*) *n.* sweetmeat.

baker *n.* one who bakes bread and the like.

bald *adj.* 1) baldheaded, bald on top, 2) forthright, outright, straightforward.

baldly *adv.* straight out, without softening one's words.

baldness *n.* baldheadedness.

bale *adj.* 1) busy with evil, 2) sorrowing.

bale *n.* evil, harm, woe.

bale-fire *n.* a great fire on open ground, a beacon-fire, bonfire.

baleful *adj.* baneful, bodeful, deadly, dreadful, evil, forbidding, frightening, threatening, wyrdful.

ball[(2)] *n.* clew, bead, drop.

ban *v.* to black, drive away/out, hunt/shut/throw out, outlaw, send away, warn off.

ban *n.* curse, doom, lock-out, spurning.

bane *n.* bitterness, blight, burden, curse, evil, woe, stone/weight about one's neck.

baneful *adj.* baleful, dreadful.

banns (for a wedding) *n.* forthtelling, making known, spreading abroad.

bare *adj.* 1) cold, dreary, empty, forsaken, hard, lonely, pathless, stony, wild, 2) naked, stripped, unclothed, unclad, naked as the day one was born, without a stitch on.

bare *v.* to strip off, unclothe.

barefoot *adj.* unshod, without shoes.

bare-headed *adj.* with the head bare, without a hat.

barely *adv.* baldly, hardly, narrowly, only.

bark *n.* the sharp *cry* of hounds, foxes.

bark *v.* to make a sharp *cry*.

barley *n.* a 'bearded' (*awned*) crop, from which ale and barley bread are made.

Barley-month (*September*) *n.* Harvest-month, Holy-month.

barm *n.* yeast, leaven.

barn *n.* byre.

barn-owl *n.* screech owl, scritch owl, lich owl.

barrow *n.* hillock, low.

barrow *n.* hand-barrow.

bat *n.* stick.

bat *v.* to strike with a bat.

bat-and-ball[(2)] (*cricket*) *n.* stockball.

batch *n.* heap, lot.

bath *n.* 1) trough of water in which to wash the body, 2) the business of bathing.

bath *v.* to give someone a bath.

bath-cloth *n.* *towel*.

bathe *v.* to wash, cleanse.

batsman *n.* *cricket* player seeking both to keep his *wicket* and to make runs.

batting *n.* the business of batting and run-making.

baxter *n.* baker.

be *v.* to become, breathe, live, be alive, come about, befall.

beach *n.* sea-rim, seaside, sands, strand.

beach *v.* to come to rest, land, run aground, run up on to the strand.

beached *adj.* aground, grounded, high and dry, stranded, stuck.

beacon *n.* 1) marker, token, 2) beacon-fire, warning-light, watch-fire.

bead *n.* dot, drip, dewdrop, drop, tear.

be-all *n.* that which makes up the whole.

beam *n.* 1) tree, 2) building timber.

beam *n.* gleam/shaft of light, light-beam.

beam and bough *adv. phr.* fully, thorough, wholly, root and rind.

beaming *adj.* aglow, glowing, gleaming, glistening, shimmering, shining.

bean *n.* the smooth seed of some plants, such as broad bean, runner bean.

bear *v.* 1) to bring, hold, shoulder, take, 2) to bear oneself, behave, 3) to abide, bear up under, bear with, brook, go through, put up with, withstand, 4) to give birth to, bring forth, give forth, yield.

bear *n.* a strong, heavily-built *beast* of the wild.

beard *n.* hair that grows about the chin and lips, bristles.

beard *v.* 1) to become bearded, 2) to go against openly, set at naught.

bearded *adj.* having a beard, bristly, hairy, shaggy, unshaven.

beardless *adj.* green, raw, underfledged.

bear down[6] **on** *v.* to come near to, draw near to.

bearer *n.* load-handler, runner, shield-bearer, word-bearer.

bearing *n.* 1) bringing, shouldering, 2) the way one holds oneself, behaviour, 3) withstanding, 4) bringing forth, yielding, 5) the *sum* of the *degrees* (of the *compass*) between one *point* within sight and another *point* set beforehand.

bearing *adj.* of that which bears.

bear in mind *v.* to bethink, think about, deem, look on as.

bear-like *adj.* strong, rough, uncouth, glowering.

bear out *v.* to back up, help, side with, stand behind, stand up for, strengthen, uphold.

bear up *v.* to abide, withstand.

bear upon *v.* to tell upon, work upon, override.

bear with *v.* to abide, brook, forbear, put up with.

bear witness *v.* to say out, say outright, set down, set forth, speak out, speak up, deem, dwell on, drive home, go as far as, highlight, hold, lay down, swear on oath.

beat *v.* 1) to beat down, cudgel, hammer, knock, pound, strike, thrash, 2) to beat back, beat off, fell, outdo, overcome, overthrow, strike down, undo, worst.

beat *adj.* work-weary.

beat about *v.* to go back and forth, hedge, hold back, hold off, play for time.

beat back *v.* to drive back/off, overcome, put to flight, withstand, worst.

beat down[6] *v.* to knock down, overcome, quell, strike down, thrash.

beaten *adj.* worsted, outdone, bowed, broken-hearted, unmanned.

beating *n.* 1) hammering, hiding, pounding, thrashing, 2) downfall, overthrow.

beat off *v.* to drive back/off, outplay, overcome, put to flight, worst.

beat up *v.* to break, knock down, overcome, strike down, thrash, throw down, worst.

beaver *n.* a *beast* of both land and water having strong biting teeth.

beaver away *v.* to keep at it, keep one's nose to the grindstone, sweat, work hard.

beck *n.* nod, bow.

beckon *v.* to nod or wave to someone (to bid him/her come or draw near).

becloud *v.* 1) to cloud over, 2) to darken, hide, hood, shade, shroud, smother.

become *v.* to arise, come about.

becoming *adj.* 1) comely, goodly, well-shaped, 2) answering to, aright, cut out for, in keeping, meet, right, the done thing, worthy.

becomingness *n.* bearing, fair-speaking, loveliness, queenliness, winning ways.

bed *n.* 1) bedstead, 2) bottom, ground, sea-bed, stream-bed, 3) (in earthlore/ *geology*) layer of *rock*.

bed-clothes *n.* bedding, linen, bed linen, sheets.

bedding *n.* bed-clothes.

bedelve *v.* to bury.

bed-fast *adj.* bedridden, crippled, laid up, sick.

bedraggled *adj.* awry, tousled, unkempt, untidy, drenched, dripping, sodden.

bedridden *adj.* bed-bound, bed-fast, crippled, laid up, on one's back.

bedroom *n.* bower, sleeping bower.

bedside 1) *n.* the floor at the side of a bed, 2) *adj.* alongside or near a bed.

bed-sitting-room, bed-sitter *n.* bedroom and living room all in one.

bedspread *n.* bed-cloth.

bedstead *n.* bed.

bedtime *n.* the time for going to bed.

bee *n.* a small *winged beast* that busily makes wax and hoards honey.

beech *n.* broad-leaved tree.

beechen *adj.* of the beech tree, made of beech wood.

beech-holt *n.* a small beech wood.

beech-mast *n.* the nut crop of the beech tree.

beech-rind (*paper*) *n.* the rind (*bark*) of the beech tree.

beech-staff (*letter*, *character*) *n.* a written mark standing for a speech-*sound*.

beehive *n.* the home of a swarm of bees.

bee-keeper *n.* one who rears bees.

beer[4] *n.* strong drink, brew, ale.

bees-wax *n.* the wax made by bees for the comb.

beetle *n.* tool for driving wedges.

beetle *n.* small *winged beast*.

befall *v.* to arise, begin, betide, come about, fall out, follow from.

befit *v.* to become, be worthy, behove, be one's right, be fair to one.

befold *v.* to lead/drive sheep into a fold.

before *adv. prep.* above, ere.

beforehand *adv.* ahead, earlier, foregoing, in the lead, further on.

beforesaid *adj.* abovesaid, aforesaid, earlier, foregoing, fore-spoken, fore-written.

beforetime *adv.* in former time.

befoul *v.* to beslime, drag down, foul, harm, mar, teach wickedness, twist, warp.

befriend *v.* to give friendship, make friends with, warm to.

beg *v.* to <u>ask</u> earnestly, beseech, crave, go down on one's knees, make bold to ask.

beget *v.* to father a child, to bring forth a child.

beggar *n.* broken man, have-not, starveling, leech, toady.

beggar *v.* to make a beggar of, cut off, fleece, leave one penniless.

beggarly *adj.* broken, idle, mean, worthless.

begin *v.* 1) to arise, make a beginning, burst forth, come into the world, come out, open, spring forth, spring up, start, go to it, set to, set to work, 2) to break new ground, bring about, lead off, lead the way, open, put to work, set about, set going, set on foot, set up, sow, start off/up.

beginner *n.* learner, follower, greenhorn.

beginning *n.* birth, cradle, opening, outset, rise, spring, springhead, start, womb.

beginningless *adj.* from before the world was made, from everlasting.

begird *v.* to gird/ring about, hedge/hem/keep/lock/shut in.

begirt *adj.* girded about.

begone 1) *adj.* gone, 2) *v.* go away!

begotten *adj.* brought into being, fathered.

behalf *n.* 1) in the name of, 2) for the sake of, for the good of, on the side of.

behave *v.* to bear oneself, behave oneself, behave towards, lead one's life.

behead *v.* to strike off the head, put to death, kill.

behest *n.* bidding, say-so, word, writ.

behind *adv.* abackwards, after, hindward.

behindhand *adv.* after time, behind time, belated, late, unready.

behither *prep. adv.* 1) on this side of, short of, 2) on the nearer side.

behold *v.* 1) to hold by, hold on, 2) to eye, look at, see, watch, witness.

behold *intj.* look now!

beholden *adj.* bound, bounden, ever thankful, sworn.

beholdenness see 'beholdingness'.

beholder *n.* one who looks/sees, watcher, witness.

beholdingness *n.* plighted word, rightly owing.

behoof *n.* 1) blessing, godsend, good, worth, 2) what is up to one.

behove *v.* to belong to, fall to, be fair to one, be owed, lie, rest on one's shoulders.

being *n.* life, living, living thing, soul.

belated *adj.* behindhand, running late, late in the day, long about it, slow.

belay (*besiege*) *v.* to begird, beset, cut off, gird/ring about, hedge/hem/shut in.

belch *n.* the belching of wind.

belch *v.* to throw out wind loudly from the belly.

beleave *v.* to <u>leave</u> behind, leave high and dry, forsake, throw over, walk out on.

belie *v.* 1) to begird, gird about, beset, hedge in, lie about, ring about, 2) to lie near.

belie *v.* 1) to lie to, tell lies about, twist, warp, 2) to gainsay, give the lie to.

belief *n.* what one believes/holds, way of thinking.

belief-some *adj.* belief-worthy, worthy of belief, likely, well-grounded.

believe *v.* 1) to believe in, be a believer, acknowledge, reckon on, swallow, take one at his word, 2) to deem, hold, hold to be true, look upon as, think, ween.

believer *n.* follower, worshipper.

belike 1) *adv.* like enough, 2) *adj.* like, likely.

belittle *v.* to look down on, pick holes in, put down, run down, <u>smear</u>.

bell *n.* cup-like hollow body which rings when struck by the hammer hanging in it.

bell-cote (*belfry*) *n.* bell-house.

bell-ringer *n.* one who rings the church or town bell.

bell-rope *n.* the rope by which a bell is rung.

bellow *v.* to blast, deafen, roar, shout, storm, thunder, yell.

bellow *n.* roar, shout.

bellows *n.* blower.

bell-wether *n.* the leading sheep of a flock, having a bell about the neck.

belly *n.* the insides, where one's food goes.

belly-ache *n.* griping ache in the belly as if it were clenched hard.

bellyache *v.* to bleat, groan, moan, whine, whinge, be sorry for oneself.

bellyful *n.* 1) one's fill of food, 2) more than enough, more than one can stand.

belong *v.* to be akin to, be one of, make one of, go with, be stamped with, tie in with.

belonging *adj.* built-in, inwrought, making up, kindred.

belongings *n.* goods, things.

beloved 1) *adj.* darling, dear, dearest, greatly loved, much loved, 2) *n.* darling, dear one, love, lover, loved one, sweetheart, truelove.

below[2] *adv. prep.* at the bottom, at the end, beneath, underneath, further on, following, less than, smaller than, not as much as, under.

bemean *v.* to bear the marks/stamp of, bespeak, betoken, foreshadow, foretell, forewarn, give one to understand, mean, show, stand for, tell.

bemean *v.* to <u>shame</u>, bring down, take down.

bemoan *v.* to bleat, groan, moan, <u>sorrow</u>, whine.

bench *n.* long settle (with or without a back), workbench.

bench-mark *n.* 1) land-reckoner's mark (cut into stone or such like) at a height from which he can take sightings to other landmarks, 2) yardstick.

bend (*angle*) *n.* elbow, knee, horn.

bend *v.* 1) to twist, bow, stoop, 2) to browbeat, override, shape.

bendsome, bendy *adj.* 1) lissom, lithe, springy, stretchy, willowy, yielding, 2) flighty, pulled this way and that, <u>two-minded</u>, unsteadfast, wieldy, yielding.

beneath *adv. prep.* under, underneath, not good enough for, unworthy of.

benighted *adj.* 1) overtaken by the darkness of night, 2) <u>bewildered</u>, blind, in the dark, groping, unseeing, unwitting, without the light, backward, heathenish, loreless.

bent *n.* 1) reed-like grass, 2) treeless field, grassland, meadow, heath.

bent *n.* 1) bend, bow, tilt, twist, 2) bent of mind, leaning, set, trend.

bent *adj.* awry, bowed, misshapen, out of shape, stooped, stooping, twisted, warped.

benumb *v.* to numb with fear, fill with <u>fear</u>, make one's blood run cold.

bequeath *v.* to bestow, give, hand on, leave, settle on, will.

bequest *n.* bestowing, handing down, willing.

bereave *v.* to bear away/off, cut off, leave fatherless/motherless, <u>sadden</u>, widow.

bereaven *adj.* heart-broken, saddened, <u>sorrowful</u>, <u>woebegone</u>, wretched.

bereft *adj.* cut off from, empty of, <u>forlorn</u>, heart-broken, <u>hopelorn</u>, <u>sorrowful</u>.

beriddle *v.* to <u>bewilder</u>, darken, fox, <u>hide</u>, make it hard for.

berimed *adj.* clothed with hoar frost.

beringed *adj.* ringed about.

berry *n.* the yield of some trees, bushes and groundlings (such as the strawberry).

berth *n.* 1) steading where a ship lies in the sea-haven, 2) sleeping-stead on a ship.

berth *v.* to bring a ship to its steading in the haven.

beseech *v.* to ask earnestly, beg, crave, make bold to ask, seek, sigh at one's feet.

beseechingly *adv.* earnestly, on bended knee, heartily.

beset (*besiege*) *v.* to begird, belay, belie, cut off, gird about, ring about, hedge in, hem in, keep in, lock in, shut in.

besetter *n.* foe, onsetter.

beshrew *v.* to accurse, blacken, blast, go for, <u>smear</u>, speak evil of, speak foully of.

beside *adv. prep.* abreast of, alongside, near, near at hand, nearby.

besides *adv. prep.* as well as, along with, also, else, more, moreover, <u>furthermore</u>, let alone, likewise, and so on, and so forth, together with.

beslime *v.* to befoul, besmear, drag down, foul, harm, mar.

besmear *v.* to <u>smear</u>, backbite, blacken, run down, speak evil of, speak foully of.

besmeared *adj.* blackened, branded, chidden, named.

besmearing *n.* <u>smearing</u>, backbiting, evil-speech, foul-speech.

besom *n.* broom (made with a bundle of rods or twigs tied about a handle).

besotted *adj.* bewitched, doting, hooked, smitten, spellbound.

bespeak *v.* to speak about, speak against, speak for, speak of.

bespoke *adj.* ready-made.

best *adj.* first, foremost, highest, leading, unmatched, outstanding, <u>worthful</u>.

bestill *v.* to make still on all sides.

bestir *v.* to be up and doing, stir up, stir oneself, busy oneself, do one's utmost, put oneself out, put one's back/heart and soul into it, put forth one's whole strength.

best man *n.* friend of the bridesman at a wedding.

bestop[(4)] (to *punctuate*) *v.* to mark.

bestow *v.* (of a woman) to give one's hand in wedlock, to give freely, hand out, make over.

bestraddle *v.* to straddle, bestride, span.

bestraught *adj.* at a loss, at one's wits' end, bereft (of one's wits), forstraught, <u>bewildered</u>, in two minds, pulled this way and that, unsettled, wayward.

bestrew *v.* to strew about, strew with.

bestride *v.* to sit upon (a horse) with shanks astride, to be in the saddle.

betell *v.* 1) to speak for, 2) to bear witness, give out, hold forth, put about, say out, set forth, <u>speak</u>, 3) to uphold one's rights, 4) to blacken, <u>smear</u>, speak against.

bethink *v.* to bestow thought upon, pull one's wits together, <u>think</u>.

betide *v.* to arise, become, befall, come about, fall out.

betimes *adv.* before long, quickly, shortly, <u>soon</u>, within a short time.

betoken *v.* to foretoken, <u>foreshadow</u>, foretell, spell, witness beforehand.

betroth *v.* to bind oneself, give one's word, plight one's word, make a match.

betrothed *n.* husband-to-be, wife-to-be.

betrothing *n.* troth, plighting, undertaking.

better *adj.* 1) healthier, more healthy, stronger, well, 2) greater, worthier.

better *adv.* more thoroughly, rather.

better *v.* to do better than, make better, beat, outdo.

between *prep.* amidst, among, betwixt, in the middle/midst of, mid.

between-whiles *adv.* from time to time.

betwixt *prep.* amidst, among, between, in the middle/midst of, mid.

beware *v.* to be careful/heedful/wary, to look out, watch out.

bewend *v.* to go about, go away, go back, go out of one's way, step/swerve aside.

bewilder *v.* to amaze, bring to a stand, darken, drive one mad, drive out of one's mind, fox, make speechless, overcome, put one off his stroke, put one out of his stride, shake, smite/strike dumb, throw one off his bearings, throw one out, unman, upset, unsettle, worry.

bewildered *adj.* all at sea, at a loss, at one's wits' end, at sixes and sevens, brought to a stand, dizzy, floored, in two minds, light-minded, lost, not know if one is coming or going, shaken, speechless, struck dumb, unsettled, wandering, wildered.

bewildering *adj.* beclouding, benumbing, misleading, upsetting, unsettling.

bewilderingly *adv.* amazingly, overwhelmingly, wonderfully.

bewitch *v.* 1) to accurse, lay a curse upon someone, bend, bind (with spells), blast, lay under a spell, spellbind, weave a spell about, bewilder, draw/fill/hold the mind, grip, madden, play upon, quell, forelay, waylay, work upon, 2) to fill with longing, set the heart on fire, steal one's heart, stir love, sweep off one's feet, take one's breath away, take someone's eye, thrill.

bewitched *adj.* spellbound, gripped, thrilled.

bewitchful, bewitching *adj.* 1) witching, 2) 'come-hither', thrilling, winning.

bewitchingly *adv.* playfully, winsomely.

bewray *v.* 1) to blacken, lay at one's door, smear, run down, speak evil of, 2) to give away, lay bare, let on, make known, tell on, spill the beans.

bewrought *adj.* worked, wrought.

bewry *v.* to belie, bend, twist, read/write into, warp.

beyond *adv.* above all, beyond telling, the more so, out of reach, over and above.

beyond belief *adj.* far-fetched, hard to swallow, utterly unlikely, wildly out.

bid *v.* 1) to say something must be done, lay upon, 2) to make a bid/offer, offer.

bidding *n.* behest, say-so, word, writ.

bide *v.* 1) to dwell, have/make one's home in, live, put up at, settle at, 2) to abide, hold one's ground, stand fast, withstand.

bide-fast *adj.* at a stand/standstill, standing, still, stock-still, settled, laid up.

biding *adj.* abiding, holding, lasting, long-standing, unshaken.

bidsale (*auction*) *n.* sale by bidding.

bier *n.* the stand on which a dead body is laid before being buried.

bight *n.* 1) bend, bending, 2) stretch of open water between two headlands.

bill *n.* weapon having a blade and a long wooden handle, or having an axe-head and a shaft ending in a spear-head.

bill *n.* 1) neb (*beak*) of a bird, 2) bill-like headland.

bill-hook *n.* a heavy knife with a hooked end, for hedging and tree-care.

bin[6] *n.* bread-bin, draff-bin, dustbin.

bind *v.* to grasp, grip, hold, hold fast, keep, lay by the heels, lay hands on.

bind *n.* tie, withe.

binding *n.* fastening, tie, withe, the binding of a book.

binding *n.* that which binds together or binds up.

bindweed *n.* withwind.

bindwith (*clematis*) *n.* a climbing plant.

birch *n.* broad-leaved tree.

birchen *adj.* birch-like, made from birch wood.

bird *n.* fowl.

birdlore *n.* bird-learning.

bird's-eye 1) *n.* the name of some plants having small, bright blossoms, 2) *adj.* of a sweeping outlook (as from a high building or a hill), of a quick overlooking of something (the business in hand, or a book).

birdwatcher *n.* bird-lover, bird-seeker.

bird-witted *adj.* addle-headed, feather-headed, goosish, thimble-witted, witless.

birth[2] *n.* 1) childbirth, child-bearing, lying-in, 2) beginning, cradle, outset, rise, start, womb, 3) background, blood, breeding, stock.

give **birth**[2] *v.* to bring forth, bring into the world, bear.

birthday[2] *n.* birth-tide.

birthmark[2] *n.* a mark (from birth) on the flesh, mole, 'strawberry mark'.

birthright[2] *n.* the rights which come to one by birth, rights of the first-born.

birth[2]**-tide** *n.* birthday.

bison *n.* wild ox, weosand.

bit *n.* 1) whit, 2) little while, spell, time.

bitch *n.* 1) she-dog, she-fox or vixen, she-wolf, 2) lewd or rough woman.

bite *n.* 1) a bite to eat, a bite of food, light meal, mouthful, 2) prick, sting, wound.

bite *v.* to eat into, rend, sink the teeth into, sting, tear, wound.

biting *adj.* 1) sharp, stinging, shrewish, waspish, withering, 2) bitter, chill, chilly, cold, cutting, freezing, icy, raw, wintry.

bitter *adj.* 1) sharp, sour, tart, unsweetened, 2) cold, hard, hoarding hatred, mean-minded, ruthless, smarting, unforgetting.

bitterly *adj.* bitingly, grimly, ruthlessly, sharply, sorely, sourly, tartly.

bitterness *n.* 1) sharpness, sourness, tartness, 2) abiding wrath, soreness.

bitter-sweet *adj.* sweet – but with a mingling or aftermath of bitterness.

bitter-tongue *n.* ne'er-do-well, stirrer, word-twister.

black *adj.* black as night, dark, sloe-black, black-locked, raven, swart.

black *n.* 1) a black man or woman, 2) black speck.

black *v.* to make black, put a black hue on, clean and smarten with blacking.

black alder *n.* foul-beam, foul-tree.

blackberry *n.* bramble apple.

blackbird *n.* ouzel, colly/coaly bird.

blackboard *n.* (in school) black drawing/writing board.

black book *n.* book in which are written the names of misdoers.

black-browed *adj.* dark-browed, glowering, wrathful.

blacken *v.* to smear, besmear, beshrew, run down, speak evil of.

blackened *adj.* booked, named, branded, besmeared, chidden.

black-hearted *adj.* evil, fiendish, sinful, ungodly, unrightwise, worthless.

black-hole *n.* 1) lock-up for misdoers, 2) bottomless pit that would swallow all. **black-horn** *n.* inkwell.

black ice *n.* frozen rain on the blackness of a road (so that it is not readily seen).

black kite *n.* glede, puttock.

black look *n.* clouded brow, dark look, glowering look, wrathful look.

black mark n a mark against the name of a misdoer.

black mood *n.* bitterness, gloom, heaviness, hopelessness.

black-mouthed *adj.* evil-tongued, foul-tongued, foul-mouthed, rough-tongued.

blackness *n.* darkness, utter darkness, swartness.

blackout *n.* 1) news blackout, 2) a widespread cut-off of *electricity*, 3) swoon.

black sheep *n.* misdoer, ne'er-do-well, sinner, 'handful'.

blacksmith *n.* iron-smith, iron-wright.

blackthorn *n.* sloe-thorn.

bladder *n.* the *bag* in man's body wherein body waters are gathered.

blade *n.* 1) leaf, 2) the broad *part* of a tool such as a spade or an oar, 3) cutting edge of a tool or weapon, the tool/ weapon itself, 3) shoulder-blade.

blain *n.* boil, swelling.

blake *adj.* wan, of a sickly hue.

blast *n.* outburst, roughness, storminess, uproar, wildness.

blast *v.* 1) to blow up, burst, shoot, 2) to wither under a blight, 3) to curse, lay into.

blaze *n.* fire, roaring fire, blaze of light.

blaze *v.* to be on fire, burn, burn bright, roar.

blazing *adj.* 1) ablaze, afire, burning, on fire, 2) fiery, quick-hearted, wild.

bleach *v.* to whiten, lighten, wash out, become white, go white.

bleat *v.* 1) (of sheep or goats) to call out, 2) to moan, bemoan, groan, whine.

bleat *n.* the calling of a sheep or goat.

bleed *v.* 1) to lose blood, shed blood, 2) to bleed dry/white, drain, fleece, milk.

blench *v.* to shrink with fear, shy away, start aside.

bless *v.* to brighten, gladden, do one's heart good, fill with wonder.

blessed *adj.* blithe, feeling right, filled, thankful.

blessedness *n.* bliss, blissfulness, blitheness, gladness, list, weal, well-being.

blessing *n.* 1) thanks, thanksgiving, 2) godsend, good, weal, wealth, welfare, well-being, 3) the go-ahead, the green light.

blight *n.* 1) mildew, 2) bane, curse, dearth, evil, harrowing, sickness, withering.

blight *v.* to mar, over-stretch, over-work, wear out, worsen.

blind *adj.* 1) sightless, unsighted, unseeing, eyeless, stark blind, stock-blind, stone-blind, 2) benighted, darkened (in mind), hard-bitten, hardened, headstrong, heedless, hidebound, loreless, narrow-minded, short-sighted, small-minded, stony, unheeding, unmindful, 3) dim, hidden, unseen, 4) dark, leading nowhere, 5) unthinking, unwitting, wilful, blind/deaf/dead to.

blind *n.* 1) hood, shade, shutter, sun-blind, 2) sham, show, shift, makeshift.

blind *v.* 1) to make/strike blind, 2) to becloud, bedim, darken, hoodwink, mislead, outwit, pull the wool over one's eyes, 3) to amaze, bewilder, overwhelm.

be **blind** to *v.* to be unaware of, be unfair, be heedless of, be unmindful of, to shut the eyes to, overlook, see one side only.

blindfold *v.* 1) to swathe the eyes with cloth, 2) to becloud, bedim, darken.

blinding *adj.* 1) blazing, bright, gleaming, shining, 2) amazing, startling, striking.

blindingly *adv.* overwhelmingly.

blindly *adv.* 1) heedlessly, recklessly, unthinkingly, witlessly, 2) madly, wildly.

blindness *n.* 1) sightlessness, 2) benightedness, hardness, narrow mindedness.

blink *n.* 1) gleam of light, twinkling gleam, 2) twinkling of an eye.

blink *v.* to twinkle with the eye or eyelids, to wink.

blinkered *adj.* hidebound, narrow, narrow-minded, one-sided, short-sighted.

bliss *n.* blissfulness, blessedness, blitheness, gladness.

blissful *adj.* blithe, blitheful, blithesome, glad, gladsome.

blissfully *adv.* blithely, gladly, gleefully.

blithe, blitheful *adj.* beaming, blessed, blissful, blithe-hearted, blithesome, bright, carefree, feeling right, filled, glad, gladsome, gleeful, gleesome, laughing, laughter-loving, light, light-hearted, lively, merry, mirthful, mirth-loving, playful, sparkling, sunny, thankful, unworried, winful, with nothing left to wish for.

blithefully *adv.* blissfully, blithely, gladly, gleefully, laughingly, winly.

blithe-hearted *adj.* blithesome, glad.

blitheless *adj.* forbidding, frowning, glowering, grim, stern, threatening, unlaughing.

blithely *adv.* blissfully, blithefully, gladly, gleefully, laughingly, winly.

blitheness *n.* blessedness, bliss, blissfulness, gladness, glee, list.

blithesome *adj.* blithe, blessed, blissful, glad, gladsome, winful.

blood *n.* 1) the red 'sap' of the bodies of men and *beasts*, 2) bloodstock.

blood-bath *n.* blood-letting, bloodshed, killing, slaying, wholesale killing/murder.

blood-guiltiness *n.* the guilt of blood-shedding/murder.

blood-guilty *adj.* red-handed, with blooded hands.

blood-heat *n.* heat of the blood in a healthy man or woman.

blood-hot *adj.* afire, fiery, headstrong, heedless, hot-hearted, quick-hearted, wild.

bloodhound *n.* keen-nosed hound.

blood-less *adj.* 1) ashen, sallow, sickly, wan, washed out, 2) without bloodshed.

blood-letting *n.* blood-bath, bloodshed, killing, slaying.

Blood-month (*November*) *n.* Windmonth.

blood-red *adj.* bright red.

bloodshed *n.* ash-play, spear-play, spear-storm, blood-bath, blood-letting, fight, field-fight, hand-to-hand fighting, running fight, stand-up fight, killing, slaying.

bloodshot *adj.* blood-red, bloody.

bloodstock *n.* blood, breed, seed, stem, stock, strain.

bloodthirsty *adj.* ready/thirsting for a fight, full of fight, fiery, wild, hot-hearted.

blood-warm *adj.* warm as blood.

bloody *adj.* 1) bleeding, blooded, blood-soaked, grisly, 2) bloodlusty, bloodthirsty, cut-throat, hot-blooded, ruthless, wild, wolfish.

bloody-minded *adj.* pig-headed, unhelpful, wilful.

blossom *n.* blowth.

blossom *v.* to grow, do well, fare well, ripen, rise, sprout, strengthen, swell, wax.

blossoming *n.* growing, doing well, looking well, ripening, shooting up, spreading, springing up, sprouting, starting up, swelling, unfolding, waxing.

blow *n.* blast, hard blow, high wind, sough, strong wind.

blow *v.* 1) (of the wind) to blow hard, drive, sough, sweep, 2) (of such as a horn) to play, 3) to live recklessly/thoughtlessly, run through everything, throw it all away.

blow *v.* to blossom.

blowing *adj.* blowy, lively, windy.

blowing *adj.* blossoming.

blown *adj.* 1) driven by the wind, 2) breathless, heaving, winded, broken-winded.

blown *adj.* that has blossomed.

blow over *v.* to be forgotten, die away/down, dwindle, ebb, end, melt away.

blowth *n.* blossom.

blow up *v.* 1) to burst, go off, 2) to become heated/wild, fly off the handle, go off the deep end.

blowy *adj.* blowing, lively, rough, stormy, wild, windy.

blue[3] *adj.* of the hue of the heavens or the deep sea.

blush *n.* flush, glow, reddening.

blush *v.* to burn, flush, glow, go red, redden, a-redden.

boar *n.* he- swine.

board *n.* 1) sawn timber, lath, 2) shield, linden-board, 3) blackboard, whiteboard, games-board, 4) stand, *table*, 5) rooms, housing, shelter, 6) board (of a body such as a business or *college*), heads, leadership, steersmanship.

board *v.* 1) to fall upon a ship, 2) to go on board, 3) to put up at another's house.

board-cloth *n.* *table* cloth, board-sheet.

boarder *n.* 1) (in sea-fighting) one who falls upon another ship, 2) one who boards at a house or school.

boarding-house *n.* rooms.

board-sheet *n.* *table* cloth, board-cloth.

boarish *adj.* bloodthirsty, cold-eyed, heartless, ruthless, tearing.

boat *n.* row-boat, rowing-boat, sailing-boat, small boat, lifeboat, long-boat.

boat *v.* to row/sail in a boat.

boat-house *n.* outhouse (for keeping a boat).

boating *n.* rowing, sailing.

boatkeeper *n.* boat-ward.

boatman *n.* oarsman, waterman.

bode *v.* 1) to speak/tell forth, 2) to bespeak, betoken, forebode, foreshadow, forewarn, spell, bid fair to, give hopes of.

bodeful *adj.* baleful, dreadful, forbidding, harmful, threatening, threatful.

bodice *n.* upper half of a shift.

bodied *adj.* having a body (as in 'great-bodied').

bodiless *adj.* having no body, ghostly, otherworldly, shadowy.

bodily *adj.* earthly, fleshly, of flesh and blood.

bodily *adv.* 1) in the flesh, 2) all together, as a whole, one and all.

body *n.* 1) the frame (flesh and bones) of man or *beast*, build, make-up, shape, 2) dead body, 3) chest, middle, 4) the main *part* of anything, framework, 5) (of a body of water or such) breadth, stretch, sweep, 6) a business seen in law as one 'body', 7) crowd, throng, body of fighting men, 8) heavenly body, other world.

body-upset (*allergy*) *n.* upset or sickness stirred up by food, drink, *pollen* or such.

boil *n.* blain, swelling.

bold *adj.* 1) daring, daring-hearted, dreadless, driving, fearless, fiery, high-hearted, full of fight, unfearing, unshrinking, knightly, manful, 2) brazen, forward, off-hand.

be bold *v.* to dare, outdare, fear nothing, set at naught, show fight, stand one's ground, stand up to.

bolden *v.* to make bold, to take heart, strengthen.

boldly *adv.* daringly, fearlessly.

boldness *n.* 1) daring, drive, fearlessness, fire, heart, steadfastness, steeliness, strength of heart/mind/will, 2) brazenness, forwardness, shamelessness, uppishness.

bolster *n.* back-rest, head-rest.

bolster *v.* to back up, hearten, help, strengthen, uphold.

bolt *n.* 1) a short arrow with thickened head, shaft, 2) thunderbolt, 3) door-fastener, lock, 4) holdfast, rod, 5) bundle of cloth of set length (such as 30 yards, 28 ells), reel, 6) burst of speed, run, spring.

bolt *v.* to flee, take to flight, take to one's heels, run for one's life, win free.

bolt-hole *n.* burrow, den, earth, fox-hole, hideaway, hide-out, lair.

bolt-upright *adj.* stiff-backed, stiff as a rod, straight-backed.

bone *n.* heel-bone, shin-bone, shoulder blade, and so on.

bone *v.* to take out the bones from.

bone-break *n.* break, crack.

bonelore (*osteology*) *n.* the lore of bones, – how made and set.

bonesetter *n.* one who sets broken or wrenched bones.

bonfire ('bone-fire') *n.* great fire out of doors.

bony *adj.* fleshless, lean, spindly, starved, thin, thin as a lath/rake, wizened.

book *n.* written work.

book *v.* to put one's name down for a seat (on a *'plane*, *train*, or such).

bookbinder *n.* one who puts the binding (boards, cloth, leather) on a book.

book-black *n.* ink.

book-craft *n.* book-learning.

booked *adj.* named, branded, blackened, besmeared, chidden.

book-ends *n.* two stands, often of wood, for holding books upright.

bookful *n.* enough to fill a book.

bookful *adj.* full of book knowledge, bookish.

bookholder (*librarian*) *n.* book-ward.

bookholding (*library*) *n.* book-house, hall/house of books, reading room/house.

booking *n.* putting one's name down for a seat (on a *'plane*, *train*, or such).

bookish *adj.* 'islanded' from daily life, in cloud-land, learned.

book-keeper *n.* reckoner, rimer, teller.

bookkeeping *n.* reckoning, weighing.

bookland *n.* (in Anglo-Saxon times) land held under rights set out in a 'book' or deed, and often freeing the owner from the burdens of 'folkland' (such as having to send food for the king's household).

book-learned *adj.* having book knowledge, bookish.

book-learning *n.* knowledge won from books (rather than from daily life).

bookless *adj.* benighted, darkened (in mind), loreless, narrow-minded, unlearned.

book-lore *n.* learning, knowledge won from books.

bookmaker *n.* one who takes *wagers* on the outcome (of a horse race or such).

bookman *n.* bookworm, learned man/woman, <u>thinker</u>.

book-read *adj.* well-read.

bookseller *n.* keeper of a bookshop.

bookstaff, bookstave (*letter* of the *alphabet*) *n.* staff, stave, beech-staff.

book-teaching *n.* teaching by following a book.

book-ward (*librarian*) *n.* bookholder.

book-wise *adj.* book-learned, bookish.

book-worm *n.* 1) *larva* of beetles given to eating the leaves of books, 2) one who is forever reading.

bookwright *n.* maker of books, <u>writer</u>, book craftsman, wordsmith, word-weaver.

boot (*profit*) *n.* winnings, yield.

to **boot** also, besides, moreover, <u>furthermore</u>, likewise.

boot *v.* to come by, come into, do well out of, <u>gather</u>, make a good thing of, pick up.

bootless *adj.* 1) hopeless, no way out, 2) empty, meaningless, worthless.

bore *v.* to cut through, drive a hole into or through.

borough *n.* burh, (walled) town.

borough-folk (*citizens*) *n.* townsfolk.

borough-man (*citizen*) *n.* town-dweller, townsman.

borough-moot *n.* town moot, folkmoot, wardmote.

borough-reeve *n.* town reeve.

borough speech *n.* town speech, long-worded speech.

borough-town *n.* town which is a borough.

borough-way *n.* street, back street, by-street, high street, side street.

borrow *v.* 1) to take out a loan/overdraft, 2) to crib.

borrower *n.* ower.

bosom *n.* 1) breast, chest, 2) feelings, heart, inward thoughts, soul.

bosom-friend *n.* dear friend.

both[2] *adj.* the one and the other, in twos, the two (and not only one).

bottom *n.* 1) bed, floor, foot, underneath, underside, 2) back end, backside, behind, buttocks, tail end, 3) depths, bed or ground of a mere/stream, sea-bottom, sea-floor, 4) broad dale or hollow, 5) end, far end, 6) ground, heart.

bottomless *adj.* fathomless, reachless, unfathomful.

bottommost *adj.* nethermost, undermost.

bough *n.* 1) shoulder, arm, 2) limb of a tree.

bought *adj.* in one's hand, in one's hold.

bough-timber *n.* wood.

bound *adj.* fastened, held, yoked together.

bounden *adj.* beholden, sworn, tied.

bourn, bourne *n.* brook, burn, stream.

bow *n.* 1) *arc*, bend, bent line, 2) rainbow, 3) longbow, 4) rod of bendsome wood (once bow-shaped) with which to play a stringed *instrument*, 5) braid, knot, tie.

bow *n.* bending, ducking, stooping.

bow *v.* 1) to bend, stoop, 2) to bow before the storm, bow one's neck to the yoke.

bow-arm *n.* arm that holds the bow (weapon, or bow for playing an *instrument*).

bow-back *n.* hunchback.

bow-backed *adj.* bowed, having a bent, misshapen, or twisted back.

bow-draught *n.* (from the thought of 'drawing' a bow) bowshot.

bowed *adj.* 1) out of shape, misshapen, stooped, stooping, twisted, warped, 2) beaten, 'down', <u>hopelorn</u>, sick at heart, listless, forlorn, wretched.

bower *n.* bedroom, inner room, love-nest.

bow-hand *n.* hand which holds the bow (the left hand for holding the weapon, the right hand for the bow *used* when playing a stringed *instrument*).

bowl *n.* drinking-bowl, hand-bowl, wash-bowl.

bowl-ful *n.* peck (fourth of a *bushel*).

bowman *n.* fighting man who shoots with a bow.

bowshot *n.* the length an arrow can be shot from a bow (up to 500-650 feet).

bowstaff *n.* staff from which a bow is made (often of yew, but also of ash or elm).

bowstring *n.* string of a bow.

bowyer *n.* 1) one who makes, or buys and sells, bows, 2) bowman.

box[5] *n.* 1) chest, 2) 'the box' – *television*.

braid *n.* binding, brede, twine, yarn.

braid *v.* to brede, knit, knot, twine, weave.

braiding *n.* braided work.

brain *n.* 1) mind, home of thought, 2) brainbox, highbrow, <u>thinker</u>, wisehead.

brain *v.* to kill by smiting out the brains.

brainchild (*invention*) *n.* outcome of one's thought and work.

brainless *adj.* <u>witless</u>, unwitful, dim, empty-headed, slow-witted, thick.

brain-pan (*skull*) *n.* head-bone.

brainsick *adj.* addled, giddy, mindsick, thoughtless, unmanned.

brainsickness *n.* mind-sickness.

brain-storm *n.* 1) outburst of thoughts and feelings, 2) madness.

brain-storm *v.* to throw out half-shaped thoughts or answers, which can then be talked through.

brainwash *v.* to make one believe, misteach, put over, shape the mind, twist, warp.

brainwave *n.* insight, mindfall, thought.

brainy *adj.* <u>awake</u>, <u>bright</u>, clever, keen-minded, <u>sharp</u>, witfast.

brake *n.* fernbrake, shaw, thicket.

bramble *n.* blackberry bush.

brand *n.* 1) naked light, 2) mark made by burning with a hot iron, 3) brand name, hall-mark, stamp, 4) ilk, kind, make.

brand *v.* 1) to burn, burn in, mark, put a mark on, stamp, 2) to blacken, give one a bad name, lay at one's door, mark out, name, smear.

branded *adj.* besmeared, blackened, booked, chidden, named.

brand-new *adj.* new, new-fangled, new-fleshed, new-made, latter-day.

brass *n.* a mingling of copper with tin.

brass-farthing *n.* a farthing (and nothing more).

brazen *adj.* bold as brass, forward, headstrong, unblushing, unbridled, uppish.

brazen it out *v.* to be unashamed, outstare.

brazenly *adv.* boldly, shamelessly, unblushingly.

brazenness *n.* boldness, forwardness, lip, overstepping, shamelessness, uppishness.

breach *n.* newly-broken-in land.

bread *n.* loaf, staff of life.

breadth *n.* 1) beam, span, wideness, width, 2) reach, spread, sweep.

breadth of mind *n.* depth of mind, reach of mind, wisdom, insight.

bread-winner *n.* earner, worker.

break *n.* 1) bone-break, crack, 2) cleft, hole, opening, rent, tear, 3) lessening, let-up, slackening, 4) away day, holiday, leave, time off, 5) sundering.

break *v.* 1) to burst, crack, 2) to break the heart, overwhelm with sorrow, 3) to bring down, tame, 4) to break the law, 5) to break into, break open, break out, 6) to come out (in the news), let out, make known, tell, 7) (of a tie such as friendship or wedlock) to break with someone, bring to an end, cut, forsunder, put an end to, stop, 8) to stop for a while (on the way to somewhere), 9) (of a fall) to lessen, lighten, soften, 10) (of the dawn) to come, 11) (of waves) to burst, 12) (of a *code*) to crack, work out, 13) (of a *sports record*) to beat, outdo, top.

break away *v.* to win free, break out, make off.

break down[6] *v.* 1) to unmake, pull down, tear down, throw down, make an end of, 2) to 'die', give out, stop working, 3) to come to nothing, fall through.

break-down[6] *n.* breaking-off, cutting out, shut-down, stop.

break even *v.* to have enough, make ends meet.

breakfast *n.* morning-meat.

breakfast *v.* to take one's breakfast.

break in *v.* 1) to housebreak, raid, steal, 2) to cut in, heckle, put/shove one's oar in.

break-in *n.* housebreaking, theft, thieving.

breakneck *adj.* headlong, heedless, high-speed, reckless, wild.

break off *v.* 1) to break with someone, forsunder, put an end to, 2) to stop talking.

break out *v.* to win free, break away.

break through *v.* to win free, break out.

breakthrough *n.* great strides, good outcome, leap forwards, step forward.

break up *v.* 1) to open up the ground, 2) (of a tie such as wedlock) to break with another, forsunder, 3) (of the *police* with a crowd) to beat/drive back, throw back.

break-up *n.* breakdown, breaking, ending, wind-up.

breaker *n.* wave, white horse.

breakwater *n.* sea wall.

breast *n.* 1) bosom, chest, 2) being, feelings, heart, soul, thoughts.

breast-board *n.* mould-board of a plough.

breastbone *n.* chest-bone.

breast-care (*anxiety*) *n.* aching, worry, burden, weight on one's mind.

breast-high *adj.* as high as the breast.

breath *n.* 1) wind, draught, 2) (of time) little while, this while, short span/time, twinkling of an eye.

breathe *v.* 1) to breathe in and out, draw breath, 2) to breathe a word, hint, whisper.

breather *n.* break, rest.

breathful *adj.* full of breath, alive, having life, in life, living.

breathing *n.* breathing in and out, living and breathing.

breathing-spell, breathing-while *n.* break, breathing time, rest, time to think.

breathless *adj.* 1) out of breath, short of breath, winded, short-winded, 2) flushed, all of a flutter, overwrought, restless.

breathlessly *adv.* earnestly, quiveringly, with a swelling heart.

breathlessness *n.* striving for breath.

breathtaking[2] *adj.* amazing, beyond belief, startling, unwonted, wonderful.

breeches *n.* knee breeches, riding breeches.

breed *n.* bloodstock, seed, stem, stock, strain.

breed *v.* to bear/have children, bear young, bring forth, bring up, rear.

breeding *n.* 1) rearing, 2) bearing, becomingness, good breeding, winsomeness.

brere *n.* the earlier spelling of briar, brier.

brethren *n.* brothers.

Bretwalda *n.* 'Britain-wielder', high king, over-king.

brew *n.* strong drink, ale, mead.

brew *v.* 1) to make strong drink, 2) to be on the way, gather, start.

brewer *n.* maker of strong drink.

brewing *adj.* at hand, coming, forthcoming, hanging over, heavy with, in the offing, in the wind, near, nearing, nigh, ready, threatening, well nigh here.

briar *n.* brere, brier.

bridal 1) *n.* wedding, wedding breakfast, 2) *adj.* of the bride, worn by the bride.
(The word is shaped from 'bride' and 'ale', and means 'ale-drinking at a wedding'.)

bride *n.* blushing bride, wife-to-be, young wife.

bride-bed *n.* bed for the man and his wife on the first night together.

bridelope[2] *n.* the oldest Germanic word for a wedding. It means 'the bridal run', speaking of the taking of the bride to her new home.

bride-night *n.* wedding night.

bridesmaid *n.* bridehelper.

bridesman *n.* best man (once named the brideleader because he led the bride to the man about to wed).

bride-song *n.* wedding song.

bridge *n.* 1) framework bearing a road over a waterway, drawbridge, footbridge, overbridge, stock-bridge, stone bridge, 2) land-bridge, (neck or tongue of land between two greater bodies of land), 3) 'stepping-stone'.

bridge *v.* 1) to bridge over, bestride, go over, span, straddle, 2) to bring two sides together, make a path for.

bridge-head *n.* land won from the foe after over-leaping a waterway, or the sea.

bridle *n.* leather-work by which a horse is held and led.

bridle *v.* 1) to put a bridle on a horse, 2) to hedge in, hem in, hinder, hold back, hold in, put a drag on, 3) to straighten up (in wrath), bristle, draw oneself up, seethe.

bridle-path, bridle-road, bridle-way *n.* horse-way (with good going for a horse, but not a wain).

bright *adj.* 1) light, aglow, glowing, beaming, blazing, gleaming, glistening, shimmering, shining, sparkling, 2) clever, keen-minded, nimble-witted, quick-thinking, quick-witted, ready-witted, sharp, sharp-witted, wide-awake, wise, 3) beaming, blithe, glad, gladsome, hearty, hopeful, in good heart, laughing, light-hearted, lively, merry, sparkling, sunny, winful.

brighten *v.* 1) to make bright/brighter, 2) to become bright/brighter, gleam, glow, lighten, light up, shine, 3) to look up, pick up, take heart.

bright-hued (*colourful*) *adj.* bright, many-hued, lively, rich.

brightly *adv.* hopefully, lightly, light-heartedly.

brightness *n.* 1) (*glory*) worthfulness, worthship, 2) quickness, readiness, insight, wisdom, 3)

blitheness, gladness, healthiness, heartiness, hopefulness, life, light-heartedness, liveliness, sparkle, sunniness, well-being.

brim *n.* sea, deep, deep sea, flood, great waters, high seas.

brim-fowl *n.* sea-bird, sea-fowl.

brimstone (*sulphur*) *n.* burning stone.

brine *n.* salt water, sea-water.

bring *v.* 1) to come with, fetch, 2) to bring in, earn, yield.

bring about *v.* to be/lie at the bottom of, bring on, make, shape, set afoot, set going.

bring-and-buy *n.* sale (of goods given to bring in *money* for some good end).

bring down[6] *v.* 1) to shame, thrust down, cut down, 2) to overcome, to overthrow, floor, outmatch, outplay, throw down, 3) (of prices) to cut, drop.

bring forth *v.* to bear, give birth.

bring forward *v.* to come up with, highlight, put forward.

bring in *v.* to let in, throw open, open the door, welcome.

bring off *v.* to bring about, fulfil, pull off, see through.

bring on *v.* to bring about, draw out, give rise to, sow, start.

bring out *v.* 1) to set forth, 2) to set up, start up, 3) to draw forth, highlight.

bring over *v.* to talk into, win over.

bring to heel *v.* to beat, bring under the yoke, overcome, put down, quell.

bring to mind *v.* to bethink, bear one's thoughts back, to bear/hold/keep in mind, hark back, keep (alive) in one's thoughts, think, think back upon, not forget.

bring under *v.* to beat, overcome, quell.

bring up *v.* 1) to care for, foster, rear, shape, teach, 2) to come up with, speak about/of.

briny *adj.* (of water) salty.

bristle *n.* one of the stiff hairs on the backs of swine and wild boar, hair, prickle.

bristle *v.* 1) (of hair) to stand up stiff and bristly, stand on end, stand up, 2) to bridle, seethe, show fight, 3) to be alive with/thick with/burst with, swarm, teem.

bristly *adj.* set with bristles/stiff hairs, brambly, briery, hairy, prickly, rough, thorny.

brittle *adj.* 1) thin, 2) edgy, prickly, stiff.

broad *adj.* 1) great, open, roomy, full-wide, wide, 2) wide open (as in 'broad daylight'), 3) (of speech) heavy, rough, strong, thick, 4) filthy, naughty, shameless, unwholesome, 5) far-reaching, full, sweeping, thorough, thoroughgoing, 6) woolly.

broad *adv.* in a broad way, fully, outspokenly, widely.

broaden *v.* to build up, fill out, <u>greaten</u>, grow, widen.

broadening *n.* 1) growing, growth, lengthening, opening out, spreading, strengthening, waxing, widening, 2) (for the mind) mind-opening.

broad land *n.* highland, upland.

broad-leaved *adj.* of a tree having broad leaves.

broadly *adv.* in a broad way, fully, widely.

broad-minded *adj.* all things to all men, free-minded/-thinking, open-minded.

broadness *n.* beam, breadth, span, spread, wideness, width.

broadsheet (*newspaper*) *n.* daily, news-sheet, morning/evening news.

broad-shouldered *adj.* great-limbed, mighty, <u>strong</u>, thickset.

broadside *n.* 1) side of a ship above water, 2) burst/hail/shower/storm of fire, 3) blast of oaths/shouts.

broadside *adv.* with the side turned full.

broadsword *n.* cutting sword with a broad blade.

broadway *n.* wide open road.

broadways, broad-wise *adv.* broadside on, on one side, sideways.

brock[6] (*badger*) *n.* grey.

broken *adj.* 1) bent, in bits, not working, worn-out, 2) beaten, heart-lorn, <u>hopelorn</u>, helpless, overcome, overwhelmed, shrinking, <u>sorry</u>, worsted, 3) badly off, hard up, narrowed, <u>needy</u>, penniless, 4) <u>fitful</u>, flickering, halting, off and on, unsteady, 5) (of the ground) ridged, rough-edged, saw-edged, uneven.

broken-backed *adj.* beaten, <u>sorry</u>, unmanned, wretched.

broken-hearted *adj.* heavy-hearted, <u>hopelorn</u>, bowed, sick at heart, <u>woebegone</u>.

broken-heartedness *n.* bitterness, heartache, heart-sickness, <u>sorrow</u>, <u>wretchedness</u>.

brokenly *adv.* forlornly, hopelessly, sorrowfully, unmanfully, wretchedly.

brokenness *n.* 1) beggardom, 2) bitter <u>sorrow</u>, shame, wretchedness.

broken-winded *adj.* blown, breathless, out of breath, short of breath, heaving.

brood *n.* 1) chicks, 2) children, offspring, young.

brood *v.* 1) to sit on eggs so as to hatch such, 2) to bethink, dwell upon, lay to heart, <u>think</u> over, think upon.

broodiness *n.* moodiness.

brooding *adj.* moody.

broody *adj.* breeding, with young.

brook *n.* bourne, burn, runnel, stream.

brook *v.* to <u>abide</u>, bear with, forbear, brook, put up with.

broom *n.* 1) shrub, 2) besom (for sweeping).

broomstaff, broomstick *n.* staff bound with broom twigs so as to make a besom.

broomy *adj.* 'clothed' with broom.

broth (*soup*) *n.* stock.

brothel *n.* brothel-house, whorehouse.

brother *n.* 1) he- sibling, 2) one who is as a brother, a near friend.

brother-child *n.* child of one's brother.

brother-daughter (*niece*) *n.* daughter of one's brother.

brotherhood *n.* brothership, brotherliness, kinship.

brother-in-law[2] *n.* brother of one's wife, husband of one's sister.

brotherliness *n.* friendship, helpfulness, kindness, neighbourliness.

brotherly *adj.* friendly, kind, neighbourly.

brothership *n.* brotherhood, brotherliness.

brother-son (*nephew*) *n.* son of one's brother.

brow *n.* 1) forehead, 2) (of a hill) height, peak, top.

browbeat *v.* to bend, fill with fear/dread, <u>hold down</u>, overbear, <u>overcome</u>, override.

browbeaten *adj.* broken, helpless, overcome, shrinking, <u>sorry</u>, wretched.

browhead *n.* the top of a hill.

brown *adj.* 1) dark, dun, dark brown, reddish-brown, hazel, nutbrown, 2) dusky, sun-brown, sunburnt, brown as a berry.

brown *v.* 1) to become brown, 2) to make brown.

brownish *adj.* light-brown, rust-hued.

brownness *n.* brown, sun-brown, sun-burn

bruise *n.* mark, black eye.

bruise *v.* 1) to blacken, mark, 2) to cut to the quick, <u>sadden</u>, sting, upset, wound.

bruisewort *n.* daisy or other plant thought to heal bruises.

brunt *n.* burden or full strength (of an onset).

brustle *v.* to sough, whisper.

buck *n.* he-fallow-deer, he-goat, he-hare.

build *n.* body, cut, frame, height, likeness, make-up, look, shape, trim.

build *v.* 1) to frame, make, put together, put up, shape, work up, 2) to broaden, deepen, greaten, heighten, lengthen, widen, 3) to forstrengthen, harden, toughen.

builder *n.* house-builder, house-wright, workman.

building *n.* dwelling house, flats, warehouse, workshop.

build-up *n.* growth, rise, spreading, strengthening, swelling, upbuilding, waxing.

build up *v.* 1) to broaden, deepen, fatten, fill, fill out, fill up, <u>greaten</u>, grow, heap on, heighten, strengthen, forstrengthen, swell, thicken, wax, widen, 2) to gather up, heap up, hoard, lay in/up, put by, stock up, stow, 3) to <u>hearten</u>, put heart into, stir up.

built-in *adj.* fitted, in-built.

built-up *adj.* town, towny.

bulk *n.* batch, great deal, heap, lot.

bulk *v.* to overtop, stand out, threaten.

bull[(2)] *n.* he- ox.

bundle *n.* armful, batch, cluster, handful, heap, sheaf.

bundle *v.* 1) to make into/tie into a bundle, 2) to gather together, gather up.

burden *n.* 1) load, weight, 2) load-bearing room of a ship (set in tons), 3) bane, care, drag, drawback, <u>hardship</u>, sorrow, weight on one's mind, <u>worry</u>, 4) heart, kernel, marrow, meaning, pith, long and the short of it.

burden *v.* to bear hard on, <u>hinder</u>, lie/weigh heavily upon, load, overload, overburden, overwhelm, saddle with, snow under, weary, weigh down, worry.

burdened *adj.* care-worn, <u>fearful</u>, laden, loaded, <u>shaken</u>, weighed down, worried.

burdensome *adj.* grinding, hard going, smothering, tiring, tough, uphill, <u>wearing</u>.

burh, burgh *n.* town, borough.

burial *n.* burying.

burial-ground *n.* burying ground, graveyard, lich-yard, lich-rest, 'God's acre'.

burly *adj.* broad-shouldered, great-limbed, heavy, mighty, <u>strong</u>, thickset.

burn *n.* bourn, bourne, brook, stream.

burn *n.* brand, mark.

burn *v.* 1) to blaze, be ablaze, be on fire, 2) to burn to ashes, burn up, fire, set on fire, light, 3) to brand, sear, singe, 4) to bite, smart, sting, 5) to give off light, gleam, glow, shimmer, shine, 6) to blaze with wrath, 7) to be beside oneself, be wild, seethe, 8) to ache, crave, hunger, itch, <u>long for</u>, lust after, thirst, yearn.

burner *n.* brand, light, rush-light.

burning *n.* craving, hungering, itching, longing, lusting, running after, thirsting.

burning *adj.* 1) fiery, full of fight, ready/thirsting for a fight, hot-headed, hot-hearted, 2) biting, burning, red-hot, stinging, throbbing.

burning stone (*sulphur*) *n.* brimstone.

burnt *adj.* blackened, overdone.

burnwater (*acid*) *n.* sourwater, firewater.

burrow *n.* den, earth, hideaway, hide-out, hole, lair.

burrow *v.* to delve.

burst *n.* 1) blast, blow-out, blow-up, outbreak, outburst, 2) flood, outflow.

burst *v.* 1) to blow up, go off, 2) to break, rend, 3) to burst on the ear.

burst forth *v.* to arise, <u>begin</u>, come out, spring forth, spring up.

burst upon *v.* to amaze, <u>bewilder</u>, come like a thunderclap, <u>overcome</u>, <u>shake</u>.

burst with *v.* 1) to be many, overflow, swarm, teem, 2) to have to overflowing.

bury *v.* 1) to lay in the grave, lay to rest, 2) to hide, keep dark, let it go no further, 3) (of former misunderstandings) to forget, think no more of.

burying-ground *n.* burial ground, graveyard, lich-yard, lich-rest, 'God's acre'.

burying-song *n.* death-song, sorrowing.

bury oneself *v.* to be held/spellbound, to busy oneself, give oneself to.

bush *n.* shrub, thicket, undergrowth, underwood.

bushy *adj.* shrubby, bristly, rough, shaggy, thick, thick-growing.

busily *adv.* earnestly, speedily.

business *n.* dealings, dealership, doings, trade, work, workings.

businesslike *adj.* hard-working, quick, ready, thorough, workmanlike, craftly.

businessman *n.* man of business, buyer, seller, dealer, middleman, salesman, trader, tradesman, wholesaler.

busy *adj.* a-doing, hard at it, hard-working, never-resting/sleeping/tiring, on the go, stirring, tireless, untiring, unsleeping, up and doing, up to one's eyes, busy as a bee.

busybody *n.* gossip, stirrer, tell-tale.

busyness *n.* always a-doing, always on the go, coming and going, having a finger in every bowl, restlessness.

but 1) *prep.* leaving out, outside of, 2) *adv.* outside, without, 3) *conj.* without, other than, otherwise than, but that, if not, however, nevertheless, yet, moreover.

butt *n.* 1) thick end, 2) haft, shaft, stock.

butt *n.* ridge of land between two furrows of a ploughed field.

butt-end *n.* butt, leftovers.

butter[(4)] *n.* fatness got from the *cream* of milk by churning.

buttock/s *n.* back, back end, backside, behind, bottom, tail, tail end.

buxom *adj.* bosomy, full-bosomed, shapely.

buy *n.* deal.

buy *v.* to come by, make one's own, pick up.

buyer *n.* bidder.

by 1) *prep.* through, with the help of, by way of, beside, near, next to, before, earlier than, no later than, 2) *adv.* at hand, handy, nearby, within reach, aside, away.

by, bye *adj.* lesser (over against the main).

by and by *adv.* anon, before long, erelong, in a while, one day, shortly, soon.

bye *n.* (in *cricket*) run given when the ball goes by the batsman and the infielders.

by-end *n.* 1) lesser end/goal, 2) hidden end/goal.

by-going *n.* going by.

bygone *adj.* erstwhile, forgotten, former, gone by, lost, of old, olden, one-time.

bygones *n.* things belonging to days now gone.

byland (*peninsula*) *n.* foreland, headland, neck of land, seagirt land.

by-lane *n.* bridle-path, by-road, by-way, side lane.

by-law, bye-law[(2)] *n.* hundred-law, town law, lesser law.

by-name *n.* name other than the main name, nickname.

bypath *n.* bridle-path, by-way, footpath, side-path.

by-play *n.* 1) doings to one side at the playhouse (often in dumb-show), 2) things that are done aside and so little seen or marked, a hint.

byre *n.* cow-house, cowshed, barn.

by-road *n.* by-lane, by-way.

by-saying (*proverb*) *n.* byspell, byword, saying, folksaying, pithy saying, stock saying, true saying, wise saying, saw, truth, word.

by-speech *n.* words spoken aside.

byspell (*parable*) *n.* teaching-tale, likening, life-tale, tale with a meaning, word to the wise.

bystander *n.* beholder, eyewitness, witness, looker-on, onlooker, watcher.

by the by, by the way *adv.* while speaking of, while on this business.

by-time *n.* spare time.

by-way *n.* way other than the highway, by-lane, by-road, short-cut.

byword *n.* saying, by-saying, folksaying, saw, word.

by-work *n.* 1) work done in by-times, 2) work done for bad ends.

calf *n.* young of the cow, deer, whale.

calf-hide *n.* leather made from calf hide.

calf-love *n.* first love, young love.

carve *v.* 1) to cleave, cut, hew, 2) to mark, 3) to cut up meat at the board, 4) to deal out, mete out, share out.

carving *n.* stone-cutting.

cat[(4)] *n.* four-footed meat-eating *beast.*

chaff *n.* 1) hulls, 2) draff, leavings, sweepings.

chaffinch *n.* a woodland, hedge and *garden* bird.

chalk[(4)] *n.* soft white limestone.

charcoal *n.* black *matter*, pocked with small holes, left after burning wood or bone in an oven from which any draught has been kept out.

call[(2)] *n.* 1) shout, word, yell, 2) ring, 3) dropping in, 4) bidding.

call[(2)] *v.* 1) to send word, shout, sing out, yell, 2) to give someone a ring, ring up, 3) to drop in, go to see, look in on, look one up, 4) to call upon someone to do something, ask, bid, 5) to waken, awaken, 6) to ask one over, ask one to come, fetch, send for, 7) to name, give a name.

calling[(2)] *n.* business, life's work, walk of life, work.

calve *v.* to give birth to a calf.

can *v.* to have it in one, to have the might of body and/or craft of mind with which to do something.

candle[(5)] *n.* tallow-candle, wax-candle.

cannily *adv.* cleverly, craftily, heedfully, knowingly, warily.

canniness *n.* cleverness, insight, knowingness, shrewdness, wisdom.

canny *adj.* clever, crafty, knowing, ready-witted, sharp-witted shrewd, wary.

care *n.* heed, watchfulness, mindfulness, readiness, forethought, foresight.

care *v.* to mind, sorrow, take thought.

care for *v.* to look after, take care of.

carefree *adj.* blithe, light-hearted, sunny.

careful *adj.* heedful, mindful, thorough, thorough-going, thoughtful, watchful.

to be careful *v.* to be heedful, watch one's step.

carefully *adv.* with care, heedfully, mindfully, rightly, truly, thoroughly, watchfully.

carefulness *n.* utmost care, heedfulness, mindfulness, thoroughness, watchfulness.

careless *adj.* heedless, light-minded, offhand, rash, reckless, slack, sloppy, thoughtless, unmindful, unthinking, ware-less, unwary.

carelessly *adv.* heedlessly, rashly, recklessly, thoughtlessly, unware-ly, unwarily.

carelessness *n.* heedlessness, rashness, recklessness, unwareness, unwariness.

carer *n.* caregiver.

caretaker[(2)] *n.* keeper, housekeeper, watchman.

careworn *adj.* bowed down, drawn, forstraught, harrowed, overburdened.

charily *adv.* carefully, heedfully, mindfully, warily, watchfully.

chariness *n.* carefulness, heedfulness, wariness, watchfulness.

chark *v.* to creak, grind, groan, screech.

charlock *n.* field *mustard*, other field-weeds.

chart *n.* rough heathland of gorse, broom and *bracken.*

charwoman *n.* woman hired by the day to do housework.

chary *adj.* careful, heedful, wary.

chavel *n.* jowl.

cheap[4] *adj.* 1) marked down, not dear, undear, two-a-penny, going for a song, 2) bad, light-weight, makeshift, mean, rough, shabby, worthless.

cheek *n.* 1) side of the *face*, 2) backtalk, brazenness, forwardness, lip.

cheeky *adj.* bold, brazen, forward, sharp.

cheese[4] *n.* curd of milk made (by the *use* of rennet) into a soft *mass*, then sundered from the whey and shaped into a 'clod'.

chesil *n.* rough sand and waterworn stones.

chest[4] *n.* 1) box, strongbox, 2) breast.

chew *v.* 1) to gnaw, grind, 2) to bethink, brood over, think about/over/upon.

chick *n.* short for 'chicken' and *used* of the newborn; also the young of other birds.

chicken *n.* 1) young of the tame fowl, 2) chicken meat.

chicken-hearted *adj.* fearful, hen-hearted.

chicken-pox *n.* sickness (mostly among children).

chickweed *n.* weed, so named as being eaten by chickens.

chidden *adj.* booked, named, branded, blackened, besmeared.

chide *v.* to give one a black mark, give one a talking-to, go on at, lay into, speak against, spurn, tell off, upbraid, bring to book.

chiding *n.* putting right/straight, talking-to, telling-off, upbraiding, word in the ear.

chidingly *adv.* upbraidingly, warningly.

chilblain *n.* swelling on the hands and/or feet after being out in the cold.

child *n.* bairn, girl, litling, little one, maid-child, man child, suckling, weanling.

child-bearing *n.* childbirth, childing, lying-in.

childbed *n.* 1) bed in which a child is born, 2) suchness of a woman in the bitterness of child-bearing.

childbirth[2] *n.* bearing or birth of a child, lying-in.

childhood *n.* early years, girlhood, youth, youthhood.

childing *n.* child-bearing, childbirth, lying-in.

childish *adj.* over-young, shallow, silly, unfledged.

childless *adj.* bairn-less.

childlessness *n.* emptiness, forlornness.

childlike *adj.* believing, lamb-like, open, open-hearted, unhardened, unworldly.

childlikeness *n.* greenness, harmlessness, openness, unworldliness.

childliness *n.* childishness, childship.

childling *n.* little child.

childly *adj.* childish or childlike.

childness *n.* childishness, childship.

childship *n.* suchness of a child before its father and mother.

chill *n.* 1) cold, coldness, rawness, sharpness, 2) goose flesh, shiver, thrill (of fear).

chill *adj.* 1) biting, cold, raw, sharp, wintry, 2) (of looks and such) baneful, icy.

chill *v.* 1) to benumb, cool, freeze, 2) to fill with fear/dread, make one's blood run cold, unhearten, unman.

chilling *adj.* dreadful, fearful, frightening, frightful, nightmarish, numbing.

chillingly *adv.* balefully, dreadfully, fearfully.

chilly *adj.* biting, chill, cold, freezing, raw, sharp, wintry.

chilver *n.* ewe-lamb.

chin *n.* foremost *part* of the lower jowl.

chin bone *n.* jowl.

chine *n.* cleft, clough, dell.

chink *n.* 1) chine, cleft, 2) break, hole, opening, rent, slit.

chip *n.* 1) small bit of wood (or such) hewn or broken off, shred, sliver, 2) break.

chip *v.* 1) to cut, hack, hew, 2) to break off.

chip-board *n.* kind of *pasteboard* made by *pressing* offcuts of *paper* and wood together.

chirk *v.* to creak, croak, grind.

chirp *n.* cheep of a bird, short sharp call of an *insect*.

chirp *v.* (of a bird) to chirrup, sing.

chirpiness *n.* brightness, light-heartedness, liveliness, sparkle, sunniness.

chirpy *adj.* blithe, bright, glad, light-hearted, lively, sparkling, sunny.

chirrup *v.* to cheep, chirp, sing.

chirt *v.* to cheep, chirp, chirrup.

choke *n.* choking, cough.

choke *v.* 1) to cut off, kill, quell, smother, throttle, 2) to bring to a stand, stop.

choose *v.* 1) to come out for, go in for, like better/best, make up one's mind, mark out, settle on/upon, think it best to, 2) to wish, be so minded, have a mind to.

choosy *adj.* hidebound, narrow, small-minded, prickly, unbending.

chosen *adj.* forechosen, picked, hand-picked, dear to one's heart.

Christian[5] *n.* Christ's man/woman, believer, follower.

Christianity[5] *n.* believing in all that God has wrought in Christ (that in oneness with Christ the sinner dies to his/her old life of sin and rises to new life in him), following in Christ's steps, the Way.

church[4] *n.* 1) the body of Christ, the Christ-folk, 2) building where Christians meet to worship God.

churchyard[(4)] *n.* burial-ground, graveyard, lich-yard, lich-rest, 'God's acre'.

churl *n.* 1) free working man, 2) clod-hopper, clout-shoe, lout, oaf, rough.

churl-born *adj.* meanly born.

churlish *adj.* loutish, oafish, rough, <u>uncouth</u>, <u>unfriendly</u>.

churlishly *adv.* roughly, shortly, uncouthly, without thanks.

churlishness *n.* loutishness, roughness, uncouthness, unthankfulness.

churn *n.* butter-maker.

churn *v.* 1) to beat/stir up milk in a churn so as to make butter, 2) to foam, seethe.

churned up *adj.* <u>shaken</u>, unsettled, upset, worried.

cinder/s *n.* ash, ashes.

clad *adj.* clothed.

clam *n.* 1) that which holds fast, 2) means of holding fast, fastener, grip.

clam *n.* shellfish.

clamber *v.* to climb by holding on with hands and feet, climb hand over fist, claw one's way up, shin up.

clammy *adj.* steamy, sticky, sweaty.

clap *n.* 1) *sound* made by striking the hands together, 2) thunderclap, afterclap.

clap *v.* to give someone a great hand.

clasp *n.* 1) clip, fastener, fastening, hasp, hook, 2) grasp, grip, hold.

clasp *v.* to fasten on to, grasp, grip, hold fast, hold on, take hold of, twine about.

clatter *n.* din.

clatter *v.* to make a din.

claw *n.* cliver, gripper, nail.

claw *v.* 1) to rend, tear, 2) to claw back, wrest/wring something of what has been lost.

clay *n.* 1) stiff and sticky earth, 2) sometimes *used* of man's body (see Genesis 2:7).

clay-cold *adj.* deathly, of a dead body.

clayey *adj.* full of clay, clay-like.

clean *adj.* 1) bright, shining, shiny, washed, 2) good, upright.

clean *adv.* 1) in a clean way, 2) fully, thoroughly, utterly, wholly.

clean *n.* cleaning, clean-up, spring clean, wash, wipe.

clean *v.* to bath, clean out/up, dust, make bright, spring-clean, sweep, wash, wipe.

cleaner *n.* soap, lye.

clean-handed *adj.* clean-hearted, fair-dealing, <u>rightwise</u>, <u>true</u>.

clean-hearted *adj.* clean-handed, high-minded, <u>open</u>, right-hearted, <u>rightwise</u>, <u>true-hearted</u>, upright, upstanding.

clean-limbed *adj.* shapely, well-shaped, becoming, fair.

cleanliness *n.* cleanness, whiteness.

cleanly *adj.* 1) bright, shining, washed, 2) good, upright.

cleanly *adv.* 1) in a clean way, 2) deftly, readily.

cleanness *n.* cleanliness, freedom from dust, shine.

cleanse *v.* to clean out, clean up, wash out.

cleanser *n.* cleaner, lye, quicklime, soap.

cleat *n.* wedge, wedge-shaped handle.

cleave *v.* to cut in two, cut through, hew asunder, open, rend, sleave, slive, sunder.

cleave to *v.* to clasp, cling like a shadow, fasten on to, hang together, hold fast, hold together, grasp, grip, stick to, stick fast, stick like a leech/limpet, twine about.

cleft *adj.* break, crack, opening, rent, slit.

clench *n.* 1) fastening, 2) last word, that which settles the thing.

clench *v.* to shut tightly (the fingers, fist, teeth).

clenched *adj.* tightly fastened.

clencher *n.* clincher.

clever *adj.* <u>bright</u>, canny, deft, good at, handy, in the know, knowing, keen-minded, quick-thinking, ready-witted, <u>sharp</u>, sharp-witted, shrewd, wide-awake.

cleverly *adv.* cannily, deftly, knowingly, shrewdly.

cleverness *n.* deftness, handiness, <u>knowledge</u>, quickness, readiness, <u>wisdom</u>.

cleverstick *n.* know-all, show-off, 'self-made man in love with his maker'.

clew *n.* 1) ball of thread or yarn, 2) that which 'threads' a way through a maze, a key, hint, lead, something to go by, tell-tale mark.

clew *v.* 1) to make up into a ball, 2) to be lead by/follow a clew.

cliff *n.* high/steep foreside of land, sheer drop, steepness.

cliff-hanger *n.* film/play/tale/match which keeps the onlookers/readers on edge right to the end.

climb *n.* climbing.

climb *v.* to clamber, go climbing, make/work one's way up, shin up.

climb-down[(6)] *n.* come-down, let-down, set-down, shame.

climb down[(6)] *v.* 1) to come downhill, 2) to back down, give in, withdraw, <u>yield</u>.

climber *n.* cliff-clinger, hill-walker.

clinch *n.* fastening, grip, way of fastening ropes on a ship.

clinch *v.* 1) to fasten a bolt or nail, 2) to make fast the end of a rope (on board ship), 3) to drive home, settle.

clincher *n.* last word, that which settles the thing.

cling to *v.* to clasp, <u>cleave to</u>, hold fast, abide by, stick like a leech/limpet, stick to.

clinker-built *adj.* of a ship or boat each of whose side-staves overlaps the one below, being fastened with clinched nails.

clip *n.* clasp, fastening, grip.

clip *v.* to clasp with the arms.

clipboard *n.* board with a spring-holder for *papers*.

clitch *v.* 1) to bend, clench one's fist, shut one's hand, 2) to grasp tightly, make fast.

cliver *n.* claw, clinger.

cloam *n.* clay, earthenware.

clock[(4)] *n.* timekeeper, timer.

clod *n.* wedge of earth, loam, and such.

clod-hopper *n.* churl, lout, oaf, wooden-head.

clod-hopping *adj.* heavy-footed, loutish, oafish, rough, slow, <u>uncouth</u>, unhandy.

clot *n.* knot (of blood or such).

clot *v.* to set in clots, thicken.

cloth *n.* woollen weave, woven *stuff*.

clothe *v.* to be-gird, fit out, put clothes on one, swathe.

clothes *n.* clothing, outfit, things, wear.

clothier (*draper*) *n.* maker of woollen cloth, cloth/clothes-dealer, cloth/clothes-seller.

clothing *n.* clothes, outfit, things, wear.

cloth-maker *n.* maker of woollen cloth, web-wright.

clotted *adj.* gathered into clots, stuck together in clots.

clotty *adj.* full of clots, ready to clot.

cloud *n.* 1) mist, 2) 'cloud' of birds, flies or such, 3) darkness, gloom.

cloud *v.* 1) to cloud over, darken with clouds, overshadow, 2) to becloud the wits.

cloud-burst *n.* drenching rain, heavy rainfall, rainstorm.

cloudless *adj.* bright, fair, set fair, sunny, unclouded.

cloudy *adj.* 1) beclouded, gloomy, leaden, overclouded, sunless, 2) darkened, dim.

clough *n.* cleft, dell, hollow, chine.

clout *n.* 1) bit of cloth, leather or *metal*, for mending work, 2) knock, stroke.

clouted *adj.* of *cream* that is thick or clotted.

clout-shoe *n.* 1) shoe studded with great-headed nails, 2) one who wears such shoes.

clove *n.* small *bulb* (of garlic and such).

cloven *adj.* cleft, hewn asunder, rent, sundered.

clover *n.* plant (grown for fodder).

clovewort *n.* buttercup.

cluck[(7)] *n. sound* made by a hen when about to sit, or when calling her chicks.

cluck[(7)] *v.* (of a hen) to chuckle.

clue, clew *n.* hint, key, lead, something to go by, tell-tale mark.

clueless *adj.* <u>bewildered</u>, in the dark, dim, groping, thick, <u>witless</u>.

cluster *n.* 1) bundle, handful, knot, 2) crowd, gathering, meeting, swarm, throng.

cluster *v.* to come together, forgather, <u>gather</u>, meet, throng.

clustered *adj.* gathered, shared.

clusterfist *n.* 1) clod-hopper, oaf, wooden-head, 2) grasper, hoarder, holdfast.

clutch/es *n.* grasp, grip, hold.

clutch *v.* to fasten on, grip, <u>gather</u>, lay hands upon.

clutter *n.* heap, untidiness.

clutter *v.* to crowd, heap, strew.

coal *n.* a hard, black ore (found in seams) burned to make heat.

coal-black *adj.* black as coal, dark black.

coal-field *n.* seams of coal.

coal-seam *n.* coal-bed.

coal-thread (*plumb-line*) *n.* righting-thread.

cob *n.* head.

cobweb *n.* thread-like network spun by a spider, in which to take flies and such.

cock[(5)] *n.* he- tame fowl (also of other birds), rooster.

cod *n.* sea-fish.

cold *adj.* 1) benumbed, numb, chilled to the bone, frozen, shivery, 2) forbidding, grim, hard, standoffish, stiff, unbending, unforthcoming, <u>unfriendly</u>, unlaughing, unsmiling, unwelcoming, warmthless, withdrawn, 3) lifeless, stiff, stone-dead.

cold *n.* 1) chilliness, coldness, frostiness, iciness, 2) chill, cough.

cold-blooded *adj.* cold-eyed, fiendish, heartless, <u>ruthless</u>, wolf-hearted, wolfish.

cold-footed *adj.* in a cold sweat, <u>fearful</u>, frightened, frozen with fear.

cold-hearted *adj.* flint-hearted, hardbitten, hardhearted, hard-fisted, stony-hearted.

cold-heartedness *n.* coldness, grimness, hardness, heartlessness, ruthlessness.

coldly *adv.* grimly, stiffly, stonily.

coldness *n.* 1) chilliness, coldness, frostiness, iciness, 2) grimness, misliking, hardness, heartlessness, off-handedness, ruthlessness, standoffishness, unfriendliness.

cold shoulder *v.* to cut dead, drive away, harden one's heart, have nothing to do with, keep at arm's length, <u>shun</u>, shut the door on, <u>spurn</u>.

cole, kale[(4)] *n.* greens.

cole mase, colemouse (*coal tit*) *n.* coalmouse.

Colemonth[(4)] (*February*) *n.* Kale-month, Sol-month, 'Fill-ditch'.

collier *n.* 1) coal-/ore-worker, 2) coal-dealer, 3) ship bearing coal for trade.

colt *n.* 1) young of the horse, 2) youth.

comb *n.* toothed length of bone, horn, wood or such (for combing the hair).

comb *v.* 1) (of the hair) to straighten out, unknot, untousle, 2) to comb through, delve deep, go into, hunt through, look into, seek out, sift through.

come *v.* 1) to near, draw near, 2) to come to, come as far as, reach, be on the doorstep, be at the threshold, fetch up at, 3) to arise, befall, come about.

comeback *n.* picking up, upswing.

come-down[6] *n.* downfall, let-down, setback.

come-hither *adj.* bewitching, fetching, spellbinding, taking, winning.

come into *v.* to come by, come into one's own, come in for, gather, make one's own.

comeliness *n.* fairhood, fairness, loveliness, winsomeness.

comeling *n.* 1) (*immigrant*) incomer, newcomer, outsider, settler, wanderer, inwanderer, 2) (*novice*) beginner, colt, greenhorn, know-nothing, learner, 3) (*parvenu*) climber, high flier, latecomer, new rich, rising man, upstart, 'not one of us'.

comely *adj.* fair, lovely, willowy, elf-fair.

coming *n.* drawing near, reaching.

cook[5] *n.* one who makes food ready.

cook[5] *v.* to bake, make ready a meal, put in the oven.

cooker[5] *n.* oven.

cool *adj.* 1) chilly, cold, on the cool side, 2) even-minded, steadfast, steady, unshaken, 3) half-hearted, laid-back, lukewarm, offhand, standoffish, stern, stiff, unforthcoming, unfriendly, unwelcoming, without warmth, 4) unfearing, 5) bold, brazen, forward, shameless.

cool *v.* 1) to cool down, cool off, lose heat, 2) to chill, freeze, make cool, 3) to hold one back, lessen, talk out of, warn.

cool-headed *adj.* steady, unshaken, unworrying.

cool-headedness *n.* steadfastness, steadiness.

coolly *adv.* 1) offhandedly, stiffly, 2) fearlessly, 3) boldly, brazenly, shamelessly.

coolness *n.* 1) chilliness, cool weather, 2) even-mindedness, steadiness, strength of mind/will, 3) coldness, frostiness, half-heartedness, lukewarmness, offhandedness, unfriendliness, 4) fearlessness, grit, manliness, steadfastness, steadiness, strength, toughness, 5) brazenness, forwardness, shamelessness.

coomb, combe *n.* dell or hollow, most often shorter and broader than a dean/dene, being bowl- or trough-shaped with three fairly steeply rising sides.

copper[4] *n.* a reddish *metal*.

corn *n.* the leading crop of a land, being wheat in England, oats in Scotland.

corn-rick *n.* corn-*stack*.

corn-worm *n.* weevil.

cot, cote (*cottage*) *n.* 1) small house, 2) bell-cote, sheepcote.

cotland *n.* land (about five acres) tilled by a cottar.

cottar, cotter *n.* land-worker/smallholder to whom a cot and a few acres are let.

couch-grass *n.* quitch, quicken, twitch.

cough *n.* 'frog' in the throat.

cough *v.* to free the throat.

coulter *n.* the sharp blade at the fore-end of a plough, which cuts a line through the ground as the plough is driven along.

couth *adj.* 1) known, well known, 2) kind, 3) bowery, homely, sheltered, warm.

couthly *adv.* forsooth, indeed, ringingly, truly, no two ways about it.

cove *n.* inlet, bight.

cow/s *n.* she- *beast* (of kine, seals, whales and others), livestock.

cowflesh (*beef*) *n.* meat, red meat, cow, cowmeat, kinemeat.

cowherd *n.* dairyman.

cow-house *n.* cowshed, byre, barn.

cowmeat (*beef*) *n.* cow, cowflesh, kinemeat, meat, red meat.

cow-pox *n.* kine-pox.

cowshed *n.* cow-house, byre, barn.

cowslip *n.* plant of meadow-land and grassy slopes.

crab *n.* small *beast* of shallow waters and the strand.

crabbed *adj.* 1) bitter, mean-minded, narrow, pigheaded, prickly, sour, uncouth, unfriendly, twisted, warped, 2) (of handwriting) badly written, hard to make out.

crack *n.* 1) sharp *sound* (of thunder), 2) break, cleft, slit.

crack *v.* 1) to make a sharp *sound*, 2) to break, break open, burst, 3) to cleave, 4) to fathom, find the key to, make out, unriddle, work out, 5) to be overcome, break down, give in, give way, yield.

crack-brained *adj.* brainsick, mazed, not right in the head, wildered in one's wits.

crackle *v.* to spit.

crackling *n.* spitting.

cradle *n.* 1) little bed for a small child, 2) beginning, spring, wellspring.

cradle *v.* 1) to lay in a cradle, 2) to hold a little child in one's arms.

cradle-child *n.* little bairn.

craft *n.* 1) clever work, 2) foul play, shift, stealth, underhand dealing.

craft *n.* 1) boat, ship, little ship, 2) flying craft.

craftful *adj.* canny, clever, craftly, deft, knowing, sharp, shrewd, witfast, witful.

craftily *adv.* cleverly, shiftily, shrewdly, stealthily.

craftiness *n.* foxiness, sharp-dealing, sharpness, shiftiness, smoothness, stealthiness.

craftly *adj.* clever, deft, good at, handy, knowing, quick, ready, sharp.

craftsman *n.* doer, maker, worker, wright.

craftsmanship *n.* cleverness, deftness, handiness, quickness (of the hand), shrewdness.

craftswoman *n.* doer, maker, worker, wright.

craft-work *n.* clever work, deft workmanship.

crafty *adj.* foxy, fox-like, knavish, misdealing, not born yesterday, not straightforward, shady, sharp, shifty, slippery, smooth, smooth-spoken, smooth-tongued, stealthy, too clever by half, two-hearted, two-tongued, truthless, underhand, up to everything, without truth.

cram *v.* 1) to fill, fill to bursting, fill up, ram down, stow, 2) to crowd, overfill, fill to overflowing, 3) to bolt, overeat, wolf, eat like a horse, 4) to pore over, read up.

crane *n.* 1) a great marsh bird, 2) *machine* for lifting heavy weights.

crank *n.* elbow-shaped tool.

crank *v.* 1) to twist about, 2) to draw up by means of a crank.

crankle *v.* to crinkle, twist.

crave *v.* to burn for, hunger/thirst/itch for, lust after/for, run after, long for.

craving *n.* burning, hungering/thirsting/lusting/running after, itching for.

craw *n.* crop (of a bird).

creak *n.* grinding, screeching.

creak *v.* to grind, groan, screech.

creaky *adj.* creaking, hoarse, rusty.

creep *n.* creeping.

creep *v.* 1) to edge forward, slither, 2) to go softly/stealthily, slink, steal along.

creeper *n.* 1) (among birds) hedge creeper, nettle creeper, tree creeper, 2) (among plants) climber, runner.

creepy *adj.* chilling, frightening, ghostly, nightmarish, threatening.

cress *n.* eatsome plant.

crib *n.* 1) feeding frame (for kine and such), 2) small bed for a child.

crib *v.* 1) to put in a crib, 2) to steal someone else's written work.

cringe *v.* 1) to draw back, fawn, keep one's head down, quake, shrink, 2) to writhe.

cringing *adj.* fawning, little in the eyes of others, mean, not thought much of, stooping, toadying, of little worth, worthless.

crinkle *n.* crumple, fold, twist, wrinkle.

crinkle *v.* to crumple, fold, twist, wind, wrinkle.

crinkly *adj.* crumpled, furrowed, gathered, wrinkled, wrinkly.

cripple *n.* lame man/woman.

cripple *v.* 1) to hamstring, lame, 2) to blight, harm, mar, unstring, warp, worsen, put a spoke in one's wheel.

crippled *adj.* bed-fast, bedridden, halt, laid up, lame, limping.

croak *n.* 1) deep, hoarse call (of frog, raven or such), 2) hoarse speech of one with a dry throat.

croak *v.* 1) to caw, 2) to speak with a hoarse, hollow *sound.*

croaky *adj.* hoarse, hollow, throaty.

crock *n.* bowl.

croft *n.* holding, small-holding, steading.

crofter *n.* acreman, smallholder.

crop *n.* 1) craw of a bird, 2) stock or handle of a *whip,* 3) harvest, yield.

crop *v.* 1) to bring home, bring in, gather, harvest, mow, pick, reap, 2) to eat, feed on, graze, 3) to cut, lop, shear, shorten, trim.

crop-lore *n.* fieldcraft, fieldlore, earth-tilling, earth tilth, tilth.

cross[5] *n.* 1) two stakes set crosswise, whereon to hang an evil-doer and so put him to death, a rood, 2) mark, 3) burden, load, woe, worry, 4) mingling.

cross[5] *v.* 1) to go from one side to the other, go over, 2) to bridge, span, straddle, 3) to hinder, forset, 4) to crossbreed, mingle.

cross[5] *adj.* put out, waspish, wrathful.

cross[5]**-roads** *n.* 1) road-meet, way-meet, leet, 2) time to make up one's mind.

crow *n.* gorcrow, gore crow, black neb.

crow *v.* 1) to screech, 2) to show off.

crowd *n.* swarm, throng.

crowd *v.* 1) to cluster, forgather, gather, stream, swarm, throng, 2) to cram into, fill to overflowing.

crowded *adj.* busy, full, overflowing, swarming, teeming, thronged.

crow's nest *n.* look-out *place* at the masthead of a ship.

crumb *n.* bit, speck.

crumble *v.* 1) to break up, break into bits, fall asunder, 2) to crumb, grind, pound, 3) to break down, crumble to dust, go downhill, sink, wither.

crumbling *adj.* broken, fallen in, in bits, moss-grown, overgrown, run-down, uncared for, weather-beaten.

crumbly *adj.* bitty, broken, 'short' (of bakemeats).

crumpet *n.* thin bakemeat.

crumple *v.* to crinkle, fold and twist in one's hand.

crutch *n.* staff for a lame man to lean on.

cud *n.* food chewed over in the mouth (by kine and such).

cuddle *v.* to clasp, fold in one's arms, hold to one's bosom, play with.

cudgel *n.* heavy staff, stick.

cudgel *v.* 1) to beat with a cudgel, beat down, fell, knock down, strike down, thrash, 2) to bend the mind to, hammer at, think hard.

cup[5] *n.* drinking cup.

cupboard[5] *n.* sideboard.

curd *n.* clotted milk.

curdle *v.* to clot, go sour, thicken.

curse *n.* 1) spell, 2) oath, swearword, 3) bane, blight, burden, ordeal.

curse *v.* to smear, besmear, beshrew, speak evil of, speak foully of.

cursing *n.* foul-speech, smearing, swearing.

cut *n.* 1) rent, slit, tear, wound, 2) deal, hand-out, lot, share, share-out, 3) mark-down, something off, 4) build, look, shape, trim, 5) cut-back, cutting, lessening, narrowing, shortening, 6) ditch, drain, furrow.

cut *v.* 1) to cleave, fell, hew, saw through, 2) to cold-shoulder, cut dead, cut out, cut to the quick, have nothing to do with, look straight through one, shun, spurn, sting, upset, wound deeply, 3) to make an opening through, 4) to cut back, lop off, shear, thin out, trim, 5) to cut down, cut short, for-hew, lessen, shorten, foreshorten, take out, whittle down, 6) to mark down, take off, 7) to carve, cut into, hollow out, rough hew, shape, 8) to cut in half, cut down the middle, cut in two, halve, cleave, 9) to cut in, break in, heckle, put/shove one's oar in, stick one's nose in, 10) to cut off, break off, shut down/off, stop, stop the flow.

cut above *adj.* better, foremost, greater, higher, matchless, unmatched, nonesuch, one up, on top, outmatching, outstanding.

cut and dried *adj.* in black-and-white, known, open and shut, settled, well-grounded.

cutback *n.* cutting, lessening, narrowing, shortening, foreshortening.

cut back *v.* to cut down/short, lessen, shorten.

cut off *v.* to sunder, come between, drive a wedge between.

cut off *adj.* sundered, broken away, islanded, alone, lonely.

cut out *v.* to shunt aside, take over, unsaddle, tread on the heels of.

cut out for *adj.* aright, right, good for, in keeping.

cut short *v.* to cut in, put a stop to, shut out.

cut-throat *n.* evil-doer, fiend, killer, lout, murderer, rough, tough.

cut-throat *adj.* ruthless, self-seeking, worldly.

cutting *n.* 1) cut, ditch, furrow, trough, 2) *railway* cutting, 3) newscutting.

cutting *adj.* 1) belittling, biting, rough, rough-tongued, sharp, short, shrewish, smearing, stabbing, stinging, waspish, withering, wounding, 2) (of wind or weather) biting, bitter, chill, freezing, wintry.

cuttingly *adv.* bitingly, bitterly, harmfully, witheringly.

cutwater *n.* wedge-shaped end of the upright of a bridge which sunders the flow of water.

daft *adj.* 1) mad, not right in the head, wildered in one's wits, witless, 2) giddy, dizzy, empty-headed, flighty, hare-brained, heedless, light-minded.

daily *adj.* day-to-day, everyday.

daily *adv.* every day, day by day, from day to day.

dairy *n.* milkhouse.

dairymaid *n.* dairy-woman, milkmaid.

dairyman *n.* man who keeps/works in a dairy, seller of milk, cheese and such.

daisy *n.* plant which 'shuts' in the evening and opens again in the morning, hence the 'day's eye'.

dale *n.* coomb, dean, dell, hollow, slade.

dalesman *n.* uplander.

dare *n.* hat in the ring, threat.

dare *v.* to be bold, outdare, fear nothing, set at naught, show fight.

daring *n.* boldness, drive, fearlessness, fire, heart.

daring *adj.* bold, fearless, daring-hearted.

daring-hearted *adj.* bold, daring, dreadless, fearless, fiery, unshrinking.

daringly *adv.* boldly, fearlessly.

dark *adj.* 1) black, coal-black, sloe-black, black as night, 2) gloomy, grey, leaden, shadowy, twilight, 3) dark-hued, raven, sunburnt, swarthy, 4) evil, foul, hellish, sinful, wicked, 5) deep, hidden, knotted, unfathomful, riddle-wrought, 6) canny, not open, not to be drawn, stealthy, unforthcoming, 7) blitheless, forbidding, frowning, glowering, grim, stern, threatening, unlaughing.

dark *n.* darkness, dimness, dusk, gloom, night, night-time, shadows.

dark brown *adj.* sallow-brown.

darken *v.* 1) to dim, shade, shroud, 2) to becloud, bedarken, beriddle, bewilder, fox, hide, hood, mask, mislead, shroud.

dark-hued *adj.* sallow, dim-hued, dun-hued.

darkly *adv.* aside, in a dark way, behind one's back,

darkness *n.* 1) blackness, thick darkness, night-gloom, shadows, 2) benightedness, blindness, narrow-mindedness, backwardness.

dark-room *n.* darkened room in which to work on *photographic* film.

dark saying *n.* knot, hard saying, deep or hidden word, riddle.

darksome *adj.* darkish, dim, dusky, gloomy, grey, misty, shadowy, smoky, thick.

darling, dearling *n.* beloved, dear, dearest, dear heart, dear one, love, sweetheart, truelove, apple of one's eye.

darling *adj.* beloved, best-loved, dearest, sweet.

darn *n.* stitch, rightening.

darn *v.* to sew up a hole (in a stocking or the like) with thread or yarn, to righten.

darning *n.* things darned or to be darned.

daughter *n.* maid-child.

daughter-in-law[2] *n.* good daughter, son's wife.

daughterly *adv.* good, loving, ready, well-behaved.

dawn[2] *n.* 1) break of day, daybreak, day-dawn, first light, sunrise, 2) beginning, dawning, rise, start.

dawn[2] *v.* to arise, begin, open, spring forth, spring up, start.

day *n.* 1) the time between sunrise and sunset, broad daylight, daytime, working day, 2) the twenty-four hours from one midnight to the next, 3) *age*, *era*, time, heyday.

daybook *n. diary, journal, log.*

daybreak *n.* break of day, dawn, dayspring, ere-day, first light, morning, sunrise.

daydream *n.* golden dream, make-believe, wishful thinking.

daydream *v.* to be far-away, be lost in thought, dream, go wool-gathering, idle, let one's mind/ thoughts wander, lose the thread, not listen, play at.

day-dreamer *n.* dreamer, thinker.

daylight *n.* broad daylight, daybreak, daytime, light of day, sunlight, sunshine.

daylong *adj.* lasting all day, lasting one day.

daylong *adv.* all through the day.

day-mare *n.* fright, onset like to a nightmare (but happening while awake).

day-meat *n.* daily food.

day old *adj.* one day old (as of chicks).

day-red *n.* dawn, day-dawn, ere-day, sunrise.

day-rime *n.* span of one's life, days of one's life.

daysman (*arbitrator*) *n.* go-between, for-speaker, spokesman.

dayspring *n.* break of day, dawn, daybreak, day-dawn, first light, morning, sunrise.

day-tale *n.* reckoning (of work, *pay*) by the day.

day-tide *n.* day-time.

day-time *n.* daylight, day-tide.

day-while *n.* span of time within a day.

day work *n.* 1) the land that can be worked in a day, 2) work for which a man is hired and *paid* by the day.

dead *n.* 1) the dead, 2) (of the night) depth, heart, middle, midst.

dead *adj.* 1) dead and gone, gone, stone dead, dead as a doornail, 2) still, 3) dreary, heavy, lifeless, 4) broken, not working, 5) died out, forgotten, long gone, lost and gone forever, old, 6) benumbed, numb, cold, deadened, frozen, stiff, stony, unfeeling, wooden, 7) downright, outright, thorough, utter.

dead-beat *adj.* dead tired, fordone, ready to drop, tired out, weary, worn out.

dead-born *adj.* born dead, still-born.

deaden *v.* to lessen, numb, benumb, smother.

dead end *n.* deadlock, standstill.

dead-end *adj.* dead, mind-numbing, wearisome.

dead-hearted *adj.* without heart or feeling for others.

dead heat *n.* race in which two or more runners reach the line together, tie.

dead lock *n.* full stop, standoff, standstill,

deadly *adj.* baleful, death-bringing, death-dealing, deathly, dreadful, harmful.

deadly *adv.* altogether, fully, thoroughly, utterly, wholly.

deadness *n.* coldness, dreariness, heaviness, lifelessness, numbness, stillness.

dead-on *adj.* true, no other, right, so, straight.

dead-reckoning *n.* working out where one's ship is by reading *log* and wayfinder (*compass*), and without the help of star-reckoning.

dead weight *n.* burden, drag, millstone, shackle.

deaf *adj.* 1) hard of hearing, stock-deaf, stone deaf, 2) deaf to, heedless, not listening, unhearing.

deafen *v.* to drown one's hearing, make deaf, roar.

deafening *adj.* dinning, ear-rending, ringing.

deafness *n.* deaf ears, hardness of hearing.

deal *n.* 1) dole, cut, lot, share, share-out, 2) a great deal, a lot, richness, wealth.

deal *v.* 1) to share, share out, carve, carve up, deal out, dole, mete, 2) to do a deal, deal with, have to deal with, clinch a deal, cut a deal, deal in, do business, have a hand in, settle for, shake hands, strike hands.

dealer *n.* one handling business for another, middleman, steward, player.

dealership business, stewardship, undertaking.

dealing/s *n.* doings, business, work, working, steps, sharing, handing or sorting out.

dean, dene *n.* coomb, dale, dell, hollow, slade. See also 'dene'.

dear *n.* beloved, darling, dearest, dearling, dear heart, dear one, love, sweetheart.

dear *adj.* 1) beloved, darling, dearest, 2) bewitching, fetching, lovely, loveworthy, winning, winsome, 3) dearly bought, pretty penny, steep, stiff.

dear *adv.* 1) at a heavy/high outlay, 2) deeply, greatly, heavily.

dear-bought *adj.* bought at a high outlay.

dearling *n.* beloved, darling, dear, first love, near friend, apple of one's eye.

dearly *adv.* deeply, greatly, heavily.

dearness *n.* high worth, pretty penny.

dearth *n.* drought, lack, leanness, want.

dearworth *adj.* 1) dearly bought, worthful, 2) (of folk) beloved, darling, dearest.

dearworthy *adj.* dearly bought, forworthy, worthful.

death *n.* 1) dying, end, forthfaring, loss, 2) downfall, ending, undoing, wiping out.

death-bed *n.* dying, dying breath, dying day, end.

death-day *n.* day of death, yearday/ yeartide (of that death).

death-dene *n. valley* of death.

deathful *adj.* 1) deadly, 2) doomed, flickering, short-lived, 3) ashen, ashy, bloodless, deathlike, deathly, ghastly, sallow, wan, white.

death knell *n.* beginning of the end, death's door, doom, hand/shadow of death.

deathless *adj.* abiding, everlasting, endless, lasting, timeless, undying, unending.

deathlike *adj.* ashen, ashy, bloodless, deathful, deathly, ghastly, sallow, wan, white.

deathling *n.* earthling, man, woman, son of Adam.

deathly *adj.* 1) ashen, ashy, bloodless, deathful, deathlike, ghastly, sallow, wan, white, 2) baleful, baneful, deadly, dreadful, harmful.

death-spear *n.* deadly spear, death-dealing spear.

death-stricken, death-struck *adj.* sick/wounded unto death.

death-throe *n.* last breath, nightmare of death.

death-trap *n.* harm, nightmare, threat.

deathward/s *adv.* in the way of death, towards death.

death-wish *n.* wish for death (for oneself or another).

death-wound *n.* deadly wound, death-bringing wound.

deave *v.* 1) to become deaf, 2) to deafen.

deck[1] *n.* (in a ship) timbers roofing in all the room below, while also being a floor; upper deck, main deck, middle deck.

deed *n.* 1) doing/s, dealings, business, handiwork, work, working, workmanship, stroke, step, 2) great strides, good ending/outcome, breakthrough, outright win.

deed-known (*abstract*) *adj.* that which is seen only in its outworkings.

deem *v.* 1) to bethink, think of/look on as, 2) to find for/against, find guilty/not guilty, reckon, see straight, settle, mete out, weigh.

deemster (*judge, critic*) *n.* bencher, deemer, dempster, doomsman, doom-sayer.

deep *adj.* 1) bottomless, deepsome, fathomless, unfathomed, yawning, 2) knotted, beyond understanding, 3) learned, wise, 4) gripped, lost, 5) deeply felt, great, heartfelt, 6) (of *sound*) full, low, mellow, 7) (of hues) dark, rich, strong, warm, 8) canny, clever, knowing, sharp, shrewd, 9) a good way, a long way, deeply, far.

deep *n.* 1) deep sea, great waters, high seas, the main, the waves, 2) (as in 'the deep of night') dead, heart, middle, midst.

deep *adv.* 1) far into, for a long time, late, 2) at heart, inside, inwardly, within.

deepen *v.* 1) to go deep, hollow out, make deeper, 2) to greaten, strengthen, forstrengthen, 3) to darken, make dark/darker, shade.

deep-fetched *adj.* fetched from deep in the bosom.

deep-freeze *n.* freezer.

deep-laid *adj.* deeply laid, crafty, knowing, sharp, shrewd, underhand.

deeply *adv.* 1) far downwards/inwards, to a great depth, 2) thoroughly, to the heart, to the quick, with deep feeling.

deepmost *adj.* deepest, farthest down.

deepness *n.* 1) depth, 2) maze, hidden depths, riddle, the unknown.

deep-read *adj.* learned, deep-thinking, book-crafty, highbrow, well-read, wise.

deep-rooted[2] *adj.* abiding, innermost, inward, inwoven, inwrought, dyed in the wool.

deep sea *n.* great waters, high seas, the main, the waves.

deepsome *adj.* bottomless, deep, fathomless, unfathomed, yawning.

deep-thinking *adj.* learned, book-crafty, highbrow, well-read.

deer *n.* 1) wild *beast*, 2) fallow deer, red deer, hart.

deer-kin *n. beast*-kind.

deer-lore (*zoology*) *n. beast*-lore, kind-craft.

deft *adj.* canny, clever, handclever, good at, handy, nimble-fingered, quick, ready.

deftly *adv.* cleverly, nimbly, quickly, readily.

deftness *n.* handcleverness, handiness, quickness, readiness.

delf *n.* ditch, shaft.

dell *n.* coomb, hollow, slade.

delve *v.* 1) to till the ground, 2) to ask, comb/rake/root/sift through, delve deep, delve into, follow up, go into/over/through, hunt, look for, look into, rake over, rake through, root through, seek out, work over.

delving *n.* asking, getting to the bottom of, going deep into, going over, hunting, looking into, rooting, seeking, sifting, threshing out, weighing, winnowing.

dempster *n.* bencher, <u>deemster</u>, doom-sayer, doomster, one laying down the law.

den (*prison*) *n.* 1) fastness, hold, keep, lock-up, stronghold, 2) bolt-hole, burrow, earth, fox-hole, hide-out, hole, lair, shelter.

dene, dean *n.* the foremost Old English word for a main *valley*, a dean being most often long, winding, and narrow with two fairly steep sides and a slight slope downward along most of its length. See also 'dean'.

denn, den *n.* woodland grazing for swine.

depth *n.* 1) deepness, deeps, 2) keenness/strength (of feelings), 3) breadth/depth of mind, <u>wisdom</u>, understanding, wit, 4) breadth/depth (of knowledge).

depthen *v.* to deepen, make deeper, <u>greaten</u>, <u>strengthen</u>, forstrengthen.

dew *n.* dewiness, wet, wetness.

dewdrop *n.* drop of dew, bead.

dew-fall *n.* 1) the alighting of dew, 2) evening (when dew-fall happens).

dew-pond *n.* water-hold.

dew-worm *n.* earth-worm, ring-worm.

dewy *adj.* sodden, watery, wet.

dewy-eyed *adj.* tearful.

die *v.* 1) to be all over/up with, breathe one's last, die untimely, drop dead, fall, forthfare (from life), give up the ghost, go under, lose one's life, meet one's end, 2) to break down, cut out, give up, stop working.

die away, die down[6] *v.* to become/grow less, <u>dwindle</u>, lessen, tail off, wane.

die-hard *n.* bitter-ender, hard-head, last-ditcher, withstander,

die out *v.* to <u>dwindle</u>, end, wane, wither.

dill *n.* plant.

dim *adj.* 1) dark, gloomy, grey, shadowy, twilight, 2) dim-witted, empty-headed, half-witted, slow-witted, thick, unwitful, <u>witless</u>.

dim *v.* 1) to bedim, darken, shade, soften, 2) to become dim, grow dark.

dim-eyed *adj.* dim-sighted, half-blind, near-sighted, short-sighted.

dim-hued *adj.* dark-hued, dun-hued.

dimly *adv.* a bit, a little, slightly.

dimness *n.* bad light, dusk, gloaming, gloom, greyness, half-light, nightfall, shades of evening, shadowiness, twilight.

dim-out *n.* lessening in the brightness of lighting in a playhouse.

dimple *n.* cleft, dent, dip, hollow.

dim-sighted *adj.* dim-eyed, half-blind, near-sighted, short-sighted.

dim-wit *n.* clod, half-wit, lackwit, <u>witling</u>, oaf.

dim-witted *adj.* empty-headed, half-witted, slow-witted, thick, unwitful, <u>witless</u>.

din *n.* clatter, loudness, much ado, screech, shouting, uproar.

din *v.* to be loud, clatter, deafen, ring in the ear, roar.

dingy *adj.* 1) dark, dim, dreary, dun, gloomy, 2) seedy, shabby.

dint *n.* hit, knock, stroke.

dip *n.* 1) bathe, dive, swim, drenching, ducking, soaking, 2) downward slope, hillside, 3) bowl, hole, hollow, 4) cut, drop, fall, going down.

dip *v.* 1) to bathe, duck, wet, 2) to drop away, drop down, slope, 3) to dive, drop, fall, sink, 4) (of lights) to dim, bedim.

dipper *n.* brook ouzel, water ouzel, water blackbird.

distaff *n.* cleft staff on which wool or flax was wound.

distaff side *n.* women, womenfolk, womankind, woman's side of the kindred (also 'spindle side').

ditch *n.* long and narrow trough dug in the ground, cutting, drain, leat, runnel.

ditch *v.* 1) to delve a ditch, clean out a ditch, 2) to axe, drop, forsake, <u>leave</u>.

ditch *v.* to bring a flying craft (*aircraft*) down in the sea.

ditcher *n.* workman who delves ditches and sees to the upkeep of such.

dive *n.* header, leap, nosedive, spring, swoop.

dive *v.* 1) to leap into the water, pitch, go/swim underwater, 2) to drop, nosedive, fall, fall off, sink, slide.

diver *n.* one who works underwater, wearing underwater clothing.

dizziness *n.* lightmindedness, rashness, <u>heedlessness</u>.

dizzy *adj.* flighty, giddy, hare-brained, empty-headed, light-minded, all at sea.

do *n.* at-home, gathering, get-together.

do *v.* 1) to work, do the work of, drive forward, earn a living at, make, 2) to bear oneself, behave, 3) to make, make ready, put together, see to, shape, 4) to learn, read, read up on.

do away with *v.* to cut down, lay in the dust, make an end of, bring to <u>naught</u>, pull up, root up, tear up, <u>undo</u>, <u>unmake</u>, wipe out.

do in *v.* to do away with, kill, murder.

do up *v.* to brighten, clean up, make better, make good, put/set right, tidy up.

do well *v.* to better oneself, blossom, bring it off, come off well, come well out of it, fare well, feather one's nest, get ahead, get on, get to the top, go on well, grow fat, have the best of, live in clover, live on the fat of the land, make a breakthrough, make good, make a go of, make great strides, make hay, make one's mark, make one's way, make short work of, pull it off, reach one's goal, ride high, rise in the world, sail before the wind, speed well, win one's spurs, work one's way up.

do without *v.* to forbear, hold back, hold off, keep from, keep away, keep back.

do-all *n.* man of all-work.

dock *n.* plant.

doe *n.* she- fallow deer, she- hare.

doer *n.* maker, man of deeds, leader, shaker, stirrer, worker, craftsman, wright.

doff *v.* 1) to do off (one's hat), take off, 2) to shed, slip out of, throw off.

dog *n.* hound.

dog *v.* to follow after, go after, hound, hunt down, shadow, sit on one's tail, stalk.

dog-eared *adj.* not new, well-thumbed, well-trodden, well-worn, worn.

dog-fight *n.* 1) fight between dogs, 2) fight between flying craft.

dog-fox *n.* he- fox.

dogged *adj.* doughty, steadfast, steady, stalwart, tough, unyielding.

doggedly *adv.* steadfastly, steadily, tirelessly, unswervingly, through thick and thin.

doggedness *n.* doughtiness, steadiness, tirelessness, toughness.

do-gooder *n.* good man, good woman, good neighbour, busybody.

dog's body *n.* drudge, hireling, maid-of-all-work, underdog, underling, wretch.

dog-sleep *n.* light or fitful sleep, sham sleep.

dog-tired *adj.* fordone, hollow-eyed, ready to drop, tired out, weary, worn.

dog-weary *adj.* done for, faltering, more dead than alive, washed out, weary.

doings *n.* dealings, deeds, handiwork, steps, works.

doingsome *adj.* busy, hard-working, lively, quick, on one's toes, on the go, tireless.

do-it-yourself doing up one's house oneself.

dole *n.* cut, deal, helping, share.

dole *v.* to deal out, fordeal, give out, hand out, mete out, share out.

do-little *n.* good-for-nothing, idler, layabout, slacker.

don *v.* to do on, clothe oneself in, get into, pull on, put on, slip on.

done *adj.* 1) ended, over, settled, through, 2) cooked, ready.

do-nothing, do-nought, do-naught *n.* good-for-nothing, idler, layabout.

doom *n.* 1) (*judgement*) doom-saying, doom-word, finding, reckoning, weighing up, 2) wyrd, foredoom, foreshadowing, foreshaping, foreweaving, hidden hand, lot.

doom *v.* to accurse, lay a curse upon someone, thunder against.

doombook *n.* law book.

doomed *adj.* 1) born to evil, stricken, undone, wretched, 2) foreshapen, fore-willed, fore-woven, fore-written, fore-wrought, willed, wyrdful.

doomfast (*just*) *adj.* aright, even-handed, fair, right, rightwise, true.

doomfastness (*justice*) *n.* fairness, fair play, folk-right, right, rightness, righting evil.

doom-house (*law court*) *n.* doom-hall, the bench.

doom-sayer (*judge*) *n.* bencher, deemster, doomsman, one laying down the law.

doom-saying (*judgement*) *n.* doom, doom-word, finding, reckoning, weighing up.

Doomsday *n.* Last Day, Great Day, Day of the Lord, end of the world.

doom-settle *n. judgement* seat.

doomsman, doomster (*judge*) *n.* bencher, deemster, one laying down the law.

door *n.* doorway, ingoing, opening, way in, back door, house-door, side door.

doorkeeper *n.* doorward, gate-ward.

door-nail *n.* heavy nail (with which doors were once studded).

door-shelter (*porch*) *n.* doorway, hall inway.

door-sill, door-step *n.* threshold.

door-stone *n.* foot-stone, step-stone before a door.

doorward *n.* doorkeeper.

doorway *n.* inway, way in, way through, way to, gateway, opening, open door.

dor, dorr *n. insect* that flies with a loud droning, bee, black dung-beetle.

dot *n.* mark, speck, stroke, stop.

dot *v.* to mark with a dot/s.

dote on *v.* to be wild about, hold dear, love madly, make much of, smother.

doting *adj.* liking, loving, smitten, sweet on.

dotted *adj.* made up of dots, marked with dots.

dough *n.* 'clod' of meal wetted and kneaded, ready to be baked into bread.

doughnut *n.* bakemeat, sweetmeat.

doughtiness *n.* backbone, doggedness, grit, heartstrength, manliness, toughness, steadiness, steeliness, sternness.

doughty *adj.* dogged, game, stalwart, steadfast, manly, tough, unquelled, unyielding.

doughy *adj.* dough-like.

dove[7] *n.* bird of the *pigeon* kind.

down,[6] **dun** *n.* open upland, hill, ridge, wold.

down[6] *adj.* 1) going down, 2) bowed, <u>forlorn</u>, heavy-hearted, <u>hopelorn</u>, listless, sick at heart, woebegone, 3) broken, broken down, not working.

down[6] *adv.* adown, downhill, downstairs, downstream, downwards.

down[6] *prep.* 1) along, to the other end of, 2) through, throughout, over.

down[6] *v.* 1) to bring down, fell, floor, throw down, 2) to drain, drink down.

down[6]**-draught** *n.* downward breath of wind.

down[6]**-elf** (*mountain fairy*) *n.* hill elf.

downfall[6] *n.* end, fall, death-knell, doom, lost game, overthrow, undoing.

downfallen[6] *adj.* brought down, fallen, fordone, lost, overwhelmed, undone.

downhearted[6] *adj.* bowed down, <u>forlorn</u>, <u>hopelorn</u>, lorn, <u>weary</u>, wretched.

downhill[6] *adv.* adown, downwards.

downland[6] *n.* hilly land.

downplay[6] *v.* to play down.

downright[6] *adj.* 1) outright, out-and-out, sheer, thorough, thorough-going, utter, 2) hidebound, narrow-minded, overbearing, stiff-backed, stiff-necked, unbending.

downside[6] *n.* 1) under side, 2) drawback.

downstairs[6] *adv.* below stairs, on/to a lower floor, down to the bottom.

down[6]**-to-earth** *adj.* true, true to life, of flesh and blood, straight, grounded.

downtown[6] *adv.* to the heart/middle of town, to the business neighbourhood.

downtrodden[6] *adj.* broken, harrowed, heavy-laden, quelled, wretched.

downward/s[6] *adv.* adown, down, earthward, heading down, netherward.

draff (*rubbish*) *n.* chaff, dross, leavings, sweepings, throw-outs, dead wood.

draff-heap (*midden*) *n.* dunghill.

draffish, draffy *adj.* broken down, good for nothing, <u>hopeless</u>, idle, loss-making, no good, not working, not worth while, unhandy, unneeded, <u>worn out</u>, <u>worthless</u>.

draff-man, draff-rake (*scavenger*) *n.* sweeper, down-and-out, street-dweller.

draft *n.* drawing, foredraft, frame, lay-out, outline, rough draft, working draft.

draft *v.* to do one's homework/spadework, draw up, frame, lay out, mark out, outline, put together, rough out, set out, think out/through/up, work out.

draftsman *n.* drafter, drawer, framer.

drag *n.* burden, dead-weight, drawback, hindering, load, millstone, shackle, weight.

drag *v.* to draw, heave, pull, tow, drag down, drag one's heels.

drain *n.* 1) cut, ditch, leat, open drain, overflow, runnel, trough, waterway, 2) burden, drag, weight.

drain *v.* 1) to empty, leak away, ooze out, 2) to drink to the last drop, knock back, put away, swallow, 3) to leach, leak into, ooze, seep, soak through, 4) to drain off, draw off, empty, free, run off, tap, unclot, 5) to bleed white, eat up, run through, suck dry, 6) to overwork, tire out, wear out, weary.

drained *adj.* aground, at a low ebb, hollow-eyed, overworked, <u>weary</u>, worn out.

draining *adj.* back-breaking, crippling, hard going, tiring, <u>wearing</u>, wearying.

draught *n.* breath, downdraught, updraught, flow, wind.

draught *v.* see 'draft'.

draughtsman *n.* see 'draftsman'.

draughty *adj.* blowy, chill, cold, windy.

draw *n.* 1) pull, winning ways, 2) gambling, gaming, 3) drawn game or match.

draw *v.* 1) to drag, pull, tow, 2) to draw a bolt, draw in a net, 3) to bend a bow and pull back the arrow on the string, 4) (of window hangings) to open, pull open, pull back, pull shut, pull together, 5) (of a ship) to sweep aside so much depth of water, 6) (of meaning) to draw out, draw forth, bring to the fore, open up, unfold, 7) to draw breath, breath in, 8) to bewitch, grip, pull, take someone's eye, win over, 9) to pull out, take out, wrench out, 10) to choose, pick, 11) to bring out, drain off, draw blood, draw out, take, 12) to draw a net along a stream for fish, to hunt through woods for game, 13) to do drawings, mark out, outline, 14) (of a *bill, paper*) to frame, write out, 15) to come, draw near, draw aside, drive, go, 16) (of a sword) to take out, unsheath, withdraw.

draw alongside *v.* to team up with, go with, walk with, be found with, be seen with, keep with, shadow, follow.

draw away *v.* to bewitch, draw/fill/hold the mind, grip, lead on, mislead, play upo.

draw back *v.* to back out, climb down, have other thoughts, withdraw.

drawback *n.* downside, shortcoming.

drawbridge *n.* bridge which may be drawn up – to shut out foes from a stronghold, or (when the bridge is over a *river*) to let ships go upstream/downstream.

drawer *n.* drafter, draftsman, framer.

drawer *n.* one of the box-shaped holders in a chest of drawers.

drawers *n.* underclothes, underwear, also (less often) breeches.

drawing *n.* line drawing, outline, rough draft, working draft.

drawing *adj.* bewitchful, bewitching, 'come-hither', taking, <u>winning</u>.

drawing-board *n.* drafting board.

draw-gate *n.* water-gate (for letting out water that has been held back, in a draining and/or water-meadow setup).

drawing-room *n.* at first the 'withdrawing room', to which one went after even-meat, or where one welcomed folk; sitting-room.

drawn *adj.* careworn, harrowed, overwrought, stricken, woebegone, wretched.

draw out *v.* 1) to drag out, lengthen, make longer, play for time, spin out, stretch, string out, 2) to pull out, take out, 3) to bring out, bring to the fore, <u>highlight</u>, open up, shed/throw light upon.

draw up *v.* to draft, frame, mark out, outline, put together, set out, shape, write out.

dray *n.* 1) wain without wheels, 2) low wain without sides, for bearing heavy loads (such as a brewer's dray).

drayman *n.* carter, driver, cart-driver.

dread *n.* <u>fear</u>, fright, affright, cold feet.

filled with **dread** <u>fearful</u>, frightened to death, frozen with fear, shrinking with fear.

dread *v.* to <u>fear</u>, fordread, shake/shiver/shrink with fear, feel one's blood run cold.

dread *adj.* dreaded, dreadful, frightening, frightful, ghastly.

dreadful *adj.* 1) baleful, baneful, chilling, fearful, fearsome, forbidding, frightening, frightful, ghastly, great, grisly, mighty, numbing, threatening, 2) bad, filthy, foul, ghastly, harrowing, hateful, hellish, <u>loathsome</u>, nightmarish, of deepest dye, shameful, sickening, too bad, woeful, worthless, wretched.

dreadfully *adv.* badly, fearfully, <u>shamefully</u>, woefully, wretchedly.

dreading *adj.* in dread, over-heedful, over-wrought, harrowed, writhing, <u>fearful</u>.

dreadingly *adv.* with dread, fearfully.

dreadless *adj.* <u>bold</u>, <u>fearless</u>, knightly, stopping at nothing, unfearing.

dreadnought *n.* 1) thick 'windbreaker' (*coat*), 2) warship.

dream *n.* dreamcraft (*music*), gladness, mirth.

dream *n.* flights of thought and make-believe, running through the mind whilst one is asleep.

dream *v.* to make *sounds* of dreamcraft and/or gladness.

dream *v.* to dream dreams, dream up, daydream, hatch, make-believe, make up, play with one's thoughts, see in the mind's eye, take into one's head, think up.

dreamcraft (*music*) *n.* song-craft, cradle-song, singing, song, love-song, undersong, burden, setting, work.

dreamer (*musician*) *n.* harper, horn-player, player, singer, songster.

dreamful *adj.* dreamy, soft, sweet.

dream-hole *n.* hole or slit left in the wall of a barn, steeple or such.

dreamless *adj.* night without dreams, restful, soothing, still, unstirring.

dream-song *n.* cradle-song, song, love-song.

dreamy *adj.* daydreaming, <u>far-away</u>, lost in thought, head in the clouds.

drear *adj.* grey, wearisome.

dreariness *n.* greyness, heaviness, slowness, tiresomeness, twice-told tale, wearisomeness, world-weariness.

dreary *adj.* dragging, dry, dry as dust, endless, grey, harping, heavy, leaden, lifeless, mind-numbing, overlong, slow, unbroken, weariful, wearing, wearisome.

dredge *n.* tool for bringing up things from a stream-bed by dredging.

dredge *v.* to clean out/deepen the bed of a stream.

dredger *n.* boat *used* in dredging.

drench *n.* drink, draught, deep draught, leech-draught (*medicine*) for a *beast*.

drench *v.* to bathe, drown, flood, soak, steep, wet through, overwhelm, whelm.

dretch *v.* to beset, give one a bad time at night, <u>goad</u>, harry, needle, <u>worry</u>.

drier *n.* tool for drying (such as a hair-drier).

drink *n.* 1) cup, draught, glass, thirst quencher, 2) brew, strong drink, ale, mead.

drink *v.* to drain, drink one's fill, drink up, quench/slake one's thirst, sip, swallow.

drink-bound *adj.* having made a plighting with drink (*Beowulf*, lines 1230-31).

drink in *v.* 1) to fill the mind, lap up, <u>learn</u>, come to know/understand, 2) to look at/on, stand and stare, stand in amaze/wonder, soak up, take in.

drinking-horn *n.* horn hollowed out to make a drinking *vessel*.

drink to *v.* to drink a health to, lift one's glass to.

drink-vat *n.* drinking bowl.

drip *n.* bead, drop.

drip *v.* to drain, drop, leach, leak into, ooze, seep, soak through.

drip (*medical*) *n.* pipe through which water (strengthened with *medicine* or food) or blood seeps into the body.

drip-dry *v.* to dry by hanging up to drip (without needing ironing afterwards).

drive *n.* 1) outing, ride, run, 2) driveway, 3) (*cricket*) a strike with the bat, sending the ball either straight back or to the off or on sides, 4) hammering away, striving, 5) boldness, earnestness, fire, go, hard work, head, life, liveliness, lustiness, might, putting one's back into it, sparkle, spring, steam, strength, life-strength, strength of heart/mind/will, warmth.

drive *v.* to drive forward, elbow, goad, play upon, shoulder, shove, spur on.

drive at *v.* to go for, go all out for, go after, bid for, make for, be minded.

drivel *n.* childish talk, empty/idle talk.

drivel *v.* 1) to ooze/run as spittle from the mouth, 2) to talk childishly.

driver *n.* one who steers a *vehicle*.

driveway *n.* drive, inway.

driving *n.* driving along, going along.

driving *adj.* bold, go-ahead, hearty, keen, lively, lusty, tireless, up-and-doing, wild.

drizzle *n.* light rainfall, spitting, wet, wetness, wet weather.

drizzle *v.* to be wet, drip, rain, spit.

drizzly *adj.* rainy, wettish.

drone *n.* the he- honey-bee.

drone *n.* hum, humming.

drone *v.* 1) (of bees) to hum, 2) to go on and on, run on, talk on and on.

drop *n.* 1) bead, teardrop, 2) sip, spot, 3) cut, cutback, fall, fall-off.

drop *v.* 1) to fall in drops, drip, leak, 2) to fall a-wearied/wounded/dead, sink down, 3) to let fall (a word, hint or such), 4) to leave hold of, let go of, 5) to leave something at someone's house, set down, unload, 6) to dwindle, fall away, lessen, slacken, 7) to axe, forsake, give up, throw over, 8) to leave out/undone, miss.

drop by, drop in on *v.* to call in, go and see, look in on,

drop off *v.* 1) to fall asleep, go off, 2) to dwindle, fall off, lessen, shrink, wane.

drop-out *n.* idler, loser, runaway, wanderer.

drop out *v.* to back out, fall by the wayside, forsake, give up, leave, pull out, stop,

drop-meal *adv.* drop by drop, in drops.

droppings *n.* dung, stool.

dropwise *adv.* drop by drop.

dross *n.* leavings.

drought *n.* 1) dryness, dry spell, dry weather, dryth, 2) dearth, lack, shortfall.

drove *n.* 1) herd, 2) crowd, gathering, swarm, throng.

drover *n.* herdsman, kinesman.

drown *v.* 1) to die under water, go down, go under, 2) to drench, flood out, soak, 3) to be louder than, overcome, overwhelm, swallow up.

drowsy *adj.* half asleep/awake, heavy-eyed, heavy with sleep, sleep-weary, sleepy.

drudge *n.* dogsbody, maid of all work, worker, hewer of wood and drawer of water.

drudge *v.* to work hard, work one's fingers to the bone.

drunk (*alcoholic*) *n.* hard drinker.

drunken *adj.* drunk, blind drunk, dead drunk, dead to the world, fighting drunk, drunk as a lord, having had a drop too much, merry, sodden, the worse for drink.

drunkenly *adv.* beerily, loutishly.

drunkenness *n.* hard drinking.

dry *adj.* 1) bone dry, dry as a bone, dried-up, rainless, sere, thirsty, waterless, withered, 2) dreary, heavy going, longsome, 3) cutting, keen, sharp, witty, wry.

dry *v.* to drain, dry up, make dry, sear, wring out.

dry-clean *v.* to clean clothes without water.

dry-eyed *adj.* cold, grim, shedding no tears, stony-hearted, heartless, ruthless.

dry-fist *n.* grasper, hoarder, holdfast.

dry-foot *adv.* without wetting the feet.

dry land *n.* the land (as against the sea).

dryly, drily *adv.* keenly, sharply, wittily, wryly.

dryness *n.* drought, dry spell, dry weather, dryth.

dry run *n.* going-over, run-through.

dry-shod *adj.* with dry shoes, without wetting the feet.

dry-stone *adj.* of a wall built without *mortar*.

dryth *n.* drought, dryness.

dry up *v.* 1) to become dry, harden, wither, wizen, 2) to die out, dwindle, ebb, lessen, run out.

duck *n.* ened, ende.

duck *n.* bow.

duck *v.* 1) to dip, drench, soak, wet, 2) to bend, bow, keep one's head down, stoop.

duck-boards *n.* wooden boards laid across wet ground, to make a pathway.

ducking *n.* drenching, soaking, wetting.

duckling *n.* young duck.

duck's bill *n.* 1) bill of a duck, 2) tool of this shape.

duckweed *n.* plant found on still water.

dumb *adj.* 1) speechless, tongueless, wordless, 2) at a loss for words, bewildered, dumb-struck, tongue-tied.

smite/strike **dumb** *v.* to cut one short, cut the ground from under, make speechless, shut one up, still, stop someone's mouth, tie up one's tongue, amaze, bewilder.

dumbly *adv.* speechlessly, wordlessly.

dumbness *n.* speechlessness, wordlessness.

dummy *n.* man-/woman-shaped likeness in a shop window, for showing clothes.

dun *adj.* of a brown or grey hue.

dung *n.* droppings.

dung *v.* to rake in dung.

dung-beetle *n.* dor-beetle.

dunghill *n.* draff-heap, mixen.

dun-hued *adj.* brown or grey.

dunnock *n.* hedge creeper, hedge chat, hedge sparrow, pinnock.

dusk *n.* dark, evening, eventide, half-light, nightfall, owl-light, sunset, twilight.

dusky *adj.* 1) darkish, darksome, dim, gloomy, grey, shades of evening, shadowy, shady, twilight, twilit, 2) dark, swarthy.

dust *n.* filth.

dust *v.* 1) to overlay with dust, 2) to clean by wiping off dust.

duster *n.* cleaning cloth with which to wipe off dust.

dusting *n.* light overlay of meal on a bakemeat or snow on the ground.

dusty *adj.* unclean, undusted, unswept.

dwarf *n.* 1) (in wonder tale) small man-like being, 2) small man or woman, halfling, hopthumb ('hop on my thumb').

dwarf *v.* to overlook, overtop, overshadow, throw into the shadow, put in the shade, stand head and shoulders above, stand over.

dwarfish *adj.* knee-high, little, short, small, slow-growing, stunted, wee, wizened.

dwarfling *n.* small dwarf.

dwell *v.* to abide, bide, live, put up at, settle.

dwell on *v.* 1) to go on (thinking) about, harp on about, 2) to highlight, drive home.

dweller *n.* indweller.

dwelling *n.* home, housing, board, rooms, shelter.

dwindle *v.* to become smaller, die away, die down, die out, dim, dwine, ebb, ebb away, grow dim, grow less, lessen, melt away, shade off, shrink, tail off, thin, wane, wear away, wear off, wilt, wither.

dwine *v.* to dwindle, die away, ebb away, shrink, wane, wear away, wither.

dye *n.* hue, shade, wash.

dye *v.* to shade with some hue.

dyeing *n.* the work of giving a new hue to cloth, leather and such.

dyer *n.* cloth-dyer, dye-worker.

dying *n.* coming to the end of life, dying breath, last breath.

dying *adj.* 1) at death's door, on one's deathbed, breathing one's last, doomed, ebbing, falling, going, near death, near the end, not long for this world, sinking, 2) last, 3) dwindling, shrinking.

each *adj.* every.

each *pron.* all, one and all, each one, each and every one, everyone.

ealdorman *n.* earl, elder, head, leader, lord.

eanling *n.* young lamb.

ear *n.* the *part* of the body by which one hears, ear-hole.

ear *n.* head of corn, corn seed.

ear *v.* to plough, till.

ear-ache *n.* upset in the ear (making it ache).

ear-finger *n.* the little finger (often put in the ear).

earful *n.* telling-off, as much talk as one can take at one time.

earing *n.* ploughing, tilling

earing *n.* (of corn) coming into ear.

earl *n.* earldorman, high lord.

ear-lap *n.* ear *flap/lobe*.

earldom *n.* the lands lorded over by an earl, the standing of an earl.

earlier *adj.* aforesaid, erstwhile, first, foregoing, former, last, one-time, sometime.

earliest *adj.* first, first in the field, opening.

earlship *n.* standing or work of an earl, lordship.

early *adj.* earliest, first, forward, in time, in good time, on time, timely, opening.

early *adv.* ahead of time, beforehand, before long, betimes, ere long, first thing, soon, too soon, with time enough, with time to spare.

earmark *n.* mark in the ear of a sheep or other *beast*, showing ownership.

earmark *v.* to hold for, keep back, mark down for, mark out, set aside.

earn *v.* to gather, build up, reap, win.

earned *adj.* bought, in one's hand, in one's hold.

earnest *adj.* aglow, burning, hearty, keen, open, steady, steadfast, thorough, thoughtful, trothful, true, warm, whole-hearted, willing, ready and willing.

earnestness *n.* steadfastness, tirelessness, warmth, whole-heartedness.

earnestly *adv.* from the bottom of one's heart, in earnest, truly, wholeheartedly.

earnings *n.* income, meed, takings.

ear-ring *n.* ring worn in the lap/*lobe* of the ear.

earshot *n.* span or sweep of one's hearing.

ear-sore *adj.* bearish, crabbed, fretful, prickly, short, shrewish, sour.

ear-speaker *n.* gossip, tale-teller, whisperer.

earth *n.* 1) middle earth, world, wide world, 2) ground, land, dry land, 3) clay, dust, 4) bolt-hole, burrow, den, fox-hole, hideaway, hide-out, hole, lair, shelter.

earth *v.* to bury, ground.

earth-bed *n.* 1) bed on the ground, 2) grave.

earth-board *n.* mould-board of a plough.

earth-born *adj.* fleshly, manlike, mannish.

earth-bound *adj.* homeborn, settled.

earth-craft (*geometry*) *n.* earth-mete, earth-reckoning.

earth-din *n.* earthquake, earth-stirring, ground wave.

earthen *adj.* 1) made of earth, 2) of flesh and blood.

earthenware *n.* crocks, pots.

earthfast *adj.* set in the ground, lasting, settled, standing fast.

earth-hem (*horizon*) *n.* earth-rim, farthest reach, outer edge.

earthiness *n.* 1) forthrightness, outspokenness, roughness, 2) lustiness, worldliness.

earth-land *n.* crop-land, tilth.

earthlight *n.* light thrown back from the earth upon the dark half of the moon, earth-shine.

earth-like *adj.* earth-kindly, earthly, this-worldly.

earthliness *n.* mannishness, worldliness.

earthling *n.* acreman, crofter, earth-tiller, smallholder, yeoman.

earthling *n.* earth-dweller, worldling.

earthlore (*geology*) *n.* stonelore.

earthly *adj.* earth-kindly, earth-like, this-worldly.

earthly-minded *adj.* fleshly, godless, lewd, lusty, shameless, worldly-minded.

earthly-mindedness *n.* fleshliness, lewdness, lust, worldliness.

earth-mete (*geometry*) *n.* earth-craft, earth-reckoning.

earthquake *n.* 1) earth-stirring, earth-din, ground wave, 2) clean sweep, landslide, overthrow, shake-up, swing, upheaving.

earth-reckoning (*geometry*) *n.* earth-craft, earth-mete.

earth-rim (*horizon*) *n.* earth-hem, sea-rim, farthest reach, field of sight, outer/ outside edge, the uttermost.

earth-stirring *n.* earth-din, earthquake, ground wave.

earth-tiller *n.* acreman, crofter, smallholder, yeoman.

earth-tilling, earth-tilth (*agriculture*) *n.* fieldcraft, fieldlore, croplore.

earthward *adv.* towards the earth.

earthwork *n.* earth ridge, ditch, outwork.

earthworm *n.* mould-worm, rain-worm.

earth-worn *adj.* hoary, old, heavy with years, worn out by long years.

earthwrit *n.* geography.

earthy *adj.* 1) down-to-earth, rough, rough and ready, straightforward, 2) bodily, fleshly, lewd, lusty, worldly, worldly-minded.

earth-yard *n.* the *metre* (more or less a yard, but meant to be one ten-*millionth* of the way from the earth's girdle/*equator* to the North Pole).

ear-wax *n.* wax which gathers in the outer *part* of the ear.

earwig *n. insect* thought to worm its way into the ear.

earwitness *n.* one who witnesses to what he/she has heard with their own ears.

east *adv.* eastwards.

east *n.* that length of the earth's rim which lies towards the rising of the sun.

east *adj.* belonging to/lying towards/of the east, looking towards the east, (of the wind) blowing from the east.

east-end *n.* east end of anything (such as a town).

Easter *n.* the *Feast* of Christ's Rising from the dead.

Easter-day *n.* the Day of Christ's Rising from the dead.

Easter eve *n.* Easter-night.

easterly *adv.* to the eastward, from the east, on the east side.

easterly *adj.* set towards the east, eastern, (of the wind) blowing from the east.

Easter-month (*April*) *n.* fourth month of the year, first month of spring/summer.

eastern *adj.* coming from/living in/lying to the east, (of the wind) blowing from the east.

easterner *n.* dweller in the east.

Easter-night *n.* Easter eve.

easternmost *adj.* set farthest to the east.

eastland/s *n.* 1) eastern land or hundred, 2) lands about the Baltic Sea.

east-right *adv.* dead/straight east.

eastward/s *adv.* to/towards the east.

eastward *adj.* that which goes or looks eastward.

eastwardly *adv.* to/towards the east, from an eastern fourthing.

eat *v.* 1) to chew, put away, swallow, wolf down, 2) to break bread, breakfast, fall to, feed, have a meal, set to, take food, 3) (of the work of frost, rust, waves and such) to crumble, gnaw, make inroads into, wear away/down.

eath, eathly (*easy*) *adj.* leaf-light, light, no sooner said than done, not hard, ready, soft, 'all in a day's work', 'a walk-over'.

eath, eathly (*easily*) *adv.* far and away, readily, smoothly, straightforwardly, swimmingly, 'with one's eyes shut'.

eat into *v.* to drain, get through, go through, run through, swallow up.

eatsome (*edible*) *adj.* good to eat, harmless, wholesome.

eat up *v.* to go through, run through, swallow up.

eaves *n.* 1) overhanging edge of a roof, 2) edge/rim of woodland.

eavesdrip *n.* dripping of rainwater from the eaves of a house.

ebb *n.* 1) ebb tide, outgoing tide, 2) drop, dwindling, flowing back, going out, falling, lessening, sinking, slackening, wane, waning, withdrawing.

ebb *adj.* shallow.

ebb *v.* 1) to flow back, go out, 2) to drop, dwindle, fall back, lessen, slacken, wane.

eddish *n.* aftermath grass, stalks left after gathering in the crop.

eddy *n.* water of a stream that runs against the flow/tide.

eddy *v.* to *swirl* about in an eddy.

eddy-wind *n.* wind that goes about in an eddy.

edge *n.* 1) eaves, lip, rim, threshold, 2) hill-slope, lith, long ridge, rise, sloping edge, steep slope, 3) bite, sharpness, sting, 4) head start, lead, upper hand.

on **edge** *adj.* edgy, treading warily, fearful, dreading, starting at a *sound*.

edge *v.* 1) to give a cutting edge (to a tool or weapon), 2) to give an edging/hem to, 3) to creep, steal towards, work edgeways/sideways, worm one's way.

edgeless *adj.* having no edge, unsharpened, unwhetted.

edgeling, edgelong *adv.* with the edge, on the edge.

edgeways, edgewise *adj.* with the edge foremost, sideways, on the edge.

edging *n.* hem, trimming.

edgy *adj.* highly-strung, on edge, restless.

eel *n.* snake-like fish.

eel-bed *n.* pond for eels.

eel-net *n.* net for taking eels.

eely *adj.* eel-like.

eerie, eery *adj.* chilling, frightening, ghostly, nightmarish, uncanny, unearthly, weird.

eft *n.* newt.

egg[2] *n. oval* body in a shell, laid by she-birds and other *beasts*, and bearing the beginnings of new life within.

eight *n. adj.* the root *number* following seven.

eighteen *n. adj.* the root *number* made of ten and eight.

eighteenth *adj. n.* 1) the marking *number* that is kin to eighteen, 2) eighteenth share of something.

eightfold *adj.* eight times as great or as many.

eighth *adj. n.* 1) the marking *number* that is kin to eight, 2) eighth share of something.

eighthly *adv.* in the eighth *place*.

eightieth *adj. n.* 1) the marking *number* that is kin to a eighty, 2) eightieth share of something.

eighty *n. adj.* the root *number* that is eight times ten.

either 1) *adj.* each (of two, or sometimes more), both, one or the other (of two), any one (of more than two), 2) *adv.* which you like, any more than the other.

eke out *v.* to be sparing, make do, make ends meet, stretch.

eke-name *n.* a further name, a nickname.

elbow *n.* 1) the bend of the arm, outer bit of the tie-up between forearm and upper arm, 2) knee, horn, bend, *angle*.

elbow *v.* to shoulder, shove.

elbow-room *n.* breathing room, field, leeway, play, free/full play.

elder *n.* a tree.

elder *n.* 1) older man/woman, 2) ealdorman, earl, head, leader, 3) church leader.

elder *adj.* earlier born, first, first-born, older.

elder-days *n.* the days of high deeds, the great days, the long-ago days.

elder-hood *n.* grey hairs, many winters.

elderly *adj.* full of years, going grey, greying, grey-haired, hoary, hoary-headed, many-wintered, old, white-haired, withered, wizened.

eldern *adj.* elderly, hoary, many-wintered, olden, belonging to earlier times.

eldern *adj.* made of elder wood.

eldership (*authority*) *n.* headship, leadership, lord-dom, lordliness, lordship.

eldest *adj.* earliest born, first, first-born, oldest.

eldritch *adj.* of the elf kingdom/land/world, unearthly, weird.

eleven *n. adj.* 1) the root *number* that is 'one left' (over ten), 2) the eleven players of a stockball/*cricket* team.

eleventh *adj. n.* 1) the marking *number* that is kin to eleven, 2) eleventh share of something.

elf *n.* dark elf, light elf.

elf-addle *n.* nightmare, bad dream, wild dream.

elf-arrow *n.* the flint-headed arrow thought to be fired by elves (see 'elf-shot').

elf-blessed *adj.* blessed by a light (good) elf.

elf-bolt *n.* the flint-headed arrow thought to be fired by elves (see 'elf-shot').

elfin, elfish *adj.* 1) of elvish being, elf-like. 2) unearthly, weird, 3) light, small.

elf-kin *n.* the elfin folk, elfin kind.

elf-sheen *adj.* fair as an elf, elf-fair, bewitching, comely, lovely, willowy.

elf-shot *n.* the flint-headed arrow thought to be fired by elves at kine, bringing on sickness.

elf-stone *n.* the flint-headed arrow thought to be fired by elves (see 'elf-shot').

elf-ward (*genius*) *n.* other self.

elk *n.* great deer.

ell *n.* a reckoning of length, namely the length of a man's forearm. The English ell is forty-five inches.

ell-mete, ell-rod *n.* ell yardstick.

elm *n.* a tree whose wood is long-lasting and can withstand wetness. From it are made such things as the naves of wheels, felloes and *axle*-tree beds.

else *adv.* as well as, also, besides, moreover, furthermore, let alone, likewise.

elsewhere *adv.* somewhere else, elsewhither.

elsewhither *adv.* elsewhere, whithersoever, in some other path, to some other *place.* **elsewise** *adv.* otherwise.

elven *adj.* see 'elfin'.

elver *n.* young eel.

elvish *adj.* see 'elfish'.

ember/s *n.* small bit/s of live coal or wood in a dying fire, ashes, cinders.

ember-day/s, ember weeks *n.* the four times of fasting and bidding/*prayer* in the church year. At a *council* in the year of our Lord 1095, these were set for the Wednesday, Friday and Seventh Day/*Saturday* next following 1) the first Lord's Day in Lent, 2) Whitsunday, 3) 14th Harvest-month/*September*, 4) 13th Ere-yule/ *December*.

emmet *n.* ant.

emmet-hill *n.* ant-heap, ant-hill, ant-hillock.

emptiness *n.* 1) being empty, nothingness, 2) hollowness, idleness, worthlessness, 3) dizzyness, light-mindedness, oafishness, unwisdom.

empty *adj.* 1) having nothing within, 2) blown out, drained, lean, 3) bare, dreary, wild, 4) childish, flighty, giddy, hollow, light-minded, shallow, thoughtless, unwitful, witless, 5) idle, worthless, 6) stony, unforthcoming, wooden.

empty *v.* 1) to drain out, draw off, run off, run through, 2) to lay bare, strip bare.

empty-handed *adj.* bootless, with nothing.

empty-headed *adj.* dim-witted, dizzy, flighty, giddy, hare-brained, light-minded.

empty-headedness *n.* carelessness, dizzyness, feather-headedness, heedlessness, light-mindedness, unwisdom.

end *n.* 1) edge, head, peak, 2) leftover, tail end, 3) ending, stop, wind-up, 4) goal, mark, outcome, upshot, 5) death, doom, dying.

end *v.* 1) to axe, leave off, put a stop to, shut down, stop, wind up, 2) to be all over, come to an end, die out, run out, 3) to do away with, put an end to, put to death.

end-all *n.* that which ends all.

end-day *n.* death, last day.

end game *n.* the last steps of a game such as *chess*, a last 'make-or-break' tussle.

ending *n.* end, outcome, upshot, wind-up.

endless *adj.* 1) abiding, deathless, everlasting, forevermore, never-ending, timeless, unending, 2) dragging, dreary, long, long-drawn-out, overlong, wearisome, 3) bottomless, far-stretching, unfathomful, 4) ever so many, ever-flowing, overflowing, swarming, teeming, unrimed, untold, 5) unbroken, without end.

endlessly *adv.* again and again, 'day in, day out', everlastingly, forever, night and day, over and over, time and again, time after time.

endlessness *n.* 1) (*eternity*) life everlasting, endless time, everlastingness, never-endingness, timelessness, 2) dreariness, slowness, wearisomeness.

endlong 1) *prep.* along, from end to end of, over/through the length of, 2) *adv.* lengthwise, on end, straight on/through, 3) *adj.* laid out lengthwise, set on end.

endly *adv.* 1) at the last, lastly, in the end, in the fullness of time, 2) for all time, for ever, once and for all.

endmost *adj.* furthest, nearest to the end.

end-rime (*number*) *n.* rime-tally, rime-tell, tale, tellship.

endsay (*epilogue*) *n.* aftersay, afterword, end-speech.

endship *n.* a small edge-of-town/out-of-town neighbourhood.

end-speech (*epilogue*) *n.* aftersay, afterword, endsay.

endways, endwise *adv.* 1) with the end foremost or uppermost, 2) end foremost, end on, lengthwise.

ened, ende *n.* duck.

English-rede *n.* the English tongue.

enough *adj.* enough to get by/live on, enough said, meeting the need, middling.

ent *n.* *giant*, oak of a man.

ere *adv.* afore, aforetime, before, beforehand, earlier, ere now, ere then, ere-while.

Ere-litha (*June*) *n.* Fore-litha, Lida ærra, Midsummer-month, Sere ('dry')-month.

erelong *adv.* before long, betimes, forthwith, now, soon, straightway.

ere-named *adj.* above named.

erenow *adv.* before now, heretofore, hitherto, till now, time out of mind.

ere-while *adv.* aforetime, erstwhile, formerly, a long time/while ago, in olden times, lately, long ago, long since, of old, some time ago/back/since, time was, years ago.

Ere-yule (*December*) *n.* Midwintermonth, Yule-month.

erne (*eagle*) *n.* a great hunting bird – golden erne, white-tailed erne.

errand *n.* 1) a word, tidings, 2) a going with tidings/business for another.

errand-bearer *n.* runner, word-bearer.

errand-writ, -writing (*letter*) *n.* line, written tidings, written word, written answer.

ersc *n.* ploughed field, stalky/stubble field (after harvest).

erst 1) *adj.* first, 2) *adv.* at first, earlier, earliest, sooner, soonest.

erstwhile *adv.* aforetime, ere-while, formerly, some time back, some while ago.

erth *n.* plough land.

eve, even *n.* evening, eventide, going down of the sun, nightfall, twilight.

even *adj.* 1) smooth, steady, unbroken, 2) flush, right, true, 3) alike, like, matching, on a like footing, 4) drawn, evenly-matched, neck and neck, tied, 5) cool, cool-headed, unshaken, 6) even-handed, fair, fair-minded, right, rightwise.

even *adv.* 1) although, though, notwithstanding, 2) all the more, much, still, yet, 3) at all, so much as, 4) indeed, in truth.

even *v.* 1) to even out, smooth down, smooth off, smoothen, 2) (in book-keeping) to make even, reckon up, get the books right/straight, 3) to liken, match.

even-fall *n.* the beginning of evening, dusk, nightfall, twilight.

even-handed *adj.* fair, fair-minded, straight, rightwise.

even-handedness *n.* fair-mindedness, fairness, uprightness.

evenhead, evenhood (*equality*) *n.* evenness, likeness, meetness.

even-high *adj.* as high, of like height.

evening *n.* eve, even, eventide, going down of the sun, nightfall, twilight.

evening *n.* the business of making even, smoothing.

evening-star *n.* even-star – the heavenly body (*planet*) *Venus*.

even-light *n.* evening light.

even-like *adj.* alike, even, matched, on a like footing.

evenlong 1) *adj.* even-sided, 2) *adv.* straight along.

evenly *adv.* even-handedly, fairly, rightly.

even-meat *n.* evening-meal.

even-minded *adj.* cool, steady, unshaken.

evenness (*equality*) *n.* evenhood, likeness, meetness.

even-night (*equinox*) *n.* one of the two times in the year (in the Lengthening Month/ *March* and in Harvestmonth/*September*) when day and night are of the like length.

even-sided *adj.* matched, rightly/truly shaped, rightly wrought, straight, true.

evensong *n.* the church worship held towards sunset.

even-star *n.* evening star – the heavenly body (*planet*) *Venus*.

eventide *n.* eve, even, evening, going down of the sun, nightfall, twilight.

even up *v.* to straighten out, set in line.

ever *n.* wild boar.

ever *adv.* 1) always, at all times, everlastingly, evermore, for ever, to the end of time, throughout all time, unendingly, 2) at all, at any time.

evergreen *adj.* always green, having green leaves all the year through.

evergreen *n.* evergreen tree (such as the holly, yew).

everlasting *adj.* <u>abiding</u>, lasting, long-standing, unending,

ever-living *adj.* <u>abiding</u>, deathless, everlasting, never-ending, timeless, undying.

evermore *adv.* always, ever, for ever, for ever and a day, to the end of time.

every *adj.* all, each, each and every.

everybody *n.* all and sundry, everyone, one and all, the world and his wife.

everyday *adj.* daily, day-to-day, homely, homespun, stock, wonted, workaday.

everydeal *n.* every whit, the whole.

everyone *n.* all and sundry, each one, everybody, one and all, the whole world.

everything *n.* all, each thing, the lot, the whole, the whole lot.

everyway *adv.* in every way.

everywhere *adv.* abroad, all over, far and near/wide, here and there, the world over.

everywhither *adv.* in every way/bearing.

evil *n.* 1) evil-doing, wickedness, backsliding, badness, misdealing, misdeed, misdoing, shamelessness, sin, besetting sin, deadly sin, sinfulness, ungodliness, unrightness, wickedness, wicked ways, wilfulness, worthlessness, 2) bane, blight.

evil *adj.* bad, baleful, baneful, black, black-hearted, evil-doing, evil-minded, fallen, fiendish, foul, godless, guilty, hateful, hellish, knavish, <u>loathsome</u>, shameful, <u>shameless</u>, lost to shame, shady, shifty, sinful, sin-laden, twisted, ungodly, unhallowed, unholy, unrightwise, warped, wicked, worthless, as bad as bad can be, utterly bad, up to no good.

evil *adv.* badly, harmfully, in an evil way.

evil-doer *n.* cut-throat, fiend, guilty man, knave, misdoer, sinner, hardened sinner, worker of evil, worldling, good-for-nothing, ne'er-do-well, fox, snake, snake in one's bosom, snake in the grass, wolf, wretch, rough, tough, twister, backslider, black sheep, lost sheep.

evil-speaking *adj.* foul-mouthed, foul-speaking, foul-tongued, evil-tongued.

evil-speech *n.* foul-speech, smearing, backbiting, cursing.

evil-tongued *adj.* foul-mouthed, foul-spoken, foul-tongued, rough-tongued.

ewe *n.* she- sheep.

eye *n.* 1) naked eye, sight, eye-sight, 2) sharp eye, watchful eye, weather eye, 3) awareness, insight, shrewdness, understanding, 4) heart, mid, middle.

eye *v.* to follow with the eyes, look at, have a look at, stare at, watch.

eyebrow *n.* brow of hair along the upper rim of the eye.

eye-draught *n.* drawing or outline made by eye alone, without taking reckonings.

eye-drop/s *n.* 1) a tear, 2) healing-draught for the eye.

eyeful *n.* look, sight, sight for the eyes.

eye-glass/es *n.* glasses, reading glasses.

eyehole *n.* 1) the hole in which the eye is set, 2) hole to look through.

eyelid *n.* one of the lids (upper, lower) of the eye.

eye-opener *n.* daylight, the lid taken off, a new insight/understanding.

eyesalve *n.* healing salve for the eye.

eye-shade *n.* shade for the eyes against strong light.

eye-shadow *n.* make-up put on about the eyes.

eyeshot *n.* reach/span/sweep of one's sight, field of sight.

eyesight *n.* seeing, dim-sight, far sight, good/keen/sharp sight, long/short sight.

eyesore *n.* blight, fright, sight.

eye-wash *n.* 1) healing draught for the eye, 2) fair-wording, honey-speech, mealy-mouthedness, smooth-lip, softened wording, soft soap, soft-speech.

eye-wise *adj.* wise-looking.

eyewitness *n.* witness (with one's own eyes), bystander, onlooker, watcher.

eye-worship *n.* looking on dotingly/yearningly, worship with the eyes.

eyot, ait *n.* small *river* island.

fain *adj.* glad, ready, ready and willing, willing.

fain *adv.* gladly, nothing loth, readily, willingly, with a will, with all one's heart.

fair *adj.* 1) comely, lovely, willowy, elf-fair, elf-sheen, fair-haired, flaxen-haired, light-haired, 2) above board, even-handed, fair-minded, rightwise, straight, true, 3) all right, middling, so-so.

fair *adv.* becomingly, well, wonderfully.

fair-haired *adj.* flaxen-haired, golden-haired, light-haired.

fair-hand (*calligraphy*) *n.* fair-writing, handwriting-craft, reedmanship.

fairhood *n.* comeliness, fairness, loveliness, shapeliness, winsomeness,

fairly *adv.* 1) becomingly, 2) even-handedly, rightly, 3) pretty well, rather, somewhat, well enough.

fair-minded *adj.* even-handed, fair, open-minded, right-minded, upright.

fairness *n.* 1) comeliness, loveliness, fairhood, 2) even-handedness, fair play, openness, open-mindedness, rightness, rightfulness, right-mindedness, uprightness.

fair-speaking *n.* good breeding, knightliness, winsomeness.

fair-spoken *adj.* well-spoken, knightly, well-behaved, winning.

fairway, fare-way *n.* 1) stretch of *river* where ships may go, 2) (in *golf*) the open, mown ground between one green and the next.

fair-weather *adj.* ready only for fair-weather.

fair-weather friend *n.* shammer, yarn-spinner, snake in one's bosom/in the grass.

fair-word *n.* smooth-speaking, soft answer, soothing speech.

fair-wording (*euphemism*) *n.* eyewash, honey-speech, mealy-mouthedness, smooth-lip, softened wording, soft soap, soft-speech, hard words in honey, sharp words in sheep's wool, salt made sweet, soft words for sooth, trim words for truth, light words for lewd, lip-salve for low talk, naming a spade a spindle.

fall *n.* 1) a dropping down to the ground, dive, nose dive, slip, 2) downhill drop, slope, 3) dip, drop, dwindling, lessening, lowering, 4) a falling into sin, 5) falling in the fight, death, downfall, overthrow, 6) waterfall, 7) the time of the falling of the leaves, 8) rod, being five and a half yards (one fortieth of a furlong).

fall *n.* something that falls (such as a trap-door), as in a 'mousefall'.

fall *v.* 1) to come down, dive, nose-dive, drop, fall down, miss one's footing, sink, go head over heels, 2) (of land) to drop, slope down/downhill, 3) to dwindle, ebb, fall away/off, go down, lessen, wane, 4) to fall into sin, 5) to fall wounded or dead in the fight, be killed, be lost, be slain, die, meet one's end, 6) to fall over, 7) (of a stronghold) to be overthrown, be taken, to give in/up/way, yield, 8) (of one's look) to show blighted hope/setback, 9) to befall, come about, fall out.

fall down[6] *v.* 1) to swoon, 2) to be found lacking, be left empty-handed, break down, come to naught/nothing, come to a bad/sticky end, come to a dead end, come unstuck, fall, fall by the wayside, fall to the ground, fall short, fall through, give out, go by the board, go downhill, go under, go wide of the mark, ground, lose, lose out, miss, misfire, miss the mark, not come up to the mark, reach the depths, run aground, sink to the bottom, bite the dust.

fallen *adj.* 1) lost, shamed, sinful, 2) dead, killed, slain.

fall for *v.* 1) to be smitten by, be swept off one's feet, lose one's heart to, 2) to be hoodwinked, misled, taken in.

fall foul of *v.* to fall out with, run foul of.

falling away *n.* wandering away from the right path, leaving the straight and narrow.

falling-sickness (*epilepsy*) *n.* fit.

fall in with *v.* to do as asked, do as others do, go along with, put up with, not mind, see no harm in, say yes to, swallow, go or swim with the stream.

fall out *v.* to fight, gainsay, have words, stand against, have a bone to pick with.

fallout *n.* outcome, upshot.

fall short of, fall through *v.* to fall down, come to nothing, come unstuck, miss.

fallow *n.* ground ploughed and harrowed, but left unsown for a year or more.

fallow *adj.* dun, light brown, reddish yellow.

fallow *adj.* (of land) unsown.

fallow *v.* to become wan or yellow, go white, wither.

fallow *v.* to plough up the land to ready it for sowing.

fallow-deer *n.* a deer of fallow hue (the he-deer is a buck, the she- deer a doe).

fall upon *v.* to bear down on, beset, fight, go for, hammer, harry, hound, have at, lay about one, lay into, make an onset, make inroads, pitch into, ride down, run down, run against, drive against, open fire, fire the first shot, set on, set upon, start a fight, storm, strike at, strike home, tear into.

falter *v.* 1) to fall, grope, miss one's footing, reel, slip, topple, 2) to mis-say, speak thickly, stammer, 3) to back away, beat about, be in two minds, blench, give way, hang back, hedge, hold back, hold off, play for time, shy away.

fane *n.* flag, streamer.

fang *n.* tooth of dog or wolf.

fang *v.* to cleave to, clutch, fasten on, grasp, grip, hold, lay hold of, take.

far *adv.* 1) afar, away, far-away, far afield, far off, a good way/great way/long way, to the back of beyond, to the ends of the earth, 2) greatly, markedly, much.

far *adj.* 1) farther, farthest, further, furthermost, furthest, not nigh, 2) far-away, far-off, outlying, out-of-the-way.

far-away 1) *adj.* lost in thought, deep in thought, sunk in thought, head in the clouds, in another world, in a world of one's own, with one's mind on other things, dreamy, daydreaming, forgetful, unheeding, unmindful, far-minded, 2) *adv.* a long way off/away, elsewhere, gone, gone away.

be **far away** *v.* to be deaf, be lost in thought, daydream, give no heed, go wool-gathering, hear nothing, let one's mind wander, lose the thread, not listen, overlook.

far-comer *n.* farfarer, newcomer, newfarer, otherlander, outsider, wanderer.

fare *n.* 1) toll, way-toll, 2) food, board, meals.

fare *v.* to go forth, go on one's way, make one's way.

farer *n.* wayfarer, pathfinder, walker, wanderer.

farewell *intj.* go well, goodbye, good day, good evening, good night, see you later.

farewell *n.* leave-taking, sendoff.

far-fetched *adj.* beyond belief, hare-brained, mad, outlandish, utterly unlikely.

far-forth *adv.* far, far on.

far-gone *adj.* a long way on, well towards the end.

faring *n.* farfaring, forthfaring, going, outfaring, outing, walking, wayfaring.

far-land *n.* far away land.

far-minded *adj.* far-away, lost in thought, daydreaming, forgetful, unmindful.

far-mindedly *adv.* dreamily, unmindfully.

farness (*distance*) *n.* length, span, spread, stretch, sweep, width.

far-reaching *adj.* far-stretching, sweeping, thoroughgoing, wholesale, widespread.

farrow *n.* young pig.

farrow *v.* (of a sow) to bring forth young.

far-seeing *adj.* far-sighted, foresighted, looking ahead, wise.

farsighted *adj.* deep, foresighted, keen-thinking, understanding, wise.

farsightedness *n.* awareness, forethought, insight, understanding, wisdom.

farther *adv.* 1) further away, further off, 2) more, 3) farthermore, also, besides.

farther *adj.* 1) greater, more, new, other, over and above, 2) faraway, far-off, farthest, further, furthest, furthermost, not nigh.

farthermore *adv.* also, besides, furthermore, moreover, likewise.

farthest *adj.* far-away, far-off, further, furthest, furthermost.

farthing (*quarter*) *n.* 1) fourth, fourthling, fourthing, 2) fourth of a penny, 3) fourth of an acre or a hide.

farthingdeal *n.* 1) fourth deal, 2) fourth of an acre, rood.

fast *n.* 1) going without food or drink, fasting, 2) fast-day.

fast *v.* to eat nothing, go without food or drink, go hungry, have no food, keep fast.

fast *adj.* 1) hard to shake, settled, steady, strong, stuck fast, well set, 2) flying, high-speed, light-footed, like an arrow, lively, nimble, nimble-footed, speedy, swift, swift-footed, as/like the wind, quick, quick-footed, quick as lightning/thought/the wind, 3) giddy, reckless, wanton, wild.

fast *adv.* 1) steadfastly, steadily, strongly, 2) at full speed, fastly, like lightning, quickly, speedily, swiftly.

fasten *v.* 1) to bolt, do up, lock, make fast, 2) to bind, bring together, bring ends together, draw together, hang on, hook on, make fast, set, stick on, tie on.

fastener, fastening *n.* binding, clasp, tie.

fasten on *v.* to cleave to, clutch, keep by one, lay hands upon, lay in, lay up, stow.

fast-held *adj.* held fast, made fast, settled, stuck fast, well set.

fasting *n.* keeping fast, not eating.

fast lane *n.* outer lane of a freeway (for faster *traffic* overtaking slower).

fastly *adv.* like lightning, quickly, speedily, swiftly.

fastness *n.* hold, stronghold, keep, ward.

fast-rede *n.* steadfast mind.

fat *adj.* fleshy, heavy, overweight, well-fed, fat as butter.

fat-head *n.* clod, half-wit, lackwit, witling, oaf.

fat hen *n.* an old food-plant (*spinach* is now eaten in its stead).

father *n.* 1) begetter of a child, 'old man', foster-father, stepfather, 2) forebear, forefather, a man of old, 3) builder, framer, maker, shaper, 4) elder, leader.

father *v.* 1) to beget a child, bring into being, give life to, 2) to begin, frame, shape.

father-half *n.* father's side (in kinlore/ *genealogy*).

fatherhood *n.* the kinship of a father to a child, the care of a father for his child.

father-in-law[2] *n.* good-father.

fatherkin *n.* kindred/kinship by the father's side.

fatherless *adj.* having no father, helpless, kithless.

fatherlike 1) *adj.* fatherly, like a father, 2) *adv.* in a fatherly way.

fatherliness *n.* fatherly care/love, kindliness.

fatherly *adj.* forbearing, kind, kindly.

fathom/s *n.* 1) the clasping/infolding arms, 2) the length of the outstretched arms, namely six feet (now *used* for depth of water).

fathom *v.* 1) to clasp, fold/hold in one's arms, grasp, hold fast, hold to one's bosom, infold, 2) to reckon depth with a fathom-line, 3) to get to the bottom of, grasp.

fathomless *adj.* bottomless, reachless, unfathomful.

fatling *n.* calf, lamb, or other young *beast* fatted for slaying.

fatness *n.* bulk, fleshiness, heaviness, weight, overweight.

fatted *adj.* fattened, made or grown fat.

fatten *v.* to grow, fill out, build up, thicken, swell.

fatty *adj.* of food that has a lot of fat in it, rich.

fat-witted *adj.* dim-witted, slow-witted, unwitful, witless.

fawn *v.* to cringe, make much of, make up to, play up to, toady to, worm one's way.

fawning *adj.* cringing, mean, stooping, toadying.

fax *n.* the hair of the head.

fear *n.* dread, fright, affright, cold feet, misgiving.

fear *v.* to be frightened to death, dread, fear for one's life, feel one's blood run cold, feel one's hair stand on end, stand in fear/dread, take fright, quake/shake/shrink with fear, shiver, think twice, start at one's own shadow.

fill with **fear** *v.* to affrighten, frighten, give one a fright, frighten one out of his wits, fill with dread, freeze the blood, shake, startle, put fear into, strike dumb, strike with fear, chill with fear, benumb, numb with fear, make aghast, make one's blood run cold, make one's hair stand on end/flesh creep/teeth chatter/knees knock, harrow, unman, put the wind up.

fearful *adj.* fear-ridden, in fear, in a fright, frightened, frightened to death, frightened out of one's wits, frozen with fear, numbed with fear, filled with dread, dreading, afeard, cold-footed, in a cold sweat, overcome, quaking, shaken, shivering, shrinking with fear, knees knocking, one's heart in one's mouth, treading warily, on edge, startled, unmanned, white as a sheet, chicken-hearted, hen-hearted, hare-hearted, little-hearted, quake-hearted, milk-livered.

fearfully *adv.* badly, dreadfully, frightfully, shamefully, woefully, wretchedly.

fearless *adj.* bold, dreadless, unfearing, stopping at nothing.

fearnought *n.* strong, thick woollen cloth for making a seaman's shirt.

fearsome *adj.* dreadful, fearful, frightful, grisly, nightmarish, numbing, startling.

feather/s *n.* the 'sheathing' of a bird's body and that of which its *wings* are wrought.

feather *v.* to line with feathers, to fit such as an arrow or hat with feathers.

feather-bed *n.* bed filled with feathers.

feather-brain *n.* feather-head, <u>witling</u>.

feather-brained *adj.* empty-headed, flighty, hare-brained, <u>light-minded</u>, unsteady.

feathered *adj.* 1) lined with feathers, 2) (of an arrow) fitted with a feather.

feather-head *n.* feather-brain, <u>witling</u>.

feather-headed *adj.* giddy, <u>heedless</u>, light-headed, <u>light-minded</u>, wayward.

featheriness *n.* 1) feathery suchness, 2) lightness, fickleness.

featherless *adj.* having no feathers.

feather-weight *n.* 1) a weight no greater than that of a feather, a truly little thing, 2) slightly-built rider in a horse race, 3) slightly-built fist-fighter (*boxer*).

feathery *adj.* feathered, light, soft, wispy.

fee *n.* livestock, goods.

feed *n.* fodder, food for livestock.

feed *v.* 1) to give food to, suckle young, fatten, fill with food, 2) to meet the hopes/ wishes of, 3) to eat, graze, take food, 4) (of inside knowledge or such) to give, send on, tell to another, 5) to bolster, foster, make stronger, strengthen.

feedback *n.* input from others (about outcomes), insights, write-up.

feeder *n.* bird-feeder.

feel *n.* 1) feeling, mood, 2) ilk, kind, make-up, weave.

feel *v.* 1) to finger, handle, run one's hands over, stroke, 2) to feel one's way, grope, 3) to feel cold/heat/a wound, to bear, go through, undergo, 4) to be aware of, 5) to feel for/with, sorrow with, understand, 6) to believe, deem, hold, know, think, feel in one's bones, have a feeling, 7) to strike one as.

feeler *n.* 1) forefinger, hair, tongue, 2) a 'fathoming' of the waters, a hint put forth.

feeling *n.* 1) awareness, care, deep feeling, love, true feeling, understanding, warm feeling, warmth, 2) hard feelings, stirred feeling, 3) flutter, goose-flesh.

feeling *adj.* caring, deeply-felt, heart-felt, strongly-felt, understanding.

feelingly *adv.* lovingly, ruthfully, understandingly, warmly, warm-heartedly.

fell *n.* 1) hide, leather, 2) fleece, hair, wool.

fell *v.* to knock down, strike down, throw down, bring down, beat down.

felloe *n.* outer rim (or length of the rim) of a wheel.

felt *n.* kind of cloth made of wool, or of wool and hair.

fen *n.* fenland, marsh, marshland, mere, moss, slough.

fen *n.* mildew.

fen-cress *n.* water cress.

fen-man *n.* fenlander, marsh-dweller.

ferling *n.* farthing, fourthing, fourthling.

fern *n.* plant.

fern-seed *n.* seed of the fern.

ferny *adj.* thick with ferns.

fetch *v.* 1) to bear, bring, pick up, 2) to bring in, earn, go for, make, sell for, yield.

fetching *adj.* bewitching, sweet, <u>winning</u>, winsome.

fetlock *n.* lower shank of a horse.

fetter/s *n.* irons, shackle.

fetter *v.* to bind, put in irons, shackle.

fettle *n.* health, shape, trim, well-being.

fettle *v.* to make ready, busy oneself.

few *adj.* few and far between, not many, one or two, short, thin, thin on the ground.

fewer *adj.* less than before, not so many.

fewest *adj.* least, littlest, smallest.

fewness *n.* a handful, not so much, one or two, two or three, spoonful, thimbleful.

fey *adj.* 1) doomed, dying, 2) accursed, bewitched, spellbound, gripped.

fickle *adj.* <u>fitful</u>, giddy, <u>light-minded</u>, shifting, trothless, <u>two-minded</u>, unsteady.

fickleness *n.* flightiness, light-mindedness, shallowness, steadlessness, unsteadiness.

field *n.* 1) open land (that is, without trees, hills or buildings), grazing, cropland, 2) greensward, mead, meadland, meadow, meadowland, 3) coal-field, *oil*-field, 4) field of war, 5) field of play, ground, pitch, playing field/ground, 6) (in foot-racing, horse-racing) running field/ground, horse-running field/ground, 7) the runners, 8) body/field of knowledge, business, life-work, setting, world.

field *v.* 1) (of a games team) to play, put up, 2) (in stockball/*cricket*) to stop/pick up the ball, 3) to answer, deal with, handle.

field-book *n.* book written up in the open, by such as a land-sighter/*surveyor*.

field breadth *n.* a short way.

fieldcraft (*agriculture*) *n.* fieldlore, croplore, earth-tilling, earth tilth, tilth.

field-day *n.* 1) gathering of a fighting body (for a work-out, or a warlike show), 2) great day, highday, holiday, holy day, 3) a day in the hunting field.

field-elf *n.* elf of the open fields.

fielden, fieldy *adj.* 1) open, out-of-town, 2) of that which grows in the fields.

fielder *n.* 1) fieldworker, 2) (in stockball/*cricket*) near fielder, outfielder.

field-fight *n.* pitched fight in the open, <u>bloodshed</u>, running fight, stand-up fight.

field-folk *n.* crofters, fieldworkers, land workers, smallholders.

field-glasses *n. binoculars.*

field-keeper (*scarecrow*) *n.* crow-fright.

field-land *n.* cropland, meadowland, open land.

field-leader, field-lord (*general*) *n. host*-lord, war-lord, fierd-lord.

fieldlore (*agriculture*) *n.* croplore, fieldcraft, knowledge won from the fields.

fieldmouse *n.* mouse of the harvest fields.

field-reeve *n.* foreman, headman, overman, overseer.

field-room *n.* open land.

fieldsman (in stockball/*cricket*) *n.* fielder.

field-word (*battle cry*) *n.* watchword.

fieldwork *n.* 1) work done out in the field, 2) work done 'on the ground' (as against work back in a seat of learning), work at the chalk side.

fieldworker *n.* 1) land worker, 2) worker at the chalk side.

fiend *n.* black/dark/night elf, hell-fiend, hell-hound, hell-wight, nightmare.

fiendful *adj.* wrought by fiends.

fiendish *adj.* baleful, black-hearted, bloodthirsty, <u>evil</u>, <u>dreadful</u>, foul, frightful, ghastly, hateful, hellish, <u>loathsome</u>, mad, nightmarish, wicked, wild.

fiendlike, fiendly *adj.* black-hearted, bloodthirsty, <u>evil</u>, <u>dreadful</u>, foul, hellish.

fiendsick *adj.* beside oneself, bewitched, cursed, elf-driven, fiend-held, fiend-indwelt, hag-ridden, horn-mad, maddened, under a spell, wild.

fierd (*army*) *n.* fighting body, weapon-lords, weapon-wielders. (A 'fierd' was a folk *army*, as against a 'here' – a striking, reaving *army*.)

fiery *adj.* <u>bold</u>, bloodthirsty, untamed, wild, hot-hearted, burning, throbbing.

fifteen *n. adj.* the root *number* made of ten and five.

fifteenth *adj. n.* 1) the marking *number* that is kin to fifteen, 2) fifteenth share of something.

fifth *adj. n.* 1) the marking *number* that is kin to five, 2) fifth share of something.

fifthly *adv.* in the fifth *place*.

fiftieth *adj. n.* 1) the marking *number* that is kin to fifty, 2) fiftieth share of something.

fifty *n. adj.* the root *number* that is five times ten.

fifty-fifty *adv.* half each, half-and-half.

fight *n.* running fight, stand-up fight, in-fighting, set-to, free-for-all, horse-play.

fight *v.* to come to grips, drive against, <u>fall upon</u>, fight hand to hand, fight it out, fight to the end, have a fight, lay about one, lock horns, make an onset, make inroads, match oneself with, pitch into, storm, strike at, take the field, take the fight to the foe, whet the sword/blade, <u>withstand</u>, unsheathe the sword, throw away the sheath.

fighter *n.* fighting man, man of blood, weapon-lord, weapon-wielder.

fighter *n.* high-speed flying-craft built for *air* warfare.

fighting *n.* <u>bloodshed</u>, stand, weapon-heat.

fighting *adj.* ready to fight, weapon-bearing.

fighting ship (*warship*) *n.* long-ship, 'sea-mare'.

file *n.* rough-edged tool for lessening or smoothing wood or *metal*.

file *v.* to file down, shape, smooth off.

file-hard *adj.* hard as a file.

filing/s *n.* 1) the work of filing, 2) the small wooden or *metal* bits filed off.

fill *n.* 1) all one could wish, enough, fullness, one's fill, 2) filling.

fill *v.* to fill out, fill up, build up, heap up, load.

fill in (for someone) *v.* to stand in for, take over from,

fill one in *v.* to fill in the background, 'bring up to speed'.

fill out *v.* to put together, put on, heap on, lay up, strengthen, swell.

'Fill ditch' (*February*) *n.* Kale-month, Sol-month.

filling *n.* 1) filling in, filling up, 2) infilling.

film *n.* 1) dusting, glaze, layer, overlaying, sheet, 2) a growth upon the eye (shrouding the sight), 3) shooting (*photographic*) film, 4) film telling a tale (from life or made-up) to be shown in the filmhouse or on 'the box', 5) cloud, mistiness.

film *v.* 1) to shroud over as with a film, become/grow dim, 2) to get a shot of, shoot, take, make into a film.

film-goer *n.* film-lover.

filmhouse *n. cinema.*

film-player *n. DVD.*

film-shot (*photograph*) *n.* shot, slide, still, lightshot, likeness.

film star *n.* leading lady, leading man, player.

filmy *adj.* gossamer, light, see-through, sheer, through-shining/-showing, wispy.

filth *n.* dung, slime.

filthiness *n.* 1) foulness, uncleanness, 2) lewdness, lust, wantonness.

filthy *adj.* foul, lewd, <u>loathsome</u>, stinking, unclean, unkempt, unwashen.

finch *n.* chaffinch, goldfinch, greenfinch, hawfinch, and such.

find *n.* 1) blessing, godsend, good buy, 2) something found in *archaeological* work.

find *v.* to come by, come upon, lay one's hands on, light upon, pitch upon, pick up.

finding *n.* insight, outcome, reckoning, weighing up.

find out *v.* to find out about, find the meaning, find the key to, become aware of/ alive to, bring to light, comb out, come up with, draw out, gather, get to hear of, get to the bottom of, get wind of, learn, make out, overhear, pick up, read the riddle, unriddle, run to ground, run to earth, unearth, unlock, untwist, unweave, work out.

finger *n.* forefinger, little finger, middle finger, ring finger, first/other/third/fourth finger.

finger *v.* to feel, handle, play with, run the hand over.

finger-apple *n. date*.

finger/s-breadth *n.* the breadth of a finger, three-fourths of an inch.

finger-end *n.* end/tip of the finger.

finger-hole/s *n.* the holes in a wind-*instrument*, being first opened, then shielded, by the fingers (to let out, or stop, *sound*).

fingering *n.* a kind of wool or yarn.

fingering *n.* 1) playing a wind-*instrument* with the fingers, 2) *guide* (in sheet *music*) as to which fingers are to play.

finger-mark *n.* the mark left by a finger on a board (or other such).

finger-nail *n.* nail shielding the end of each finger.

fingerspeech *n. braille*.

fire *n.* 1) coal fire, wood fire, heater, 2) blaze, bonfire, wild-fire, 3) life, sparkle, warmth, 4) firing, burst of fire, shelling, shooting, 5) beacon fire, watch-fire.

fire *v.* 1) to light, make up the fire, feed the fire, 2) to set ablaze, set alight, set fire to, 3) to awaken, fire up, quicken, stir up, spur on, 4) to fire at, fire off, let off, open fire, set off, shell, shoot, 5) to fire clay (in the making of crocks).

fire-brand *n.* 1) length of wood lit at the fire, 2) fighter, fire-eater, thunderer.

fire-eater *n.* fire-brand, rough.

fire-eyed *adj.* having eyes glowing as with fire.

fire-fang *v.* to burn, sere, singe.

fire-fighter *n.* fireman.

fire-fly *n. insect* which shines in the dark.

fire-hot *adj.* hot as fire, red-hot.

fire-light *n.* the light given out by a fire.

fire-lighter *n.* 1) one who makes a fire, 2) firesome *matter* for lighting a fire.

fireman *n.* 1) the man who feeds the fire of a steam *engine*, 2) fire-fighter.

fire-ship *n.* ship filled with goods that readily burn, sent in among ships of one's foe (in the hope of setting such on fire).

fireside *n.* 1) hearth, 2) home, home-life.

firestarting (*arson*) *n.* forburning.

fire-stone *n.* flint.

fire-storm *n.* great fire set off in an onset by fighter-craft (*bombers*).

fire up *v.* to bestir, fire, awaken, liven up, quicken, stir up, madden, spur on.

fire-watcher *n.* 1) one who feeds a fire, 2) one who watches for fires started in an onset by fighter-craft (*bombers*).

firewater (*acid*) *n.* sourwater, burnwater.

firewood *n.* wood for burning.

firework/s *n.* 1) firework show, 2) storm, uproar.

first 1) *adj.* earliest, first in the field, foremost, maiden, opening, 2) *n.* the beginning, the best, greatest, head, highest, key, leading, overriding, top, winning, 3) *adv.* at the beginning, at the outset, before all else, beforehand, earlier in time, firstly, to begin with, to start with.

firstborn *n.* eldest, first-birth, forerunner, forebear, first man.

First-day *n.* Sunday.

first dweller (*aboriginal*) *n.* folklander, homelander.

first-floor *n.* the floor next above the ground floor, upper floor.

first hand 1) *adj.* seen, heard, witnessed, 2) *adv.* straight from the horse's mouth.

first light *n.* break of day, daybreak, day-dawn, dawning, sunrise.

firstling *n.* first of its kind, first-born of a *beast*.

first love *n.* calf love, dawn of love, young love.

firstly *adv.* before all else, to begin with, to start with.

first name *n.* forename, given name.

firstnight *n.* opening night of a play.

first strike *n.* a first onset in war (before the foe is ready).

firth, frith *n.* wooded land.

firwood *n.* evergreen tree.

fish *n.* cod, eel, pike, smelt, swordfish.

fish *v.* 1) to angle, fly-fish, net, 2) to delve, go into, look for, look into, seek.

fishdealer *n.* fish seller.

fisher, fisherman *n.* angler.

fish-hook *n.* angle.

fishing *n.* angling.

fishing *adj.* of that which is for taking fish (as 'fishing net').

fish-mere *n.* fishpond.

fishpond *n.* pond in which fish are kept, fish-mere.

fish-tail wind *n.* a shifting wind (blowing now on one side, now on the other).

fishwife *n.* bitter tongue, redhead, shrew, vixen.

fishy *adj.* 1) rich in fish, 2) fish-like, fish-smelling, 3) shady, shifty, slippery.

fisk *v.* to fly, go about busily/nimbly.

fist *n.* clenched hand (so as to threaten or to strike).

fistful *n.* handful.

fit, fytte *n.* one 'head' (*part*) of a long song or *poem*.

fit *n.* 1) bout, falling sickness, stroke, the shakes, 2) bout, outburst, outbreak, spell.

fit *v.* 1) to be the right shape for, 2) to match, make right, shape, 3) to belong to, go with, match, meet, 4) to fit out, fit up, get ready, lay the groundwork, make ready.

fit *adj.* 1) becoming, fitting, good enough, meet, ready, right, worthy, 2) hale, healthy, in good health, in good shape, strong, well.

fitful *adj.* flickering, flighty, fluttering, light-minded, moody, off and on, once in a while, restless, shiftful, shifting, steadless, stop-go, stopping and starting, straggling, uneven, unsettled, unsteadfast, unsteady, wayward, blowing hot and cold.

fitfully *adv.* at times, by fits and starts, every so often, every now and then, first one and then the other, from time to time, now and then, off and on, once in a while.

fitness *n.* 1) becomingness, readiness, rightness, 2) health, good health, health and strength, strength, healthiness, heartiness, weal, well-being, wellness,

fitted *adj.* 1) shaped, 2) built-in.

fitting/s *n.* built-in cupboards and such.

fitting *adj.* becoming, good, in keeping, meet, right, aright, worthy.

fittingly *adv.* becomingly, meetly, rightly, worthily.

five *n. adj.* the root *number* following four.

fivefold *adj.* made up of five together, five times as great or as many.

flat *n.* rooms (on one floor).

flax *n.* plant, *fibres* of the plant.

flaxen 1) *adj.* made of flax, of the hue of flax, yellow, 2) *n.* linen, linen cloth.

flax wench *n.* woman working with flax.

flay *v.* 1) to rend, tear to shreds, 2) to storm against, tear into, upbraid, weigh into.

flea *n.* small *insect* that feeds on the blood of man and *beasts*.

flea-bite *n.* 1) bite of a flea, 2) hardly anything, next to nothing, nothing to speak of.

flea-bitten *adj.* bitten by fleas, full of fleas.

fleawort *n.* plant once thought to be the death of fleas.

fledge *adj.* ready to fly (having feathers full-grown).

fledge *v.* to become fully feathered.

fledgeling 1) *n.* nestling, young bird, 2) *adj.* beginning, maiden, new, new-made.

flee *v.* to fly, take to flight, win free, make off, run for one's life, bolt.

fleece *n.* wool, hair.

fleece *v.* 1) to shear the wool from a sheep, 2) to steal heartlessly, bleed white.

fleecy *adj.* shaggy, soft, woolly.

fleet *n.* fighting ships.

fleet *n.* inlet, mouth, roadstead, small stream, tidefleet.

fleet *v.* 1) to float, go by water, sail, swim, 2) to flow, glide away, slip away, 3) (in a ship) to shift (a rope or such).

fleeting *adj.* fair weather, flying, overnight, shifting, short-lived.

fleetingly *adv.* for a little/short while, for a time/short time, for the time being.

flesh *n.* 1) the soft bits of the body about the framework of the bones, 2) fat, fatness, meat, weight, 3) the soft bits of a *fruit* about the stone or kernel, 4) mankindly being (having bodily needs), 5) mankind's fallen and sinful being.

flesh and blood *n.* 1) the body, 2) mankind, 3) one's near kindred.

flesh-eating (*carnivorous*) *adj.* meat-eating.

fleshed *adj.* clothed with flesh.

flesher (*butcher*) *n.* meat seller, meat trader.

fleshhood (*incarnation*) *n.* infleshness, mannishness.

fleshly *adj.* 1) of flesh and blood, 2) earthy, lewd, lustful, wanton, wolfish, worldly.

flesh-wound *n.* wound that does not go deep (beyond the flesh).

fleshy *adj.* bosomy, fat, goodly, lusty, meaty, overweight, well-fed.

flicker *n.* gleam, play of light, spark.

flicker *v.* 1) (of birds) to flutter, quiver, shake out the feathers, 2) (of a light) to burn fitfully, shimmer, sparkle, twinkle.

flickering *adj.* fluttering, shimmering, twinkling.

flickeringly *adv.* fleetingly, unsteadily.

flight *n.* 1) flying, 2) swift going (of such as an arrow), 3) (of birds) cloud, flock, 4) the stairs between two landings.

flight *n.* fleeing, headlong flight, running away.

flight arrow *n.* light and well-feathered arrow (for shooting afar).

flight-hub[1] (*airport*) *n.* landing ground, runway.

flightiness *n.* dizziness, giddiness, heedlessness, lightmindedness.

flight path *n.* the path to be followed by a flying craft (drawn up before take-off).

flight-shot *n.* 1) the span an arrow is shot, 2) shot fired at wildfowl in flight.

flighty *adj.* 1) swift, 2) dizzy, empty-headed, fickle, hare-brained, light-minded.

flimsily *adv.* lightly, wispily.

flimsiness *n.* lightness, shakiness, slightness, thinness.

flimsy *adj.* 1) makeshift, shaky, slight, 2) (of clothing) light, sheer, wispy, 3) (of grounds/ *evidence*) thin, woolly.

flint *n.* a hard stone, most often of a grey hue.

flint-grey *adj.* grey as flint.

flint-hearted *adj.* flinty, hard-hearted, hardened, stony-hearted, unfeeling.

flinty *adj.* 1) of flint-strewn ground, 2) hard, hard as nails, tough, gritty, unyielding.

flinty-hearted *adj.* hard-hearted, stony-hearted.

flitch *n.* side of pig (salted and smoked).

flitter[(2)]**-mouse** (*bat*) *n.* rearmouse/reremouse.

float *n.* 1) floating, 2) *cork* tied to a fishing-line (quivering when a fish bites).

float *v.* 1) to set afloat, glide, ride, sail, slide, 2) to hang in the wind, 3) to put forward a thought (for others to answer), 4) to set a new business going, set up.

floating *adj.* 1) resting on water, 2) hanging back, not knowing one's own mind, pulled this way and that, two-minded, unsettled, 3) free, rootless, wandering.

flock *n.* 1) drove, herd, flight, 2) crowd, gathering, throng, 3) church gathering.

flock *v.* to flock together, crowd, forgather, gather, herd, stream, swarm, throng.

flood *n.* 1) the flowing in of the tide, 2) overflowing waters, swollen stream, 3) (of folk fleeing war or other threat) flow, stream, tide.

flood *v.* 1) to drown, overflow, 2) (of folk fleeing) to overwhelm, swarm into.

flood-gate *n.* watergate, the lower gate of a lock.

flood-hatch *n.* hatch-door in a flood-gate, lifted in time of flood.

flood-light *n.* lights shone from two or more ways (so that there are no shadows).

flood-tide *n.* the flowing in of the tide, high tide.

floor *n.* 1) the ground of a room, 2) set of rooms on the one floor, 3) the floor of a *parliament* house (where a speaker 'takes the floor').

floor *v.* 1) to lay a floor, 2) to knock down, knock over, 3) to bewilder, bring up short, fell, overcome, overthrow, strike dumb, throw.

floor-cloth *n.* cloth for washing floors.

floored *adj.* amazed, bewildered, overcome, shaken, speechless, thunderstruck.

flooring *n.* 1) the work of laying a floor, 2) the floor of a room, 3) the boards, stones or such of which it is made.

floor show *n.* show given on the floor of a night *club* or such.

flow *n.* 1) flood, mill-stream, tide, 2) (of wind) indraught, inflow, outflow.

flow *v.* 1) to flood, overflow, run, stream, sweep, well forth, 2) to arise, spring.

flowing *adj.* 1) bursting, falling, flooding, full, overflowing, rich, running over, streaming, swarming, teeming, 2) sleek, smooth, unbroken, 3) (of speech) free-flowing, rich, speechful, wordful, 4) (of clothing) hanging, loose.

flush *n.* 1) strong flow, 2) the work of cleansing a drain by flushing, 3) glow of light or hue, 4) reddening, redness, rosiness.

flush *adj.* 1) full, in flood, 2) rich, wealthy, well-off, 3) of like height, even.

flush *v.* (of birds) to fly up quickly, to make to fly up.

flush *v.* 1) to flow strongly, 2) to cleanse a drain or ditch by a flood of water, 3) (of light or hue) to glow brightly all at once, 4) to blush, burn, go red, redden.

flush *v.* to make even/flush.

flutter *n.* 1) a fluttering, 2) flush, heaving, restlessness, throbbing, unsettledness, 3) quiver, quivering, shaking, shiver, twitching.

flutter *v.* 1) (of birds) to shake out the feathers, to make short, quick flights, 2) to fly here and there, go about restlessly, 3) to flicker, quiver, shiver.

fly *n.* flying *insect* (greenfly, horse-fly and such).

fly *v.* 1) to fly through the *air*, 2) to flee, win free, take to flight, run for one's life.

flyer, flier *n.* 1) (*pilot*) flight-man, 2) handout.

flying *n.* flight.

flying *adj.* 1) gliding, wind-borne, 2) fast, speedy, 3) fleeting, short-lived.

flying boat *n.* flying craft that takes off and lands on water.

flying craft *n.* aircraft.

flying start *n.* fair wind, following wind, tail wind, having the edge/the upper hand.

fly-leaf *n.* leaf at the beginning of a book (and sometimes at the end as well).

fly-net *n.* net to keep away flies.

fly-over *n.* *railway* bridge over another line, road bridge over another road.

fly-wheel *n.* wheel with a heavy rim (in the working of some *machinery*).

foal *n.* young horse, colt.

foal *v.* to bear a foal.

foam *n.* head, lather, sea-foam, spray.

foam *v.* 1) to lather, 2) to go wild, seethe, throw fits.

fodder *n.* food (such as hay, straw) for stall-fed kine.

foe, foeman *n.* bitter foe, bitter-ender, die-hard, fighter, hard-head, last-ditcher.

fold *n.* pen (for sheep or other *beasts*), sheepfold.

fold *n.* 1) a bend in something that may be turned over upon itself (such as cloth, a folding door, *paper*), a gather, layer, overlap, 2) the mark left by a fold.

fold *v.* to put sheep (or others) in a pen or sheepfold.

fold *v.* 1) (of cloth, *paper* and such) to bend over upon itself, gather, overlap, 2) (of a business) to go under, shut down.

folder *n.* binder.

folding-door *n.* door with two halves (which fold back).

fold-stool *n.* folding stool, *camp* stool.

folk *n.* 1) men and women, mankind, 2) house, kin, kindred, stock.

folk-body *n.* 1) gathering, folk-gathering, 2) (of a folkdom) eldership, leadership.

folkcraft *n.* making/setting right, leadership, steersmanship.

folkdom *n.* 1) folk-body, shared weal, 2) land, homeland, kingdom, motherland.

folk-gathering *n.* folk-body, folk-meeting, folkmoot.

folkhood *n. ethnicity.*

folkland *n.* hearthland, homeland, forefathers' land, land of one's forebears.

folklore *n.* folk tales, old-lore, tales of the long-ago.

folkmeeting, folkmoot (*conference, parliament*) *n.* 1) body, folk-body, folk-gathering, gathering, meeting, law-body, steering body, 2) house, house of law-making, speech-house.

folk-reckoning (*census, referendum*) *n.* reckoning, telling.

folk-right *n.* fairness, fair play, <u>right</u>, rightfulness, <u>rightness</u>, righting evil.

folksaying (*proverb*) *n.* <u>by-saying</u>, pithy saying, stock saying, wise saying.

folkspeech *n.* 1) (*language*) speech, ready speech, tongue, living-tongue, mother tongue, spoken word, wording, 2) (*dialect, idiom*) *n.* folkwording, home speech, home-tongue, household speech, kailyard speech.

folk-spelling (*orthography*) *n.* right spelling, (that is, the long-held spelling).

folk-stock (*race, tribe*) *n.* blood, breed, kindred.

folk-tale (*genealogy*) *n.* 1) <u>kinlore</u>, 2) dream-tale, knightly tale, wonder tale, tale of old/of the long-ago days/of the elder-days.

folkway *n.* lore, way, wont, done thing, the old way.

folk-weal *n.* the *common* weal, shared weal.

folkwealth (*heritage*) *n.* kin-wealth.

folkwording (*dialect, idiom*) *n.* folk-speech, home speech.

follow *v.* 1) to come/go after, come behind, 2) to come next, step into the shoes of, take over from, tread on the heels of, 3) to arise from, flow/spring from, follow as night follows day, follow on, 4) to follow as helper/hanger-on/worshipper, 5) to dog, hound, hunt, run after, shadow, stalk, tail, 6) to follow the lead of, follow in the footsteps of, take a leaf out of someone's book, 7) to bow to, fall in with, listen to, mind, stick to, yield to, 8) to fathom, keep up with, see, take in, <u>understand</u>, 9) to follow a way of life, 10) to follow things arising, to look on, watch, witness.

follow on *v.* (*cricket*) to go in again (being 150/200 runs behind on first innings).

follower *n.* backer, <u>friend</u>, henchman, hanger-on, believer, learner, worshipper.

following *n.* 1) the business of following, 2) backing, hangers-on.

following *adj.* coming, later, next.

follow through *v.* to follow up on, see something through.

food *n.* meat, board, bread, fare, meals.

foot *n.* 1) lowest *part* of the shank (on which one treads and walks), forefoot, hindfoot, 2) bottom, end, 3) length-mete (of twelve inches).

football[2] *n.* game in which each team seeks to put the ball into the other's goal, while keeping it out of *their* own.

foot-bath *n.* 1) bowl in which to bathe one's feet, 2) the deed of bathing the feet.

footboard *n.* board to stand on.

foot-breadth *n.* (in width-mete) breadth of the foot.

foot-bridge *n.* small bridge for those on foot, going over a *river*, *railway* or road.

footfall *n.* footstep, tread.

foothill/s *n.* hill lying before much higher hills.

foothold *n.* footing, grip, standing, toehold, bridge-head.

foot-hot *adv.* without stopping, hard on the heels.

footing *n.* 1) ground, groundwork, 2) standing, 3) foothold, hold, grip, toehold.

footkey *n. organ pedal.*

footlights *n.* lights set along the forward edge of the boards (*stage*) in a playhouse.

footmark *n.* footstep, mark, tread, hoof-mark.

foot-path *n.* footway, sidewalk.

footsore *adj.* dead tired, foot-weary, fordone, tired, <u>weary</u>, way-weary, worn out.

footstall (*pedestal*) *n.* foot-stone, stand, staddle-stone.

footstep *n.* 1) footfall, step, tread, 4) mark, footmark.

foot-stone (*pedestal*) *n.* footstall, stand, staddle-stone.

footstool *n.* stool on which to rest one's feet.

foot-swell *n.* swelling of the foot

footway *n.* foot-path, sidewalk.

foot-work *n.* (in football) clever play with the feet.

foot-worn *n.* footsore, foot-weary, way-worn, weary, worn out.

for *prep.* 1) before, 2) on behalf of, on the side of, 3) over a span of, throughout, 4) to, towards, 5) because of.

for *conj.* because, seeing that, since.

forbear *v.* 1) to forgo, break off, do without, hold back, hold off, keep (oneself) from, keep away, keep back, leave off, 2) to bear with, brook, put up with.

forbearing *adj.* forgiving, kind-hearted, kindly, ruthful, understanding.

forbid *v.* to ban, stop, say no, shut the door on, warn off.

forbidden *adj.* banned, outlawed, stopped.

forbidding *adj.* dark, frightening, grim, threatening, unwelcoming.

for-bind *v.* to fasten, tie up, tie on, yoke.

forboding *adj.* doomed, overshadowing, wyrdful.

forcarve *v.* to cut asunder, cut down, cut in two, cut through.

forcut *v.* to cut into, cut up.

ford *n.* crossing, way over/through.

ford *v.* to go over, go/wade through.

fordo, foredo *v.* 1) to do away with, put an end to, undo, 2) to break down, pull down, tear down, throw down, unmake.

fordone *adj.* drained, more dead than alive, tired out, weary, worn out, foreworn.

fordread *v.* to dread, fear, shake/shiver/shrink with fear.

fordrive *v.* to drive forth, drive about.

fordrunken *adj.* overcome with drink.

fore *adj./n.* foreside, head, top.

fore *adv.* aforetime, before, beforehand, before now, earlier, ere now, ere then.

forearm *n.* lower arm (between elbow and wrist).

forebear *n.* begetter, forefather, forerunner, elder-father.

forebears (*ancestors*) *n.* forefathers, forekin, forerunners, house, kin, kindred, stock.

forebode *v.* to bespeak, bode, foreshadow, give warning, warn of, threaten.

foreboding *n.* foresight, foreknowledge, heed, long-sightedness, forewarning.

forechoose *v.* to foredoom, foresay, foreshape, fore-weave.

forechosen *adj.* doomed, foreshadowed, foreshapen, fore-willed, fore-woven.

foredeem *v.* to blind oneself to, make one's mind up beforehand, see one side only.

foredeeming (*prejudice*) *n.* mind made up, set mind.

foredo *v.* to bring to naught/nothing, do away with, put an end to, undo, unmake.

foredoom *n.* doom, foreshadowing, foreweaving, hidden hand, lot, wyrd.

foredoom *v.* to doom, foresay, foreset, foreshadow, foreweave, will beforehand.

foredooming (*predestination*) *n.* doom, foreweaving, hidden hand, lot, wyrd.

forefather *n.* forebear, forerunner, fore-elder, elder-father.

forefatherlore *n.* kinlore, forekinlore, kinsfolklore, kindred-lore, kinship-lore.

forefeel *v.* to feel beforehand, have a foreboding.

forefeeling *n.* foreboding, foreglimpse, foreknowledge, foresight, forewarning.

forefinger *n.* first finger, the finger next the thumb.

fore-foot *n.* one of the *front* feet of a four-footed *beast.*

foreganger *n.* forerunner, pathfinder.

foregate *n.* the main inway.

forego *v.* to go before, go first, lead off.

foregoing *adj.* above-written, abovesaid, aforesaid, beforehand, going before, earlier.

foregone *adj.* that has gone before/gone by.

foreground *n.* the ground straight before, and nearest to, the onlooker.

forehand *adj.* (in *tennis*) of a stroke played with arm outstretched (as against 'backhand', where the arm is set before the body).

forehanging (*curtain*) *n.* hanging, window hanging.

forehead *n.* brow.

forehear *v.* to hear beforehand.

forekinlore (*genealogy*) *n.* kinlore, forefatherlore, kinsfolklore, kindred-lore.

foreknow *v.* to foresee, think ahead, see something coming, aread/arede.

foreknowing *adj.* foreseeing, farsighted, foresighted, understanding, wise.

foreknowledge *n.* foresight, forethought, long-sightedness, watchfulness.

foreland *n.* bill, headland, ness, sea-ness, spit.

forelay *v.* 1) to waylay, 2) to draw up a way of doing something beforehand.

foreleader *n.* one who leads the way forward.

Fore-litha (*June*) *n.* Ere-litha, Lida ærra ('joy time'), Midsummer-month, Sere ('dry')-month.

forelock *n.* lock of hair growing from the upper brow.

forelook *n.* forward look, foresight.

forelook *v.* to look ahead, see beforehand.

foreman *n.* head, headman, overseer, steward.

fore-marking (*chapter*) *n.* heading.

fore-mighty *adj.* 1) truly mighty, stalwart, strong, 2) great, lordly, nonesuch.

foremost *adj.* best, first, headmost, highest, leading, top.

foremother *n.* forebear, forerunner, elder-mother.

forename *n.* first name.

forenamed *adj.* named above/before.

forenight *n.* last night, the night before.

fore-rider *n.* one who rides before, outrider, pathfinder.

foreright *adv.* forward, straight ahead.

foreright *adj.* 1) straight forward, 2) headstrong, forthright, outspoken.

fore-run *v.* to be before, go before, go first, lead, lead off, open, show the way.

forerunner *n.* 1) forefather, forebear, fore-elder, elder-father, ere-father, 2) early leader, the first, pathfinder.

foresay (*preface*) *n.* first word, foreword, forespeech, foretale, heading, lead-in.

foresay *v.* to forebode, foresee, foreshadow, foretell, forewarn.

fore-sayer *n.* fore-teller, fore-thinker, seer, loreman, watcher, wise man/woman.

foresee *v.* 1) to see ahead, look ahead, think ahead, think likely, foreglimpse, foreknow, foretell, forewarn, see something coming, feel it in one's bones, look for, look forward, look out for, watch out for, forween, aread/arede, 2) to be beforehand, be ready for, lay up for a rainy day.

foreseeing *adj.* farsighted, foresighted, insightful, understanding, wise.

foreseer *n.* fore-sayer, fore-teller, long-seer, loreman, star-teller.

fore-send *v.* to send ahead/before.

fore-set *v.* to lay/set before.

foreshadow *v.* to shadow forth, betoken, forebode, foreshow, foretell, foretoken, forewarn, mark out, spell, witness beforehand.

foreshadowed *adj.* foreshapen, fore-willed, fore-woven, fore-written, wyrdful.

foreshape (*paradigm, prototype*) *n.* forerunner, framework, pathfinder.

foreshape *v.* to forestall, fore-weave, fore-will, fore-write.

foreshapen *adj.* doomed, fore-woven, fore-written, fore-wrought, wyrdful.

foreship (*prow*) *n.* bows, head.

foreshorten *v.* to cut down/short, lessen, shorten.

foreshow *v.* to show beforehand, betoken, foresee, foreshadow, foretell, foretoken.

foreside *n.* forward side, upper side.

foresight *n.* foreknowledge, forethought, long-sightedness, watchfulness, heed, care,

mindfulness, readiness, foreboding, forewarning, forewit, insight, long-sightedness.

foresighted *adj.* farsighted, forseeing, insightful, understanding, wise.

foresleeve *n.* the fore-length of a sleeve.

forespeak *v.* to speak of beforehand, foretell, forewarn.

forespeech (*preface*) *n.* first word, foretale, foreword, lead-in, opening.

forespell (*prescribe*) *v.* to lay down, set.

fore-spoken *adj.* foregoing, fore-written, abovesaid, aforesaid, beforehand, earlier.

forestall *n.* trap, waylaying, stealth-work.

forestall *v.* 1) to waylay, 2) to get in first, be beforehand, be ready for, stop.

fore-steerer *n.* helmsman, steersman.

forestep (*premise*) *n.* belief, ground.

fore-step *v.* to go before, step ahead.

fore-stepping (*anticipating, preventing*) *n.* 1) foreseeing, getting ahead, 2) forestalling, heading off, staving off, warding off.

fore-stick *n.* stick laid on the fire-dogs, to hold back the other sticks.

foretale (*preface*) *n.* first word, foreword, foresay, forespeech, lead-in.

foretell *v.* to forebode, foresay, foresee, forewarn.

forethink *v.* to think ahead, think out beforehand.

forethinking *adj.* farsighted, forseeing, foresighted, insightful, understanding, wise.

forethought *n.* awareness, farsightedness, foresight, understanding, wisdom.

foretime *n.* former times, heretofore time, bygone days, long-ago days, old days.

foretoken *n.* foreshadowing, foreshowing, forewarning, gathering clouds.

foretoken *v.* to foreshadow, foreshape, forewarn.

fore-tokening *n.* doom, foreshadowing, foreweaving, foreworking, wyrd.

fore-tooth *n.* 1) one of the teeth to the fore of the mouth, 2) a first or milk-tooth.

forever, forevermore *adv.* 1) evermore, for ever and a day, for good, for all time, till Doomsday, to the end of time, 2) always, all the time, endlessly, everlastingly.

foreward (*vanguard*) *n.* fore-watch.

foreward (*covenant, contract*) *n.* understanding, deal, undertaking.

forewarn, forwarn *v.* to warn, forebode, give fair warning, foresay.

forewarning *n.* foresight, foreboding, foreknowledge, watchfulness, heed.

fore-willed *adj.* forechosen, foreshadowed, foreshapen, fore-written, wyrdful.

forewit *n.* 1) farsightedness, foreknowledge, foresight, understanding, wisdom, 2) awareness, forethought, heedfulness, wariness.

forewit *v.* to know beforehand, foreknow, foresee.

foreword (*preface*) *n.* first word, foresay, forespeech, foretale, heading, lead-in.

foreworn, forworn *adj.* drained, fordone, tired out, weary, worn out.

fore-woven *adj.* forechosen, foreshapen, forewrought, inwrought, wyrdful.

fore-written *adj.* above-written, abovesaid, aforesaid, beforehand, earlier, foregoing, 2) forewoven, fore-wrought, willed, wyrdful.

fore-wrought *adj.* forechosen, foreshadowed, forewritten, wyrdful.

fore-wyrd (*predestination*) *n.* doom, wyrd, foreworking, hidden hand, lot.

fore-yard *n.* (on a sailing ship) the lowest yard on the foremast.

forfear *v.* to fill with fear, frighten, numb with fear, make one's blood run cold.

forfill *v.* to bring to a stand, hinder, hold back, hold up, stop up.

forgather, foregather *v.* 1) to come/flock/gather together, 2) to meet with.

forget *v.* 1) to clean forget, let in one ear and out of the other, 2) to overlook, let bygones be bygones, put out of one's mind, think no more of.

forgetful *adj.* head in the clouds, with one's mind on other things, far-away.

forgetfulness *n.* daydreaming, dreaminess, heedlessness.

forget-me-not *n.* plant with blue blossom and a yellow eye.

forgive *v.* to bear with, forbear, bury one's wrath, forgive and forget, give back good for evil, heap coals of fire, hold back, hold off, let off, let bygones be bygones, not be too hard upon, overlook misdoing, put behind one, set the guilt aside, set free, shake hands, spare, unbend, understand, write off what is owed, be ruthful.

forgiveness *n.* forbearing, kindness, overlooking, setting free, unshackling, write-off.

forgiving *adj.* forbearing, kind, understanding.

forgivingness *n.* kindness, mildheartedness, ruth.

forgo *v.* to yield, give up, hand over, leave hold of, let go, withdraw.

forgotten *adj.* clean forgotten, gone out of one's head/mind, well forgotten.

for-hard *adj.* hard as flint/nails, tough, unbending, unyielding.

for-harden *v.* to harden, strengthen, toughen.

for-hew *v.* to cut down, cut to the bone.

forhold *v.* to bridle, fetter, hedge in, hem in, hinder, hold back.

forholding *adj.* careful, forgoing, giving little away, heedful, sparing, steady.

fork[4] *n.* 1) tool with two or more tines, for delving, lifting or throwing, 2) elbow, knee, horn, bend, *angle*.

forleave *v.* to give up, leave behind.

forlessening *n.* drop, dwindling, dying down, ebb, fall, falling off, losing ground, narrowing, shortening, shrinking, slackening, waning.

forlet *v.* 1) to let go by, look the other way, not be hard upon, overlook, put up with, whitewash, wink at, 2) to forsake, ditch, leave behind, leave high and dry, walk out on, 3) to drag the heels, let slide, not follow through, slack, go woolgathering.

forlikening (*allegory*) *n.* other-speaking, othertelling, under-telling, undersong.

forloned *adj.* 1) forlorn, hopelorn, friendless, alone, lonely, 2) bare, dreary, empty, godforsaken, wild.

forlorn *adj.* hopelorn, lonesome, sad, sick at heart, sorrowful, wretched.

forlornly *adv.* gloomily, hopelessly, sadly, sorrowfully.

for-many *adj.* more than enough, over-many, overmuch, too many, too much.

formarked *adj.* black-and-white, cut and dried, known, well-marked, settled.

former *adj.* earlier, erstwhile, one-time, once upon a time.

formerly *adv.* aforetime, in olden times, long ago, long since, of old, time was.

fornaughten *v.* to bring to naught, undo, unmake.

for-nigh *adv.* almost, full-nigh, more or less, nearly, not far off, well-nigh.

for-oft *adv.* many a time and oft, oft-times, oftentimes, too often, time after time.

forsake *v.* to leave, ditch, throw aside/away/off/over, walk out on.

forsaken *adj.* left, stranded, thrown aside, thrown away, thrown off, thrown over.

forsakenness *n.* 1) forlornness, hopelessness, lonesomeness, sorrow, wretchedness, 2) dreariness, loneliness, wildness.

for-sear *v.* to die away, dry up, dwindle, shrink, for-shrink, wilt, wither.

for-set *v.* to hedge in, hinder, make it hard for, put a drag on, stand in the way.

forshamed *adj.* ashamed, put to shame, shamefast, shown up, sunk low.

forshape *v.* 1) to hew into shape, make into, make something of, make/shape anew, work anew, 2) to make worse, make the bad worse, deepen, undo.

for-shrink *v.* to die away, dry up, dwindle, shrink, wilt, for-sear, wither.

forslow, foreslow *v.* 1) to be slow, put off, 2) to make slow, hinder.

forsooth *adv.* indeed, no two ways about it, truly, couthly.

forspeak *v.* to speak for, speak up for, stand up for, help.

for-speaker (*advocate*) *n.* friend in need, go-between, spokesman, spokeswoman, right-hand man, backer, oath-helper.

for-speaking (*advocacy*) *n.* speaking/standing up for, making/setting right, helping.

for-stand *v.* to fight back, hold back, hold out against, stand against, withstand.

forstraught *adj.* harrowed, bewildered, shaken, upset.

forsunder (*divorce*) *v.* to put away, put asunder, unthread, untie the knot, unweave.

forsundering (*divorce*) *n.* broken word, forsaking, leaving, oath forsworn, putting away, sundering, unthreading, untroth.

forswear *v.* to go back on one's word, unsay, withdraw, throw over.

forth *adv.* ahead, away, forward, into the open, out, outward, onward.

for that *conj.* because, in that.

forthcoming *adj.* about to be, at hand, brewing, in the wind, near, nearing, nigh.

forthcoming-time *n.* aftertime, aftertide, hereafter, hither days, coming days, what lies ahead, outlook.

forthfare (from life) *v.* to breathe one's last, die, meet one's end.

forthfaring *n.* death, dying, end, loss.

forthgo *v.* 1) to go forth, 2) (of day, night) to end, go by, wane, wear away.

forthgoing *n.* a going forth, setting forth, setting out.

forthright *adj.* bald, bold, downright, free, free-spoken, making no bones, open, outright, outspoken, stark, straight, straightforward, straight-speaking, straight from the shoulder, truly-spoken, truth-telling, unshrinking, no beating about the bush.

forthrightly *adv.* freely, openly, with an open heart, not seeking to hide or mislead, readily, straightforwardly, in straight words, trothfully, truly, with an open heart.

forthrightness *n.* boldness, openness, outspokenness, straightforwardness.

forthward/s *adv.* onward/s.

forthwith *adv.* anon, at once, betimes, now, shortly, soon, straightway.

fortieth *adj. n.* 1) the marking *number* that is kin to forty, 2) fortieth share.

fortnight *n.* fourteen nights, two weeks.

fortnightly *adv. adj.* once in a fortnight, done once in a fortnight.

fortread *v.* to tread down.

forty *n. adj.* the root *number* that is four times ten.

forwander *v.* to wander far and wide, weary oneself with wandering.

forward *adj.* 1) first, fore, foremost, head, leading, 2) early, forward-looking, onward, timely, 3) bold, brazen, overweening, shameless, wayward, wilful.

forward *adv.* 1) ahead, forth, 2) on, onward/s, 3) into the open, out.

forward *v.* 1) to further, help, help forward, lift, make better, 2) to send on, ship.

forwards *adv.* straight ahead, straight on.

forwarn, forewarn *v.* to warn, give fair warning, forebode, foresay.

forwearied *adj.* dead tired, fordone, drained, way-worn, weary, worn out.

forweary *v.* to overweary, tire out, wear down, wear out, weary.

forween *v.* to foreknow, foresee, foretell, see something coming.

forweep *v.* to wear oneself out with weeping.

for-well *adj.* bursting with health, hale and hearty, truly well.

forwhy 1) *adv.* why, wherefore, 2) *conj.* because, for.

forworn, foreworn *adj.* dead tired, drained, fordone, tired out, weary, worn out.

foster *n.* 1) food, 2) wardship, keeping, 3) foster-child.

foster *v.* to bring into one's kindred, take on, rear, bring up, take care of.

foster-brother *n.* 1) he-child of others suckled at one's mother's breast, 2) he-child from another kindred reared among one's own kin.

foster-child *n.* fosterling.

foster-daughter *n.* she-child from another kindred reared as one's own daughter.

foster-father *n.* one who stands in as father to another's child.

fosterling *n.* foster-child.

foster-mother *n.* one who stands in as mother to another's child.

foster-sister[(2)] *n.* 1) she-child of others suckled at one's mother's breast, 2) she-child from another kindred reared among one's own kin.

foster-son *n.* he-child of others brought up as one's own son.

foul *adj.* loathsome, rank, stinking, unhealthy, unwholesome.

foul *v.* 1) to make filthy, smear, besmear, 2) (of a ship's steering and such) to be hindered, stuck, wedged, 3) (in football) to drive into, run against, run into.

foul-beam *n.* black alder.

foully *adv.* dreadfully, hatefully, shamefully, unrightfully, wickedly, wretchedly.

foulmew (*fulmar*) *n.* a sea bird.

foul-mouthed *adj.* foul-speaking, foul-spoken, foul-tongued, evil-speaking, evil-tongued, rough-tongued, black-mouthed.

foul play *n.* evil-doing, misdeed, sharp/underhand dealing, unrightness, wickedness.

foul-speaking, foul-spoken *adj.* foul-mouthed.

foul-speech *n.* smearing, besmearing, backbiting, cursing, evil-speech, swearing.

foul-tongued *adj.* cursing, filthy, foul-mouthed, loud, rough, swearing, uncouth.

foundling *n.* forsaken child.

four *n. adj.* the root *number* following three.

fourfold *adj.* made up of four together, four times as great or as many.

four-footed *adj.* having four feet.

fourling *n.* one of four children born at the one time.

foursome *n.* four folk together.

fourteen *n. adj.* the root *number* made of ten and four.

fourteenth *adj. n.* 1) the marking *number* that is kin to fourteen, 2) fourteenth share.

fourth *adj. n.* 1) the marking *number* that is kin to four, 2) fourth share.

fourthing, fourthling (*quarter*) *n.* fourth, farthing, ferling.

fourthly *adv.* in the fourth *place.*

four-wheeler *n.* four-wheeled *carriage.*

fowl *n.* greater bird ('bird' being a small bird).

fowler *n.* one who hunts wild fowl (mostly with nets).

fowl-kin *n.* bird kind.

fox *n.* 1) *beast* of the wild, reddish and having a long bushy tail, 2) knave, sharper.

fox *v.* to hoodwink, mislead, play the fox, pull the wool over someone's eyes.

foxiness *n.* craftiness, knowingness, sharp-dealing, sharpness, stealthiness.

fox-hole *n.* bolt-hole, den, earth, hideaway, hide-out, hole, lair, shelter.

fox-hound *n.* hound reared to hunt foxes.

fox-hunt *n.* the hunting of a fox with hounds.

fox-like *adj.* crafty, foxy, knowing, sharp, shrewd, slinking, stealthy, underhand.

fox-sleep *n.* sham sleep.

foxtail *n.* 1) fox's tail, 2) kind of grass.

fox-whelp *n.* young of the fox.

foxy *adj.* 1) fox-hued, reddish brown, 2) crafty, fox-like, sharp, shifty, slippery.

frame *n.* 1) draft, first draft, rough draft, framework, layout, outline, shell, 2) backing, rim, setting, 3) body, build, cut.

frame *v.* 1) to build, find a way, hammer out, hew, ready, make ready, make up, set up, shape, work up, 2) to set (a *picture* in a frame), set off, 3) to begin, bring about, come up with, draft, draw up, dream up, hatch, lay out, mark out, outline, put together, shape, set out, think out/through/up, 4) to word, put into words, 5) to ring about, 6) to blacken, lay at one's door, lay guilt, name.

framer *n.* builder, craftsman, doer, draughtsman, maker, shaper, wright.

frame-up *n.* shift, underhand dealing, web, web-weaving.

framework *n.* draft, drawing, layout, outline, shape, weave.

free *adj.* 1) free-born, free-bred, freed, free as the wind, 2) free-handed, free-hearted, great-hearted, open-handed, open-hearted, room-hearted, handsome, lordly, overflowing, unselfish, unsparing, unstinting, 3) unbound, unfettered, unhindered, unshackled, 4) heart-whole, unwed, unwedded, unwived, 5) unbridled, wanton, 6) bold, brazen, downright, forthright, forward, off-handed, sharp, short, straight-speaking, uncouth, 7) for nothing, for love, for the asking, 'on the house'.

free *v.* 1) to set free, come to the help of, send help to, get one out of, let out, take by the hand, throw a life-line to, 2) to lighten, unbind, unbridle, unburden, unclasp, undo, unfasten, unfetter, unhook, unknot, unlock, unshackle, unstick, unstring, untie.

free-born *adj.* free, free-bred, free as the wind.

freedman *n.* a man who has been a thrall and has been set free, freeman.

freedom *n.* free-hand, free play, free speech, freedom of thought, freewill, opening, rights, room.

freedom fighter *n.* fighter, underground fighter.

free fall *n.* 1) falling with nothing to break one's fall, 2) (of *prices* in trading) sharp falls when sellers have cold feet and flood the *markets.*

free-for-all *n.* fight, hell let loose, horse-play, madhouse, storm, to-do, upheaving.

free hand *n.* free field, full play, leave, leeway, one's head, room.

free-hearted *adj.* free-handed, friendly, great-hearted, hearty, kind, open-handed, open-hearted, unsparing, unstinting, warm, welcoming.

freehold *n.* 1) land/buildings held by the owner without ties, 2) a field of work freely held (for life – as long as the work is rightly done).

freeholder *n.* holder of lands/buildings which may be freely sold or handed on.

freely *adv.* 1) handsomely, open-handedly, unstintingly, widely, with a free hand, with both hands, with open hand, 2) openly, straightforwardly, 3) readily, willingly, of one's own free will, 4) without let, cleanly, smoothly.

freeman *n.* free-born man, freedman.

free-minded *adj.* free-souled, free-speaking, free-thinking, open-minded.

free oneself *v.* to <u>win free</u>, win one's freedom, throw off the yoke.

free-right *n.* the rights of a free man.

free-spoken *adj.* downright, forthright, free, open, straightforward.

free-thinker *n.* one who will not blindly believe (as he/she sees it) Christian teaching.

free-thought *n.* free-thinking, freedom to believe as one chooses.

freeway (*motorway*) *n.* fast road, highway, mainway.

freewheel *v.* to glide, go smoothly, rest on one's oars.

free will *n.* 1) free choosing, strength of will, 2) (in Christian teaching) the belief that a man or woman may freely choose whether or not to follow God's way (as against a belief in God's forechoosing).

freeze *n.* 1) freeze-up, frost, 2) hold, standstill,

freeze *v.* 1) to ice over, ice up, 2) to benumb, chill, 3) to cut short, hold, stop.

freeze-drying *n.* the drying of food, blood, and other things by first freezing such and then warming again in an 'emptiness'/ *vacuum*.

freezer *n.* cold-chest, cooler, deep-freeze, ice-chest.

freezing *adj.* 1) of the weather) biting, bitter, chill, frosty, icy, numbing, wintry, 2) (of one who is cold) benumbed, numb, chilled, chilly, frozen, frozen to the marrow.

fret *v.* 1) to gnaw, wear away, 2) to goad, nettle, 3) to be in two minds, be on edge, brood, follow one's own tail, lose sleep, twitch, upset oneself, <u>worry</u>.

fretful *adj.* brooding, edgy, restless, twitchy, worried.

fretfully *adv.* broodily, edgily, restlessly.

fretfulness *n.* edginess, restlessness, sleeplessness, twitchiness, unsettledness, <u>worry</u>.

Friday (Friga's day) *n.* sixth day of the week.

friend *n.* best/bosom/dear/fast/good/near/warm friend, friend in need, near friend, backer, brother, follower, helper, helpmeet, helping hand, henchman, mainstay, right-hand man, one's other self, upholder, well-wisher.

friendless *adj.* alone, lonely, <u>forlorn</u>, unfriended.

friendlessness *n.* forsakenness, loneliness, lonesomeness, lostness, wretchedness.

friendliness *n.* heartiness, kindliness, kindness, open arms, warmth, welcome.

friend-lord *n.* one's good lord (*Beowulf*, line 3175).

friendly *adj.* hearty, kind, kindly, kind-hearted, lively, loving, neighbourly, sweet, warm, warm-hearted, winning, well-wishing, word-winsome.

friendship *n.* brotherhood, understanding, liking, warmth, kindness.

fright *n.* <u>fear</u>, affright, cold feet, dread.

frighten *v.* to fill with fear, frighten one out of his wits, strike with fear.

be frightened *v.* to dread, <u>fear</u>, fear for one's life, quake/shake/shrink with fear.

frightened *adj.* <u>fearful</u>, fear-ridden, frightened to death, frozen with fear.

frightening <u>fearsome</u>, dreadful, fearful, startling, nightmarish.

frightful *adj.* baleful, chilling, <u>dreadful</u>, ghastly, hellish, nightmarish, numbing.

frightfully *adv.* fearfully, foully, hatefully, <u>shamefully</u>, unrightfully, woefully.

frith (*peace*) *n.* weal, well-being, wholeness, friendship, fighting forsworn, understanding, hand of friendship, sword-sheathing.

frith *n.* land overgrown with underwood and scrub on the edge of a weald.

frithfen *n.* fen where underwood was found.

frith-weaver *n.* 1) bridge-builder, healer, frith-maker, weal-weaver, 2) woman.

frog *n. creature* of ponds and cool and wet shelters.

frogman *n.* man who swims/works under water, clad in tight *rubber*-wear and having *oxygen-bottles* on his back.

from *prep.* away, onward, out of.

frost *n.* hoarfrost, hard frost, sharp frost, rime, hoar-rime.

frost-bite *n.* scathing of bare flesh after being out in biting cold.

frost-bitten *adj.* frost-scathed.

frosted *adj.* 1) frost-bitten, frozen, 2) overspread with frost, 3) glass or silver or such made to look as if overspread with frost.

frostiness *n.* chilliness, coldness, iciness, wintriness.

frost-mist *n.* mist arising from the freezing of wetness in the *air*.

frosty *adj.* 1) cold, frozen, hoar, icy, rimy, wintry, 2) unfriendly, unwelcoming.

froward *adj.* headstrong, pigheaded, wayward, <u>wilful</u>.

frozen *adj.* a-cold, chilled to the bone, shivering, shivery, stone-cold.

frozen with fear *adj.* <u>fearful</u>, numbed with fear, white as a sheet.

fulfil *v.* to do well, do the deed, do thoroughly, earn, bring about, bring off, get the thing done, make a breakthrough, make good, make a go of, make one's mark, make short work of, not do by halves, reach one's goal, reap the harvest, put through, see through, be as good as one's word, work one's way up, come off well, come out on top, have the best of it, pull off, win one's spurs.

full *adj.* 1) bursting at the seams, crammed, crowded, filled to <u>overflowing</u>, loaded, rich in, stocked, well-stocked, thronged, well-filled, 2) (of eating) full-fed, having had enough, 3) greatest, highest, top, utmost, 4) (of life) busy, lively, 5) bosomy, buxom, goodly, shapely, 6) (of clothing) full-shaped, 7) (of the *voice*) deep, loud, rich, strong, swelling, 8) thorough, thoroughgoing.

full *adv.* fully, right, straight, thoroughly.

full-blooded *adj.* full, hearty, lusty, sweeping, thorough, wholehearted.

full-blown *adj.* full, fully-fledged, full-shaped, whole.

full-flood *n.* high tide.

full-foul *adj.* utterly foul.

full-grown *adj.* full-fledged, grown-up, manly, womanly, ripe.

full-hearted *adj.* 1) <u>bold</u>, daring-hearted, fearless, self-believing, 2) full of feeling.

full house *n.* crowd, houseful, not a seat empty (in a playhouse), sell-out, throng.

full length *adj.* 1) the whole length of something, 2) long-drawn, unshortened.

full-mighty *adj.* broad-shouldered, <u>stalwart</u>, <u>strong</u> as an ox.

full moon *n.* the moon wholly seen, the time when this comes about.

fullness *n.* broadness, greatness, richness, strength, wealth, wholeness.

full-nigh *adv.* almost, more or less, nearly, not far off, roughly, well-nigh.

full-weaponed *adj.* bristling with weapons, weaponed from head to foot.

full-wide *adj.* broad, far-reaching, far-stretching, sweeping, widespread.

fully *adv.* above all, altogether, <u>greatly</u>, at great length, handsomely, highly, markedly, overly, richly, strongly, thoroughly, to the full, truly, unstintingly, utterly, wholly, widely, indeed, inside out.

fulsome *adj.* 1) foul, <u>loathsome</u>, rank, 2) fawning, smooth spoken, toadying.

furlong *n.* a furrow's length, being forty poles or 220 yards.

furrow *n.* 1) cutting made by a plough (for putting in seed), 2) drain, hollow, line, seam, trough, 3) crinkle, crow's foot, fold, gather, wrinkle.

furrow *v.* 1) to plough, 2) to make wrinkles, to knit (the brow), line, seam.

further *adj.* 1) greater, more, new, other, over and above, 2) far-away, far-off, farther, farthest, furthest, furthermost, not nigh.

further *adv.* 1) further away, further off, 2) more, 3) also, as well as, besides, furthermore, moreover, on top of, over and above, to boot, what's more, yet.

further *v.* to forward, foster, <u>help</u>, speed.

furthermore *adv.* as well as, also, besides, more, moreover, let alone, likewise, else, and so on, and so forth, along with, together with, too.

furthermost *adj.* farthest, furthest, lost to sight.

furthersome *adj.* helpful, helping forward.

furthest *adj.* farthest, furthermost, lost to sight.

furze *n.* gorse.

furzy *adj.* of furze, overgrown with furze.

gad *v.* to gad about, wander.

gadabout *n.* wanderer, wayfarer.

gadling *n.* down-and-out, outsider.

gaffer ('godfather') *n.* goodman (as a way of speaking to an old man), old man.

gaingiving *n.* 1) giving again to a giver, 2) misgiving, looking twice, wariness.

gainsay *v.* 1) to speak against/out/up, answer back, belie, give the lie to, have words, say no, say outright, shake one's head, withsay, 2) to go against, make it hard for, set at naught, set oneself against, stand against, stand out, take one up on.

gainsayer *n.* 1) (*accuser*) tell-tale, withstander, 2) heckler, misbeliever.

gainsaying *n.* 1) bearing witness against, speaking against, branding, <u>smearing</u>, bringing home-truths, one word against another, 2) knock-down answer, thorough answer, truth made fast, whole answer.

gainstand *v.* to <u>withstand</u>, hold out against, stand against, for-stand.

gamble *n.* leap/shot in the dark, long shot, throw, last throw.

gamble *v.* to buy blind, make up a book, spin the wheel, have a flutter.

gambler *n.* bookmaker, gamester, player, sharper.

game *n.* 1) play, 2) field games, head-to-head, match, meeting, 3) business, line, 4) blind, makeshift, <u>shift</u>, step, web, 5) wild fowl that are hunted.

game *adj.* <u>bold</u>, daring, dogged, doughty, gritty, steady, <u>steadfast</u>, steely, tough, true.

gamekeeper *n.* man whose work is to keep watch against unlawful hunting of game.

gamely *adv.* doggedly, doughtily, manfully, steadfastly, through thick and thin.

gameness *n.* backbone, grit, stalworthness, steadfastness, steeliness, toughness.

gamesmanship *n.* seeking to win at any *cost*, shift, underhand dealing.

gamester *n.* bookmaker, gambler, player, sharper.

gaming *n.* having a flutter, laying *wagers*.

gammer ('godmother') *n.* old woman.

gander *n.* he-goose.

gang *v.* to fare, go, leave home/neighbourhood, make one's way, walk, wend.

ganger *n.* strider, walker, wayfarer.

gangway *n.* opening, thoroughfare, way in, way through, way up.

gannet *n.* a great seabird.

garlic ('spear-leek') *n.* plant with a strong smell and *taste*.

gate *n.* 1) opening in the wall of a town or fastness or greenyard (for comings and goings), 2) way between hills, way through highlands, 'saddle', 3) the door/s (of wood or iron) with which the gateway is shut.

gatehouse *n.* housing at or over a town/fastness gate.

gate-keeper, gateward *n.* doorkeeper, doorward.

gateway *n.* inway, doorway, way in, way through, way to, opening, open door.

gather *n.* fold.

gather *v.* 1) to forgather, come together, flock together, meet, 2) to bring together, draw together, gather together, foregather, hold a meeting, 3) to put together, bring ends together, build up, come by, come into, come into one's own, come in for, earn, fill up, find, get hold of, get in one's hand, set up, lay hands upon, lay together, light upon, make one's own, pick up, pitch upon, reap, heap up, hoard.

gathered (*collective*) *adj.* clustered, shared.

gathered works/writings (*anthology, corpus*) *n.* body of written works, writings.

gathering *n.* at-home, crowd, meeting, swarm, throng.

gather up *v.* to heap up, keep by one, lay in, lay up, put by, stock up, stow.

get$^{(2)}$ *v.* to get hold of, get one's hands on, gather.

get$^{(2)}$ **at** *v.* to have a go at, pick on.

get$^{(2)}$ **away** to win free, to fly, break away, break through, make off.

get$^{(2)}$ **hold of** *v.* to gather, clutch, lay hands upon, take hold of.

get$^{(2)}$ **the better of** *v.* to overcome, rise above.

get$^{(2)}$ **out** *v.* 1) to win free, to win one's freedom, break out, be off, bolt, 2) to bear witness, give out, put about, say out, set forth, lay down.

get$^{(2)}$ **over** *v.* to feel oneself again, get better, get back on one's feet, get well, make a come-back, pick up, pull through.

get$^{(2)}$**-rich-quick** *adj.* marked by hopes of/the seeking for quickly-won wealth.

get$^{(2)}$ **through to** *v.* to bring home to, bring over, make one believe, win over.

get$^{(2)}$**-together** *n.* gathering, forgathering, meeting, at home, drinks, sing-song.

get$^{(2)}$ **up** *v.* to get to one's feet, arise, rise up, stand up.

ghastful, ghastly *adj.* 1) filled with fear, 2) baleful, chilling, dreadful, fearsome, frightening, frightful, grisly, hellish, nightmarish, numbing.

ghost *n.* shade, shadow, soul of one dead.

ghost *v.* 1) to give up the ghost, to die, 2) to indwell and harrow a house, 3) to write a book for the named writer.

ghostlike *adj.* 1) like a ghost, 2) having the feel of a ghost-dwelt house.

ghostly *adj.* 1) bodiless, 2) eerie, hag-ridden, nightmarish, uncanny, unearthly.

ghost writer *n.* one who writes a book for the named writer.

giddily *adv.* dizzily, light-headedly, unsteadily.

giddiness *n.* dizziness, flightiness, heedlessness, lightmindedness.

giddy, giddybrained *adj.* empty-headed, flighty, hare-brained, light-minded.

gift$^{(2)}$ *n.* 1) deftness, 2) bequest, dole, hand-out, windfall.

gild *v.* to put on a thin layer of gold.

gilded *adj.* brightened with a layer of gold, gilden, gilt.

gilden *adj.* golden, gilded.

gilding *n.* thin layer of shining gold on the outside of something.

gird *v.* 1) to gird oneself with a girdle (in readiness for deed-doing), to fasten with a girdle, to gird on such as a sword, to bind on, 2) to gird about, hem in, pen, ring.

girder *n.* main beam in a framed floor, beam of iron or steel in the framework of a building.

girdle *n. belt.*

girdle v. to gird about, hem, ring.

girdle ring *n.* clasp, fastener.

girl *n.* daughter, maid, maid-child, maiden, wench, young woman.

girl Friday *n.* a ready-witted young woman helper.

girlfriend *n.* beloved, love, lover, truelove, sweetheart.

girlhood *n.* childhood, youth.

girlish *adj.* childish, growing, maidenly, youthful.

girth$^{(2)}$ *n.* 1) girdle of cloth or leather set about the body of a horse, to which a saddle or a load is fastened, 2) <u>greatness</u>, thickness, rimreach (of a man's body, or of the stock of a tree), land-girth (*area*, length and breadth).

give *v.* to give away, give freely, give out, bestow, deal out, hand out, hand over, make over, mete out, open one's hand, share out, shower upon.

giveaway *n.* 1) little outlay asked for goods, 2) hint, tell-tale mark.

give in, give up *v.* 1) to back down, have had enough, throw in one's hand, withdraw, <u>yield</u>, 2) to be <u>hopelorn</u>/without hope, give up hope, lose hope/heart.

given *adj.* marked out, set, settled, spelled out.

given-meaning (*metaphor*) *n.* forlikening.

give out *v.* to <u>bear witness</u>, get out, put about, say out, set forth, lay down.

giver *n.* bestower, good neighbour, helper.

give way *v.* to bend, break, fall, sink.

glad *adj.* <u>blithe</u>, blithe-hearted, laughing, light-hearted, lively, sparkling, thankful.

gladden *v.* to bless, brighten, <u>hearten</u>, lighten, quicken, thrill, warm the heart.

glade *n.* woodland meadow, opening in woodland.

gladly *adv.* blithely, blithefully, heart and soul, heartily, laughingly, nothing loath, readily, willingly, with all one's heart, without asking, with open arms.

gladness *n.* bliss, blissfulness, blitheness, gladness, glee, list.

gladsome *adj.* blissful, <u>blithe</u>, blithesome, gleeful.

glass *n.* 1) see-through sheet (hard and brittle) made by mingling sand with *soda* and/or *potash*, 2) drinking glass, sand-glass, weather-glass.

glass *v.* to glaze.

glasses *n.* eyeglasses, reading glasses, dark glasses, sunglasses.

glass-house *n.* greenhouse or hothouse, in which young plants are brought on.

glass-vat *n.* glass drinking bowl.

glass-work *n.* 1) glass-works (where glass is made), 2) the making of glass and glass-ware, things made of glass.

glass-worker *n.* one who works in glass.

glassy *adj.* 1) see-through, through-shining, gleaming, shining, 2) (of a look) cold, empty, lacking fire, lifeless, 3) smooth, still, 4) icy, slippery.

glaze *n.* 1) shine, 2) icing, topping.

glaze *v.* 1) to put glass into windows, 2) to ice.

glazed *adj.* (of someone's look) cold, empty, lifeless, stony.

glazer *n.* 1) glazier, 2) a tool for glazing.

glazier *n.* glass-maker, one who glazes windows.

glazing *n.* the business of putting glass into windows, or of putting on a glaze.

glazy *adj.* glass-like, glassy, looking like a glaze.

gleam *n.* beam, flicker/play of light, shimmer, shine, sparkle, twinkle.

gleam *v.* to be bright, burn, glisten, glow, shimmer, shine, twinkle.

gleaming afire, <u>bright</u>, burning, glistening, glowing, shimmering, shining.

glee *n.* liveliness, merry-making, mirth, sparkle, thrill.

glee-beam, glee wood (*musical instrument*) *n.* harp, pipe.

glee-craft, glee-dream (*music*) *n.* dreamcraft, song-craft, singing, setting, work.

gleeful *adj.* beaming, <u>blithe</u>, <u>bright</u>, crowing, giddy, glad, laughing, light-hearted, light-minded, <u>lively</u>, merry, mirthful, playful, sparkling, sunny.

gleefully *adv.* giddily, laughingly, light-heartedly, merrily, playfully.

gleeman, glee-singer (*minstrel, musician*) *n.* dreamer, harper, horn-player, player, singer, songster, songstress, songwright, song-writer, wordwright, wordcraftsman, wordcrafter, wordshaper.

glee-word *n.* song, cradle-song, dream-song, love-song, undersong.

glidder *adj.* glassy, icy, slidder, slithery, slippery, smooth.

glide *n.* a floating/flowing by, sailing by.

glide *v.* to float by, flow, go by, go/run smoothly, sail, slide, stream.

glimpse *n.* 1) look, quick look, sight, sighting, half an eye, 2) insight.

glimpse *v.* to sight, have a sight of.

glisten *v.* to gleam, shimmer, shine, sparkle, twinkle.

glistening *adj.* aglow, glowing, beaming, gleaming, shimmering, shining, sparkling.

gloaming *n.* dusk, eventide, half-light, nightfall, shades of evening, twilight.

gloom *n.* 1) blackness, darkness, dimness, greyness, shadow, shadowiness, twilight, 2) downheartedness, gloominess, heaviness, sadness, <u>sorrow</u>, woe, wretchedness.

gloominess *n.* 1) dimness, gloom, greyness, shadowiness, 2) heaviness, <u>sorrow</u>.

glooming *n.* 1) dark/glowering look, 2) gloaming, twilight.

gloomy *adj.* 1) dark, dim, dreary, grey, shadowy, 2) <u>forlorn</u>, <u>hopelorn</u>, sad, <u>sorrowful</u>, 3) dreary, saddening.

glove *n.* hand-wear (for shielding from cold, thorns or such).

glow *n.* 1) brightness, gleam, light, afterglow, sunset glow, 2) blush, flush, reddening, ruddiness, warmth.

glow *v.* 1) to brighten, burn, gleam, shimmer, shine, 2) to blush, flush.

glower *v.* to breathe fire, knit one's brows, look black/wrathful, look like thunder.

glowing *adj.* afire, aglow, bright, gleaming, glistening, shimmering, shining.

glowingly *adv.* fulsomely, warmly.

glow-worm *n. insect* – the she- glow-worm gives out a shining green light.

gnat *n.* small fly.

gnaw *v.* 1) to bite, chew, eat away, fret, 2) to harrow, harry, wear down, worry.

gnawing *n. adj.* aching, biting, harrowing, wearing.

go *n.* 1) bid, shot, stab, spell, 2) drive, life.

go *v.* to fare, go forth, go on one's way, make one's way.

goad *n.* 1) stick sharpened at the end, for driving oxen at ploughing, 2) prick, spur.

goad *v.* to drive, fire, harrow, harry, hound, needle, nettle, prick, put up to, quicken, spark, spur, sting, stir up, unsettle, upset, worry, wring, be a thorn in one's flesh.

go after *v.* to follow, hunt for, ride down, run/after, seek, shadow, stalk, tail.

go-ahead (*ambitious*) *adj.* keen, up-and-coming, seeking, bent/set upon, would-be.

goal *n.* end, mark, seeking.

goalkeeper *n.* player in a football team whose work is to keep the goal.

go along with *v.* to fall in with, put up with, do as asked, not mind, see no harm in, say yes to, swallow, throw open, welcome, go/swim with the stream.

goat *n.* 1) horned *beast* of the steading or the wild, he-goat or buck, she-goat, 2) lady-killer, wolf, woman-hunter, womaniser.

go-between *n.* dealer, middleman.

god *n.* 1) heavenly being, 2) (*idol*) stone god, wooden god.

God *n.* All-Father, All-holy, All-wielder, All-wise, God Almighty, the Almighty, God of our fathers, Maker of all things.

god-child *n.* god-daughter, godson.

god-daughter *n.* daughter in God, to whom one becomes as a father/mother at baptism, and who one is bound to teach the things of God.

godfather *n.* father in God, godsib.

god-fearing *adj.* godly, holy-minded, holy, right-hearted, rightwise, upright.

godforsaken *adj.* bare, dreary, empty, wild.

godhead, godhood *n.* godkindness, godship.

God-learned *adj.* learned in the lore of God.

godless *adj.* evil, evil-living, evil-speaking, fallen, hard-bitten, heathen, shameless, blind/deaf/dead to, trothless, truthless, unbelieving, ungodly, worldly-minded.

godlessness *n.* evil, sinfulness, trothlessness, ungodliness, unholiness, worldliness.

godlike *adj.* holy, all-holy, all-knowing, all-seeing, almighty, all-wise, everlasting, great, good, heavenly, overwhelming, timeless, worshipful.

godliness *n.* goodness, holiness, righteousness, sinlessness, true-heartedness.

godling (*idol*) *n.* sham god, stone god, wooden god.

Godlore (*theology*) *n.* God-learning.

godly *adj.* believing, earnest, God-fearing, God-filled, good, holy, holy-minded, rightwise, upright, worthy.

God-man *n.* God in man-likeness, God in flesh, the Son (Jesus Christ).

godmother *n.* mother in God, godsib.

God's acre *n.* burial-ground, churchyard, graveyard.

godsend *n.* blessing, great help, windfall.

godship *n.* godhead, godhood, godkindness.

godson *n.* son in God, to whom one becomes as a father/mother at baptism, and who one is bound to teach the things of God.

Godspell-book *n.* the Gospels.

godwards *adv.* towards God.

goer *n.* race-horse, thoroughbred.

go for *v.* to go after, go all out for, bid for, mean to, drive at.

go forward *v.* to make good ground, make headway, make inroads, step forward.

going *n.* 1) the width of a hall-way or stair, 2) suchness of the ground for driving, hunting, walking and so on.

going *adj.* 1) latest, ongoing, today's, 2) working.

gold *n.* 1) *metal* of most high worth, 2) riches, wealth, wherewithal, the needful.

gold-bright *adj.* bright with gold.

gold dust *n.* small motes/specks of gold.

golden *adj.* 1) bright, flaxen, yellow, 2) (of an opening) best, fair, hopeful, rich, 3) (of good times) blessed, blissful, cloudless, fair.

golden-fax, golden-haired *adj.* fair-haired, flaxen, flaxen-haired.

golden wedding *n.* the fiftieth yearday after one's wedding.

goldfinch *n.* thistle finch, thistle tweaker, thistle warp.

gold-hoard *n.* 1) mathom-hoard, wealth-heap, wealth-hoard, 2) strong room, wealth-hold, mathom-hold.

gold-hue *adj.* flaxen, old gold, yellow-red.

gold leaf *n.* small lot of gold, beaten thin for gilding.

goldsmith *n.* one who shapes gold and fairstones into *jewellery.*

gold-ward (*dragon*) *n.* great fire-snake, great wyrm (worm).

gold-weight/s *n.* 1) truthfast weight, 2) scales for weighing gold.

good *n.* weal, welfare, wellbeing, what is good for one.

good *adj.* blessed, goodly, great, heaven-sent, outstanding, wonderful, worthwhile.

good at *adj.* handy, clever, knowing, quick, ready.

good-bye 1) *intj.* farewell, see you later, 2) *n.* saying farewell, leave-taking.

good-daughter *n.* daughter-in-law.

good day *intj.* 1) (on meeting) how are you? 2) (on going) farewell, good-bye.

good-doer *n.* backer, friend, good neighbour, helper, upholder, well-wisher.

good enough *adj.* all right, middling, pretty good, worthwhile, worth having.

good-father *n.* father-in-law.

good-for-nothing *adj.* idle, shiftless, slack, slothful, slow, workshy.

good-for-nothing *n.* foot-/heel-dragger, layabout, ne'er-do-well, slow-bones, wretch.

Good Friday *n.* Long Friday.

good-liking *n.* kindly feeling towards someone, goodwill.

good-looking *adj.* 1) (of a man) handsome, manly, striking, 2) (of a woman) comely, fair, lovely.

goodly *adj.* 1) becoming, comely, handsome, well-made, well-shaped, 2) great, marked, much, weighty.

goodly *adv.* 1) becomingly, winsomely, wonderfully, 2) kindly, warmly.

goodman *n.* the husband as head of a household.

good-mother *n.* mother-in-law.

goodness *n.* 1) cleanness, goodness, righteousness, rightwiseness, sinlessness, uprightness, 2) good name, good standing, greatness, standing, worth, worthiness, 3) wholesomeness, 4) friendliness, goodwill, kind-heartedness, kindliness, kindness.

good night *intj.* good-bye, see you tomorrow, sleep well!

goods *n.* 1) belongings, things, 2) stock, wares.

goods-house *n.* stockroom, warehouse.

goodwife *n.* the lady of the house.

goodwill *n.* kindness, readiness, understanding, willingness.

goose *n.* 1) a great waterfowl, 2) the she- goose (the he- being 'gander').

goose-flesh *n.* little pimples over the flesh (arising from cold, fear or such).

goose-grass *n.* plant, at times given to geese as food.

goosish *adj.* goose-like, empty-headed, flighty, hare-brained, heedless, light-minded.

gore *n.* blood that has been shed and thus thickened.

gore ('gar' – spear) *n.* three-sided stretch of land.

gorse *n.* furze.

gory *adj.* bloody.

goshawk *n.* goose hawk.

go-slow *n.* a going-slow by workers seeking a better deal.

Gospel ('good spell/news') *n.* Christ-book, Godspell-book, that is, 1) the books of Matthew, Mark, Luke and John, 2) the tidings of what God has done in Christ (buying men back from the hold of sin).

gospel-true *adj.* wholly true.

gospel-truth *n.* the full, utter truth.

gossamer *n.* filmy cobwebs seen floating in the *air*, or spread over the grass, in the fall-time ('goose-summer' or Saint Martin's summer).

gossip *n.* 1) busybody, tell-tale, 2) hearsay, idle talk, smearing, tongue-wagging.

gossip *v.* to smear, tell tales.

gossiping *n.* smearing, backbiting, running someone down, tale-telling.

gossipy *adj.* newsy, long-winded, long-tongued, ready-tongued, running on, windy.

go with *v.* to go along with, go together, walk with, be found with, be seen with, keep with, team up with, draw alongside, shadow, follow.

go with the stream *v.* to fall in with, go along with, put up with, see no harm in.

grasp *n.* 1) clasp, clutches, grip, hold, 2) awareness, ken, knowledge, understanding, 3) reach, sweep.

grasp *v.* 1) to clasp, clutch, fasten on to, grip, 2) to follow, see, take in, understand,

grasping *adj.* craving, greedy, griping, mean, mean-minded, selfish, stingy, wolfish.

grass *n.* the green crops of the field, on which horses, kine and sheep feed.

grass *v.* to lay down grass, to become overgrown with grass.

grass-eating (*herbivorous*) *adj.* plant-eating.

grass-green *adj.* of the hue of grass, green with grass.

grasshopper *n. insect* known for its leaping and its chirruping.

grassland *n.* fields, grazing land, meadland, meadow, meadowland, water-meadows.

grass-snake *n.* the everyday ringed snake.

grass widow *n.* woman whose husband is much away from home.

grassy *adj.* 1) rich in grass, overgrown, 2) soft under foot, springy.

grave *n.* burial spot, last rest, long home.

grave-clothes *n.* shroud, winding-sheet.

grave-delver *n.* one who delves graves.

gravestone *n.* stone marking a grave, bearing the name and years of the one buried.

graveyard *n.* burial-ground, churchyard, lich-yard, lich-rest, 'God's acre'.

graze *n.* a light wound, pin-prick.

graze *v.* to crop, feed.

graze *v.* to draw blood, wound lightly.

grazier *n.* one who fattens up kine for sale.

grazing *n.* grazing ground, grassland, meadland, meadowland, outleas (meadland away from the house), water meadow.

great *adj.* 1) broad, far-reaching, far-stretching, high, lengthy, roomy, tall, thick, full-wide, wide, widespread, 2) many, overflowing, swarming, sweeping, teeming, 3) broad-shouldered, entish, great-limbed, heavy, mighty, strong, thickset, 4) amazing, breathtaking, foremost, high, high and mighty, in the news, in all mouths, in the eye of, on the every tongue, leading, lordly, kingly, queenly, main, of mark, not like the rest, not as others are, outstanding, starring, talked of, weighty, well-known, well-seen, wonderful, worshipful.

great bee *n. bumble* bee.

greaten *v.* 1) to build up, broaden, deepen, fatten, fill out, fill up, grow, heap on, heighten, lengthen, strengthen, forstrengthen, stretch, thicken, widen, 2) to look up to, make much of, speak highly of, swear by.

greater *adj.* ahead, better, cut above, more, further, higher, marked, one up, outmatching, outstanding, over, over and above, overtopping, on top, upper.

greatest *adj.* best ever, far ahead, first, foremost, most, highest, matchless, more than a match for, unmatched, nonesuch, outstanding, topmost, utmost, uppermost.

great-eyed *adj.* far-seeing, having a wide outlook on life.

great-hearted *adj.* great-minded, high-minded, kind, open-handed, selfless.

great-heartedness *n.* goodness, open-handedness, open-heartedness, unselfishness.

great king (*emperor*) *n.* high king, over-king, overlord, all-wielder.

great-limbed *adj.* broad-shouldered, heavy, mighty, strong, thickset.

greatly *adv.* amazingly, deeply, ever so, ever/never so much, fully, great deal, highly, mainly, markedly, mightily, more than enough, mostly, much, overly, richly, strongly, thoroughly, truly, right well, utterly, wholly, widely, wonderfully, worthily.

great-minded *adj.* far-seeing, high-minded, open-minded, selfless, unsparing.

great-mouthed *adj.* 1) loud-speaking, 2) loud-mouthed, swollen-headed.

greatness *n.* 1) fullness, more than enough, roominess, strength, thickness, breadth, depth, height, length, 2) high name, highness, high standing, standing, kingliness, lordliness, queenliness, leadership, overlordship, might, mightiness, undying name, deathlessness, weightiness, worth, worthfulness, worthiness, worthship.

greave *n.* thicket, underwood.

greed *n.* craving, hungering/thirsting/lusting/running after, itching for.

hungering/ thirsting for, burning, itching, wolfishness, lust.

greedily *adv.* graspingly, hungrily, piggishly, selfishly, wolfishly.

greediness *n.* 1) greed, piggishness, 2) graspingness, meanness, stinginess.

greedy *adj.* 1) all-swallowing, belly-worshipping, hungry, never full, overfed, quenchless, piggish, wolfish, 2) clinging, grasping, griping, hoarding, mean, selfish.

green *adj.* 1) hue between blue and yellow, grass-green, hedge-green, leaf-green, sea-green, 2) grassy, leafy, 3) new, raw, unhewn, 4) childish, clueless, goosish, over-ready to believe, readily taken in, born yesterday, unfledged, unwary, 5) green-eyed, 6) sick, unhealthy, under the weather, wan, 7) earth-caring (*eco*-friendly).

green *n.* grass sward in the middle of a ham or small town.

green *v.* to become green as plants come up, give a green hue to, clothe with green.

green-eyed *adj.* bitter (against one who has what one lacks), mean-minded, restless.

greenfinch *n.* green-hued bird of the finch kind.

greenfly *n.* plant-louse (of a green hue).

greenhorn *n.* beginner, clod, colt, goose, know-nothing, learner, newling.

greenhouse *n.* glass-house in which young plants are brought on.

green-hued *adj.* greenish.

greenish *adj.* somewhat green.

green man *n.* 1) man clad with green boughs, in the likeness of a wild man of the woods, 2) one who is raw and new to things.

greenness *n.* 1) the suchness of being green, 2) cluelessness, newness, rawness.

greens *n.* kale, leeks, sprouts, and such.

greensand *n.* a kind of sandstone.

greensward *n.* grassland, green, mead, meadow.

greenwood *n.* weald or woodland in leaf.

greenyard *n.* kitchen yard for growing greens.

greet *v.* to bid/say good morning, send greetings, shake hands, welcome.

greet *v.* to groan, moan, shed tears, sorrow, weep.

greeting/s *n.* welcome, best wishes, good wishes.

grey *adj.* 1) ashen, ash-hued, grey-hued, hoar, 2) cloudy, gloomy, 3) dreary, grim.

grey *n.* 1) brock, 2) grey horse.

greybeard *n.* elder, old man, old timer.

grey goose *n.* greylag goose, fen-goose, wild goose.

greyhound *n.* hound with lithe body and long shanks, swift and keen-sighted.

grey-hue *n.* greyish.

greyish *adj.* somewhat grey.

greyness *n.* the suchness of being grey, hoarness.

grey-ware *n. pewter.*

grim *adj.* cold, forbidding, gloomy, heavy, leaden, stern, stiff, unlaughing.

grim *adv.* bitterly, grimly, in a grim way/mood, dreadfully.

grimly *adj.* dreadful, grim-looking, hateful.

grimly *adv.* dreadfully, in a grim way, with a grim look.

grimness *n.* deadliness, dreariness, heaviness.

grin *n.* beam, smirk.

grin *v.* to beam, smirk.

grind *n.* hard work, hard-going, spadework, uphill work.

grind *v.* 1) to mill, pound, 2) to grind away, hammer away, work hard.

grinder *n.* upper millstone or runner, pounder.

grinding *n.* the work of grinding, grinding barley (or such) readily ground.

grinding *adj.* of that which wears down (such as hardship or overwork).

grindle stone *n.* grindstone, stone good for making a grindstone.

grindstone *n.* millstone.

grip *n.* 1) clasp, handclasp, grasp, hold, 2) clutch, iron hand, iron heel, 3) haft, handgrip, handle, helve, hilt, 4) clip, fastening, hair-grip.

grip *n.* small open furrow, ditch, drain, drain in a cowhouse.

grip *v.* 1) to grasp, clasp, fasten on, take hold of, lay hands upon, 2) to spellbind.

grip *v.* to delve out a ditch or drain.

gripe/s *n.* 1) grasp, grip, hold, 2) belly-ache.

gripe *v.* to clasp, clutch, fasten on to, grasp, grip, lay hold of.

griping *adj.* grasping, hard-fisted, mean, mean-handed, stingy, gripple.

gripingly *adv.* meanly, stingily.

gripple *adj.* grasping, griping, hard-fisted, mean, mean-handed, stingy.

grisly *adj.* dreadful, fearful, fearsome, frightening, nightmarish.

grist *n.* corn ready to be gound, a batch of such corn.

grist-bite *n.* gnashing the teeth

gristing *n.* the business of grinding corn.

gristle *n. cartilage.*

gristly *adj.* hard, leathery, tough.

grit *n.* 1) little bits of sand or stone (the outcome of wearing down by water and/or wind), 2) rough sandstone of the kind that is good for making grindstones and millstones, 3) backbone, doggedness, doughtiness, steadiness, toughness.

grit *n. husks* of barley/oats/wheat and such, chaff, mill-dust, rough oatmeal.

grit *v.* to put down grit or salt on the road in icy weather (for a better grip).

gritstone *n.* rough sandstone.

gritty *adj.* doughty, flinty, hard as iron/nails/steel/stone, tough, unyielding.

groan *n.* moan, sigh.

groan *v.* to moan, bemoan, sigh, sorrow.

groaner *n.* bleater, moaner.

groats *n.* hulled corn (most often oats, but also barley or wheat).

groin *n.* the fold on either side of the body between the belly and the upper thigh.

grope *v.* to feel one's way, grope in the dark, have nothing to go on, inch forward.

grot *n.* bit, mite, mote, speck, whit.

ground/s *n.* 1) earth, land, dry land, 2) clod, dust, loam, mould, 3) pitch, playing field/ground, 4) footing, grounding, groundwork, standing, 5) grounds (*estate*), acres, fields, holding, land, 6) grounds (*reason, basis*), why and wherefore.

ground *v.* 1) to set, settle, 2) to teach, 3) (of a ship) to run aground, become stranded, 4) (of flying craft) to be brought down to land, stopped from taking off.

ground-ash *n.* ash sapling.

ground-breadth (*area*) *n.* ground-width, land-breadth/-width, length and breadth.

grounded *adj.* aground, beached, high and dry, stranded, stuck.

ground-floor *n.* the floor of a building which is of like height with the ground.

grounding *n.* 1) footing, groundwork, 2) teaching, 3) grounding of a ship in the shallows.

groundless *adj.* 1) bottomless, unfathomful, 2) far-fetched, flimsy, wildly out.

groundsman *n.* one who looks after the ground for stockball/*cricket*.

groundsel, ground-sill (*foundation*) *n.* footing, grounding, ground-wall.

groundstone (*foundation* stone) *n.* bottom stone, footing stone.

ground-swell *n.* deep swell of the sea after a storm or earthquake faraway, sea-wave.

groundward *adv.* towards the ground.

ground wave *n.* earthquake, earth-stirring, ground wave.

ground-width (*area*) *n.* ground-breadth, land-breadth/-width, length and breadth.

groundwork *n.* 1) footing, readying, spadework, 2) forethought, homework.

grout *n.* 1) rough meal, stripped corn seeds, 2) grounds, settlings.

grove (*copse*) *n.* holt, holt-wood, wood-holt, shaw, thicket, thorn-grove, underwood.

grow *v.* 1) to grow up, grow in strength, become taller, blossom, fledge, ripen, spring up, sprout, shoot up, build up, gather up, heap up, 2) to spread, thicken, widen, 3) to bring on, seed, sow, till, 4) to arise, become, come to be.

grower *n.* acreman, earth-tiller, smallholder.

grown-up *n.* grown man, grown woman, grown to full/riper years.

growth *n.* 1) broadening, growing, heightening, lengthening, 2) headway, rise, spreading, strengthening, upbuilding, unfolding, waxing, widening, 3) swelling.

grub *n.* mad, mathe, worm.

grub *v.* to grub out, delve out roots, pull up.

grubbiness *n.* dust, filth, slime.

grubby *adj.* filthy, foul, unwashen.

grunt *n. growl.*

grunt *v.* to speak low, talk under the breath.

gruntle *v.* to bellyache, bemoan, have a chip on one's shoulder.

guest[2] *n.* boarder, caller.

guilt *n.* guiltiness, blood guiltiness, red-handedness, sinfulness, wickedness.

guiltless *adj.* clean, clean-handed, free from guilt, not guilty, unguilty, upright.

guiltily *adv.* shamefastly, unrightfully, untruly.

guiltiness *n.* blood guiltiness, red-handedness, sinfulness, wickedness.

guilty *adj.* black-hearted, evil, sinful, sin-laden, unrightwise, wicked, blood-guilty.

gum *n.* fleshy inside of the mouth in which are set the teeth.

gut/s *n.* 1) belly, insides, 2) backbone, boldness, daring, grit.

gut *v.* 1) to clean, draw, 2) to clean out, empty.

gut *adj.* heartfelt, unthinking.

hab or nab, hab nab *adv.* anyhow, get or lose, hit or miss.

hack *v.* to cut down, hew.

hack-saw *n.* tool.

hacker *n.* 1) tool for hacking a tree (so as to draw off the sap or such), 2) one who breaks into another's main-reckoner/*computer*.

hackle (*cloak*) *n.* 1) overhood, riding hood, 2) straw roofing of a beehive.

hackle *n.* 1) comb for cleaving and combing out the 'threads' of flax or hemp, hatchel, heckle, 2) the long shining feathers on the neck of the cock.

hackle *v.* to cut roughly, hack.

hackle *v.* to comb flax or hemp with a hackle.

haft *n.* grip, handle, handgrip, helve, hilt, hold, stock.

haft *v.* to fit with a haft or handle.

hag *n.* 1) night-hag, witch, 2) churlish old woman.

hag-ridden *adj.* in the grip of a hag.

hail *n.* 1) hailstones, hailstorm, 2) broadside, burst/shower/storm of fire.

hail *v.* to send down, shower, throw down.

hailstone *n.* icestone.

hailstorm *n.* wild storm of hail.

hair *n.* head/shock of hair, locks, flowing locks, mane.

hairbreadth, hair's-breadth *n.* breadth of a hair, truly narrow.

hair-do *n.* cut, set, trim, wave.

hair-grass *n.* kind of grass likened to hair.

hair-needle *n.* pin for fastening up the hair.

hair-stroke *n.* thin line made in drawing or writing.

hairy *adj.* fleecy, shaggy, unshaven, unshorn, woolly.

hale *adj.* healthy, in good health, strong, well, whole.

half *n.* 1) side, left/right side, father's/mother's side, this/that side, 2) one of two bits into which something is sundered.

half *adj.* halved, not whole, half-done.

half *adv.* all but, barely, pretty nearly.

half-and-half *adj.* lukewarm, neither one thing nor the other, watered down.

half-arm *n.* half an arm's length.

half-baked *adj.* 1) half-done, underdone, leathery, tough, 2) makeshift, raw, unhewn, unripe, 3) harebrained, short-sighted, unthought out.

half-blood *n.* the kinship between folk who have the *same* father but not the *same* mother (or the other way about).

half-bold *adj.* unsteady, making to be strong (but too often giving up).

half-breed *n.* one whose father and mother are not of the like folk-stock.

half-brother *n.* son of one's father but not one's mother, or son of one's mother but not one's father.

half-dead *adj.* dead tired, half-quick, nigh dead, worn out.

half-ebb *n.* the suchness or time of the tide when it is half out.

half-flood *n.* the suchness or time of the tide half-way between low and high water.

half-hearted *adj.* cool, dragging heels, leaden, listless, lukewarm, slow, wooden.

half-heartedly *adv.* coolly, listlessly, lukewarmly, slowly, unreadily, unwillingly.

half-holiday *n.* half a day's holiday.

half-island (*peninsula*) *n.* foreland, headland, horn, near-island, seagirt land.

half-length *n.* a likeness (*portrait*) of half the full length.

half-light *n.* dusk, gloaming, nightfall, shades of evening, twilight, waning light.

halfling *n.* dwarf, small man or woman.

halfly *adv.* by halves, halfway, not wholly, somewhat.

half-mast *n.* the half of a mast, half the height of a mast.

half-moon *n.* the moon when only half its shape is seen shining.

halfpenny *n.* *coin* of half the worth of a penny.

halfpennyworth *n.* as much as a halfpenny will buy.

half-red *adj.* reddish.

half-sister[(2)] *n.* daughter of one's father but not one's mother, or daughter of one's mother but not one's father.

half-tide *n.* the suchness of the tide half-way between flood and ebb.

half-timber *adj.* building of stonework in a timbered frame.

half-time *n.* 1) half the full time in which work is done, 2) the break at the end of the first half of a football match.

half-timer *n.* one who works half-time.

half-truth *n.* half-lie, playing with words, sidestep, twisted saying, untruth.

half-way *adj.* mid, middle, middling, midway.

half-way *adv.* 1) in/to the middle, midway, 2) nearly, rather.

half-white *adj.* whitish.

half-wit *n.* clod, lackwit, witling.

half-witted *adj.* backward, clod-hopping, dim-witted, slow-witted, thick, witless.

half-word *n.* word/speech which tells only half, hint, aside, clue, word in the ear.

half-year *n.* six months.

half-yearly (*biannual*) twice a year, twice-yearly.

hall *n.* 1) a great house, 2) great meeting room, 3) dwelling hall for the learners at a seat of learning/*university*, 4) hallway of a house.

hall-door *n.* door of a hall, door leading into the hall.

hall-mark *n.* 1) mark of the Goldsmiths *Company* stamped on things of gold or silver, 2) mark or stamp of worth in other fields.

hall of books (*library*) *n.* bookhoard, house of books, reading room, reading house.

hall of learning (*academy, college, university*) *n.* house/seat of learning.

hallow *v.* to make holy, keep holy, to bless a thing, sunder from the world.

Hallow-e'en *n.* All-hallow-even, the eve of All Hallows (*Saints*) Day.

Hallow-tide *n.* the time of All Hallows, the first week of Wind-month/*November*.

hallway *n.* inway of a house, way through to the rooms of the house.

halt *adj.* bed-fast, bedridden, crippled, laid up, lame, limping.

halter *n.* 1) rope with a headstall by which horses or kine are led and fastened up, 2) rope with a headstall for hanging evil-doers.

halting *adj.* 1) fitful, groping, limping, off and on, straggling, unsteady, 2) (of speech) faltering, shamefast, stammering, tongue-tied.

halve *v.* to cleave/cut in half, cut in two, go halves, lessen by half.

ham *n.* that bit of the shank at the back of the knee, the back of the thigh.

ham *n.* small town, thorp, wick.

hamble *v.* to cripple, lame.

ham-fisted, ham-handed *adj.* all thumbs, thick-fingered, unhandy, unwieldy.

hamm *n.* land hemmed in by water or marsh (or may be by high ground), water-meadow, tilled land on the edge of woodland or moor.

hamm *n.* land reaching out like a bent shank into a winding stretch of a *river*, or into the sea or a marsh.

hammer *n.* tool with a hard and heavy head (for driving in nails and such).

hammer *v.* 1) to beat, drive, knock, strike, 2) to din into, drive home, 3) to beset, have a go at, lay into, pitch into, 4) to hammer out, give shape to one's thoughts.

hammer-beam *n.* short beam set into the wall of an *aisled* timber building and holding the upright hammer *post*.

hammer-head *n.* 1) head of a hammer, 2) thick-head, witling.

hammer-stone *n.* stone tool for hammering.

hammer-work *n.* work done with a hammer, something shaped with a hammer.

hamstring *n.* one of the sinews at the sides of the ham and the back of the knee.

hamstring *v.* 1) to cut the hamstrings so as to cripple or lame, 2) to fetter, hinder.

hand *n.* 1) the end bit of the arm by which man grasps and handles things, fist, 2) side, right-hand, left hand, 3) share, 4) help, helping hand, 5) craftsman, hired man, worker, workman, sailor, 6) the hand (of another) by which a deed is done, 7) writing, handwriting, longhand, 8) the hand of a clock, 9) a handbreadth of four inches (now *used* only in giving the height of horses), 10) hand (at *cards*).

hand *v.* 1) to give, hand over, 2) to help, lead.

handbell *n.* small hand-held bell.

handbill *n.* light bill or lopping knife.

handbook *n.* lorebook, workbook.

hand-breadth *n.* *measure* of length, namely, four inches.

handclever *adj.* clever, deft, good at, handy, nimble, quick, ready.

handcleverness *n.* deftness, handiness, quickness, readiness.

hand-cloth *n.* *towel*.

handcraft *n.* handicraft.

handfast *n.* 1) strong grip or hold, 2) taking hands in making a deal, betrothing.

handful *n.* 1) one or two, two or three, thin house, 2) as much as one can handle.

hand-glass (*magnifying* glass) *n.* reading-glass.

handgrip *n.* clasp, clutch, grasp, grip, hold.

handhold *n.* 1) hold for the hand when climbing, 2) hold for a tool.

handicraft *n.* craftsmanship, handcraft, handiwork.

handicraftsman *n.* craftsman, handcraftsman.

handily *adv.* 1) helpfully, readily, 2) cleverly, deftly, nimbly, quickly.

handiness *n.* deftness, handcleverness, quickness, readiness.

handiwork *n.* 1) craftsmanship, workmanship, 2) deed, doings.

handle *n.* grip, haft, handgrip, helve, hilt, hold, stock.

handle *v.* 1) to feel, finger, hold, run the hand over, play about with, stroke, 2) to wield, work, 3) to steer, 4) to deal in, sell, trade in, 5) to deal with, write about.

handled *adj.* having a handle/s.

handling *n.* running, overseeing, steering, stewarding.

handlock *v.* to fetter, shackle.

hand-loom *n.* weaver's loom worked by hand.

hand-made *adj.* crafted, done by hand, hand-wrought.

handmaid *n.* maid, maid-of-all-work, woman follower/helper.

handout *n.* 1) dole, 2) sheet, write-up.

hand out *v.* to deal out, dole out, give out, open one's hand, share, bestow.

hand-picked *adj.* carefully/thoughtfully chosen, well-chosen, worthful.

hand-play *n.* striking with the fists in hand-to-hand fighting.

hand-quern *n.* hand-mill.

hand-reading *n.* hand-telling, soothsaying.

hand-saw *n.* small saw wielded in one hand.

hand-setting (*signature*) *n.* hand, mark, underwriting.

handsome *adj.* 1) good-looking, manly, striking, 2) free, free-handed, unstinting.

handsomely *adv.* freely, fully, greatly, readily, richly, willingly.

handsomeness *n.* 1) good looks, manly looks, 2) open-handedness, unselfishness.

hand-staff *n.* that half of a flail by which it is wielded.

handstroke *n.* dint or stroke with the hand.

hand-tame *adj.* truly tame.

handwork *n.* 1) work done by hand and arm, 2) (*surgery*) bodycraft, cutwork.

handwrit *n.* deed, written deal/understanding.

handwriting *n.* 1) fair hand, flowing/running hand, longhand, down-stroke, up-stroke, 2) someone's writing as belonging to his/her being, 3) written work, writing.

handy *adj.* 1) deft, good at, clever, quick, ready, 2) at hand, on hand, to hand, ready to hand, near, nearby, within reach.

handyman *n.* worker good at many kinds of work about the house.

hang *v.* 1) to drop, hang down, 2) to bend forward/downward, lean over, 3) to hang upon, rest on, 4) to hang by the neck, put to death, 5) to hang oneself.

hang back *v.* to be loath/unwilling, hang fire, hold back, shrink back.

hanger *n.* wood on a slope.

hanger-on *n.* fawner, follower, leech, toady, tool, yes-man.

hang fire *v.* 1) (of a *gun*) to not go off, misfire, 2) to bide one's time, put off.

hanging (*curtain*) *n.* forehanging, window hanging.

hangman *n.* the man whose work it is to hang those sent to the *gallows*.

hang on *v.* 1) to fasten, set, stick on, hook on, tie on, tie up, yoke, 2) to bide, hold out, 3) to hang on to, hold on to, keep hold of.

hangover *n.* 1) feeling the outcome of drinking too much, aching head, 2) throwback from childhood.

hang together *v.* 1) to hold together, cleave to, stick to, stick together, 2) to match.

hang up *v.* 1) to hang up on a hook, 2) to put the 'phone down.

happen[2] *v.* to arise, befall, betide, come about, come off, fall out, work out.

happening[2] *n.* arising, outcome, showing, upshot.

happily[2] *adv.* blithely, gladly, light-heartedly, merrily.

happiness[2] *n.* blessedness, blitheness, gladness, sunniness, wellbeing.

happy[2] *adj.* blithe, glad, blessed, feeling right, filled.

hard *adj.* hard as nails/steel/stone, stiff, stony, tough, unbending, unyielding.

hard *adv.* 1) earnestly, 2) fast, 3) near in time or steading.

hard and fast *adj.* abiding, hardened, hidebound, unbroken, timeless, unyielding.

hardbeam *n.* hornbeam.

hard-bitten *adj.* down-to-earth, hard-headed, hardened, shrewd, tough.

hardboard *n.* stiff board made from wood leftovers.

hard by 1) *prep.* alongside, at hand, beside, right beside, in the neighbourhood of, near, near at hand, nearby, next to, nigh, not far, 2) *adv.* near at hand in time.

hard drinker (*alcoholic*) *n.* drunk.

harden *v.* to give strength/heart to one, put heart into, steel, strengthen, toughen.

hardened 1) given to, wont, 2) flinty, stiff, stony, unyielding.

hard-fisted *adj.* grasping, hard-handed, mean, selfish, stingy, tight-fisted.

hard-going *n.* grind, hardship, hard life, hard work, heavy work, weary way.

hard-handed *adj.* 1) hard-fisted, mean, stingy, 2) flinty, grim, stern, stony-hearted.

hard-headed *adj.* 1) unbending, unyielding, 2) down-to-earth, shrewd, tough.

hard-hearted *adj.* flinty, stony-hearted, ruthless, stiff, unfeeling, unmelting.

hardhew *n.* chisel, edged tool, quern-bill.

hardly *adv.* 1) against the stream/wind, in the teeth of, the hard way, uphill, with much ado, 2) barely, no more than, only, 3) by no means, not at all, no way.

hard-mouthed *adj.* 1) (of a horse) having a hard mouth, and not so readily handled with bit and bridle, 2) headstrong, self-willed, wayward, wilful.

hardness *n.* sternness, stiffness, toughness, stoniness.

hard saying *n.* a dark/deep saying or word, hard nut to crack, a knotted or hidden saying, riddle, twisted saying, two-edged saying.

hard sell *n.* driving salesmanship.

hard-set *adj.* 1) beset by much ado, 2) pig-headed, stiff-necked, unbending.

hardship *n.* dearth, grinding hardship, hard-going, hard life, hard times, hard way, bad times, bitterness, bitter draught, blight, burden, dreariness, evil plight, harm, heart-ache, lack, leanness, load, loss, utter loss, need, neediness, ordeal, running sore, slough, sorrows, weariness, woe, wretchedness, hand-to-mouth life, wolf at the door.

hard shoulder *n.* hardened land beside the highway, where *vehicles* may pull over.

hard up *adj.* badly off, needy, not making ends meet, not well-off, penniless, short.

hardware *n.* 1) household goods such as nails, pots and pans, 2) the 'body' of a main reckoner/*computer* (as against its 'software' or running setup).

hard-wearing *adj.* strong, tough, well-made.

hardwood *n.* the wood of broad-leaved, leaf-shedding trees such as ash and oak.

hard work *n.* grind, grindstone, hammering away, hard-going, heavy work, long pull, spadework, uphill/warm work.

hard-working *adj.* busy, horny-handed, steady, tireless, untiring, sweating.

hare *n.* *beast* with long ears and hind shanks, buck (he-hare), doe (she-hare).

hare-brain *n.* addle-head, feather-head, giddy-head, lackwit.

hare-brained *adj.* dizzy, empty-headed, flighty, giddy, light-minded, mad-headed.

harecleft *n.* hare-lip.

hare-eyed *adj.* having eyes that look all about and/or are never shut.

harefoot *n.* 1) narrow foot, 2) nickname for one who is quick on his feet.

hare-hearted *adj.* fearful, chicken-hearted.

hareling (*rabbit*) *n.* little hare.

hare-lip *n.* cleft in the upper lip.

hare's eye *n.* sickness of the upper eyelid (making one to sleep with eye/s half-open).

hare-sighted *adj.* short-sighted.

hare-sleep *n.* a light sleep.

hare's tail *n.* a kind of grass.

harish *adj.* dizzy, empty-headed, mad, thimble-witted, unwitful, <u>witless</u>.

hark *v.* to give ear, give a willing ear, give heed, hearken, listen to, mark.

harm *n.* 1) foul play, evil-doing, 2) threat, death-trap, shadow of death.

harm *v.* to bite, cut, gnaw at, harrow, tear, wind, work/wreak evil, <u>worry</u>, wound.

harmful *adj.* baleful, baneful, blighting, deadly, dreadful, tearing, threatening, undoing, unwholesome, withering.

harmfully *adv.* balefully, dreadfully, witheringly.

harmless *adj.* 1) wholesome, 2) lamb-like, mild, mouselike, soft, tame.

harmlessly *adv.* mildly, softly, tamely.

harm-speaking, harm-speech *n.* backbiting, blackening, gossiping, lying, <u>smear</u>.

harm-spell *n.* curse, spell-weaving, witching.

harp *n.* stringed *musical instrument*.

harp *v.* 1) to play the harp, 2) to harp on, dwell on, go on and on, weary.

harper *n.* harp player.

harping *n.* bellyaching, moaning, whinging.

harp-song *n.* song to the playing of the harp.

harrier *n.* hawk.

harrow *v.* to harry, unman, fill with <u>fear</u>.

harrowed *adj.* <u>careworn</u>, over-wrought, in dread, dreading, writhing, <u>fearful</u>.

harrowing *adj.* worrying, worrisome, making one fearful of an outcome.

harry *v.* to <u>goad</u>, harrow, hound, heckle, needle, sting, stir up, worry someone.

harsh[1] *adj.* 1) churlish, cold-eyed, flint-hearted, <u>grim</u>, hard-hearted, heartless, <u>ruthless</u>, stony-hearted, thoughtless, <u>uncouth</u>, <u>unfeeling</u>, wolf-hearted, wolfish, 2) heavy-handed, overbearing, threatening, 3) (of words) belittling, biting, cutting, hard, stinging, unsparing, withering, 4) (of *sound*) creaky, grinding, screeching, 5) (of the weather) biting, bitter, foul, freezing, rough, stormy, wild, wintry.

hart *n.* he- red deer, stag.

harvest *n.* 1) crop, full growth, output, year's growth, yield, 2) gathering, ingathering, harvesting, mowing, reaping, 3) harvest-tide, harvest time, reaping-time.

harvest *v.* to bring in, gather in, pick, reap.

harvester *n.* 1) reaper, 2) reaping *machine*, 3) harvester ant.

harvest-field *n.* corn-field in harvest.

harvest home *n.* thanksgiving/merrymaking to mark a good end to the harvesting.

Harvest-month (*September*) *n.* Barley-month, Holy-month.

harvest moon *n.* the moon which is full within a fortnight of the even-night (*equinox*) of leaf-fall (*autumn*) time.

harvest mouse *n.* small mouse which nests among the stalks of growing corn.

harvest queen *n.* young woman chosen from among the reapers to take the high settle at the harvest home.

harvest-tide (*autumn*) *n.* harvest time, fall, fall of the leaf/year, leaf-fall.

harvest-wet *n.* wet weather at the time of leaf-fall.

has-been *n.* someone who shone in former days but whose time is now gone by.

hasp *n.* hinged clasp for fastening a door, gate or the lid of a chest.

hassock *n.* 1) thick clump of grass or sedge, 2) footrest, kneeler (in church).

hat *n.* cloth cap, deerstalker, straw hat, sunhat, top-hat.

hatch *n.* half-door, hatchway.

hatch *v.* 1) to breed, bring forth, 2) to brew, dream/think up, frame, put together.

hatchel *n.* comb for cleaving and combing out the 'threads' of flax or hemp, heckle.

hatchway *n.* hatch, trap-door.

hate *v.* to loathe, mislike, shrink from, not like the look of, shun, <u>spurn</u>.

hateful *adj.* <u>loathsome</u>, accursed, <u>dreadful</u>, foul, sickening, wretched.

hatefully *adv.* dreadfully, foully, frightfully, <u>shamefully</u>, unrightfully.

hatless *adj.* bare-headed.

hatred *n.* bitter feelings, bitterness, coldness, hard/bad feelings, loathing, misliking, bad blood, no love lost.

haugh *n.* 1) the smallest hollow with shelter enough for a ham (*village*) or steading, 2) land between *rivers*, or within a *river*-bend or slightly uplifted ground in a marsh.

haulm, halm *n.* stalks of beans, *hops*, peas, and sometimes corn, *used* as straw bedding for *beasts*, or for thatching.

have *v.* 1) to have to one's name, hold, keep, own, 2) to bear, bring forth, bring into the world, give birth to, 3) to have folk to one's house (to eat and drink).

haven[2] *n.* 1) hythe, roadstead, 2) shelter.

haven[2] *v.* to bring a ship into a haven.

have-not/s *n.* the have-nothings, the needy, those elbowed out, those on the edge.

haw *n.* 1) hedge, 2) ground/yard with a hedge about it.

haw *n.* berry of the hawthorn.

hawfinch *n.* bird of the finch kind.

hawk *n.* 1) hunting bird, 2) war-lord.

hawk *v.* to hunt with hawks.

hawkbill *n.* 1) hawk's bill, 2) *pincers* having a hooked nose.

hawk-billed *adj.* having a mouth like a hawk's bill.

hawked *adj.* hooked like a hawk's bill.

hawkish *adj.* fiery, hot-hearted, ready/thirsting for a fight.

hawk-moth *n.* a moth which hangs in the wind and then swoops like a hawk.

hawk-nose *n.* hooked nose (shaped like the bill of a hawk).

hawthorn *n.* small tree often *used* for making hedges, quickthorn, white-thorn.

hay *n.* grass cut or mown and dried as feed for *beasts*.

hay *n.* hedge, ground with a hedge about it.

hay *v.* to lay a hedge, set a hedge about.

hay field *n.* field in which grass is grown for hay.

hay-maker *n.* man or woman on a steading whose work is in making hay.

hay-making *n.* the business of cutting and drying grass for hay.

hay-rake *n.* hand-rake used in hay-making.

hayrick *n.* *haystack.*

hayward *n.* 1) one who looks after hedges so that kine kept on the *common* land cannot break into hedged fields, 2) the herdsman of kine grazing on the *common.*

hazel *n.* broadleaved tree.

hazel-nut *n.* the nut of the hazel.

hazel-wood *n.* 1) holt or shaw of hazel trees, 2) the wood of the hazel.

he *pron.* the 'spear-kin' (*male*) *pronoun.*

head *n.* 1) that bit of the body wherein are the eyes, ears, nose, mouth and such, set within the head-bone/*skull*, 2) the seat of the mind/thought/understanding – hence brain, wisdom, wits, 3) the ball-shaped 'crown' of a plant at the top of the stem, the leafy top of a tree, 4) the foam on the top of a drink of ale, 5) beginning or springhead of a *river*, headwaters, 6) foreland, headland, height, spur, 7) elder, head teacher, leader, lord, overseer, 8) end, peak.

head *v.* 1) to be/go first, lead/show the way, steer, take the helm, 2) to top, 3) (in football) to shoot or strike the ball with one's head.

headache *n.* 1) head, sick headache, 2) burden, care, weight on one's mind, worry.

headboard *n.* board at the head end of a bedstead.

head-bolster *n.* headrest.

head-bone (*skull*) *n.* brain-pan.

head-cloth *n.* bit of clothing for the head.

header *n.* 1) reaping-*machine* that cuts the heads off the corn, 2) (in building) stone laid with its head or end to the fore of the wall, 3) (in football) a strike of the ball by a player, with his head.

head first *adv. phr.* 1) head foremost, headlong, 2) recklessly, without thinking.

head for *v.* to bend one's steps to, go towards, make for, steer for.

head-foremost *adv. phr.* with the head first or foremost, headlong.

head-gate *n.* upper gate at a *canal* lock.

head-guilty *adj.* guilty of a deed deemed worthy of death.

head-hunt *v.* to seek out and offer work to one deemed well-matched for that work.

head-hunter *n.* one who takes the heads of slain foes.

headily *adv.* in a heady way, heedlessly, rashly, readily, recklessly, thoughtlessly.

heading *n.* name.

headland *n.* bill, foreland, ness, sea-ness, spit.

headless *adj.* 1) leaderless, 2) empty-headed, slow-witted, thick, unwitful, witless.

headlight *n.* light set on the fore-end of a *vehicle*.

headlong 1) *adv.* headfirst, head foremost, heedlessly, rashly, thoughtlessly, wildly, without forethought, 2) *adj.* breakneck, heedless, rash, reckless, wild.

headman *n.* foreman, leader, overseer.

headmost *adj.* foremost, topmost.

head-on *adj.* head-to-head.

headship *n.* leadership, lordship.

head-sill *n.* upper frame of a door or window.

headsman *n.* hangman.

head-spring *n.* springhead, wellhead, wellspring.

headstall *n.* the length of a bridle or halter that goes about the head of the horse.

head start *n.* edge, help, start, upper hand.

headstone *n.* 1) main stone or *cornerstone* in the grounding of a building, 2) upright stone at the head of a grave.

headstrong *adj.* fiery, heedless, hot-headed, pig-headed, prickly, quick-hearted, rash, reckless, self-willed, thoughtless, unthinking, unwary, wayward, wild, wilful.

head-water/s *n.* streams flowing from a springhead.

headway *n.* break-through, forward step/way, making strides, upswing, uptrend.

head-wind *n.* 1) fore wind going against one, 2) hindering, hold-up, let, setback.

head-word *n.* word making a heading.

head-work *n.* brain work.

heady *adj.* going to the head, lively, soul-stirring, overwhelming, strong, thrilling.

heal *v.* 1) to bind up, make better/well/whole, 2) to become whole, heal over, heal up, 3) to help, lessen, salve, soothe, 4) to bridge over, put right, settle, win over.

heal-all (*panacea*) *n.* allheal.

healer *n.* helper, frith-weaver.

healing *adj.* mild, soothing.

health *n.* health and strength, soundness, weal, well-being, wholeness.

healthful *adj.* hale, healthy, hearty, ruddy, <u>strong</u>, whole.

healthsome *adj.* healthful, healthy, wholesome.

healthy *adj.* hale and hearty, bursting with health, fit, ruddy, <u>strong</u>, well, whole.

heap *n.* batch, great deal, hoard, lot, manyness.

heap *v.* to heap up, heap on, build up, <u>gather</u> up, hoard, lay in, lay up, put by, stow.

hear *v.* 1) to be all ears, give ear, hearken, heed, lend an ear, listen to, 2) to listen in, overhear, put one's ear to, 3) (in law) to hold a hearing, go into, weigh, 4) to be told of, find out, gather, get wind of, hear tell of, learn, pick up.

hearer *n.* listener.

hearing *n.* 1) *sense* of hearing, 2) (*trial* in law) doom-/meed-weighing, 3) earshot.

hearken *v.* to give a willing ear, hang on the lips, heed, listen to, mark, yield to.

hearsay *n.* gossip, idle talk, talk of the town, tidings, whisper, word of mouth.

heart *n.* 1) that *part* of the body which sends the blood through it, 2) heart of hearts, inmost being, innermost being, mind, soul, heart and soul, inmost soul, 3) beating heart, breast, bosom, feelings, kindness, understanding, 4) <u>boldness</u>, fearlessness, <u>steadfastness</u>, strength, will, 5) the middle *part* of something, heartland, heart of a tree, kernel, marrow, root.

heart-ache *n.* aching, heart-break, harrowing, heaviness, <u>sorrow</u>, wretchedness.

heart-beat *n.* breath, 'prick' in time, little while, short span, twinkling of an eye.

heart-blood, heart's blood *n.* life, life-blood.

heart-break *n.* aching, heart-ache, harrowing, heaviness, <u>sorrow</u>, wretchedness.

heart-breaking *adj.* bitter, harrowing, heart-rending, sad.

heart-broken *adj.* bowed down, overcome, overwhelmed, sick at heart, <u>sorrowful</u>.

heartburn *n.* 1) upset inside, 2) bitterness of heart.

hearten *v.* to allay (fears), give hope, give strength to, give heart to one, make a man of, put heart into, put/set the mind at rest, quicken, stir up, strengthen.

heartfelt *adj.* deeply-felt, hearty, stirring, strong, truly felt, warm, wholehearted.

heart-free *adj.* free, free to choose, floating, unsmitten.

hearth *n.* 1) the floor of the firestead, 2) the fireside, the home, hearth and home.

heart-high *adj.* glad (about something done well), thrilled.

hearthland *n.* folkland, homeland,' land of one's forebears/forefathers, motherland.

hearth-stead (*focus*) *n.* heart, kernel.

hearthstone *n.* 1) firestead stone, 2) soft stone for whitening hearths, door-steps.

heartily *adv.* 1) deeply, warmly, 2) earnestly, gladly, thoroughly, willingly.

heartiness *n.* 1) brightness, friendliness, keenness, liveliness, lustiness, warmth, 2) earnestness, wholeheartedness, 3) healthiness, strength.

heart-led *adj.* afire, earnest, quick, warm, whole-hearted.

heartless *adj.* bitter, cold-blooded, hard, <u>ruthless</u>, unforgiving, wolfish.

heart-lorn *adj.* bitter, forlorn, <u>hopelorn</u>, saddened, <u>sorrowful</u>, wretched.

heart-quake *n.* 1) racing of the heart, 2) dreadful fright/start, thunderbolt.

heart-rending *adj.* harrowing, heartbreaking, sad.

heart-shaped *adj.* having the shape of a heart.

heart-sick *adj.* bowed, broken-hearted, heavy-hearted, <u>hopelorn</u>, <u>forlorn</u>.

heart-sore *adj.* bitter, deeply upset, heart-lorn, sick at heart, soured.

heart-stricken *adj.* cut to the heart, smitten, stricken, stung.

heartstrength *n.* fearlessness, manliness, <u>steadfastness</u>, strength, toughness.

heart-strings *n.* 1) the sinews thought to hold and keep the heart, 2) the deepest feelings (of bliss, love, woe).

heart-strong *adj.* dogged, doughty, <u>fearless</u>, gritty, <u>steadfast</u>, tough, <u>unyielding</u>.

heart-struck *adj.* struck/stung to the heart, heart-broken, smitten with sorrow.

heart-to-heart *adj.* man-to-man, woman-to-woman, one-to-one, forthright, open.

heart-warming *adj.* heartening, heart-stirring, soul-stirring, warming, winning.

heart-whole *adj.* free, heart-free, unsmitten,

heart-wood *n.* inmost timber of a tree, hardened by the years.

hearty *adj.* 1) beaming, <u>bright</u>, <u>friendly</u>, heart-warming, in good heart, keen, <u>lively</u>, lusty, outgoing, warm, 2) earnest, heartfelt, true, wholehearted, 3) bursting with health, hale, hale and hearty, healthy, in good health, strong, well.

heat *n.* 1) blood heat, body heat, hotness, swelter, warmth, white heat, 2) heatwave, hot spell, hot/warm weather, summer heat, 3) heat in a race, run-off, 4) warmth of feeling, 5) drive, fire, high words, wrath, wrathfulness, 6) *animal* craving, lust.

heat *v.* to become hot, get hotter, grow hot, make hot, seethe, warm up.

heated *adj.* 1) seething, stormy, wrathful, wroth, 2) keyed up, on fire, worked up.

heatedly *adv.* bitterly, sharply, wrathfully.

heater *n.* fire, stove.

heat-stroke *n.* breakdown in bodily well-being (through being in/by too great heat).

heath *n.* open untilled land, heathland, moor, moorland, upland.

heathen *n.* misbeliever, unbeliever.

heathen *adj.* godless, heathenish, unbelieving.

heathendom *n.* 1) worshipping gods of wood and stone, 2) the heathen world.

heathenish *adj.* godless, misbelieving, unbelieving.

heathenly *adv.* after the way of the heathen.

heathenness *n.* heathendom, hollow/warped worship, unbelief, worldliness.

heathenry *n.* 1) heathen belief, heathen ways, 2) heathen folk.

heather *n.* heathland plant, *ling*.

heathery *adj.* clad with heather, heather-like.

heathy *adj.* clad with heathland plants, heath-like, heathery.

heating *n.* the network of heaters in a building.

heatwave *n.* hot spell, hot/warm weather, summer heat.

heave *n.* heaving, shove.

heave *v.* 1) to bear up, drag, draw, heave up, pull, 2) to breathe hard/heavily, fight for breath, lose one's wind, 3) to pitch, send flying, send headlong, throw, 4) to retch, throw up, 5) to rise, swell, 6) to heave the lead, fathom, mark off, reckon, 7) (of a ship) to heave and pitch in heavy seas, heel over, thresh about, wallow.

heaven *n.* 1) abode of the blest, everlasting home, everlasting rest, the afterlife, life everlasting, the life to come, the heavenly kingdom, the hereafter, the next world, 2) blessedness, bliss, wonder.

heaven-born *adj.* readied by heaven for some work (now often said waspishly).

heaven-gate *n.* the gates of heaven.

heaven-hall *n.* the halls of heaven.

heaven-high *adj.* as high as heaven, reaching to heaven.

heaven-light *n.* the light of heaven.

heaven-like *adj.* heavenly.

heavenly *adj.* 1) starry, 2) beyond words, blessed, blissful, blitheful, hallowed, holy, light, lithe, lovely, overwhelming, unearthly, winsome, wonderful, 3) bewitching, fetching, 4) honeyed, mouthwatering, rich, sweet as honey.

heavenly *adv.* by/from heaven, in a heavenly way.

heavenly-bow *n.* rainbow.

heavenly-minded *adj.* godly, good, holy, otherworldly, rightwise, unworldly.

heaven-sent *adj.* blessed, goodly, helpful, of help, timely, well-timed, welcome.

heavenwards *adv.* towards heaven.

heavily *adv.* 1) a great deal, overmuch, 2) greatly, mightily, strongly, thickly, 3) slowly, wearily, 4) gloomily, sorrowfully.

heaviness *n.* 1) heftiness, weight, 2) deadness, dreariness, lifelessness, listlessness, numbness, stiffness, 3) gloom, heavy-heartedness, sadness, weariness, wretchedness.

heaving *n.* heave, shove.

heavy *adj.* 1) broad, broad-shouldered, great, great-limbed, hefty, strong, thickset, 2) fat, fleshy, overweight, well-fed, 3) top-heavy, unwieldy, 4) deadly, drearisome, dreary, lifeless, overlong, tiresome, wearing, wearisome, dry as dust, 5) cloudy, dark with clouds, gloomy, leaden, 6) bitter, dreadful, grim, hard, harrowing, heart-breaking, woeful, 7) meaty, weighty, 8) heady, honeyed, strong, sweet-smelling.

heavy-eyed *adj.* drowsy, half-awake, half-asleep, heavy with sleep, sleepy.

heavy-footed *adj.* clod-hopping, leaden, loutish, oafish, rough, slow, stiff, uncouth.

heavy-going *adj.* deadly, dreary, dry as dust, hard going.

heavy hand *n.* high-handedness, long arm, strong grip.

heavy-handed *adj.* high-handed, overbearing, rough, strong-arm, unkind,

heavy-headed *adj.* dim-witted, slow-witted, thick, unwitful, witless.

heavy-hearted *adj.* heart-sick, forlorn, hopelorn, listless, sorrowful, wretched.

heavy-heartedness *n.* gloom, gloominess, listlessness, sadness, weariness of heart.

heavy-laden *adj.* bowed down, overburdened, weighed down.

heavy sea *n.* rough sea, stormy sea.

heavyweight *n.* 1) he-man, strong man, wrestler, 2) man to be reckoned with.

heckle *n.* comb for cleaving and combing out the 'threads' of flax or hemp, hatchel.

heckle *v.* to give one a bad time, make it hard for, needle, shout down, sting.

heddle *n.* small wires in a loom through which the warp-threads are drawn.

hedge *n.* 1) a row of bushes and/or low trees (such as the hawthorn, hazel) set near together to make a sundering between fields, or running alongside a road, hedgerow, quickset hedge, 2) shelter, shield, windbreak.

hedge *v.* 1) to lay a hedge, 2) hedge in, hem in, ring about, begird, 3) to back away, beat about, be careful/wary, be all at sea, be at a stand, be at one's wits' end, be in two minds, be in a maze, become lost, blow hot and cold, come to a stand, draw back, fall back, falter, grope, grope in the dark, hang back, have no answer, have nothing to go on, lose the clue, lose the thread, miss one's way, not give a straight answer, play for time, rest on one's oars, see how the land lies, see-saw, shift, shrink from, shy away, sidestep, stand by, think twice, tread warily, 4) to shield against.

hedge-bird *n.* 1) any bird that lives in or feeds in hedges, 2) down-and-out.

hedge-born *adj.* of unknown birth.

hedge-green *n.* the green headland in a ploughed field.

hedgeling (*urchin*) *n.* whelp.

hedgepig (*hedgehog*) *n.* small *beast* often found under hedges.

hedger *n.* one who lays, makes good, and trims hedges.

hedgerow *n.* the line of bushes and trees that make a hedge. (The Anglo-Saxons also had hazel-rows, thorn-rows, willow-rows, rush-rows, stone-rows.)

hedge sparrow *n.* dunnock, hedge chat, hedge creeper, pinnock.

hedging *n.* the business of laying hedges.

heed *n.* awareness, care, carefulness, foresight, hearkening, listening, readiness.

heed *v.* to be all ears/eyes, have one's wits about one, hearken, listen hard, look to, mark, mind, miss nothing, prick up one's ears, sit up and listen, think through.

heedful *adj.* canny, careful, chary, cool-headed, listful, wary, awake, watchful, mindful, thorough, thorough-going, keeping a weather eye on, looking all ways.

to be **heedful** *v.* to be careful/mindful/wary, feel one's way, hedge, heed, keep well out of, leave well alone, let sleeping dogs lie, look/think ahead, look out, look/think twice, see how the land lies, tread warily, watch, watch one's step.

heedfully *adv.* cannily, carefully, charily, mindfully, thoroughly, warily, watchfully.

heedfulness *n.* carefulness, foresight, thoroughness, wariness, watchfulness.

heedless *adj.* careless, dizzy, giddy, headstrong, headlong, hot-headed, over-bold, over-daring, rash, reckless, redeless, short-sighted, silly, thoughtless, unheedful, unthinking, unwise, unwitful, ware-less, wild, unwary.

heedlessly *adv.* carelessly, thoughtlessly, unheedingly, unware-ly, unwarily.

heedlessness *n.* 1) carelessness, dizziness, dreaminess, empty-headedness, feather-headedness, flightiness, giddiness, light-mindedness, 2) hot-headedness, over-daring, playing with fire, rashness, recklessness, unwariness, wildness, unwisdom.

heel *n.* the hinder bit of the foot, the heel of a shoe or stocking.

heel *v.* to put a heel on a shoe, to put a spur on a fighting cock.

heel *n.* (of a ship) leaning to one side.

heel *v.* to heel over, lean over, lean to one side.

heel-bone *n.* bone of the heel.

heelless *adj.* (of a shoe) having no heel.

heft *n.* bulk, weight.

heft *v.* to lift up (to reckon the weight).

hefty *adj.* heavy, meaty, strong, weighty.

he-goat *n.* goat buck.

heifer *n.* young cow that has not had a calf.

height *n.* 1) build, tallness, 2) hill-top, horn, peak, tip, 3) fullness, highlight.

heighten *v.* 1) to build up, greaten, make higher, 2) highlight, make the most of.

hell *n.* 1) bottomless pit, everlasting fire, fire and brimstone, hellfire, nether world, outer darkness, underworld, 2) nightmare, ordeal, wretchedness.

hell-bent *adj.* recklessly or doggedly set on something, stopping at nothing.

hell-fiend *n.* nightmare.

hell-fire *n.* the fires of hell.

hell-gate *n.* gateway of hell.

hell-hound *n.* hound of hell, fiend.

hellish *adj.* 1) fiendish, nightmarish, 2) accursed, dreadful, wicked.

hell-mere *n.* mere of fire in hell.

hellward 1) *adv.* towards hell, 2) *adj.* leading to hell.

helm (*helmet*) *n.* ward-wear for the head.

helm *n.* tiller, wheel.

helm *n.* corn-stalk, straw.

helm *v.* to don a helm.

helm *v.* to steer with the helm.

helmed *adj.* wearing a helm.

helmless *adj.* without a helm.

helmless *adj.* without tiller or steerman's wheel.

helmsman *n.* 1) sealord, steersman, 2) head, leader.

helmsmanship *n.* seacraft, seamanship, ship-handling, steering.

helm-wind *n.* a wild wind in the Pennines.

help *n.* willing help, helping hand, backing, friendship, stay, upholding.

help *v.* to back up, bear/give/lend a hand, come to the help of, forward, further, send help to, side with, speed, stand by, stand up for, strengthen, take up the cudgels for.

helper *n.* backer, friend, friend in need, helping hand, henchman, right-hand man.

helpful *adj.* 1) caring, friendly, kind, neighbourly, thoughtful, timely, willing, 2) good for one, healing, soothing.

helpfully *adv.* readily, thoughtfully, well, willingly, with a will.

helpfulness *n.* friendliness, goodness, goodwill, helping hand, kindness, readiness.

helping *n.* 1) the deed of helping, 2) share of food given out.

helping *adj.* of that by which help is given (as in 'a helping hand').

helping hand *n.* helper, helpmeet, friend in need.

helpless *adj.* forlorn, kinless, mightless, strengthless, wretched.

helplessly *adv.* forlornly, hopelessly, sadly, wretchedly.

helplessness *n.* forlornness, hopelessness, wretchedness.

helpmeet *n.* husband, wife of one's bosom, friend, other self.

helve *n.* handle of axe or hammer, haft, stock.

hem *n.* edge, edging, trimming.

hem *v.* 1) to sew an edge, 2) to hedge in, hem in, hold back, keep in.

hemlock *n.* a baneful, even deadly, plant.

hemp *n.* plant grown for its *fibre*, from which is made rope and rough cloth.

hempen *adj.* made of hemp.

hem-stitch *v.* to hem with a pretty stitch, giving the look of a row of stitching.

hen *n.* she-bird of that fowl kept on a steading for its eggs and young and its meat.

henbane *n.* 1) weed having deadening/numbing ways, 2) draught made therefrom.

hence *adv.* so, thus, therefore.

henceforth *adv.* from now on, from today.

henceforward, henceforwards *adv.* from this time forward, henceforth.

henchman *n.* backer, follower, friend, hanger-on, right-hand man, upholder,.

hen-hearted *adj.* fearful, chicken-hearted.

hen-house *n.* shed where hens are housed.

hen-roost *n.* shelter where hens roost at night.

her *pron.* 1) the 'she' spoken of, 2) belonging to her, of her.

herd *n.* 1) drove, flock, 2) crowd, swarm, throng.

herd *v.* 1) to drive/gather into a herd, 2) to bed down, lead, shepherd.

herdsman *n.* cowherd, cowman, stockman, drover, shepherd, shepherdess, goatherd.

here *adv.* 1) hereabout, 2) hither, 3) at hand, 4) at this time, now.

hereabout/s *adv.* 1) here, 2) almost, nearabouts, nearly, well-nigh.

hereafter *adv.* after this, from now on, from this time forth, hence, henceforth.

hereafter *n.* the afterlife, the beyond, life after death, life to come, next world.

hereafterward/s *adv.* after this, from now on, hence, henceforth, henceforward.

hereat *adv.* hereabout.

hereaway *adv.* away in this path, hereabouts, hither.

hereby *adv.* 1) nearby, 2) by this, from this, through this.

here-hence *adv.* through this, from henceforth, from here.

herein *adv.* 1) here within, in here, 2) in this.

hereof *adv.* 1) as to this, of this, 2) from here, from this.

hereon *adv.* herein, on this business.

hereout *adv.* on this grounding.

hereright *adv.* straightway.

hereto *adv.* to this, hitherto.

heretofore *adv.* before now/this, formerly, hitherto, time out of mind, until now.

heretofore *n.* the time gone by, the long-ago days.

hereunder *adv.* under this.

hereunto *adv.* to/unto this.

hereupon *adv.* upon this business, straight after this, following from this.

herewith *adv.* with this, at the like time with this.

hern, hirn *(corner)* *n.* 1) bend, 'elbow', 'knee', 2) hideaway, *nook*.

herring *n.* sea-fish.

herring-bone 1) *n.* bone of the herring, 2) stonework of walls or flooring wherein the stones are set in rows atilt (*slantwise*) – first one way then the other.

hers *pron.* her one/s, belonging to her.

herself *pron.* that woman above all.

hest *n.* behest, bidding, will.

hew *v.* 1) to cut down, 2) to cleave, rend, 3) to carve, make, rough-hew, shape.

hewer *n.* one who cuts down, one who delves out coal from a seam.

hewn *adj.* made by hewing with an axe or quern-bill/*chisel*, hollowed out by hewing.

hickock[7] *n.* hiccup, hiccough.

hid, hidden *adj.* buried, dark, <u>knotted</u>, masked, stealthy, unbeknown, unseen.

hiddenly *adv.* in a hidden way, by stealth, stealthily.

hide *n.* cowhide, fell, leather, woolfell.

hide *n.* a reckoning of land, being enough for one kindred to make a living – about 60 acres of good ground, or as much as 120 acres where the ground was not rich.

hide *n.* (for watching birds), look-out.

hide *v.* 1) to shade, shelter, shield, keep watch over, ward, 2) to be stealthy, breathe not a word, bury, darken, keep dark, hide from the light, hide the truth, hold one's tongue, keep one's mouth shut, keep back, let it go no further, <u>mislead</u>, not give a straight answer, shroud, spin, stow away, becloud, withhold.

hide-and-seek *n.* children's game in which some hide and others seek for them.

hideaway *n.* bolt-hole, den, earth, fox-hole, hide-out, nest, shelter.

hidebound *adj.* 1) of badly-fed kine whose skin clings to the back and sides, 2) (of a book) bound in/with leather, 3) narrow, narrow-minded, set, set in one's ways.

hide-out *n.* bolt-hole, burrow, den, earth, fox-hole, hideaway, hole, lair, shelter.

hiding *n.* 1) beating, flaying, thrashing, 2) downfall, overthrow, shipwreck.

high *adj.* 1) tall, 2) high-born, high-up, leading, main, outstanding, 3) <u>great</u>, strong, weighty, 4) (of meat) gone bad, gone off, strong-smelling, 5) (of singing) high-pitched, loud, sharp, 6) (of *prices*) dear, steep, stiff, 7) high and mighty, lordly, overbearing, 8) light-hearted, merry.

high *adv.* far up, way up, to a great height.

high and dry *adj.* aground, grounded, beached, stranded, stuck.

high-blooded *adj.* high-born, of high kindred, well-born.

high-born, high-bred *adj.* <u>great</u>, lordly, queenly, well-born, <u>worthful</u>, top-drawer.

highbrow, high-browed *adj.* <u>learned</u>, deep-thinking, deep-read, lorewise.

high-craft *n.* <u>deftness</u>, <u>knowledge</u>, quickness.

highday *n.* 1) field day, great day, holiday, 2) mid-day (when the sun is high).

higher *adj. adv.* higher up, taller.

highermost, highest *adj.* greatest, highmost, matchless, unbounded, utmost, whole.

high-father (*patriarch*) *n.* forbear, forefather.

high-flood *n.* high tide.

high-flown *adj.* (of speech) long-worded, overblown, overplayed, windy, wordy.

high-flyer *n.* 1) go-getter, 2) high-churchman.

high-flying *adj.* 1) (of birds) flying high up, 2) holding the high church line.

high ground *n.* edge, lead, upper hand.

high-handed *adj.* high and mighty, off-handed, on one's high horse, <u>overbearing</u>.

high-handedly *adv.* overbearingly, overweeningly, uppishly, witheringly.

high-handedness *n.* high mightiness, pigheadedness, uppishness, wilfulness.

high-hearted *adj.* <u>bold</u>, doughty, fearless, daring, steely, <u>unyielding</u>.

high-heartedly *adv.* boldly, daringly, fearlessly.

high-heartedness *n.* <u>boldness</u>, daring, fearlessness.

high kindred *n.* atheldom, high blood, high kinsfolk.

high king (*emperor*) *n.* great king, over-king, overlord, all-wielder.

highland/s *n.* heights, hills, moorlands, uplands.

highlander *n.* hill dweller, hillman, uplander.

highlight *n.* 1) brightest bit of a *painting*, 2) the best/peak (of a play, tale or such).

highlight *v.* to bring/draw forth, bring forward, bring out, bring to the fore, draw out, drive home, dwell on, give weight to, make much of, mark out, set forth.

high-love *n.* burning love, great love, strong love.

highly *adv.* 1) high up, on high, 2) greatly, strongly, high-heartedly.

high-minded *adj.* fair-dealing, great-minded, knightly, right-hearted, <u>rightwise</u>, selfless, straightforward, <u>true</u>, truly good, <u>upright</u>, upstanding, worthy.

highmost, highest *adj. adv.* greatest, matchless, utmost, whole.

high-name *n.* good/great name, worthy name.

highness *n.* 1) height, top, tallness, 2) greatness, overbearingness.

high-pitched *adj.* high, loud, sharp.

high-reaching *adj.* 1) reaching high, 2) itching for, reaching up for.

high-rise *adj.* (of a building) many-floored, tall.

high road *n.* highway, roadway, main road, thoroughfare.

high sea *n.* deep sea, great waters, the main, the waves.

high settle *n.* high seat, king's/queen's seat, lord's seat.

high speed *adj.* <u>fast</u>, fast-going, flying, quick, speedy, swift.

high-stepping *adj.* (of a horse) lifting high the hooves when going, lordly.

high-talking *adj.* high-flown, high-flying, high-speaking, overdone, windy, wordy.

high tide *n.* full-flood, high-flood.

high-ups *n.* chosen few, men/women of mark, the top drawer/set, the haves.

high water *n.* the time when the tide is at the full.

high-water mark *n.* the highest line reached by the tide at high water.

highway *n.* high road, roadway, main road, thoroughfare.

highwayman *n.* raider, reaver, way-reaver, thief.

high-wrought *adj.* 1) high-strung, overwrought, worked up, 2) deftly wrought.

hill *n.* foothill, height, hillock, hilltop, knoll, peak, ridge, rise, rising ground, spur, upland, wold.

hill-folk *n.* hill-dwellers, uplanders.

hilliness *n.* the suchness of being hilly, wildness.

hill-man *n.* hill-dweller, uplander.

hillock *n.* little hill, knap, knoll, rise.

hillside *n.* rise, rising ground, slope of a hill.

hilltop *n.* height, knap, peak, ridge.

hilly *adj.* steep, upland.

hilt *n.* handgrip of a sword or knife, grip, haft, handle, helve.

him *pron.* the 'he' spoken of.

himself *pron.* that man above all.

hind *n.* she- red deer.

hind *adj.* set behind, at the back.

hind-berry *n.* raspberry.

hind-calf *n.* fawn.

hinder *adj.* after, hind, hindermost, set behind, at the back, latter, last.

hinder *v.* to come between, get in the way, hamstring, head off, hedge in, hold, hold back, hold in, hold down, keep a tight hold on, keep back, keep one in play, make it hard for, put a drag on, bridle, fetter, saddle with, shackle, stand in the way, stop.

hinderland *n.* the land further in from the seaboard, the backwoods, outlands.

hindermost *adj.* after, furthest behind, hind, hindmost, last come to.

hinderward *adj.* creeping, heel-dragging, long about it, slow, snail-like.

hindmost *adj.* after, furthest behind, hind, hindmost, last come to.

hindsight *n.* after-knowledge, afterthought, later thought.

hindward *adv.* abackwards, behind.

hinge[(1)] *n.* 1) the tie by which a door or gate is hung (that door/gate being opened or shut as it is turned upon it), 2) that which binds on the lid of a box.

hint *n.* aside, clue, foreshadowing, half-word, sideways word, something to go on.

hint *v.* to breathe a word, drop a hint/word, give one to understand, leave one to gather, let

drop/fall, make an aside, put in one's head, say by the way, whisper.

hip/s *n.* 1) the outmost sides of the body between ribs and thighs, 2) outhanging (*projecting*) sloping edge on a roof, reaching from ridge to eaves.

hip *n.* the yield of the wild *rose*.

hip-bone *n.* bone of the hip.

hip-girdle *n.* *pelvic* girdle.

hipped *adj.* (of a roof) having hips (sloping edges).

hip-roof *n.* roof with hips, the ends being sloped as well as the sides.

hire *n.* 1) hiring, 2) outlay.

hire *v.* 1) to take on (a worker/workers), 2) to take on, 3) to hire out, let out.

hireling *n.* hand, hired man/woman, man, underling, worker.

his *pron.* his one/s, belonging to him, of him, that man's.

hit[(2)] *n.* knock, stroke.

hit[(2)] *v.* 1) to beat, knock, smite, strike, strike hard, thrash, 2) to meet head-on, run into, 3) to harm, leave a mark on, overwhelm, 4) to come to, dawn on, strike one, 5) to find, hit the mark, make, reach, win to.

hithe, hythe *n.* landing-stead on a *river*, berth, wharf.

hither *adv.* here, over here, near, nearer, nigh, towards.

hither days *n.* aftertime, aftertide, hereafter, coming days, what lies ahead, outlook.

hithermost *adj.* nearest.

hitherto *adv.* before this, before now, formerly, heretofore, so far, thus far, till now.

hitherward/s *adv.* 1) hither, 2) on this side of, 3) hitherto, until now.

hive *n.* 1) roofed box for a swarm of bees, 2) house/neighbourhood of 'busy-ness'.

hive *v.* to gather bees into a hive.

hoar *adj.* 1) old, many-wintered, 2) grey, greying, greyish white, hoary, silvery.

hoard *n.* fulness, gathering, growth, heap, more than enough, stock.

hoard *v.* to build up, fasten on, gather up, heap up, lay up, stow.

hoared *adj.* grown or made hoary.

hoar-frost *n.* white frost.

hoarhead *n.* a hoary head, an old grey-haired man.

hoariness, hoarness *n.* the suchness of being hoary, greyness, grey/white hairs.

hoarse *adj.* croaky, rough, throaty, hoarse as a raven.

hoarsely *adv.* throatily.

hoarsen *v.* to become hoarse, make hoarse.

hoarseness *n.* croakiness, throatiness.

hoar-stone *n.* 1) old/grey standing stone, 2) merestone, landmark, marker.

hoar tree *n.* tree wreathed with beard-like lichens.

hoary *adj.* 1) old, old as the hills, long-standing, many-wintered, 2) grey, greying, grey-haired, greyish white, hoar, hoary-headed, silvery, white, white-haired.

hock *n.* hollyhock.

hock, hough *n.* the hinge in the hinder shank of a four-footed *beast*.

hock *v.* to cripple, hamstring, lame.

hoe *n.* bill, foreland, headland, height, ness, ridge.

hoh (hoo, howe) *n.* heel, hill-spur.

hold *n.* 1) clasp, clutch, grasp, grip, 2) foothold, footing, 3) having a hold on someone, 4) (*prison*) lock-house, lockup, 5) fastness, stronghold.

hold *n.* the hold of a ship, holl.

hold *v.* to hold one's ground, <u>abide</u>, hold fast, stand fast.

holdall *n.* overnighter.

hold back *v.* to forbear, hold off, keep oneself from, do without.

hold down[6] *v.* to bear hard on, be down on, be heavy-handed, be tough with, break, bring under the yoke, browbeat, burden, come down on, deal hardly with, have it all one's own way, have the upper hand over, have under one's thumb, hold in the hollow of one's hand, hold under, keep down, keep under one's thumb, lay a heavy hand on, lay under the yoke, lead, lead by the nose, lord it over, <u>overcome</u>, override, put down, put upon, quell, ride roughshod over, stamp on, tame, tread down, tread underfoot, wear the breeches.

holdfast *n.* 1) grasper, hoarder, 2) bolt, clasp, fastening, hook, staple.

hold fast, hold on to *v.* 1) to cleave to, clasp, cling to, stick fast, grasp, grip, stick together, 2) to <u>abide</u>, die fighting, die hard, fight on, hold out, stand fast, stick it out.

hold forth *v.* to bear witness, dwell on, give out, say out, speak out, set forth.

hold good *v.* to be so, hold together, hold true, hold water, ring true, stand.

hold hard *v.* to pull on the bridle to stop the horse, stop (most often *used* in bidding, as in 'Hold hard!').

hold in *v.* to keep back, keep in, keep a hold on oneself, stop oneself.

holding *n.* holding of land, shares or other goods.

holding *adj.* <u>abiding</u>, lasting, long-lasting, long-standing, unending.

holding-ground *n.* ground in a haven, or off-shore, where an anchor will hold.

hold off *v.* 1) to hold back, keep away/from/off, 2) to forbear, do without.

hold on *v.* to bide, cling on, hang on, keep going, keep on, stand fast.

hold one's own *v.* to do well, keep in play, keep up, stand one's ground.

hold one's tongue *v.* to breathe not a word, bridle one's tongue, keep one's mouth shut, keep under one's hat, let it go no further, not be drawn, say nothing, withhold.

hold out *v.* to hold one's ground, hold fast, <u>abide</u>, <u>withstand</u>.

hold over *v.* to lay over, put off, keep on ice.

hold to *v.* to abide by, stand by, swear by, mean what one says, truly mean.

hold together *v.* to cling to, clasp, hang together, hold good, hold up, stick together.

hold true *v.* to ring true, hold good, hold up, hold water.

hold up *v.* to hold good, hold water, hold true, ring true, stand up.

hold-up *n.* 1) reaving, stealing, theft, thieving, 2) setback, taking time.

hold water *v.* to hold true, hold good, hold up, be so, ring true, stand up.

hold with *v.* to fall in with, go along with, see eye to eye, take kindly to.

hole *n.* 1) a hollow, opening, shaft, 2) break, outlet, rent, tear, 3) bolt-hole, burrow, earth, fox-hole, lair, nest, shelter, 4) (*loophole*) makeshift.

hole *v.* to make a hole in, cut through, knock holes in, riddle, run through, stave in.

holiday *n.* away day, break, day off, half-holiday, leave, rest, time off.

holiness *n.* godliness, goodness, holy-mindedness, rightwiseness.

holl *n.* 1) ditch, hole, 2) hold of a ship.

hollin, hollen *n.* holly, holm.

hollow *n.* 1) dip, hole, trough, 2) bowl, coomb, dale, dean, dell, slade.

hollow *adj.* 1) having a hole inside, empty, having nothing within, 2) deep-set, sunken, 3) meaningless, worthless, 4) lying, sham, shifty, <u>smooth-tongued</u>, two-tongued, two-hearted, underhand, untrue, untruthful, 5) (of *sound*) deep, low.

hollow *adv.* altogether, fully, out-and-out, root and rind, thoroughly, utterly, wholly.

hollow *v.* to delve out, hollow out.

hollow-eyed *adj.* having deep-sunk eyes.

hollow-hearted *adj.* <u>crafty</u>, shallow, sham, slippery, smooth-spoken, truthless.

hollowness *n.* craft, emptiness, empty speech/talk/words, fawning, half-truth, hollow words, honeyed words, idle speech, lightwords, lying, pretty speeches, shallowness, shiftiness, show, outward show, soft nothings, soft soap, stealth, toadying, trothlessness, two-talking, underhand dealing, untruthfulness, wind, worthlessness.

holly *n.* hollin, holm.

hollyhock *n.* hock.

holm *n.* sea, wave.

holm *n.* 1) holly, 2) holm-oak.

holm-oak *n.* evergreen oak, having leaves like those of the holly.

holm-tree *n.* hollin, holly.

holmward (*coastguard*) *n.* sea-ward, sea-watchman.

holt *n.* wood (often of one tree-kind), holt-wood, wood-holt, shaw.

holy *adj.* godly, good, guiltless, hallowed, holy-minded, rightwise, sinless, upright.

holy-day/ Holy Day *n.* 1) *feast* day, 2) Sunday, First Day.

Holy Ghost *n.* the Third Being (with the Father and the Son) within the Godhead.

Holy-month (*September*) *n.* Barley-month, Harvest-month.

Holy Rood *n.* the cross on which Jesus Christ was put to death.

holy stone *n.* a soft sandstone *used* for cleaning the deck of a ship.

holystone *v.* to clean with a holy stone.

holy tide *n.* the time of one of the great *feasts* of the Church, such as Easter.

Holy Week *n.* week before Easter Sunday.

holy well *n.* well or spring whose water is believed to bring healing.

Holy Writ *n.* the Book, the Word, the Word of God, Writings.

home *n.* abode, homestead, home from home, dwelling, fireside, hearth, house.

home *adj.* 1) done at home, 2) neighbouring, 3) inland (as against overseas).

home *adv.* 1) to one's home, 2) as far as it will go, 3) to the heart/root of the business, thoroughly.

home *v.* to go home, home in on something, highlight.

homeborn *adj.* born in the land/neighbourhood.

home-bred *adj.* bred/reared at home, homegrown.

home-brew *n.* home-brewed ale.

home-brewed *adj.* 1) brewed at home and/or for drinking at home, 2) homegrown.

home-coming *n.* coming, coming back, landfall.

homefast *adj.* abiding, settled, well-grounded, long-standing, unshaken.

home ground *n.* (in field games) ground or playing field where the team of one's town or neighbourhood are housed (*based*) and where they play home matches.

homegrown *adj.* 1) of food grown in one's own greenyard or at a neighbouring steading, 2) of that which has arisen/sprung up in one's homeland.

home-keeping *adj.* keeping/taking care of a home, abide-at-home, unstirring.

homeland *n.* fatherland, folkland, hearthland, land of one's forebears, motherland.

homelander *n.* folklander, homeling, inlander.

homeless *adj.* floating, kinless, on the road, roofless, wandering, wayfaring.

homelessness *n.* kinlessness, rooflessness, rootlessness.

home-like *adj.* bowery, homely, restful, sheltered, warm.

homeling *n.* folklander, homelander, inlander.

home-loving *adj.* home-keeping, homely, housely, housewifely.

homely *adj.* 1) bowery, home-like, restful, sheltered, warm, 2) everyday, home-made, homespun, rough and ready, 3) uncomely, unhandsome.

homely *adv.* 1) kindly, 2) forthrightly, freely, openly, straightforwardly, tellingly.

home-made *adj.* everyday, homespun, rough and ready.

home-sick *adj.* forlorn, heart-sick, sad, sighing, wretched.

home-sickness *n.* forlornness, loneliness, sadness, sorrow, weariness of heart.

home speech (*dialect*) *n.* folkspeech.

homespun *adj.* 1) childlike, everyday, homely, home-made, unlearned, untaught, workaday, 2) open, straightforward, truth-telling, unhardened, unworldly.

homestall, homestead *n.* abode, cot, cote, dwelling-house, home, house, steading.

home-truth *n.* chiding, stern truth, talking-to, upbraiding, word in one's ear.

homeward *adj.* going homeward, leading home, homing.

homeward/s *adv.* towards one's home or homeland.

home-work *n.* work done at home (as against work done in a workshop or such), reading and writing to be done at home by a schoolchild.

hone, hone-stone *n.* whetstone for giving a keen edge to cutting tools.

hone *v.* 1) to put an edge on, file, sharpen, whet, 2) to bring to the highest pitch.

honey *n.* sweet sticky 'sap' (*fluid*) made by honey-bees.

honey-bee *n.* bee that gathers and hoards honey, hive-bee.

honeycomb *n.* wax framework made by hive-bees (to hoard honey and lay eggs).

honeycombed *adj.* riddled with holes (like honeycomb).

honey-dew *n.* sweet sticky 'sap' (*fluid*) found on the leaves of trees and plants. It is left by plant-lice, but was once thought to be akin to dew.

honey-drop *n.* drop of honey.

honeyed *adj.* 1) laden with honey, honey-sweet, 2) mellow, smooth, soothing.

honeying *n.* flirting, love-making, love-play (often short-lived).

honey-lipped (*euphemistic*) *adj.* smooth-lipped, soft-lipped, soothing but soothless.

honey-month *n.* the first month of living together as man and wife.

honeymoon *n.* the honey-month, the holiday that a man and his new wife take together before settling down at home.

honey-mouthed *adj.* honey-lipped, honey-tongued, smooth-tongued, soft-lipped.

honey-speech (*euphemism*) *n.* fair-wording, smooth-lip, soft soap, soft-speech.

honeysuckle *n.* woodbine, suckling.

honey-sweet *adj.* sweet as honey.

honey-tongued *adj.* honey-mouthed, speaking sweetly/smoothly, smooth-tongued.

honey-words *n.* sweet words, smooth words, winning words.

hoo (hoh, howe) *n.* heel, hill-spur.

hood *n.* clothwear for the head, neck and (sometimes) shoulders.

hooded *adj.* half-hidden, masked, shrouded.

hoodwink *v.* to hide, mislead, make game of, play the fox, take in.

hoof *n.* the horny sheath over the end of a horse's foot.

hook *n.* 1) fastener, fastening, 2) angle, fish-hook, 3) hook-shaped tool, such as a reaping-hook, 4) sharp bend, 5) (in fist-fighting) hit, 6) (in stockball) the shot by which a batsman hits a fast ball rising to shoulder or head height.

hook *v.* to lay hold of with a hook, land, net, trap, waylay, win.

hook and eye *n.* clasp, clip, fastener, grip.

hook-bill *n.* 1) billhook, 2) hooked bill of a hunting fowl.

hooked *adj.* 1) bent, hooklike, hook-shaped, 2) having a hook/s, 3) besotted, bewitched, doting, smitten, spellbound, taken.

hooker *n.* one who hooks, tool which hooks.

hook-nose *n.* hook-shaped nose.

hook-nosed *adj.* having a hook-nose.

hook on *v.* to fasten, make fast, set, stick on, hang on, tie on, tie up, yoke.

hook up *v.* to link together, link up, tie up with.

hook-wrench *n.* hand-tool having a bent end for grasping and tightening a nut.

hoop *n.* ring, ring-shape.

hooper *n.* one who puts hoops on tuns (*barrels*).

hop *n.* 1) leap, spring, springy step, step, 2) short drive/flight/ride/run.

hop *v.* to leap, leap-frog, leap over, spring, spring over,

hop, hope *n.* land that is out-of-the-way (as in a fen or a 'blind' coomb).

hope *n.* beam/gleam of hope, good/high/well-grounded hope, looking forward.

hope *v.* to be in hopes, live in hopes, cling to hope, hope against hope, hope for, hope for the best, hope and believe, hope in, keep hope alive, dream of, look forward, look on the bright side, never say die, set one's heart on, wish for, yearn for.

hopeful *adj.* dreaming, in good heart, longing, looking forward to.

hopefully *adv.* 1) brightly, dreamily, longingly, 2) all being well, it is hoped.

hopefulness *n.* brightness, good/high hope, liveliness, sunniness.

hopeless *adj.* 1) forlorn, hopelorn, without hope, sorrowful, 2) all thumbs, butter-fingered, clueless, helpless, no good at, rudderless, slow, unhandy, unworkmanlike.

to be **hopeless** *v.* to give up hope, give up on, lose hope, lose heart, to be crushed.

hopelessly *adv.* forlornly, listlessly, sorrowfully, woefully, wretchedly.

hopelessness *n.* forlornness, last hope gone, loss of hope, overthrow of hope, sorrow.

hopelorn *adj.* borne down, brooding, forlorn, without hope, broken-hearted, bereft, forsaken, heartbroken, beaten, down, downhearted, bowed down, filled with heaviness, friendless, gloomy, heartbroken, heart-lorn, heart-sick, sick at heart, heavy-hearted, hopeless, listless, lost, overborne, sad, saddened, sorrowful, unblithe, unmanned, woebegone, wretched.

hopper *n.* 1) (in a mill) bowl with narrowing sides through which runs the corn to be ground, 2) bowl with narrowing sides, taking rainwater from a down-pipe.

hopthumb *n.* dwarf, truly little being.

horn *n.* 1) hard growth on the heads of goats, kine and such, 2) something made from horn, 3) hunting-horn, wind-*instrument*, horn of a *vehicle*.

hornbeam *n.* broad-leaved tree, giving a truly hard wood.

hornblower *n.* horn-player.

hornbook *n.* a first 'learning-book', being a leaf of paper shielded by a thin layer of horn, with the staves (*letters*) of the *alphabet* set thereon, the whole being framed in wood with a handle.

hornet *n.* *insect* of the wasp kind.

hornless *adj.* without horns.

horn-mad *adj.* maddened, seeing red, seething, wild with wrath.

horn-rimmed *adj.* of glasses having rims made of horn.

hornwork *n.* 1) work wrought in horn, 2) outwork of a stronghold.

horny *adj.* hard, hardened, horny-handed, tough.

horse *n.* four-footed *beast* with flowing mane, steed, drafthorse, hunter, saddle-horse, shaft-horse, shire-horse, thoroughbred.

horse *v.* to give one a horse to ride on, set on horseback.

horseback *adv.* on horseback, riding a horse.

horseflesh *n.* horse, horse-meat.

horse-fly *n.* fly (such as the horse-tick) that worries horses.

horsehair *n.* hair from the mane or tail of a horse.

horse hand, horse-herd (*groom*) *n.* horse-ward, horse-worker.

horse-hoof *n.* hoof of a horse, horse-foot.

horse-laugh *n.* loud uncouth laugh.

horse-load *n.* weight of goods that a horse can bear.

horse-lord (*cavalryman*) *n.* horse-fighter, knight.

horseman *n.* rider, huntsman, man on horseback,

horsepath *n.* path wide enough for a man on horseback, horse-way.

horse-play *n.* free-for-all.

horse-pond *n.* pond for watering horses, and for ducking lesser misdoers.

horse-pox *n.* horse-sickness.

horseshoe *n.* strip of iron bent into a half-ring and nailed to a horse's hoof.

horse-tail *n.* tail of a horse.

horse-wain *n.* *chariot.*

horse-ward *n.* one who cares for horses.

horse-way *n.* bridle path, bridle way, horsepath.

horse-whale (*walrus*) *n.* sea-horse.

horsewoman *n.* rider, huntswoman, woman on horseback.

horsy *adj.* of horses, loving to be with horses and forever talking about such.

hose *n.* stocking/s, tights.

hose *v.* to give out hose.

hot *adj.* 1) burning, fiery, red-hot, searing, white-hot, 2) heated, seething, steaming, 3) baking, sweltering, warm, 4) flushed, aglow, glowing, 5) (of food) stinging, 6) heated, hopping mad, quick-hearted, stormy, wild, wrathful, wroth.

hotbed *n.* 1) earth-bed heated by heaving dung, 2) breeding ground, seedbed.

hot-blooded *adj.* fiery, headstrong, heedless, hot-headed, hot-hearted, wild.

hot-foot *adv.* quickly, speedily, swiftly.

hothead *n.* fire-eater, madman, ne'er-do-well.

hot-headed *adj.* headlong, hot-blooded, quick-hearted, unsteady, wayward.

hot-headedly *adv.* heatedly, stormily, unthinkingly, waywardly, wildly.

hot-headedness *n.* heedlessness, playing with fire, recklessness, storminess.

hot-hearted *adj.* hot-blooded, bloodthirsty, burning, fiery, throbbing.

hot-house *n.* 1) glasshouse, greenhouse, 2) breeding ground, hotbed, seedbed.

hotly *adv.* 1) heatedly, wrathfully, 2) keenly, hard on the heels.

hotness *n.* heat, wrath.

hot water *n.* 1) heated water, seething water, 2) stir, to-do, upset.

hough, hock *n.* the hinge in the hinder shank of a four-footed *beast*, hollow bit behind the knee-hinge in man.

hough-sinew *n.* one of the sinews at the sides of the ham and the back of the knee, hamstring.

hound *n.* 1) dog, hunting dog, bloodhound, deer-hound, fox-hound, wolfhound, 2) sleuth, 3) cut-throat, evil-doer, good-for-nothing, knave, swine, tough, wretch.

hound *v.* to goad, harry, needle, sting, stir up, or worry someone.

house *n.* 1) abode, cot, cote, dwelling, dwelling-house, dwelling-stead, hall, home, homestead, household, living-stead, roof over one's head, steading, town house, 2) kindred ties, roots, stock, 3) business house, 4) house of law-making, 5) the gathering in a playhouse.

house *v.* to find/give a house or housing for someone, give shelter, put up.

house-boat *n.* boat with a roof and living-rooms.

housebreaker *n.* picklock, thief.

housebreaking *n.* break-in, raiding, theft, thieving.

house-builder *n.* one whose business is the building of houses, house-wright.

house-dog *n.* watch-dog, house-taught dog.

house-father *n.* father of a household, head of those living together in a household.

household *n.* 1) house, kindred, one's nearest and dearest, brood, offspring, 2) followers, following, hangers-on, henchmen.

householder *n.* head of a household, deed holder, freeholder, owner.

housekeeper *n.* 1) one who keeps open house, 2) woman who runs a house and is head over the household workers.

housekeeping *n.* the business of running a household, homemaking, housecraft.

houseless *adj.* homeless, shelter-less.

house-lore *n.* kinlore, kinship-lore.

housemaid *n.* maid working in a house, maid-of-all-work.

houseman *n.* newly taught *doctor* working in a sickhouse.

house-mother *n.* the mother in a household, woman heading up those living together in a household.

house of learning (*academy, college, university*) *n.* hall/seat of learning, school.

house-room *n.* room in a house for a man/woman, room enough to hold goods.

house sparrow *n.* eavesing sparrow, sparr, thack sparrow.

house-stead *n.* ground or pitch for a building.

house-top *n.* roof ridge, roof top, top floor.

house-warming *n.* having friends and kin to eat and drink in one's new house.

housewife *n.* wife of a householder, house-mother.

housewifely *adj.* careful/mindful/sparing in running a household.

housewright *n.* house-builder, house-crafter.

housing *n.* dwelling, home, board, rooms, shelter.

how *adv.* in what way? on what lines? how come?

howbeit *adv. conj.* be that as it may, however it may be, nevertheless, although.

howe (hoh, hoo) *n.* heel, hill-spur.

however *adv.* 1) in whatever way, however much, although, 2) be that as it may, but, even though, for all that, nevertheless, nonetheless, anyhow, notwithstanding, on the other hand, still, though, yet, 3) how? how on earth?

howsoever, howsomever *adv.* however.

hue (*colour*) *n.* 1) dye, shade, loud/soft hue, 2) light, look.

hue-less *adj.* sickly, wan.

hull *n.* shell.

hull *n.* body or frame of a ship.

hull *v.* to take off the hull.

hulled *adj.* stripped of the hull.

hundred *n.* 1) the root *number* that is ten times ten, 2) *part* of a shire, most likely of one hundred hides (the hide being land enough for one kindred to make a living).

hundredfold *adj.* hundred times as great or as many.

hundredth *adj. n.* 1) the marking *number* that is kin to a hundred, 2) hundredth share of something.

hundredweight *n.* reckoning of weight, being 112 pounds or one twentieth of a ton. (It was likely 100 pounds at the first, hence the name.)

hundredyear (*century*) *n.* one hundred years, yearhundred.

hunger *n.* 1) emptiness, hungriness, 2) blight, dearth, hardship, hard times, lack, wolf at the door, wretchedness, 3) ache, burning, craving, itch, longing, yearning.

hunger *v.* 1) to be empty/hungry, have no strength left, starve, 2) to crave, burn for, eat one's heart out over, hunger/thirst/itch for, long for, sigh for, yearn for.

hunger-bitten *adj.* careworn, drawn, starved, thin, worn.

hunger-strike *n.* saying 'no' to food, to back up one's stand.

hungrily *adv.* greedily, keenly, nothing loth, readily, wolfishly, yearnfully.

hungry *adj.* 1) empty, starving, 2) craving, itching, longing, restless, yearning.

hunt *n.* 1) hounding, hunting, run, boar-hunt, deer-hunt, deer-stalking, fox-hunt, stag-hunt, 2) delving deep, going into, rooting.

hunt *v.* 1) to be hard on the heels of, follow, go after, harry, ride down, ride to hounds, run down, stalk, tail, 2) to comb, delve into, go deep into, seek.

hunter *n.* huntsman, huntress, horse ridden in the hunt.

hunting *n.* 1) following the hounds, stalking, 2) combing, delving, going deep into, reading, looking into, rooting, seeking, sifting.

hunting-ground *n.* hunting lands.

huntsman *n.* hunter.

hurdle *n.* 1) wooden frame *used* to pen sheep, once made of boughs woven together or wattled with withes (of hazel, willow and such), but now often an open gate-like frame, 2) drawback, let.

hurdle *v.* 1) to make like a hurdle, pen with hurdles, 2) to run in a hurdle-race.

hurdler *n.* 1) one who makes hurdles, 2) runner in a hurdle-race.

hurst *n.* 1) wooded hillock or knoll, 2) grove, holt, shaw, thicket.

husband[(2)] *n.* household head, goodman, helpmeet.

hussy *n.* quean, wanton.

hwilpe (*curlew*) *n.* whaup.

hythe *n.* landing-stead on a *river*, berth, wharf.

I *pron.* self, myself.

ice *n.* frozen water, layer of ice on a mere, stream or the sea.

ice *v.* 1) to ice over, freeze, 2) to ice the top of a *cake*.

ice-axe *n.* ice wielded by climbers in cutting steps.

ice-bound *adj.* frozen in, held fast by ice, hemmed in by ice.

ice-breaker *n.* ship for beaking a sea-way through ice.

ice-cold *adj.* biting, bitterly cold, freezing, frozen, icy, raw.

ice-field *n.* wide stretch of ice.

ice-house *n.* small building or roomwhere ice can be kept through the year.

ice-mere *n.* frozen mere.

ice-sheet *n.* sheet of ice over a wide stretch of land.

icily *adv.* 1) freezingly, 2) coldly, coolly, frostily.

icing *n.* the glaze on a *cake*.

ickle *n.* icicle.

icy *adj.* 1) biting, bitter, chill, ice-cold, freezing, frozen over, 2) glassy, rimy, slippery, 3) cold, forbidding, frosty, stony, unfriendly, unwelcoming.

idle *adj.* slothful, shiftless, slack, slow, unthorough, unwilling.

idle *v.* to daydream, go wool-gathering, let slide, let one's mind wander, slack.

idle-handed *adj.* slothful, shiftless, slack, slow, unthorough, unwilling.

idle-headed *adj.* addle-headed, empty-headed, witless.

idleness *n.* sloth, slothfulness, do-nothingness, slackness, slowness.

idler *n.* good-for-nothing, foot-dragger, heel-dragger, layabout, lie-abed, slacker, slow-body, slow-bones, slow-foot.

idly *adv.* carelessly, slackly, slothfully, slowly, creepingly.

if *conj.* 1) if so be, should it be that, taking it that, 2) if not, unless, 3) as long as, given that, 4) any time, every time, when, whenever, 5) although, though, but, yet.

ilk (*same*) *adj.* brand, breed, kind, stamp.

impound *v.* 1) to gate, keep in, pen, shut up, 2) to lay hold of.

in *prep.* 1) inside, into, within, 2) by, with, 3) after, following, 4) out, out of.

in *adv.* at home, indoors, inside, within, within doors.

inarm *v.* to fold/hold in one's arms, grasp, hold to one's bosom, infathom, infold.

inasmuch[(2)] *adv.* in so far as, because, in that, seeing that, since.

inbeing (*immanence*) *n.* indwelling, inwovenness.

inblow *v.* to blow or breathe into, put life into, stir.

inblowing *n.* leading, stirring, inbreathing.

inboard *prep.* inside/within a ship.

inborn *adj.* inbred, deep-rooted, inbuilt, in one's blood.

inbreathing *n.* leading, stirring, inblowing.

inbred *adj.* inborn, bred in the bone, inwoven, inwrought.

inbreeding *n.* breeding only within the kinsfolk, not drawing on any other stock.

inbuilt *adj.* inborn, inbred, bred in the bone, deep-rooted, inwoven, inwrought.

inch[(5)] *n.* the length of three *grains* of barley, or one twelfth of a foot.

inch[(5)] *v.* to feel one's way, creep, go slowly, inch along.

income *n.* cut, earned income, earnings, growth, meed, rake-off, takings, yield.

incomer *n.* late-comer, newcomer, otherlander, outsider, settler, homeless wanderer.

incoming *adj.* 1) homeward, homing, (of the tide) flooding, 2) following, next, new.

indeed *adv.* fully, overly, truly, in truth, utterly, wholly, strongly.

indoors *adv.* at home, inside, within, within doors, withinside.

indraught *n.* letting in, bringing in, inflow.

indrawn *adj.* drawing from one's own wellsprings, inward-looking, withdrawn.

indrench *v.* to drench/drown in something.

indwell *v.* to abide, dwell in, have/make one's home in, live in, settle at.

indwelling (*immanence*) *n.* inbeing, inwovenness.

infall *n.* breakthrough, drive, inroad, onset.

infathom *v.* to fold/hold in one's arms, grasp, hold to one's bosom, inarm, infold.

infelt *adj.* inwardly felt/known.

infield *n.* 1) the land of a *farm* which lies near the homestead, 2) (in stockball) that stretch of the field of play which is near to the *wickets*, the fielders set therein.

infighting *n.* strife of words between the insiders of a set or team.

inflesh *v.* to take on flesh and blood, put flesh on.

infleshness (*incarnation*) *n.* fleshhood, mannishness.

inflow *n.* indraught, letting in, bringing in.

inflow *v.* to drain/flow/stream into, break through, flood, to empty/seep/soak into.

infold *v.* 1) to bundle up, sheathe, shroud, swathe, 2) to fold/hold in one's arms, grasp, hold fast, hold to one's bosom, inarm, infathom.

infolding *n.* 1) background, setting, 2) (*envelope*) holder, sleeve.

infolding *adj.* begirding, infathoming.

ingather *v.* to bring in, gather in, harvest, pick, reap.

ingathering *n.* 1) harvest, picking, reaping, 2) harvest-tide, harvest time.

ingirdle *n.* to begird, gird about, ring about.

ingoing *n.* 1) a going in, way in, 2) *sum* given by a hirer or buyer for the fittings in a workroom or other buildings.

ingrave *v.* to carve in stone, cut, grave.

ingraving *n.* 1) the craft of the ingraver, 2) ingraved drawing or writing, carving.

ingrowing *adj.* of that which is growing inwards or within – such as a finger-nail or toe-nail growing into the flesh.

ingrown *adj.* of that which has grown into the flesh.

ingrowth *n.* the growing inwards, that which grows inwards.

inhive *v.* to put into a hive.

inlaid *adj.* inset, set.

inland *n.* 1) the land about a homestead, infield, 2) heart-land, the midlands.

inland *adj.* girt about by land (such as an inland sea, inland waterway).

inlander *n.* 1) homelander, 2) one who knows nothing of the sea and its ways.

inlaw[(2)] *v.* to bring again within the law and its shield (as against 'outlaw').

-in-law[(2)] *n.* kindred through wedlock (father-in-law, mother-in-law, and such).

inlay *n.* inlaid work, *material used* for inlay.

inlay *v.* to inset, put in.

inlet *n.* 1) cove, arm of the sea, roadstead, fleet, tidefleet, 2) hole, inway, opening.

inlook *n.* looking within, looking inwards, brooding.

inly *adj.* inward, inwardly felt.

inly *adv.* 1) inwardly, in the heart, 2) heartily, thoroughly.

inlying *adj.* lying inside.

inmost *adj.* innermost, deep, deepest, hidden.

inn *n.* alehouse, roadhouse, roadside house, wayside house.

inner *adj.* 1) inside, inward, middle, midmost, 2) (of a well-knit set) belonging, bosom, friendly, near, 3) deep, hidden, underlying.

innerly *adv.* inwardly, more within.

innermost *adj.* 1) inmost, middle, midmost, 2) deeply-felt, heartfelt,.

innholder *n.* alehouse keeper, innkeeper.

innings *n.* 1) lands taken in from former marsh or flooded land, 2) (in stockball) the play of the batting side, the play of any one batsman, a knock.

innkeeper *n.* alehouse keeper, innholder.

input *n.* feedback.

input *v.* to put in, set.

inroad *n.* breakthrough, drive, onset, raid, strike, swoop.

inrunning *n.* 1) breakthrough, drive, 2) inflowing, flooding.

ins and outs *n.* 1) windings, 2) bit, dot, every last word, every whit and word.

inset *v.* to drive/hammer/knock/put in, set in.

inside 1) *n.* indoors, inner side, heart, 2) *adj.* inner, innermost, inward, 3) *adv.* in, within, indoors, deep down, at heart, in one's inmost being/heart, inwardly.

inside out *adv.* at great length, fully, thoroughly, utterly, wholly, beam and bough, root and rind.

insider *n.* one of a well-knit set, one in the know, one of an inner ring.

insight *n.* farsightedness, forethought, reach of mind, understanding, <u>wisdom</u>.

insightful *adj.* long-headed, sharp-witted, shrewd, <u>wise</u>, aware, witful, quick.

insomuch[(2)] *adv.* 1) inasmuch as, seeing that, since, 2) insomuch that, so that.

instead *phr.* for, in room of, the stead of, in its stead, rather than.

inswathe *v.* to clothe, bind up, infold, overlay, shroud, swathe.

into *prep.* bringing/coming/going/putting into a steading or thing.

intwine *v.* to bind, braid, inweave, twine about, twist, weave, wind, wreathe.

intwined *adj.* <u>knotted</u>, twining, twisted, winding.

inward *adj.* 1) incoming, inflowing, ingoing, 2) inner, inside, inmost, innermost.

inwardly *adv.* at heart, deep down, deeply, inly, in one's inmost heart.

inwardness *n.* inner *part/s*, inbeing, depth of feeling/thought.

inwards *adv.* inside, inward.

inway *n.* gateway, way in, way through, way to, doorway, opening, open door.

inweave *v.* to weave in, weave things together, intwine.

inwith 1) *prep.* within, inside of, 2) *adv.* inwardly, inwards.

inwitness (*conscience*) *n.* inner warning, inward word, inwit, telling good from evil.

inwoven *adj.* foreshadowed, fore-willed, fore-woven, wyrdful.

inwrought *adj.* fore-shapen, fore-written, fore-wrought, wyrdful.

iron[6] *n.* 1) wrought iron, 2) smoothing iron, steam iron, smoother, 3) fetters.

iron[6] *adj.* 1) wrought in iron, 2) hard, steely, strong, tough, unbending, unyielding.

iron[6] *v.* 1) to smooth clothes with a heated iron, 2) to iron out, put right, set right, settle, smooth over, smooth the path/way of, straighten out.

iron[6]**-hard** *adj.* steely, tough, truly hard/strong.

ironing[6] *n.* smoothing clothes with a heated iron, batch of clothes for ironing.

island *n.* land girt about by water (in the sea, or in a *river* or marsh).

islander *n.* island-dweller.

it *pron.* the *pronoun used* 1) for things without life, 2) often for *beasts*, 3) sometimes for little children.

itch *n.* 1) prickling, 2) craving, longing, restlessness, yearning.

itch *v.* 1) to prickle, 2) to crave, long for, lust after/for, yearn after.

itching *n.* craving, longing, yearning.

itchy *adj.* edgy, restless, unsettled.

itself *pron.* that one above all.

ivied *adj.* clothed/overgrown with ivy.

ivy *n.* creeping evergreen plant.

jowl (*jawbone*) *n.* chin bone.

kail, kale, cole[4] *n.* greens.

Kale[4]**-month** (*February*) *n.* Colemonth, 'Fill-ditch', Sol-month.

kechel *n.* a little *cake*, kichel.

keen *adj.* 1) biting, cutting, edged, searing, sharp, stinging, 2) keen-thinking, keen-witted, quick-witted, sharp-witted, wise, witful.

keenly *adv.* bitterly, sharply, tellingly.

keen-minded *adj.* bright, clever, nimble-witted, quick-thinking, sharp, wise, witfast.

keenness *n.* 1) earnestness, 2) canniness, cleverness, insight, shrewdness.

keep *n.* 1) fastness, stronghold, 2) board, food, livelihood, living, upkeep.

keep *v.* 1) to grasp, grip, hang on to, hold fast to, hold on to, keep in one's own hands, 2) to hold off, keep/hold/stand one's ground, 3) to abide, go on being, not stir, 4) to heap up, hoard, house, lay up, put by, stow, 5) to keep going, keep on, outlast, 6) to abide by, follow, fulfil, heed, 7) to hold up, be long about it, 8) to bring up, care for, feed, foster, look after, shelter, 9) to handle, oversee, run.

keep at *v.* to grind/hammer away, keep on, not give up, work at, work night and day.

keep down[6] *v.* to hold down, keep under, lord it over, tread underfoot.

keep from *v.* to forbear, hold back, hold off, keep away, keep back, do without.

keep going, keep on *v.* to abide, go on, hold out, outlast.

keep in *v.* to begird, cut off, gird about, ring about, hedge in, hem in, lock in, shut in.

keep in mind *v.* to bear in mind, bethink, give thought to, think about/over.

keep off *v.* to beat/fight/stave/ward off, withstand.

keep to *v.* to abide by, be true to, cling to, hold to, stand by, truly mean.

keep under *v.* to hold down, keep down, lord it over, tread underfoot.

keep up *v.* to keep going, keep in the running.

keeper *n.* 1) caretaker, overseer, steward, watchman, 2) bee-keeper, boatkeeper, book-keeper, doorkeeper, field-keeper, gamekeeper, gate-keeper, goalkeeper, housekeeper, innkeeper, time-keeper, wealth-keeper.

keeping *n.* 1) holding, 2) care, wardship.

keepsake *n.* something given by one to another and kept for the sake of the giver.

ken *n.* 1) reach of sight, sight of something, 2) awareness, understanding.

ken *v.* 1) to make known, show the way to, teach, 2) to look at, 3) to acknowledge, get to know, have knowledge of, make out, pick out.

kenning *n.* 1) reach of one's sight, a sea *measure* of about 20/21 miles, 2) awareness, knowledge, understanding, 3) *roundabout* way of naming someone or something (in Old Norse songcraft).

kernel *n.* 1) seed, stone, 2) heart, key, main thing, marrow, pith.

kettle[4] *n.* heater, seether.

key *n.* 1) tool that shifts the bolts of a lock to fasten or shut it, door key, 2) list, listing, 3) answer, clue, path, token, 4) key of a *piano*.

key *adj.* far-reaching, foremost, greatest, highest, leading, main, telling, weighty.

key bearer *n.* key holder, key keeper.

keyboard *n.* *piano*, keyboard of a main-reckoner (*computer*).

keyhole *n.* hole by which a key is put into the lock.

keystone *n.* 1) headstone, horn-stone, springer, 2) ground, mainspring.

key word (*password*) *n.* watchword.

kichel *n.* small *cake*, kechel.

kill *n.* stroke, the deed of killing, a killed *beast*.

kill *v.* to fell, make an end of, murder, overcome, put an end to, slay, smite.

killer *n.* man of blood, murderer, slayer.

killing *n.* bloodshed, manslaying, murder, putting to death.

killing *adj.* backbreaking, draining, grinding, hard, tiring, tough, uphill, <u>wearing</u>.

kiln[5] *n.* great oven for baking, burning or drying, such as a lime-kiln.

kin *n.* <u>kindred</u>, kinsfolk, kith and kin, kinsmen, one's own flesh and blood.

kincraftlore (*ethnology*) *n.* folklore.

kind *n.* brand, breed, hue, ilk, make, make-up, stamp, strain.

kind *adj.* good, great-hearted, kind-hearted, kindly, loving, soft-hearted, sweet, unselfish, warm, warm-hearted, brotherly, fatherly, motherly.

kind-hearted *adj.* good, great-hearted, kindly, loving, warm-hearted.

kind-knowing the knowledge of birds, *beasts* and *plants*.

kindliness *n.* <u>kindness</u>, kindheartedness, loving-kindness, warmth, winsomeness.

kindly *adj.* good, <u>kind</u>, soft-hearted, sweet, unselfish, warm.

kindly *adv.* lovingly, in kindness, out of kindness.

kind-name *n.* kind, breed.

kindness *n.* kindliness, kindheartedness, loving-kindness, brotherliness, friendliness, great-heartedness, helpfulness, open-handedness, open-heartedness, thoughtfulness, warmth of heart, warm-heartedness, friendship, goodwill, softness, unselfishness.

kindness *n.* kindliness, kindheartedness, loving-kindness, brotherliness, friendliness, helpfulness, open-handedness, warmth of heart, warm-heartedness, friendship, goodwill, softness, unselfishness, heart of gold.

kindred *n.* 1) house, household, kin, kinfolk, kinsfolk, folk, next of kin, kith and kin, kinsman, kinswoman, kinsmen, one's nearest and dearest, one's own flesh and blood, stock, 2) forebears, forefathers, forekin, blood, line, 3) brood, children, little ones, offspring, young, aftercomers, afterkin.

kindred-land *n.* folkland, hearthland, homeland, land of one's forebears.

kindred word (*cognate*) *n.* kinword.

kine *n.* cows, livestock.

kinemeat (*beef*) *n.* cow, cowflesh, cowmeat.

kine-pox *n.* cow-pox.

king *n.* lord, hoard-ward, ethel-ward, folk-king, land-ward, mathom-giver, theoden

kingcraft *n.* 1) the craft of kingship, 2) craftiness of a king in his dealings.

kingdom *n.* 1) folkdom, 2) fatherland, motherland, homeland, 3) field, world.

kinghood *n.* kingship, leadership, lordship, overlordship.

king-like *adj.* highborn, lordly, of high worth, of mark.

kingliness *n.* high bearing, high birth, knightliness, lordliness, worth.

kingly *adj.* great, high, highborn, lordly, of high worth, of mark, <u>worthy</u>.

king-maker *n.* one who makes kings and seeks to lead such, wire-puller.

kingship *n.* kinghood, kingly house, lordship, overlordship.

kinless *adj.* roofless, rootless, unfriended.

kinlore (*genealogy*) *n.* forefatherlore, forekinlore, house-lore, kinsfolklore, kindred-lore, kinshiplore, kin-tree.

kin-reckoning (*lineage, pedigree*) *n.* blood, bloodstock, breed, house, kindred ties, kin-tree, line, roots, shoots, offshoots, seed, stem, stock, strain, 'crane's foot'.

kinsfolk *n.* kin, <u>kindred</u>, kinfolk, folk, kith and kin.

kinsfolklore *n.* kinlore, forefatherlore, house-lore.

kinship *n.* 1) kindred, roots, ties of blood, stem, stock, 2) alikeness, fair/near likeness, good/striking likeness, nearness.

kinshiplore *n.* <u>kinlore</u>, <u>kin-reckoning</u>, kindred-lore.

kinsman *n.* father's brother, mother's brother, kith and kin, one's flesh and blood.

kinsmanship *n.* kinship, ties of blood.

kinswoman *n.* father's sister, mother's sister, kith and kin, one's flesh and blood.

kin-tree *n.* <u>kinlore</u>, <u>kin-reckoning</u>, forefatherlore, house-lore.

kin-wealth (*heirloom*) *n.* bequest, birthright.

kinword (*cognate*) *n.* kindred word.

kiss *n.* light stroke with the lips as a token of warmth, farewell kiss, kiss of greeting.

kiss *v.* to blow a kiss, kiss one's fingers.

kitchen[4] *n.* bake-house, cookhouse, cooking room.

kite *n.* glede, puttock.

kith *n.* 1) knowledge, 2) homeland, 3) kith and kin, kindred, kinsfolk, friends.

kithless *adj.* alone, forsaken, friendless, kinless, rootless, unfriended.

kitish *adj.* like a kite, greedy.

knap *n.* top of a hill or hillock.

knave *n.* <u>evil-doer</u>, fox, good-for-nothing, shammer, <u>sharper</u>, ne'er-do-well, twister.

knavish *adj.* <u>crafty</u>, fox-like, shady, <u>sharp</u>, shrewd, slippery, stealthy, underhand.

knead *v.* to shape, work, work up into.

kneading-trough *n.* wooden trough in which to knead dough.

knee *n.* 1) the hinge between the thigh and the lower shank, 2) bend, bend in a stream, elbow, horn.

knee *v.* to shove with the knee.

knee-cloth (*napkin, serviette*) *n.* lap-cloth.

knee-deep *adj.* 1) deepish, up to the knees, 2) sunk up to the knees.

kneel *v.* to fall on one's knees, kneel to, throw oneself at the feet of, worship.

kneeler *n.* hassock.

knell *n.* ring, toll.

knell *v.* to toll a bell.

knife[2] *n.* blade, cold steel, bread-knife, carving knife, clasp-knife, sheath-knife.

knight *n.* deed-doer, fighting man, horse-lord, lord, man of mark, worthy.

knighthood *n.* 1) the standing of a knight, 2) knightliness, 3) a body of knights.

knightliness *n.* 1) boldness, daring, doughtiness, fearlessness, 2) good breeding, high-mindedness, lordliness, manliness, rightwiseness, selflessness, steadfastness, straightforwardness, thoughtfulness, true-heartedness, uprightness, worthiness.

knightly *adj.* 1) bold, daring-hearted, doughty, fearless, 2) fair, fair spoken, high-minded, high-wrought, kind-hearted, manly, self-forgetful, selfless, thoroughbred, thoughtful, unselfish, unsparing of self, upright, well-born, well-spoken, winning.

knit *v.* 1) to twine, weave, 2) to draw together, knot, wrinkle, 3) to bind, tie.

knitch *n.* bundle (of corn, hay, wood or such).

knitting *n.* knitted work.

knitting-needle *n.* long straight needle for knitting.

knitwear *n.* knitted clothing.

knock *n.* 1) hammering, 2) dint, hit, stamp.

knock *v.* to beat, hammer, hit, strike.

knock about *v.* to wander.

knock down[6] *v.* to beat down, fell, strike down, thrash, throw down, worst.

knocked back *adj.* amazed, bewildered, floored, shaken, speechless, struck dumb.

knocker *n.* door knocker.

knock-kneed *adj.* having the shanks bent inwards so that the knees knock together.

knock off *v.* to break off, down tools, leave off, stop work.

knock-out *n.* one's doom/end/undoing.

knoll *n.* hillock, low hill, spur.

knot *n.* 1) tie, twining, 2) hard saying, brain teaser, maze, riddle, web.

knot *v.* to bind, knit, tie, twine, twist, weave.

knotted, knotty *adj.* bewildering, dark, deep, hard to fathom/grasp/understand, hidden, hooded, riddle-wrought, shrouded, thorny, unfathomful.

knotwork *n.* kind of needlework.

know *v.* to be aware, feel in one's bones, find out, have a grasp, ken, know all the answers, know backwards, know by heart, know full well, know inside out, know down to the ground, know one's way about, know what's what, understand, ween.

know-all *n.* swollen-head, wiseacre.

know-how *n.* understanding, lore, long-headedness, wisdom.

knowing *adj.* 1) shrewd, canny, clever, quick-thinking, ready-witted, sharp-witted, in the know, 2) having knowledge, all-knowing, aware, alive to, bookish, book-learned, bookwise, learned, well-read, well up in, widely-read, wise.

knowingly *adv.* 1) knowing well what one is doing, wilfully, wittingly, 2) shrewdly.

knowingness *n.* being in the know, canniness, shrewdness.

knowledge *n.* knowing, learning, book-learning, ken, lore, awareness, insight, grasp, wit, wisdom, understanding, know-how.

known *adj.* 1) understood, heard, seen, 2) settled, cut and dried, in black-and-white.

know-nothing *n.* clod, goose, greenhorn, oaf.

knuckle[1] *n.* the bone at a finger-hinge.

lack *n.* dearth, drought, hardship, leanness, need, pennilessness, shortfall, unweal.

lack *v.* to be in need of, be short of, have not a penny, live from hand to mouth.

lackadaisical *adj.* dreamy, half-hearted, idle, lifeless, limp, listless.

lackadaisy, lackaday *intj.* welladay! sadly! woe!

lackbrain *n.* witling, half-wit, clod, addle-head.

lacking *adj.* 1) down and out, empty of, needy, penniless, 2) below strength, half-done, lean, light-weight, makeshift, middling, shallow, short, unfilled.

lackwit *n.* witling, half-wit, clod, addle-head.

ladder *n.* steps, set of steps.

lade *n.* mill-race, runnel, water-leat.

lade *v.* to load up, put goods on board a ship, stow.

laden *adj.* burdened, full, weighed down, weighted.

ladle *n.* dipper, spoon,

ladleful *n.* spoonful.

ladle *v.* to spoon out.

lady *n.* high-born lady, woman, frith-weaver.

lady-bird *n.* *insect.*

Lady day *n.* *Feast* of the 25th Lengthening-month (*March*) marking the tidings brought to Mary of the birth of the Christ-child. Lady-day is one of the four days marking the four fourths of the year (when the letting of houses begins and ends).

ladyhood *n.* the suchness of being a lady, the standing/worth of a good lady.

lady-killer *n.* heartbreaker, ladies' man, wolf, woman-hunter, womanizer.

ladylike *adj.* becoming, fair spoken, queenly, right-hearted, well-bred, well-spoken.

lady-love *n.* beloved, betrothed, bride-to-be, darling, lover, true-love, sweetheart.

ladyship *n.* 1) the suchness of being a lady, 2) kindness of the lady of the house.

laid-back *adj.* carefree, cool, offhand, unworrying.

lair *n.* bolt-hole, burrow, den, earth, fox-hole, hideaway, hide-out, hole, shelter.

lamb *n.* 1) young of the sheep, ewe lamb, lambling, 2) little child, unworldly soul.

lamb *v.* 1) to bring forth, drop a lamb, 2) to care for ewes at lambing-time.

lamb's tails *n.* hazel catkins.

lamb-like *adj.* childlike, harmless, lowly, mild, sinless, soft, sweet, unhardened.

lambling *n.* lambkin, little lamb.

lamb's-wool *n.* the wool of lambs wrought into clothing.

lame *adj.* bent, halt, marred, mightless, misshapen, shaky, strengthless, withered.

lame *v.* to cripple, hamstring, harm, mar, twist, warp, wound.

lame-duck *n.* also-ran, has-been, loser, write-off.

land *n.* 1) dry land, ground, 2) clay, earth, loam, new tilled land broken in from marsh/moor/heath/wood, 3) hearthland, heartland, homeland, fatherland, motherland, kingdom, 4) acres, broad acres, holding, steading, 5) (as against the town) back of beyond, middle of nowhere, outdoors, outlands, out-of-town.

land *v.* 1) to hook, net, win, 2) to bring to land, come to land, make a landing.

land-book *n.* 1) (*charter*) deed, 2) (*gazetteer*) handbook, stow-book.

land-bridge *n.* neck of land.

landed *adj.* owning land.

landfall *n.* coming, sighting land.

land-flood *n.* drowning of land by overflowing *rivers* or other inland waters.

landfolk *n.* (*country* folk) folklanders, homelanders.

landholder *n.* landowner, landlord, landlady.

land-hungry *adj.* hungry for land to till and so make a living.

landing *n.* 1) coming in, making land, 2) stair-head.

landing craft *n.* craft that brings fighting men and their *gear* to land.

landing ground (*airport*) *n.* runway, flight-hub.

landlady *n.* 1) owner, house-owner, 2) innkeeper.

landless *adj.* having no land to till and from which to make a living.

land-line[4] *n.* 1) outline of the land at the edge of one's field of sight, 2) '*phone* line to one's house or business.

landlocked *adj.* ringed about with land (as of a land with no seaboard).

landlord *n.* 1) owner, landowner, landholder, 2) innkeeper.

landlore (*cartography*) *n.* the craft of setting forth (on cloth or *paper*) the shape of land and seas – *charting*, *chart*-making, *mapping*, *map*-making, rindlore (marking the outlinesof the land on a *strip* of beech-rind).

landman (*countryman*) *n.* crofter, smallholder.

landmark *n.* 1) merestone, hoar-stone, standing stone, waymark, 2) milestone.

landowner *n.* landholder, landlord, landlady.

land-reckoner (*surveyor*) *n.* reckoner, house-reckoner, land-sighter.

land-right *n.* the rights and undertakings that go with the ownership of land.

landship (*landscape*) *n.* backcloth, background, outlook, broad outlook, setting.

landslide *n.* 1) sliding of earth and stones down a hillslope or cliff slide, land which has so fallen, 2) beating, hiding, thrashing, walkover.

landsman *n.* 1) smallholder, 2) no seaman, one who knows nothing of life at sea.

land-steward *n.* overseer, reeve.

landstretch (*continent*) *n.* mainland, wide-lands, great-land.

landswoman *n.* land-worker, smallholder.

landtrothen (*nationalistic*) *adj.* father/motherland loving, homeland-loving.

landward 1) *adv.* towards the land, 2) *adj.* out-of-town.

land-wind *n.* wind blowing from the land seawards.

lane *n.* 1) narrow way between hedges or houses, back street, by-street, narrow street, side street, thoroughfare, wynd, 2) the hollow way cut by water overflow in meadow-land, a brook whose flow is hardly to be seen, the smooth and slowly flowing *part* of a stream.

lank *adj.* 1) lean, shrunken, spare, thin, 2) (of hair) *flat* and straight, limp.

lanky *adj.* tall and lean, bony, fleshless, long-shanked, rawboned, thin as a rake.

lap *n.* the fore *part* of someone seated.

lap *n.* 1) overlap, 2) (in a race) stretch.

lap *v.* 1) to drink, lap up, wet one's lips, 2) (of water) to wash about.

lap *v.* to bind up, fold, fold up, swathe, wreathe.

lap-cloth (*napkin, serviette*) *n.* knee-cloth.

lap-dog *n.* small dog, such as may sit or lie in a lady's lap.

lapful *n.* so much as will fill someone's lap.

lapwing, lapwinch *n.* pewit.

lark *n.* field-lark, laverock, skylark.

larkspur *n.* plant.

last *n.* wooden likeness of a foot, on which the shoemaker shapes shoes.

last *n.* 1) burden, load, 2) weight-mete, being two tons or 4,000 pounds (in wool weight 4,368 pounds or twelve sacks, in corn weight ten fourths or 80 *bushels*).

last *adj.* 1) aforesaid, foregoing, latest, 2) aftermost, furthest, furthest behind, hindmost, latest, 3) thorough, utmost, 4) least likely, most unlikely.

last *adv.* after, behind, at the end, in the end.

last *v.* to abide, hold out, keep on, last out, outlast, outlive, stand fast.

last-ditch *adj.* holding out to the last, all-out, forlorn, hopeless, true to the last.

lasting *n.* shaping a shoe on the last.

lasting *adj.* abiding, everlasting, longlived, lifelong, livelong, undying, unending.

lastly *adv.* all in all, at the last, at long last, at length, endly, in the end.

last-word *n.* 1) after-word, end-say, 2) best, first, foremost, highest, leading.

last-wright *n.* shoemaker, shoe-wright.

latch *n.* door-latch.

latch, letch *n.* stream flowing through marshland, a slime-filled hole or ditch.

latch *v.* to clutch, get hold of, hold fast, grip, lay hands upon, take hold of.

latch *v.* to fasten with a latch.

late *adj.* 1) behindhand, behind time, belated, never on time, not on time, too late, 2) dead, former, one-time, sometime, 3) like new, new-looking, new-made.

late *adv.* 1) after time, last thing, late in the day, 2) in the night, late at night.

latecomer *n.* aftercomer, incomer, newcomer.

lately *adv.* latterly, not long ago, of late, latewardly.

lateness *n.* belatedness, unreadiness.

later *adv.* after, afterwards, by and by, in a while, in time, later on, next, thereafter.

latest *adj.* brand new, new, like new, new-looking, new-made, upstart.

lateward *adj.* backward, late, slow.

latewardly *adv.* lately, of late.

lath *n.* thin *strip* of wood used in roofing and walling.

lathen *adj.* made of lath.

lather *n.* 1) foam from soap and water, 2) foamy sweat of a horse.

lather *v.* 1) to put on a lather of soap and water, 2) (of a horse) to be *flecked* with lather, 3) to make a lather of soap and water.

lathing *n.* lath-work.

lathy *adj.* 1) tall and thin like a lath, lanky, 2) made of lath and *plaster*.

latish *adj.* somewhat late, a little bit late.

latter 1) *adj.* ending, last, later, latest, 2) *pron.* last, last-named.

latterly *adv.* hitherto, lately, newly, of late, a short time ago.

lattermath *n* aftermath, latter mowing, the crops then reaped.

lattermost *adj.* aftermost, hindmost, last, latest.

laugh *n.* laughter, roar/shout of laughter,

laugh *v.* to burst out laughing, laugh in one's sleeve, laugh one's head off.

laughing *adj.* 1) of that which laughs, 2) (of the eyes) bright, shining, sparkling.

laughingly *adv.* lightly, playfully.

laughing-stock *n.* by-word, fair game.

laughter *n.* 1) laughing, hearty laughter, loud laughter, 2) glee, mirth.

laughterless *adj.* dreary, gloomy, mirthless.

laughter-loving *adj.* mirth-loving, playful.

laughworthy *adj.* beyond belief, far-fetched, utterly unlikely, wildly out.

laverock *n.* lark, field-lark, skylark.

law *n.* hill, low.

law/s[2] *n.* 1) behest, bidding, say-so, word, writ, 2) body of law, settled/written law.

law[2]**-abiding** *adj.* high-minded, rightwise, steady, true-hearted, upright.

law[2]**-body** *n.* house of law-making, steering body.

law[2] **book** (law *code*) *n.* doombook.

lawbreaker[2] (*criminal*) *n.* evil-doer, guilty man, knave, outlaw, rough, tough.

lawful[2] *adj.* meet and right, right, rightful, rightwise, rightly/truly-grounded.

law[2]**-giver** *n.* law-maker, law-writer, steersman.

lawless[2] *adj.* a law to oneself, hot-blooded, reckless, self-willed, threatening, wilful.

lawlessness[2] *n.* free for all, storm, unrest, upheaving, wildness, writ not running.

law[2]**-maker** *n.* law-giver, law-writer, steersman.

lawyer[2] *n.* man of law.

lax (*salmon*) *n.* leax, lox.

lay *n.* lay of the land.

lay *v.* 1) to put, set down, 2) to lay a trap, hatch, work out, 3) to lay (eggs), 4) to draw up, make, put forward, put together, set out, 5) to lay a *bet*, gamble.

layabout *n.* good-for-nothing, foot-/heel-dragger, idler, slacker, slow-bones.

lay aside *v.* to have done with, put aside, put off.

lay-by *n.* 1) slack stretch of a *river* where boats are laid up, 2) stead beside a road where *vehicles* can pull off.

lay down[6] *v.* 1) (of one's life) to give up, yield, 2) to hand over, make way for, stand aside, 3) to deem, say outright, set down, set forth, speak.

layer *n.* 1) bed, seam, thickness, underlayer, 2) dusting, film, sheet.

lay hands on *v.* to fasten on, gather up, get hold of, pick up, take hold,

lay in *v.* to buy in, gather in, heap up, hoard, lay by, put by, stock up, stow away.

lay into *v.* to beshrew, blast, chide, flay, go for, have words with, upbraid.

lay off *v.* to axe, drop, let go.

lay out *v.* 1) to put out, spread out, 2) to set out, show, unfold.

lay up *v.* to gather up, heap up, build up, hoard, fill up, put by, stock up.

lea *n.* 1) wood-leas, woodland meadow, 2) open land, grassland, meadow.

lea, ley, lay *n.* fallow land, tilled land now under grass.

lea, ley, lay *adj.* fallow, untilled.

leach *v.* to drain, seep.

lead *n.* grey-hued heavy *metal* that is soft and readily shaped.

lead *n.* 1) clew/clue, hint, 2) leadership, 3) edge, start, 4) line.

lead *v.* 1) to go before, lead on, lead/open the way, lead through, show the way, 2) to head, head up, steer, take the helm, 3) to be at the head of, be first, be winning, come first, lead off, outdo, 4) to lead to, bring about, bring on, give rise to.

leaden *adj.* 1) made of lead, 2) heavy, unwieldy, weighty, 3) dreary, dry, lifeless.

leaden hued *adj.* ashen-hued.

leader *n.* 1) doer, head, 2) leading light, 3) groundbreaker, pathfinder, shaper.

leaderless *adj.* lord-less, shepherd-less.

leadership *n.* 1) headship, lordship, steersmanship, 2) inner ring, leaders.

leader-writer *n.* gossip writer, newshound, writer.

leading *adj.* ahead, first in the field, foremost, greatest, highest, outstanding.

leading lady *n.* player, playwoman, showwoman, star player.

leading man *n.* player, playman, showman, star player.

leaf *n.* 1) blade, 2) sheet.

leafen *adj.* leaf-like.

leaf-fall (*autumn*) *n.* harvest, harvest-tide.

leaf-green *adj.* light green.

leafiness *n.* green, leafed, leaved, leafy.

leafless *adj.* bare, bare-boughed, stripped of leaves.

leaf-light *adj.* not hard, straightforward, 'all in a day's work'.

leaf-shedding (*deciduous*) *adj.* of a tree that sheds its leaves every year.

leafy *adj.* green, leafed, leaved, shaded, shady, springlike, summery.

leak[2] *n.* 1) drip, giving off/out, outflow, 2) give-away, lid taken off.

leak[2] *v.* to drain, drip, empty, give off, leach, ooze out, seep, sweat, well forth.

lean *n.* tilt, warp.

lean *adj.* bony, drawn, fleshless, half-starved, shrunken, spare, spidery, spindle-shanked, spindly, thin, withered, wizened, thin as a lath/rake, worn to a shadow.

lean *v.* to lean over, heel over, tilt.

leaning *n.* 1) leaning over to one side, 2) bent (of mind), liking, one-sidedness.

leanly *adj.* slightly, sparely, thinly.

leanness *n.* lankiness, thinness.

lean-to *n.* shelter built against the side of a another building.

leap *n.* 1) hop, spring, springy step, 2) sharp rise, upswing.

leap *v.* 1) to hop, leap-frog, leap over, spring, 2) to to climb/rise sharply, shoot up.

leap-frog *n.* children's game.

leap-frog *v.* 1) to leap over the back of another child, in the game of leap-frog, 2) to overleap some hurdle (fairly or unfairly) and so get on faster.

leap year *n.* year having one day (29th Kale-month) more than other years.

learn *v.* to awaken to, bend one's mind to, bury oneself in one's books, come to know, come to understand, delve into, delve deep, drink in, fathom, find out, follow up, give one's mind to, go into, look into, look through, pore over, read up, seek for truth, sift, sit at the feet of, thirst after knowledge, thresh out, winnow, work through.

learned *adj.* book-learned, deep-thinking, thinking, well-read, book-crafty.

learner *n.* beginner, bookworm, follower, greenhorn.

learning *n.* book-craft, book-learning, book-lore, book work, head work, mind work, knowledge, lore, reading, wisdom, learning-craft.

lease *n.* land that has been 'let alone', not tilled, meadowland.

least *adj.* fewest, lowest, meanest, smallest.

leastways, leastwise *adv.* at least, in the least.

leat *n.* ditch, drain, overflow, runnel, water-leat.

leather *n.* fell, hide.

leather *v.* to beat, flay, lay on one, strike, thrash.

leathern *adj.* hard, leathery, tough.

leather worker, leather-wright *n.* craftsman/worker in leather.

leathery *adj.* hard, hardened, leathern, leather-like, tough.

leave *n.* 1) freedom, 2) break, holiday, time off, 3) farewell, going, leaving.

leave *v.* 1) to bequeath, bestow, give, hand down, hand on, settle on, will, 2) to leave behind, forget, mislay, 3) to give over, hand over, have done with, leave off, 4) to bid farewell, flee, forsake, go away/out from, leave home, leave the nest, leave the neighbourhood, pull out of, run away from, set out from, take oneself off, take one's leave, withdraw from, 5) to drop out of, get away, get out of, 6) to ditch, drop, give up, leave high and dry, throw aside/away/off/over, walk out on.

leave *v.* to come into leaf, put forth leaves.

leaved *adj.* 1) (of a tree) in leaf, 2) (of a door) having two folding leaves.

leave hold of *v.* to drop, forgo, give up, hand over, let go, yield.

leaveless *adj.* bare, leafless, without leaves.

leave off *v.* to break off, end, give up, stop.

leaver *n.* school leaver, fledgling.

leave-taking[2] *n.* farewell, going, leaving, sendoff.

leave-word (*password*) *n.* key word, watchword.

leavings *n.* bits, crumbs, left-overs, sweepings.

leax (*salmon*) *n.* lax, lox.

ledge *n.* ridge, sill, step.

ledger *n.* the main reckoning (*accounts*) book in which *monies* coming in and going out, and *monies* owed, are written.

lee *n.* 1) leeside or leeward side of a ship, 2) shade, shadow, shelter.

leech *n.* 1) a water-dwelling, blood-sucking worm, 2) hanger-on, toady, yes-man.

leek *n.* plant akin to the *onion*.

leer *n.* a shifty or lustful sideways look.

leer *adj.* crafty, foxy, knowing, shady, sharp, shifty, slippery, underhand.

leer *v.* to eye, make eyes, wink.

lee side *n.* the side of a ship away from the wind (as against the weather side).

leet *n.* cross-roads, road-meet, way-meet.

leeward *adj.* riding or sailing downwind (as against to windward).

lee-way *n.* 1) the sideways going of a ship to leeward, 2) free hand/play, room.

left 1) *adj.* name for the hand which (with most folk) is less deft, left-hand, nearside, on-side, 2) *n.* (in *politics*) those who believe in folk-will (*democracy*) and wide ownership of goods.

left-handed *adj.* having a left hand stronger than the right.

left-hander *n.* 1) one whose left hand is stronger than his right, 2) (in stockball) player who bats and/or *bowls* with the left hand.

leftmost *adj.* set furthest to the left.

left-over/s *n.* bits, crumbs, leavings, sweepings.

leftward 1) *adv.* on or towards the left hand, 2) *adj.* set on the left.

lench *n.* wide hill-slope.

lend *v.* 1) to let out/loan, 2) to back.

lender *n.* one who lends, loan-wolf.

lending *n.* the letting out of *money*.

length *n.* 1) the mete (*measure*) of anything from end to end, longness, span, stretch, full length, over-all length, 2) (in a race) the length of a boat, horse or such, as a *measure* of the greatness of the win, 3) (in stockball) the right pitch for the ball.

lengthen *v.* to draw out, let out, pull out, sprawl, spread out, stretch out, unfold.

lengthening *n.* growth, spinning out, strengthening, waxing.

Lengthening *n.* Lent (the time of lengthening days).

Lengthening-month (*March*) *n.* Loud-month, Rough-month.

lengthful *adj.* long, of great length.

length-mete *n.* one foot of twelve inches.

lengthways, lengthwise *adv.* in the set of the length of something.

lengthy *adj.* long, long-drawn, long as my arm, long-winded, wordy.

Lent *n.* the forty days from Ash Wednesday to Easter Eve (calling to mind Jesus Christ's forty days in the wilderness), kept as a time of fasting and sorrow for sins.

lenten *adj.* of the time of Lent, of something that is fitting for Lent.

Lent-tide *n.* spring-tide, the time of the Lenten fast.

less 1) *adj.* not so much, shorter, smaller, 2) *adv.* barely, little, not so much.

less-born *adj.* of lower birth.

lessen *v.* 1) to make less/smaller, lighten, cut back, cut short, cut down, narrow down, shorten, trim, whittle, 2) to become less, die down, drop, dwindle, fall back, grow less, shrink, slacken, wane.

lessening *n.* downgoing, down-trend, drop, dwindling, dying down, ebb, fall, falling off, loss, losing ground, narrowing, shortening, shrinking, slackening, waning.

lesser *adj.* lower, slighter.

lest *conj.* for fear that, lest that.

let *n.* drag, drawback, hindering, hurdle.

let *v.* to say yes to, give one's blessing, give the green light for, make a path for, open the door to, not stand in the way, smooth the way.

let *v.* to hinder, hold back, make it hard for, put a drag on, saddle with.

let alone *phr.* besides, moreover, furthermore, likewise.

letch *n.* stream flowing through marshland (see 'latch').

let down[(6)] *v.* to fall short.

let drop, let fall *v.* to let on, let fall, come out with, spill the beans.

let fly *v.* to break out, fall upon, lay into, run wild, set upon.

let go *v.* to leave hold of, drop.

let in *v.* to open the door, throw open, bring in, show in.

let off *v.* 1) to forgive, let go, 2) to fire, fire off, let fly, shoot.

let on *v.* to let drop/fall/out, make known, speak of, tell all, tell on, come out with.

let out *v.* to free, set free, get one out of.

let-up *n.* break, falling off, lessening, slackening.

letting *n.* hiring out.

lewd *adj.* churlish, lustful, oafish, rough, wanton, wild, wolfish, uncouth.

lewdness *n.* craving, lust, wantonness, wildness, wolfishness.

liar *n.* one who tells lies, shammer, twister.

lich-gate *n.* roofed gateway into a churchyard, where the body (in a chest) is set down for a while.

lich-way *n.* path along which a dead body is borne for burial.

lich-yard *n.* burial-ground, graveyard, 'God's acre'.

lick *n.* 1) deed of licking, 2) bit, little.

lick *v.* 1) to run the tongue over something (to *taste* it, or wet it, or to lick something off), 2) to lap with the tongue, drink, sip, 3) (of fire) to flicker, play over, 4) to lick into shape, 5) to beat hollow, thrash, outdo, undo, blow out of the water.

licking *n.* beating, hiding, thrashing.

lickpenny *n.* one who or that which 'licks up pennies' (that is, runs through *money*).

lid *n.* 1) hinged top of a bowl, box or such, 2) eyelid.

lidded *adj.* 1) having a hinged top, 2) (of the eyes) having lids, heavy-lidded.

lidless *adj.* 1) without a lid, 2) without eyelids, 3) watchful.

lie *n.* less than the truth, untruth, downright lie, shameless lie, white lie, unsooth.

lie *v.* to tell a lie, forswear oneself, mislead, misteach, not speak/tell the truth.

lie *v.* 1) to lie down, rest, stretch out, 2) to be, sit, stand, 3) to be found, dwell, lie in, 4) to be buried, 5) to be a burden on, weigh on, 6) to lie with, bed, know, live with, sleep with, 7) to waylay.

life *n.* 1) being, living being, soul, living soul, 2) breath, living, 3) living things, wildlife, 4) drive, liveliness, sparkle.

life-blood *n.* heart, heart's blood, heart and soul.

life-giving *adj.* livening, quickening.

lifeless *adj.* 1) cold, dead and gone, stiff, stone dead, 2) bare, empty, forsaken, lonely, 3) deadly, drearisome, dreary, heavy, wearing, wearisome.

life-like *adj.* true-to-life.

lifelong *adj.* abiding, longlasting, for all one's life, for life, lifetime.

lifelore *n.* *biology.*

lifemanship *n.* craft, gamesmanship, one-upmanship, wit.

lifetale (*biography*) *n.* life, life-writing.

life-thread *n.* the 'thread' of life (cut through at the time deemed for death).

life-theatening *adj.* baleful, deadly, deathly, dreadful, harmful.

lifetime *n.* days, length of days/life, a long time, all one's born days, life span.

life-way *n.* behaviour, way of life.

life-weary *adj.* tired of living, way-weary, wretched.

life-writing (*biography*) *n.* lifetale.

lift[(2)] *v.* 1) to draw up, heave up, 2) to end, stop, withdraw.

light *n.* 1) broad day, daybreak, daylight, sunlight, 2) brightness, gleam, sparkle, 3) beacon, fire-light, naked light, 4) lighter, match, spark, 5) insight, understanding.

light *adj.* 1) aglow, bright, glowing, shining, sunny, unclouded, undimmed, well-lighted, well-lit, 2) fair, light-hued.

light *adj.* 1) flimsy, lean, not heavy, of little weight, leaf-light, lightweight, thin, 2) mild, soft, 3) lightweight, nigh worthless, 4) elf-like, lithe, nimble, willowy, 5) filmy, see-through, sheer, thin, thread-like, through-showing, wispy.

light *v.* 1) to brighten, light up, 2) to fire, set fire to, set alight, start a fire.

light-bringing (*educational*) *adj.* life-learning, mind-growing.

light-brown *adj.* brownish, yellowish brown.

lighten *v.* to brighten up, light up, throw light upon, shine upon.

lighten *v.* 1) to lessen, make less, take off one's shoulders, trim back, unburden, unload, free, 2) to allay, brighten, gladden, hearten, take the load off one's mind.

light elf (*fairy*) *n.* fair one, wight.

lightener (*leaven*) *n.* barm, yeast.

lightening *n.* lessening, smoothing, softening, stilling.

lighter *n.* flat-bottomed boat for unloading ships that are of too great a draught to be brought alongside a wharf.

lighter *n.* match.

lighterman *n.* one who works a lighter, waterman.

light-fingered *adj.* 1) nimble-fingered, quick-fingered, 2) shifty, thievish.

light-fingeredness *n.* 1) deftness, 2) shadiness, thefting.

light-footed *adj.* lissom, lithe, lively, light of heel, nimble, quick, swift.

lightful *adj.* bright, full of light, well-lighted, well-lit.

light-handed *adj.* 1) deft, nimble, mild, soothing, 2) short-handed.

light-headed *adj.* dizzy, featherbrained, flighty, giddy, playful, shallow, unsteady.

light-hearted *adj.* blithe, bright, carefree, laughing, lively, merry, playful, sunny.

light-heartedly *adv.* blithely, gleefully, merrily.

light-heartedness *n.* brightness, liveliness, merry-making, mirth, sparkle, sunniness.

light-heeled *adj.* light-footed, nimble, quick, swift.

light horse *n.* body of light horsemen, horse-lords.

lighthouse *n.* tall building, having a strong light to lead and warn ships at sea.

light-hued *adj.* fair, flaxen, light, soft-hued.

lighting *n.* lights.

light-limbed *adj.* lissom, lithe, lively, light-footed, light-heeled, nimble, quick.

lightly *adv.* 1) barely, hardly, sparingly, thinly, ever so little, 2) mildly, softly, 3) carelessly, heedlessly, thoughtlessly, 4) readily, with hardly a thought.

light-minded *adj.* addle-headed, bird-witted, careless, dim-witted, dizzy, empty-headed, far-away, feather-brained, feather-headed, fickle, fleeting, flighty, forgetful, giddy, hare-brained, lightweight, shallow, shallow-minded, shiftful, thoughtless, unsettled, unsteady, unwitful, wandering, wayward, wildered, witless, woolly-headed.

light-mindedness *n.* flightiness, heedlessness, unsteadiness, waywardness.

lightness *n.* 1) brightness, 2) litheness, nimbleness, quickness.

lightness *n.* 1) little weight, hollowness, 2) flightiness, shallowness, worthlessness.

lightning *n.* flicker of lightning, sheet-lightning, summer lightning.

lightship *n.* ship (anchored where there is no lighthouse) bearing a light to warn and lead other ships.

lightshooter (*photographer*) *n.* one who takes *photographs.*

lightshooting (*photography*) *n.* filming, shooting.

lightshot (*photograph*) *n.* shot, film-shot, slide, still, likeness.

light-stepping (*dance*) *n.* reel, quickstep, lithe-step, lithe weaving.

light upon *v.* to come upon, find.

lightweight *adj.* 1) light in weight (of cloth, *coins* and such), 2) filmy, sheer, thin, thread-like, wispy, 3) mightless, nigh worthless, strengthless, shallow.

lightweight *n.* man of straw, nobody, small game, small man.

lightwords *n.* empty words, honeyed words, pretty speeches, soft soap, toadying.

like *n.* liking for.

like *n.* match, twin.

like *adj.* akin to, alike, matching, twin, much like, something like, such like.

like *adv.* 1) in the like way, 2) even as, 3) as well as, like as, 4) likely.

like *v.* 1) to be keen on, go for, hold dear, like well, love, take to, think well of, think the world of, warm to, 2) to care, choose, set one's heart/mind on, wish for.

likelihood, likeliness *n.* well-grounded hope.

likely *adj.* 1) in a fair way, most likely, well-grounded, 2) bright, fair, hopeful.

likely *adv.* like enough, like as not.

like-minded *adj.* answering, in step, of like mind, of one mind.

liken *v.* to match, set beside, set side by side.

likeness *n.* 1) alikeness, speaking/striking likeness, 2) (*parable*) likening, life-tale.

likewise *adv.* 1) in the like way, 2) as well as, also, besides, more, moreover, furthermore, let alone, else, and so on, and so forth, along with, together with.

liking *n.* bent, friendship, kindness, leaning, love, warmth.

limb *n.* 1) arm, shank, forelimb, hinder-limb, nether limb, 2) bough, offshoot, spur.

limbless *adj.* armless, shankless, one-armed, one-shanked, marred.

limb-weary *adj.* dead tired, done in, fordone, ready to drop, way-worn, weary.

limb-whole *adj.* sound in limb, healthy, strong, unharmed.

lime *n.* 1) bird-lime, 2) limestone.

lime *v.* 1) to smear boughs with bird-lime (to take birds), 2) to do over with lime-wash.

lime *n.* lime-tree, lind, linden.

limelight *n.* 1) white light made by heating lime, 2) footlight, stardom.

limestone *n.* a kind of stone which yields lime when burnt.

lime-wash *n.* a mingling of lime and water, for whitewashing walls.

limp *n.* lameness.

limp *adj.* 1) loose, slack, 2) strengthless, tired, worn out.

limp *v.* to drag one's steps, falter, walk lamely.

limpet *n.* *creature* with a shell which holds fast to *rocks*.

limpingly *adv.* falteringly, haltingly, lamely.

limply *adv.* slackly.

limy *adj.* besmeared with bird-lime.

linch *n.* hill, ledge, link, ridge, rising ground, slope.

lind, linden *n.* lime-tree.

linden *adj.* of lime wood.

linden board *n.* shield.

line[4] *n.* 1) rope, thread, string, tow-line, wire, 2) fishing-line, 3) mark, streak, stroke, 4) cut, outline, shape, 5) edge, mark, 6) row, 7) firing line, first line, 8) forebears, forefathers, house, stock, strain, 9) path, road, way, 10) business, field, livelihood, trade, walk of life, work, 11) way of doing things, lifemanship, 12) brand, goods, kind, make, stock, wares, 13) *railway* line, main line, 14) crow's foot, furrow, wrinkle, 15) clue, hint, lead, 16) line/s of a play/song.

line[4] *v.* to line with linen or such, fill, inlay, put in.

line[4] *v.* 1) to cut, draw a line, furrow, mark, underline, 2) to edge.

linen[4] *n.* cloth woven from flax.

link *n.* ledge, linch, ridge, rising ground, slope.

link[2] *n.* 1) ring, 2) tie-up, 3) tie.

link[2] *v.* to bind, fasten, hook up with, tie up with, yoke.

lip/s *n.* 1) the upper and lower lips of the mouth, speech, 2) answering back, backtalk, brazenness, forwardness, uppishness, 3) (of a cup, bell or such) edge, rim.

lip-read *v.* to 'read' what another is saying by watching the lips.

lipstick *n.* stick of *cosmetic* for giving a redder hue to the lips.

lipsalve *n.* 1) salve for the lips, 2) empty words, hollowness, honeyed words.

lipwisdom *n.* wisdom in one's talk without deeds to match.

lisp *n.* 1) lisping, 2) *sound* of water, or leaves.

lisp *v.* to speak with something near a 'th' *sound* instead of 's' and 'z' (either through a speech shortcoming or for show), to mis-say, speak thickly.

lissom, lissome *adj.* lithe, light, light-footed, nimble, trim, willowy, elfin, elf-like.

list *n.* hearing.

list *n.* 1) edging, 2) the *fence* about a field where tilting is to happen.

list *n.* blessedness, bliss, blissfulness, blitheness, gladness.

list[3] *n.* black list, list of names, reading list, short list, sick list, stock-list, word list.

list *v.* to wish for, long for, set one's heart or mind on, yearn after, yearn for.

list *v.* to give ear, hear, hearken, lend an ear, listen.

list *v.* to put an edge on something.

list[3] *v.* to book, make a list, set down, write down.

listen *v.* 1) to be all ears, give ear, hang on the lips of, hear, hearken, keep one's ears open, lend an ear, listen in, miss nothing, 2) to do as one is told, heed.

listener *n.* hearer.

listful *adj.* all ears, heedful, mindful.

listless *adj.* forlorn, hopelorn, without hope, bowed, 'down', unmanned, woebegone.

lit *adj.* lighted.

lith *n.* slope, hill-slope, hill, hillside.

lith *n.* 1) limb, 2) hinge (*joint*).

lith and limb *n.* the whole body.

lithe *adj.* lissom/lissome, lithesome, light-footed, light of heel, nimble, nimble-footed, quick, quick-footed, sparkling, willowy.

lither *adj.* 1) bad, evil, wicked, 2) withered, 3) bendsome, yielding.

lithesome *adj.* lissom, lithe, light, light-footed, willowy, elf-like.

litling *n.* 1) little one, child, 2) narrowling (*bigot*).

little *adj.* dwarfish, light, knee-high, lightweight, mean, short, small, thumb-nail.

little *adv.* a little time (before), not many, not much, in a nutshell.

little *n.* a bit, drop, thimbleful.

little-hearted *adj.* fearful, chicken-hearted.

little man *n.* 1) little finger, 2) small businessman or landowner.

littleness *n.* 1) dwarfishness, smallness, 2) meanness, shallowness, unworthiness.

little-worth *adj.* 1) cheap, empty, nigh worthless, two a penny, 2) good for nothing.

live *adj.* 1) alive, breathing, living, quick, 2) afire, go-ahead, lively, sparkling, up-and-doing, 3) (of a shell) still working, 4) (of a fire) ablaze, blazing, alight, burning, glowing, red hot, 5) (of something talked about) hot, news-worthy, startling.

live *v.* 1) to be alive, breathe, draw breath, have being/life, still be, 2) to abide, dwell, 3) to behave, lead a life, live one's life, 4) to earn/make a living, make ends meet, 5) to live life to the full, make the most of life.

live-birth *n.* a child being born alive (as against a still-birth).

livelihood *n.* business, daily work, life's work, line, living, trade, walk of life, work.

liveliness *n.* quickness, readiness, sleeplessness, tirelessness.

livelong *adj.* abiding, lasting, lifelong, longstanding.

lively *adj.* 1) alive, awake, quick, keen, ready, willing, astir, stirring, up-and-doing, a-doing, never-resting, never-sleeping, never-tiring, restless, sleepless, tireless, unsleeping, unwearied, busy, hard at it, hard-working, on one's toes, full-blooded, light-footed, light of heel, nimble, nimble-footed, on the stretch, go-ahead, go-getting, on the go, up to one's eyes, 2) blithe, bright, carefree, laughing, laughter-loving, light-hearted, merry, playful, sparkling, sunny.

liven *v.* to breathe life into, brighten, fire, liven up, make lively, stir, quicken.

liver *n.* a *part* of the body which gives out *bile* and cleanses the blood.

liver-sickness *n.* *hepatitis.*

livestock *n.* cows, kine, goats, sheep.

living *n.* 1) business, line, trade, 2) behaviour, way of life, ways.

living *adj.* 1) alive, breathing, in the land of the living, 2) adoing, in the news.

lo *intj.* behold! look! look now! see!

load, lode *n.* small waterway in fenland, ditch, drain, leat, runnel.

load *n.* 1) goods, heap, lading, wainload, 2) burden, millstone, weight.

load *v.* 1) to fill up, load up, stow, 2) to burden, overload, saddle with, weigh down.

loaded *adj.* 1) burdened, full, laden, weighed down, 2) (of a *gun*) ready to fire, 3) one-sided, twisted, unfair, warped, weighted.

loading *n.* weighting.

load-shedding *n.* cutting *electricity* to one neighbourhood (because of short *supply*).

loadstone, lodestone *n.* 1) waystone, 2) draw, pull.

loaf *n.* loaf of bread.

loaf-oven *n.* baker's oven.

loam *n.* clay, clayey earth.

loam-wright *n.* potter.

loan[2] *n.* borrowings, overdraft.

loan[2] *v.* to lend, let out.

loan[2]**-wolf** *n.* lender, *money*-lender, loan-*shark*.

loath, loth *adj.* against, backward, dragging heels, half-hearted, hanging back, holding back, not in the mood, shrinking, shrinking back, slow, unminded, unwilling.

to be loath *v.* to be unwilling, not hear of, not hold with, set oneself against.

loathe *v.* to find loathsome, hate, shrink from with misliking, shun, spurn.

loathful *adj.* 1) hateful, loathsome, 2) backward, shamefast, sheepish, shrinking.

loathing *n.* hatred, misliking, shrinking from, shunning, spurning.

loathly *adj.* accursed, baleful, baneful, foul, ghastly, hateful, hellish, loathsome.

loathly *adv.* 1) in a way to stir loathing, foully, hatefully, 2) unreadily, unwillingly.

loathsome *adj.* accursed, foul, as bad as bad can be, too bad, baleful, baneful, dreadful, filthy, fulsome, ghastly, hateful, hellish, rank, sickening, stinking, unwholesome, wretched.

lock *n.* flowing locks, lovelock.

lock *n.* clasp, fastening.

lock *v.* 1) to fasten, bolt, shut, 2) to clasp, grasp, infathom.

lockfast *adj.* fastened by a lock, locked up, made fast.

lock-out *n.* shutting strikers out until they fall in with the business-owner's *terms.*

locksmith *n.* craftsman who makes locks and puts right broken locks.

lockup *n.* hold for misdoers, lockhouse, wardhouse.

lodestar *n.* 1) star that shows the way (above all the ship-star/*pole-star*), 2) draw, pull.

loft[(2)] *n.* roof room.

lone *adj.* 1) by oneself, on one's own, out on a limb, 2) friendless, lonely.

loneliness *n.* 1) forlornness, forsakenness, lonesomeness, 2) emptiness, wildness.

lonely *adj.* alone, lonesome, forlorn, forsaken, unfriended.

loneness *n.* aloneness, friendlessness, loneliness, lonesomeness.

lonesome *adj.* forlorn, friendless, gloomy, lone, lonely, sad.

long *adj.* 1) full-length, lengthy, lengthened, long as my arm, 2) drawn out, long-drawn-out, endless, long-lasting, longsome, never-ending, no end to, overlong, spun out, strung out, too long, unending, wearisome, without end, long as a wet week.

long *adv.* for a long time, long after/before/since.

long *v.* to ache for, dream of, list, long for, yearn after.

long-acre *n.* long narrow field of one acre.

long ago *adv.* aforetime, in bygone times, in olden times, long since, of old.

long-ago, long-ago days *n.* bygone days, old days, olden times,

long-boat *n.* the greatest boat belonging to a sailing ship.

long-bow *n.* great bow.

long-drawn, long-drawn-out *adj.* lengthy, never-ending, overlong, spun out.

longer *adv.* any longer, no longer, much longer.

longest *adj.* the longest time/way.

long for *v.* to ache for, burn for, dream of, hope for, hunger for, thirst for, list, long to see, set one's heart/mind on, wish for, yearn after, yearn for.

long forefathers *n.* forebears, forefathers, forerunners, kindred, stock.

Long Friday *n.* Good Friday.

long-glass (*telescope*) *n.* spy-glass.

long gone *adj.* dead and buried, died out, ended, lost, no more, over and done with.

long-hand *n.* handwriting in full (as against short-hand).

long-headed *adj.* aware, farsighted, forethinking, thinking, shrewd, wise, witful.

long-headedness *n.* wisdom, insight, understanding, sharpness, shrewdness.

longing *n.* aching, burning, dreaming, gnawing ache, heartache, hope, hungering/thirsting after, itching for, weariness of heart, yearning.

longing *adj.* hungry, thirsty, wishful, yearning.

longing while *n.* time of longing or weariness, heaviness.

longish *adj.* fairly long, somewhat drawn-out.

long-lasting *adj.* abiding, everlasting, longstanding, timeless, undying, unending.

long-lived *adj.* full of years, long-lasting, many-yeared.

longness *n.* length, drawn-outness.

(in the) **long run** *adv.* after many days, at last, in the end, in the fullness of time, in time, not before it was time, sooner or later.

longshanks *n.* nickname for one who is long-limbed.

long-ship *n.* war-ship, 'sea-mare'.

long-shot *n.* 1) shot fired from a long way off, 2) a shot in the dark.

long-sighted *adj.* seeing things a way off (while not seeing near things so well).

long-sightedness *n.* 1) the suchness of seeing things a way off, 2) foresight.

longsome *adj.* dreary, endless, lengthy, long-winded, wearing, wearisome, wordy.

long-standing *adj.* abiding, everlasting, holding, lasting, long-lasting, unending.

long sword *n.* sword with a long cutting blade.

long time (*age*) *n.* a great stretch of time, timestretch, time span, stream of time, 'day', long years, years on end, many lives long.

long-tongued *adj.* flowing, gossipy, long-winded, smooth-spoken.

longways *adv.* along, endlong, head to heels, lengthways, lengthwise, longwise.

long-winded *adj.* going/running on, gossipy, high-flown, lengthy, long-drawn-out, long-tongued, long-worded, many-worded, never-ending, overlong, overwordy, speechful, ready-worded, spun out, wandering, winding, windy, wordful, word-spinning, wordy.

longwise *adv.* along, at full length, end to end, endlong, head to foot/heels, lengthways, lengthwise, longways.

look *n.* 1) glimpse, sight, 2) bearing, the way one holds oneself.

look *v.* 1) to eye, look ahead, look before one, look down, look over, look up, see, stare, watch, 2) to delve into, follow up, go into, hunt, look into, look over, seek, 3) to give onto, overlook, 4) to hope, reckon on, 5) to look like, strike one as.

look after *v.* to care for, keep an eye on, mind, sit with, watch.

look down[(6)] **on** *v.* to look one up and down, look down one's nose at, spurn.

looking-glass *n.* mirror.

look in on *v.* to drop in on, go to see, look someone up, stop by.

look now! *intj.* behold! see!

look out for *v.* to be careful/wary of, keep an eye out for, watch out for.

look-out *n.* 1) watch, watch and ward, weather-eye, 2) watchman, watcher.

on the **look-out** keeping a look-out, awake, on the watch, all ears, all eyes.

loom *n.* web-beam on which yarn or thread is woven into cloth.

loose[(2)] *v.* to free, set free, let go, let off, unbind, undo, unfasten.

loose[(2)] *adj.* 1) free, not tied up, not bound together, unbound, unfastened, unfettered, untied, 2) broad, hit or miss, slack, woolly, 4) careless, heedless, unmindful, thoughtless, 5) earthy, fleshly, lewd, lustful, thrill-seeking, wanton, wolfish, worldly.

loosen[(2)] *v.* to free, set free, slacken, unbind, undo, unfasten, unfetter, unloose, unknot, unshackle, untie, unyoke, work loose.

loose[(2)]**-tongued** *adj.* gossipy, newsy, long-winded, long-tongued, ready-tongued, running on, windy.

lop *n.* spider.

lop *n.* small boughs and twigs of trees, loppings, firewood.

lop *v.* to cut off the boughs of a tree, cut back, shorten, trim,

lopping/s *n.* small boughs and twigs lopped from a tree.

lord *n.* ealdorman, earl, great man, head, high lord, leader, overlord, gold-giver, ring-giver, horse-lord, sea-lord, ship-lord (*captain*), field-lord (*general*), weapon-lord.

lord-dom (*authority*) *n.* headship, leadership, lordship.

lord it over *v.* to bring to heel, do what one likes with, have eating out of one's hand, lead by the nose, make one's plaything, override, play the lord, quell, tame.

lordless *adj.* without a lord, leaderless.

lordlessness *n.* outlawship, wretchship.

lord-like *adj.* lordly.

lordliness *n.* greatness, highness, high standing, knightliness, worship, worth.

lordling *n.* little lord, lightweight, nobody.

lordly *adj.* 1) foremost, great, high, highborn, well-born, knightly, matchless, unmatched, outmatching, mighty, nonesuch, of mark, open-handed, strong-handed, weighty, worthy, worthful, 2) high and mighty, high-handed, high-stepping, off-handed, overbearing,

overweening, standoffish, uppish, on one's high horse.

Lord's Day *n.* First Day, Sunday.

Lord's Day Eve (*Saturday*) *n.* Seventh Day, Weekend-day.

Lord's Meal *n.* meal of bread and wine tokening the body and blood of Jesus Christ.

lordship (*authority*) *n.* 1) lord-dom, lordliness, kingship, leadership, overlordship, standing, 2) arm of the law, long arm, might, right, strength, weight.

lore *n.* teaching, wit, wisdom, understanding, awareness, worth-weighing.

lore-book *n.* lore-work, wisdom book.

lorecraft *n.* body/field of knowledge, know-how, lore, world-wisdom.

lorehall (*academy, college, university*) *n.* hall/seat of learning, house of learning.

lorehouse *n.* hall/house/seat of learning, school.

loreless *adj.* benighted, blind, bookless, clueless, darkened (in mind), in the dark, groping, narrow-minded, short-sighted, unaware, unknowing, unlearned, unseeing, unthinking, without the light.

loreman, loreseeker, lore-smith *n.* great mind, learner, thinker, truthseeker.

loreway (*course, curriculum*) *n.* path of learning.

lorewise *adj.* learned, deep-thinking, highbrow, deep-read, well-read.

lorn *adj.* 1) doomed, lost, 2) bowed down, forlorn, heart-lorn, hopelorn, sorrowful.

lose *v.* 1) to mislay, miss, not find, have nothing to show for, spill the milk, 2) to be beaten, be the loser, be worsted, lose ground, lose out, lose the day, lose the match, lose hands down, 3) to lose/miss one's way, become lost, wander, 4) to shed.

lose heart/hope *v.* to be hopelorn/forlorn, bereft of hope, bowed down, broken-hearted, of heavy heart, sick at heart, filled with sorrow, listless, wretched.

loser *n.* also-ran, has-been, lame duck, underdog.

loss *n.* 1) losing, mislaying, 2) drain, outfall, outflow, 3) harm, utter loss, 4) death.

lost *adj.* 1) gone forever, lost to sight, mislaid, missing, 2) dead, died out, forgotten, 3) at sea, bewildered, having lost one's bearings, helpless, 4) dreamy, lost in thought, spellbound, 5) fallen, hardened, hopeless, shiftless, wanton, wayward.

lot *n.* 1) share, share-out, cut, deal, batch, bulk, great deal, heap, 2) doom, wyrd.

loth *adj.* see 'loath'.

loud *adj. adv.* deafening, dinning, ear-rending, thundering.

loudly *adv.* deafeningly, dinningly, lustily.

Loud-month (*March*) *n.* Lengthening-month, Rough-month.

loudness *n.* bellow, clatter, din, knocking, roar, uproar, scream, screech, shout, stamping, thunder, thunderclap.

lour *v.* 1) to glower, look like thunder, 2) (of clouds) to look dark and threatening.

louse *n.* *insect* that besets the hair and skin of folk.

lousy *adj.* 1) full of lice, overrun with lice, 2) filthy, foul, loathsome, stinking, 3) sick, unwell, under the weather, 4) bad, dreadful, no good.

lout *n.* churl, oaf, rough.

loutish *adj.* bearish, churlish, oafish, rough, uncouth.

love *n.* 1) friendship, heart, liking, warmth, 2) bent for, leaning, 3) beloved, darling, dear, dearest, lady-love, loved one, lover, sweet, sweetheart, truelove.

love *v.* to hold dear, hold in one's heart, care for, cling to, set one's heart/mind on, lose one's heart to, live only for, warm to, think the world of, worship, burn for, fall for, sigh for, yearn for.

love-begotten *adj.* born out of wedlock, without a father/name.

love-child *n.* child born out of wedlock.

love-drink *n.* a drink to stir love.

love-driven *adj.* driven by a blind/burning love.

love-hate *n.* strong feelings of mingled love and hate.

love-knot *n.* knot of *ribbon* tied in an 'unalike' (*special*) way (as a love token).

love-led *adj.* led on by a burning or yearning love.

loveless *adj.* 1) cold-hearted, hard, heartless, heart-whole, icy, uncaring, unfeeling, unfriendly, unloving, 2) forsaken, lovelorn, unchosen, unloved, unmissed.

loveliness *n.* comeliness, shapeliness, winsomeness, fairhood, fairness.

love-longing *n.* care, kindness, love, sweetness, warmth, warm-heartedness.

lovelorn *adj.* forsaken by one's love, aching or longing for him/her, lovesick.

lovely *adj.* becoming, comely, bewitching, fair, goodly, pretty, shapely, willowy, elf-fair, elf-sheen (fair as an elf), sun-sheen (fair as the sun), winsome.

love-making *n.* love-play, honeying.

love-match *n.* wedlock for love and not for worldly wealth or standing.

love-play *n.* love-making, honeying.

lover *n.* love, true love, sweetheart, wooer, young man.

lovesick *adj.* besotted, bewitched, bitten, lovelorn, smitten, yearning for one's love.

love-song *n.* song-dream of love.

lovethought *n.* love-play in the mind.

loveworthy *adj.* worthy of love, lovely, warm, winning, winsome.

loveworthiness *n.* true-heartedness, winsomeness, worthiness.

loving *adj.* caring, kind, kindly, kind-hearted, motherly, soft-hearted, sweet, thoughtful, warm, warm-hearted.

low (*tumulus*) *n.* barrow, burial-*mound*, grave-*mound*.

low[2] *adj.* 1) forlorn, hopelorn, sorrowful, listless, 2) beaten, cringing, mean.

low[2] *adv.* in a low standing, on the ground, unworthily.

low *v.* (of kine) to bellow.

lower[2] *adj.* 1) lesser, lower down, nether, smaller, under, 2) cut, lessened, worse.

lower[2] *v.* 1) to drop, let down, let fall, make lower, 2) to cut, lessen, make less, mark down, worsen, 3) to belittle, cheapen, run down, 4) (of speech) to soften.

lowermost, lowest[2] *adj.* nethermost, undermost.

lowly[2] *adj.* shrinking, shy, blushing, shamefast, maidenly, unheard, unseen.

lowly[2] *adv.* metely, mildly, shamefastly, shrinkingly, shyly.

lox (*salmon*) *n.* lax, leax.

lukewarm *adj.* cool, half-hearted, off-hand, unstirred, without warmth.

lung *n.* one of the two breathing *organs* (in man and many *beasts*).

lurk *v.* to go stealthily, hide, play hide-and-seek, slink, stalk, steal along.

lust *n.* lewdness, craving, wantonness, wolfishness.

lust *v.* to crave much, be dying for, burn for, hunger/thirst for, lust after/for, make eyes at, run after.

lustful *adj.* lewd, wanton, wolfish.

lustfulness *n.* burning, craving, wantonness, wolfishness.

lustihood *n.* 1) drive, overdrive, fire, lustiness, 2) lustfulness.

lustily *adv.* heartily, mightily, willingly, hammer and tongs, with might and main.

lustiness *n.* 1) drive, fire, lustihood, might, strength, 2) lustfulness.

lusty *adj.* 1) burly, hearty, hefty, meaty, mighty, strong, 2) lewd, wanton, wolfish.

lych-gate *n.* see lich-gate.

lye (*detergent*) *n.* cleaner, cleanser, quicklime, soap.

lying *adj.* laid out, lying down, lying on one's back, sprawling, stretched out.

lying *n.* forswearing, telling lies, untruthfulness.

lying *adj.* crafty, shifty, smooth-tongued, truthless, untruthful.

lying-in *n.* birth-throes, the being in child-bed.

mad *n.* grub, mathe, worm.

mad *adj.* brain-sick, daft, having lost one's wits, horn-mad, mad-headed, mazed, moonmad, moonstricken, moonstruck, not in one's right mind, not right in the head, off one's head, stark staring mad, unstrung, wandering, wildered in one's wits.

mad-brained *adj.* far-fetched, hare-brained, mad-headed, outlandish.

madden *v.* to drive one mad, goad, stir one's wrath, make one's blood seethe, make one seethe with wrath, make one see red, stir the blood, set by the ears.

maddened *adj.* burning, hot-blooded, hot-hearted, quick-hearted, red-hot, wild.

maddening *adj.* goading, teasing, tiresome, wearisome.

madder *n.* climbing plant (grown for the dye won from it).

made-up *adj.* 1) dreamed-up, make-believe, wild, 2) overdone, put-on, showy.

mad-headed *adj.* far-fetched, hare-brained, mad-brained, outlandish.

madhouse *n.* 1) haven for the mad, 2) din, free for all, to-do, storm, uproar.

madly *adv.* hell for leather, quickly, recklessly, speedily, wildly.

madman, madwoman *n.* crack-brain.

madness *n.* mind-sickness, clouded mind, mind-darkening, mind overthrown, wandering of the mind.

maid *n.* 1) girl, maiden, wench, young woman, 2) handmaiden, housemaid.

maid-child *n.* girl, maid, maiden-child.

maiden *n.* daughter, girl, maid, maid-child, maiden-child, wench, young woman.

maiden *adj.* 1) unwed, unknown by man, 2) of that which is *untested* or has brought no outcome (as, in stockball, an over in which no runs are made).

maiden-child *n.* girl, maid, maid-child.

maidenhair *n.* name for some kinds of fern.

maidenhead, maidenhood *n.* childlikeness, goodness, maidhood, wholesomeness.

maidenlike *adj.* befitting a maiden, blushing, maidenly, shamefast, shy.

maidenliness *n.* shyness, troth, wholesomeness.

maiden name *n.* the father's/kindred name of a wife before she was wedded.

maidenly *adj.* blushing, shamefast, shy, sweet, true, wholesome, winning, winsome.

maiden's blush *n.* a soft, light-red hue.

maidhood *n.* childlikeness, goodness, maidenhood, wholesomeness.

main *n.* 1) main-craft, main-strength, might, might and main, strength, 2) water (or *gas, electricity*) main.

main *n.* the deep, great deep, the sea, high sea, the waves.

main *adj.* 1) foremost, head, leading, outstanding, 2) sheer, utmost, utter.

main *adv.* truly, utterly, wholly.

mainfast *adj.* astir, bold, hearty, keen, lively, lusty, quick, tireless, up-and-doing.

main-hard *adj.* main-strong, manful, manly, mighty, sinewy, strong, thickset.

mainland (*continent*) *n.* landstretch, wide-lands, great-land.

mainly *adv.* above all, first and foremost, most of all, on the whole.

mainmast *n.* the great mast of a sailing ship.

mainreckoner *n. computer*.

main-sail *n.* the great sail of a sailing ship.

mainspring *n.* beginning, drive, ground, root, spring, spur.

mainstay *n.* 1) the stay which runs from the maintop to the foot of the foremast, 2) backbone.

main stream 1) *n.* the main stream of a *river*, 2) *adj.* broad, over-all, widespread.

main-strength *n.* main-craft, might, might and main, strength.

main-strong *adj.* lusty, main-hard, manful, manly, mighty, sinewy, strong, thickset.

mainway (*motorway*) *n.* fast road, freeway, highway, throughway.

make *n.* brand, build, kind, mark, stamp.

make *v.* 1) to bring about, build, do, frame, put together, set up, shape, shapen, hew into shape, 2) to draft, draw up, lay down, think up, write, 3) (of making up one's mind) to come to, reach, settle on, 4) to bend, browbeat, drive, override, twist one's arm, 5) to bring in, earn, fetch, net, win, 6) to be, become, come to be, grow into, make up, 7) to come to, fetch up at, get as far as, get to, reach, 8) to reckon, ween.

make away with *v.* to bear away, make off/run off/walk off with, steal away.

make-believe 1) *n.* daydream, dream, dream land, dream world, wild dream, shadow, wishful thinking, wonderland, 2) *adj.* dreamed-up, made-up, shadowy.

make do with *v.* to do what one can with, make a shift with, make the best/most of.

make fast *v.* to bind, bolt, fasten, stick, strengthen, tie.

make for *v.* to drive at, go for, go all out for, go after.

make game of *v.* to have one on, <u>mislead</u>, outwit, play with, take in.

make headway *v.* to do well, make good ground, make one's way.

make known *v.* to be open about, open up, bring into the open, bring light to bear, lay open, bring out, come out with, din into one's ears, fill one in, give away, give one to understand, give out, give to the world, lay bare, lay before the world, tell the world, let fall, let in daylight, let one know, let on, let out, make aware, make a clean breast of, make much of, make news of, open one's mind, open the eyes, put out, put about, send word to, show for what it is, show up, speak about, spread abroad, speak of, talk about/of, tell the world, throw light on, unbosom oneself, unburden oneself, unfold, unshroud, spill the beans.

make out *v.* 1) to do, fare, 2) to draft, draw up, fill in/out, write out, 3) to glimpse, pick out, see, sight, 4) to fathom, follow, gather, grasp, put two and two together, take in, think through, <u>understand</u>, unriddle, work out, 5) to make as if.

make over *v.* to give into the hands of, hand over, hand to, put into the hands of.

maker *n.* builder, craftsman, doer, worker, wright.

make ready *v.* to draw up, lay the groundwork, put in readiness, sow the seed.

make right (for the work to be done) *v.* to match, put right, set right, pitch anew, shape anew, work anew, straighten out, tidy up, trim, bend, bring in step with.

makeshift *adj.* half-baked, half-done, home-made, offhand, rough and ready.

make up *v.* 1) to even up, make good, make up for, offset, set off, set against, 2) to build, frame, put together, 3) to dream up, shape, spin, think up, weave, write, 4) to fawn on, make up to, toady to, 5) to brew, mingle, put together, shake/stir together.

make-up *n.* 1) build, make, stamp, 2) eye shadow, lip-stick and such.

make way *v.* to give way, stand down, withdraw, <u>yield</u>.

makeshift *n.* fill-in, shift, way to an end.

makeweight *n.* 1) a small bit thrown in to make up the weight of something, 2) someone or something reckoned as of little worth.

making-up *n.* 1) mingling, putting together, 2) reckoning up of the books.

malm *n.* light loamy earth made by the breaking down of chalk.

malt *n.* barley or some other crop made ready for brewing.

malt *v.* to make barley or some other crop into malt.

malt-house *n.* building in which malt is made ready and stowed.

maltster *n.* one whose work is to make malt.

malty *adj.* of a drink with malt in it.

man *n.* 1) mankind, folk, 2) being, body, somebody, soul, 3) he, 4) husband, lover, 'old man', 5) hand, hireling, worker, working man, workman.

man *v.* 1) to fill, staff, 2) (in war) to man a ship/walls.

man-child *n.* bairn, little one, suckling, weanling.

mane *n.* long hair on the back of the neck and the shoulders of a horse.

man-eater *n.* 1) (*cannibal*) man-hunter, 2) *beast* that eats or may eat men.

manful *adj.* broad-shouldered, dogged, doughty, game, manly, stalwart, tough.

manhandle *v.* 1) to handle roughly, rough up, 2) to heave, pull, shift, shove, wield.

man-hole *n.* hole in the floor/pathway/road by which a man may get to pipes and such below.

manhood *n.* 1) full years, grown-upness, 2) manfulness, manliness, strength.

manifold *adj.* many, many-headed, many-sided.

manifold *adv.* in many ways.

manifoldly *adv.* in manifold ways.

mankind *n.* everybody, everyone, flesh and blood, man, the living, the world.

manlihood *n.* manliness, backbone, grit.

manlike *adj.* 1) manly, mannish, 2) of a woman who behaves as a man.

manliness *n.* <u>boldness</u>, fearlessness, manhood, manlihood, backbone, grit.

manling *n.* little man, small-minded man.

manly *adj.* <u>bold</u>, broad-shouldered, doughty, manful, <u>strong</u>, tough.

man-made (*artificial*) *adj.* made by man from God-made things.

mannish *adj.* 1) manlike, 2) unladylike, unwomanly.

mannishness *n.* (*incarnation*) *n.* fleshhood, infleshness.

man of the world *n.* man about town, man of business, worldly man.

manslayer *n.* killer, murderer.

man-stealer *n.* one who steals away a woman/child/other, a man-thief.

manswear *v.* to swear truthlessly.

mansworn *adj.* forsworn.

man-thief *n.* one who steals away a woman/child/other, a man-stealer.

man-trap *n.* trap for taking men who come to fish or hunt unrightly.

manward *adv.* towards man.

many *adj.* a thousand and one, ever so many, manifold, not a few, untold.

many-acred *adj.* owning wide lands.

many-hued (*variegated*) *adj.* rainbow-hued, streaked.

many-like *adj.* ever so many, manifold, many-headed, manykind, many-sided.

manyness *n.* 1) great deal, heap, hoard, lot, 2) many-sidedness, maze, web.

many-sided *adj.* 1) manifold, many-fielded, sundry, 2) clever, deft, ready.

many-sidedness *n.* 1) otherness, sundriness, 2) cleverness, deftness.

many-wintered *adj.* many-yeared, hoary-headed, old as the hills, old as time.

maple *n.* tree, often grown for its shade or for its light, hard wood.

mar *v.* to blight, cripple, eat away, gnaw at the roots, hamstring, lame, rot, rust, undo, warp, wear down, worsen, make things worse, make the bad worse.

march *n.* wild *celery*.

mare *n.* she- horse.

mare's nest *n.* a wonder.

mare's tail *n.* 1) marsh plant, 2) streaks of cloud thought to foretoken bad weather.

mark *n.* 1) mere or mear, 2) landmark, merestone, 3) earmark, hallmark, stamp, token, 4) dent, streak.

mark *v.* 1) to mark out the edges, set out the grounding of a building, mark off, 2) to betoken, show, 3) to brand, put a mark on, stamp, 4) to dent, streak, 5) (of some markworthy happening) to acknowledge, 6) to hearken to, mind.

marked *adj.* markworthy, outstanding, striking.

markedly *adv.* greatly, outstandingly, strikingly.

marker *n.* tool for marking/writing, marker-stone.

marking/s *n.* hallmark, spots.

mark-land *n.* *border*-land.

marksman, markswoman *n.* dead shot, good shot, sharpshooter.

marksmanship *n.* deftness in shooting.

mark-up *n.* the *sum* which a trader puts on to the *cost* of his goods, so that the sale thereof gives him enough for his overheads and income.

markworthy *adj.* leading, marked, outstanding, striking.

marrow *n.* 1) soft, fatty 'mush' inside bones, 2) kernel, pith, the great/main thing.

marrowbone *n.* bone in which there is eatsome marrow.

marsh *n.* marshland, salt-marsh, mere, fenland, moorland, moss, slough, wetland.

marsh-fire, marsh-light *n.* will o' the wisp.

marshland *n.* marsh, salt marsh, mere, fen, moor, moss, slough, wetland.

marshy *adj.* fenny, undrained, wet.

mash *n.* mush.

mash *v.* to beat, grind, pound, soften.

mask *n.* 1) hood, 2) blind, show.

mask *v.* to becloud, bedim, darken, hide, hood, overlay, shroud, smother.

masked *adj.* having or wearing a mask, hidden, shrouded.

mast *n.* 1) ship's mast (the upright pole from which the sails of a sailing ship are hung), 2) wireless mast.

mast *v.* to put a mast in a ship.

mast *n.* the crop of the beech, oak and other trees (being food for swine).

masted *adj.* (of a ship) having a mast or masts.

mast-head *n.* the head or top of a ship's mast.

mat[4] *n.* 1) rough web of woven rushes or sedges or such (to put down on the floor), doormat, 2) knot/mane/shock/thatch of hair.

match *n.* 1) lookalike, twin, 2) game, head-to-head, tie, 3) wedlock.

match *v.* 1) to go with, belong/hang/hold together, team with, 2) to answer, meet, twin, 3) to pit oneself against, 4) to bring together, wed, yoke.

matching *adj.* like, of like mind, twin.

matchless *adj.* greatest, highest, unmatched.

matchlessly *adv.* fully, thoroughly, truly, utterly, wholly.

matchmaker *n.* go-between.

math *n.* a mowing, the heap of mowings.

mathe *n.* grub, mad, worm.

mather *n.* one who mows grass, mower.

mattock *n.* tool for loosening hard ground or for grubbing up the stocks of felled trees. The head has an adze-shaped blade on one side and a pick on the other.

maw *n.* belly, inside/s, craw, crop, mouth, throat.

may *v.* maybe, might be, could/should/might have been.

maybe *adv.* it could be, it may be, if so be, for all one knows.

maze *n.* network, web.

me *pron.* I myself.

mead *n.* strong drink made from honey and water.

mead, meadland *n.* meadow, meadowland, water-meadow.

meadow *n.* mead, meadland, meadowland, water-meadow, grassland, grazing land.

Meadow-month (*July*) *n.* After-litha.

meadow-sweet *n.* plant of the meadows and stream edges.

meadowy *adj.* grassy.

meal *n.* the eatsome *part* of barley, corn, oats, rye, wheat and such, after being ground up, oatmeal, wholemeal.

meal *n.* board, something to eat, full meal, heavy meal, light meal, spread.

meal-time *n.* eating time, meat-tide.

mealy *adj.* like meal, made up of meal.

mealy-mouthed *adj.* honey-lipped, honey-mouthed, smooth-lipped, soft-lipped.

mealy-mouthedness *n.* fair-wording, honey-speech, soft soap, soft-speech.

mean *adj.* 1) cringing, low, not thought much of, of little worth, 2) flint-hearted, grasping, greedy, griping, hard-fisted, hard-handed, hoarding, mean-handed, penny-wise, selfish, self-seeking, shabby, sparing, stingy, tight-fisted.

mean *v.* to bear/have a meaning, mean to say, speak of, spell, stand for, tell of.

mean-hearted *adj.* hard-hearted, mean, mean-minded, narrow-minded, selfish, shabby, small-minded, unworthy.

meaning *n.* bearing, burden, flow, pith, thread, long and the short of it.

meaning, meaningful *adj.* 1) weighty, worthwhile, 2) pithy, striking, telling.

meaningfully *adv.* earnestly, forthrightly, tellingly.

meaningless *adj.* empty, hollow, unmeaning, without meaning, worthless.

meanly *adv.* badly, shamefully, unrightfully, unworthily, underhandedly.

meanness *n.* greed, greediness, selfishness, stinginess, tight-fistedness.

meat *n.* 1) fare, flesh, food, 2) heart, kernel, marrow, pith.

meat-dealer (*butcher*) *n.* meat seller.

meat-eating (*carnivorous*) *adj.* flesh-eating.

meatiness *n.* 1) fleshiness, 2) richness.

meaty *adj.* 1) full of meat, fleshy, 2) heavily built, heavy, 3) hearty, rich, weighty.

meed *n.* earnings, winnings, windfall, wish/dream come true.

meedful *adj.* worthwhile.

meet *n.* gathering of men and hounds (to go hunting).

meet *v.* 1) to come upon, fall in with, find, light upon, run into, see again, 2) to come/flock together, forgather, gather, throng, 3) to get to know, 4) to answer, fulfil, match up to, 5) to bear, go through, undergo, 6) (of *paying*) to settle.

meet, meetful *adj.* becoming, in keeping, right, aright.

meet *adv.* in a meet or becoming way, arightly.

meeten *v.* to make meet or right for.

meeting *n.* gathering, forgathering, meet, putting heads together, talks.

meeting-house *n.* 1) folkmoot, speech-house, 2) God's house.

meetly, metely *adv.* 1) fairly, rightly, 2) mildly.

meetness, meteness *n.* becomingness, rightness, timeliness, what should be.

mellow *adj.* 1) ripened, weathered, 2) kind-hearted, warm-hearted, 3) (of *flavour*) rich, smooth, sweet, 4) (of hues) deep, rich, soft, warm, 5) (of *sound*) full, rich, soft.

mellow *v.* 1) to ripen, 2) to settle, soften, sweeten.

melt *v.* 1) to melt down, run, soften, thaw, unfreeze, 2) to melt away, be gone, be lost to sight, melt into the mist, 3) to soften, unbend, warm.

men-folk *n.* men, the spear side.

mere *n.* land-locked water, pond, pool, inland sea.

mere, mear *n.* edge.

merestone *n.* landmark, hoar-stone, standing stone.

mermaid, mermaiden *n.* sea-being thought of as having the head and upper body of a woman and the tail of a fish.

merman *n.* he- sea-being.

merrily *adv.* blithely, gleefully, laughingly, light-heartedly.

merry *adj.* blithe, glad, gleeful, laughing, light-hearted, lively, sunny.

make merry *v.* to have a good time, have a night out, drive care away, drown care.

merry-hearted *adj.* blithe, bright, glad, gleeful, light-hearted, lively, sunny.

merry-maker *n.* drinker, night-outer.

merrymaking *n.* eating and drinking, mirthmaking, night out, playing.

merse *n.* low land beside a stream or the sea, a marsh.

mete (*measure*) *n.* reckoning, taking stock, weighing.

mete (to *measure*) *v.* 1) to deem, eye up, mark off, read off, reckon up, take stock, tell, weigh, weigh up, work out, 2) to mete out, hand out, share out, weigh out.

metely *adv.* see 'meetly'.

meteness *n.* see 'meetness'.

meteyard *n.* bench-mark, straight edge, yardstick.

mew (*gull*) *n.* cob.

mew[7] *v.* (of sea-birds, cats) to call.

mewl[7] *v.* to mew.

mid *adj.* middle, midmost, middlemost, middling.

mid *adv.* in the middle.

midday (*noon*) *n.* twelve o'clock, the middle of the day.

mid-daytide (*noon*) *n.* full-time of the day, middle day.

middle *adj.* halfway, inner, inside, mid, midmost, middlemost, middling.

middle *n.* 1) heart, inside, midst, the thick of things, 2) belly, midriff, waist.

middle *v.* 1) (in stockball) to strike the ball with the middle of the bat, 2) (in football) to send the ball from the edge of the field of play to the mid-field.

middle day (noon) *n.* full-time of the day, mid-daytide.

middle ear *n.* middle bit of the ear.

middle earth *n.* earth (as set between heaven and hell).

middle finger *n.* the other (*second*) finger.

middle ground *n.* 1) the ground between, 2) the middle stretch of a *painting*.

middleman *n.* one handling business for another, dealer, go-between.

middlemost *adj.* midmost, true middle, nearest the middle.

middlesharing *adj. concentric.*

middle way *n.* path between two that are over against each other.

middling *adj. adv.* all right, better than nothing, betwixt and between, fair, fairish, fair to middling, enough, good enough, barely good enough, half and half, lukewarm, middle-of-the-road, neither good nor bad, neither hot nor cold, neither one thing nor the other, neither too much nor too little, not bad, not striking, nothing to speak of, pretty good, so-so, up to the mark.

mid-field *n.* the middle of a football field.

midge *n.* gnat, small fly.

midge-net *n. mosquito* net.

mid-heaven *n.* 1) the height/utmost height (of the sun), 2) the midst of the heavens.

midland *n.* the middle stretch of a land, land that is far from the sea.

Mid-lent *n.* the fourth Sunday in Lent.

midmost *adj.* middlemost, true middle, nearest the middle.

midnight *n.* twelve o'clock at night, the middle of the night, the dead of night.

mid-off *n.* fielder on the off side, before the batsman and fairly near the *bowler.*

mid-on *n.* fielder on the on side, before the batsman and fairly near the *bowler.*

midriff *n. diaphragm.*

mid-sea *n.* the open sea.

midst *n.* bosom, depths, heart, middle, the middle stretch, thick.

midstream the middle of a stream.

midsummer *n.* midsummer's day, high summer, summertide, summertime.

Midsummer-month (*June*) *n.* Ere-litha, Fore-litha, Lida ærra, Sere ('dry')-month.

mid-ward *adv.* in the middle.

midway halfway, in the middle of, betwixt and between.

mid-week *n.* the middle of the week, Wednesday.

midwife *n.* 1) woman who helps another in childbirth, 2) one who helps bring new things to be.

midwifery *n.* the craft of helping women in childbirth.

midwinter *n.* the middle of winter, depths of winter, winter-tide, winter-time.

Midwintermonth (*December*) *n.* Ere-yule, Yule-month.

midwintry *adj.* biting, bitterly cold, freezing, icy, raw, rime-cold, winter-bitter.

might *n.* main-strength, mightiness, strength, strong right arm/hand.

mightful *adj.* full-mighty, main-hard, stalwart, strong, thickset.

mightily *adv.* greatly, lustily, strongly, with might and main.

mightiness *n.* 1) might, stalworthness, strength, 2) highness, worship.

mightless *adj.* helpless, kinless, weaponless, wretched.

mighty *adj.* broad-shouldered, burly, great-limbed, main-strong, strong, well-built.

milch *adj.* milk-giving, kept for milking.

milch-cow *n.* 1) cow kept for its milk, 2) one from whom *money* is readily drawn.

mild *adj.* harmless, sheepish, overshy, unheard, unknown, unsung, yielding.

milden *v.* 1) to become mild/milder, 2) to lessen, lighten, slacken, unburden.

mildew *n.* growth on plants/leather/wood and such, blight.

mildewy *adj.* overspread with mildew.

mildhearted *adj.* forbearing, forgiving, kindly, ruthful, sparing, understanding.

mildheartness *n.* forgivingness, kindness, mildness, ruth, understanding.

mildness *n.* kindness, mellowness, softness, warmth.

mildly *adv.* lightly, softly, soothingly, sweetly, whisperingly, yieldingly.

mile[4] *n.* length of eight furlongs or 1,760 yards.

mile[4]**-mark, milestone**[4] *n.* 1) stone at the wayside marking one mile from the last such stone, or telling the miles to the next town, 2) landmark.

milk *n.* cow's/goat's/sheep's milk, breast milk, mother's milk, curds, whey.

milk *v.* 1) to draw milk from, 2) to bleed, drain, fleece, suck dry, wring.

milk-and-water *n.* 1) milk thinned with water, hue of milk and water, 2) goosish talk or thoughts.

milk-and-waterish *adj.* wishy-washy.

milkhouse *n.* dairy.

milkiness *n.* the suchness of being milky.

milk-livered *adj.* fearful, chicken-hearted, frightened to death.

milkmaid *n.* woman who milks cows, dairymaid, dairy-woman.

milkman *n.* man who sells milk door-to-door.

milksop *n.* 1) bit of bread soaked in milk, 2) softling, weakling.

milk-tooth *n.* one of a short-lived set of teeth in young children.

milk-white *adj.* white as milk, clean white.

milky *adj.* milk-white, clouded, cloudy, white, whitish.

mill(4) *n.* 1) water-mill or windmill where corn is ground into meal, 2) grinder, hand-mill, quern, 3) works where goods are wrought (such as a steel-mill).

mill(4) *v.* to grind corn at the mill, to pound.

miller(4) *n.* workman who works a mill.

mill(4) **leat** *n.* drain or runnel cut to bring water to the mill.

mill(4) **pond**, **mill**(4)-**pool** *n.* water held back by dam (for driving the mill-wheel).

millstone(4) *n.* 1) grindstone, quernstone, 2) drag, heavy burden, load, dead weight.

mind *n.* 1) brain/s, head, thinking, thoughts, understanding, wits, 2) inner mind, heart, soul, 3) bent, leaning, readiness, will, wish, 4) belief, feeling, outlook, way of thinking, 5) scholar, thinker.

mind *v.* 1) to mislike, take amiss, 2) to be careful/wary, care about, keep an eye on, look after, look to, see to, watch, 3) to bethink, bring to mind, not forget to, see that, 4) to bend the mind to, give one's mind to, follow, heed, listen to, mark.

to be **minded** *v.* to have a mind to, set one's heart or mind on, long for.

minder *n.* keeper.

mindful *adj.* careful, heedful, wakeful, ready.

mindfully *adv.* carefully, with care, heedfully, thoroughly, watchfully.

mindfulness *n.* carefulness, foresight, forethought, heed, readiness, watchfulness.

mind-help *n.* *mnemonic.*

mind-hoard (*memory*) *n.* mind, mind-stock.

mind itch (*curiosity*) *n.* itch/thirst for finding out, mind thirst, nosiness.

mindless *adj.* 1) empty-headed, narrow-minded, small-minded, unsteady, unseeing, unthinking, unwise, wild, witless, 2) careless, heedless, thoughtless, unmindful.

mind-reader *n.* thought-reader, man/woman of insight, seer.

mind-set *n.* frame of mind, make-up, outlook, way of thinking.

mindsight *n.* inmost thoughts, insight, thought, mind's eye, thought-life, wisdom.

mind-strength *n.* breadth/depth of mind, insight, understanding, wisdom.

mind thirst (*curiosity*) *n.* thirst for finding out, seeking mind, wishing to know.

mind-wit *n.* insight, quickness, readiness, sharpness, shrewdness, wisdom.

mine *pron.* my, my own.

mingle *v.* 1) to make as one, put together, shake/stir together, weave in, 2) to be found/seen with, go about together, keep in/up with.

mingled *adj.* 1) all anyhow, upside down, 2) deep, knotted, thorny, winding.

mingle-mangle *n.* clutter, heap, mingling, mish-mash, brew, untidiness.

mingler (*extrovert*) *n.* showman.

mingling *n.* making one, putting together.

minnow *n.* small fish.

mirth *n.* gladness, glee, laughter, merrymaking.

mirthful *adj.* blithe, laughter-loving, light-hearted, lively, merry, playful.

mirthless *adj.* brooding, gloomy, grim, moody, sour, unlaughing.

misbear *v.* to behave badly.

misbecome *v.* to fall short, misbeseem.

misbecoming *adj.* unbecoming, shabby, shameful, shame-making, unworthy.

misbeget *v.* to beget unrightly.

misbegotten 1) unrightly begotten, without a name, 2) badly thought out.

misbehave *v.* to behave badly, be bad/naughty, misdo, sow one's wild oats.

misbelief *n.* benightedness, blindness, unbelief, ungrounded belief.

misbelieve *v.* to believe amiss, believe what is untrue, be blind to the truth.

misbeliever *n.* gainsayer, unbeliever, outsider.

misborn *adj.* 1) born misshapen, 2) born out of wedlock.

mis-calve *v.* to bear a still-born calf.

mischoose *v.* to choose unwisely.

misdeal *v.* to share out unfairly.

misdealing *n.* evil, foul play, sin, sinning, wickedness.

misdeed *n.* foul play, misdoing, sin, wicked deed.

misdeem *v.* to deem mistakenly, to think evil of.

misdoer *n.* knave, sinner, hardened sinner, worldling, black sheep.

misdoing *n.* evil, foul play, misdealing, sin, sinning, wickedness.

misfall *v.* to fall out amiss.

misfallen (*accidental*) *adj.* miswrought, not meant, unforeseen, unlooked for.

misfalling (*accident*) *n.* befalling.

misfare *v.* to do badly, go awry.

misfire *v.* to come to naught/nothing, fall through, go amiss/awry/badly, not go well.

misfit *n.* one-off, outsider, fish out of water.

misgive *v.* to be at a stand, falter, feel foreboding, have fears, worry.

misgiving *n.* cold feet, fear, fighting shy, wariness.

misgotten *adj.* evil-gotten, unrightly gotten.

misgrounded *adj.* groundless, ungrounded, mistaken, untrue.

mishandle *v.* to handle badly, make sad work of, misfire.

mishear *v.* to hear amiss.

mish-mash ('mash' twyfolded) *n.* heap, mingling, brew, witches' brew.

mislay *v.* to forget the whereabouts of, lose, miss, not find.

mislead *v.* to be too clever/quick for, be up to something, blindfold, hide, hoodwink, know all the answers, lie, live by one's wits, outwit, make game of, mistell, play a deep game, play the fox, play with words, pull a fast one, pull the wool over one's eyes, shift, spin a web, take in, throw dust in the eyes, twist, waylay, weave a web.

misleading *adj.* truthless, underhanded, unstraightforward.

mislearn *v.* to learn amiss, learn badly.

mislike *n.* coolness, misliking, shunning, spurning, no love lost.

mislike *v.* to hate, have no time for, loathe, not abide, shrink from, shun, spurn.

misliking *n.* coldness, hatred, loathing, shrinking from, shunning, spurning.

mismake *v.* to make badly, to unmake.

mismatch *n.* bad match.

mismatch *v.* to make a bad match.

mismatched *adj.* badly-matched, out of keeping, unlike, at sixes and sevens.

misname *v.* to misname oneself, mistake the name of.

misread *v.* to mistake the meaning, misdeem, misreckon, misunderstand, read into.

misreckon *v.* to be mistaken, make a mistake, misread.

miss *n.* misthrow, mistake, oversight, shortcoming.

miss *v.* 1) to come/fall short of, go wide of, miss the mark, 2) to mistake, overlook, 3) to lose out on, 4) to be without, lack, 5) to be late for, not go to, 6) to miss hearing/seeing, 7) to mishear, misunderstand, 8) to feel the loss of, long for.

mis-say *v.* 1) to say something amiss, 2) to blacken, speak evil against/of.

missaying *n.* miswording, slip of the tongue.

mis-see *v.* to see with warped look.

mis-send *v.* to send amiss.

mis-set *v.* 1) to forget the whereabouts of, lose, mislay, miss, 2) to upset.

misshapen *adj.* bowed, out of shape, unshapely, stooped, stooping, twisted, warped.

misshapenness (*deformity*) *n.* twisting, unsightliness, warp.

missing *adj.* 1) gone, lost, mislaid, nowhere to be found, 2) lacking, left out.

mis-speak *v.* to speak evil of, to speak shabbily/unrightly/unworthily.

misspell *v.* to spell badly/amiss.

mis-step *v.* to wander from the path.

mis-sworn *adj.* forsworn.

mist *n.* greyness, low cloud.

mistake$^{(2)}$ *n.* oversight, shortcoming.

make a **mistake**$^{(2)}$ *v.* to give oneself away, misread, put one's foot in it.

mistaken$^{(2)}$ *adj.* misled, misread, misunderstood, wide of the mark.

mistaught *adj.* kept in the dark, misled, unlearned, unread, unrightly taught.

misteach *v.* to bend the truth, mislead, teach badly, throw one off his bearings, twist.

misteaching *n.* clever (but truthless) words, hollowness, warped teaching.

mistell *v.* 1) to reckon amiss, 2) to mislead, misteach.

misthink *v.* to have sinful thoughts, to think badly of, think mistakenly.

mistime *v.* to happen amiss, time amiss, misreckon the time.

mistimed *adj.* badly timed, not in time, out of time, too soon/late for, untimely.

mistiming (*anachronism*) *n.* out of step with the times, untimeliness.

mistle thrush *n.* hollin thrush.

mistletoe *n.* plant that lives on apple trees and, sometimes, oaks.

mis-treading *n.* mis-step, misdeed.

misty *adj.* clouded, dusky, grey, shadowy, thick.

misunderstand *v.* to misdeem, misread, not see beyond one's nose, not see the wood for the trees, twist the words, read into, write into.

misunderstanding *n.* 1) misreading, misreckoning, 2) falling-out, strong words.

miswandering *adj.* missing the path.

miswedded *adj.* misbound in wedlock, misyoked.

miswend *v.* to lead aside, go from the right path, wander away.

mis-word *v.* to mis-say.

miswording *n.* missaying, miswriting, slip of the *pen*/tongue.

miswrite *v.* to mis-spell.

miswrought *adj.* misfallen, not meant, wrought awry/amiss.

misyoke *v.* to misbind in wedlock, wed amiss, wed unwisely.

mite *n.* small *insect* (such as the cheese-mite, tick).

mixen *n.* dunghill.

mizmaze *n.* maze, <u>knot</u>, weavings and windings, web.

moan *n.* 1) groan, 2) bleating, whine, 3) (of the wind) sigh, whisper.

moan *v.* 1) to bemoan, groan, 2) to bellyache, bleat, whine, whinge, be sorry for oneself, have a chip on one's shoulder, 3) (of the wind) to sigh, sough, whisper.

mole *n.* spot on the skin.

molten *adj.* aglow, melted, runny.

Monday (Moon day) *n.* Other (*Second*) day of the week.

month *n.* stretch of time of about four weeks or thirty days.

monthly *adj.* done or happening each month,

monthly *n.* *magazine* that comes out each month.

monthly *adv.* in each/every month, month by month, once a month.

mood *n.* 1) frame of mind, 2) feeling.

moody *adj.* 1) <u>fitful</u>, fretful, restless, shiftful, 2) brooding, gloomy, unforthcoming.

moon *n.* the lesser heavenly body that goes about the earth, from which light (from the sun) is thrown on to the earth.

moon *v.* to go about in a dreamy/idle/listless way (as though moonstruck).

moonbeam *n.* beam of moonlight.

moonless *adj.* black as night, dark, pitch-dark, starless, unlit.

moonlight *n.* moonshine.

moonlighting *n.* 1) slipping away by night, 2) misdoing in the shadow of night.

moonlit *adj.* lit up by the moon, flooded with moonlight.

moonmad *adj.* brain-sick, <u>mad</u>, mazed, moonstruck.

moonrise *n.* the rise of the moon, the east.

moonset *n.* the setting of the moon.

moonshine *n.* 1) moonlight, 2) unrightly traded strong drink, 3) empty/idle talk.

moonsickness *n.* <u>madness</u>, mind-sickness, clouded mind, mind-darkening.

moonstone *n.* stone through which light shines.

moonstricken, moonstruck *adj.* brain-sick, daft, <u>mad</u>, mad-headed, mazed.

moor *n.* marsh, heath.

moor-beam *n.* *mulberry* tree.

moor-dene *n.* marshy dean/dell.

moorhen *n.* a water-bird, water hen.

moorland *n.* moor, high land, upland, wild land.

moot *n.* folkmoot, gathering, meeting.

moot *adj.* bewildering, <u>knotty</u>, left open, unsettled.

moot *v.* to put forward a thought (that it might be talked through), to bring up.

moot-hall *n.* meeting hall, rede-hall, shire-hall, speech-house.

more *adj.* further, greater, new, new-found, other, over and above.

moreover *adv.* besides, furthermore, likewise, and so on, and so forth.

morn *n.* break of day, daybreak, dayspring, dawn, dawning, first light, sunrise.

morning *n.* first half of the daytime, until mid-daytide (*noon*) or the midday meal.

morning-meat *n.* breakfast.

morning-sickness *n.* a feeling sick in the morning (as for one with child).

morning-star *n.* 1) star or heavenly body seen in the morning, 2) Jesus Christ (see Revelation 22:16), 3) any forerunner of some 'dawn'.

morning-tide *n.* morning, the earlier half of the day.

morning-watch *n.* 1) (in Jewish and Roman time-keeping) the last of the three (or four) watches of the night, 2) (on ship-board) the watch between the fourth and eighth hours of the morning.

morrow *n.* 1) the day after today/a named day, 2) the time after some happening.

morrowtide *n.* morning-tide.

moss *n.* 1) marsh, marshland, moor, moorland, slough, wetland, 2) soft plant of wet lands, growing on the ground, stones, or trees.

moss-grown *adj.* overgrown with moss.

moss-oak *n.* *bog*-oak.

mossy *adj.* 1) marshy, 2) overgrown/ringed about with moss, 3) moss-like.

most *adj.* almost all, nearly all.

mostly *adv.* above all, mainly, most often, on the whole.

mote *n.* bit of dust, such as one of the specks seen floating in a sunbeam, mite, spot.

moth *n.* small *insect* which breeds in cloth.

moth-eaten *adj.* 1) eaten away by moths, 2) in holes, threadbare, well-worn.

mother *n.* 1) woman who has given birth to a child, birth mother (also foster mother, stepmother), 2) beginning, root, wellspring.

mother *v.* 1) to bear, bring forth, give birth to, 2) to care for, rear.

mothercraft *n.* craft of caring for young children as a mother.

mother earth *n.* the earth as 'mother' of all that grows and all that dwells thereon.

motherhood *n.* the suchness of being a mother, the warm feelings of a mother.

mothering *n.* 1) motherly care, 2) the wontedness (*custom*) of going to see one's mother and father on Mid-lent (Mothering) Sunday.

mother-in-law[2] *n.* the mother of one's husband/wife, good-mother.

mother-kin *n.* blood ties on the mother's side, spindle-kin.

motherland *n.* folkland, hearthland, homeland, kindred-land, land of one's forebears.

motherless *adj.* without a mother.

motherlike *adj.* like a mother, motherly, caring, kind.

motherliness *n.* motherly care, kindness, loving kindness, warmth.

motherly *adj.* caring, kind, loving, motherlike, sheltering, warm.

mother naked *adj.* as naked as at birth.

mother's son *n.* a man.

mother tongue *n.* one's birth tongue, folk speech, hearth speech, home speech.

mother wit (*common sense*) *n.* awareness, insight, quickness, quick thinking, ready wit, sharp wit, shrewdness, understanding, wisdom, wit.

mothy *adj.* overrun with moths.

mould *n.* 1) loose crumbly earth, loam, 2) the earth of the grave.

mould-board *n.* the head-board of a plough which turns over the furrow.

mould-worm *n.* earthworm, rain-worm.

mourn *v.* to bemoan, groan, shed bitter tears, sigh, sorrow, weep over.

mourner *n.* one who mourns the loss of kindred or friend.

mournful *adj.* bowed, heart-broken, saddened, sorrowful, tearful, wretched.

mourning *n.* 1) sorrowing, weeping, woe, 2) the wearing of black clothes in token of mourning over a death, widow's weeds.

mouse *n.* 1) small *beast*, field mouse, harvest mouse, house mouse, wood mouse, 2) mouse-shaped tool for working a main-reckoner (*computer*).

mouse *v.* to hunt or take mice (by cats, owls).

mouse-dun *adj.* mouse-hued.

mousefall *n.* mousetrap.

mouse-hole *n.* dwelling hole of mice, hole by which mice go in and out.

mouselike *adj.* mousy, shrinking, shy, shamefast.

mouser *n.* *beast* (such as a cat, owl) that hunts and takes mice.

mousetail *n.* stonecrop.

mousetrap *n.* trap for taking mice, mousefall.

mousing *n.* hunting and taking mice.

mousle *v.* to pull about roughly.

mousy *adj.* 1) brownish, dun, 2) hanging back, mild, mouselike, overshy.

mouth *n.* 1) lips, 2) door, gateway, opening, 3) inlet, tidefleet, outlet, outfall.

mouth *v.* to give tongue, hold forth, say, speak.

mouthfriend *n.* no true friend.

mouthful *n.* 1) bite, drop, little, 2) long name which 'fills' the mouth when said.

mouthy *adj.* loud, windy, wordy.

mow *v.* 1) to crop, cut, scythe, shear, trim, 2) to cut down, mow down.

mower *n.* 1) one who mows grass, mather, 2) mowing-*machine*.

much[2] *adj.* great, a lot of, untold.

much[2] *adv.* 1) amain, greatly, 2) a great/good deal, a lot, many times, often.

mulch *n.* wet straw, leaves and loose earth spread on the ground to shield new plants.

murder *n.* killing, shedding blood, slaying, taking life.

murder *v.* to kill, do to death, slay.

murderer *n.* cut-throat, killer, man of blood, slayer.

mush *n.* mash.

mushy *adj.* doughy, soft.

must *n.* a need, something one cannot get by without.

must *v.* to have to, have got to, need to, ought to, should.

my *adj.* of or belonging to me.

myself *pron.* me, my own self.

nail *n.* 1) fingernail, thumbnail, toenail, 2) fastening, 3) a *measure* of cloth, being 2¼ inches or one sixteenth of a yard.

nail *v.* to fasten, drive/hammer in.

nail-head *n.* the broadened head of a nail.

naked *adj.* 1) bare, mother naked, stark naked, start-naked, stripped, unclothed, shorn, unclad, in the raw, naked as the day one was born, without a stitch on, 2) helpless, shelterless, unshielded, weaponless, wide open, 3) open, stark.

name *n.* 1) first name, fore-name, father's name, kindred name, last name, couth-name, by-name, nickname, 2) bad name, fair name, good name, high name, standing, weight, worth, worthship.

name *v.* 1) to call by name, give one a name, 2) to lay at one's door, speak against.

name-book *n.* day-book, list.

name-child *n.* one named after another who is near to, or looked up to, by the namer.

named *adj.* 1) called, known as, 2) booked, branded, chidden, chosen.

name-day *n.* the day of the holy man or woman (*saint*) whose name one bears.

name-dropping *n.* naming leading folk as if well-known to one.

nameless *adj.* 1) unknown, unnamed, unheard-of, 2) dreadful, frightful, hateful.

namely *adv.* that is to say, to wit.

namesake *n.* one sharing the name of another.

nap *n.* light sleep, rest, sleep, shuteye.

nap *v.* to catnap, drop off, fall asleep, take a nap.

narrow *adj.* 1) not wide, tight, 2) lean, thin, 3) narrow-minded, small-minded.

narrow *v.* 1) to lessen, make smaller, narrow down, 2) to get narrower, shrink.

narrow-boat *n.* boat of inland waterways.

narrow-eyed *adj.* of a wary or unbelieving look.

narrowling (*bigot, racist*) *n.* hate-hound, litling.

narrowly *adv.* 1) carefully, 2) barely, hardly, 3) coldly, sternly, unbendingly.

narrow-minded *adj.* mean-minded, of set mind, small-minded, stiff, unbending.

narrow-mindedness *n.* hardness, set mind, small-mindedness, unyielding mind.

narrowness *n.* 1) smallness, 2) narrow-mindedness.

naught *n.* nothing, nought.

to bring to **naught** *v.* to make nothing, bring to nothing, put an end to, do away with, benaughten, set aside, tear up, undo, unmake, wipe out.

naughtily *adv.* 1) badly, wickedly, wilfully 2) lewdly, wantonly.

naughtiness *n.* misdoing, sinfulness, sinning, waywardness, wildness, wilfulness.

naught-like *adj.* 1) beggarly, shabby, worthless, 2) shameful, unworthy.

naughtship *n.* emptiness, hollowness, nothingness, shamelessness, wickedness.

naughty *adj.* 1) badly behaved, self-willed, wayward, 2) lewd, wanton.

nave *n.* the middle *part* of a wheel.

navel *n.* 1) small dip in the middle of the belly, 2) eye, heart, middle.

neap *n.* a tide happening shortly after the first and third fourthings of the moon, in which high water is at its lowest.

near *adj.* in the neighbourhood of, beside, nearby, next to, beside, not far.

near *v.* to come to, draw near, come on, make towards, reach, tread on one's heels.

near *adv.* nigh.

nearabouts *adv.* hereabouts, more or less, near enough, well-nigh.

nearby 1) *adv.* near at hand, not far away, within reach, 2) *adj.* neighbouring.

nearly *adv.* about, almost, more or less, nearing, near upon, not far off, roughly.

near miss *n.* a miss by only a little way.

nearness *n.* 1) anigh-ness, handiness, 2) (of time) drawing near, coming, oncoming.

near-sighted *adj.* dim-eyed, dim-sighted, groping, short-sighted.

near thing *n.* near miss, near shave.

neb, nebb *n.* bird's bill.

neck *n.* 1) the *part* of the body between the head and the shoulders, 2) the neck of a *bottle*, shirt or such, 3) land-bridge, tongue of land.

need *n.* 1) must, 2) longing, wish, 3) hardship, hunger, lack, neediness.

need *v.* 1) to behove, have to, 2) to lack, miss.

needful *adj.* needed, needwise, bound to be, binding, overriding.

needfully *adv.* all along of, because of, willy-nilly.

needle *n.* small and narrow steel tool (for sewing)

needle *v.* to goad, harry, hound, nettle, prick, spur, sting, stir up, or worry someone.

needless *adj.* beyond one's needs, not needed, on one's hands, over and above.

needle match *n.* a match on which much is seen to hang and which is keenly fought.

needlewoman *n.* seamstress.

needlework *n.* needlecraft, sewing, stitching.

needwise *adj.* needed, needful, bound to be, binding, overriding.

needy *adj.* badly off, beggared, hard put to it, hard up, in need, not blest with this world's goods, not making ends meet, not well-off, short, penniless, sore put to it, up against it, down to one's last penny, down at heel, in the red, on one's beam-ends.

ne'er *adv.* never, nevertheless.

ne'er-do-well *n.* black sheep, good-for-nothing, gossip, idler, knave, wretch.

neigh *n.* the *whinny* of a horse.

neigh *v.* (of a horse) to *whinny*.

neighbour *n.* near-dweller.

neighbour *v.* 1) to live near to, 2) to lie near/next to.

neighbourhood *n.* neck of the woods, setting, ward.

neighbouring *adj.* in the neighbourhood of, near, near at hand, nearby.

neighbourly *adj.* friendly, hearty.

neither 1) *adv.* and not, nor, nor yet, 2) *adj.* not the one or the other.

neithersome *adj.* middle-of-the-road, in between, neither one nor the other.

ness *n.* head, headland, foreland, spur, tongue of land.

nest *n.* 1) birds' nest, rats' nest, wasps' nest, 2) burrow, 3) breeding ground, den.

nest *v.* to build a nest, roost.

nestle *v.* to cuddle up, nuzzle.

nestling *n.* chick, fledgling, young bird.

net *n.* netting, network, trap, web.

net *v.* to hook, land, reap, win, gather, heap up, lay in, stow, swell.

nether *adj.* bottom, lower, underground.

nethermost *adj.* bottom most, furthest down, undermost.

netherstock *n.* stocking.

netherward *adv.* downward.

netherworld *n.* hell, lower world, underworld.

netting *n.* network.

nettle *n.* wayside plant having stinging hairs.

nettle *v.* to goad, harry, hound, needle, prick, spur, sting, stir up, or worry someone.

network *n.* 1) netting, web, 2) maze of link roads/*railways*/waterways.

networking *n.* folk with like work/cares linking up with each other (to share news).

net-yarn *n.* string for making nets.

never *adv.* 1) at no time, nevermore, never again, not ever, 2) no way, not at all.

never-ending *adj.* endless, going on and on, unbroken, unending, without end.

nevermore *adv.* never again.

never-never *n.* hire-buying, that is, buying goods with a loan which, with the *interest*, takes a long time to settle.

nevertheless *adv.* even so, however, nonetheless, notwithstanding, still, yet.

new *adj.* 1) brand-/bran-new, ground-breaking, latest, new-fangled, new-looking, 2) green, new-found, new-made, 3) new to, never seen before, unknown.

new-blown *adj.* (of *flowers*) newly opened.

new-born *adj.* born but now.

new broom *n.* hard worker, tireless worker.

new-come *adj.* but lately come.

newcomer *n.* incomer, latecomer, new broom, outsider, settler.

newfangled *adj.* latter-day, outlandish, unwonted.

newfarer *n.* newcomer, incomer, latecomer.

new-found *adj.* but lately found (as of lands over the sea) or thought up.

newish *adj.* fairly/pretty well/somewhat new.

new-laid *adj.* laid but now.

newly *adv.* anew, lately, latterly.

newlywed *n.* young husband, young wife.

newly-wed *adj.* wed but now, honeymooning.

new moon *n.* 1) the moon when first seen, 2) the time of the new moon.

new-mown *adj.* newly cut, mown but now.

newness *n.* greenness, unlikeness.

news *n.* gossip, hearsay, the latest, tidings, word.

newshound n. gossip writer, writer.

newsman *n.* gossip writer, newshound, one in the know.

news-writer *n.* leader-writer, writer, newshound.

newsy *adj.* full of news, gossipy, windy, wordful.

newt *n.* eft, water *creature*.

new wording (*paraphrase*) *n.* bewording, unfolding.

new-year *n.* the coming year, the beginning of another year, the first days of the year.

next *adj.* following, later, nearest, neighbouring.

next *adv.* afterwards, then, thereafter.

next door *adv.* 1) the door of the neighbouring house, 2) almost, near to, nigh.

nickname *n.* a name given laughingly or indearingly.

nickname *v.* to give someone a nickname.

nigh *adj.* at hand, near, next, upcoming.

nigh *adv.* 1) about, alongside, at one's door/elbow/feet, at the threshold, fast by, hard by, next door, not far, under one's nose, within earshot/hearing/sight of, within a stone's throw, 2) all but, almost, in a fair way to, nearly, near upon.

nigh hand *adv.* 1) near at hand, nearby, 2) almost, nearly.

night *n.* dark, darkness, dead of night, night-time, night-tide, night watches.

night-bird *n.* 1) bird of the night (owl, nightingale), 2) one who reads/works late at night, 3) house-breaker, thief.

night-clothes *n.* nightwear.

night-crow *n.* bird (owl or nightjar) thought to croak in the night as a warning of death or other evil.

nightfall *n.* dusk, evening, eventide, gloaming, sunset, twilight.

night-gloom *n.* darkness of night.

nightingale *n.* a bird of thickets and overgrown *gardens*.

night-life *n.* night-meeting (at a 'watering hole') to drink with friends, high life.

night-light *n.* short thick candle kept burning all night to give light in a sick-room.

night-long *adj. adv.* 1) lasting all night, 2) through the whole night.

nightly *adj.* coming by night, done by night, dark as the night, of the night-time.

nightly *adv.* at/by night, each night, every night, night after night, through the night.

nightmare *n.* 1) dark elf that falls upon the sleeping, hell-fiend, 2) bad dream, wild dream, 3) bad time, hell on earth, ordeal, thin time.

nightmarish *adj.* dreadful, frightening, frightful, ghastly, grisly, harrowing.

night-old *adj.* a day old.

night-owl *n.* 1) owl that comes out at night, 2) one who reads/works late at night.

nightshade *n.* plant with bitter and harmful berries.

night-shift *n.* 1) nightwear, 2) shift of men who work by night.

night-shirt *n.* nightwear.

night-song *n.* 1) the last worship-time of the day (*compline*), 2) cradle-song.

night-spell *n.* spell wrought either to keep away or wreak harm at night.

night-tide, night-time *n.* dark, darkness, dead of night, night watches.

night-walker *n.* one who walks out by night (most often to do evil).

night-watch *n.* 1) watch and ward by night, 2) one of the watches of the night.

night-watchman *n.* watchman.

night-work *n.* work set to be done by night.

nimble *adj.* light-footed, lively, quick.

nimble-come-quick *adj.* of quick growth.

nimble-fingered *adj.* handclever, handy, deft, quick, ready.

nimble-footed *adj.* light-footed, on one's toes, quick, quick-footed, speedy.

nimbleness *n.* lightness, quickness.

nimble-witted *adj.* quick-thinking, ready-witted, sharp-witted, shrewd, witful, wise.

nimbly *adv.* busily, quickly, readily, smartly.

nine *n. adj.* the root *number* following eight.

ninefold *adj.* made up of nine together, nine times as great or as many.

nineteen *n. adj.* the root *number* made of ten and nine.

nineteenth *adj. n.* 1) the marking *number* that is kin to nineteen, 2) nineteenth share of something.

nine-tenths *n.* nine tenths of the whole, almost the whole of something.

ninety *n. adj.* the root *number* that is nine times ten.

ninth *adj. n.* 1) the marking *number* that is kin to nine, 2) ninth share of something.

ninthly *adv.* in the ninth *place*.

nipple *n.* tip of a woman's breast, tit.

nit *n.* 1) the egg of a louse or such that lives on man and beast, 2) the *insect* itself.

nitty *adj.* full of nits, overrun with nits.

no *adj.* hardly any, not any.

no *intj.* nay! never! nothing of the kind!

no *n.* a gainsaying, saying no, thumbs down.

nobody 1) *pron.* no one, not a soul, 2) *n.* lightweight, man of straw, small man.

noll *n.* top of the head, the head as a whole.

none *pron.* 1) not any, nothing, not a bit, 2) nobody, no one, not a soul, not one.

nonesuch, nonsuch *n.* match-winner, one in a thousand, the best, wonder, worthy.

nonesuch, nonsuch *adj.* greatest, matchless, one and only, wonderful, worthful.

nonetheless *adv.* even so, nevertheless, notwithstanding, still, whether or no, yet.

nor *conj.* *negative* link-word.

north *adv.* in/towards the north, northwards.

north *n.* that length of the earth's rim which lies on the left-hand when looking towards the rising sun.

north *adj.* 1) belonging to/lying towards/of the north, looking towards the north, 2) (of the wind) blowing from the north.

north about *adv.* by a northerly way (such as about the north of Scotland).

north-east *adv.* in that path lying midway between north and east.

north-east *n.* that length of the earth's rim which lies between north and east.

north-east *adj.* 1) set in/towards the north-east, 2) blowing from the north-east.

northeaster *n.* wind or storm blowing from the north-east.

north-easterly *adj.* lying towards the north-east, blowing from the north-east.

north-easterly *adv.* towards the north-east.

north-eastern *adj.* of the north-east, lying on the north-east side.

north-eastward *adv.* towards the north-east.

north-eastward *n.* the north-east fourthing.

north-eastward *adj.* set towards the north-east.

north-eastwardly *adv.* towards the north-east.

north-eastwardly *adj.* 1) set/leading towards, 2) blowing from the north-east.

northerly *adv.* to the northward, from the north, on the north side.

northerly *adj.* 1) set towards the north, northern, 2) blowing from the north.

northern *adj.* 1) coming from/living in/lying to the north, 2) blowing from the north.

northerner *n.* dweller in the north.

northernmost, northmost *adj.* set farthest to the north.

northing (or southing) *n.* *latitude*.

northland *n.* northern land or hundred.

north-right *adv.* dead/straight north.

North Sea *n.* the sea between the British Islands, Scandinavia and Holland.

north star *n.* the *pole* star.

northward/s *adv.* to/towards the north.

northward *adj.* that which goes or looks northward.

northwardly *adv.* to/towards the north, from a northern fourthing.

north-west *adv.* in that path lying midway between north and west.

northwester *n.* wind or storm blowing from the north-west.

northwesterly *adj.* 1) lying towards the north-west, 2) blowing from the north-west.

northwesterly *adv.* towards the north-west.

northwestern *adj.* of the north-west, lying on the north-west side.

north-westward *adv.* towards the north-west.

north-westward *n.* the north-west fourthing.

north-westward *adj.* set towards the north-west.

north-westwardly *adv.* towards the north-west.

north-westwardly *adj.* 1) set/leading towards, 2) blowing from the north-west.

nose *n.* bill, neb.

nose *v.* 1) to nose out, smell out, pick up news, 2) to edge/inch forward, shove.

nosedive *n.* dive, drop, header, sharp fall, swoop.

nosedive *v.* to dive, drop, fall sharply, go down, go under, sink.

nose-wise *adj.* full of oneself, looking down on one, too clever by half.

nosey, nosy *adj.* busybody, gossiping.

nostril *n.* one of the openings in the nose.

not *adv.* the *adverb* of *negation*.

nothing *n.* 1) naught, nought, 2) nothingness, 3) no great deal, nothing to it.

bring to **nothing** *v.* to bring to naught, make nothing, undo, unmake, wipe out.

nothingness *n.* emptiness, hollowness, nothing at all, unmeaningness, worthlessness.

no-thoroughfare *n.* lane/path/road from which there is no way out at one end.

notwithstanding 1) *prep.* even if, even though, 2) *adv.* however, nevertheless, nonetheless, still, though, yet, 3) *conj.* although.

nought *n.* naught, nothing, nothingness.

now *adv.* anon, at once, betimes, forthwith, soon, straightway.

nowadays *adv.* in these times, now, these days, today.

noway/s *adv.* in no way.

nowhere *adv.* not anywhere, no-whither.

no whit *adv.* not at all, not the least.

nowhither to no *place*, nowhere.

nowise *adv.* in no way, not at all.

nozzle *n.* small *spout*.

numb *adj.* benumbed, deadened, frozen, unfeeling.

numb *v.* 1) to benumb, deaden, freeze, 2) to knock out, unman.

numbed with fear *adj.* frozen with fear, in a cold sweat, fearful.

numbing *adj.* dreadful, frightening, ghastly, fearsome.

nut *n.* 1) kernel, seed, stone, hazel-nut, walnut, 2) small bit of (holed) iron or wood, by which a bolt is made fast.

nut-beam *n.* nut-tree.

nut-brown 1) *adj.* of the hue of a ripe hazel-nut, of a warm reddish-brown hue, brown as a nut, 2) *n.* brown hue as of nuts.

nutshell *n.* the hard outside of a nut.

nutting *n.* the business of gathering nuts.

nut-tree *n.* a tree that bears nuts, nut-beam.

nutty *adj.* 1) having lots of nuts, nut-like, 2) mad, out of one's mind.

nuzzle *v.* to cuddle up, nestle.

oaf *n.* churl, clout-shoe, lout, rough.

oafish *adj.* churlish, clod-hopping, lewd, loutish, rough, short, uncouth.

oafishness *n.* backwardness, slowness, thick-headedness, unwisdom.

oak *n.* tree from which comes the strongest, toughest and most long-lasting wood.

oak-apple *n.* the oak-*gall* which grows on the leaf-*bud* of the oak.

oak-beam *n.* oak tree.

oaken *adj.* made of oak wood.

oak-meal *n.* acorn meal.

oak-rind (*bark*) *n.* the 'skin' of the oak tree.

oakum *n.* 'off-combings', that is, the threads of unpicked rope.

oar *n.* strong pole with a blade at one end, for driving a boat through the water.

oarlock *n.* rowlock.

oarsman *n.* rower.

oast *n.* kiln for drying *hops*.

oast-house *n.* building housing a kiln for drying *hops*.

oats *n.* a *hardy grain* crop.

oaten *adj.* made from oatmeal.

oath *n.* 1) plighted word, sworn word, 2) curse, filthy/foul speech, swear word.

oatmeal *n.* meal made from oats.

o'clock[(4)] *n.* of the clock, that is, the time as shown by the clock.

o'er *adv.* over.

of *prep.* about, by, from, of late, on, out of.

off *adv.* aside, away, elsewhere, from here, hence, out.

off *adj.* 1) flown, gone, 2) all off, 3) bad, foul, high.

off and on *adv.* by fits and starts, first one and then the other, fitfully, sometimes.

offbeam *adj.* outlandish, out of the way, unearthly, unheard of, weird.

offcut *n.* a bit cut off (from wood or such), left-over.

offer *n.* 1) bid, fair offer, feeler, 2) (in shopping) deal, giveaway, good buy.

offer *v.* to bid, come up with, hold out, put forward, put in for, speak to, talk to.

offering *n.* 1) gift, 2) burnt-offering, sin-offering, thank-offering.

offhand, off-handed *adj.* 1) light-minded, thoughtless, 2) unfeeling, uncouth.

offing *n.* the sea some way out from the shore.

offish *adj.* cool, standoffish, unforthcoming, unfriendly, unwelcoming.

offlet *n.* drain-pipe, water-pipe, water outlet.

off-line[(4)] *adj.* not on-line, not linked-up (and therefore not working).

offload *v.* to see the back of, shift, 2) to take off, unload, unship.

off-peak *adj.* happening outside peak times (such as faring by train, or buying *electricity* for the home, outside busy times).

off-putting *adj.* upsetting, unsettling.

offset (*compensate*) *v.* to even up, make good, make up for, set against, set off.

offshoot *n.* 1) offspring, seed, stem, stock, 2) outgrowth, spin-off.

off side 1) (in football, *hockey*) on the *wrong* side, 2) (in stockball/*cricket*) the side of the field over against that on which the batsman stands.

offspring *n.* afterkin, brood, children, one's flesh and blood, young.

off-the-tongue word (*exclamation*) *n.* screech, shout, yell.

off-white *adj.* greyish.

oft *adv.* many a time and oft, oft-times, oftentimes, time after time, time and again.

often *adv.* again and again, every day, oftentimes, oft-times, over and over again.

oftentime/s *adv.* many a time, often, oft-times, time after time.

oft-time/s *adv.* many a time and oft, often, oftentimes, time and again.

old, olden *adj.* elderly, full of years, grey, grey-haired, hoary, hoary-headed, many-wintered, old as the hills, old as time, one foot in the grave, timeworn, toothless.

olden *v.* to grow old, go grey, wither, show one's years.

older *adj.* earlier born, elder.

old-fangled *adj.* behind the times, of other times, old world, timeworn, outworn.

old-lore (*mythology*) *n.* elder-saying/s, tales of the long-ago days.

old maid *n.* elderly spinster.

oldness *n.* eldership, ripeness.

old-right *n.* long-held right.

old-saying/s *n.* elder lore, old-lore, words of the forefathers.

old-tale (*myth*) *n.* folk tale, dream-tale.

old-time *adj.* bygone days, old/olden days, when time began, yesteryear.

old-world *n.* behind the times, of other times, of old, of yore, old-fangled.

on 1) *prep.* on top of, resting on, 2) *adv.* at length, for a long time.

on *adj.* working.

on and off see 'off and on'

onblowing (*inspiration*) *n.* leading, stirring, inblowing, inbreathing, on-breathing.

once *adv.* 1) once in a way, once only, one time only, 2) at any one time, at all, ever, only, 3) once for all, for all time, for ever, for good, 4) formerly, long ago, in the old days, in times gone by, once upon a time.

one *n. adj.* the lowest of the root *numbers* – one thing, without any more.

onefold *adj.* lone, one, one-off, only, only one, only one of its kind, one and only.

one-handed *adj.* 1) having only one hand/good hand, 2) done with only one hand, 3) by oneself, without help.

one-hearted *adj.* 1) bound together, like-minded, of one mind, well-knit, 2) knightly, manly, straightforward, true-hearted, upright.

one-horn *n.* unicorn.

one-eyed *adj.* blind in one eye, having only one eye.

one-minded *adj.* 1) (*united*) like-minded, one-hearted, of one mind, well-knit, 2) (*single*-minded) steadfast, strong-minded, unshaken, unshrinking, unyielding.

one-mindedness *n.* 1) (*unity*) oneness, wholeness, holding together, meeting of minds, understanding, 2) (*single*-mindedness) doggedness, one-mindedness, <u>steadfastness</u>, steadiness, strength of mind/will, tirelessness.

oneness *n.* 1) (*individuality*) bent, kind, make-up, selfhood, 2) (*unity*) one-mindedness, wholeness, holding together, meeting of minds, understanding.

one-off *adj. n.* 1) the only one made, 2) one and only, matchless, unmatched.

one-rede (*unanimous*) *adj.* at one, one-hearted/-minded, of like mind, of one mind.

oneself, one's self *pron.* one's own self, no other.

one-sided *adj.* 1) uneven, unfair, unrightwise, 2) narrow-minded, weighted.

onesome *adj.* full, uncut, whole.

one-someness (*virginity*) *n.* maidenhead, maidenhood.

one-up *adj.* better, cut above, <u>greater</u>, higher, outmatching, outstanding.

one-upmanship *n.* craft, gamesmanship, lifemanship, wit.

ongoing *n.* 1) goings-on, 2) going ahead, headway.

ongoing *adj.* 1) growing, unfolding, 2) endless, never-ending, unending, unbroken.

on-line[4] *adj.* linked-up (and therefore working).

onlooker *n.* beholder, bystander, eyewitness, look-out, looker-on, watcher.

only *adj.* one, one and only, lone, first and last.

only *adv.* at most, no more than, but, nothing but, barely, hardly.

only-begotten *adj.* begotten as an only child, one and only.

onset *n.* 1) drive, strike, swoop, 2) beginning, coming, nearing, rise, start.

onset *v.* to beset, <u>fall upon</u>, harry, make an onset, set upon, storm, strike at.

onsetter *n.* foe.

on side *n.* 1) (in football, *hockey*) one's true/right side, 2) (in stockball) that side of the field which is behind the batsman's back when he stands at the *wicket*.

onto *adv.* to a *place* on/upon.

onward/s *adv.* ahead, beyond, forth, forward/s, on.

onwardness *n.* forward steps, making headway, making great strides, ongoing.

on-writing (*inscription*) *n.* carved writing, wording, words.

ooze *n.* slime.

ooze *v.* to bleed, drip, give off, give out, leak, overflow with, seep, sweat, weep.

oozy *adj.* slimy.

open *adj.* 1) ajar, unbolted, undone, unfastened, unlocked, wide open, opened out, unfolded, 2) above board, open and above board, bald, aright,

downright, forthright, forthcoming, outspoken, straight, straightforward, <u>true</u>, truthful, truth-telling, <u>upright</u>, 3) friendly, open-handed, open-hearted, open-minded, welcoming, ready and willing.

open *v.* to throw open, unbolt, unclasp, unfasten, unlock, undo, untie.

open door *n.* 1) openness to free trade, 2) freedom, free hand, free field, opening.

open-ended *adj.* open to more than one meaning/reading/understanding.

opener *n.* 1) tool for opening (such as a tin-opener), 2) (in stockball) one of the two batsmen who open the innings for the batting side.

open-eyed *adj.* alive to, all eyes, missing nothing, wide <u>awake</u>.

open field *n.* broad field that is neither hedged nor walled, held and tilled in *strips* by the ham-dwellers (*villagers*).

open-handed *adj.* free-handed, great-hearted, unselfish, unsparing, unstinting.

open-hearted *adj.* 1) childlike, <u>open</u>, straightforward, truth-telling, 2) friendly, hearty, great-hearted, kind, kind-hearted, kindly, warm, warm-hearted, welcoming.

opening *n.* inway, doorway, gateway, way in, way through, way to, open door.

openly *adv.* 1) forthrightly, above-board, 2) shamelessly, wantonly.

open-minded *adj.* broad-minded, fair-minded.

open-mouthed *adj.* amazed, bewildered, filled with wonder.

openness *n.* forthrightness, outspokenness, straightforwardness, truthfulness.

open out *v.* to lay open, open up, spread before one, undo, unfold.

open sea *n.* the deep, fathomless deep, great deep, great sea, high seas, great waters, the main, the sea, the waves, wide sea.

open time *n.* time in which an inn, shop or such is open.

open up *v.* to bring to light, lay open, say what is on one's heart, throw open.

open-work *n.* wrought work (such as iron-work, netting) with in-between *spaces*.

or[2] *conj.* a word set between that on the one hand and that on the other.

ordeal *n.* bitterness, grind, hard going, <u>hardship</u>, load, nightmare.

ore *n.* *mineral* in which there is enough iron, lead or such to make it worth working.

other *adj.* 1) one of the two, *second*, 2) further, new, 3) another, far from it, unlike.

otherlander (*alien, foreigner*) *n.* outsider, outlander, wanderer, incomer, newcomer.

otherly *adv.* otherwise, in another way.

otherness *n.* the suchness of being other, unlikeness.

othersome *adj.* some other.

other-speaking, other-telling (*allegory*) *n.* under-telling, undersong, forlikening.

otherwhere *adv.* elsewhere.

otherwhile/s *adv.* 1) at one time or other, sometimes, 2) at other times.

otherwise *adv.* 1) or, or else, if not, 2) in other ways, 3) in another way.

otherworld *n.* 1) heaven, the world to come, the unseen world, 2) underworld.

otherworldliness *n.* 1) ghostliness, shadowiness, unearthliness, 2) earnestness, godliness, godly fear, goodness, hallowedness, holiness, heavenly-mindedness.

otherworldly *adj.* 1) dark, ghostly, shadowy, uncanny, unearthly, weird, 2) godly, good, heavenly-minded, holy-minded, holy, not of this world, unworldly.

otter *n.* fur-bearing water *beast*, which swims strongly as it hunts for fish.

ought *n.* right thing, what ought to be done, what is owing, what is up to one.

ought *v.* 'helping' (*auxiliary*) word for speaking of that which is right/should be.

our *pron.* our own, of or belonging to us.

ours *pron.* our one/s, that or those belonging to us.

ourself, ourselves *pron.* us, our own selves.

ousel, ouzel *n.* blackbird, coaly bird, colly bird.

out *adv.* 1) abroad, from home, gone away, not in, out of doors, 2) cold, dead, ended, 3) in full blossom, 4) (of goods for sale) in the shops, on sale, 5) wide of the mark, wildly out, 6) (of a clock) fast, slow, losing, 7) out in the open, shown up.

out *v.* 1) to drive out, put out, send out, smoke out, throw out, 2) to speak out.

out and out *adj.* downright, outright, sheer, thoroughgoing, utter, 'dyed-in-the-wool'.

outbid *v.* 1) to outdo in bidding, 2) to go one better, outdo, outmatch, outplay.

outboard *adj.* set on the outside of a boat or ship.

outborn *adj.* born outside the homeland, otherlandish, outlandish.

outbreak *n.* 1) burst, outburst, break-out, 2) onset, uprising, 3) outcrop.

outbuild *v.* to outdo in building, to overbuild.

outbuilding *n.* a building outside the main building, outhouse.

outburst *n.* blast, bluster, roughness, storminess, uproar, wildness.

outcome *n.* end, ending, fall-out, upshot.

outcrop *n.* the cropping out of a stone-layer above ground.

outdare *v.* to be bold, dare, fear nothing, set at naught, show fight.

outdo *v.* to beat all comers, be more than, be too much for, be better at, go beyond, go one better, leave standing, outbid, outmatch, outplay, outride, outrun, outshine, overshadow, put in the shade, throw into the shade, top, overtop.

outdoor *adj.* outlying, outside.

outdoors *adv.* out of doors, outside.

outdraught *n.* outward draught, backwash of a wave.

outdrink *v.* to drink dry, drink more than.

outer *adj.* outdoor, outermost, outlying, out-of-the-way, outside, outward.

outermost *adj.* farthest out from the inside or middle, most outward.

outfall *n.* outlet or mouth of a *river* or drain, outflow.

out-field *n.* 1) outlying land of a steading, 2) (in stockball) that stretch of the field of play furthest away from the pitch.

out-fielder *n.* (in stockball) one of the fielding side who watches a stretch of out-field.

outfight *v.* to fight better than, beat, outmatch, overcome, put to flight, worst.

outfit *n.* 1) clothes, clothing, things, wear, 2) loads, stock, wherewithal.

outfitter (*tailor*) *n.* clothes-maker, clothier, breeches-maker, seamstress, seamer.

outflow *n.* flow, outfall, overflow, stream.

outfly *v.* to outdo in flight, to fly beyond.

outfoot *v.* to outdo in footing it, outrun.

outgate *n.* way out.

outgoing *n.* going out, withdrawing.

outgoing *adj.* 1) former, late, one-time, 2) friendly, open, warm.

outgoings *n.* outlay, overheads.

outgrow *v.* 1) to grow faster than, grow taller, 2) to grow out of.

outgrowth *n.* 1) limb, outcrop, shoot, 2) offshoot, outcome, spin-off, upshot.

outhouse *n.* outbuilding (barn, horse-stall, wash-house or such).

outing *n.* day out, drive, ride, run.

outknave *v.* to outdo in wreaking evil.

outland/s *n.* 1) another land (other than one's homeland), 2) outlying land/s.

outland *adj.* 1) outborn, outlandish, otherlandish, 2) outlying.

outlander *n.* otherlander, outsider, incomer, newcomer.

outlandish *adj.* 1) (*foreign*) rootless, kinless, wandering, unfriended, 2) offbeam, out of the way, unheard of, <u>weird</u>.

outlast *v.* to <u>abide</u>, last longer than, live longer than, live on after, outlive.

outlasting *adj.* <u>abiding</u>, everlasting, long-lasting, unending.

outlaugh *v.* to laugh at, laugh down.

outlaw[(2)] *n.* lordless man, outlander, outsider, wanderer, wretch.

outlaw[(2)] *v.* to ban, lay under a ban, drive away/out, send away, throw out, warn off.

outlay *n.* outgoings, overheads.

outleap *n.* to leap further than, leap beyond or over.

outleas *n.* meadland away from the house.

outlet *n.* 1) shop, 2) opening, outgate, way out.

outlier *n.* an outlying *part* of anything, such as a stone outcrop some way from the main outcropping.

outline[(4)] *n.* a drawing out of the key goals and findings of a work, pith.

outlive *v.* to abide, keep going, live longer than, live on after, outlast.

outlook *n.* 1) frame of mind, mood, way of looking at things, 2) forelooking, foreseeing, looking forward, 3) setting, sight.

outlying *adj.* faraway, far-off, outer, out-of-the-way.

outmatch *v.* to be more than a match for, beat hollow, better, leave behind, <u>outdo</u>.

outmost *adj.* farthest off/out, most outward, outermost.

out of *prep. phr.* from within, outside.

out-of-door/s 1) *adj.* outside, 2) *n.* the world outside the house.

out-of-the-way *adj.* 1) far, in the middle of nowhere, lonely, outlying, 2) far-fetched, outlandish, unwonted, <u>weird</u>.

outplay *v.* to beat, outmatch, <u>overcome</u>, overwhelm, sweep aside/away, worst.

output *n.* growing, making, shaping, yield.

outreach *v.* 1) to go one better, go beyond, leave standing, <u>outdo</u>, outgo, outmatch, 2) to overreach, outwit, 3) to reach out to, reach out for.

outride *n.* 1) to ride out, 2) to ride better/faster/farther than.

outrider *n.* forerunner, pathfinder.

outright *adj.* out-and-out, sheer, thoroughgoing, utter, 'dyed-in-the-wool'.

out-room *n.* an outlying room, outbuilding, outhouse.

outrun *v.* 1) to beat, leave behind, leave standing, outmatch, 2) to <u>outdo</u>, outreach.

outrunner *n.* forerunner, pathfinder.

outsail *v.* to outdo in sailing, to sail faster or farther than.

outsee *v.* to see beyond, see further.

outsell *v.* to sell more than.

outset *n.* a setting out, beginning, early days, opening, start, starting out.

outsettler *n.* one who settles in outlying lands, outsider.

outshine *v.* to be head and shoulders above, leave standing, <u>outdo</u>, outmatch.

outshoot *v.* to shoot beyond/farther, to shoot better than.

outside *n.* outer side, shell, topside.

outside *adj.* 1) abroad, outer, outermost, outdoor, outward, 2) unlikely.

outside *adv.* out, outdoors, out-of-doors, out of the house, without.

outsider *n.* fish out of water, wanderer, widefarer.

outsmart *v.* to be too clever for, be too quick for, outfox, outthink, outwit.

outspin *v.* to spin a thread to its full length.

outspoken *adj.* downright, <u>forthright</u>, free-spoken, <u>open</u>, straightforward.

outspread *n.* field, spread, stretch, sweep.

outspread *v.* to open out, spread out, stretch, stretch out, unfold.

outspreading *n.* broadening, growing out, stretching, unfolding, widening.

outstanding *adj.* 1) cut above, good, great, well-known, 2) marked, matchless, outmatching, stirring, striking, 3) (of a reckoning) ongoing, owing, unsettled, 4) left, not done, undone, unfulfilled.

outstare *v.* to brazen it out, browbeat, look one up and down.

outstep *v.* to overstep, step outside of, step beyond.

outstretch *v.* to stretch out, stretch forth, outspread, stretch beyond.

outstretched *adj.* lengthened, opened out, spread, stretched, unfolded.

outstride *v.* to take a longer stride, outgo, leave standing.

outthink *v.* to be too clever for, be too quick/sharp for, outfox, outwit.

outwalk *v.* to walk faster/farther than, to walk beyond.

outward *adj.* outer, outermost, outside.

outwardly *adv.* as far as one can see, at first sight, on the outside, to the eye.

outwards *adv.* towards the outside.

outway *n.* way out, outgate.

outweary *v.* to forweary, overweary, tire out, wear down, wear out, weary.

outweigh *v.* to override, overweigh, weigh heavy.

outwit *v.* to <u>hide</u>, hoodwink, live by one's wits, outfox, outthink, <u>mislead</u>, take in.

outwork *n.* 1) outer shield of a stronghold, 2) work done outside the workshop.

outworking *n.* end, handiwork, outcome, upshot.

outworn *adj.* 1) threadbare, tired, worn-out, 2) behind the times, timeworn.

outwrought *adj.* done thoroughly, wrought well.

oven *n.* baking-oven.

ovenware *n.* the bowls, pots and pans *used* for baking in an oven.

over *n.* 1) *flat*-topped ridge or hill-spur, tongue of uplifted ground in marshland, 2) (in stockball/*cricket*) the six balls *bowled* by one player from one of the *wickets* (another player then *bowling* from the other *wicket*).

over *adj.* greater/higher (in standing), upper.

over *adv.* above, atop, on top of, on high, upon.

over *prep.* above, higher than, more than, upwards of.

overall/s *n.* clothing worn over one's everyday clothes to keep the latter clean.

overall *adv.* 1) all over, all through, everywhere, 2) <u>above all</u>, above all things, beyond everything, beyond telling, the more so, utterly, 3) all in all, in the main, mostly, on the whole.

overall *adj.* full, whole

over and above *adv.* <u>above all</u>, beyond, over the mark, the more so.

over-arm *adj.* (in stockball/*cricket*) *bowling* done with the hand above the shoulder, over-hand.

overbear *v.* to bend, browbeat, override.

overbearing *adj.* over-mighty, overweening, grinding, hard, heavy-handed, high and mighty, high-handed, iron-handed, iron-heeled, threatening, unsparing.

overbid *v.* to bid more than the worth of a thing, outbid.

overboard *adv.* over the side of a ship, over the side and into the water.

over-bold *adj.* <u>heedless</u>, hot-blooded, hot-headed, over-daring, quick-hearted.

overbuild *v.* 1) to build over/upon, 2) to put up more buildings than are needed.

overburden *v.* to load, overload, saddle with, snow under, weigh down.

overburdened *adj.* careworn, harrowed, laden, loaded, <u>shaken</u>, weighed down.

overbuy *v.* 1) to buy for more than the worth, 2) to buy more than one can afford.

over-cliff *n.* overhanging cliff.

overcloud *v.* 1) to become cloudy, cloud over, 2) to throw a shadow over.

overcome *v.* 1) to overmatch, override, overrun, overthrow, overwhelm, beat, beat down, beat hollow, be more than a match for, benumb, browbeat, be too good for, be too much for, break, bring down, bring to naught, cut the ground from under one's feet, fell, fill with fear/dread, get the upper hand, have a walkover, <u>hold down</u>, knock down, lay by the heels, outdo, do for, outmatch, outplay, outshine, put an end to, put to flight, put down, quell, send to the bottom, strike down, swallow up, sweep aside/ away, thrash, throw down, tread under foot, undo, wind about one's little finger, wipe out, worst, 2) to <u>bewilder</u>, startle, strike dumb, take aback, take one's breath away.

overcome *adj.* amazed, <u>bewildered</u>, knocked back, numbed, <u>shaken</u>, thunderstruck.

over-crafty *adj.* <u>crafty</u>, knavish, misdealing, <u>sharp</u>, too clever by half.

overcrowded *adj.* choked, crammed, overflowing, overloaded, seething, teeming.

over-dare *v.* 1) to dare too much, be headstrong, 2) to overcome by great daring.

over-daring *adj.* headlong, <u>heedless</u>, hot-hearted, over-bold, quick-hearted.

over-dear *adj.* dear, dearly bought, pretty penny, steep, stiff, worthly.

overdo *v.* to go too far, make overmuch of, make too much of, not know when to stop, overwork, take too far, 'do to death', lay it on thick.

overdone *adj.* 1) burnt to a cinder, overcooked, leathery, 2) far-fetched, overblown, over much, too much, overplayed, put on, showy.

overdraft *n.* *sum* borrowed from the *bank* by drawing over and above what one has put by there, borrowing, owings.

overdraught *n.* draught going over a fire, or let in from above the fire.

overdraw *v.* 1) to draw from a *bank* more than one has put by there, 2) to blow up, greaten, heighten, make too much of, overdo, overplay, <u>overreckon</u>, stretch the truth.

overdrive *n.* (within the workings of a *vehicle*) way of making the *propeller* shaft turn more quickly than the output shaft of the *gearbox*, so getting a higher *gear ratio*.

over-drunk *adj.* utterly drunk.

over-earnest *adj.* too hearty, too keen.

overeat *v.* to cram, fill oneself, make oneself sick, not know when to stop, overdo it.

overfall *n.* breakers, broken water, foaming sea, sea-foam, spray, swell, white horses.

over-far *adj.* long way away, too far away, too far to go.

over-fare *v.* 1) to go over, go from one side to the other, 2) to bridge, span.

over-fat *adj.* much too fat, overweight, pot-bellied.

over-fed *adj.* fleshy, overweight, pot-bellied.

over-feed *v.* to eat too much, cram, wolf.

overfill *v.* to fill to overflowing, fill up.

over-fish *v.* to fish beyond what can be put back through breeding.

overflood *n.* drowning, flood, flooding, overflow, welling over.

overflow *n.* flood, flooding, spill, overspill.

overflow *v.* to be many, burst with, run over, spill over, swarm, teem, well over.

overflowing *adj.* bursting, coming thick and fast, filled to overflowing, flooding, full, rich, running over, streaming, swarming, teeming.

overfly *v.* to fly over or beyond, to fly faster or higher than.

overfold (in earthlore/ *geology*) *n.* folding over of stone layers until such are upside down.

overfold *v.* 1) to fold over, 2) (in earthlore/ *geology*) to drive stone layers over until these overhang or overlie what were formerly the upper layers.

overforward *adj.* brazen, overfree, over-weening, shameless, uppish.

overforwardly *adv.* brazenly, shamelessly, uppishly.

overforwardness *n.* brazenness, shamelessness, uppishness.

overfree *adj.* too free, brazen, shameless.

overfreely *adv.* brazenly, shamelessly, uppishly.

overfull *adj.* bursting, filled to overflowing, more than enough, overmuch, too many, running over, streaming, too much.

over-greedy *adj.* craving, grasping, greedy, wolfish.

overground *adj.* being above ground.

overgrow *v.* to grow over, grow too great, choke, overrun, overspread.

overgrown *adj.* choked, overrun, weed-ridden.

overgrowth *n.* too great or too quick growth, growth over/upon something.

overhand *adv.* 1) upside down, 2) out of hand, 3) with the hand above/over that which it holds.

overhang *n.* 1) overhanging (of a ledge or such), 2) outreaching of the upper *parts* of a ship beyond the bows and stern.

overhang *v.* 1) to overtop, stand out, stick out, 2) to overshadow, threaten.

over-hard *adj.* stone-hard, too hard, truly hard.

overhead 1) *adv.* above, on high, up above, 2) *adj.* overhanging.

overheads *n. costs* over and above the bare *costs* of making goods.

overhear *v.* to come to know, gather, get wind of, listen in.

over-heat *v.* to become too hot, burn, seethe.

over-heated *adj.* 1) flushed, glowing, 2) overwrought, seething, worked up.

over-heedful *adj.* overwrought, harrowed, in dread, dreading, writhing, fearful.

over-high *adj.* high up, truly high.

over-keen *adj.* over-earnest, too keen by half.

overkill *n.* doing much more than is needed to win some end, going too far.

over-king *n.* great king, high king, overlord, all-wielder.

overlade *v.* to burden, overload.

overlaid *adj.* 'clothed', overspread.

overland *adv.* by land.

overland *adj.* (of the way to somewhere) faring/going over land.

overlap *n.* the edge of one thing overlying the edge of another.

overlap *v.* to lap over, overlie somewhat, run against/into.

overlay *n.* overlap, top-layer.

overlay *v.* to 'clothe', hide, overspread.

overleaf *adv.* on the other side of the leaf (of *paper*).

over-leap *v.* to leap over, leap to the other side of, leap too far.

overleather *n.* the upper leather of a shoe.

overlie *v.* to lie over/upon, overhang.

over-lip *n.* the upper lip.

overload *n.* too great a load/burden.

overload *v.* to burden, overburden, saddle with, snow under, weigh down.

overloaded *adj.* burdened, laden, loaded, snowed under, weighed down.

overlong 1) *adv.* for too long a time, 2) *adj.* too long, late, wearisome.

overlook *v.* 1) to have no time for, have nothing to do with, 2) to be blind to, shut the eyes to, 3) to overshadow, overtop, stand over.

overlord *n.* head, leader, high king, over-king, over-wielder.

overlordship *n.* headship, leadership, lordship, wieldship.

over-loud *adj.* deafening, dinning, ear-rending, full-throated, loud, lusty.

overly *adv.* above all, fully, indeed, over and above, strongly, truly, utterly, wholly.

overman *n.* foreman, overseer.

over-many *adj.* more than enough, overmuch, too many, too much.

overmatch *v.* to be more than a match for, outmatch, outplay, overcome.

over-mighty *adj.* high and mighty, high-handed, overbearing, overweening.

overmuch[(2)] 1) *adj.* more than one looked for, overhigh, too many, too much, 2) *adv.* needlessly, overly, too much.

overnight 1) *adv.* through the night (until the following morning), 2) *adj.* of/ belonging to the evening before, done overnight.

overpitch *v.* (of the *bowler* in a game of stockball/*cricket*) to pitch the ball too far, that is, beyond a good length.

overplay *v.* to overdo, overdraw, overplay one's hand, overreach, overreckon.

overreach oneself *v.* to be too clever by half, bite off more than one can chew, have too many irons in the fire, overbid, overdo, overplay one's hand, overstep.

overreckon *v.* to give too much weight to, make much ado, make overmuch of, make/think too much of, overdo, overdraw, make heights out of hillocks.

over-rede *v.* to bring over, make one believe, put over, settle, talk into, win over.

override *v.* to bend, browbeat, drive into, overbear.

over-ripe *adj.* gone beyond its best, too ripe.

overrun *v.* to overcome, overthrow, overwhelm, put to flight.

over-sail *n.* topsail.

oversale *n.* playing the *market* by the forward selling of more goods than can be made over.

oversaying (*hyperbole*) *n.* overshooting, truth-stretching, word-stretching.

oversea/s 1) *adv.* abroad, beyond the sea, 2) *adj.* across the seas.

oversee *v.* to handle, head, lead, keep an eye on, look after, run, see to, steer.

overseer *n.* foreman, hard driver, head, headman, hirer, overman, steward.

over-sell *v.* 1) to sell at more than the true worth, 2) to sell more than one can make over, or more than there is.

overset *v.* to knock down/over, spill, upend, upset.

oversew *v.* to sew overhand, sew together two bits of cloth or leather.

overshadow *v.* to outdo, put in the shade, throw into the shadow.

overshine *v.* to shine over/upon, outshine.

overshoe *n.* a shoe worn over one's everyday shoe (to keep it from wet or filth).

overshoot *v.* 1) to go beyond, 2) to shoot an arrow beyond, overshoot the mark.

overside *adv.* over the side of a ship (into the sea or into a smaller boat).

oversight *n.* 1) care, handling, overseeing, running, steering, steersmanship, stewardship, 2) misdoing, misreckoning, mistake, carelessness, forgetfulness.

oversleep *v.* to sleep beyond the time.

oversleeve *n.* outer sleeve over one's everyday sleeve.

overslide *v.* to slide away, glide over.

oversow *v.* to sow other seed in a field already sown.

overspan *v.* to bridge over, bestride, go over, straddle.

over-speak *v.* to drone on, go on and on, go on too long, talk too much.

overspill *n.* overflow, the folk of an overcrowded town who need to be housed somewhere else.

overspread *v.* 1) to spread something over, overlay, smear on, 2) to spread out/over.

overstep *v.* to go beyond, go too far, not know when to stop, overplay.

overstock *v.* to lay in too much stock, overfill.

overstretch *v.* to over-work, mar, run through.

overstrew *v.* to strew something over something else.

overstride *v.* to stride over, to take long strides.

overstrung *adj.* highly strung, overquick.

overswell *v.* to swell so as to overflow.

overtake[(2)] *v.* 1) to go beyond/by, leave behind/standing, outgo, 2) to go one better, outdo, outmatch, 3) to befall, come upon, 4) to overwhelm, swallow up.

overthrow *n.* downfall, tearing down, undoing, unmaking, wiping out.

overthrow *v.* to overcome, overwhelm, outmatch, outplay, throw down, undo.

overtime *n.* time put in beyond the day's work, overwork.

overtire *v.* to drain, tire out, weary.

overtop *v.* 1) to dwarf, overlook, rise above, 2) to better, come out on top, go beyond, leave/put in the shade, outdo, outmatch, outshine, overshadow, top.

over-tread *v.* 1) to tread under foot, 2) to hold down, quell, ride roughshod over.

overturn *v.* to overcome, undo, unmake, bring to naught.

overwash *v.* to wash or flow over something, to wash by flowing over.

overwatch *v.* to keep watch over, keep watch all through the night.

overweary *v.* to outweary, tire out, wear down, wear out, weary.

overweening *adj.* above oneself, high-handed, overbearing, over-mighty.

overweeningly *adv.* high-handedly, overbearingly, uppishly.

overweigh *v.* 1) to outweigh, 2) to weigh down, overburden.

overweight *adj.* fat, fleshy, heavy, pot-bellied, well-fed, broad in the beam.

overweight *v.* 1) to overburden, overload, weight too heavily, 2) to give too much weight to, make too much of.

overwhelm *v.* to overcome, overthrow, outmatch, outplay, overrun, put to flight.

overwhelmed *adj.* amazed, bewildered, overcome, shaken, speechless.

overwhelming *adj.* amazing, bewildering, gripping, overriding, striking, telling.

over-wield *v.* to have the upper hand over, override, oversee, steer.

over-wielder *n.* high king, over-king, leader, overbearing lord.

over-wind *v.* (of such as a clock) to wind too far.

overwinter *v.* to bide through the winter, get through the winter.

over-wise *adj.* too wise, putting on a show of wisdom, wearing one's wisdom.

overword *n.* word or saying said or sung again and again.

overwork *n.* work over and above one's time and/or strength

overwork *v.* 1) to over-stretch, wear out, 2) to work hard, overdo it.

overworked *adj.* driven into the ground, ground down, hard-driven, worn out.

overworked words (*cliché*) *n.* well-worn saying, worn-out saying.

overworn *adj.* much worn, worn out, the worse for wear, threadbare.

over-wreak *v.* to outmatch, outplay, overcome, overrun, overthrow, overwhelm.

overwrite *v.* 1) to write over, write something over other writing, 2) to write too much about something, wear oneself out with writing.

overwrought *adj.* forstraught, harrowed, high-strung, high-wrought, worked up.

owe *v.* to be beholden to, be overdrawn, be in the red.

owing *adj.* outstanding, owed, unsettled.

owl *n.* a night hunting bird.

owlish *adj.* one who reads/works/goes about late at night, one who is wise-looking.

owl-light *n.* the dim light in which owls go forth, half-light, nightfall, twilight.

own *adj.* one's own, belonging, in one's hand/hold, owing nothing to, unshared.

own *v.* 1) to be the owner of, have to one's name, 2) to acknowledge, bear witness.

owner *n.* holder, deed holder, freeholder, landlord, landlady, landowner.

ownership *n.* grasp, holding, rightful ownership.

own-speech (*idiom*) *n.* folk-speech, folkwording, heart-speech, home speech.

ox *n.* *beast* of the steading, the he- ox being a 'bull' and the she- ox a 'cow'.

ox-bow *n.* a bend in a *river* making a half-ring, also the land within the bend.

ox-eye *n.* the ox-eye daisy (and other plants).

oxherd *n.* keeper of oxen, cowherd, herdsman.

ox-horn *n.* horn of the ox, sometimes *used* as a drinking horn.

oxlip *n.* plant sprung from a mingling of the cowslip and the *primrose*.

ox-stall *n.* stall for oxen.

ox-tail *n.* tail of the ox, taken for food.

oxter *n.* arm-pit, underside of the upper arm.

ox-tongue *n.* 1) tongue of the ox, 2) tongue-shaped plant.

paddock *n.* field, meadow, parrock, pen.

pail *n.* milk-pail.

pailful *n.* as much as will fill a pail.

pan *n.* bowl, pot.

parrock *n.* paddock, pen, small field/meadow.

path *n.* bridle-path, bypath, byway, footpath, towpath, walk, footway, pathway.

pathfinder *n.* forerunner, leader, way-leader, wayfinder.

pathless *adj.* lonely, untrodden, wayless, wild.

pathway *n.* bridle-path, bypath, byway, footpath, towpath, walk, footway.

peak *n.* 1) brow, high land, hilltop, horn, ridge, 2) height, highwater mark, pitch, top, 3) peak for a cap (to shade the eyes).

peak *v.* to be at its height, come to a head, reach the top.

peaked *adj.* having a peak, rising to a peak.

pebble *n.* small *round* stone worn down by water (in a stream or on the strand).

pebble *v.* to strew with pebbles, to roughen leather (so that it looks as if pebbles have been rammed down on it).

pebbled *adj.* strewn with pebbles, pebbly.

pebble-stone *n.* pebble.

pen *n.* fold, pinfold, pound.

pen *v.* to gate, impound, keep in, shut up.

penniless *adj.* down and out, empty of, needy.

penny *n.* English *coin* (there being 240 to the pound).

pennyweight *n.* weight-mete, being at first 1/240 of a Tower pound and reckoned at 22½ *grains* (the weight of a silver penny). Later, in Troy weight, there were 24 *grains* to a pennyweight, and twenty pennyweights made one *ounce* Troy weight.

penny-wise *adj.* sparing, stinting.

pennyworth *n.* 1) the goods which might be bought for a penny, 2) that which is of little worth.

penstock *n.* 1) water-gate for holding back water, then freeing it to flow from the pen to the water-mill, 2) pentrough.

pent *adj.* 1) penned in, shut in, 2) pent up (as of sorrow, wrath 'penned' within).

pentrough *n.* trough or leat taking water from the pen (where it has been held) to the wheel of a water-mill.

pewit *n.* lapwing, lapwinch.

pick *n.* tool for breaking up the ground, pickaxe, mattock.

pick *n.* 1) choosing, picking out, 2) the chosen few, salt of the earth.

pick *v.* 1) to wield a picking tool (as in 'to pick the teeth', 'pick holes in'), 2) to gather, harvest, 3) to choose, handpick, pick and choose, settle on/upon, 4) to pick a *pocket*, pick open a lock, break into, break open, 5) to pick/start a fight. stir up.

pickman *n.* (*miner*) one who hews with a pick.

pick on *v.* to give the rough edge of one's tongue, curse, run down, smear.

pick out *v.* to choose, mark out, settle on/upon.

pick up *v.* to gather, lay in, lay up, put by, stock up.

pig *n.* 1) swine, boar, sow, 2) greedy pig, 3) fiend, hound, rough, wretch.

piggish *adj.* belly-worshipping, overfed, swinish, wolfish.

pig-headed *adj.* headstrong, self-willedstiff-necked, wilful.

pigsty *n.* 1) pen or sty for pigs (with a shed), swine-cote, 2) filthy house/hole.

pigtail *n.* braid of hair hanging down from the back of the head.

pike *n.* pick, pickaxe.

pike *n.* fish.

pike *n.* weapon with a wooden shaft and a sharp head of iron or steel.

pikeman *n.* fighting man wielding a pike.

pikeman (*miner*) *n.* pickman, one who hews with a pick.

pill, pyll *n.* pool or wide inlet.

pimple *n.* boil, pock, swelling.

pin[4] *n.* nail, needle.

pinfold *n.* fold, pen, pound.

pinner *n.* a reeve having the work of impounding *beasts* that have wandered.

pintle *n.* 1) *penis*, 2) bolt.

pipe[4] *n.* drain, main, outlet, shaft, drain-pipe, water-pipe, windpipe.

pit[4] *n.* 1) hole, hollow, 2) coal-pit, shaft.

pitch *n.* tar.

pitch *n.* 1) pitching forward of a ship in heavy seas, 2) (in stockball) the sending down of the ball and the way it lands, 3) field of play, ground, 4) height, peak, top, 5) (in songcraft) key, 6) slope.

pitch *v.* 1) to heave, send flying, shoot, throw, 2) (in stockball) to pitch up.

pitched *adj.* 1) (in war) of a hard-fought field-fight (as against a raid or running fight), 2) (of the slope of a roof), high-pitched, low-pitched.

pith *n.* 1) soft inside of plants, 2) burden, main thing, heart, kernel, marrow.

pithy *adj.* not long in telling, put in a nutshell, in a few well-chosen words.

plant[5] *n.* 1) wort, meadwort, moorwort, 2) stock, tools, mill, workshop.

plant[5] *v.* to bed out, grow, root, seed, sow, till.

plash *n.* a shallow stretch of standing water, a marshy pool, a puddle.

plashy *adj.* fenny, marshy, undrained, wet.

play *n.* 1) the play of light (on leaves, water and such), 2) freedom, free play, full play, free field, give, leeway, room, elbowroom, slack, sweep, swing, 3) children's play, 4) the playing of a game, 5) gambling, gaming, 6) show, playcraft.

play *v.* 1) (of the sunlight) to alight on/play on (leaves, water and such), 2) to play a game, play against, match oneself, 3) to finger, make love to, play games with, play with, while away the time, 4) to play songcraft (on harp, pipe or such), 5) to play a *part*, tread the boards, make a show of, put on.

play-book *n.* book of plays.

playcraft (*acting*) showmanship.

play-day *n.* day for play, school holiday.

player *n.* (*actor, actress*) player, playman/woman, star player, leading man/lady, showman/woman.

playful *adj.* light-hearted, lively, merry.

playfully *adv.* light-heartedly, lightly, merrily.

playgoer *n.* follower, onlooker, first-nighter

playground *n.* playing-field, school playground.

playhouse (*theatre*) *n.* show hall/house.

playing-field *n.* school field for games.

play-off *n.* a game played again after a draw or tie.

plaything *n.* 1) children's *toy*, 2) one who is played with (by another, or by the foreweaving of life) then lightly thrown off.

playtime *n.* 1) time for children's play, 2) holidaying, holiday-making.

play-tired *adj.* of children tired in the evening after a day's play.

playwright *n.* writer of plays.

plight *n.* 1) death-trap, harm, shadow, threat, 2) oath, plighted word, troth-word, a word given to another.

plight *v.* to bind oneself, give/plight one's word, mean what one says, take oath.

plough[(2)] *n.* tool for breaking up the ground ready for sowing, sullow.

plough[(2)] *v.* to break up the ground, furrow, till.

pock *n.* boil, pimple, swelling.

pockmarked *adj.* pitted, pocked.

pocky *adj.* pimply.

pole[(4)] *n.* 1) post, stake, 2) rod (five and a half yards).

poll *n.* 1) head, top of the head, 2) the reckoning of heads, 3) taking stock of what folk think about some business (by asking such), 4) the choosing of a spokesman/ spokeswoman at the polls.

poll *v.* to give one's *vote*, to win *votes* at the polls.

pond *n.* dew-pond, fish-pond, millpond, pool, mere, water-hole.

pondweed *n.* weed that grows in ponds and still waters.

pool *n.* 1) land-locked water, mere, pond, water-hole, fish-pool, millpool, swimming pool, 2) wide inlet, haven.

pore *v.* to delve into, give one's mind to, <u>learn</u>, read up, bury oneself in one's books.

pot[(4)] *n.* bowl, crock, pan.

potter *v.* to potter about, do nothing much.

pound[(4)] *n.* 1) weight-mete, being sixteen *ounces* (or twelve *ounces* Troy weight), 2) English *money* reckoning, being at first one pound weight of silver of the worth of 240 pence.

pound *n.* pen, fold, pinfold, yard.

pound *v.* 1) to beat, crumble, grind, mill, 2) (of the heart) to heave, quake, quiver.

pound *v.* to gate, impound, infold, keep in, pen, shut in, shut up.

pounding *n.* 1) cudgelling, hammering, thrashing, 2) beating.

pout *v.* to make the lips swell out as a mark of being put out.

pox *n.* a sickness marked by pocks on the skin (such as chicken-pox, small-pox).

prettily *adv.* bewitchingly, becomingly, sweetly, winningly, winsomely.

prettiness *n.* comeliness, fairness, loveliness, winsomeness.

pretty *adj.* bewitching, comely, fair, <u>lovely</u>, shapely, willowy.

pretty *adv.* fairly, rather, somewhat.

prick *n.* cut, light wound, stab wound, pin prick, smart, sting, prickle.

prick *v.* 1) to cut, spear, stab, stick into, sting, wound, 2) to harrow, unsettle, upset.

prick-eared *adj.* <u>awake</u>, on the watch, all ears, missing nothing, <u>heedful</u>, ready.

prickle *n.* prick, smart.

prickle *v.* to itch, smart, sting, twitch.

prickly *adj.* 1) brambly, briery, bristly, comblike, rough, sharp as a needle, spear-like, swordlike, thistly, thorny, 2) bearish, churlish, crabbed, fiery, roughly-spoken, sharp-tongued, shrewish, <u>unfriendly</u>, vixenish, waspish.

puddle *n.* 1) small body of slimy standing water, 2) a mingling of clay, sand and water, making a water-tight lining for *canals*.

puddle *v.* to make puddle, line with puddle.

puff *n.* 1) blast, breath of wind, draught, 2) a smoke.

puff *v.* 1) to breath hard/heavily, fight for breath, 2) to smoke, blow smoke-rings.

pull *n.* 1) drag, heave, tow, 2) draw, spell, witchery, 3) (in stockball) a shot which sends a ball pitched on the off side over to the on side, 4) short spell of rowing.

pull *v.* 1) to draw out, gather, pick, pull out, take out, uproot, 2) to drag, draw, heave, tow, 3) to rend, stretch, tear, wrench, 4) to row.

pull down[(6)] *v.* to <u>undo</u>, <u>unmake</u>, bring to <u>naught</u>, put an end to.

pull out *v.* to back out, draw back, leave, pull back, withdraw.

pullover *n.* sweater, woolly.

pull through *v.* to be all right, come through, live to fight another day.

pull up *v.* to draw up, <u>stop</u>.

put *v.* 1) to lay out, set down, set out, settle, 2) to frame, say, word, 3) to lay/set before, 4) to reckon.

put about *v.* 1) to lay a sailing ship on a new *tack*, 2) to give out, say out.

put asunder, put away *v.* (of breaking wedlock) to come between, drive a wedge between, <u>sunder</u>, unthread, unweave.

put back *v.* to give back, hand back, make good, put/set right.

put by *v.* to <u>gather</u>, hoard, lay in, lay up, stock up, stow.

put down[(6)] *v.* to <u>overcome</u>, overthrow, quell, put an end to, lay in the dust.

put-down[(6)] *n.* belittling, shaming, showing up.

put forth *v.* 1) to come up with, moot, put forward, set forth, 2) to blossom, unfold.

put forward *v.* to bring up, come up with, put forth, set forth.

put it about *v.* to give out, make known, put over, spread the word, tell the world.

put off *v.* 1) to lay over, play for time, sidestep, 2) to shake, throw, unsettle.

put on *v.* to heap on, strengthen, yoke to.

put out *v.* 1) to drive away, throw out, 2) to put someone out, nettle, unsettle, upset, 3) to quench, smother, stamp out.

put over *v.* to put it about, spread the word abroad, get the word out.

put straight *v.* 1) to straighten out, tidy up, 2) to put/set right, righten, upbraid.

put through *v.* to deal with, get something done, take steps.

put to *v.* to make an offer, moot, put forward.

put together *v.* to bring/draw together, draft, draw up, gather, lay together, set up.

put up *v.* 1) to build, run up, set up, 2) to put up at, dwell in, live in, take rooms.

put upon *v.* to bear hard on, burden, lean hard on.

put up with *v.* to abide, forbear, go along with, swallow.

putt *n.* (in *golf*) a stroke which sends the ball along the putting-green to the hole.

putt *v.* (in *golf*) to strike the ball lightly and carefully on the putting-green.

quake *n.* earthquake, quaking.

quake *v.* 1) to shake, 2) to shake/ shrink with fear, stand in dread.

quake-hearted, quaking *adj.* fearful, shaking, shivering, shrinking with fear.

quaking-grass *n.* kind of grass.

quaky *adj.* given to quaking.

quaver *n.* a shake or quivering of the *voice*.

quaver *v.* to flicker, flutter, quiver, shake, thrill.

quean *n.* 1) a strong, healthy young woman, 2) over-bold woman, hussy, wanton.

queen *n.* 1) one who is the wife of a king, or queen in her own right (as eldest daughter of a king who had no son to follow him), 2) leading lady, leading light.

queenhood *n.* queenship.

queenlike *adj.* great, high, queenly, worthful, worthy.

queenliness *n.* bearing, becomingness, greatness, highness, worth, worthship.

queenly *adj.* 1) great, high, worthful, worthy, 2) comely, ladylike, winsome.

queen-mother *n.* widow of the late king and mother of the new king/queen.

queenship *n.* queenhood.

quell *v.* to overcome, overwhelm, kill, put an end to, put down, strike down.

quelm *n.* sickness.

quench *v.* 1) to end, put out, smother, stamp out, 2) to allay, slake.

quencher *n.* a good drink (that thoroughly quenches one's thirst).

quern *n.* hand mill.

quern-bill (*chisel*) *n.* edged tool, hardhew.

quern-stone *n.* one of the two stones of a quern, millstone.

quern-teeth *n.* grinding (*molar*) teeth.

quick *adj.* 1) lively, nimble, light-footed, swift-footed, 2) quick-witted, quick-thinking, keen-witted, nimble-witted, ready-witted, sharp-witted, shrewd, wise.

quick-beam *n.* aspen, upland (*mountain*) ash.

quicken *n.* upland (*mountain*) ash.

quicken *n.* couch grass, quitch, twitch.

quicken *v.* 1) to speed up, 2) to breathe new life into, stir into life, strengthen.

quick-fire *n.* brimstone, *sulphur*.

quick-hearted *adj.* burning, hot-blooded, hot-hearted, maddened, wild.

quick-lime *n.* lye, cleaner, cleanser, soap.

quickly *adv.* before long, betimes, forthwith, shortly, soon, straightway.

quickness *n.* 1) liveliness, lightness, nimbleness, readiness, 2) sharpness, shrewdness, readiness, cleverness, wisdom, insight.

quicksand *n.* 1) bed of loose wet sand which will readily swallow up anything that rests on it, 2) trap for the unwary.

quickset *n.* 1) cuttings of plants set in the ground to grow, 2) quickset hedge.

quick-sighted *adj.* awake, far-sighted, keen-minded, sharp, sharp-witted.

quicksilver *n.* *mercury.*

quick step *n.* the step *used* when going at quick time (which see).

quick-thinking *adj.* bright, keen-witted, quick-witted, sharp, wise, witfast, witful.

quick-thorn *n.* hawthorn.

quick time *n.* stepping out at 128 steps of 33 inches (118 yards) every *minute*, or four miles every *hour*.

quick-tree *n.* aspen.

quick-witted *adj.* bright, quick-thinking, ready-witted, sharp, wise, witful.

quitch *n.* couch grass, quicken, twitch.

quiver *v.* to flicker, flutter, quake, quaver, shake, thrill.

quoth said.

race[2] *n.* 1) a run, foot-race, horse-race, boat-race, 2) mill-race.

rack[1] *n.* frame, framework, holder, stand.

rafter *n.* roof-beam.

raid *n.* break-in, breakthrough, inroad, onset, storm, swoop.

raid *v.* to housebreak, make off with, reave, steal from, thieve.

raider *n.* night-runner, reaver, <u>thief</u>, wolf.

rain *n.* cloudburst, drenching rain, drizzle, raindrops, rainfall, showers.

rain *v.* to be wet, drizzle, rain hard, come down in sheets.

rainbow *n.* heavenly-bow, shower-bow.

raindrop *n.* a drop of rain.

rainfall *n.* 1) shower, 2) reckoning (in inches) of the rain that has fallen in the year.

rain-water *n.* water that has fallen as rain.

rain-worm *n.* earthworm, mould-worm.

rainy *adj.* drizzly, showery, wet.

rake[2] *n.* tool having teeth and a long handle, *used* for drawing together grass, hay and such, or for smoothing over broken up ground.

rake *v.* 1) to draw/gather together, rake in, 2) to go over with a rake so as to make smooth, 3) to rake through, <u>seek</u>, 4) (in war) to fire upon, straddle, sweep with shot.

ram *n.* 1) he- sheep, 2) striking (*battering*) ram, ram set at the bows of a warship.

ram *v.* to drive into, hammer, hit, run against, run into.

rammer *n.* wooden tool with a heavy head, for ramming down earth and/or driving stones into the ground.

ramrod *n.* rod for ramming down the *charge* in a mouth-loading *gun*.

ramson *n.* wild garlic.

rank *adj.* 1) froward, high and mighty, showy, strutting, 2) (of growth) rich, thick, 3) bad, foul, high, off, sickening, stinking, strong-smelling, unwholesome.

rare *adj.* (of meat) underdone.

rash *adj.* headstrong, <u>heedless</u>, hot-blooded, hot-headed, hot-hearted, reckless, wild.

rashness *n.* <u>heedlessness</u>, recklessness, unwariness, wildness.

rat[4] *n.* 1) black rat, brown rat, 2) bad lot, knave, tell-tale, twister.

rather *adv.* 1) a little, fairly, somewhat, 2) more truly, 3) instead, sooner.

raven *n.* a great bird of the crow kind.

raw *adj.* 1) uncooked, 2) green, <u>unfledged</u>, unhewn, unwrought.

raw-boned *adj.* bony, fleshless, half-starved, <u>lean</u>, shrunken.

reach *n.* 1) grasp, stretch, sweep, 2) straight stretch of *river* between two bends.

reach *v.* to reach one's goal, come to, fetch up at, make land.

reachless *adj.* bottomless, fathomless, unfathomful.

read *n.* spell of reading.

read *v.* 1) to read up, 2) to read dreams/riddles, 3) to put a meaning on, understand by, 4) to delve into a field of learning at a seat of learning.

reader *n.* book lover, book reader, bookworm.

readership *n.* following.

readily *adv.* 1) freely, gladly, heartily, willingly, 2) at once, in no time, quickly, right away, smoothly, speedily, straight away.

readiness *n.* 1) forethought, <u>foresight</u>, heed, watchfulness, 2) deftness, awareness, cleverness, insight, liveliness, quickness, sharpness, <u>wisdom</u>, wit, 3) willingness.

reading *n.* 1) reading up, 2) knowledge, learning, book learning, lore, wide reading, wisdom, 3) reading out loud, giving a reading from a written work, 4) reading of a draft law in *parliament*, 5) the wording of a written work.

reading-glass *n.* a greater hand-glass.

reading-room *n.* room set aside for reading, bookroom.

reading-stand *n.* *desk*, writing-board, writing-stand.

ready *adj.* 1) at the ready, in readiness, readied, ready saddled, in the saddle, <u>awake</u>, foreseeing, forewarned, keyed up, on the look-out, on the watch for, standing by, 2) aware, businesslike, keen-thinking, quick, quick-thinking, ready-witted.

ready-witted, aware, quick, quick-thinking, keen-thinking.

ready *v.* to make ready, put in readiness, do one's homework/spadework, lay the groundwork, draft, draw up, lay out, mark out, put into shape, straighten out.

be **ready** *v.* to <u>foresee</u>, look ahead, take steps, think ahead, think out, think through.

ready-made *adj.* ready-to-wear, off-the-rack.

ready-reckoner *n.* small book of lists that help with everyday rime-telling.

ready-to-wear *adj.* ready-made, off-the-rack.

ready-witted *adj.* <u>bright</u>, quick-witted, <u>sharp</u>, sharp-witted, shrewd, <u>wise</u>.

ready-worded *adj.* flowing, ready, running on, smooth, smooth-spoken.

ream *n.* *cream*, milk-ream.

reap *v.* to gather up, heap up, lay in, lay up, put by, stock up, stow.

reaper *n.* harvester.

reaping-iron[6] *n.* sickle.

reaping-time *n.* harvest time.

rear *v.* 1) (of children) to bring up, care for, foster, 2) (of *beasts*) to breed, keep.

rearmouse, reremouse (*bat*) *n.* flitter-mouse.

reave, reive *v.* to bear off, cut out, make off with, steal, swoop on, thieve, waylay.

reaver, reiver *n.* night-runner, raider, wolf.

reaving *n.* raiding, theft.

reck *n.* care, heed.

reck *v.* 1) to be heedful, 2) to be worried.

reckless *adj.* headstrong, heedless, hot-headed, hot-hearted, rash, wild.

recklessly *adv.* heedlessly, hot-headedly, rashly, wildly, hand over head.

recklessness *n.* heedlessness, over-daring, rashness, unwariness, wildness.

reckon *v.* to answer for, to hold a thing to be such and such, to work out.

reckoner *n.* 1) *calculator*, 2) bookkeeper, rimer, teller.

reckoning 1) bookkeeping, reckoning (of the worth of work done, or of *monies* coming in and going out), riming, telling, weighing, 2) *revenge*

reckon up *v.* to rime, tell, work out, take stock.

red *adj.* of the hue of berries/blood/fire, ruddy.

redbreast *n.* reddock, ruddock

red deer *n.* a kind of deer, of a reddish-brown hue.

redden *v.* 1) to dye/make red, 2) to go red (with wrath or shame), blush.

reddish *adj.* half-red, somewhat red.

reddle, ruddle *n.* red *ochre* dye, once widely *used* by shepherds to mark sheep.

reddle, ruddle *v.* to wash over with reddle.

reddleman *n.* dealer in reddle.

rede (*advice*) *n.* word/words of wisdom, input, steer, warning, word of warning.

rede (*advise*) *v.* to give rede, open the mind, put right, warn, give warning, forewarn, steer, help, hint, give one to understand, have one know, put it to one.

redecraft (*logic, rhetoric*) *n.* 1) redelore, wisdom, 2) redespeech, speech-weaving.

rede-fast *adj.* deep, farsighted, shrewd, thinking, understanding, wise, witful.

rede-giver *n.* redesman, thinker, wiseman.

rede-hall *n.* meeting hall, moot-hall, shire-hall, speech-house.

redeless *adj.* 1) unwise, unwitful, witless, 2) bewildered, forstraught.

redelore (*logic*) *n.* redecraft, thinking, understanding, wisdom.

redesman (*adviser, councillor*) *n.* rede-giver, wiseman, thinker, far-seer, long-head.

redespeech (*rhetoric*) *n.* redecraft, speech-weaving.

redewise *adj.* deep-thinking, farsighted, thoughtful, understansing, wise.

red-handed *adj.* in the midst of misdoing, having yet the marks thereof.

redhead *n.* having a head of red hair.

red heat *n.* the suchness of being red-hot, that heat which makes something red-hot.

red herring *n.* 1) herring that has become red by being smoked, 2) that which misleads or makes for loss of time, sideshow.

red-hot *adj.* 1) afire, burning, glowing, searing, seething, white-hot, 2) hot-blooded, in the glow of heightened/quickened/stirred feelings, on fire, thrilling.

red-tape *n.* the hedges and hurdles made by reevedom and its *paperwork*.

reechy *adj.* reeky, smoky.

reed/s *n.* the tall straight stems of some water plants.

reed-bird *n.* bird living in reedbeds.

reeden *adj.* made of reeds, reed-like.

reedmanship (*calligraphy*) *n.* fair-hand, fair-writing, handwriting-craft.

reed name (*alias*) *n.* *pen*-name.

reed-water *n.* reedy stretch of water.

reed-writ (*pen*) *n.* reed-*pen*, writing-reed, writing-feather.

reedy *adj.* stretch of water that is full of reeds.

reek *n.* 1) smoke from burning *stuff*, 2) smell, strong smell, stench, stink.

reek *v.* 1) to give off smoke, 2) to smell, stink, 3) to bear the stamp/mark of.

reeky *adj.* smoky, blackened with smoke.

reel *n.* small wheeler (*roller*) for winding such as thread/a fishing line.

reel *n.* a fall, topple.

reel *n.* a lively quickstep or lithe-step (*dance*).

reel *v.* to wind thread or such on a reel, to wind a fishing line in or out.

reel *v.* to be thrown, falter, slip, topple.

reel *v.* to step out in a reel (*dance*).

reeve *n.* steward, overseer, one handling business for another.

reevedom *n.* 1) cluster of hundreds, in the stewardship of a reeve, 2) (*bureaucracy*) the unbending ways of reeve-lings (bound to little laws and *paperwork*).

reeve-ling *n.* a lesser reeve who is yet high and mighty and unbending.

reft *adj.* bereft of something.

reive *v.* see 'reave'.

rend *v.* 1) to bite, claw, cut, tear, wound, 2) to cleave, sunder, 3) to cut to the quick, draw tears, harm, harrow, tear the heart-strings, wrench, wring.

rennet *n.* 'clod' of *curdled* milk found in the belly of a calf (*used* for *curdling* milk in making cheese).

rent *n.* hole, opening, slit, tear.

rest *n.* 1) break, breather, lie-down, sleep, time off, 2) standstill, stop.

rest *v.* 1) to break off, have a break, lie down, sit down, sleep, 2) to be founded on.

restful *adj.* sleepy, soothing.

restless *adj.* astir, busy, churned up, lively, shifting, sleepless, unsettled, unstill.

restlessness *n.* edginess, fretfulness, flightiness, sleeplessness, wakefulness.

retch *v.* to be sick, heave, spew, throw up.

rib/s *n.* 1) chest bone/s (set in twos), half-ring in shape, shielding the heart, lungs and such, 2) ridge of upland, 3) narrow *strip* of land between furrows, 4) the frame-timbers (half-ring shaped) of a wooden ship, 5) roof timber (now known as a *purlin*) laid length-wise and giving strength to the rafters.

rich[6] *adj.* wealthy, well-off, well-to-do, well-feathered, well-heeled.

riches[6] *n.* richness, untold riches, gold, wealth, weal.

richly[6] *adv.* 1) unstintingly, worthily, 2) fully, greatly, thoroughly, well.

richness[6] *n.* fullness, a lot, more than enough, wealth.

rick *n.* hayrick.

rick-yard *n.* yard (at a steading) where ricks stand.

riddle *n.* a hard saying, dark saying or word, a deep/knotted/hidden saying.

riddle *n.* sieve for sundering chaff from corn, sand from stones, ashes from cinders.

riddle *v.* 1) to speak in riddles, 2) to unweave a riddle.

riddle *v.* 1) to put something through a riddle, 2) to honeycomb with holes like those of a riddle.

riddled *adj.* knotted, dark, shadowy, shrouded, thorny.

riddled *adj.* 1) holed, honeycombed, shot through, 2) beset, marred, overrun.

riddle-wright *n.* know-all, word-weaver, word-wiseman/*sophist*.

ride *n.* 1) drive, outing, 2) bridle-path, rideway, bridleway, greenway.

ride *v.* to ride/handle a horse, ride a two-wheeler.

rider *n.* horse-rider, horseman, horsewoman.

ride-weary *adj.* weary from riding, fordone, limb-weary, way-worn.

ridge *n.* 1) height, highland, moorland ridge, sow-back, upland, wild-land, 2) earthwork, 3) the peak of the roof where the two sloping sides meet.

ridge-bone *n.* backbone.

ridgeway *n.* way or road along a ridge of downland.

riding *n.* way or road for horse-riders, greenway.

riding-hood *n.* overhood, bell-hood.

rife *adj.* full-wide, in everyone's mouth, on all tongues, widespread, worldwide.

right *n.* 1) birthright, freedom, rightfulness, 2) fairness, good, goodness, truth.

right *adj.* aright, fair, fair-minded, meet and right, rightwise, straight, true.

right *v.* 1) to bring a ship back to the upright after it has heeled over, 2) to make good, put right, set to rights, straighten, 3) to right an evil.

right *adv.* 1) straight, upright, 2) all the way to/into/through, 3) right off, right out.

right about *n.* about turn.

righten *v.* 1) to make good, put right, set right, set to rights, 2) ('*justify*' in Christian Godlore) to free from the guilt of sin.

rightening ('*justification*' in Christian Godlore) *n.* making right before God, that is, God deeming believing men and women right and guiltless before his law (through their oneness with Christ in his true law-keeping).

righteous *adj.* clean, right-hearted, rightwise, sinless, upright.

righteously *adv.* right-heartedly, rightly, trothfully, well.

righteousness *n.* cleanness, goodness, rightwiseness, sinlessness, uprightness.

right forth *adv.* at once, right away.

rightful *adj.* 1) meet and right, true, 2) coming to one, well-earned.

right hand *n.* 1) that hand which is most often the stronger of the two, 2) token of friendship or ties, 3) a strong helper, right arm, right-hand man, 4) the right side.

right-handed *adj.* having the right hand/arm stronger than the other.

right-hander *n.* 1) one whose right hand is stronger than his left, 2) (in stockball) player who bats and/or *bowls* with the right hand.

right-hand man *n.* backer, follower, friend, henchman.

right-hearted *adj.* godly, good, rightwise, true, true-hearted, upright, upstanding.

righting-thread (*plumb-line*) *n.* coal-thread.

rightly *adv.* aright, fairly, meetly, truly.

right-minded *adj.* 1) even-minded, fair-minded, rightly believing, right thinking, upright, 2) in one's right mind, right in the head.

rightness *n.* 1) right, truth, sooth, 2) fairness, fair-mindedness, fair deal, fair play, folk-right, right, rightfulness, right-mindedness, uprightness.

right of way *n.* path or way over someone's land, by which all may rightly go.

right-tide *n.* the right time.

rightwise *adj.* above board, childlike, lamb-like, clean, clean-handed, even-handed, fair, fair-minded, good, guiltless, heavenly-minded, high-minded, holy-minded, right, righteous, right-hearted, right-minded, sinless, sterling, straight, true, upright.

rightwiseness *n.* cleanness, goodness, righteousness, sinlessness, uprightness.

rim *n.* edge, outer edge, hem, lip, side.

rime *n.* hoar-frost, hard frost, rime frost, sharp frost, frozen mist.

rime *n.* rerckoning.

rime *v.* to reckon up, rime-tell, take stock, tell, work out.

rime-cold *adj.* bitter, cold with frost, icy cold.

rimecraft (*arithmetic*) *n.* talecraft, tell-craft.

rimecrafty *adj.* good at riming/telling.

rime-frost *n.* rime, hard frost, hoar frost.

rime-hard *adj.* hard frozen, stone hard, winter hard.

rime or rede *phr.* (as '*rhyme* or *reason*') ground, meaning, why and wherefore.

rimer *n.* bookkeeper, reckoner, teller.

rime-tally (*sum*) *n.* end-rime, tale, tellship, worth.

rime-tell *v.* to reckon up, rime, take stock, tell, work out.

riming *n.* reckoning, telling.

rimreach (*circumference*) *n.* edge, outer edge, girdle, rim.

rind *n.* *bark* of a tree.

rindle *n.* runnel, small stream, small waterway.

ring *n.* 1) earring, gold ring, nose-ring, wedding ring, 2) fastening, hoop, 3) tree ring, 4) inner ring, 5) field, ground, 'bowl', 6) (*circle*) trendle, trundle, girdling.

ring *n.* the ringing of a bell, bell-ringing, 'phone call.

ring *v.* 1) to beset, ring about, 2) to ring a bird (to learn more of its goings).

ring *v.* 1) to ring a bell, ring out, toll, 2) to 'phone, ring up, give someone a ring.

ringer *n.* bell-ringer.

ring-finger *n.* third finger of the hand (most often the left hand).

ringleader *n.* firebrand, leader, stirrer, workers' leader.

ring-lock, ring-net *n.* *chainmail*.

ring-road *n.* road about the outside of a town, which can be followed by *traffic* which does not need to go into the middle of the town.

ring-straked *adj.* having rings of this and that hue about the body.

ring true *v.* to have the ring of truth, hold good, hold up, hold water, be so, stand up.

ring-wise (*circular*) *adj.* ringlike, ring-shaped.

ringworm *n.* dew-worm, tetterworm.

ripe *adj.* 1) fully-grown, ready, ripened, 2) hoary, mellow, old, 3) right, timely.

ripen *v.* to grow, blossom, broaden, fill out, swell, thicken, wax.

rise *n.* growth, strengthening, waxing.

rise *v.* 1) to go up, go/grow/rise higher, 2) to do well, go up in the world.

rise up *v.* to come out against, take to the streets, take up weapons.

rising *n.* 1) (*resurrection*) rising again, rising from death, 2) outbreak, uprising.

rising *adj.* 1) having an upward slope, upgoing, 2) (of the sun, moon) rising above the earth's rim, 3) going up in the world (in wealth and/or standing).

rith, rithy *n.* small stream.

rivelled *adj.* 1) withered, wizened, wrinkled, writhled, wrizzled, 2) shrunken.

road *n.* by-road, high road, highway, main road, roadway, side road, lane, street, thoroughfare, through road, throughway, way.

roadhouse *n.* alehouse, inn, roadside house, wayside house.

road-maker *n.* road builder.

roadside *n.* road edge, side of the road, hard shoulder, wayside.

roadstead *n.* water where ships may ride at anchor near the shore, haven.

roadway *n.* road, highway, lane, main road, thoroughfare, way.

roadworthiness *n.* suchness of being fit for the road.

roadworthy *adj.* (of a wain/*vehicle*) fit for the road, kept in good running *order*.

roar *n.* 1) bellow, shout, yell, 2) thunder, thundering.

roar *v.* 1) to bellow, shout, yell, 2) to roar with laughter, 3) to thunder.

roaring *adj.* (of a fire) blazing, burning.

rock *v.* 1) to rock a cradle (to soothe the child or send it to sleep), 2) to reel in walking, 3) to shake.

rod *n.* 1) staff, stick, 2) pole (five and a half yards) – one fortieth of a furlong.

roe, roe-deer *n.* a small deer.

roebuck *n.* he- roe-deer.

rood *n.* 1) cross (of Christ), 2) forty *square* poles, or one fourth of an acre.

roof *n.* the 'shield' over the top of a building.

roof *v.* to put a roof on a building.

roof-bow (*arch*) *n.* bow-shaped work in a building (weight-bearing or there 'for the look of it').

roofed *adj.* having a roof.

roofer *n.* roof-wright, one who puts a roof on a building or makes it good.

roofing *n.* the work of putting a roof on a building, the wood/stone/thatch/tiles of which a roof is made.

roofless *adj.* homeless, kinless, rootless, unfriended, wandering.

rooflessness *n.* homelessness, kinlessness, rootlessness.

roof-room (*attic*) *n.* loft.

roof-stone *n.* roof tile.

roof-top *n.* roof-ridge.

roof-tree *n.* main beam or ridge-pole of a roof.

roof-wright *n.* roofer.

rook *n.* bird of the crow kind.

rook *v.* to do out of, fleece, hoodwink, steal from, take in.

room *n.* 1) bathroom, bedroom, drawing room, living room, playroom, reading room, sitting room, wardroom, workroom, 2) breathing room, elbow room, headroom, sea room, standing room, 3) freedom, leeway, opening, play.

room-hearted *adj.* free, open-handed, great-hearted, unsparing, unstinting.

room-heartedness *n.* great-heartedness, open-handedness, unselfishness.

rooms *n.* board, home, shelter.

roomy *adj.* broad, wide.

roost *n.* a rest for chickens in a hen-house.

roost *v.* (of hens) to settle on the rest for the night.

rooster *n.* cock.

root/s[(2)] *n.* 1) the underground stock of a tree or plant, 2) beginning, heart, mainspring, seed, 3) kin-reckoning, line, stem, stock.

root[(2)] *v.* 1) to root in the ground, 2) to put down roots, strike root, 3) to settle, 4) to pull up, tear, outroot, uproot.

root *v.* (of swine) to delve with the *snout* looking for food, delve, hunt, nose.

root and rind *adv. phr.* (as 'root and *branch*') fully, thorough, wholly, beam and bough.

rootless[(2)] *adj.* homeless, kinless, wandering, unfriended.

root[(2)] **out** *v.* to root up, tear out/ up, wipe out, bring to naught, undo, unmake.

rope *n.* line, tow-line, tow-rope, twine.

rope *v.* to bind, fasten, rope/string together, tie up.

rot *v.* to become rotten, go bad, moulder, rot down, wither away.

rough *n.* 1) fire-eater, 2) draft, outline.

rough *adj.* 1) bristly, hairy, uneven, unsmooth, 2) (of the ground) broken, wild, 3) (of sea or weather) blowy, stormy, 4) churlish, clod-hopping, lewd, oafish, short, uncouth, 5) rough-hewn, unhewn, unworked, unwrought.

rough *adv.* carelessly, in a rough way, roughly.

rough *v.* 1) to make rough, 2) to deal roughly with, 3) to rough it.

rough-and-ready *adj.* 1) about good enough, home-made, makeshift, thrown together, 2) (of folk) ready to take what comes along, working in a rough way.

rough-draw *v.* to make a rough draft or outline.

roughen *v.* 1) to make rough, 2) (of sea or weather) to become rough.

rough-hewn *adj.* 1) roughly shaped/wrought, unworked, unwrought, 2) (of folk) downright, forthright, making no bones, outspoken, straightforward, uncouth.

roughly *adv.* 1) heavy-handedly, 2) about, more or less, nearly, not far off.

Rough-month (*March*) *n.* Lengthening-month, Loud-month.

roughness *n.* 1) bristliness, unevenness, 2) stoniness, wildness, 3) broken water, storminess, 4) churlishness, uncouthness.

rough-rider *n.* horse-breaker, horseman undertaking rough work.

roughshod *adj.* (of a horse) having shoes with the nail-heads sticking out.

rough-tongued *adj.* foul-mouthed, foul-tongued, evil-speaking, evil-tongued.

rough up *v.* to handle roughly, harm, knock about, manhandle, twist, warp.

rover *n.* raider, reaver, sea-rover.

row *n.* line, run, set, string.

row *n.* spell of rowing, faring over the water in a row-boat.

row *v.* to drive a boat through the water with oars.

row-boat *n.* boat driven by oars, rowing-boat.

rower *n.* oarsman, oarswoman.

rowers' bench *n.* ship-settle.

rowlock *n.* oarlock.

rudder *n.* 1) oar for steering a boat, steer-oar, 2) steer-rudder.

rudderless *adj.* crippled, helpless, redeless.

ruddock *n.* redbreast, reddock.

ruddy *adj.* 1) red, reddish, 2) glowing, healthy, bursting with health.

rue *v.* to be sorry about, sorrow, be ashamed, think better of, wish undone.

rueful *adj.* sad, sadder and wiser, sorrowful, sorry, woebegone, woeful.

ruff *n.* *frill* on a sleeve, neckwear.

run *n.* 1) race, 2) unbroken run, 3) flow, path, stream, tide, trend, way, 4) drive, outing, ride, spell, stretch, string, 5) (for chickens and such) pen, 6) (in stockball) the running (by each batsman) from one *wicket* to the other, thus making one run.

run *v.* 1) to run like a hare, run like the wind, speed, 2) to bolt, break away, cut and run, flee, make off, make a run for it, run away, run for one's life, take flight, take to one's heels, 3) to flow, go, leak, spill, stream, 4) to go soft, melt, 5) to handle, head, lead, look after, oversee, 6) to drive, keep, own.

run-about *n.* 1) wanderer, way-wender, 2) small *car* for short farings.

run after *v.* to angle, hunger/thirst/itch for, <u>long for</u>, woo.

run away *v.* to run for one's life, fly, flee, take to flight, <u>win free</u>, make off, bolt.

runaway *n.* someone who is on the run.

run down[6] *v.* 1) to run down one's stocks, 2) to blacken, <u>smear</u>, speak evil of.

run-down[6] *adj.* 1) broken, crumbling, rusting, shabby, weather-beaten, worn, 2) drained, tired, under the weather, weary, worn-out.

rune[2] *n.* *letter* of the runic *alphabet*, sometimes wielded in the weaving of spells.

rung *n.* stave of a ladder.

run into *v.* 1) to drive into, 2) to come upon, meet.

runnel *n.* ditch, drain, leat, rindle, overflow.

runner *n.* 1) errand-bearer, word-bearer, 2) miler, 3) stem, shoot, offshoot, sprout.

runner-up *n.* runner or team beaten into *second place*.

running *n.* 1) running a race, 2) handling, overseeing, 3) working, 4) oozing.

running *adj.* flowing, overflowing, spewing, streaming.

runny *adj.* flowing, melted, running, thawed, watery.

run off with *v.* to make/walk off with, run away with, <u>steal</u>.

run-out *n.* (in stockball) the putting out of a batsman when the *wicket* is hit with the ball before he has made the run.

run out of *v.* to be out of, be cleaned out, have no more, have none left.

run over *v.* 1) to overflow, spill over, 2) to go over the top of, 3) to go over, go through, look over, run through, 4) to hit, knock down/over, run down.

run through *v.* 1) to over-stretch, over-work, 2) to run through with a sword.

run together *v.* to make one, mingle, put together.

run-up *n.* build-up, time leading up to, readying time.

runway *n.* landing ground, flight-*hub*.

rush *n.* plant which grows in marshy ground, and at the edges of streams and ponds.

rush-bed *n.* bed of rushes.

rush garlic, rush-leek *n.* sedge-leek.

rush-grass *n.* kind of grass that looks like rushes.

rushlight *n.* light made by dipping the pith of a rush in *tallow*-fat, rush-candle.

rush-mere *n.* rushy pond.

rush toad *n.* *natterjack* toad.

rushen *adj.* made of rushes.

rushy *adj.* full of rushes, made of rushes, looking like a rush/rushes.

rust *n.* rustiness.

rust *v.* 1) to become rusty, 2) to go downhill, run down, wear out, worsen.

rusty *adj.* 1) rusted, 2) not what it was, 3) (of hue) reddish-brown, rust-hued.

ruth *n.* forgivingness, kindness, understanding.

ruthful *adj.* forbearing, forgiving, kind-hearted, kindly, sparing, understanding.

ruthless *adj.* 1) bloodthirsty, boarish, cold, cold-blooded, cold-eyed, cut-throat, fiendish, flint-hearted, grim, hard, hardened, hard-hearted, stony-hearted, heartless, hellish, iron-heeled, tearing, tearless, unfeeling, unforgiving, unmelting, unsparing, wolf-hearted, wolfish, 2) set upon, bent upon, unbending, <u>unyielding</u>.

ruthlessly *adv.* bloodily, cold-bloodedly, heartlessly, ruthlessly.

ruthlessness *n.* bloodthirstiness, coldness, fiendishness, hardness, heartlessness.

rye *n.* food crop.

rye-bread *n.* bread made from rye.

sack[4] *n.* 1) holdall, 2) (in everyday speech) lay-off, 'the axe', 3) fire and slaying.

sad *adj.* forlorn, <u>hopelorn</u>, heart-sick, listless, wretched.

sadden *v.* to make sad, break one's heart, bring sorrow, bring tears to one's eyes, cut to the quick, draw tears, make the heart bleed, overcome, overwhelm, prick the heart, rend/tear the heart-strings, upset, wound, bereave.

saddened *adj.* sore, woeful.

saddle *n.* 1) seat for a rider (of a horse, two-wheeler), 2) ridge between two hills.

saddle *v.* 1) to put a riding saddle upon a horse, 2) to burden, overload, saddle with.

saddle-bow *n.* the bow-shaped foreside of a saddle tree or saddle.

saddle-cloth *n.* cloth laid on a horse's back under the saddle.

saddle-horse *n.* riding-horse.

saddler *n.* maker of saddles, dealer in saddles.

saddle-sore *adj.* stiff and sore from long riding.

sadly *adv.* forlornly, hopelornly, sorrowfully, listlessly, wretchedly.

sadness *n.* <u>sorrow</u>, forlornness, heavy-heartedness, sighing, <u>weariness</u> of heart.

said *adj.* 1) abovesaid, aforesaid, named before, 2) spoken.

sail *n.* sheet, foresail, mainsail, staysail, topsail.

sail *v.* to handle/work a ship, put to sea, set afloat, set sail.

sail-arm *n.* one of the beams of a windmill.

sailcloth *n.* stretch of cloth from which to make a sail for a ship or a windmill.

sailing *n.* helmsmanship, seacraft, seafaring, seamanship, ship-handling, steering.

sailing-boat, sailing-ship *n.* sailboat, sailer, sailing-craft.

sail-maker *n.* one whose work is to make sails, and to make good rent sails.

sailor *n.* sailor-man, seafarer, seafaring man, seaman, sea-dog, shipman, hand.

sailor-like *adj.* sailorly, seamanlike.

sailyard *n.* one of the yards on which sails are spread.

sake *phr.* because of, in the name of, on behalf of.

sale[2] *n.* dealing, putting on sale, selling, trading.

salesman[2] *n.* businessman, businesswoman, man/woman of business, buyer, seller, dealer, door-to-door salesman, middleman, trader, wholesaler.

salesmanship[2] *n.* sales talk, waresmanship, winning ways.

sallow *n.* willow.

sallow *adj.* ashen, off-hued, sickly, unhealthy, wan, washed-out, yellowish.

sallow-brown *adj.* dark-brown.

salt *n.* 1) white *stuff* that gives a sharper *taste* to food and keeps it from going off, 2) that which gives greater liveliness to one's being, or sharper wit to one's words.

salt *adj.* salted (to keep from going off).

salt *v.* to put salt on.

salted *adj.* salty.

salter *n.* dealer in salt, workman at a salt-works.

saltern *n.* building in which salt is made (by seething or wind-drying salt water).

saltings *n.* salt lands.

salt marsh *n.* marsh flooded by the sea from time to time.

salt-mere *n.* salt water pool.

salt water *n.* water with salt in it, sea-water.

salty *adj.* briny, salt, salted.

salve *n.* eye-salve, hand-salve, tooth-salve.

salve *v.* to put salve on a sore or wound, allay, soothe, still.

sand *n.* little bits of waterworn or wind-worn stone.

sand *v.* 1) to overlay with sand, 2) to grind down, smooth, wear away, wear down.

sand-bed *n.* a layer of sand.

sand-glass *n.* timer, timekeeper.

sand-hill *n.* sandy hillock or ridge on the strand.

sand-ridge *n.* heaped up sand on the strand.

sandstone *n.* stone wrought from sand whose *grains* have become bound together.

sand-storm *n.* storm of wind and wind-driven sand in the drylands (*deserts*).

sandy *adj.* 1) sand-strewn, dusty, grassless, 2) of yellowish-red hue.

sap *n.* the life-giving 'water' in trees and plants.

sapling *n.* young tree.

sap-wood *n.* the softer and newer wood between the rind and the heart-wood.

saw *n.* cutting tool with teeth, for sawing through wood, *metal* or stone.

saw *n.* <u>by-saying</u>, byword, pithy saying, stock saying, wise saying, truth, word.

saw *v.* to cut with a saw.

sawdust *n.* the wood dust made when cutting with a saw.

saw-edged *adj.* having a 'toothed' edge, as a saw.

sawmill[4] *n.* mill where felled trees are sawn into boards.

sawyer *n.* workman who saws timber, often in a saw-pit.

say *n.* 1) speech, word, 2) weight,

say *v.* to <u>speak</u>, say outright, speak out, to mean what one says, <u>bear witness</u>.

saying *n.* <u>by-saying</u>, byword, byspell, folksaying, pithy saying, saw, stock saying.

say no to *v.* to be unwilling, give a deaf ear to, harden one's heart, not hear of, <u>spurn</u>, withhold, <u>withstand</u>, send one about his business, send one off with a flea in the ear.

say-so *n.* behest, bidding, word.

scale/s[2] *n.* weigh beam, weighing bowl, steelyard.

scathing[2] *adj.* biting, bitter, burning, cutting, sharp, stinging.

school[4] *n.* 1) hall/house/seat of learning, 2) following, set.

scream *n.* screech, shout, whine, yell.

scream *v.* to bellow, screech, shout, sing out, whine, yell.

screech *n.* roar, scream.

screech *v.* to bellow, scream, yell.

screed *n.* 1) *strip* of wood or cloth, 2) long list, long speech (spoken or written).

scritch *n.* scream.

scritch *v.* to scream.

scrub *n.* briars, brambles, low stunted trees, undergrowth, underwood.

scruffy *adj.* down at heel, out at elbows, seedy, shabby, sloppy, unkempt, untidy.

scurfy *adj.* scurvy.

scurvy *n.* sickness marked by sore gums, foul breath and bodily weariness – the outcome of not having enough *fresh* food.

scurvy *adj.* 1) scurfy, 2) shabby, sorry, worthless, wretched.

scythe *n.* long-bladed, long-handled tool for mowing grass and other crops.

scythe-stone *n.* whetstone for sharpening a scythe.

scythe *v.* to cut/mow with a scythe.

scytheman *n.* 1) worker with a scythe, 2) Death, Time.

sea *n.* 1) deep, deep sea, flood, great waters, high seas, main, (and, among Old Englsi given names, 'seal-bath', 'swan-road', 'whale-mere') 2) crowd, throng.

sea-bird *n.* brim-fowl, sea-fowl.

seaboard *n.* land by the sea, sea-land, sea-rim, seaside, strand, sea-strand.

sea-borne *adj.* of goods brought by sea.

sea-calf *n.* seal.

sea-cliff *n.* cliff overlooking the sea.

sea-coal *n.* *jet*, coal.

sea-cob *n.* cob, mew, seamew.

seacraft *n.* helmsmanship, seamanship, ship-handling, steering.

sea-dog *n.* sailor, sailor-man, seafarer, seafaring man, seaman.

sea-elf *n.* sea *nymph*, water-elf.

seafarer *n.* seafaring man, seaman, sailor, sailor-man, sea-dog, shipman.

seafaring *n.* faring by sea, the life of a sailor.

sea-faring *adj.* of faring oversea, following the sea as a way of life.

sea-fight *n.* fight between warships.

sea-fishing *n.* the business of hunting for fish in the sea.

sea-foam *n.* breakers, broken water, foaming sea, overfall, spray, white horses.

sea-food *n.* food from the sea (crabs, fish, shell-fish).

sea-fowl *n.* brim-fowl, sea-bird.

sea-girt *adj.* girt about by the sea.

sea-god *n.* god of the sea.

sea-going *adj.* of ship that goes over the sea (as against one that sails near the shore or follows inland waterways).

sea-green *adj.* green hue (as the sea).

sea-horse (*walrus*) *n.* horse-whale.

sea-king *n.* leader of sea reavers.

seal *n.* sea-calf.

sea-land *n.* land by the sea, seaside, sea-strand.

sea-lark *n.* a name for small birds often found on the strand.

sea-lord *n.* sea *captain*, shiplord.

seam *n.* 1) the binding where two stretches of cloth, leather or such have been sewn together, 2) (in *geology*) thin layer (of coal or such) between two thicker layers.

sea-maid (*mermaid*) *n.* sea-elf.

seaman *n.* seafarer, seafaring man, sailor, sailor-man, sea-dog, shipman.

seamanlike *adj.* sailorly, seacraftly, seamanly.

seamanship *n.* helmsmanship, seacraft, ship-handling, steering.

'sea-mare' *n.* craft, long-ship, sea-boat, ship.

sea-mark *n.* landmark that can be seen from out at sea, marker, warning-mark.

seamer (*tailor*) *n.* clothes-maker, clothier, outfitter.

seamew (sea-*gull*) *n.* cob, mew, sea-cob.

seamless *adj.* of cloth woven without a seam.

seamster *n.* needlewoman, clothes-maker, clothier.

seamy *adj.* 1) of the underside of clothing where the edges of the seams can be seen, 2) of the roughest and worst side of life.

sea-ness (*cape*) *n.* headland.

sea-path (*course*) *n.* line/way set by the *captain* of a ship.

sea-quake *n.* undersea earthquake or upheaving from an undersea *volcano*.

sear *v.* 1) to blight, burn, wither, 2) wilfully to numb one's inner witness (*conscience*) so as to drive away shame.

sea raider, sea-reaver *n.* sea-thief, sea wolf.

sea-rim *n.* 1) seaboard, sea-strand, seaside, 2) (*horizon*) earth-hem, earth-rim.

sea-room *n.* open sea where a ship can be *safely* steered.

sea-salt *n.* salt taken from sea-water by seething.

sea-shell *n.* shell of a salt-water *creature*.

sea-shift (sea-*change*) *n.* shake-up, shift, swing, upheaving, upset.

sea-sick *adj.* feeling sick through the pitching of a ship at sea.

seaside *n.* sea-rim, sea-strand.

sea-snake *n.* harmful snake living in some warm seas.

sea-star *n.* 1) star which leads seamen, 2) starfish.

sea-strand *n.* seaboard, sea-rim, seaside.

sea-stream (sea *current*) *n.* flow, stream-faring.

seat[(2)] *n.* bench, settle, stool.

sea-thief *n.* sea raider, sea reaver, sea wolf.

seat[(2)] **of learning** (*academy, college, university*) *n.* hall/house of learning, school.

sea-ward (*coastguard*) *n.* holmward, sea-watchman.

seaward/s *adv.* towards the open sea.

sea-ware *n.* seaweed thrown up on the shore by the sea and taken for dung.

sea-water *n.* the water of the sea, water taken from the sea.

sea-wave (*tsunami*) *n.* ground-swell.

sea-way *n.* a way over the sea, the sea as a way of faring to other lands.

sea-weary *adj.* weary of the sea, fordone, foreworn, worn down.

seaweed *n.* plant found in the sea.

sea-wolf *n.* sea raider, sea reaver, sea thief.

seaworthy *adj.* (of a ship) good for seafaring (even through storms).

sea-wrack *n.* goods or seaweed thrown on the land's edge.

sedge *n.* rough rush-like plant growing in wetlands.

sedge-leek *n.* rush garlic.

see *v.* 1) to behold, make out, watch, witness, 2) understand, see it all, see through.

see about *v.* to deal with, see what can be done, see to.

see through *v.* to be wise to, fathom, not fall for, read someone like a book.

see to *v.* to look after, take care of.

seed *n.* 1) *grain*, kernel, 2) beginning, start, wellspring, 3) mannish seed (*semen, sperm*), 4) children, kin-reckoning, offspring, shoots, offshoots, sons and daughters.

seed *v.* 1) to run to seed, 2) to sow seed.

seed-bed *n.* bed for seeds and seedlings.

seeder *n.* self-working tool for sowing seed.

seedling *n.* young plant grown from a seed.

seed-lip *n.* windle or *basket* borne by one sowing seed by hand.

seed-time *n.* time for sowing.

seedy *adj.* down at heel, out at elbows, run-down, scruffy, shabby, unkempt, untidy.

seeing *conj.* because, inasmuch as, since.

seek *v.* to delve into, delve deep, be after, comb, follow up, go into/over/through, hunt, look for, look into, rake over, rake through, root through, steer for, work over.

seeker *n.* asker, seeker for truth, thinker.

seeking *n.* delving, burrowing, combing, hunting, rooting.

seep *v.* to drip, leak into/through, ooze, seep into/through, soak into/through, weep.

seer *n.* 1) fore-sayer, foreseer, fore-teller, 2) hand-reader, soothsayer, star-teller.

see-saw *n.* 1) board set over a tree-stock, with children seated at each end making the board go up and down, 2) ups and downs, ebb and flow.

see-saw *v.* to go up and down, swing.

seethe *v.* 1) to be hot, spit, steam, 2) to be wrathful, become heated, storm.

seething *adj.* burning, heated, hopping mad, wrathful, wroth.

see-through *adj.* filmy, light, sheer, thin, through-shining, through-showing.

seldom 1) *adv.* almost never, hardly ever, not often, once in a way/while, only now and then, only sometimes, 2) *adj.* almost unheard of, few and far between.

seldom-seen *adj.* little known, unknown, unbeknown, unwonted, weird.

self *n.* 1) being, innermost being, inner self, selfhood, 2) heart of hearts, innermost feelings, soul, inmost soul.

selfdom *n.* being, 'kingdom' of the mind.

self-drive *adj.* of a hired *car* driven by the hirer.

self-feeling *n.* awareness of one's being and one's own feelings.

self-forgetful *adj.* selfless, thoughtful for others, unselfish.

self-heal *n.* plant believed to heal sickness.

self-help *n.* seeking to meet one's needs.

selfhood *n.* being, innermost being, self, inner self.

selfish *adj.* cold-hearted, flint-hearted, hard-hearted, hard-fisted, mean, mean-hearted, mean-minded, self-seeking, stingy, unhandsome, worldly.

selfishness *n.* greed, greediness, hard-fistedness, meanness, self-seeking.

self-killer *n.* self-murderer, self-slayer.

self-knowing *adj.* knowing oneself, having self-knowledge,

self-knowledge *n.* knowing oneself, awareness of one's shortcomings, knowing what one can and cannot do.

selfless *adj.* forgoing, heedless/unsparing of self, self-forgetful, thoughtful, unselfish.

selflessly *adv.* taking no thought for oneself, unselfishly.

selflessness *n.* forgoing, rising above oneself, thought for others, unselfishness.

self-life *n.* 1) being, innermost being, self, inner self, 2) life lived for oneself.

self-love *n.* 1) a right love for oneself (as made by God), 2) selfishness.

self-made *adj.* of one who has lifted up himself or herself by hard work.

self-murder *n.* self-killing, self-slaying, taking one's own life, ending it all.

selfness *n.* selfishness, self-seeking.

self-righteous *adj.* righteous in one's own eyes, 'holier-than-thou'.

self-righteously *adv.* uppishly.

self-righting *adj.* of a boat which rights itself after being upset.

self-seeker *n.* one who is always seeking his or her own well-being first, worldling.

self-seeking 1) *n.* selfish seeking of one's own well-being, 2) *adj.* selfish, mean.

self-sown *adj.* of that which has sown itself, without any work of man.

self-taught *adj.* of one who has taught himself or herself, without help from others.

self-will *n.* one's own will, following one's own way.

self-willed *n.* froward, headstrong, prickly, stiff-necked, wilful.

self-wisdom *n.* narrow wisdom, shallow wisdom.

self-wise *adj.* wise in one's own eyes, leaning to one's own understanding.

sell *v.* 1) to be in the business of, deal in, handle, have for sale, hold a sale, offer for sale, put up for sale, stock, trade in, sell off, sell out, sell up, 2) to be bought, be traded at, bring in, fetch, go for, sell at, sell for, sell dear, undercut, 3) to sell someone into the hands of his/her foes, 4) to sell a thought, put over, win over.

seller *n.* dealer, salesman, saleswoman, tradesman, wholesaler.

sell off, sell up *v.* to sell off everything, sell the whole of one's stock.

send *v.* 1) to forward, send off/on/out, ship, 2) to send flying/headlong, shoot.

send away *v.* to drive away/out, lay off, see off, send flying, send one about his business, send one away with a flea in the ear, show out, show the door, spurn.

sender *n.* shipper.

send-off *n.* farewell, leave-taking.

sengreen *n.* houseleek.

sennight *n.* seven nights, a week.

sere, sear *adj.* dried-up, dry, rainless, thirsty, waterless, withered.

Sere-month (*June*) *n.* Ere-litha, Fore-litha, Lida ærra, Midsummer-month.

set *n.* 1) sunset, setting of the moon, 2) a dead set, a strong onset, 3) the way in which something 'hangs' (as in the set of a ship's sails), 4) a run of games in *tennis*, 5) burrow or earth of a brock, 6) tool for setting.

set *v.* 1) to lay, leave, put, rest, stick, 2) to fasten, hang on, hook on, tie on, tie up, yoke, 3) to set on its feet, set up, 4) to give, name, settle, 5) to harden, stiffen, thicken, 6) to dip, go down, sink, 7) to lay, lay down, lay out, make ready, set out.

set *adj.* abiding, cut and dried, in black and white, settled, well-grounded.

set about *v.* 1) to begin, set to, start, make a start on, wade into, 2) to fall upon someone, go for, lay into, let fly at, pitch into.

set against *v.* to drive a wedge between, set by the ears, sow wrath between.

set aside *v.* 1) to earmark, put on one side, 2) to not listen, think nothing of.

setback *n.* blighted hope, hold-up, let-down.

set forth *v.* to put forward, set down, say/speak out, say outright, speak up.

set off *v.* 1) to be on one's way, fare forth, make a start, 2) to light, set going.

set-off *n.* offset, makeweight.

set out *v.* 1) to be off, make a start, 2) to lay out, set forth, 3) to put forward.

set sail *v.* to go on board, put out to sea, spread sail, leave the land behind.

setter *n.* hound taught to 'set' game.

setting *n.* backdrop, background, frame, lay of the land, set.

settle *n.* seat, high settle.

settle *v.* 1) to settle on, acknowledge, bring to a head, cut through, fall in with, go along with, hold with, make a deal, override, say yes, see eye to eye, set one's heart on, stand with, steel oneself, 2) to abide, make a new home, put down roots, 3) to settle with, get even with, have one's head for.

settled *adj.* abiding, cut and dried, in black and white, known, lasting, no getting away from it, open and shut, set, unshaken, well-grounded.

settler *n.* incomer, newcomer, inwanderer.

settling *n.* 1) clinching, reckoning up, thrashing out, 2) dropping, falling, sinking.

settling in *n.* finding one's feet.

settlings (*sediment*) *n.* grounds.

settling with *n.* reckoning, day of reckoning, wrath-wreaking, an eye for an eye.

set-to *n.* fight, free-for-all, head-to-head, sparring match.

set-up *n.* framework, lay-out, make-up, setting.

set upon *v.* to fall upon, beset, storm, strike at.

seven *n. adj.* the root *number* following six.

sevenfold *adj.* made up of seven together, seven times as great or as many.

seven-night *adj.* seven days old (of the moon).

seventeen *n. adj.* the root *number* made of ten and seven.

seventeenth *adj. n.* 1) the marking *number* that is kin to seventeen, 2) seventeenth share of something.

seventh *adj. n.* 1) the marking *number* that is kin to seven, 2) seventh share of something.

Seventh Day (*Saturday*) *n.* Weekend-day, Lord's Day Eve.

seventhly *adv.* in the seventh *place*.

seventy *n. adj.* the root *number* that is ten times seven.

sew *v.* to hem, seam, stitch.

sewing *n.* sewing/sewn work, needlecraft, needlework, stitching.

sewn *adj.* fastened by sewing, stitched.

shab *n.* skin-blight, the itch.

shabby *adj.* down at heel, out at elbows, run-down, scruffy, seedy, unkempt, untidy.

shackle *n.* 1) fetter, irons, 2) burden, dead-weight, drag, millstone.

shackle *v.* 1) to bind, bridle, fetter, handlock, 2) to hamstring, hedge in, <u>hinder</u>.

shade *n.* 1) shadiness, shadow/s, 2) hue, 3) hint, shade of meaning, 4) blind, shield, sunshade, 5) ghost, soul of one dead.

shade *v.* 1) to cloud, darken, dim, shadow, overshadow, shut out the light, 2) to hide, shelter, shield, 3) to shade into night.

shadeless *adj.* without shade or shelter from the brightness and heat of the sun.

shading *n.* slight shift/s of hue.

shadow *n.* 1) darkness, gloom, shade, shelter, 2) outline, shape, 3) ghost, hint.

shadow *v.* 1) to darken, overhang, shade, shield, 2) to dog, follow, tail.

shadowing *n.* foreshadowing, foreshowing, forewarning, foreweaving.

shadowy *adj.* 1) dark, gloomy, shaded, shady, 2) dim, ghostly.

shady *adj.* 1) cool, dim, leafy, shaded, 2) <u>crafty</u>, slippery, stealthy, underhand.

shaft *n.* 1) arrow, arrow-/spear-shaft, staff, 2) beam of light, gleam, 3) cross-shaft, 4) shaft of an axe or other tool, handle, 5) the shafts of a wain, 6) crank-shaft, 7) (in weaving) one of the two long laths between which the heddles are stretched).

shaft[1] *n.* *mine*-shaft, pit.

shaftment *n.* a hand-breadth, about six inches.

shaft-right *adv.* in a straight line.

shag *n.* rough hair/wool, matted hair.

shaggy *adj.* hairy, long-haired, rough, shock-headed, unkempt, unshorn, woolly.

shake *n.* handshake, quaking, shaking, shiver.

shake *v.* to <u>bewilder</u>, fill with <u>fear</u>, make speechless, <u>overcome</u>, put one off his stroke, put one out of his stride, smite/strike dumb, startle, take aback, take one's breath away, throw one off his bearings, unman, upset, unsettle.

shaken *adj.* aghast, amazed, <u>bewildered</u>, <u>fearful</u>, filled with dread, numbed with fear, floored, overcome, overwhelmed, speechless, startled, struck dumb, struck hard, taken aback, thunderstruck, unmanned, unsettled, upset, worried.

shake off *v.* to leave behind, lose, throw off,

shake out *v.* to straighten out by shaking(of crumpled cloth or such).

shake-out *n.* upheaval or 'spring-clean' within a body, shake-up.

shaker *n.* believer (such as a Quaker) who shakes as he/she feels God's nearness at a church meeting.

shake up *v.* 1) to shake something together so as to stir up and mingle, 2) to frighten, unsettle, upset.

shake-up *n.* 1) fright, upset, 2) upheaval or 'spring-clean' within a body, shake-out.

shaking *adj.* <u>fearful</u>, knees knocking, quaking, shrinking with fear, shivering.

shaky *adj.* crumbling, <u>shifting</u>, unsettled, unsteady.

shale *n.* kind of *rock*.

shale *n.* shell.

shale *v.* to shell.

shall *v.* (with an *infinitive*) am to/is to, must, ought, will.

shallow *adj.* 1) not deep, shoaly, 2) flimsy, light-weight, meaningless.

shallow-brained *adj.* bird-witted, not bright, slow-witted, unwitful, <u>witless</u>.

shallow-minded *adj.* childish, empty-headed, goosish, light-minded, <u>witless</u>.

shallows *n.* shoal/s, shoal water.

shaly *adj.* of or like shale.

sham *n.* empty words, whitewash, wolf in sheep's clothing.

sham *adj.* hollow, make-believe, shallow, truthless, underhand.

sham *v.* to hide the truth, make a show of, put on.

shame *n.* burning shame, bad name.

shame *v.* to put to shame, bring shame upon, heap shame upon, show up, <u>smear</u>.

shamed *adj.* brought down, shown up, withered.

shamefast *adj.* 1) blushful, shrinking, shy, 2) ashamed, forshamed, sunk low.

shamefastly *adv.* 1) blushingly, meetly, mildly, shyly, 2) shamelessly, wantonly.

shameful *adj.* mean, unworthy, unbecoming, shame-making, beneath one.

shamefully *adv.* badly, dreadfully, foully, frightfully, hatefully, meanly, sinfully, trothlessly, underhandedly, unfairly, unrightfully, unrightly, untruly, unworthily, wickedly, woefully, wretchedly.

shameless *adj.* lost to shame, given up to evil, godless, hardened, headstrong, lewd, unbridled, wanton, wild, worldly-minded, worthless.

shamelessly *adv.* wantonly, wildly, heedlessly, carelessly.

shamelessness *n.* careless freedom of bearing, wantonness, wildness, worthlessness.

shaming *n.* besmearing, blackening, lowering.

shammer *n.* fair-weather friend, yarn-spinner, snake in the grass.

shank *n.* the lower *leg* (the upper *leg* being the thigh or ham).

shank-bone *n.* shin-bone.

shape *n.* 1) build, cut, frame, likeness, 2) fettle, health, trim.

shape *v.* to bend, bring about, build, carve, frame, make, put into shape.

shapeless *adj.* misshapen, unshaped, unshapen.

shapeliness *n.* comeliness, fairness, loveliness, winsomeness.

shapely *adj.* clean-limbed, comely, lovely, willowy.

shapen *adj.* hewn, made.

shapen *v.* to hew into shape, make into.

shapening *n.* building, framing, making, shaping.

shaper *n.* 1) God as maker, 2) one who carves/frames/hews something into shape.

shaping (*creation*) *n.* building, carving out, framing, making.

shard, sherd *n.* bit of broken earthware.

share *n.* iron blade of a plough.

share *n.* share-out, fair share, cut, deal, halves, lot.

share *v.* to carve up, cut into bits, cut off.

share, share out *v.* 1) to bestow, deal out, dole out, earmark, give out, give away, go halves, halve, hand out, mete out, settle, weigh out, share and share alike, 2) to have a hand in, be in on, share the load.

shareholder *n.* owner of shares in a business, stockholder.

shareholding *n.* a holding of shares in a business, stock.

sharing *n.* dealing, handing out, bestowing.

sharp *adj.* 1) sour, tart, bitter, stinging, unsweetened, 2) keen, biting, cutting, burning, edged, sharp-edged, knife-edged, sword-sharp, whetted, 3) awake, bright, canny, clever, deft, far-sighted, foreseeing, forward, having one's wits about one, heedful, insightful, keen, keen-minded, keen-sighted, keen-thinking, keen-witted, knowing, missing nothing, nimble-witted, quick, quick-sighted, quick-thinking, quick-witted, ready, ready-witted, sharp-sighted, sharp-witted, shrewd, witfast, witful, not born yesterday.

sharp *adv.* sharply, stingily.

sharp-edged *adj.* biting, bitter, cutting, keen-edged, knife-edged.

sharpen *v.* 1) to hone, whet, 2) to give an edge to, 3) to fire, quicken, stir.

sharpener *n.* shaped stone for giving an edge to cutting tools, grindstone, hone-stone, knife-sharpener, whetstone.

sharper *n.* evil-doer, fox, knave, shammer, snake, twister, fair-weather friend.

sharp-eyed *adj.* awake, open-eyed, sharp-seeing, all eyes, missing nothing.

sharply *adv.* 1) tartly, bitterly, heatedly, 2) betimes, forthwith, soon, straightway.

sharpness *n.* 1) sourness, tartness, bitterness, 2) shrewdness, wisdom, wit.

sharp-nosed *adj.* having a sharp nose, quick to find out any shortcoming.

sharp-seeing *adj.* sharp-eyed, sharp-sighted, keen-sighted.

sharp-set *adj.* craving food, hungry.

sharpshooter *n.* marksman, markswoman.

sharp-sighted *adj.* sharp-eyed, sharp-seeing, all eyes, wide awake, missing nothing.

sharp-tongued *adj.* biting, cutting, prickly, shrewish, stinging, vixenish, waspish.

sharp-witted *adj.* wide awake, on one's toes, having one's wits about one, wise.

shave *n.* the business of shaving off the beard.

shave *v.* 1) to scrape the hairs off a hide, 2) to cut off thin bits or shavings, 3) to cut off the beard with a shaver or *razor*, trim, 4) to graze.

shaver *n.* 1) (*plane*) drawing-knife, spokeshave, 2) driven (*electric*) shaver.

shaw *n.* grove, holt, small wood, thicket, underwood (most often long and narrow, as at the edge of a field).

she *pron.* the 'spindle-kin' (*female*) *pronoun.*

sheaf *n.* bundle, heap (of corn and, later, other things).

shear *v.* 1) to fleece, shave 2) to shear off, cut off.

shearers (*scissors*) *n.* shears.

shear-grass *n.* a sharp-edged grass or sedge.

shearing *n.* the business of shearing off the fleece of a sheep.

shearling *n.* 1) sheep that has been once shorn, 2) fleece of such a sheep.

shears *n.* blades, cutters, trimmers.

sheath *n.* sleeve for a knife or sword.

sheathe *v.* to put a knife or sword in its sheath.

sheathing *n.* shielding layer of *copper* over the outside of a ship's bottom.

sheave *n.* wheel having a *groove* in its rim, either to take a small rope or to make it so that the wheel can run on a *rail*.

sheave *v.* to gather reaped corn into sheaves.

shed *n.* byre, cot, cowshed, lean-to, outhouse, shelter.

shed *v.* 1) to shed/spill blood, 2) to shed tears, weep, 3) to shed light on something, 4) (of trees) to shed leaves, drop leaves, let fall.

sheel *v.* to shell.

sheen *n.* brightness, glaze, gleam, glow, shimmer, shine, sparkle.

sheen *adj.* bewitching, comely, elf-fair, elf-sheen, fair, light, lovely, willowy.

sheep *n.* *beast* of the steading reared for its meat/fleece/milk.

sheepcote *n.* rough shed for sheltering sheep.

sheep-dip *n.* water-trough where sheep are washed, sheep-wash.

sheep-dog *n.* dog taught to gather and drive sheep for the shepherd.

sheepflesh (*mutton*) *n.* sheepmeat.

sheepfold *n.* sheep-pen, sheep-wick.

sheepish *adj.* backward, blushing, mild, shamefast, shrinking, shy.

sheepishly *adv.* mildly, shrinkingly, yieldingly.

sheep-mark *n.* the mark a sheep-owner puts on his sheep to tell such from others.

sheepmeat (*mutton*) *n.* sheepflesh.

sheep-pen *n.* sheepfold, sheep-wick.

sheep-pox *n.* a kind of smallpox which besets sheep.

sheep's eyes *n.* love-lorn look, lovesick look, come hither look.

sheep-shearer *n.* one who shears sheep, *machine* for shearing sheep.

sheep-shearing *n.* the shearing of sheep.

sheep-wash *n.* 1) the washing of sheep before shearing, 2) sheep-dip.

sheep-wick *n.* sheepfold, sheep-pen.

sheer *adj.* 1) downright, outright, out-and-out, thorough, thorough-going, utter, 'dyed-in-the-wool', 2) steep, 3) gossamer, see-through, thin.

sheer *adv.* altogether, steeply up or down, straight up or down, wholly.

sheet/s *n.* 1) bedding, bed-clothes, cloth, winding-sheet, 2) sail, 3) sheet of *paper*, leaf, 4) film, layer, overlay, 5) stretch, sweep.

sheet *n.* ship's rope.

sheeting *n.* 1) strong linen cloth for bed-clothes, 2) timber or *metal* laid down for shielding.

shelf[1] *n.* bookshelf, shelving.

shelf *n.* sand-ridge in the sea or in a *river*, making the water shallow.

shell *n.* 1) the shell of some *creatures* such as the crab, snail, 2) egg-shell, 3) nutshell, 4) frame, framework, 5) (*ammunition*), shot, shells, 6) mousiness, shamefastness, shyness.

shell *v.* 1) to take the *husks* off, 2) to fire, shoot, strike.

shell-fish *n.* water *creature* (such as the crab, *oyster*) having a shell as a shield.

shell-lore (*conchology*) *n.* knowledge of shells.

shelter *n.* 1) shade, shield, windbreak, 2) home, a roof over one's head, 3) bolt-hole, burrow, den, earth, fastness, fold, fox-hole, hideaway, hide-out, hole, lair.

shelter *v.* 1) to shield, take care of, watch over, 2) to hide, take shelter.

sheltered *adj.* bowery, homely, out of harm's way, shielded, warm.

shelterless *adj.* homeless, kinless, unready, unshielded, wide-open.

shelve[1] *v.* to lay aside, set aside, hold over, put on hold, put aside, put off.

shelve *v.* to lean, slope, tilt.

shepherd *n.* 1) drover, herdsman, stockman, 2) church leader, elder.

shepherd *v.* to care for/look after sheep, herd, lead, watch over.

sherd, shard *n.* bit of broken earthware.

sheriff *n.* shire reeve, shire lord, folk-reeve.

sheriffdom *n.* the shire overseen by a sheriff, reeve-dom, reeveship.

shield *n.* 1) linden board, 2) shelter, shield against heat/sun/wind/sight, windbreak.

shield *v.* 1) to hold off, ward off, withstand, 2) to hide, shade from the sun.

shift *n.* 1) blind, game, little game, gamesmanship, lifemanship, makeshift, net, sham, web, 2) woman's smock, 3) (*change* of *position*) shake-up, upset.

shift *v.* to shift one's ground, be fickle/shifty, blow hot and cold, come and go, ebb and flow, go up and down, flicker, flutter, rise and fall, see-saw, swing.

shiftful *adj.* fickle, fitful, forstraught, light-minded, shifty, slippery, wayward.

shifting *adj.* fitful, flighty, fluttering, light-minded, shifty, two-minded, unstill.

shiftless *adj.* idle, never on time, slack, slothful, unwilling, workshy.

shiftlessly *adv.* idly, slothfully.

shifty *adj.* crafty, foxy, knavish, not straightforward, shady, slippery, underhand.

shilling *n.* English *coin* (there being twelve pence to the shilling, and twenty shillings to the pound).

shillingsworth *n.* that which may be bought for a shilling.

shilly-shally *v.* to be in two minds, blow hot and cold, not know what to do, see-saw.

shimmer *n.* gleam, play of light, sheen.

shimmer *v.* to gleam, glisten, twinkle.

shimmering *adj.* aglow, glowing, beaming, gleaming, glistening, shining, sparkling.

shin *n.* the foreside of a man's shank (from knee to ankle).

shin *v.* to climb up (without steps or ladder), shin up.

shin-bone *n.* shank-bone.

shine *n.* brightness, glaze, light, sheen, sparkle,

shine *v.* 1) to beam, be bright, give off light, gleam, glisten, glow, shimmer, sparkle, twinkle, 2) to put a shine on, wax, 3) to do well, have one's wits about one, stand high, stand out in a crowd, star, 'steal the show', throw into the shade.

shining *adj.* bright, gleaming, glistening, glowing, shimmering.

shiny *adj.* agleam, bright, gleaming, glistening, sheeny, sparkling.

ship *n.* great ship, little ship, sea-boat, steamer, steamship.

ship *v.* 1) to put on board ship, to send by ship, to bring or run goods by sea, 2) to take on water in a heaving sea, 3) to ship one's oars.

shipboard *n.* 1) the side of a ship, 2) 'on shipboard', that is, on board ship.

shipbuilder *n.* ship-wright.

shipbuilding *n.* the craft and business of building ships.

shipcraft (*naval power*) *n.* strength for sea-warfare.

ship-fight *n.* fight between warships.

ship-load *n.* the load of goods or folk being borne by ship.

shiplord *n.* sea *captain*, sea-lord.

shipman *n.* sailor, sailor-man, seafarer, seafaring man, seaman, sea-dog, hand.

shipper *n.* one who ships goods.

shipping *n.* ships thronging a haven or sea-way.

shippon, shippen *n.* cowhouse, cowshed.

ship-settle *n.* rowers' bench.

shipshape *adj.* businesslike, straight, tidy, trim, uncluttered, well-kept, workmanlike.

ship-star *n.* *Pole* star.

shipwreck[2] *n.* 1) the loss of a ship in a storm at sea or when driven on shore and broken up, 2) downfall, end, overthrow, setback, undoing, utter loss.

ship-wright *n.* ship-builder.

shipyard *n.* yard where ships are built, cleaned and made good.

shire *n.* cluster of hundreds headed by a sheriff, earldom, sheriffdom.

shire-hall *n.* meeting hall, moot-hall, speech-house.

shire horse *n.* a heavy, strong horse bred for draught.

shire-moot (*county council*) *n.* folkmoot, shire gathering.

shire-oak *n.* oak tree marking a shire *border* or a meeting *place* of the shire moot.

shire-reeve *n.* sheriff, the leading law-man of the shire.

shire-town *n.* head town of a shire.

shirt *n.* hair shirt, nightshirt, undershirt.

shirt-sleeve *n.* the sleeve of a shirt.

shiver *n.* flutter, quiver, shake, thrill,

shiver *v.* 1) to shake with cold, 2) to shiver with fear, quake, dread.

shivery *adj.* chilled, cold, quaking, quivery, shaky.

shoal *n.* stretch of sea-bed or *river*-bed where the water is shallow.

shoal *adj.* shallow, shoaly.

shoal *v.* (of a stretch of water) to become shallow or more shallow.

shoaling *n.* the becoming shallow or more shallow.

shoal-mark *n.* float or marker showing where the water is shallow.

shoaly *adj.* shallow.

shock *n.* a heap of sheaves of corn set upright (to dry and ripen).

shod *adj.* having shoes, badly shod, well-shod.

shoe/s *n.* footwear, overshoe/s.

shoe *v.* to put one's shoes on, to shoe a horse.

shoeblack *n.* one who makes a living by cleaning *boots* and shoes.

shoe-horn *n.* length of horn or such *used* to help get one's heel into a shoe.

shoe-leather *n.* leather for making shoes.

shoeless *adj.* without shoes.

shoemaker *n.* last-wright, shoe-wright.

shoemaking *n.* the making of shoes.

shoe-string *n.* a string for fastening a shoe, shoe-thong.

shoe-thong *n.* shoe-string.

shoe-wright *n.* shoemaker, last-wright.

shoon *v.* shoes.

shoot *n.* offshoot, sprout.

shoot *v.* 1) to fire upon, let fly, loose an arrow, open fire, 2) to bring down, hit, kill, pick off, shoot down, 3) to bolt, fly, shoot through, speed, spring, streak, tear, 4) to shoot up, grow, 5) to film, make a film of.

shooter *n.* trout.

shooting *n.* the right to shoot game on a stretch of land.

shooting star *n.* *meteor.*

shop[(3)] *n.* neighbourhood shop, shopping haven (*supermarket*).

shopping[(3)] *n.* the business of going from shop to shop to get the things one wants.

shore[(1)] *v.* sands, sea-rim, strand, waterside,

short *adj.* 1) dwarfish, little, not high/tall, stocky, thick-set, 2) not long in telling, pithy, short and sweet, sparing of words, 3) churlish, lewd, oafish, rough, uncouth.

short *adv.* 1) without warning, 2) on the hither side of one's goal (fallen short).

short *v.* to cut off the *current* by making a short *circuit*.

short-bread *n.* hard *flat* bakemeat (*cake*).

short-breathed *adj.* short of breath, finding it hard to breath, short-winded.

shortcoming *n.* drawback, falling short, shortfall.

short cut *n.* path or way that is shorter than the better known way, short way.

shorten *v.* 1) to make shorter, lessen, cut short, trim, 2) to become shorter, dwindle.

shortfall *n.* dearth, lack, loss.

shorthand *n.* speed writing through the *use* of tokens for *letters* and words.

short-handed *adj.* short-staffed, below strength, undermanned, understaffed.

shorthorn *n.* breed of kine having short horns.

shortish *adj.* somewhat short, dwarfish, stocky.

short-lived *adj.* fair-weather, fleeting, flickering, flighty, flying, for the time being, homeless, makeshift, restless, rootless, shifting, short and sweet, swiftly gliding, time-bound, unsettled, wandering, here today and gone tomorrow, whilen.

shortly *adv.* 1) pithily, in a few words, 2) roughly, sharply, tartly, 3) soon.

short-mete *n.* short weight, under-weight.

shortness *n.* 1) dwarfishness, littleness, smallness, stockiness, 2) dearth, thinness.

shorts *n.* short breeches.

short sight *n.* dim-sightedness, near blindness, near sight, near-sightedness.

short-sighted *adj.* 1) dim-eyed, dim-sighted, half-blind, near-sighted, 2) heedless, unforeseeing, unthinking, unwise, seeing no further than the end of one's nose.

short-staffed *adj.* short-handed, below strength, undermanned, understaffed.

short time *n.* heart-beat, twinkling of an eye.

short-tongued *adj.* 1) faltering, halting, lisping, stammering, 2) not ready with words, unready in speech, tongue-tied.

short way *n.* short cut, short step, arrow-shot, bowshot, short span, stone's throw.

short-winded *adj.* short of breath, finding it hard to breath, short-breathed.

shot *n.* 1) arrow-shot, bowshot, *gun*-shot, bolt, 2) *ammunition*, lead, shells, 3) marksman, markswoman, shooter, sharpshooter, 4) hit, strike, 5) film-shot.

shot *adj.* of cloth woven with warp-threads in one hue and weft-threads in another (the look of it shifting in the light).

shot-free (*scot-free*) *adj.* 1) free of any reckoning, 2) unharmed, unscathed.

shotten *adj.* over-tired, run down, the worse for wear, thin, worn out.

shoulder/s *n.* 1) uppermost *part/s* of the arm/s and of the back (to either side of the neck), 2) slope on the side of a hill, near the top, 3) the hard shoulder of a road.

shoulder *v.* 1) to bear, heave, stoop one's back to, 2) to crowd, drive, elbow, shove.

shoulder-blade/s, shoulder-bone/s *n.* bone/s of the upper back.

shoulder-high *adj.* as high as one's shoulder.

shout *n.* bellow, roar, scream, yell.

shout *v.* to bellow, roar, scream, sing out, yell.

shove *n.* heave, knock, shunt.

shove *v.* to crowd, drive, elbow, knock, manhandle, ram, shoulder, shunt.

shove-halfpenny *n.* a game like shovel-board.

shovel *n.* spade.

shovel *v.* to dredge, heap, heave, load, shift.

shovel-board *n.* a game in which a *coin* is knocked by the hand along a marked board.

shovelful *n.* load, spadeful.

show *n.* 1) hollowness, sham, showiness, 2) play, showing, sight, street show.

show *v.* 1) to make a show of, put on a show, make known, make one see, set before one's eyes, set forth, show off, show over, 2) to lead, show the way, steer, teach.

show-business *n.* the business of putting on plays and such.

shower *n.* 1) light rainfall, 2) shower bath, cold/hot shower, 3) burst/hail of fire.

shower *v.* 1) to have a shower, wash, 2) to bestrew, strew, let fly, 3) to shower gifts upon, give freely, open one's hand.

shower-bath *n.* shower, cold/hot shower, wash.

shower-bow *n.* rainbow, heavenly-bow.

showery *adj.* rainy, raining off and on.

showfolk *n.* players, stars.

showman *n.* 1) player, playman, 2) show-off.

showmanship *n.* 1) (*acting*) barnstorming, playcraft, 2) brazenness, idle show, showing-off, showiness, tall talk.

show off *v.* to be showy, make a show of, put on a show, overdo things.

show-room *n.* shop-room where goods are set out for buyers to see.

show up *v.* 1) to be seen, show up well, stand out, 2) to bring to light, lay bare, lay open, let in daylight, put to shame, show for what it is, 3) to come, fetch up at.

showy *adj.* brassy, gilded, hollow, loud, made-up, overdone, put on, shallow.

shred *n.* bit, shard, sliver, whit.

shred *v.* to cut up, tear up.

shredding/s *n.* 1) the work of lopping and cutting back, 2) loppings, shreds.

shrew *n.* shrewmouse.

shrew *n.* fishwife, quean, redhead, spitfire, vixen.

shrew *v.* to beshrew, accurse, curse, lay a curse upon someone, bewitch, blast.

shrewd *adj.* long-headed, keen-witted, ready-witted, sharp-witted, wise.

shrewdness *n.* sharpness, quickness, insight, wisdom, wit, awareness.

shrewish *adj.* biting, cutting, stinging, waspish, withering.

shrewishness *n.* prickliness, waspishness.

shrewmouse *n.* shrew.

shrink *v.* to dwindle, grow smaller, lessen, narrow, shorten, wither.

shrink back *v.* to cringe, draw back, hide, keep one's head down, quake, shy away.

shrink from *v.* to fight shy of, shun, spurn, shy away from, think twice about.

shrink with fear *v.* to dread, fear, quake/shake/shiver with fear.

shroud *n.* sheet in which to lay a dead body, grave clothes, winding sheet.

shroud *v.* 1) to bury, hide, keep dark, 2) to lay in a shroud, put a shroud on a dead body, to make the body ready for burying.

shroud/s *n.* a set of ropes leading from the masthead of a sailing ship (helping the mast to bear the pulls upon it).

shrouded *adj.* dark, hidden, hooded, knotted, unfathomful.

shrub *n.* woody bush.

shrubby *adj.* overgrown with shrubs.

shrunk, shrunken *adj.* dwarfish, dwindled, narrowed, stunted, withered, wizened.

shun *v.* to back away, draw back, fight shy of, shy away, give a wide berth to, hang back, hold off, keep away from, keep oneself from, keep oneself to oneself, keep at arm's length, keep out of the way, let alone, not go near, sidestep, spurn, stand off.

shunt *n.* heave, knock, shove.

shunt *v.* to shift, shoulder, shove.

shut *v.* to draw to, fasten, lock, stop up.

shut down[6] *v.* to go out of business, wind up a business, put an end to, stop work.

shut-eye *n.* a light sleep, short sleep.

shut off *v.* to cut off, stop.

shut out *v.* to ban, keep out, lock out, shut the door on.

shutter/s *n.* blind, shade.

shuttle *n.* weaver's shuttle, which takes the threads of the weft to and fro from one edge of the cloth to the other between the threads of the warp.

shuttle *n.* floodgate set in a mill-stream (shut, and then opened, to even the flow of water to the mill-wheel).

shuttle *v.* to go back and forth, go to and fro, seesaw.

shut up *v.* to shut someone away, to shut up shop (for the night, or for good), to stop talking or stop someone else talking.

shy *adj.* 1) backward, blushing, hanging/holding back, mousy, shamefast, sheepish, shrinking, 2) heedful, mindful, watchful.

shy *v.* 1) to draw back, shrink/start back (in fear or loathing), sidestep, 2) (of a horse) to sheer off, swerve, wheel.

shyness *n.* mousiness, shamefastness.

sibling *n.* brother, sister.

sick *adj.* ailing, unwell.

sick at heart bowed, broken-hearted, careworn, hopelorn, forlorn, wretched.

sick-bed *n.* bed on which someone who is sick lies.

sicken *v.* 1) to ail, be unwell, 2) to fill one with loathing, make one sick, put one's back up, set against, stick in the throat, stink in the nostrils, upset.

sickening *adj.* 1) sickly, 2) dreadful, foul, frightful, hateful, loathsome, stinking.

sickle[4] *n.* tool for reaping (having a toothed cutting edge), reaping-iron.

sickly *adj.* 1) unhealthy, washed-out, 2) ashen, off-hued, sallow, wan, yellowish.

sickness *n.* bad health, being unwell, upset, waning health.

side *n.* 1) the side of a man or *beast* from shoulder to hip, 2) the side of a ship, lee-side, weatherside, 3) hill-side, 4) roadside, wayside, seaside, waterside, 5) (in stockball) off side, on side, 6) one's own side, set, 7) father's/mother's side of the kindred.

side *adj.* long.

side *adv.* wide and side (that is, far and wide).

side *v.* to side with, back, choose, come down on one side, take sides.

sideboard *n.* cupboard set in the meal-room of a house.

side-door *n.* a lesser door (set in the side of a building).

sidegate *n.* a lesser gate into the grounds of a house.

side-land *n.* *strip* of land along the side of a ploughed field.

side-light *n.* 1) window in the side of a building or to one side of a door, 2) light on either side of a wain, 3) some further light or insight into a *matter*.

sideling *n.* *strip* of land beside a greater *strip* or beside a stream.

sideling 1) *adv.* sideways, on a side-saddle, 2) *adj.* going sideways, sloping, steep.

sidelong 1) *adv.* to the side of, towards the side, sideward, sideways, side by side, 2) *adj.* leaning to one side, lying on the side, sloping, not straightforward or open.

side-look *n.* a sideways look at someone, come-hither look, stealthy look, wary look.

side-road *n.* byway, lesser road.

side-saddle *n.* saddle for a woman, having horns to give a hold to the knees of the rider, so that she can sit with both feet on one side of the horse.

side-show *n.* 1) a lesser show going on besides the main one, 2) lesser business of no great weight.

sidesman *n.* helper for a churchwardman at times of worship.

side-step *n.* a step to one side.

sidestep *v.* to step aside so as not to meet someone, seek not to answer.

side-stream *n.* bourne, brook, feeder stream.

side to side (*across*) *adv.* from side to side, on the other side, through.

side to side (*across*) *prep.* from one side to the other, to/from the other side of, over.

sidewalk *n.* path for folk on foot along the side of a road, footway, sideway.

sideward/s 1) *adv.* sideways, sidewise, 2) *adj.* going towards one side.

sideway *n.* 1) byway, 2) footway beside a road, sidewalk.

sideways *adv.* alongside, beside, by the side of, sidewards, sidewise, on one side.

sideways word (*allusion*) *n.* aside, alighting, half-word, hint, word-play.

side-wind *n.* 1) wind blowing from the side, 2) a stealthy step towards some end.

sidewise *adj.* sidewards, sideways.

siding *n.* 1) taking sides, 2) stretch of line where *rail*-wains can be parked.

sidle *v.* to edge along (stealthily or while looking another way), to go sideways.

sieve *n.* sifter, riddle.

sift *v.* to comb, delve into, rake over, root through, seek out, thresh, winnow.

sifter *n.* sieve, riddle.

sifting *n.* delving, going deep into, hunting, looking into, seeking, threshing out.

sift through *v.* to delve into, go through, seek out, weigh, winnow.

sigh *n.* 1) groan, moan (out of sorrow or longing), 2) the moaning of the wind.

sigh *v.* 1) to breathe out heavily, groan, heave a sigh, moan, sithe, sorrow, 2) (of the wind) to make a moaning/sighing *sound*.

sight *n.* 1) eyes, eyesight, seeing, far/good/keen/long/sharp sight, dim/short sight, 2) sighting, glimpse, 3) landmark, wonder, 4) eyeshot, 5) belief, outlook, thinking, 6) blight, eyesore, fright.

sight *v.* 1) to behold, make out, see, 2) to set one's sights.

sighted *adj.* having sight, long-sighted, short-sighted, dim-sighted, sharp-sighted.

sight-hole *n.* hole to see through (as with a tool for land-sighting/*surveying*).

sighting *n.* readying a *gun* so that it is set to hit the goal or mark.

sightless *adj.* blind, eyeless, stone-blind, unseeing, unsighted.

sightly *adj.* 1) for all to see, in broad daylight, 2) good to look on, fair, handsome.

sight-read *v.* to read *music* at sight.

sight-seeing *n.* faring from one land or town to another, to see the sights.

sight-seer *n.* one who goes about to see the sights of a land or town, holiday-maker.

sight-shot *n.* eyeshot.

sight-singing *n.* the craft of singing at sight.

sike, syke *n.* 1) small stream flowing through marshy ground and often dry in summer, 2) ditch or runnel.

sill *n.* door-sill, door-step, threshold, window-sill.

silliness *n.* empty-headedness, heedlessness, light-headedness, unwisdom.

silly *adj.* addle-headed, goosish, flighty, heedless, light-headed, light-minded.

silver *n.* 1) a *metal* of worth, 2) silver *coins*, silverware.

silver *adj.* grey, greyish-white, white, whitish-grey, silvery, snowy.

silver *v.* 1) to put on a thin layer of silver, 2) (of the hair) to become silvery or white.

silver-grey *adj.* of a silvery hue, having silvery-grey hair.

silver-haired *adj.* having hair silvered or hoary through weight of years.

silvern *adj.* made of silver.

silversmith *n.* a worker in silver, maker of silverware.

silver-tongued *adj.* dreamy, silvery, spellbinding, sweet-spoken, true, word-wieldy.

silverware *n.* things made of silver, most often things for the board (such as bowls).

silver wedding *n.* the twenty-fifth yearday of a wedding.

silver weight *n.* silver-mete, weight in silver.

silver-work *n.* things made of silver, silverware.

silvery *adj.* silver-hued, silver-*toned*.

sin *n.* besetting sin, deadly sin, evil, misdeed, unrightness, wickedness.

sin *v.* to do evil, work evil.

since 1) *adv.* then, thereupon, straight afterwards, thereafter, after that time, from that time, 2) *prep.* ever since, since the time that, 3) *conj.* because, inasmuch as.

sinew *n.* one of the 'strings' that tie *muscle* to bone, hamstring, hough-sinew.

sinewy *adj.* lean, spare, strong, tough, wiry.

sinful *adj.* bad, evil, evil-minded, fallen, godless, shameless, sin-laden, ungodly.

sinfully *adv.* black-heartedly, dreadfully, foully, shamefully, unrightfully, wickedly.

sing *v.* to lift up the *voice* in song, to tell of in song.

singe *n.* slight burn.

singe *v.* to blacken, burn, sear.

singer *n.* songster, nightingale, song-bird.

sing-song *n.* a gathering with a time of singing.

sink *n.* kitchen sink, wash-bowl.

sink *v.* 1) to go down, go under, 2) to drown, send to the bottom, 3) to dwindle, go downhill, lessen, wane, worsen, 4) to bore (a hole), drive, lay, put down, 5) (of the *voice*) to become softer, 6) to stoop.

sink-hole *n.* 1) hole or hollow into which filth runs or is thrown, 2) swallow-hole.

sinker *n.* weight of lead or stone for sinking a fishing-line into the water, weight of lead or other *metal* for sinking a *sounding*-line in water.

sinless *adj.* clean-handed, guiltless, free from guilt, not guilty, in the right.

sinner *n.* evil-doer, hardened sinner, knave, misdoer, wicked man/woman.

sip *n.* drop, mouthful, thimbleful.

sip *v.* to drink a little, take sips, wet one's lips.

sister[(2)] *n.* 1) she- sibling, 2) a near friend, 3) woman who is a Christian believer.

sister-in-law[(2)] *n.* wife of one's brother, sister of one's wife, wife-sister.

sit *n.* a spell of sitting down.

sit *v.* 1) to sit down, be seated, take a seat, settle down, take the weight off one's feet, 2) to sit for (a likeness, *photograph* or such), 3) to sit as a deemster/*judge*, sit on the bench, 4) to have a seat on a steering body or such.

sith 1) *adv.* afterwards, after that time, then, thereafter, thereupon, from that time, since, 2) *prep.* ever since, since the time that, 3) *conj.* because, inasmuch as.

sithe *v.* 1) to sigh, groan, moan, sorrow, 2) (of the wind) to make a sighing *sound*.

sithen *adv.* afterwards, since, thereafter, thereupon, from that time, then.

sit-in *n.* folk sitting tight in a workshop (to make a stand against what is done there).

sitter *n.* one who sits for a *painter* or such.

sitting *n.* hearing, meeting.

six *n.* the root *number* following five.

six-edged (*hexagonal*) *adj.* six-sided.

sixfold *adj.* made up of six together, six times as great or as many.

sixteen *n. adj.* the root *number* made of ten and six.

sixteenth *adj. n.* 1) the marking *number* that is kin to sixteen, 2) sixteenth share of something.

sixth *adj. n.* 1) the marking *number* that is kin to six, 2) sixth share of something.

sixthly *adv.* in the sixth *place*.

sixty *n. adj.* the root *number* that is ten times six.

sixtyfold *adj.* sixty times as great or as many.

skin[(2)] *n.* 1) the outer 'clothing' of the flesh and bones of the body, 2) fell, fleece, hide, 3) hull, outside, rind, 4) film.

sky[(2)] *n.* the blue, the heavens.

slack *n.* 1) overflow, over-fulness, overspill, 2) give, leeway, play, room.

slack *adj.* 1) careless, heedless, idle, light-minded, offhand, shiftless, sloppy, slothful, slow, unthorough, untidy, 2) hanging, limp, not tight.

slack *v.* to idle, leave undone, let slide, not follow through/up, overlook.

slacken *v.* 1) to drop off, lessen, let up, slow down, slow up, 2) to loosen, unstring.

slackening *n.* dwindling, dying down, ebb, falling off, lessening, waning.

slacker *n.* foot-dragger, good-for-nothing, idler, layabout, lie-abed, slow-bones.

slackness *n.* sloth, slowness.

slack-water *n.* 1) the time at high or low water when the tide is not seen flowing either way, 2) stretch of a stream outside the water-flow, 3) stillish stretch of sea (where there are no sea-streams/*currents*).

slade *n.* dell.

slake *v.* to quench one's thirst.

slay *v.* to kill, cut down, do to death, fell, murder, overcome, quell, take the life of.

sleave *v.* to cleave, rend, slive, <u>sunder</u>, tear.

sledge-hammer *n.* heavy hammer wielded by a blacksmith.

sleech *n.* slime left by the sea or by a *river*.

sleechy *adj.* filthy, oozy, slimy.

sleek *adj.* 1) shiny, smooth, 2) lithe, willowy.

sleep *n.* rest, shuteye, slumber, sweet dreams/sleep, deep/heavy/light sleep.

sleep *v.* to drop off, fall asleep, go to sleep, go out like a light, slumber.

sleeper *n.* dreamer, lie-abed, sleepy-head.

sleepful *adj.* drowsy, half-awake, half asleep, heavy-eyed, ready for bed, sleepy.

sleepfulness *n.* drowsiness, sleepiness.

sleepgiving *adj.* bringing on sleep.

sleepiness *n.* drowsiness, heaviness, sleepfulness, tiredness, weariness.

sleepless *adj.* 1) restless, unsleeping, wakeful, 2) tireless, watchful, wide awake.

sleeplessness *n.* tirelessness, liveliness, quickness, readiness.

sleep-walker *n.* one who walks while yet asleep.

sleep-weary *adj.* done in, fordone, overtired, tired out, <u>weary</u>, dead to the world.

sleepy *adj.* drowsy, half-awake, half asleep, heavy with sleep, sleepful, tired.

sleet *n.* snow that has thawed a little in falling.

sleety *adj.* (of a storm or wind) laden with sleet.

sleeve *n.* that bit of a shirt or such which goes over the arm.

sleeved *adj.* having sleeves.

sleeveless *adj.* without sleeves.

sleeve-shoe *n.* light indoor shoe, step-shoe.

slench *v.* to creep, go stealthily, sidle, slink, steal along, steal by.

slick *n.* smooth streak in the water (where there is *oil*).

slick *adj.* 1) sleek, shiny, smart, smooth, streamlined, 2) clever, <u>deft</u>, nimble, quick.

slickstone *n.* stone for smoothing.

slidder *adj.* glassy, glidder, slippery, slithery, smooth.

slidder *v.* to slide, slither.

slide *n.* 1) slip, 2) clasp, fastener, 3) film-shot that can be shown on a *screen*.

slide *v.* 1) to go smoothly, glide, 2) to slidder, slither, 3) to drop, fall, <u>worsen</u>.

sliding *adj.* of that which slides, hence sliding-door/s and such.

slight[(2)] *adj.* 1) light, lissome, shapely, trim, willowy, 2) lightweight, little, small.

slightly[(2)] *adv.* 1) lightly, 2) a bit, a little, a shade, somewhat.

slime *n.* clay, ooze, sleech.

slime *v.* to smear with slime.

slimy *adj.* filthy, foul, oozy, sleechy.

slink *v.* to creep, go stealthily, sidle, slench, steal along, steal by.

slinker *n.* busybody, <u>evil-doer</u>, fox, gossip, ne'er-do-well, shrew, twister, undoer.

slip[(1)] *n.* 1) slipway, 2) woman's shift, 3) mistake, oversight, slip of the tongue.

slip[(1)] *v.* 1) to fall, miss one's footing, slide, slither, 2) to creep, go stealthily, sidle, slench, slink, steal along, steal by, 3) to drop, fall, sink, wane, <u>worsen</u>, 4) to slip up, put one's foot in it, 5) to slip away, steal away, <u>win free</u>.

slippery *adj.* 1) glassy, glidder, icy, slidder, slithery, smooth, 2) <u>crafty</u>, knavish, knowing, shady, sharp, shrewd, stealthy.

slit *n.* opening, rent, tear.

slit *v.* to cut open, rend, tear.

slither *v.* 1) to slidder, slide, 2) to creep, glide, slink, snake.

slithery *adj.* sliddery, slippery.

slive *v.* to cleave, hew asunder, rend, <u>sunder</u>, tear.

slive *v.* 1) to slip on clothing, 2) to slide, 3) to hang about, idle.

sliver *n.* bit, chip, cut, shard, shaving, shiver, shred, wedge.

sloe *n.* berry of the blackthorn.

sloe-thorn *n.* blackthorn.

sloom *n.* a light sleep, slumber.

slop/s *n.* outer clothing of a wide and loose kind, and cheap.

slop/s *n.* 1) slimy ground, slime-hole, 2) a spill, 3) leavings, leftovers, watery food.

slop *v.* to spill, slop over, overflow.

slope *n.* hillside, hill-slope, lith, rise, rising ground, sloping edge, steep slope.

slope *v.* to drop away, rise, slope up/down, lean, tilt.

sloppy *adj.* careless, <u>heedless</u>, <u>light-minded</u>, makeshift, <u>untidy</u>, upside down.

sloth *n.* slothfulness, do-nothingness, idleness, slackness, slowness, unwillingness.

slothful *adj.* do-nothing, good-for-nothing, foot-dragging, half-hearted, idle, leaden, lifeless, listless, not stirring, shiftless, sitting still, slack, slackful, slow, unthorough, unwilling, workshy, resting on one's oars.

slothfully *adv.* half-heartedly, idly, slackly, unwillingly.

slough *n.* 1) marsh, mere, moss, 2) a cleft, deep coomb, a waterway running in a deep hollow or ditch.

slow *adj.* 1) creeping, heel-dragging, idling, leaden-footed, long about it, slack, snail-like, slow-footed, 2) unwilling, loath/loth, not so minded, unminded, 3) half-witted, slow-witted, unwitful, witless, wooden-headed.

slow *adv.* creepingly, slowly.

slow *v.* 1) to slow down, slow up, 2) to hinder, hold back, hold up, put a drag on.

slow body, slow-bones, slow-foot *n.* foot-dragger, good-for-nothing, heel-dragger, idler, layabout, slacker, snail.

slow-footed *adj.* creeping, heel-dragging, idling, leaden-footed, slack, snail-like.

slowly *adv.* creepingly, idly, steadily, in one's own good time, taking one's time.

slowness *n.* 1) slackness, 2) backwardness, thick-headedness, unwisdom.

slow-witted *adj.* dim-witted, empty-headed, half-witted, thick, unwitful, witless.

slow-worm *n.* small *lizard*, blindworm.

slumber *n.* rest, shuteye, sweet dreams.

slumber *v.* to drop off, fall asleep, go to sleep, sleep.

smack (*flavour, tr*ace) *n.* smatch.

smack *v.* to beat, hit, strike.

small *adj.* dwarfish, lean, lightweight, little, narrow, not much, short, thin, wee.

small *adv.* in a small way, not much, lightly, softly.

small-clothes *n.* breeches, knee-breeches.

small glass *n.* *microscope*.

smallholder *n.* acreman, crofter, earth-tiller, grazier, herdsman, stock-breeder/ rearer, wool-grower, yeoman.

smallholding *n.* croft, holding, steading.

smallpox *n.* sickness that brings up pocks on the skin.

small talk *n.* gossip, light talk.

smart *n.* 1) sore, soreness, sting, wound, 2) heartache, sorrow.

smart *adj.* 1) biting, cutting, sharp, stinging, 2) bright, clever, keen, lively, quick, quick-witted, sharp, 3) clothes-aware, showy, sleek, trendsetting, trim.

smart *v.* 1) to stab, sting, 2) to be bitter about, be sore, feel wounded, seethe.

smarten *v.* to brighten up, do up, make clean and smart.

smartly *adv.* busily, nimbly, quickly, readily.

smatch (*flavour, tr*ace) *n.* smack.

smear *n.* cutting words, gossip, hard words, the rough edge of one's tongue.

smear *v.* to backbite, belittle, besmear, beshrew, blacken, blast, brand, curse, flay, give a dog a bad name, give one a bad name, give the rough edge of one's tongue, go for, gossip, hammer, harry, hound, lay into, pick holes in, pick on, pitch into, pull asunder, put down, put in a bad light, rend, run down, speak evil of, speak foully of, storm against, talk behind one's back, tear into, throw the first stone, thunder against, weigh into, whisper.

smearing *n.* backbiting, besmearing, blackening, cursing, evil-speaking, foul-speaking, foul-speech, gossiping, swearing, whispering.

smearing *adj.* foul-mouthed, foul-tongued.

smeary *adj.* besmeared, filthy, grubby, unwashen.

smell *n.* 1) *sense* of smell, 2) reek, stench, stink, strong smell.

smell *v.* 1) to get wind of, smell out, 2) to give off a smell, reek, smell strong, stink.

smell-less *adj.* 1) giving out no smell, 2) having no *sense* of smell.

smelly *adj.* high, reeking, evil-smelling, foul-smelling, strong-smelling, stinking.

smirk *n.* grin, belittling or teasing smile.

smirk *v.* to grin, laugh at, laugh in one's sleeve.

smite *v.* to beat, cudgel, fell, hit, knock down, lay in the dust, strike, thrash.

smiter *n.* beater, striker.

smith *n.* worker in iron (and other *metals*), blacksmith, brass-smith, goldsmith, locksmith, silversmith, tinsmith, whitesmith.

smith *v.* to beat out, hammer out.

smith-craft *n.* the business of smithing.

smith-crafty *adj.* handclever in the business of smithing.

smithing *n.* the work of a smith.

smitten *adj.* 1) floored, overwhelmed, 2) bewitched, swept off one's feet.

smittle (*infectious, contagious*) *adj.* spreading, taking, deadly, foul, harmful.

smock *n.* 1) woman's shift, slip, 2) the smock-*frock* once worn by landworkers.

smoke *n.* 1) reek, 2) *cigarette*.

smoke *v.* 1) to give forth smoke, 2) to smoke out (*fumigate*), smoke-dry.

smoke-dry *v.* to dry fish or meat in smoke.

smoke-hole *n.* hole in the roof of a building for letting out smoke.

smokeless *adj.* giving off no smoke, free from smoke.

smoker *n.* 1) one who smoke-dries fish or meat, 2) one who smokes *tobacco*.

smoke out *v.* 1) to cleanse with smoke, 2) to find out.

smokestead (*chimney*) *n.* smoke-*stack*.

smoky *adj.* filthy, reeky, thick.

smooth *adj.* 1) even, steady, 2) glassy, shiny, sleek, smooth as glass, smooth-haired, 3) beardless, hairless, clean-shaven, 4) soft, soothing, straightforward.

smooth *v.* 1) to iron, smoothen, 2) to iron out, smooth over, smooth the way.

smooth-lip *n.* fair-wording, honey-speech, soft soap, soft-speech.

smooth-lipped, smooth-spoken, smooth-talking *adj.* honey-lipped, lying, not straightforward, sham, shifty, soft-lipped, smooth-tongued, two-tongued.

smooth-tongued *adj.* fawning, fulsome, hollow, honey-lipped, honey-mouthed, honey-tongued, shallow, sham, shiftful, slick, slithery, smooth-lipped, smooth-spoken, smooth-talking, truthless, two-tongued.

smoothly *adv.* evenly, steadily, straightforwardly.

smother *n.* thick and choking smoke.

smother *v.* 1) to choke off, put out, quell, quench, stamp out, 2) to choke to death, throttle, 3) to becloud, hide, hood, mask, shroud, 4) to hold back/in, keep back.

snail *n.* 1) small *creature* with a shell, 2) foot-dragger, slow body, slow-bones.

snail-like *adj.* creeping, heel-dragging, idling, leaden-footed, slack, slow-footed.

snake *n.* 1) adder, nadder, worm/wyrm, 2) great fire-snake (*dragon*), 3) evil-doer, fox, knave, sharper, slinker, twister.

snake *v.* to bend, bow, twist, wander this way and that, wind.

snake-like *adj.* like a snake, long and sinewy.

snakish *adj.* snake-like, snaky.

snaky *adj.* 1) snake-like, 2) crafty, lying, shifty, slippery, stealthy.

sneeze *n.* sneezing.

sneeze *v.* to drive out breath sharply through the nose and mouth.

snell 1) *adj.* bold, quick, smart, clever, keen-witted, sharp, (of the weather) bitter, 2) *adv.* keenly, quickly, strongly, swiftly.

snow *n.* snowfall, snow-leaves, snowstorm, sleet.

snow *v.* to let fall as snow.

snow-blind *adj.* blind or half-sighted through the snow's whiteness.

snow-blindness *n.* loss of sight (halfly or wholly) through the blinding whiteness of snow.

snow cold *adj.* biting, bitter, freezing, icy, raw, rime-cold, winter-bitter, wintry.

snowdrop *n.* an early white *flower*.

snowfall *n.* 1) a fall of snow, 2) the *amount* of snow falling at one time.

snow-field *n.* wide stretch of snow-bound land.

snow-leaf *n.* snow-*flake*.

snowman *n.* snow heaped up into a man-shape.

snow-sheen *n.* the throwing back of sunlight from snow or ice-fields in the far north and the far south.

snow-shoe *n.* footwear for walking over snow-bound land (being a frame of light wood strung with lengths of hide).

snow-storm *n.* storm bringing a heavy fall of snow.

snow-white *adj.* white as snow.

snowy *adj.* 1) (of time or weather) marked by lots of snow, 2) clothed or shrouded in snow, 3) snow-white.

so *adv.* hence, in such wise, thence, thereby, therefore, thus, whence, wherefore.

soak *n.* a soaking.

soak *v.* 1) to drench, wet through, 2) to steep, put in soak, 3) to get in, seep into.

soaker *n.* cloud-burst, drencher, drenching rain, heavy shower.

soaking *n.* drenching, ducking, thorough wetting.

soak up *v.* to drink in, swallow, take in/up.

so-and-so *n.* 1) what's his/her name, 2) good-for-nothing, ne'er-do-well.

soap *n.* lye, cleaner, cleanser.

soap *v.* to lather, put soap on.

soapiness *n.* the suchness of soapy water.

soap-stone *n.* *mineral* with a smooth feel (sometimes *used* as a soap).

soapy *adj.* smeared with soap.

sodden *adj.* drenched, soaked, sopping wet, wet through.

soft *adj.* 1) fleecy, light, lithe, soothing, woolly, 2) forbearing, kindly, mild as milk, over-kind, ruthful, soft-hearted, warm-hearted, yielding, 3) weak-willed, 4) empty-headed, feather-headed, goosish, light-minded, slow-witted, shallow-minded, witless, 5) (of *sound*) barely heard, half-heard, dying away, silvery, sweet, whispered.

soften *v.* to lessen, lighten, mellow, spare, unbend.

softening *n.* lessening, lightening, soothing, sparing.

soft-eyed *adj.* doe-eyed, mild-eyed, kindly.

soft-footed *adj.* light-footed.

soft-head *n.* feather-head, goose, know-nothing, lackwit, witling.

soft-headed *adj.* addle-headed, feather-headed, goosish, shallow-brained, witless.

soft-hearted *adj.* forbearing, kind-hearted, kindly, ruthful, sweet, warm-hearted.

softish *adj.* somewhat soft, rather soft.

softling *n.* runaway, weakling.

soft-lipped (*euphemistic*) *adj.* honey-lipped, honey-mouthed, smooth-lipped, soothing but soothless, soothing more than sooth.

softly *adv.* lightly, lithely, mildly, soothingly, sweetly, whisperingly, yieldingly.

softness *n.* 1) lightness, litheness, 2) kindness, over-kindness, 3) weakness, weak will, unsteadiness, 4) empty-headedness, feather-headedness, lightmindedness.

soft-soap, soft-speech (*euphemism*) *n.* fair-wording, honey-speech, smooth-lip.

soft-spoken *adj.* fair spoken, knightly, well-spoken.

software *n.* the driving setup or *programme* for a main-reckoner (*computer*).

soft-wood *n.* wood that is readily cut and worked.

softy *n.* weakling, weak-minded man or woman.

Sol-month (*February*) *n.* Kale-month.

some 1) *indef. pron.* a few, one or two, two or three, 2) *adj.* any, more or less, this or that, 3) *adv.* a bit, a little, ever so little, not fully, not wholly, somewhat.

somebody *n.* 1) one, someone, so and so, such a one, 2) heavyweight, man/woman of mark, name, household name, star, rising star.

some day *adv.* in the fullness of time, one day, one of these days, sooner or later.

somehow *adv.* come what may, in some way, one way or another, somehow or other.

someone *n.* one, somebody, so and so, such a one.

something 1) *adj.* thing, something between, something else, something or other, something over, 2) *adv.* a bit, a little, rather.

sometime 1) *adv.* by and by, once upon a time, one of these days, some day, somewhen, sooner or later, 2) *adj.* erstwhile, former, late, one time.

sometimes *adv.* at times, every so often, once in a while, otherwhile/s, somewhile/s.

someway *adv.* in some way, somehow.

somewhat a bit, a little, fairly, rather.

somewhen *adv.* at some time, by and by, once upon a time, one day, some day.

somewhere *adv.* here and there, wherever it may be.

somewhile/s *adv.* at one time or other, formerly, in some former time, once.

somewhither *adv.* to somewhere.

somewise *adv.* in some way.

son *n.* man-child, spear-side child.

song *n.* 1) cradle-song, dream-song, song-dream, love-song, 2) birdsong.

song-bird *n.* singing bird, songster, chirruper.

song-book *n.* book of songs.

song-craft *n.* 1) (*music*) dreamcraft, 2) (*poetry*) wordcraft.

song-dream *n.* song, cradle-song, dream-song, love-song.

songful (*lyrical*) *adj.* given to singing.

song-shaper *n.* singer, song-smith, songwright, song-writer.

song-smith *n.* singer, song-shaper, songwright, song-writer.

songster *n.* singer, nightingale, song-bird, song-writer.

son-in-law[2] *n.* daughter's husband.

sonless *adj.* having no son.

sonlike *adj.* right-hearted towards one's father and mother.

sonship *n.* the suchness of being a son.

soon *adv.* anon, at once, before long, betimes, erelong, forthwith, in a little while, now, quickly, shortly, straightaway, straightway, within a short time.

soon *adj.* coming about soon or quickly, early, speedy.

sooner *adv.* 1) ahead of time, before, earlier, 2) more readily/willingly, rather.

soot *n.* black bits made by the burning of a coal, *oil* or wood fire.

sooth *n.* truth, rightness.

sooth *adj.* right, aright, true, truthful.

sooth *adv.* rightly, truly, truthfully, thoroughly.

soothe *v.* to allay (fears), lighten, put/set the mind at rest, settle, smoothe, soften, still, take away fear, unburden, warm, wipe away the tears.

soothfast *adj.* earnest, true, true-hearted, truthfast, truthful, unswerving, upright.

soothfastly *adv.* aright, fairly, meetly, rightly, soothly, truly.

soothfastness *n.* high-mindedness, knightliness, steadfastness, troth, truth.

soothing *adj.* restful, softening, smoothing, stilling.

soothly *adv.* aright, fairly, meetly, rightly, soothfastly, truly.

soothsay *v.* to read one's hand, read the stars, read the tokens.

soothsayer *n.* hand-reader, seer, spell-weaver, wise man/woman, witch.

soothsaying *n.* foretelling, hand-reading, hand-telling, witchcraft.

sooty *adj.* filthy with soot.

sop *n.* bit of bread or such dipped in water or wine.

sop *v.* 1) to dip bread or such in water or wine, 2) to drench, soak.

sopping *adj.* soaking wet, sopping wet, wet through, sodden.

soppy *adj.* 1) soaked, 2) daft, silly, weepy.

so-put *adj.* *hypothetical*.

sore *n.* cut, harm, smart, sting, swelling, <u>wound</u>.

sore *adj.* 1) burning, raw, reddened, searing, sharp, shooting, smarting, stabbing, stinging, tearing, 2) bitter, heart-sore, stung, wroth.

sore *adv.* badly, dreadfully, greatly, sorely.

to be sore *v.* to ache, be sick at heart, be upset, <u>sorrow</u>.

sorely *adv.* badly, dreadfully, greatly, sadly, woefully.

soreness *n.* 1) aching, bruising, rawness, smarting, 2) bitterness, grief, heartache, <u>sorrow</u>, sourness, upset, wretchedness, chip on the shoulder.

sorrow, sorrowness *n.* ache, bitterness, black mood, blight, broken-heartedness, burden, care, down-heartedness, forlornness, forsakenness, gloom, gloominess, heartache, heartbreak, heart-sickness, sickness of heart, heavy-heartedness, heaviness, hopelessness, loneliness, sadness, sighing, soreness, strickenness, woe, depths of woe, tale of woe, weariness of heart, wretchedness.

sorrow *v.* to sigh for, weep over, beat one's breast, be bowed down, break one's heart, groan, moan, bemoan, shed bitter tears, wring one's hands.

sorrowful *adj.* forlorn, <u>hopelorn</u>, burdened, care-worn, cut up, gloomy, glum, lorn, down at heart, down-hearted, heavy-hearted, sick at heart, heart-sore, listless, not oneself, sad, saddened, soul-sick, weighed down, woebegone, woeful.

sorrowfully *adv.* brokenly, forlornly, heavily, sadly, wearily, wretchedly.

to be sorry *v.* to be ashamed, <u>sorrow</u>, rue, wish undone.

sorry *adj.* 1) beaten, bowed down, broken, heart-lorn, <u>hopelorn</u>, listless, woebegone, woeful, wretched, 2) light-weight, mean, not good enough, not worth a thought, shallow, unmanned, worthless.

so-so *adj.* fair, middling, fair to middling, not bad.

sough *n.* 1) the sighing or moaning of the wind, 2) a deep sigh or breath, a moan.

sough *v.* 1) (of the wind) to make a moaning/sighing *sound*, 2) to draw breath heavily, sigh deeply, 3) to sough away, breath one's last.

soul *n.* 1) breath, heart of hearts, inmost soul, inner self, innermost being, life, life-hoard, mind, 2) being, living being, living soul, man, woman, 3) feeling, mood.

soulful *adj.* heartfelt, meaningful, mournful.

soulless *adj.* 1) cold, dead, heartless, lifeless, unfeeling, unkind, 2) dreary, grey.

soul-sick *adj.* burdened, down at heart, sick at heart.

soulsight *n.* inner awareness, mindsight, true insight.

soul-stirring (*exciting*) *adj.* gripping, heady, heart-stirring, heart-swelling, heart-thrilling, thrilling, sparkling, stirring, striking.

soul-truth *n.* heavenly truth, insight into heavenly things.

sound *n.* arm of the sea, narrows, waterway.

sound, soundful *adj.* 1) hale and hearty, healthful, healthy, ruddy, <u>strong</u>, well, 2) right-thinking, true, well-grounded, <u>wise</u>, 3) unbroken, 4) downright, thorough.

sound, soundly *adv.* 1) deeply, restfully, without waking, 2) thoroughly, wholly, 3) carefully, shrewdly, wisely.

soundness *n.* 1) health and strength, wholeness, 2) depth of thought, <u>wisdom</u>.

sour *adj.* sharp, tart, bitter, biting, cutting, stinging, unsweetened.

sour *adv.* bitterly, gloomily, grimly, sourly.

sour *v.* to blight, make bitter, upset, warp, wound.

sour appletree *n.* apple-thorn (*crab* apple), apple-thorn tree, wild apple tree, wilding, wood-apple.

sour-dough (*leaven*) *n.* barm, lightener, yeast.

sourly *adv.* bitingly, bitterly, grimly.

sourness *n.* bitterness, sharpness, tartness.

sour-sweet *adj.* sweet with a mingling of sourness.

sourwater (*acid*) *n.* firewater, burnwater.

south *adv.* in/towards the south, southwards.

south *n.* that length of the earth's rim which lies over against the north.

south *adj.* belonging to/lying towards/of the south, looking towards the south, (of the wind) blowing from the south.

south-east *adv.* in that path lying midway between south and east.

south-east *n.* that length of the earth's rim which lies between south and east.

south-east *adj.* set in/towards the south-east, blowing from the south-east.

south-easter *n.* wind or storm blowing from the south-east.

south-easterly *adj.* lying towards the south-east, blowing/running from there.

south-easterly *adv.* towards the south-east.

south-eastern *adj.* of the south-east, lying on the south-east side.

south-eastward/s *adv.* towards the south-east.

south-eastward *n.* the south-east fourthing.

south-eastward/s *adj.* set towards the south-east.

south-eastwardly *adv.* towards the south-east.

south-eastwardly *adj.* set/leading towards, blowing from the south-east.

southerly *adv.* to the southward, from the south, on the south side.

southerly *adj.* set towards the south, southern, blowing from the south.

southern *adj.* coming from/living in/lying to the south, blowing from the south.

southerner *n.* dweller in the south.

southernmost, southmost *adj.* set farthest to the south.

southing (or northing) *n. latitude.*

southland *n.* southern land or hundred.

southly *adj.* southern.

southly *adv.* in/towards the south, looking towards the south, from the south.

south-right *adv.* dead/straight south.

south-rim *n.* south shorelands.

South Sea *n.* the sea to the south of England, the English *Channel.*

south-side the side set/lying towards the south.

southward/s *adv.* to/towards the south.

southward *adj.* that which goes or looks southward.

southwardly *adv.* to/towards the south, from a southern fourthing.

southwest *adv.* in that path lying midway between south and west.

southwester *n.* wind or storm blowing from the south-west.

southwesterly *adj.* lying towards the south-west, blowing/running from there.

southwesterly *adv.* towards the south-west.

southwestern *adj.* of the south-west, lying on the south-west side.

south-westward/s *adv.* towards the south-west.

south-westward *n.* the south-west fourthing.

south-westward *adj.* set towards the south-west.

south-westwardly *adv.* towards the south-west.

south-westwardly *adj.* set/leading towards/ blowing from the south-west.

sow *n.* she- pig.

sow *v.* 1) to seed, strew, 2) to begin, bring about, give rise to, set afoot, set going.

sow-back *n.* ridge, height, highland, upland.

sower *n.* one who sows seed.

spade *n.* shovel.

spade *v.* to delve, ditch, till the ground.

spadeful *n.* enough earth to fill a spade.

spadework *n.* hard work, grind, hard-going, uphill work, warm work.

span *n.* 1) the stretch of the hand from the top of the thumb to the top of the little finger (taken to be nine inches), 2) the span of life.

span *v.* 1) to *measure* with the outstretched hand, 2) to straddle, to throw a bridge over a *river.*

span-long *adj.* having the length of a span, short.

spar *v.* 1) to step and weave, strike and step back, 2) to fall out, throw words about.

spare *adj.* 1) above one's needs, enough and to spare, over and above, leftover, on one's hands, 2) (of speech) sparing with words, unforthcoming, 3) lean, thin, thin as a lath/rake, 4) careful, forgoing.

spare *v.* 1) to be forbearing/ruthful, forgive, 2) to be sparing, be penny-wise, forgo.

sparely *adv.* 1) carefully, sparingly, 2) shortly, in a few words, in a nutshell.

spareness *n.* carefulness, holding back.

sparing *adj.* canny, careful, forgoing, minding the pence.

sparingly *adv.* carefully, sparely.

spark *n.* 1) flicker, gleam, glow, light, 2) bit, hint, mark.

spark *v.* 1) to give forth sparks, to sparkle, 2) to spark off, awaken, fire up, quicken, put life into, set going, spur, start, stir up.

sparkle *n.* 1) brightness, fire, flicker of light, gleam, play of light, sheen, shimmer, shine, 2) beating heart, life, light-heartedness, liveliness, sunniness.

sparkle *v.* 1) to flicker, gleam, glisten, glow, shimmer, shine, twinkle, 2) to be lively/merry/witty, to shine.

sparkler *n.* a sparkling firework.

sparkling *adj.* 1) aglow, bright, gleaming, shimmering, shining, 2) blithe, full of life, glad, laughing, light-hearted, lively, merry, playful, sunny.

sparrow *n.* house sparrow, eavesing sparrow, thack sparrow.

spattle *n.* spettle, spit, spittle.

spattle *v.* to spit.

speak *v.* to say, say out, say outright, speak out/up, talk, hold forth, set forth, bear witness, betell, give tongue, bring out, come out with, give out, get out, put about, have one's say, open up, put in a word or two, put it over, talk one's fill.

speaker *n.* speech-maker, spokesman, spokeswoman, talker.

speaking *adj.* 1) (of the eyes) quick, ready, 2) (of a likeness) true.

spear *n.* ash-holt, shaft, death-spear, light spear, stabbing spear, throwing-spear,

spear *v.* to run through, spit, stick, kill.

spear bearer *n.* ash-bearer, ash-man, spearman.

spear-hand *n.* the hand with which a spear is held and thrown.

spearhead *n.* 1) iron (or other) head of a spear, 2) forward line, forerunner, leader.

spearhead *v.* to head, lead the way.

spear-kin *n.* he-kind.

spear-like *adj.* sharp, sharp-edged, sharp as a needle, needlelike, thorny.

spearman *n.* ash-bearer, ash-man, spear bearer.

spear-play (*battle*) *n.* ash-play, bloodshed, fight, spear-storm.

spear-shaft *n.* the shaft of a spear.

spear-shaped *adj.* like a spear in shape, tipped like a spear.

spear-side *n.* men, menfolk, man's side of the kindred.

spear-storm (*battle*) *n.* ash-play, blood-bath, bloodshed, blood-letting, spear-play.

spear-swift (*peregrine falcon*) *n.* spear-hawk.

speck *n.* dot, mark.

speckless *adj.* clean, unmarked.

specky *adj.* marked with specks.

speech *n.* 1) talk, one's say, spoken word, word of mouth, ready speech, set speech, thing said, greeting, 2) the tongue of a folk, mother tongue, folk speech.

speech-craft (*linguistics*) *n.* speechlore, word-craft.

speech-craftsman (*linguist*) *n.* word-craftsman.

speech-day *n.* day at the end of the school year when good work is acknowledged and speeches are made.

speechful *adj.* gossipy, long-winded, newsy, windy, wordful, wordy.

speech-house (*parliament* house) *n.* elder-house, folkmoot, gathering, rede-hall.

speechless *adj.* bewildered, floored, overcome, quoth-less, shaken, struck dumb.

speechlore (*grammar, linguistics, philology*) *n.* speech-craft, love of words, wordlore.

speech-maker *n.* speaker, word-wielder.

speech-reading *n.* lip-reading.

speed *n.* liveliness, quickness, speediness, breakneck speed, fair speed, full speed, headlong speed, lightning speed, reckless speed, utmost speed, full steam, swiftness.

speed *v.* to drive, fly, go all out, go full steam, leap, make the running, outdrive, quicken one's speed, ride hard, run like mad, run like the wind, spring, spur on, step out, storm along, sweep along, tear along, tear up the ground, thunder along.

speedily *adv.* all out, at speed, at full speed, like an arrow/lightning/a shot, swiftly.

speedster *n.* one who drives at high speed.

speed up *v.* to gather speed, pick up speed, put on speed, quicken, spur on, drive forward/onward, push forward/onward, swiften, 'open up the throttle', 'step on it'.

speedy *adj.* fast, flying, light-footed, like an arrow, lively, nimble, nimble-footed, swift, as/like the wind, quick, quick-footed, quick as lightning/thought/the wind.

spelk *n.* chip, thatching-rod.

spell *n.* 1) byspell, gospel, tale, tidings, 2) curse, spell-weaving, witching.

spell *n.* span, stint, stretch, tide, time, while.

spell *v.* to speak, talk, tell.

spellbind *v.* to bewitch, bind, draw, grip, hold spellbound, play upon, trap.

spell-binding *adj.* bewitchful, bewitching, 'come hither', holding, winning.

spell-bound *adj.* bewitched, far-away, gripped, smitten, thrilled, under a spell.

spellcraft *n.* tale-weaving and telling.

spell-weaver *n.* soothsayer, wise man/woman, witch.

spellweaving *n.* foretelling, soothsaying, spell-making, witchcraft.

spend[5] *v.* 1) to buy up, lay out, 2) to drain, empty, run through, wear out, 3) to spend time, fill the time, while away.

spettle *n.* spattle, spittle, spit.

spew *v.* 1) to be sick, bring up, retch, spit out, throw up, 2) to send out, throw out.

spider *n.* attercop, spinner.

spider-like *adj.* 1) long and thin, spidery, 2) crafty, sharp, shifty.

spider-web, spider's web *n.* knot, maze, net, weavings and windings.

spidery *adj.* fleshless, lean, long and thin, thin as a lath/rake.

spill *n.* flood, leak, overspill,

spill *v.* to overflow, run over, shed, slop over, well over.

spilth *n.* that which has been spilt.

spin *n.* 1) drive, outing, ride, 2) bent, leaning, one-sidedness.

spin *v.* 1) to draw out and twist the thin lines of wool or flax (to make thread), 2) to reel, twist, wheel, 3) to spin a tale, make up, tell, 4) (in stockball) to make the ball spin (in flight and so off the pitch).

spindle *n.* ax-tree, pin, pintle, rod.

spindle-kin *n.* she-kind, womanhood.

spindle-shanked *adj.* bony, raw-boned, lean, spindly, thin-shanked.

spindle-side *n.* women, womenfolk, womankind, woman's side of the kindred (also 'distaff side').

spindle tree *n.* louse-thorn.

splindling *adj.* 1) (of plants)growing up into long stalks, 2) spindly.

spindly *adj.* bony, lean, spindle-shanked, thin as a lath/rake.

spin-drier *n.* *machine* for drying washing through the spinning of it.

spinner *n.* 1) spider, 2) spinner of wool, 3) (in stockball) one who spins the ball, off-spinner, *leg*-spinner.

spinning-house *n.* room or building for the work of spinning wool.

spinning-wheel *n.* wheelwork for the spinning of wool.

spin-off *n.* a welcome unlooked-for outcome from some work that has been done.

spin out *v.* to drag out, draw out, lengthen, string out.

spinster *n.* 1) a woman spinner, 2) woman who is unwed.

spinsterhood *n.* maidenhood, spinsterdom.

spire *n.* 1) the tall and narrow growth of a plant, 2) tall work rising from the top of a church *tower* and narrowing to a tip.

spire-steeple *n.* steeple with a spire on the top of it.

spiry *adj.* (of grasses) rising in narrow shoots.

spit *n.* 1) sharp-ended bit of wood, 2) foreland, tongue of land.

spit *n.* spattle, spettle, spittle.

spit *v.* 1) to prick, riddle, run through, spear, stab, stick, 2) (of fish) to put on a spit, for drying or smoking.

spit *v.* 1) to spattle, 2) (of a fire) to seethe, 3) to spit with rain.

spitfire *n.* fire-eater, hell-cat, redhead, shrew, vixen.

spittle *n.* spattle, spettle, spit.

spoke *n.* one of the strengthening staves of a wheel, set into the nave at one end and into the rim of the wheel at the other.

spokeshave *n.* a kind of drawing knife for shaping spokes.

spokesman *n.* for-speaker, henchman, right-hand man, word-bearer, word-bringer.

spokeswoman *n.* backer, for-speaker, friend in need, word-bearer, word-bringer.

spoon *n.* eating tool with bowl and handle.

spot[(1)] *n.* 1) mark, smear, speck, streak, 2) bit, dot, drop, hint, whit, 3) neck of the woods, neighbourhood, setting, 4) plight, tight spot.

sprat *n.* small sea-fish.

sprawl *n.* an untidy spreading out of the limbs.

sprawl *v.* to lie down, stretch out in 'any old way'.

spray *n.* shoot/s and twig/s wreathed together to put on one's clothing.

spread *n.* broadening, making headway, making strides, unfolding, widening.

spread *v.* 1) to go forward, grow, make strides, ripen, rise, 2) to spread the word, get the word out, put it about, put it over, make much of.

spreadsheet *n.* lined sheet wherein *figures* can be set down and worked on.

spring *n.* 1) head-waters, springhead, wellhead, wellspring, 2) the time of new growth, seed-time, springtide, springtime, Lent-tide, 3) beginning, rise, start, 4) hop, leap, springy step, 5) drive, life, springiness, 6) hairspring, mainspring.

spring *v.* 1) to flow out of the ground, overflow, well up, 2) to grow, put forth, shoot up, spring forth, spring up, sprout, swell, 3) to arise from, begin from, come of/from, flow/grow/spring/stem from, 4) to hop, hurdle, leap, leap-frog, leap over, spring to one's feet, spring back/ forward/ over, 5) to fall upon, set upon, strike, swoop, 6) to spring something on one, startle, take unawares.

spring-board *n.* 1) board from which a swimmer may dive into the water, 2) stepping stone, flying start, head start.

spring-clean *n.* shake-up, uplift.

spring-cleaning *n.* cleaning right through the house (most often in the spring).

springe *n.* lime-twig, net, trap.

springe *v.* 1) to lime, net, take in a trap, 2) to set traps.

springer *n.* 1) a kind of fish which leaps, 2) spur set in the wall of a building from from a roof-bow (*arch*) springs.

spring-flood *n.* 1) tide coming shortly after the new and full moon in which the water rises to its highest reach, 2) *river*-flood in spring-time.

spring-head *n.* the wellhead from which a *river* begins.

springiness *n.* bendiness, litheness, willowiness.

spring-lock *n.* a kind of lock in which a spring drives the bolt.

spring-tide, spring-time *n.* the time of new growth, seed-time, Lent-tide.

spring-water *n.* water taken straight from a spring.

springy *adj.* lissom, lithe, stretchy, willowy, yielding, bendsome.

sprout *n.* shoot.

sprout *v.* to be out, blossom, grow, put forth, shoot up, spring up, swell.

spun-yarn *n.* yarn made by spinning.

spur *n.* 1) a sharp end fitted to a rider's heel with which to prick the horse's side and drive it forward, a goad, 2) headland, height *thrusting* out from a main ridge, peak.

spur *v.* to awaken, drive, goad, hound, prick, quicken, stir up.

spurn *v.* to be deaf to, cold-shoulder, cut, cut dead, find loathsome, give one a black mark, harden one's heart, hate, have no time for, have nothing to do with, keep at arm's length, keep out, leave out in the cold, loathe, look down one's nose at, mislike, not abide, not hold with, not think much of, set at naught, shake one's head, shrink from, <u>shun</u>, shut the door on, strike off, think little of, think the worse of, throw aside, throw away, <u>upbraid</u>, warn off, wash one's hands of.

spurred *adj.* 1) wearing spurs, 2) fanged, saw-edged, sawtoothed, <u>prickly</u>.

squench *v.* 1) to quench, quell, put out, smother, stamp out, 2) to allay, slake.

stab *n.* prick.

stab *v.* to cut, run through, spear, wound.

staddle *n.* 1) root or stock of a tree after it has been felled, 2) a stand of wood or stone on which a rick is set.

staff *n.* 1) rod, stick, walking stick, 2) (*letter* of the *alphabet*) beech-staff, book-rune, bookstaff, bookstave, stave, writing-mark, 3) hands, workers, workfolk.

staff *v.* to hire, take on, man.

stag *n.* he- red deer, hart.

stag-beetle *n.* a kind of beetle.

stag-headed *adj.* (of a *beast*) having a head like that of a stag.

stag-horn *n.* horns of a stag.

staghound *n.* deer-hound.

stair/s *n.* flight of steps, stairway.

stair-foot *n.* the foot of a stairway, the standing before the lowest step.

stair-head *n.* the standing at the head of a flight of steps.

stairway *n.* stairs, flight of steps.

stake *n.* shaft, stave, stick, stock.

stake *v.* to drive a stake into the ground so as to a) hinder an onset, b) hold up a young plant, c) mark out the ground.

stale *n.* 1) one of the sides of a ladder, 2) long, narrow handle (of a rake or such).

stalk *n.* shoot, stem, stock.

stalk *n.* a striding walk.

stalk *v.* 1) to angle, be after, creep up on, follow, go softly/stealthily, hunt, run after, shadow, tail, 2) to stride, strut.

stalker *n.* one who stalks game.

stalking-horse *n.* 1) horse taught to let the fowler hide behind it and work his way near to the game, 2) one whose *part* in an undertaking hides its true end.

stalky *adj.* having a cluster of stalks.

stall *n.* 1) standing-stead for horses or kine, horse-stall, horse-stand, 2) seat/s in a church, 3) seat/s in a playhouse, 4) stand (where goods for sale are laid out).

stall-fed *adj.* (of horses, kine and such) fed in the stalls.

stallion[3] *n.* steed, stud-horse.

stalwart, stalworth *adj.* doughty, <u>steadfast</u>, steady, steely, unshaken, unshrinking.

stammer *n.* faltering or lameness of speech, mis-saying, a slip in one's words.

stammer *v.* to falter, mis-say, speak thickly, slip on one's words.

stamp *n.* 1) brand, mark, earmark, hallmark, 2) heavy tread, 3) breed, kind, make.

stamp *v.* 1) to brand, mark, 2) to step/tread heavily.

stamp out *v.* to bring to <u>naught</u>, do away with, quell, quench, <u>undo</u>, <u>unmake</u>.

stand *n.* 1) holding one's ground against the foe, 2) a standstill, 3) a stand where goods for sale are laid out, stall, 4) uplifted steading for onlookers at a games meeting, 5) a rest to stand things on.

stand *v.* 1) to get to one's feet, rise, spring up, stand up, straighten up, 2) to be on one's feet, be upright, keep one's feet, stand still, 3) to hold fast, hold good, 4) to bear, hold/stand one's ground, hold out against, put up with, stand up to, <u>withstand</u>, 5) to put, set, 6) to stand for a seat in the folkmoot (*parliament*), 7) to <u>abide</u>, be, sit.

stand aside *v.* to bide one's time, let well alone, look on, sit tight.

stand by *v.* 1) to stand ready, 2) to look on, not lift a finger, not stir, watch, 3) to back, speak up for, stand up for, uphold.

stand-by *n.* 1) a boat kept ready to give help if needed, 2) someone or something that one has to fall back on.

stand down[6] *v.* to call it a day, give up, have done with, leave, step down.

stand fast *v.* to <u>abide</u>, hold fast, stand shoulder to shoulder, <u>withstand</u>.

stand in *v.* to do another's work, step into the shoes of.

stand-in *v.* a stand-by, another of like worth/weight, steadman.

standing *n.* name, fair name, good name, high name, footing, weight, worth.

standing *adj.* 1) upright, 2) still, 3) abiding, lasting, longstanding, settled.

standing stone *n.* great stone set upright in long-ago days.

stand-off *n.* deadlock, standstill.

standoffish *adj.* cold, cool, frosty, icy, unforthcoming, <u>unfriendly</u>, unwelcoming.

standoffishness *n.* coldness, coolness, frostiness, stiffness, unfriendliness.

stand out *v.* 1) to be seen, be striking, leap to the eye, show up, stand forth, stand out a mile, 2) to be better, outshine, overshadow, 3) to hold out, swim against the tide.

standstill *n.* at a standstill, on hold, left hanging.

stand up for *v.* to back, side with, stand by/with, take up the cudgels for, uphold.

stand up to *v.* to not take it lying down, stand one's ground, set at naught, withstand.

stand with *v.* to side with, speak up for, stand by, take up the cudgels for, uphold.

stanniel *n.* kestrel.

staple *n.* 1) stake, stock, upright, 2) holdfast, hook, 3) thin bit of wire by which *papers* are fastened together.

staple *v.* to clip *papers* together with staples.

stapler *n.* tool for clipping *papers*.

star *n.* 1) heavenly body, 2) *asterisk*, starkin, 3) draw, name, lead, leading light, leading man/lady.

star *v.* 1) to highlight a word or name by putting a star against it, 2) to play the lead.

starboard 1) *n.* the right-hand side of a ship (where once the 'steering board' was set), 2) *adj.* on or of the right side of a ship.

star-bright *adj.* bright as a star, bright with stars.

starch *n.* something got from meal and *used* to stiffen cloth goods.

starch *v.* to stiffen with starch.

starchy *adj.* hard, set, starched, stern, stiff, unbending.

starcluster *n.* constellation.

starcraft (*astronomy*) *n.* starlore, star-watching.

star-delver (*astrologer*) *n.* tide-shewer.

stardom *n.* a name, name-worth, standing.

stare *n.* look, long look, steady look.

stare *v.* to be all eyes, stand and stare, stare at, stare hard, stare in wonder.

starfish *n.* sea *creature*.

stark *adj.* 1) stiff, unyielding, 2) bald, bare, cold, dreary, forsaken, grim, hard, harsh, 3) sharp, striking, 4) downright, out-and-out, sheer, straightforward, utter.

stark *adv.* altogether, thoroughly, utterly, wholly.

stark blind *adj.* stock-blind, stone-blind, utterly blind, wholly blind.

stark dead *adj.* dead and gone, stone dead, dead as a doornail.

stark-hearted *adj.* doughty, stalworth, steadfast, steely.

stark-naked *adj.* bare, mother naked, start-naked, stripped, unclothed, unclad, in the raw, naked as the day one was born, without a stitch on.

stark naught *adj.* lost to shame, shameless, utterly bad, utterly worthless.

starkin *n.* asterisk, star.

starless *adj.* without stars or starlight, black as night.

starlight *n.* the light of the stars.

star-like *adj.* shining like a star, shaped like a star.

starling *n.* stare.

starlit *adj.* lit by the stars, starry, cloudless.

starlore (*astronomy*) *n.* starcraft, star-watching.

starn (*tern*) *n.* kipp, kirr mew.

starred *adj.* 1) studded with stars, starry, 2) (of a horse or cow) having a star on the forehead, 3) marked with a starkin/*asterisk* against some word or name.

starry *adj.* 1) full of stars, lit up with stars, starlit, unclouded, 2) bright as a star, shining like a star, 3) star-shaped.

starry-eyed *adj.* dreaming, ever hoping, hopeful.

start *n.* tail (of a bird).

start *n.* 1) twitch, 2) beginning, first step/s, opening, outset, 3) a headstart.

start *v.* 1) to shy, start at one's own shadow, twitch, 2) to begin, make a beginning, set about, take the first step, 3) to arise, come into being, first see the light of day, 4) to get something going, start something, start up, set up.

starter *n.* 1) food set before folk before the main meal, 2) thing that sparks a *vehicle-engine* into life.

startle *v.* to burst upon, give one a fright, fill with fear, overcome, shake.

startled *adj.* on edge, shaken, starting at a sound, fearful, unsettled, upset.

startling *adj.* fearsome, frightening, nightmarish.

startlingly *adv.* amazingly, bewilderingly, strikingly.

start-naked *adj.* bare, stark naked, stripped, unclothed, unclad, without a stitch on.

starve *v.* 1) to have no food, die from lack of food, 2) to hold/keep back, stint.

starveling *n.* a starving man/woman/child (shrunken through lack of food).

star-watcher (*astronomer*) *n.* star-seeker, star-wit.

star-watching (*astronomy*) *n.* starcraft, starlore.

starwort *n.* plant with white starry blooms.

starwrit *n.* astrology.

stave *n.* 1) narrow, shaped length of wood which with others (set side by side and hooped) makes up a tun/*barrel*, 2) rod, 3) (*letter* of the *alphabet*) staff, beech-staff, bookstaff, bookstave, writing-mark, 4) stave or *stanza* of a poem, 5) set of lines for written *music*.

stave *v.* 1) to break into and empty, stave in, 2) to stave off, hold off, ward off.

stave-fast (*literal*) *adj.* word for word.

stave-hoard (*alphabet*) *n.* horn-book, stave-row.

stave-likeness (*alliteration*) *n.* *sound*-likeness (in the first staves or *letters* of words).

stave-mark (*character, letter*) *n.* beech-staff/stave, mark.

stay *n.* a main rope of a ship, from a mast-head to mast-head or down to the deck.

stead *n.* 1) *place*, steading, stow, 2) 'room'.

steadfast *adj.* dogged, doughty, dreadless, fearless, high-hearted, lasting, knightly, manful, settled, stalwart, stalworth, stead-hard, steady, steely, strong-minded, strong-willed, tireless, undying, unfearing, unshaken, unshifting, unshrinking, unswerving, untiring, unyielding, unwearying, true to the end.

be **steadfast** *v.* to abide, bear, forbear, hold fast, stand fast, stand.

steadfastly *adv.* come what may, doggedly, fearlessly, manfully, unswervingly.

steadfastness *n.* backbone, doggedness, doughtiness, grit, manliness, mind made up, one-mindedness, stalworthness, steadiness, steeliness, sternness, strength of heart/mind/will, tirelessness, true-heartedness, whole-heartedness.

stead-hard *adj.* abiding, steadfast, steady, steely, strong, unshaken.

steadily *adv.* doggedly, steadfastly, unfalteringly.

steadiness *n.* doggedness, backbone, grit, manliness, toughness.

steading (*farmstead*) *n.* holding, smallholding, croft, fields, meadland.

steadless *adj.* fitful, flighty, light-minded, shaky, unsteady, unsettled, unsteadful.

steadlore (*topography*) *n.* landshape, lie of the land.

steady *adj.* 1) fast, still, unshaking, 2) even, unbroken, unfaltering, 3) settled, steadfast, having two feet on the ground, 4) dogged, stalwart, stalworth.

steady *v.* 1) to hold/make steady, make fast, 2) to settle, set one's mind at rest.

steal *v.* to be light-fingered, house-break, make off with, reave, fleece, strip, thieve.

steal away *v.* to slip away, slip through, win free, make off.

stealth *n.* craftiness, foxiness, knowingness, shiftiness, stealthiness.

stealthful *adj.* crafty, not straightforward, shady, sharp, shifty, stealthy, underhand.

stealthily *adv.* carefully, hiddenly, shiftily, warily, watchfully.

stealthiness *n.* stealth-work, web, web-weaving, underhand dealing.

stealthy *adj.* awake, canny, crafty, fox-like, heedful, like a thief, wary.

steam *n.* 1) the 'mist' given off by seething water, 2) drive, 'go', strength.

steam *v.* 1) to give off steam, 2) (of a ship) to steam ahead, 3) to cook with steam.

steamboat *n.* boat driven by steam.

steamer *n.* steamboat, steamship.

steamship *n.* ship driven by steam.

steamy *adj.* clammy, hot, sticky, sweaty.

steed *n.* stud-horse, bold horse, great horse.

steel *n.* 1) hardened iron, 2) cold steel (bladed weapons).

steel *v.* to harden, give heart/strength to, put heart into, stiffen, strengthen, toughen.

steeliness *n.* backbone, grit, manliness, sternness, toughness

steel oneself *v.* to abide, be one-hearted, burn one's boats/bridges, clench/grit one's teeth, cut through, dare, give oneself to, give up everything for, go to all/any lengths, not yield, put one's heart into, put one's shoulder to the wheel, see it through, set one's heart on, stand one's ground, throw away the sheath.

steely *adj.* hard/tough as steel, hardened, strong-minded, strong-willed, unyielding.

steelyard *n.* weigh-beam, weight-mete.

steep *adj.* 1a) sheer, straight up/down, headlong, 1b) marked, sharp, 1c) dear, pretty penny, stiff, worthly, 2) *n.* hill-slope, sloping edge, steep slope, 3) *adv.* with a steep slope, steeply.

steep *v.* 1) to drench, soak, 2) to go deeply into, bury oneself in, steep oneself in.

steepen *v.* to become steep or steeper.

steeple *n.* tall church *tower* (often housing the bells).

steer *n.* young ox (most often meaning one that has been *gelded*).

steer *n.* a lead.

steer *v.* 1) to steer a boat or ship, handle a ship, hold the helm, put the helm up/down, 2) to lead on/through.

steerer *n.* helmsman, steersman.

steering *n.* handling, overseeing, running, stewarding.

steering *adj.* of that which takes a lead and shows the way (as in 'steering body').

steerless *adj.* unwilling to be led, wayward, wilful.

steer-rudder *n.* rudder, steer-oar.

steersman *n.* helmsman, steerer, ship-steerer.

steersmanship *n.* headship, leadership.

stem *n.* 1) stalk/shoot of a plant, stock of a tree, 2) blood line, kin-reckoning, stock.

stem (of a ship) *n.* 1) bows, foreship, head, 2) the stern.

stem *v.* 1) (of a ship) to make headway against tide or wind, 2) (of a swimmer) to breast the waves, swim against the stream, 3) (of a bird) to fly against the wind.

stem *v.* 1) to rise straight up as a stem, 2) to spring from/of.

stench *n.* a bad smell, foul stink, foul smell, reek.

step *n.* 1) footstep, footfall, stride, tread, 2) the stride as a *measure* of length, 3) step of a stairway or ladder, 4) doorstep, sill, 5) (in a sailing ship) the stand in which is set the heel of a mast, 6) a step towards some outcome.

step *v.* 1) to take a step, tread, 2) to step out somewhere, walk, 3) to *measure* length by reckoning steps, 4) to set a mast into its step.

stepbrother *n.* son of one's stepfather or stepmother.

stepchild *n.* stepson or stepdaughter.

stepdaughter *n.* daughter of one's wife or husband from her/his former wedlock.

step down *v.* to bow out, make way for, yield up.

stepfather *n.* husband of one's mother by later wedlock.

step-ladder *n.* folding ladder having *flat* steps instead of rungs.

stepmother *n.* wife of one's father by later wedlock.

stepping-stone *n.* bridge, short cut.

step-shoe *n.* light indoor shoe, sleeve-shoe.

stepsister[(2)] *n.* daughter of one's stepfather or stepmother.

stepson *n.* son of one's wife or husband from her/his former wedlock.

sterling 1) *n.* the English silver penny, true English *money*, 2) *adj.* manly, true-hearted, upright, worthful, worthy.

stern[(2)] *n.* steer-settle, stern-sheet/s, after-ship.

stern *adj.* cold, forbidding, gloomy, grim, stark, tough, unbending, unyielding.

stern-like *adj.* hard as iron, heartless, iron-handed, ruthless, stony-hearted.

sternly *adv.* coldly, grimly, starkly.

sternness *n.* grit, steadiness, steeliness, toughness.

steward *n.* one handling business for another, keeper, overseer, reeve.

stewardship *n.* the care and oversight of lands and goods belonging to another.

stick *n.* cudgel, rod, staff, stake, stave.

stick *v.* 1) to prick, spear, spit, stab, stick into, 2) to bind, fasten, make fast, hold, hook on, stick on, tie on, 3) to cleave to, hold together, stand shoulder to shoulder, stick together, 4) to stick

out, stand out, 5) to stand up for, side with, stand by.

sticker *n.* marker.

stickiness *n.* 1) *glueyness*, 2) clamminess, steaminess, wetness.

stickleback *n.* small fish.

stickler *n.* litling, narrowling, narrow mind.

sticky *adj.* 1) *gluey*, 2) clammy, steamy, sweaty, sweltering.

stiff *adj.* hard, flinty, unbending, unyielding.

stiffen *v.* to give heart to one, put heart into one, harden, steel, strengthen, toughen.

stiffly *adv.* coldly, sternly, unbendingly.

stiff-necked *adj.* hardened, headstrong, self-willed, stiff-backed, unbending, wilful.

stiffness *n.* hardness, sternness, stoniness, toughness.

stile *n.* steps (of stone or wood) by which walkers can get over or through a *fence* or hedge from one field into the next.

still *n.* 'still' shot from a film.

still *adj.* 1) at rest, glassy, smooth, stock-still, unstirring, windless, 2) stilly.

still *v.* to allay fears, settle, smooth, soothe, steady.

still *adv.* 1) even now, up until now, yet, 2) but, nevertheless, notwithstanding.

still-birth[(2)] *n.* bringing forth of a child that has died in the womb.

still-born *n.* born dead, dead-born.

still life *n.* drawing/line-drawing/likeness (of 'breath-less'/*inanimate* things such as dead game, apples and such).

stillness *n.* windlessness.

still-water *n.* slack-water (which see).

stilly *adj.* still.

stilly *adv.* mildly, softly.

sting *n.* 1) prick, wound, 2) bite, sharpness.

sting *v.* to goad, harry, hound, needle, stir up or worry someone.

stinging *adj.* biting, bitter, burning, cutting, shrewish, waspish, withering.

stingy *adj.* hard-fisted, hard-handed, hard-hearted, mean, mean-hearted, tight-fisted.

stink *n.* bad smell, foul smell, reek, stench, strong smell.

stink *v.* to give off a bad smell, reek, stink in the nostrils, stink to high heaven.

stinking *adj.* foul-smelling, high, rank, reeking, smelling, evil-smelling, unhealthy.

stint *n.* share, shift, span, spell, stretch, time.

stint *v.* to be mean, be penny-wise, be sparing, be careful, hold back, withhold.

stir *n.* ado, to-do, upheaving, uproar.

stir *v.* 1) to come, go, come and go, 2) to flutter, quiver, shake, 3) to beat, stir up (seething broth or such), 4) to bestir oneself, be up and about, look lively, 5) to awaken, drive, fire, goad, prick, quicken, spur, thrill.

stirrer *n.* 1) doer, driver, fighter, firebrand, shaker, 2) busybody, gossip.

stirring *adj.* heady, heart-warming/-stirring/-swelling/-thrilling, soul-stirring.

stirrup/s *n.* foothold/s for a horse-rider.

stitch *n.* 1) prick, stab, twinge, 2) the working of a threaded needle in and out of cloth or (in bodycraft/*surgery*) of the edges of a wound, needlework, stitchery.

stitch *v.* to hem, seam, sew together, stitch up.

stitch-craft *n.* needlecraft, needlework, sewing, stitchery.

stitching *n.* seam-work, sewing, stitch-craft, stitchery.

stock/s *n.* 1) stem of a tree, 2) house, kindred ties, kin-reckoning, 3) tool for making a reckoning (*punishment*) with a misdoer, in which the ankles are held in holes in two locking beams of wood, 4) framework for holding a ship while it is being built, 5) the body or handle of a weapon (as in 'lock, stock and *barrel*'), 6) goods or wares stowed, 7) holdings, shares, 8) livestock, 9) *railway* wains, 10) the 'sap' from seething bones and meat, from which broth is made.

stock *v.* to deal in, handle, keep, sell, trade in.

stock *adj.* everyday, run-of-the-mill, set, well-worn.

stockball[(2)] (*cricket*) *n.* bat-and-ball.

stock-blind *adj.* as blind as a stock, stone-blind, utterly blind, wholly blind.

stock-book *n.* book in which the wares held by a business are written up.

stock-dead *adj.* dead and gone, dead as a doornail, stark dead, stone-dead.

stock-deaf *adj.* deaf as a stock, stone-deaf, wholly deaf.

stockholder *n.* owner of shares (in a business or of *government* owings).

stocking/s *n.* tights, shank-wear, netherstock.

stockman *n.* one who looks after and rears livestock.

stock-room *n.* room where goods are stowed, ready for sale.

stock-still *adj.* frozen, still as the grave, stone-still, unstirring.

stock up *v.* to build up stocks, gather up, fill up, heap up, lay in, lay up, put by, stow.

stock-weight *n.* *standard* weight (as against *Troy* weight).

stocky *adj.* short, thick-set.

stone *n.* 1) building stone, 2) *jewel*, 3) the stone of a *fruit*, kernel, seed, 4) weight (being fourteen pounds, or one eighth of a hundredweight).

stone *v.* to throw stones, to stone to death.

stonebill *n.* stone-cutter.

stone-blind *adj.* stark blind, stock-blind, utterly blind, wholly blind.

stone-bow *n.* stone *arch.*

stone-craft *n.* the stone-wright's craft.

stonecrop *n.* plant which grows on stones and old walls.

stone-cutter *n.* 1) one who cuts and/or carves stone, stoneworker, stone-wright, 2) tool for cutting or shaping stone, stonebill.

stone dead *adj.* dead and gone, dead as a doornail, stark dead, stock-dead.

stone-deaf *adj.* stock-deaf, wholly deaf.

stone-hard *adj.* overhard, too hard, truly hard, flinty, gritty, unyielding.

stone-like *adj.* flinty, gritty, hard as stone, tough, unbending, unyielding.

stone-lith *n.* stony slope.

stonelore (*geology*) *n.* earthlore.

stone's throw *n.* short way.

stone-still *adj.* as still as a stone, still as the grave, stock-still, unstirring.

stoneware *n.* a kind of hard pot-ware.

stone-way *n.* stone-street (laid down by the Romans).

stonework *n.* work of stone, the business of working with stone.

stoneworker *n.* stonecutter, stone-wright.

stonewort *n.* a fern, stone fern.

stone-wright (*stonemason*) *n.* stonecutter, stoneworker.

stoniness *n.* hardness, stiffness, sternness, toughness.

stony *adj.* flinty, gritty, hard as stone, stone-like, tough, unbending, unyielding.

stony-hearted *adj.* flinty, forbidding, gloomy, iron-handed, ruthless, unlaughing.

stool *n.* 1) seat for one, faldstool, footstool, 2) the sawn-off stock of a felled tree.

stoop *n.* bow.

stoop *v.* 1) to bend down, bow, be bowed, walk with a stoop, 2) to stoop down, go more than half-way, unbend, 3) to stoop to anything, bow one's neck to the yoke.

stooping *adj.* cringing, fawning, mean, worthless.

stop[(4)] *n.* break, breaking-off, deadlock, full stop, shut-down, stand, standstill.

stop[(4)] *v.* 1) to break off, knock off, leave off, bring to an end, end, come to a stop, die away/down/out, down tools, dry up, give over, hold, hold one's hand, let up, pull up, run out, stop short, stop work, wind up, 2) to bridle, bring to a stand/standstill, cut short, draw the ends together, forbid, forfill, have done with, hinder, hold back/up, make an end of, put an end/stop to, put the lid on, quell, see the last of, shut, shut down, stop the flow, stop up, warn off, 3) to abide, be at a stand, stand, hang fire, not stir, not stir a step, rest, rest on one's oars, settle down, stay put, stop for breath.

stopper[4] *n.* cap, lid, top, wedge.

stork *n.* a great wading bird.

storm *n.* 1) blast, cloudburst, hailstorm, high wind, rainstorm, rough weather, sou'wester, storm wind, strong wind, thunder and lightning, wild storm, windstorm, 2) din, fit, hell let loose, outburst, upheaving, uproar.

storm *v.* 1) to be wrathful, bellow, blaze, glower, go off the deep end, grind one's teeth, let fly, quiver with wrath, roar, run wild, seethe, fly off the handle, 2) to beset, fall upon, make an onset, overfall, set upon, strike at, take by storm.

stormily *adv.* heatedly, madly, wildly, wrathfully.

storminess *n.* blast, bluster, outburst, roughness, upheaving, uproar, wildness.

stormy *adj.* blowy, rough, wild.

stove[1] *n.* burner, cooker, oven.

stow (*place*) *n.* stead, steading.

stow *v.* to fill up, gather up, heap up, hoard, lade, lay in, lay up, load up, put by.

stowaway *n.* one who hides in a ship (for lack of the fare).

straddle *v.* 1) to bestraddle, bestride, sit astride, 2) to bridge, span.

straight 1) *adj.* straightforward, above board, dead on, open, true, aright, upright, 2) *n.* straight stretch (of such as a *racecourse*) 3a) *adv.* in a straight line/way, straight to a mark, all the way to the end, 3b) upright.

straight away *adv.* anon, at once, betimes, forthwith, now, soon, straightforth.

straight-edge *n.* length of wood, steel or such, with one true edge for reckoning straightness, or for *guiding* a cutting tool.

straighten *v.* to make/put/set straight, set right, straighten out, unbend, unwarp.

straightforth *adv.* 1) straight onwards, 2) at once, straight away.

straightforward *adj.* straight, open, true, forthright, upright.

straightly *adv.* 1) in a straight line, in a straight way, 2) shortly, straightway.

straightness *n.* the suchness of being straight.

straightway *adv.* at once, betimes, forthwith, now, right now, right away, quickly, shortly, soon, speedily, straightly, there and then, there-right.

strain *n.* breed, bloodstock, stock.

strake *n.* 1) a stretch of the iron rim of a wain-wheel, 2) a streak of some hue other than that of the rest of something.

strake *v.* to mark with lines, to streak.

strand *n.* land by the sea, sea-land, sea-rim, seaboard, seaside, sea-strand.

strand *v.* to drive aground, run aground.

stranded *adj.* 1) aground, grounded, beached, 2) forsaken, helpless, high and dry.

straw *n.* 1) stalks of barley, oats, rye or wheat taken as bedding for livestock, 2) something of little worth, wisp.

strawberry *n.* earth-berry.

straw's breadth *n.* breadth of a straw, next to nothing.

strawy *adj.* draffish, nigh worthless, not worth a thought, two a penny.

streak *n.* 1) layer, line, smear, stroke, 2) bent of mind, make-up, mark, strain.

streak *v.* 1) to smear, 2) to fly, speed, sweep, tear, whistle.

streaked, streaky *adj.* ringed.

stream *n.* 1) bourne, burn, brook, rith/rithy, 2) flow, run, tide, 3) (in school) set.

stream *v.* 1) to burst out, flood, flow, overflow, run, shed, spill, 2) to fly, speed, swarm, tear, teem, 3) to float behind, flutter, swing.

stream-faring (*current*) *n.* flow, flood, sea-stream, stream.

streamer (*flag*) *n.* fane.

street[4] *n.* (Roman) road, roadway, borough-way, lane, thoroughfare, way.

strength *n.* heart of oak, lustiness, main-craft, might, might and main, toughness.

strengthen *v.* 1) to build up, deepen, harden, steel, stiffen, thicken, toughen, 2) to give strength to, give heart to one, put heart into one.

strengthening *n.* growth, rise, broadening, lengthening, widening, waxing.

stretch *n.* 1) stretching out, 2) give, springiness, stretchiness, 3) sweep, 4) run, span, spell, stint, time.

stretch *v.* 1) to stretch one's limbs, straighten out, unbend, 2) to put forth, reach, spread, unfold, 3) to draw out, greaten, lengthen, widen, pull out of shape, spread out, 4) to go on, last, 5) to drive oneself to do better.

stretcher *n.* *litter* for bearing a sick or wounded man or woman.

stretcher-bearer *n.* one who helps bear a stretcher.

188

strew *v.* to bestrew, send all ways, shower, sow, spread, spread abroad.

stricken *adj.* bowed down, careworn, drawn, forstraught, harrowed, heavy-laden, overburdened, sick at heart, woebegone, worn out, wretched.

stride *n.* step, footstep, tread.

stride *v.* to stalk, step out, tread, walk.

strife[(3)] *n.* fight, head-to-head, infighting, set-to, sparring match, storm, to-do, unrest.

strike *n.* 1) drive, onset, 2) walk-out, wild-cat strike, 3) a find (of *oil* or such).

strike *v.* 1) to beat down, fall upon, fell, hit, knock down, smite, thrash, throw down, 2) to come out on strike, stop/strike work, walk out, 3) to come upon, find, light upon, unearth, 4) to dawn on one, come to one, make one think, 5) (in stockball) to drive, hit, take a *wicket*, 6) to ring, toll, 7) to strike out, 8) to strike a light.

strike-breaker *n.* workman who goes on working when others are out on strike.

strike hands *v.* to make/strike a deal, fall in with, settle on, settle with.

striker *n.* 1) (in stockball) the batsman who is taking the *bowling*, 2) workman who downs tools to back a call for more *money* or for a better shape of things at work.

striking *adj.* amazing, great, outstanding, startling, stirring, wonderful.

string *n.* 1) rope, thread, twine, wire, yarn, bowstring, 2) line, row, run.

string *v.* 1) to string a bow, 2) to hang, stretch, thread, 3) to string someone along, have one on, mislead, outwit.

stringy *adj.* 1) chewy, gristly, leathery, sinewy, tough, wiry, 2) lank, straggly, thin.

strip *v.* 1) to strip off, unclothe, shed, take off, 2) to bear away/off, beggar, empty, lay bare, strip bare, fleece, steal, tear down, tear off, tear to shreds, wrench off.

strive[(3)] *v.* 1) to fight, match oneself with, withstand, 2) to bend over backwards, bestir oneself, do one's best/utmost, do something about, get to grips with, give it one's all, go for, go all out for, keep at it, sweat, work hard.

stroke *n.* 1) dint, hit, knock, 2) fit, 3) (in writing) line, mark, down-stroke, up-stroke, 4) knell, ring, 5) (in stockball) cut, drive, pull.

stroke *n.* soft running of the hand over cloth, the skin and such.

stroke *v.* to feel, finger, play with, run the hand over, smooth.

strong *adj.* 1) broad-shouldered, burly, ent-strong, great-limbed, iron-hard, main-hard, main-strong, manful, manly, mighty, full-mighty, more than a match for, sinewy, stalwart, steely, strong as an ox/horse, thickset, tough, well-built, well-knit, 2) feeling good, hale, hale and hearty, healthy, in good heart/shape, lusty, 3) hard-wearing, hefty, meaty, tireless, unwithered, weighty.

strong-arm *adj.* heavy-handed, rough and ready, threatening.

strong drink *n.* ale, beer, brew, mead.

strong-handed *adj.* high and mighty, high-handed, overbearing, overweening.

strong-headed *adj.* 1) fiery, headstrong, hot-headed, quick-hearted, rash, reckless, wilful, 2) clever, sharp, thinking.

stronghold, stronghouse (*fortress*) *n.* fastness, keep, ward.

strongly *adv.* truly, indeed, utterly, fully, wholly, overly.

strong-minded *adj.* strong-willed, steadfast, unbending, unshaken, unyielding.

strong room *n.* wealth-hold.

strong water *n.* *whisky* and such.

strong-willed *adj.* doughty, steadfast, tough, unshrinking, unblenching, unyielding.

strut *n.* a strengthener (of wood, iron or such) in the framework of a building.

strut *n.* a way of walking with stiff steps and head up.

strut *v.* to step stiffly with head up, to show off, stalk, strut about.

stub *n.* 1) the sawn-off stock of a felled tree, 2) a bit left of something that has been broken or worn down, end, tail end.

stub *v.* 1) to cut down a tree near the bottom of the stock, 2) to grub up a tree by the roots, 3) to strike one's toe when walking or running.

stubbed *adj.* 1) (of trees) cut off near the ground, 2) short.

stubby *adj.* short, stocky, thickset.

stuck *adj.* 1) aground, high and dry, stranded, 2) landed, loaded, saddled.

stuck-up *adj.* full of oneself, high and mighty, looking down on one, overbearing, standoffish, swollen-headed, uppish, on one's high horse.

stud *n.* 1) *knob* (such as a nail-head) driven into a door or such, as a strengthener or for the look of it, 2) upright timber in the wall of a building, 3) fastener for a shirt-sleeve.

stud *n.* 1) steading where stallions and mares are kept for breeding, 2) the horses kept at the stud.

studding *n.* the woodwork of a lath and *plaster* wall.

stud-fold *n.* stud-field, stud-paddock, stud-yard.

stud-horse *n.* stallion kept for breeding.

stud-mare *n.* brood mare.

stunt *v.* to slow the growth of, to stop growing.

stunted *adj.* dwarfish, little, short, small, slow-growing, wizened.

sty *n.* pen (with a shed) for pigs, pigsty.

sty *n.* a swelling on the eyelid.

such 1a) *adj.* the like, 1b) as to such, such as, such a thing as, so great, 1c) such and such, 2) *pron.* such folk as, such a thing.

such-like 1) *adj.* of a like kind, 2) *pron.* such-like folk/things.

suchness *n.* being-ness.

suchwise *adv.* in such a way.

suck *n.* the deed of sucking milk from the breast, the sucking out of *air*.

suck *v.* 1) to drink, sip, 2) to draw, pull, take.

sucker *n.* 1) a youngling (of man or *beast*) before it is weaned, sucking-pig, 2) beginner, goose, greenhorn, know-nothing, newling, 3) one who lives off another, hanger-on, leech, 4) shoot thrown out from the foot of a tree or plant.

sucking-pig *n.* young milk-fed pig seen as good for spitting and eating.

suckle *v.* 1) to give suck to, feed a little one at the breast, 2) to bring up on.

suckling *n.* little one, weanling.

suckling *n.* honeysuckle, woodbine.

sullow *n.* plough.

sultry *adj.* hot, sticky, sweaty, sweltering.

summer *n.* summertide, summertime, high summer, midsummer.

summer *v.* to settle somewhere for the summer.

summer-bird *n.* bird that comes to Britain for the summer.

summer-cloud *n.* a fleeting cloud on a summer's day.

summer-fallow *n.* land left fallow through the summer.

summer-house *n.* a 'houseling' in the grounds of a dwelling (giving shade in the height of summer), bower.

summer-lightning *n.* sheet lightning with loud thunder.

summer-like *adj.* like that of summer.

summer-long *adj.* long as a summer's day.

summerly *adj.* of the summer, summer-like, happening in summer.

summer's day *n.* a day in summer, a long day.

summertide, summertime *n.* summer, high summer.

summer-weight *adj.* of light clothing for summer wear.

summery *adj.* summer-like, cloudless, warm.

sun *n.* 1) the star about which go the earth and other heavenly bodies, the day-star, 2) daylight, light, sunlight, sunshine, warmth.

sun *v.* to sun oneself, soak up the sun.

sun-baked *adj.* (of *bricks* and such) baked hard by being left out in the sun.

sunbathe *v.* to sun oneself, soak up the sun, get brown.

sunbeam *n.* beam of sunlight.

sun-bow *n.* a flicker of rainbow hues as sunlight is 'bent' in spray.

sun-bright *adj.* bright as the sun, bright with sunshine, truly bright.

sunburn *n.* brownness, sun-brown,

sunburn *v.* to 'burn' through being out in the sun for too long.

sunburnt *adj.* brown as a berry, burnt, red, ruddy.

sunburst *n.* burst of sunlight as the sun comes out from behind a cloud.

Sunday *n.* Holy Day, First Day (of the week).

Sunday best *n.* one's best clothes, kept for wear on Sundays.

sunder *adj.* asunder.

sunder *v.* 1) to cleave, cut away, cut off, cut through, hew asunder, hew in two, rend, sleave, slive, tear, 2) to come between, drive asunder, drive a wedge between, make bad blood, make foes, put asunder, put off, put one's back up, set against, stand between, stir hatred/loathing, unbind, undo, unhook, unknot, untie, upset, unstitch.

sundered *adj.* cleft, cloven, hewn in half, rent, torn, islanded, alone, lonely.

sundering *n.* break-up, rending, tearing, undoing, unthreading, untying.

sundew *n.* marshland plant that oozes drops which sparkle in the sun as dew.

sun-dried *adj.* (of *bricks*, clay, food) dried by being left out in the sun.

sundries *n.* many small things set together, as not being worth naming one by one.

sundry *adj.* manifold, many, manykind, many-sided, other, some.

sun-dry *v.* (of *bricks*, clay, food) to dry in the sun.

sun-glasses *n.* dark glasses.

sun-glow *n.* 1) a glow of sunlight, 2) a *hazy* light about the sun when there are bits floating in the upper *air* (thrown from a firepeak/*volcano*).

sun-going *adv.* clockwise, sunwise.

sun-hat *n.* broad-rimmed hat shielding the head from hot sun.

sunk *adj.* done for, lost, overwhelmed, shotten.

sunken *adj.* 1) (of land at the sea) drowned, flooded, 2) fallen in (as of ground sunken with the settling of a burial), 3) (of eyes, cheeks) drawn, hollow.

sunless *adj.* without the sun, beclouded, cloudy, dark, dreary, gloomy, grey.

sunlike *adj.* gleaming, shining, truly bright.

sunlight *n.* broad day, daylight, light of day, sunshine.

sunlit *adj.* lighted by the sun, bathed in sunshine.

sunny *adj.* 1) cloudless, dry, set fair, summery, 2) blithe, lively, merry, sparkling.

sunrise, sunrising *n.* 1) break of day, daybreak, dawn, day-dawn, day-red, first light, morn, 2) beginning, dawning, start.

sunset, sunsetting *n.* dusk, eventide, going down of the sun, nightfall, gloaming.

sunshade *n.* sun-blind, sun-shield.

sun-sheen *adj.* fair as the sun.

sunshine *n.* broad day, daylight, sunlight, warmth.

sun-smitten *adj.* sunstruck.

sun-stead (*solstice*) *n.* midsummertide, midwintertide, summer's height, winter's depth.

sunstroke *n.* fit or breakdown coming after being out in the sun too long.

sunstruck *adj.* sun-smitten.

sun-trap *n.* sheltered spot in one's grounds which gets lots of sunshine.

sun-trendle (*halo*) *n.* ring of light, glow of light, sheen.

sunward/s 1) *adv.* toward the sun, 2) *adj.* headed/looking toward the sun.

sunwise *adv.* clockwise, sun-going.

sup *n.* drop, mouthful, sip, thimbleful.

sup *v.* to drink a little, take sips, wet one's lips.

swaddle *v.* 1) to bind a little one in swaddling-clothes, 2) to swathe in cloth-*strips/ bandages*.

swaddling-clothes, swaddling-clouts *n.* cloth-*strips* swathed about a newborn.

swallow *n.* house swallow (also a name of the house *martin*).

swallow *v.* 1) to down, drink, eat, put away, swallow up, wash down, 2) to fall for, go along with, readily believe, take as gospel, 3) (of wrath or such) to bite back, choke back, hold back, hold in, overcome, smother.

swallow-hole *n.* deep hole in the earth (most often in limestone lands).

swallow-tail *n.* *forked* tail like that of a swallow.

swallow-tailed *adj.* having a *forked* tail like that of a swallow.

swan *n.* the lesser wild (Bewick's), tame (*mute*), or whistling/wild (*whooper*) swan.

swan-like *adj.* like a swan, above all in singing its death song ('swan-song').

swanling (*cygnet*) *n.* young swan.

swan neck, swan's neck *n.* long neck, sinewy and white.

swan-song *n.* 1) (in long-held belief) song said to be sung by a dying swan, 2) the last deed or work of one before making way for another, or before his/her death.

swan-upping *n.* the 'upping' and marking of swans on the bill, to show the king's/queen's ownership.

sward *n.* the 'rind' of the earth, green grass, greensward.

swarm *n.* crowd, drove, flood, sea of, stream, throng, the world and his wife.

swarm *v.* 1) to flock, flood, overflow, stream, throng, 2) to have to overflowing.

swarming *adj.* alive with, full, overflowing, rich, thick on the ground, untold.

swart *adj.* black, dark, darksome, dusky, raven, swarth, swarthy.

swarth *n.* 1) rind, the outside, 2) green grass, greensward.

swarth *adj.* black, dark, darksome, swarthy.

swart-hue (*violet*) *n.* deep-blue.

swarthy *adj.* black, dusky, swarth.

swartness *n.* 1) blackness, darkness, utter darkness, 2) (*ink*) book-black.

swath, swathe *n.* 1) the width of grass or corn cut by the mower's scythe, 2) stretch, sweep.

swathe *n.* cloth-*strip* in which something is swathed.

swathe *v.* to bind, bundle up, fold, infold, sheathe, shroud, swaddle, wind.

swear *v.* 1) to swear by, swear on oath, bear witness, give one's word, mean what one says, plight one's troth, take oath, truly mean, 2) to be foul-mouthed, curse.

swearer *n.* 1) one who takes an oath, witness, 2) one given to cursing.

swearing *n.* cursing, evil-speech, the rough edge of one's tongue, smearing.

swear-word *n.* curse, foul word, four-stave ('four-*letter*') word.

sweat *n.* 1) wetness, 2) worry.

sweat *v.* 1) to break out in a sweat, steam, swelter, 2) to lose sleep over, worry.

sweat-cloth (*handkerchief*) *n.* hand-cloth.

sweater *n.* pullover.

sweat-house *n.* hot-house, hotroom, steam room.

sweat-shirt *n.* thin *cotton* sweater.

sweaty *adj.* bathed/drenched/soaked in sweat, clammy, sticky, sweating.

sweep *n.* 1) a clean, 2) span, spread, stretch, 3) combing, going-over, hunt, look.

sweep *v.* 1) to clean, clean up, sweep up, wipe, 2) to look over, run the eye over, 3) to drive, sweep along, 4) to glide, sail, 5) to spread/sweep through, overwhelm.

sweeper *n.* smokestead/*chimney*-sweep, road-sweeper.

sweeping/s *n.* bits, chaff, draff, dross, leavings, throw-outs.

sweeping *adj.* broad, far-reaching, thorough, thoroughgoing, wholesale, wide.

sweet *n.* 1) sweetmeat, 'afters', 2) beloved, darling, dearest, honey, sweetheart.

sweet *adj.* 1) honeyed, sweet as honey, sweet-smelling, 2) sweet to the ear, silvery, 3) kind, soft, soft-hearted, 4) winning, winsome, 5) beloved, darling, dear, dearest.

sweet-brier, -briar *n.* a kind of *rose* having strong prickles.

sweeten *v.* 1) to put in a sweetener, to honey, 2) to smooth over, soften up, soothe.

sweetening *n.* a sweetener.

sweetheart *n.* beloved, darling, lover, true-love, lady-love, young man.

sweet-lipped *adj.* speaking sweetly.

sweetly *adv.* lovingly, softly, winningly, winsomely.

sweetmeat *n.* bakemeat (*pastry*), sweet.

sweet-mouthed *adj.* 1) liking sweet things, 2) speaking sweetly (not truly).

sweetness *n.* sweetening, sweet smell.

sweet-smelling *adj.* smelling sweet, heady.

sweet-spoken *adj.* speaking sweetly.

sweet-toothed *adj.* having a liking for sweet things.

sweet water *n.* *fresh* water.

swell *n.* the heaving of the sea after a storm (making long waves).

swell *v.* 1) to broaden, grow, rise, strengthen, well up, widen, 2) to become louder.

swelling *n.* blain, boil, growth.

swelter *v.* to sweat, break out in a sweat, steam, be hot.

sweltering, sweltry *adj.* clammy, hot, steaming, steamy, sticky, sweaty.

swerve *n.* bend, sidestep, twist.

swerve *v.* to bend, sheer off, shift, sidestep, swing, wheel about.

swift *adj.* fast, flying, quick, speedy, as the wind, quick as lightning/thought.

swift-foot *n.* fast runner, light-foot, quick-foot.

swift-footed *adj.* light-footed, nimble-footed, quick-footed, quick as the wind.

swiften *v.* 1) to make swift/swifter, quicken, spur on, 2) to go swiftly, run, speed.

swiftly *adv.* at full speed, like an arrow, quickly, speedily.

swiftness *n.* quickness, speed, lightning speed.

swill *n.* pigwash, pigswill, slops.

swill *v.* 1) to clean out, flush, wash down, wash out, 2) to shake and stir water or such in a bowl, 3) to drink down, drink freely, drink one's fill.

swim *n.* bathe, dip.

swim *v.* 1) to bathe, go swimming, take a dip, 2) (of the head or brain) to become giddy, to reel, spin, 3) to swim with tears.

swimmer *n.* one who goes out swimming.

swimmingly *adv.* like a dream, like clock-work, readily, smoothly, well.

swine *n.* 1) pig, boar, sow, 2) filthy hound, knave, wretch.

swine-cote *n.* pen or sty for pigs (with a shed), swine-sty, pigsty.

swine-denn *n.* grazing for swine in weald-land.

swineherd *n.* herdsman who cares for swine.

swine-sty *n.* pen or sty for pigs (with a shed), swine-cote, pigsty.

swing *n.* 1) shift, 2) about-turn, 3) full swing (at full speed), 4) swing for children in a playground, swing-boat.

swing *v.* 1) to wave, 2) to see-saw, shift, 3) to sheer off, swing away, swivel, twist, 4) to shake, wave about, wield, 5) to ride in a swing, 6) to hang down, 7) to hit out, strike, 8) (in stockball) to swing the ball into or away from the batsman.

swing-bridge *n.* a kind of drawbridge which swings *round* rather than being lifted up and down.

swingeing *adj.* heavy.

swinish *adj.* belly-worshipping, overfed, piggish.

swipple *n.* that half of the flail which beats the corn in threshing.

swive *v.* to go to bed with, have one's way with, lie with, make love with, sleep with.

swivel *n.* ax-tree, pintle, shaft, spindle.

swivel *v.* to spin, wheel.

swivel-bridge *n.* swing-bridge.

swollen *adj.* puffy, puffed up.

swollen-headed *adj.* above oneself, high and mighty, overbearing, overweening.

swoon *n.* black-out, fit.

swoon *v.* to black out, fall down, have a fit.

swoop *n.* 1) dive, nosedive, drop, 2) drive, inroad, onset, raid.

swoop *v.* 1) to dive, drop, sweep down, 2) to fall upon, set upon, spring from hiding, spring upon, strike, waylay.

sword *n.* blade, broadsword, short sword, two-handed sword, two-edged sword.

sword-arm *n.* arm with which the sword is wielded.

sword-bearer *n.* one who bears a sword before a high reeve or deemster (*judge*) as a mark of the dread hand of the law.

sword-bite *n.* sword cut, sword-stroke.

sword-blade *n.* blade of a sword.

sword-grass *n.* plant with sword-shaped leaves.

sword-hand *n.* hand with which the sword is wielded.

sword-play *n.* 1) fight, field-fight, 2) the wielding of the sword in a one-to-one fight, 3) the quick give and take of a lively war of words.

sword-sharp *adj.* biting, cutting, keen, two-edged, whetted.

sword-smith, sword-wright *n.* maker of swords.

swordfish *n.* a great fish of the deep, having a long, sword-like upper *jaw*.

swordless *adj.* without a sword.

sword-sheathing (*peace*) *n.* hand of friendship, fighting forsworn, understanding.

swordsman *n.* one deft in wielding a sword.

sworn *adj.* bounden, on oath, plighted.

tadpole *n.* the young of the frog (or toad) when it is little more than a head and tail.

tail *n.* 1) end, tail-end, back-end, backside, behind, bottom, 2) shirt tail, 3) the other side of a *coin* (as against the 'head'), 4) braid of hair, pigtail, *ponytail*, 5) (with birds) start, 6) (in stockball) the players in the bottom half of the batting.

tail *v.* to dog the footsteps of, follow, keep an eye on, shadow, stalk.

tail-board *n.* the board at the hinder end of a wain, hinged so that it can be lowered and goods loaded in.

tail-end *n.* the hindmost end, the last stretch of a span of time or of some work.

tailless *adj.* having no tail.

tail off *v.* to die away, fall away.

take[2] *v.* 1) to clutch, fasten on, gather up, grasp, grip, hold fast, lay hands on, lay hold of, pick up, 2) to hook, net, land, trap, 3) to take after, bear a likeness to, look like, 4) to take away, make away with, make off with, run away with, run off with, steal away, 5) to take off.

take[2] **aback** *v.* to amaze, bewilder, floor, leave speechless, overcome, shake.

take[2] **in** *v.* 1) to give shelter to, open the door to, 2) to have one on, mislead, outwit, string one along, 3) (of clothing) to shorten, 4) to look over, take stock of.

take[2]**-off** *n.* chaffing, playing another.

take[2] **on** *v.* 1) to fight, match oneself against, withstand, 2) to hire, 3) to put one's hand to, set about, shoulder, take upon oneself.

take[2]**-over** *n.* buy-out.

take[2]**-over bid** *n.* bid, offer.

take[2] **stock** *v.* to reckon up, rime, tell, work out.

take[2] **to** *v.* to be taken with, become friendly with, like, warm to.

take[2] **up** *v.* 1) to begin, start, 2) to say yes to an offer, 3) to take up someone's time, 4) to begin something again, go on with, pick up, 5) to take

up with someone, become friends with, fall in with, start seeing.

takings[2] *n.* cut, earnings, rake-off, winnings, yield.

tale *n.* 1) telling, word-weaving, 2) reckoning, tally, 3) lie, tall tale, untruth.

talebearer *n.* busybody, gossip, tell-tale.

talecraft (*arithmetic*) *n.* rimecraft, tellcraft.

tale-teller *n.* tale-weaver, wordsmith, writer.

talk *n.* 1) heart-to-heart, one's say, set speech, word of mouth, 2) gossip, hearsay.

talk *v.* 1) to come out with, give tongue, have one's say, hold forth, open up, put in a word or two, say, speak, talk one's fill, 2) to give the game away, tell all.

talker *n.* 1) speaker, speechmaker, spokesman, spokeswoman, 2) gossip.

talk out of *v.* to steer one away from, stop someone from, throw cold water on.

talk over *v.* to go into, talk about, talk through, thrash out.

talks *n.* dealings, wheeling and dealing.

talksome *adj.* gossipy, long-winded, newsy, tongueful, tongue-wagging.

tall *adj.* 1) long-shanked, 2) far-fetched, high-flown, overblown, 3) hard, steep.

tallish *adj.* rather tall, somewhat tall.

tallness *n.* height.

tallow *n.* fat of *beasts*, used for making candles and soap, also for working leather.

tame *adj.* 1) broken in, 2) dry, lifeless, wearisome.

tame *v.* to break in, bridle, bring to heel, make tame, quell, take in hand.

tameless *adj.* untamed, wild, that may not be tamed.

tamer *n.* one who tames, breaker-in.

tap *n.* stopper.

tap *v.* to draw off, milk.

tape *n.* binding.

tape *v.* to bind, do up.

tapeworm *n.* worm that lives in, and off, the insides of other *creatures*.

tap-room *n.* room in an alehouse where strong drink is kept on tap.

tapster *n.* alehouse keeper, innholder, innkeeper.

tar *n.* a thick, black 'sap' got from wood or coal.

tar *v.* to smear with tar.

tarry *adj.* black with tar, smeared with tar, sticky.

tart *adj.* bitter, biting, sharp, sour, stinging, unsweetened.

tartness *n.* sourness, sharpness, bitterness.

tatty *adj.* shabby.

taut *adj.* stretched, tight, tightly-drawn,

tauten *v.* to make taut, tighten.

teach *v.* to open up, set forth, set out, throw light on, unfold.

teacher *n.* way-leader.

teaching *n.* lore, <u>wisdom</u>, wit.

teachsome *adj.* open to learning something new.

team *n.* 1) body, knot, set, 2) side.

team *v.* 1) to yoke horses or oxen in a team, 2) to team up with, clasp hands, do a deal, go hand in hand, go together, lay heads together, link up, pull together, stand shoulder to shoulder, understand one another.

team-leader *n.* set leader, head.

teamwork *n.* working together.

tear *n.* teardrop.

tear *n.* hole, rent, slit.

tear *v.* 1) to rend, shred, slit, sunder, 2) to claw, cut, wound, 3) to tear along, fly, run like the wind, speed, storm along, sweep along, tear up the ground.

tearaway *n.* fiend, good-for-nothing, knave, ne'er-do-well, rough, tough.

tearful *adj.* 1) in tears, weeping, wet-eyed, 2) sad, <u>sorrowful</u>, woeful.

tearfully *adv.* sadly, sorrowfully.

tearless *adj.* dry-eyed, shedding no tears, unfeeling, unruthful.

tear up *v.* to undo, unmake, bring to nothing, do away with, wipe out.

tease *n.* 1) the work of teasing out, 2) a teaser, a wit.

tease *v.* 1) to comb out wool to make it ready for spinning, to comb cloth so that all the hairs stand one way (so as to make a *nap*), 2) to chaff, <u>goad</u>, play with.

teasel *n.* a plant with prickly leaves and heads.

teaser *n.* 1) one given to teasing, 2) brain teaser, dark saying, <u>hard saying</u>, knot.

teem *v.* 1) to <u>overflow</u>, to be many, swarm, 2) to have to overflowing.

teeming *adj.* alive with, full, <u>overflowing</u>, swarming, <u>untold</u>, unrimed.

teens *n.* the years of one's life from thirteen to nineteen winters.

teethe *v.* to 'cut' one's milk-teeth.

teething *n.* the cutting of one's milk-teeth.

tell *v.* 1) to reckon up, rime, work out, take stock, 2) to let know, <u>make known</u>, <u>speak</u> about, talk, tell tales, 3) to see, understand, 4) to take its toll, weigh.

tell-craft *n.* 1) *arithmetic,* rimecraft, talecraft 2) *chronology,* time-craft, timelore.

teller *n.* bookkeeper, reckoner, rimer.

telling *n.* 1) reckoning, riming, 2) word-weaving, a witness to.

telling *adj.* amazing, key, marked, overriding, striking, weighty, <u>wonderful</u>.

tell-mark (*date, period*) *n.* length of time, run, shift, span, spell, stint, stretch, time.

tell on *v.* to let on, let fall, <u>make known</u>, tell all, come out with, spill the beans.

telltale *n.* tale-bearer.

telltale *adj.* giveaway, bewraying.

tell-truth *n.* one who tells the truth.

tell-wise *adj.* good at rimecraft.

ten *n. adj.* the root *number* following nine.

tenfold *adj.* ten times as great or as many, many times as great.

tenth *adj. n.* 1) the marking *number* that is kin to ten, 2) tenth share of something.

tenthly *adv.* in the tenth *place.*

Tenth-month (*October*) *n.* Winter-fulleth.

tenyear, tenyears *n. decade.*

tetter *n.* skin sickness.

tetterworm *n.* dew-worm, ringworm.

tetter-wort (*celandine*) *n.* swallow-wort.

thack *n.* 1) roof of a building, thatched roof, 2) thatch.

thack *v.* to roof a building with thatch.

than *conj.* 1) else than, more than, other than, 2) besides, but.

thane, thegn *n.* king's man, knight, lord.

thane-born *adj.* highbred, thoroughbred, well-born.

thanedom *n.* the lands or lordship of a thane.

thanehood *n.* the standing of a thane.

thane-like, thanely *adj.* 1) <u>bold</u>, doughty, fearless, manly, 2) fair spoken, well-spoken, knightly, thane-born.

thane-right *n.* the rights held by a thane.

thaneship *n.* the lordship wielded by a thane.

thank *v.* to <u>acknowledge</u>, give thanks, heap/shower thanks upon, say thank you.

thankful *adj.* knowing oneself beholden.

thankfully *adv.* with thanks.

thankfulness *n.* thanks, hearty thanks, thanksgiving.

thankless *adj.* 1) unthankful, 2) of work that brings no thanks, bootless.

thanklessly *adv.* unthankfully.

thanklessness *n.* unthankfulness.

thanks *n.* giving thanks, hearty thanks, thanksgiving.

thanksgiving *n.* giving of thanks, blessing, harvest home.

thankworthy *adj.* worthy of thanks, goodly, worthful.

thank you *phr.* a speaking one's thanks.

that, those 1) *dem. pron.* that which has but now been spoken of, 2) *adj.* of someone or something known already, of that which is further away (as against 'this'),   3) *adv.*   so, so much, that far/high/much.

that *rel. pron.*   1) who, which,   2) as far as, at, in, on which.

that *conj.*   but that, in that, seeing that.

thatch *n.*   1) heather, reeds or straw for thatching,   2) thack, thatched roof, thatching.

thatch *v.*   to roof a building with thatch, to thack.

thatchen *adj.*   thatched.

thatcher *n.*   one who makes, or makes good, roofs with thatch.

thaw *n.*   melting, unfreezing.

thaw *v.*   to melt, soften, unfreeze, warm.

the *dem. adj.*   marker for someone or something named next.

the *adv.*   by that, in that, by how much, by so much, in so much.

thee *pron.*   you, yourself.

theft *n.*   housebreaking, raiding, reaving, stealing, thieving.

thefting *n.*   fleecing, light-fingeredness, reaving, stealing, theft, thieving.

then *adv.*   1) at that time, in those days,   2) after that, afterwards, later, next,   3) it follows that, that being so,   4) also, as well, besides, furthermore, what is more.

then-a-days *adv.*   at that time, in those days.

thence *adv.*   from there, from that time, from that, therefrom.

thenceforth, thenceforward/s *adv.*   from that time/*place*/beginning onward.

thence-from *adv.*   thence, from that *place*/beginning.

there *adv.*   over there, here and there, thereabout, thither.

thereabout/s *adv.*   about, give or take a little, hereabouts, more or less, nearabouts, near enough, roughly, somewhere about, well-nigh.

thereafter *adv.*   after a time/while, afterwards, from that time, soon after, thereupon,

thereat *adv.*   because of that, there, thereupon,

therebeside *adv.*   by the side of that, next to that, near by.

thereby *adv.*   1) because of, by that, through that,   2) beside, near that,   3) besides.

therefore *adv.*   because, for, hence, so, thanks to, thence, thus, whence, wherefore.

therefrom *adv.*   away from there, from that.

therein *adv.*   in that *place*/thing/time, there, wherein.

thereinto *adv.*   into that *place*.

thereness *n.*   the suchness of being there.

thereof *adv.*   of that, of it/s, from/out of that.

thereon *adv.*   on/upon that, on to that, thereupon.

thereout *adv.*   in the open, out of doors, from/out of that, thence.

thereover *adv.*   above that, over that.

there-right *adv.*   forthwith, right now, right away, straight away, there and then.

therethrough *adv.*   through it, through that, through such, thereby.

thereto *adv.*   1) to that *place*/thing, therewith,   2) also, besides, moreover.

theretofore *adv.*   before that time.

thereunder *adv.*   below that, beneath that, under that.

thereunto *adv.*   to that *place*/thing, thereto.

thereupon *adv.*   after that, following that, on that ground, thereafter, thereat.

therewith, therewithal *adv.*   besides, that being said/done, thereat, thereupon.

therewithin *adv.*   into/within that *place*, within there.

these   see 'this'.

thew/s *n.*   lustihood, lustiness, might, strength.

thick *adj.*   1) broad, deep, fat, hefty, stocky, thickset, wide,   2) bushy, heavy, thick-growing,   3) alive with, bursting, crowded, full, seething, swarming, teeming, thronged,   4) clotted, mushy,   5) misty,   6) (of speaking) hoarse, rough, throaty,   7) thick-headed, witless,   8) friendly with, at home with, hand in glove, thick as thieves.

thick *adv.*   1) deep,   2) thickly, thick and fast, in crowds, in throngs,   3) quickly.

thicken *v.*   to broaden, build up, grow, strengthen, swell, widen.

thicket *n.*   brake, fernbrake, grove, hurst, shaw, underwood.

thick-head *n.*   clod, half-wit, lackwit, oaf, witling.

thick-headed *adj.*   dim-witted, empty-headed, slow, witless, wooden-headed.

thick-headedness *n.*   backwardness, oafishness, slowness, unwisdom.

thickish *adj.*   somewhat thick.

thick-leaved *adj.*   thickly set with leaves.

thickly *adv.*   thick and fast, in crowds, in throngs.

thickness *n.*   1) breadth, broadness, depth, greatness, width,   2) bed, seam.

thickset *adj.*   heavy, lusty, mighty, stocky, strong as an ox/horse, well-built, entish.

thick-witted *adj.*   half-witted, slow-witted, unwitful, witless, wooden-headed.

thief *n.*   highwayman, house-breaker, night-runner, raider, reaver, sharper, wolf.

thieve *v.*   to house-break, make off with, reave, steal, strip, fleece.

thievish *adj.*   crafty, light-fingered, sharp, shady, shifty, stealthy, underhand.

thigh *n.*   upper half of the shank from hip to knee.

thigh-bone *n.* the bone of the thigh.

thimble *n.* a small sheath worn on the tip of the finger when working with a sewing needle.

thimbleful *n.* as much as a thimble will hold, a drop, a little, a spoonful.

thin *adj.* bony, lean, spindly, withered, wizened, thin as a lath/rake.

thin *v.* 1) to cut back, lessen, thin out, weed out, 2) to water down.

thine *pron.* yours, your own.

thing *n.* 1) being, body, 2) tool, 3) something.

things *n.* belongings, clothes, goods, tools.

think *n.* thinking, thought/s.

think *v.* to bend the mind to, bethink, think about, think hard, think on/upon, think over, think through, think up, ask oneself, be mindful, bear in mind, beat one's brains, bend the mind, bestow thought upon, believe, brood upon, chew over, cudgel one's brains, deem, gather one's thoughts, give one's mind to, give thought to, hammer at, hold that, look on as, pull one's wits together, reckon, sleep on it, think about, think hard/out/over, trow, ween, weigh up, wonder, work over.

think ahead *v.* to foresee, look ahead, be ready for, look out for, watch out for.

thinker *n.* thinking man/woman, great mind, man/woman of learning, bookworm, deep-thinker, seeker after truth, wiseman, wisewoman, wisehead, world-wit, learned man/woman, loreman, loreseeker, lore-smith.

think highly of *v.* to think much/well of, think the best/everything of, think the world of, know/mark/see the worth of, see the good in one, look up to, make much of.

thinking *n.* thought/s, a think.

thinking *adj.* deep, keen-sighted, thoughtful, wise, understanding, witfast, witful.

thinking man, thinking woman *n.* thinker, man/woman of learning.

think through *v.* to chew over, give thought to, go over, weigh up.

think up *v.* to dream up, find a way, hatch, draw up, shape, be up to something, play a deep game, play the fox, spin a web, work out.

thinly *adv.* lightly, slightly, sparely.

thinness *n.* leanness, spareness, slightness.

thin-spun *adj.* drawn out to a thin thread, spun thinly.

third *adj. n.* 1) the marking *number* that is kin to three, 2) third share of something.

third hand *adv. phr.* heard from one who himself heard it from someone else (thus, not from an eyewitness or ear-witness).

thirdly *adv.* in the third *place*.

thirdsman *n.* for-speaker, go-between, middleman, spokesman, spokeswoman.

thirst *n.* 1) drought, dryness, thirstiness, 2) craving, itching, longing, yearning.

thirst *v.* 1) to be thirsty, 2) to crave, burn for, hunger for, itch for, long for.

thirstily *adv.* greedily.

thirsty *adj.* 1) dry, bone dry, dry as a bone, dried-up, sere, waterless, withered, 2) athirst/burning for, dying for, greedy/hungry for, itching for, longing for, yearning for.

thirteen *n. adj.* the root *number* made of ten and three.

thirteenth *adj. n.* 1) the marking *number* that is kin to thirteen, 2) thirteenth share of something.

thirty *n. adj.* the root *number* that is thrice ten.

this, these 1) *dem. pron.* that which is before one (in the flesh or in thought) or is nearby, 2) *adj.* of that which is nearer (as against 'that' which is further away).

this *adv.* 1) in this way, like this, thus, 2) as much as this.

thistle *n.* prickly plant, thornkin.

this world *n.* the world of flesh and blood, this life (as against the next world/life).

thither 1) *adv.* to or towards that *place* or end, there, 2) *adj.* lying on that side, the farther (of two things).

thitherto *adv.* up to that time, until then, to that end.

thitherward/s *adv.* thither, towards that *place*, going thither, on the way thither.

thole *n.* 1) upright pin in the side of a boat against which the oar is set (so that the oarsman may pull on it), oarlock, rowlock, thole-pin, 2) pin by which the shafts of a wain are fastened to the ax-tree.

thong *n.* narrow length of leather for a shoe-string.

thorn *n.* 1) prickle, 2) blackthorn, hawthorn, quickthorn, whitethorn, bramble, brier, thistle, 3) the 'th' stave in Old English.

thorn-bush *n.* bramble, hawthorn.

thorn-grove *n.* shaw, holt or thicket of thorns, underwood.

thorn-hedge *n.* hedge of hawthorns.

thornkin *n.* thistle.

thornless *adj.* without thorns.

thorn-tree *n.* blackthorn, hawthorn, quickthorn, whitethorn.

thorny *adj.* 1) bristling with thorns, prickly, thistly, 2) knotted, unfathomful.

thorough 1) *prep.* from beginning to end, from end to end, over the whole of, 2) *adv.* through.

thorough *adj.* 1) full, in-depth, sweeping, 2) careful, thoroughgoing, 3) downright, out-and-out, outright, sheer, utter.

thoroughbred 1) *adj.* high-born, knightly, ladylike, well-born, well-bred, 2) *n.* blood-horse, blood-stock.

thorough-bright *adj.* truly bright.

thoroughfare *n.* high road, highway, road, roadway, lane, street, through road, way.

thoroughgoing *adj.* downright, outright, out-and-out, sheer, utter.

thorough-hearted *adj.* hearty, ready and willing, whole-hearted.

thoroughly *adv.* at great length, carefully, inside out, utterly, wholly.

thoroughness *n.* care for truth, carefulness, steadiness, whole-heartedness.

those see 'that'.

thou *pers. pron.* you (*vocative*).

though[2] 1) *adv.* for all that, nevertheless, notwithstanding, 2) *conj.* although, even though, while.

thought *n.* deep thought, hard thinking, hard thought, insight, mindsight, brooding, head-work, brain-work, inmost thoughts, the mind's eye, thinking, thinking out, thoughtfulness, thought-life, wit.

thoughtful *adj.* 1) dreamy, deep in thought, lost in thought, wise, wistful, 2) kind, mindful, understanding, 3) (of a line of thought) deep, meaty, pithy, weighty.

thoughtfully *adv.* carefully, heedfully, lovingly, mindfully, thoroughly, wisely.

thoughtless *adj.* 1) heedless, unthinking, 2) unfeeling, unkind, unmindful.

thought-out *adj.* thoroughly thought through.

thought-reading *n.* mind-reading.

thought-theft (*plagiarism*) *n.* 'borrowing', writing-theft.

thought-worn *adj.* worn-looking (through worry), careworn, drawn, hollow-eyed.

thousand *n. adj.* the root *number* that is ten times one hundred.

thousandfold *adj.* one thousand times as much or as many.

thousandth 1) *adj.* the marking *number* that is kin to thousand, 2) *n.* one of a thousand bits into which something is sundered.

thrall[2] *n.* hewer of wood and drawer of water.

thrash *v.* 1) to thresh, 2) to thrash about, flail, heave, writhe, 3) to beat, flay, leather, give one a hiding, 4) to beat hollow, hammer, outplay, overwhelm.

thrashing *n.* 1) beating, hiding, 2) beating, hammering, overthrow, walkover.

thrash out *v.* to have it out, talk over, talk through, weigh the fors and againsts.

thread *n.* line, rope, string, twine, yarn.

thread *v.* 1) to string, work, 2) to inch, pick one's way.

threadbare *adj.* in holes, rundown, shabby, well-worn, worn-out, worse for wear.

threaden *adj.* made of thread/linen thread.

thread-like *adj.* gossamer, light, sheer, slight, thin, wispy.

threat *n.* black cloud, shadow of death, threatfulness, hollow threat, idle threat.

threaten *v.* 1) to breathe out threats, give fair warning, speak threateningly, 2) to under-delve, work against, 3) to be at hand, be brewing, be in the wind.

threatening *adj.* dreadful, forbidding, frightful, grim, overbearing, threatful.

threateningly *adv.* balefully, grimly, overbearingly, threatfully.

threatful *adj.* baleful, dreadful, frightful, threatening.

three *n. adj.* the root *number* following two.

threefold *adj.* made up of three together, three times as great or as many.

three-horned (*triangular*) *adj.* three-sided, wedge-shaped.

three-ling *n.* one of three children born at the one time.

Three-milkings (*May*) *n.* Thry-milchmonth, the month when grass is so rich that cows may be milked three times in the day.

Three-ness *n.* the *Trinity*, Threefoldness.

three-sided *adj.* three-horned/*triangular*, wedge-shaped, having three outlooks.

threesome *n.* three folk together, three making a set together.

thresh *v.* to flail, winnow.

threshing-floor *n.* hard ground (often in a barn where there is a draught through open doors) where corn is threshed.

threshold *n.* 1) doorway, door-sill, door-step, 2) beginning, opening, outset, start.

thrice *adv.* three times, three times as much.

thrill *n.* 1) flutter, quiver, 2) 'glow', 'high'.

thrill *v.* to awaken, fire, set on fire, quicken, startle, stir, warm the blood, work up.

thriller *n.* book, play or film that is breathtaking, heady, startling, thrilling.

thrilling *adj.* gripping, heady, heart-stirring, stirring, soul-stirring, striking.

throat *n.* weasand, windpipe.

throaty *adj.* 1) deep, deep-throated, 2) 'coldy', hoarse, sore.

throe/s *n.* 1) fit, twitch, 2) the bitterness of childbirth, 3) death-throes.

throng *n.* crowd, drove, herd, swarm, the world and his wife.

throng *v.* to crowd, flock, flood, forgather, gather, stream, swarm.

throttle *n.* throat.

throttle *v.* to choke, cut off, smother.

through *adj.* done with, ended, having had enough of.

through 1a) *prep.* between, by way of, 1b) because of, 1c) wherewith, 1d) in the middle of, throughout, 2a) *adv.* from one end/side to the other, 2b) all the time, the whole time, from start to ending, throughout, 2c) by the hand of.

through-draught *n.* draught of wind through open doors or windows.

throughletting (*pervious*) *adj.* leachy, leaking.

throughout 1) *prep.* all over, all through, over the length and breadth of, right through, 2) *adv.* all the time, the whole time, from the start, from the word 'go'.

throughput *n. matter* that is drawn out or shaped anew by being put through some working *process*.

through-seeing *adj.* keen-minded, sharp, sharp-witted, witfast, witful.

through-shining, through-showing *adj.* glassy, see-through, sheer, thin.

throughway *n.* fast road, freeway, highway, mainway, thoroughfare.

throw *n.* heave, pitch, put, throw-in.

throw *v.* 1) to heave, pitch, put, send, 2) to floor, upset, 3) to throw one, put one off his stroke, throw one off his stride, unsettle.

throw away *v.* to ditch, throw out.

throw-away *adj.* 1) one-*use*, 2) careless, offhand, thoughtless, unthinking.

throw-back *n.* going back, an arising again of some earlier suchness among one's forebears.

throw off *v.* to throw over, forsake, forswear, free oneself from, leave, unsay.

throw open *v.* to open the door, welcome, let in, bring in, show in.

throw out *v.* 1) to bring to naught, throw away, undo, unmake, 2) to give off.

throw over *v.* to forsake, forswear, leave, withdraw, yield up.

thrower *n.* pitcher.

thrown *adj.* 1) shaped on the loamwright's wheel, turned on a woodworker's wheel (*lathe*), twisted into thread, 2) thrown from one's horse, 3) bewildered, on one's beam ends.

throw up *v.* 1) to bring to light, 2) to give up, leave, 3) to be sick, heave.

thrum/s *n.* the ends of the warp-thread left on the loom when the web is cut off, bits and ends of thread.

thrush *n.* hollin/mistle thrush.

Thry-milchmonth (*May*) *n.* Three-milkings.

thud *n.* knock.

thud *v.* to knock.

thumb *n.* the thick inner 'finger' of the hand.

thumb *v.* to finger, handle, leaf through, mark.

thumb-marked *adj.* (of the leaves of a much-read book) marked by being often thumbed through.

thumbnail *adj.* pithy, quick, short.

thunder *n.* thunderbolt, thunderclap, thunder-storm, thunder and lightning.

thunder *v.* 1) to clap, roar, 2) to bellow, roar, shout, storm, threaten, yell.

thunderbolt *n.* thunder-clap, something frightening or startling, bolt from the blue.

thunderclap *n.* 1) crack/roar of thunder, 2) bolt from the blue, eye-opener.

thunder-cloud *n.* heavy storm-cloud.

thunder-storm *n.* storm of thunder, lightning and heavy rain.

thunderstruck *adj.* amazed, bewildered, floored, overcome, shaken, speechless.

thundery *adj.* betokening thunder, threatening.

Thursday (Thunor's day) *n.* fifth day of the week.

thus *adv.* 1) hence, so that, thus far, 2) in such wise, in this way, like so, like this.

thuswise *adv.* thus, likewise.

thy *poss. adj.* your.

thyself *pron.* yourself.

tick *n.* mite.

tick[1] *n.* 1) the tick of a clock, 2) line, mark, stroke.

tick[1] *v.* 1) (of a clock) to mark the time, 2) to mark, mark off, tick off.

tickle[1] *n.* itch.

tickle[1] *v.* 1) to itch, 2) to stroke lightly, 3) to awake/stir laughter, make one laugh.

tide *n.* time, span, while, even-tide, morning-tide, spring-tide, Whitsuntide and such.

tide *n.* ebb, flood-tide, flow, high tide, low tide, stream, tideway, undertow.

tide *v.* to befall, betide, come about.

tidefleet *n.* fleet, inlet, mouth, roadstead.

tide-shewer (*astrologer*) *n.* star-delver.

tide-writer (*annalist, historian*) *n.* time-writer, year-writer.

tidily *adv.* in a tidy way, trimly.

tiding/s *n.* 1) something that has befallen, 2) gossip, hearsay, news, the latest, word.

tidy *adj.* 1) clean, shipshape, trim, well-kept, 2) fair, good, goodly.

tidy *v.* to clean, put in trim, put to rights, straighten.

tie *n.* 1) binding, fastening, fetter, knot, knotting, link, tying, drawing together, threading together, 2) necktie, 3) hindering, 4) (in games) deadlock, draw.

tie *v.* 1) to bind, do up, knot, link, 2) to make fast, 3) to <u>hinder</u>, hold, 4) (in games) to be even, draw, match, neck and neck.

tie-beam *n.* cross-beam at eaves height, helping to tie the framework of a building together.

tie-in *n.* hook-up, tie-up.

tie on *v.* to fasten, stick on, hang on, tie up, yoke.

tie-stroke (*hyphen*) *n.* link-mark.

tie up *v.* to fasten, for-bind, hook on, set, tie on, yoke.

tie-up *n.* hook-up, tie-in.

tight[(2)] *adj.* 1) drawn tight, fast, taut, wedged, 2) (of clothing) too narrow, too small, 3) (of *money*) hard to come by or borrow, 4) (of a game) even, hard-fought.

tighten[(2)] *v.* 1) to <u>fasten</u>, strengthen, 2) to stiffen, tauten, 3) to become narrow.

tight[(2)]**-fisted** *adj.* grasping, hard-fisted, hard-hearted, <u>mean</u>, selfish, stingy.

tight[(2)]**-lipped** *adj.* not open, not to be drawn, sparing with words, unforthcoming.

tightly[(2)] *adv.* narrowly, stintingly, tautly.

tile[(4)] *n.* floor-tile, roof-tile, wall-tile.

till *v.* to delve, harrow, work.

till 1) *prep.* until, up to, 2) *conj.* so long as, to the time that.

tiller *n.* acreman, crofter, earth-tiller, smallholder.

tilt *n.* heel, lean, pitch, slope.

tilt *v.* to heel over, lean, lean over, tilt over.

tilth (*agriculture*) *n.* 1) fieldcraft, fieldlore, croplore, earth tilth, 2) crop-land.

timber *n.* beams, boards, wood, hardwood, softwood.

timbered *adj.* 1) built of wood, wooden, 2) tree-clad, wooded.

timbering *n.* 1) building in wood, 2) building wood, timber-work.

timberman *n.* dealer in timber.

timber-tree *n.* tree yielding timber that is good for building.

timber-wood *n.* beams, boards, hardwood, softwood.

timber-work/s *n.* work wrought in timber, yard where timber is worked up.

timber-yard *n.* yard where felled timber is kept.

time *n.* 1) length of time, span, spell, stint, stretch, tide, while, 2) days, stream of time, year, 3) best days/years, life, life span, lifetime, 4) beat, timing.

time *v.* 1) to clock, watch the clock, beat time, keep time, 2) to book, set up.

time-craft *n.* understanding the times and the deeds of men, tell-craft, timelore.

timeful *adj.* early, timely, well-timed.

timekeeper *n.* 1) time-teller, timer, 2) one who keeps time and writes it down.

timeless *adj.* <u>abiding</u>, lasting, outlasting, undying.

timelike (*temporal*) *adj.* in/of time.

timelore (*chronology*) *n.* tell-craft, time-craft.

timely *adj.* early, timeful, well-timed.

timely *adv.* betimes, soon enough, in/on time, in good time.

timer *n.* timekeeper, time-teller.

time-reckoner (*calendar*) *n.* year-book, year-clock, year-reckoner, time-marker.

time span, timestretch *n.* <u>long time</u>, long years, years on end, many lives long.

time-teller (*chronometer*) *n.* timekeeper.

timeworn *adj.* crumbling, moss-grown, moth-eaten, old as time, outworn, worn-out, run down, rotting, rusting, withering.

time-writer (*historian*) *n.* tide-writer, yearbook-keeper, year-wright, year-writer.

time-writing (*history*) *n.* tales of the elder days, tales of the long ago days/of the olden days, tales of the years, time-delving, year-writings.

timing *n.* the time when something happens or is set to happen.

tin *n.* 1) a whitish *metal*, 2) a box or pot made of tin or tinned iron.

tin *v.* to *seal* fish, meat or other food in a tin.

tinder *n.* lighter, firelighter.

tine *n.* 1) the sharp 'tooth' of a harrow and other tools, 2) each of the sharp stems of a deer's horn.

tinman *n.* man who works with tin, tinsmith, whitesmith.

tinned *adj.* betinned (with a layer of tin), *sealed* in a tin.

tinner *n.* 1) delver after tin, 2) one who works with tin, tinman, tinsmith.

tinning *n.* 1) delving for tin, 2) layering with tin, the making of tin-ware, 3) *sealing* fish, meat or other food in tins.

tinny *adj.* 1) brassy, sharp-pitched, 2) cheap, draffish, flimsy, thin, two-a-penny.

tinsmith *n.* worker in tin, tinman, tinner, whitesmith.

tin-stone *n.* tin ore.

tip[(2)] *n.* 1) end. sharp end, head, 2) brow, peak, top.

tiptoe[(2)] *v.* to go stealthily, play hide-and-seek, slink, stalk, steal along.

tire *v.* 1) to become tired, 2) to weary to death, 3) to drain, overwork, <u>weary</u>.

tired *adj.* dog-tired, tired out, <u>weary</u>, fordone, heavy-eyed, overdriven, worn.

tiredness *n.* overtiredness, aching all over, heaviness, <u>weariness</u>.

tireless *adj.* ready, sleepless, unresting, unsleeping, untiring, unwearied.

tirelessness *n.* sleeplessness, liveliness, readiness, quickness.

tiresome *adj.* burdensome, longsome, weariful, wearing, wearisome, wearying.

tit *n.* tip of a woman's breast, nipple.

tithe *n.* a tenth of one's yearly earnings given for the work of the church.

tithe *v.* to give a tenth of one's yearly earnings.

tithe-days *n.* the thirty-six tithing days (one tenth of the year) in Lent.

to 1) *prep.* as far as, beside, towards, 2) *conj.* till, until, 3) *adv.* to and fro.

toad *n.* 1) *creature* that lives both on land and in the water, 2) a loathsome *creature*.

toadstool *n.* a kind of *fungus*.

toady *n.* fawner, hanger-on, leech, toad-eater, tool, yes-man.

toady *adj.* toad-like.

toady *v.* to be the tool of, creep, cringe, do one's foul work, knuckle under, stoop to anything, worm oneself in with, run with the hare and hunt with the hounds.

to and fro *adv.* backwards and forwards, in and out, side to side, up and down.

today 1) *adv.* at this time, in these times, nowadays, these days, 2) *n.* this day.

to-do *n.* ado, much ado, madhouse, stir, unrest, unstillness, upheaving, uproar, upset.

toe *n.* great toe, little toe, middle toe.

toe-hold *n.* 1) a hold in wrestling, 2) a slight grip or hold on something.

together *adv.* 1) hand in hand, in a body, 2) all at once, all together.

together with *adv.* as well as, besides, moreover, furthermore, likewise, along with.

token *n.* 1) brand, clue, hint, mark, marker, tell-tale mark, 2) earnest, foretoken.

token *adj.* hollow, in name only, lightweight, shallow, small.

token *v.* to bear the marks/stamp of, bespeak, forebode, foreshadow, tell its own tale.

tokening *n.* bespeaking, foreshadowing, forewarning, shadowing forth.

toll[(5)] *n.* tax.

toll *n.* knell, ring, ringing, tolling.

toll *v.* to ring, strike, toll the knell.

tomorrow 1) *n.* the morrow, 2) *adv.* on the day after today, on the morrow.

ton[(6)] *n.* reckoning of weight, being twenty hundredweight or 2,240 pounds.

tongs *n.* tool with two hinged shanks, with which one may grip things (such as burning coals) which cannot be picked up with the hand, or which may more readily be so picked up.

tongue *n.* 1) the tongue on the floor of the mouth, 2) speech, folk speech, ready speech, home-speech, home-tongue, household speech, living-tongue, mother tongue, talk, 3) neck/tongue of land, foreland, headland, spur.

tongueful *adj.* <u>long-winded</u>, newsy, ready with words, windy, wordful, wordy.

tongueless *adj.* dumb, shy, tongue-tied, unforthcoming, unspeaking, wordless.

tongue-tied *adj.* a-dumb, halting, shamefast, shy, stammering, tongueless, wordless.

tongue-wagging *n.* gossip, hearsay, idle talk, small talk.

tonight 1) *n.* this night, 2) *adv.* on the night following this day.

too *adv.* 1) also, furthermore, likewise, moreover, 2) more than enough, overmuch.

tool *n.* 1) adze, bill-hook, edged tool, hammer, rake, saw, scythe, spade, wrench, 2) fawner, hanger-on, plaything.

tool *v.* to cut, make, shape, work.

tooth *n.* back tooth, fore tooth, milktooth, fang.

toothache *n.* an ache in a tooth/teeth.

tooth-drawer (*dentist*) *n.* gum-smith, gum-wright, tooth-smith, tooth-wright.

toothless *adj.* 1) having no teeth, 2) <u>old</u>, timeworn, 3) lacking bite.

tooth-salve (*toothpaste*) *n.* tooth-cleaner.

tooth-smith, tooth-wright (*dentist*) *n.* gum-smith, gum-wright, tooth-drawer.

toothsome *adj.* full-bodied, good to eat, honeyed, mouthwatering, rich, strong, sweet as honey, out of this world.

toothy *adj.* having broad and striking teeth, toothed.

top *n.* a child's spinning *toy*.

top *n.* 1) the hair on the top of the head, 2) upper layer, 3) lid, stopper, 4) brow, head, height, peak, ridge, 5) shirt, sweat-shirt, sweater.

top *adj.* 1) furthest up, highest, topmost, uppermost, 2) best, <u>greatest</u>, head, leading.

top *v.* 1) to cut off the top of a growing tree, to break off the heads of plants, 2) to put a top on, 3) to beat, best, better, go beyond, go one better than, outdo, outshine, overtop, 4) to be at the top of, be first in, head, lead, 5) to climb, reach the top of.

top brass *n.* the heads of the fighting bodies (land, sea) of a folkdom.

top-drawer *n.* 1) the top drawer of a chest, 2) the chosen few, the pick, top folk.

top flight *adj.* of mark, outstanding.

top-hat *n.* man's high hat.

top-heavy *adj.* over-weighted, unsteady, unwieldy.

topmast *n.* a smaller mast set on the top of a greater mast.

topmost *adj.* highest, top, upper, uppermost.

topple *v.* 1) to be thrown, fall, fall over, fall headlong, falter, miss one's footing, 2) to knock down, knock over, upset, 3) to bring down, overthrow.

topsail *n.* sail set above a lower sail, over-sail, upper topsail, lower topsail.

top-sawyer *n.* 1) the sawyer who wields the upper handle of a pit-saw, 2) the leading or most knowing hand.

topside *n.* the upper side of anything, the outer side of the flesh-meat of the cow.

topsy-turvy *adv.* all anyhow, inside out, untidy, upside down.

top up *v.* to fill up, make up.

tough *n.* cut-throat, fiend, hell-hound, knave, lout, rough, wolf, wreck-all.

tough *adj.* 1) chewy, gristly, hard, leathery, sinewy, stringy, wiry, 2) dogged, doughty, flinty, gritty, hard as iron/nails/steel/stone, hardened, manly, stalworth, steadfast, steely, stern, strong, toughened, unbending, unyielding, 3) grinding, hard, steep, tiring, tough going, uphill, wearing, wearisome.

toughen *v.* to give strength to, harden, steel, stiffen, strengthen.

toughness *n.* grit, hardness, heart of oak, leatheriness, steadfastness, sternness.

touse *v.* 1) to handle roughly, 2) (of a dog) to tear at, worry, 3) to leave all anyhow.

tousle *v.* to untidy.

tousled, tousy *adj.* all anyhow, rough, uncombed, unkempt, untidy, windblown.

tout *n.* dealer, seller.

tout *v.* to bid for business, look out for or seek business.

tow *n.* a pull.

tow *v.* to draw, pull.

toward *adj.* 1) being done, coming, going on, willing, 2) *adv.* forward, onward.

towardly *adj.* 1) bright, fair, looking good/hopeful, timely, 2) wieldy, willing.

towards *adv.* 1) almost at, nearing, shortly before, 2) to, on the road/way to.

town *n.* borough, burh, township.

town-dweller (*citizen*) *n.* townsman, townswoman, town mouse, borough-man.

town-end *n.* the end of the main street of a town.

town hall *n.* hall where the town leaders meet and talk through town business.

town-house *n.* 1) town hall, 2) a landowner's house in town.

town-living *n.* town life.

town-meeting *n.* meeting of all the folk of a town (to talk through town business).

town-mouse *n.* town-dweller (knowing little of life on the land).

townsfolk *n.* town-dwellers, townsmen, townswomen, borough-folk.

township *n.* a small town and the land about it, having its own church and *priest*.

townsman (*citizen*) *n.* town-dweller, borough-man.

townswoman *n.* town-dweller.

town-talk *n.* the gossip going about town.

townward *adj.* going towards the town/s.

tow-path *n.* path beside a *canal* or shipping *river*, once *used* by the horses that towed boats along.

tow-rope *n.* rope for towing.

trade[1] *n.* business, buying and selling, dealing, shipping.

trade[1] *v.* to buy and sell, deal, cut a deal, have dealings, do business, handle.

trademark[1] *n.* brand mark, hallmark, stamp, trade name.

trader[1] *n.* businessman, businesswoman, man/woman of business, buyer, seller, dealer, middleman, salesman, saleswoman, wholesaler.

tradesman[1] *n.* craftsman, middleman, workman, wright.

trap *n.* net, deathtrap, honey trap, trap for the unwary.

trap *v.* to lay a trap for, lay hold of, run to earth/ground, hook, land, net, waylay.

trap-door *n.* small door in a floor or roof.

trapper *n.* hunter, huntsman, stalker.

tray *n.* 1) board with a rim about its edge, on which bowls and such may be borne from one room to another, 2) (in a business house) in-tray/out-tray where *papers* are left until dealt with.

tread *n.* footfall, footstep, step, stride.

tread *v.* 1) to stamp, step, stride out, walk, 2) to tread water, mark time.

treadle *n.* footkey by which a *machine* is worked, footkey of a two-wheeler.

tread-wheel *n.* wheel worked by the tread of men or *beasts* (to draw up water).

tree *n.* beam, stock, alder, apple, ash, aspen, beech, birch, blackthorn, elm, field maple, hawthorn, hazel, holly, hornbeam, lime, oak, sallow, spindle, whitebeam, willow, yew.

treeless *adj.* bare, dreary, forlorn, lonely, stark, wild.

tree rat[(4)] (*squirrel*) *n.* aquerne/acwern.

tree sparrow *n.* a bird of *farm*land and woodland edges.

tree-top *n.* uppermost boughs of a tree, the head.

tree-work *n.* wooden building.

tree-worm (*caterpillar*) *n.* leaf-worm.

tree-wright (*carpenter*) *n.* woodwright, woodcraftsman, woodworker.

trend *n.* the way something trends or bends away.

trend *v.* 1) to turn *round, revolve*, 2) to make something turn *round*, 3) to wind *partly* cleaned wool into tops for spinning, 4) to turn off and go another way.

trendle *n.* 1) *circle*, ring, ball, 2) wheel, 3) bundle of *partly* cleaned wool that has been 'trended'.

trendle, trundle *v.* to go or run on a wheel or wheels, to walk unsteadily.

trim *n.* 1) edge, edging, hem, trimming, 2) crop, shearing, tidying up, 3) fettle, health, shape, wellness, 4) build, cut, likeness, lines, outline, look.

trim *adj.* 1) shipshape, smart, tidy, well-kept, 2) elfin, lissom, shapely, willowy.

trim *v.* 1) to edge, hem, 2) to crop, lop, shave, shear, tidy, 3) to lessen, shorten, make cutbacks in.

trimmer *n.* knave, rat.

trimming *n.* braid, edging.

trindle *n.* wheel, the trundle or *lantern*-wheel of a mill, the wheel of a wheelbarrow.

trindle *v.* to make something go *round*, to *revolve* or turn *round*.

troth *n.* rightness, trothfulness, trothworthiness, truth, truthfulness, uprightness.

troth-breaker *n.* forswearer, knave, snake in the grass, tell-tale, twister.

troth-breaking *n.* forswearing, misdealing, trothlessness, unplighting.

trothen *adj.* knightly, steadfast, true, upright.

trothfast *adj.* steadfast, true, true-hearted.

trothful *adj.* knightly, steadfast, true, upright.

trothfulness *n.* goodness, worthiness, knightliness, troth, uprightness.

trothless *adj.* fickle, forsworn, truthless, untrothful, shifting, unsteady, wayward.

trothlessly *adv.* shamefully, unrightfully, unworthily, underhandedly.

trothlessness *n.* fickleness, truthlessness, untrothfulness, untruth.

troth-plight *n.* plight, plighting, plighted word, troth-word, undertaking.

troth-plight *adj.* 1) bound, plighted, tied, 2) betrothed.

troth-plight *v.* 1) to bind oneself, give /plight one's word, plight one's troth, take oath, 2) make a match.

troth-word *n.* given word, plight-word.

trothworthy *adj.* true, truthful, upright, word-fast.

trough *n.* 1) crib, feeding-trough, drinking-trough, water-trough, kneading-trough, 2) ditch, drain, leat, overflow, runnel, 3) hollow, 4) (in weather-lore) 'low'.

trow *v.* to believe in, deem, hold, think, ween.

truce *n.* break (in fighting), let-up, rest, standstill.

true *adj.* 1) aright, right, open, straight, straightforward, thorough, thorough-going, true to life, truthful, upright, word for word, above board, 2) dead on, dead straight, straight as an arrow, as the crow flies, unbent, unswerving, unwarped.

be **true** to *v.* to abide by, be as good as one's word, be true to, hold to, stand by.

true-hearted *adj.* as good as one's word, high-minded, knightly, manly, open, open-hearted, right-hearted, soothfast, stalworth, steadfast, straightforward, trothfast, trothful, trothworthy, truthful, truth-speaking, true, true as steel, upright.

true-love *n.* beloved, darling, dearling, lady-love, sweetheart.

truepenny *n.* true-hearted man or woman.

true to life *adj.* true, of flesh and blood, down to earth, straight, well-grounded.

truly *adv.* above all, indeed, in truth, rightly, truthfully, to a hair, word for word.

trundle *n.* small wheel, *lantern*-wheel.

trundle, trendle *v.* to go or run on a wheel or wheels, to walk unsteadily.

truth *n.* 1) rightness, sooth, thoroughness, gospel truth, light of truth, 'warts and all', 2) care for truth, truthfulness, mindfulness, 3) high-mindedness, knightliness, open-heartedness, steadfastness, straightforwardness, troth, trothfulness, uprightness.

truthfast *adj.* aright, right, dead-on, earnest, lifelike, settled, straightforward, thorough, thorough-going, true, careful, watchful, well-pitched, word for word.

truthful *adj.* not lying, open, telling the truth, true-hearted, soothfast, upright.

truthfully *adv.* carefully, rightly, soothfastly, truly, thoroughly.

truthfulness *n.* care of/love of the truth, openness, straightforwardness.

truthless *adj.* smooth-tongued, two-hearted, crafty, underhand, untruthful.

truthlessness *n.* hollowness, shallowness, two-heartedness, untroth, untruthfulness.

truth-stretching (*hyperbole*) *n.* oversaying, overshooting, word-stretching.

Tuesday (Tiw's day) *n.* third day of the week.

tug *n.* 1) pull, wrench, 2) small, strong boat which tows greater ships within a haven.

tug *v.* to drag, draw, heave, pull, tow, wrench.

tun[6] (*cask, barrel*) *n.* fourthing (*firkin*), vat.

turf *n.* 1) grass, green, sward, greensward, 2) home ground, stamping ground, 3) the grassy stretch where horses run in a race.

turf *v.* to lay down turf.

turn[5] *n.* 1) bend, shift, spin, swivel, swing, twist, 2) drive, ride, walk, 3) road turning, 4) go, spell, stint, time, 5) show, star turn.

turn[5] *v.* 1) to go back, shift, spin, swerve, swivel, wheel, wind, 2) to go out of one's way, 3) to twist, wrench, 4) to curdle, go bad/off/sour, 5) to frame, make, shape, work, 6) to become, reach, 7) to thumb through, 8) to sicken, upset, 9) to turn tail, fly, run away, run for one's life, 10) to turn up, come up.

tusk *n.* long tooth reaching beyond the mouth.

tusker *n.* *beast* (such as the wild boar) that has tusks.

tussle *n.* fight, set-to.

tussle *v.* to fight, handle roughly, set to.

twain *adj.* asunder, twifold, twofold.

twain *n.* two, team of two.

tweak *n.* pull, twist, twitch.

tweak *v.* to pull, put right, set right, straighten out, twist, twitch.

twelfth 1) *adj.* the marking *number* that is kin to twelve, 2) *n.* twelfth share of something.

Twelfth-day *n.* twelfth (and last) day of Christmas, *Feast* of the Making Known of the Christ-child (*Epiphany*).

twelfth man *n.* that one of twelve named for an eleven-strong stockball (*cricket*) team who is not, in the end, chosen to play.

Twelfth-night *n.* the night of the twelfth day after Christmas.

Twelfthtide *n.* Twelfth-night and Twelfth-day, Making Known-tide (*Epiphany*).

twelve *n. adj.* the root *number* that is 'two left' (over ten).

twelvefold *adj.* twelve times as great or as many.

twelvemonth *n.* year.

twentieth *adj. n.* 1) the marking *number* that is kin to twenty, 2) twentieth share of something.

twenty *n. adj.* the root *number* that is twice ten.

twentyfold *adj.* twenty times as great or as many.

twice *adj.* twicefold, twofold, two-edged, two-sided, matching, twin.

to think **twice** to fear, take fright, stand in dread, shrink with fear.

twice-told tale *n.* well-worn saying, worn-out saying, old saw.

twice-yearly (*biannual*) twice a year, half-yearly.

twifold, twyfold *adj.* 1) twofold, 2) crafty, hollow, two-spoken, smooth-tongued.

twig *n.* offshoot/shoot from the bough of a tree, stick.

twiggen *adj.* made of twigs.

twiggy *adj.* 1) like a twig, slight, 2) having many twigs.

twilight *n.* dusk, even-gloom, eventide, gloaming, half-light, nightfall.

twilight *adj.* darkish, dim, gloomy, grey, shades of evening, shadowy, shady, twilit.

twill *n.* kind of cloth.

twin *adj.* of a child born at the one birth with oneself.

twin *n.* another child brought forth at the one birth with oneself.

twin-born *adj.* born a twin, born at the one birth with oneself.

twin-brother *n.* brother brought forth at the one birth with oneself.

twine *n.* line, rope, string, strong thread, yarn.

twine *v.* to braid, knit, swathe, twist together, weave, wind, wreathe.

twinge *n.* prick, stab, sting.

twinge *v.* to prick, stab, sting, tweak, twitch.

twinkle *n.* flicker, gleam, light, shimmer, shine, spark, sparkle, wink.

twinkle *v.* to flicker, gleam, glisten, shimmer, shine, sparkle, wink.

twinkling *n.* twinkle, twinkling of an eye.

twinned *adj.* 1) born two at one birth, 2) matched, tied.

twinship *n.* twin-being, the kinship between twins.

twin-sister[2] *n.* sister brought forth at the one birth with oneself.

twist *n.* 1) bend, 2) spin, swivel, 3) pull, wrench.

twist *v.* 1) to braid, twine, weave, wind, wreathe, 2) to bend, warp, 3) to spin, swivel, writhe, 4) to pull, wrench, 5) (of meaning) to leave out, read into, twist the words, wrest the meaning.

twisted *adj.* 1) bent, misshapen, warped, 2) evil, unhealthy, wicked.

twister *n.* evil-doer, fox, good-for-nothing, knave, sharper, ne'er-do-well.

twisty *adj.* marked by twists and bends, winding.

twit *v.* to chide, lay at the door of, upbraid.

twitch *n.* flutter, shake, throe, twinge.

twitch *n.* couch-grass, quicken, quitch.

twitch *v.* to flutter, shake, thrash about, writhe.

two *n. adj.* the root *number* next after one.

two-edged *adj.* two-tongued, having two meanings, cutting two/both ways.

twofold *adj.* made up of two together, twice as great or as many, twain, twifold.

two-handed *adj.* 1) (of a sword, axe) wielded with two hands, (of a great saw) worked by the hands of two men, 2) handy with either hand (*ambidextrous*).

two-hearted *adj.* crafty, forsworn, hollow, lying, shallow, two-tongued, untruthful.

two-heartedness *n.* fickleness, shallowness, shiftiness, untroth, worldliness.

two-leaved *adj.* (of a door) having two hinged or folding leaves, (of a plant) having two leaves, or leaves growing in twos.

two-minded *adj.* in two minds, at a loss, at one's wits' end, bereft (of one's wits), bestraught, forstraught, bewildered, blowing hot and cold, brought to a stand, fickle, flighty, giddy, hanging back, holding back, pulled this way and that, shifty, shrinking from, slow, soft, two-reded, unsettled, unsteadfast, wayward, wieldy, yielding.

two-mindedness *n.* not knowing one's mind, hedging, looking twice, unsteadiness.

twopenny *adj.* of little worth.

two-pennyworth *n.* a little, nothing much to speak of.

two-reded *adj.* forstraught, two-minded, restless, unsettled.

two-sided (*bilateral*) *adj.* twin, having two outlooks.

twosome *n.* two folk together.

two-spoken *adj.* crafty, empty, hollow, smooth-tongued, two-tongued, truthless.

two-stroke *adj.* of an *engine* working with one downward and one upward stroke of the *piston.*

two-tongued *adj.* crafty, fickle, hollow, lying, not straightforward, shiftful, shifty, smooth-spoken, smooth-tongued, trothless, two-hearted, underhand, untruthful.

two-way *n.* meeting of two roads, road-meet.

two-wheeler (*bicycle*) *n.* twywheel, wheelsaddle.

two-wordy (*contradictory*) *adj.* ungrounded, woolly.

twybake *n.* biscuit.

twybill *n.* two-edged axe.

twyspeaking (*bilingual*) *adj.* speaking two tongues/*languages.*

udder *n.* (of some kinds of she- *beast*) the hanging *organ* with nipples by which milk is given.

unanswered *adj.* open, open and shut, ungainsaid, unsettled.

unasked *adj.* unbidden, unsought, willing.

unaware *adj.* in the dark, unforewarned, unknowing, unmindful, unwitting.

unawares *adv.* 1) without warning, 2) unknowingly, unwittingly.

unbaked *adj.* uncooked.

unbeaten *adj.* unbowed, unquelled, unwearied, winning.

unbecoming *adj.* misbecoming, shameful, unknightly, unladylike, unworthy.

unbefriended *adj.* friendless, lonely.

unbegotten *adj.* not begotten, self-living.

unbegun *adj.* 1) that has had no beginning, always being, 2) not yet begun.

unbeholden *adj.* owing nothing to another.

unbeknown 1) *adv.* without the knowledge of, 2) *adj.* unbeheld, unseen.

unbelief *n.* freethinking, godlessness, heathenness.

unbeliever *n.* misbeliever, outsider.

unbelieving *adj.* freethinking, godless, heathen.

unbeloved *adj.* forsaken, loveless, unloved, uncared for.

unbend *v.* 1) to unstring (a bow), 2) to let up, slacken, unwind, 3) to set straight.

unbending *adj.* hard, stone-like, unyielding.

unbethought *adj.* not meant, unforeseen, unthought of, without forethought.

unbidden *adj.* 1) free, unsought, willing, 2) unasked, unwelcome.

unbind *v.* to free, set free, get one out of, unyoke.

unblenching *adj.* dreadless, fearless, unshrinking, steely, stalwart, unyielding.

unblessed *adj.* 1) doomed, stricken, wretched, 2) evil, unhallowed, wicked.

unblithe *adj.* forlorn, heart-lorn, hopelorn, listless, sad, sorrowful, wretched.

unbloodied *adj.* unwounded, whole.

unblown *adj.* not yet open, not yet in blossom.

unblushing *adj.* brazen, forward, lewd, shameless, unashamed.

unbolt *v.* to unfasten by drawing back a bolt, unlock.

unbone *v.* to take the bones out of fish or meat.

unborn *adj.* not yet born, yet in the womb, as yet unshaped, unwrought.

unbosom *v.* to open one's mind, unburden oneself, come out with, speak of, tell all.

unbound *adj.* 1) freed, 2) (of a book) having no binding.

unbridled *adj.* headstrong, self-willed, steer-less, untamed, wayward, wild, wilful.

unbroken *adj.* 1) whole, 2) ever-flowing, ongoing, steady, unending, 3) untamed, wild, 4) unbroken ground, 5) (of fighting men) unbeaten, unbowed, unyielding.

unbrotherly *adj.* cold, uncaring, unfeeling, unkind, unloving, unthoughtful.

unburden *v.* 1) to free, come to the help of, unyoke, 2) to unburden oneself, tell all, open one's mind, unbosom oneself.

unburied *adj.* not buried.

uncanny *adj.* chilling, nightmarish, other, unearthly, weird and wonderful.

uncared for *adj.* out in the cold, overlooked, unloved, unmissed, unthought of.

uncareful *adj.* 1) careless, heedless, over-bold, reckless, thoughtless, 2) unworried.

uncaring *adj.* careless, cold, cold-blooded, cool, cold-hearted, half-hearted, heartless, heart-whole, heedless, listless, lukewarm, off-hand, reckless, soulless, thoughtless, unforthcoming, unhearing, unheeding, unloving, unmindful, unshaken, unsmitten, unstirred, unwilling, unwondering, without warmth, wooden.

unchidden *adj.* badly brought up, headstrong, untaught, wayward.

unclad *adj.* bare, stark naked, unclothed, without a stitch on.

unclasp *v.* 1) to unfasten the clasps of, undo, 2) to let go, slacken one's grasp.

unclean, uncleanly *adj.* 1) evil, lewd, unholy, 2) foul, filthy, unwholesome.

unclench *v.* to leave hold of, let go, unclinch, unhand.

unclew *v.* 1) to unwind, undo, 2) to bring to nothing, unmake.

unclinch *v.* to let go, slacken one's grasp, unclench.

unclothe *v.* to strip, strip naked, strip off, strip/take off one's clothes.

unclouded *adj.* bright, cloudless, fair, set fair, sunny.

uncomely *adj.* 1) misbecoming, unbecoming, unmeet, 2) misshapen, unlovely.

uncouth *adj.* 1) unknown, 2) bearish, churlish, clod-hopping, cursing, foul-mouthed, foul-spoken, grunting, lewd, loud, loutish, oafish, off-handed, rough, rough-tongued, sharp-edged, short, swearing, unhewn, unknightly, unladylike, withering.

uncouthly *adv.* churlishly, loudly, loutishly, roughly, shortly.

uncouthness *n.* churlishness, loudness, loutishness, off-handedness, roughness.

uncrafty *adj.* 1) uncraftful, 2) goosish, green, unwary, witless.

uncut *adj.* 1) unwounded, 2) not mown or lopped, unmown, 3) (of a book, film, play and such) not shortened.

undear *adj.* 1) unbeloved, unloved, uncared for, 2) not dear, two-a-penny.

undelved *adj.* not dug over, unharrowed, untilled, unworked.

under *adj.* 1) set lower, lying beneath/under, 2) (of *sound*) low, 3) lesser, nether.

under *prep.* 1) below, beneath, underneath, on the bottom of, 2) bound by, 3) belonging to, 4) less than, not as much as, 5) undergoing.

under *adv.* at the foot of, below, adown, down, downward, beneath, underneath.

underbear *v.* 1) to bear with, brook, forbear, put up with, 2) to back up, uphold.

underbid *v.* 1) to make a low offer, 2) to undercut.

underboard *adv.* underhand, not openly or rightly.

underbough *n.* one of the lower boughs of a tree.

under-breath 1) *n.* a whisper, 2) *adj.* whispered, 3) *adv.* in a whisper.

underclothes, underclothing *n.* drawers, underdrawers, netherbreeches, underbreeches, undershirt, underthings, underwear, smalls.

undercut *v.* 1) to cut away below or beneath, 2) to sell at a loss, undersell,

under-delve *v.* to delve a pit, play a deep game, spin/weave a web, work against.

underdo *v.* to do less than is needed, to work less than well, to undercook.

underdog *n.* loser, outsider.

underdone *adj.* half-baked, half-cooked, half-done.

underdraw *v.* 1) to underline, 2) to lay boards on the inside of a roof or under the floor, 3) to draw only a middling likeness.

under-earth *n.* the underworld.

under-earth *adj.* underground, unfathomed, underlying, unseen, deep, hidden.

underfed *adj.* half-starved, hungry, lean, sharp-set, starved, underweight.

underfeed *v.* to keep short of food, starve.

under-floor *adj.* of that which is under the floor (such as heating pipes).

underflow *n.* underswell, undertow.

underflow *v.* to flow under.

underfoot *adj.* beaten down, downtrodden, quelled.

underfoot *adv.* adown.

undergird *v.* to bolster, strengthen, underset.

undergo *v.* to bear, go through, weather, withstand.

underground *adj.* deep, hidden, under-earth, underlying, unfathomed, unseen.

underground *adv.* below ground, in hiding, under the earth, out of sight.

undergrowth *n.* briars, brambles, low stunted trees, scrub, thicket, underwood.

underhand *adj.* crafty, knavish, shady, sharp, shifty, slinking, stealthy,

underhand *adv.* stealthily.

underhand dealing (*conspiracy, plot*) *n.* buying and selling on the side, shady business, sharp-dealing, shift, web-weaving.

underhanded *adj.* low, mean, shabby, shameful, unrightful, unworthy.

underhandedly *adv.* foully, meanly, shamefully, unrightfully, unworthily.

under-king *n.* a lesser king under a high king.

underlay *n.* that which is laid under another thing, such as felt under *carpet*.

underlay *v.* to put something beneath.

underlie *v.* 1) to lie under, be beneath, 2) to be the grounding of.

underline[(4)] *v.* to go over again, go through again, highlight, mark, say again/over.

underling *n.* dogsbody, drudge, hanger-on, hireling, nobody, tool, underdog.

underlying *adj.* 1) lying beneath, lying under, 2) deep down, root, hidden.

undermanned *adj.* not having enough folk for the work, short-handed, understaffed.

undermost *adj.* holding the lowest *place*, bottom, nethermost.

undernamed *adj.* named below.

underneath 1) *prep.* below, beneath, 2a) *adv.* on the underside, 2b) in one's heart of hearts, in one's innermost thoughts, inside, 3) *n.* bottom, underside.

underplay *v.* to play a lesser game than one can do.

under-reckon *v.* to hold cheap, look down on, misdeem, misread, think too little of.

underripe *adj.* unripe, half-blown, unblown, half-grown.

undersea *adj.* deep-sea, underwater.

undersell *v.* to give away, mark down, undercut, let go for a song.

underset *v.* to bolster, strengthen, undergird, uphold.

undershirt *n.* underclothing worn under a shirt.

undershoot *v.* to shoot short of, to shoot too low for.

undershot *adj.* of a mill-wheel driven by water flowing under it.

underside *n.* bottom, underneath.

underslinking *n.* blind, game, shift, makeshift, dust in the eyes.

undersong *n.* 1) background song that is set with the main song, 2) (*allegory*) *n.* other-speaking, other-telling, under-telling, forlikening.

understaffed *adj.* below strength, short-handed, undermanned.

understand *v.* to see, fathom, find out, follow the thread, grasp, know, learn, to follow one, have it dawn on one, have one's eyes opened, put one's finger on, read between the lines, see it all, sift out.

understanding *n.* 1) awareness, insight, mother-wit, wisdom, 2) of one mind.

understanding *adj.* aware, deep, farsighted, thinking, wise, witfast, witful.

understood *adj.* known, settled, unsaid, unspoken.

undertake[(2)] *v.* 1) to put one's hand to, shoulder, take on, 2) to bind oneself, give/plight one's word, mean what one says, underwrite.

undertaking[(2)] *n.* business, dealership.

under-telling (*allegory*) *n.* other-speaking, other-telling, undersong. forlikening.

underthings *n.* drawers, underclothes, underclothing, underwear.

underthought *n.* hidden thought, other thought.

undertow *n.* underflow, underswell.

underwater *n.* underground water.

underwater *adj.* sunken, undersea.

underway *adv.* afoot, begun, going on, in business, started.

underwear *n.* drawers, netherbreeches, underbreeches, underclothes, underclothing, undershirt, underthings.

underweight *adj.* below weight, half-starved, light, underfed.

underwood *n.* brambles, small stunted trees, scrub, thicket, undergrowth, frith.

underwork *n.* 1) undergirding, 2) underhand work.

underwork *v.* 1) to do little work, 2) to work against in hidden ways.

underworld *n.* 1) abode of the dead, halls of death, hell, lower world, nether world, land of the shades, world of the dead, 2) the world of thieves.

underwrite *v.* 1) to put/set one's hand to, write (*sign*) one's name, 2) to back, lend one's name, put one's name down, stand behind, undertake.

underwriter *n.* backer, loss-bearer.

underwriting (*signature*) *n.* hand, hand-setting, mark.

underwritten *adj.* following upon what is already written, written below, written out.

undo *v.* 1) to loosen, open, unclasp, unbind, unbolt, unfasten, unhook, unlatch, unlock, unloose, untie, 2) to axe, do away with, end, bring to an end, bring to naught, unmake, fordo, overcome, overwhelm, put an end to, put away, quell, root out, root up, strike out, swallow up, tear down, throw down, uproot, wipe out.

undoing *n.* downfall, end, ending, tearing down, unmaking, uprooting, wiping out.

undone *adj.* half-done, hardly begun, left, not done.

undone *adj.* broken down, brought to nothing, ended, fallen, overthrown, unstuck.

undraw *v.* to draw back (a bolt and such), unfasten by pulling something.

undreamed of, undreamt of *adj.* unheard of, unthought of.

undying *adj.* 1) abiding, deathless, 2) unswerving, unwearying, true to the end.

unearned *adj.* not rightly won.

unearth *v.* 1) to dredge up, open up, 2) to bring to light, come upon, find out.

unearthed *adj.* 1) unburied, 2) without an earth wire.

unearthly *adj.* offbeam, outlandish, out of the way, unheard of, weird.

unending *adj.* abiding, everlasting, lasting, long-lasting, long-standing.

uneven *adj.* 1) one-sided, unfair, 2) broken, fitful, not smooth, rough, unsteady.

unevenly *adv.* 1) unfairly, 2) fitfully, not smoothly, unsteadily.

unfain *adj.* half-hearted, loath, not glad, unminded, unwilling, unwishful.

unfair *adj.* one-sided, unright, unrightwise, warped.

be **unfair** *v.* to be one-sided, lean to one side, see one side only, twist, warp, bend.

unfairly *adv.* meanly, shamefully, trothlessly, underhandedly, unrightly, untruly.

unfairness *n.* leaning (to one side), one-sidedness, unrightness, withholding the right.

unfasten *v.* to loosen, open, unbind, unbolt, unclasp, undo, unlatch, unlock, untie.

unfatherlike *adj.* in an unfatherly way, cold, unkind.

unfathomed *adj.* 1) deep, unfathomful, 2) dark, hard to fathom, knotted, thorny.

unfathomful *adj.* bottomless, fathomless, reachless.

unfearful *adj.* bold, daring-hearted, fearless, steely.

unfearing *adj.* bold, daring, doughty, fearless, unshrinking.

unfed *adj.* starved, half-starved, hungry, lean, sharp-set, underweight.

unfeeling *adj.* blind/deaf/dead to, cold, cool, hard-bitten, hardened, off-handed, unbrotherly, uncaring, unkind, unruthful, without feeling or understanding, wounding.

unfetter *v.* to free, set free, unbind, unfasten, unlock, unshackle, untie, unyoke.

unfettered *adj.* freed, unbound, unshackled, untied.

unfired *adj.* (of pots) not fired in a kiln.

unfit *adj.* 1) not fit, unfitted, untaught, unworthy, 2) out of shape, sallow, sickly, unhealthy, unwell, wan, washed-out, 3) no good, not cut out for, not up to.

unfledged *adj.* 1) unfeathered and so unready to leave the nest, 2) backward, beardless, childish, green, ungrown, unripened, unhewn, untimely, over-young.

unfold *v.* 1) to spread open, straighten out, stretch out, 2) to lay bare, make known, tell, aread/arede, 3) to blossom, grow, work out.

unfolding *n.* broadening, growing, ripening, rising, spreading, swelling, widening.

unforeknown *adj.* unforeseen, out of one's reckoning, unlooked for.

unforeseeing *adj.* heedless, short-sighted, thoughtless, unseeing, unwary, unwise.

unforeseen *adj.* dropped from the clouds, startling, out of one's reckoning, unheard of, unforeknown, unlooked for, without warning.

unforewarned *adj.* redeless, unseeing, unwary, unwise.

unforgetting *adj.* bitter, hard, hoarding wrath, ruthless, unforgiving, unkind.

unforgiven *adj.* not forgiven.

unforgiveness, unforgivingness *n.* bitterness, hardness.

unforgiving *adj.* bitter, heartless, hoarding wrath, ruthless, unforgetting, unkind.

unforgot, unforgotten *adj.* hoarded in the heart, not laid to rest.

unfound *adj.* not found, lost.

unfreeze *v.* to melt, thaw.

unfriended *adj.* friendless, alone, lonely, homeless, kinless.

unfriendliness *n.* churlishness, coldness, prickliness, standoffishness, stiffness.

unfriendly *adj.* all edges, churlish, cold, frosty, icy, moody, off-handed, prickly, standoffish, stern, stiff, uncouth, unforthcoming, unneighbourly, unwelcoming.

unfriendly *adv.* churlishly, unkindly.

unfrighted, unfrightened *adj.* bold, daring, high-hearted, unfearing, unshrinking.

unfrozen *adj.* melted, thawed.

ungainsaid *adj.* unanswered.

ungilded *adj.* not overlaid with gold, ungilden, ungilt.

ungirdled, ungirt *adj.* not wearing a girdle, not girt about.

unglad *adj.* forlorn, hopelorn, heart-sick, listless, sad, sorrowful, unblithe.

unglazed *adj.* without glass in the windows.

unglove *v.* to take off one's gloves.

ungodliness *n.* evil, godlessness, shamelessness, unrightness, wickedness.

ungodly *adj.* evil, godless, hardened, shameless, sinful, unholy, wicked, worldly.

ungrounded *adj.* groundless, on shaky ground.

unguilty *adj.* clean-handed, guiltless, free from guilt, not guilty, sinless, upright.

unhale *adj.* sallow, sickly, unwell.

unhallowed *adj.* heathen, unblest, unclean, unholy.

unhand *v.* to leave hold of, let go, set free, slacken one's grip, unclench, unclinch.

unhandsome *adj.* 1) grim, uncomely, unlovely, 2) hard, mean, selfish.

unhandy *adj.* all thumbs, thick-fingered, slow.

unharmed *adj.* unmarked, unmarred, unscathed, unwounded, whole.

unhasp *v.* to unclasp, unfasten, unlock.

unhealthy *adj.* in bad health, off-hued, sallow, sickening, sickly, unfit, unhale, unwell, wan, washed-out, like death warmed up.

unheard *adj.* not heard, not having been given a hearing, unheeded.

unheard of *adj.* 1) ground-breaking, new, undreamed of, wonderful, 2) frightful, outlandish, startling, 3) little known, unknown, unsung.

unhearing *adj.* 1) deaf, deaf to, 2) unheeding, unmindful, 3) stony, unfeeling.

unheated *adj.* cold, stone-cold, unwarmed.

unheeded *adj.* forgotten, overlooked, unheard.

unheedful *adj.* headstrong, heedless, hot-headed, hot-hearted, rash, reckless, wild.

unheedfully *adv.* carelessly, heedlessly, rashly, recklessly, unwarily, wildly.

unheedfulness *n.* carelessness, heedlessness, recklessness, unwariness, unwisdom.

unheeding *adj.* far-away, forgetful, far-minded, lost in thought, head in the clouds.

unheedingly *adv.* heedlessly, rashly, recklessly, thoughtlessly, unwarely, unwarily.

unhelm *v.* to take off one's helm, to strike off another's helm in a fight.

unhelmed *adj.* without one's helm, helmless.

unhelpful *adj.* hindering, mean, unforthcoming, unkind, unneighbourly, unwilling.

unhelpfulness *n.* hardness, meanness, unkindness, sourness, unwillingness.

unhewn *adj.* 1) rough, unshapen, unwrought, 2) earthy, rough-edged, uncouth.

unhid, unhidden *adj.* for all to see, in the limelight, in the open, standing out.

unhindered *adj.* free, free as the wind, unbound, unfettered, unshackled.

unholy *adj.* evil, fallen, foul, godless, sinful, unclean, ungodly, unhallowed, wicked.

unhook *v.* to unclasp, undo, unloose.

unhopeful *adj.* fearing the worst, forboding, gloomy, hopeless, hopelorn, listless.

unhorse *v.* 1) to throw a rider from his horse, 2) to loose the horses from a wain.

unkempt *adj.* bedraggled, sloppy, tousled, uncombed, untidy, unwashen.

unkind *adj.* hard-hearted, rough, shrewish, stony-hearted, thoughtless, unfeeling, unforgiving, unfriendly, unhelpful, unloving, warmthless, waspish, wounding.

unkindly *adv.* thoughtlessly, unfeelingly, unlovingly.

unkindness *n.* hard-heartedness, lovelessness, meanness, unfeelingness.

unkingly *adj.* unknightly, unlordly, unworthy.

unknightly *adj.* bearish, churlish, rough-edged, rough-hewn, uncouth, unhewn.

unknit, unknot *v.* to undo a knot, loosen a tie, unknot a riddle.

unknotted *adj.* undone, untied, loosened, unriddled.

unknowing *adj.* benighted, in the dark, loreless, unlearned.

unknown *adj.* 1) unbeheld, unbeknown, 2) dark, deep, knotted, unfathomed.

unladylike *adj.* brazen, forward, misbecoming, unbecoming, unworthy.

unlatch *v.* to undo, unfasten, unlock.

unlawful[2] *adj.* against the law, forbidden, outside the law, unrightwise.

unleaded *adj.* not weighted with lead.

unlearn *v.* to give up or set aside the knowledge of something.

unlearned *adj.* backward, benighted, blind, bookless, book-starved, darkened (in mind), in the dark, groping, heathenish, loreless, narrow-minded, unaware, unbookish, unknowing, unread, unseeing, untaught, unthinking, without the light.

unless *prep. phr.* if not, without.

unlifelike *adj.* untrue to life, wide of the truth, wooden.

unlighted *adj.* dark, unlit, black as night.

unlike 1a) *adj.* anything but, far from, far above/below, not like, unalike, 1b) unlikely, 2) *n.* someone or something unlike any other.

unlikely *adj.* beyond belief, far-fetched, hard to believe, not likely, unheard of.

unlikeness *n.* bad likeness, no match, otherness.

unlit *adj.* dark, unlighted, black as night.

unload *v.* to empty, lighten, off-load, unburden.

unlock *v.* to open, unbolt, undo, unfasten, unhasp, unlatch.

unlooked for *adj.* startling, undreamed of, <u>unforeseen</u>, unthought of.

unloose, unloosen[(2)] *v.* to <u>free</u>, set free, get one out of, unbind, unyoke.

unlordly *adj.* unknightly, unmanly.

unloved *adj.* forsaken, loveless, unbeloved, uncared for, undear.

unloveliness *n.* frightfulness, uncomeliness, unshapeliness, unsightliness.

unlovely *adj.* misshapen, uncomely, unhandsome.

unloverlike *adj.* backward, clod-hopping, cool, heavy, lifeless, slow.

unloving *adj.* cold-hearted, thoughtless, uncaring, unkind.

unlovingly *adv.* coldly, coolly, uncaringly, unkindly.

unmaidenly *adj.* brazen, forward, <u>shameless</u>, unblushing, wanton.

unmake *v.* to axe, end, bring to an end, bring to <u>naught</u>, cut down, fell, grind, knock down, lay in the dust, make an end of, mow down, <u>overcome</u>, pull down, put down, quell, quench, stamp out, tear down, tear to shreds, throw down, <u>undo</u>, wipe out.

unman *v.* to <u>bewilder</u>, unsettle, upset, shake, fill with <u>fear</u>.

unmanly *adj.* <u>fearful</u>, soft, womanish.

unmanly *adv.* fearfully, unmanfully.

unmanned *adj.* 1) without men to drive (a flying-craft, ship and such), 2) beaten, bowed, down, <u>hopelorn</u>, <u>shaken</u>, undone, woebegone, wretched.

unmarked *adj.* bearing no mark, unmarred.

unmarred *adj.* less, unscathed, unharmed, unmarked, unwounded, whole.

unmatched *adj.* foremost, <u>greatest</u>, makeless, matchless, nonesuch, not as others are, one and only, outmatching, outstanding, out of this world, wonderful.

unmeaning *adj.* empty, lightweight, meaningless, without meaning, shallow, windy.

unmeaningness *n.* emptiness, meaninglessness, soft nothing, wind.

unmeet *adj.* not right, out of keeping, unbecoming, <u>uncouth</u>, unworthy.

unmeetly *adv.* unbecomingly, unrightly, unworthily.

unmeetness *n.* unrightness, unworthiness.

unmelting *adj.* cold, grim, heartless, <u>ruthless</u>, stony-hearted, wolf-hearted.

unmighty *adj.* mightless, strengthless.

unminded *adj.* <u>loath</u>, unfain, unforthcoming, unready, unwilling.

unmindful *adj.* <u>heedless</u>, <u>light-minded</u>, offhand, reckless, thoughtless, unthinking.

unmingled *adj.* strong, whole, wholesome.

unmirthful *adj.* cold, cool, forbidding, sour, stern, stiff, unlaughing.

unmissed *adj.* overlooked, uncared for, unloved, unthought of.

unmothered *adj.* uncared for, unloved, untaught.

unmotherly *adj.* uncaring, unkind, unloving.

unmourned *adj.* hated, loathed, unmissed, unwept.

unmown *adj.* not mown, uncut.

unnamed *adj.* nameless, shadowy, shrouded, unfathomful, unknown,

unneeded *adj.* not needed.

unneedful *adj.* needless.

unneighbourly *adj.* churlish, crabbed, mean, unfriendly, unkind, unwelcoming.

unoften *adv.* few and far between, hardly ever, not often, once in a way.

unopened *adj.* not opened, shut.

unpathed *adj.* pathless, untrodden, wayless, wild.

unpen *v.* to let livestock out of a pen.

unpick *v.* to unbind, undo, unknit, unknot, unsew, unstitch, unthread, untie.

unplighting (*adultery*) *n.* guilty love.

unqueenly *adj.* unladylike, unworthy.

unquelled *adj.* doughty, stalwart, <u>steadfast</u>, tough, <u>unyielding</u>.

unquenched *adj.* 1) (of thirst) quenchless, unmet, 2) (of fire) blazing, burning.

unreached *adj.* not reached.

unread *adj.* 1) not read, 2) bookless, book-starved, loreless, unbookish, <u>unlearned</u>.

unreadiness *n.* backwardness, greenness, unripeness,

unready *adj.* 1) behindhand, not yet ready, 2) half-hearted, <u>loath</u>, slow, unminded.

unreckoned *adj.* unrimed, untold.

unredely *adv.* heedlessly, recklessly, thoughtlessly, unheedingly, unwisely, witlessly.

unrest *n.* restlessness, stir, unstillness, upheaving, upset, uproar.

unrestful *adj.* draining, grinding, hard-going, tiring, tough, weariful, wearing.

unresting *adj.* giving oneself no rest, keeping at it, not stopping, restless.

unridden *adj.* (of a horse) not broken in.

unriddle *v.* to unrime a riddle, find the key/meaning, make out, read, unknot.

unriddler *n.* one who unweaves a riddle.

unright *n.* misdeed, misdoing, sin, wicked deed.

unright *adj.* 1) <u>evil</u>, misdone, unrightwise, 2) not right, wide of the mark/the truth.

unrighteous *adj.* bad, <u>evil</u>, evil-minded, <u>godless</u>, unrightwise, wicked.

unrighteously *adv.* sinfully, wickedly.

unrighteousness *n.* <u>evil</u>, godlessness, sinfulness, unrightwiseness, wickedness.

unrightful *adj.* mean, shameful, untrothful, unworthy, wicked.

unrightfully *adv.* badly, meanly, <u>shamefully</u>, trothlessly, unworthily.

unrightly *adv.* foully, hatefully, meanly, <u>shamefully</u>, sinfully, unfairly.

unrightness *n.* 1) <u>evil</u>, foul play, shamefulness, sinfulness, unfairness, ungodliness, wickedness, 2) unmeetness, unworthiness.

unrightwise *adj.* <u>evil</u>, fallen, ungodly, unrighteous, unfair, wicked,

unrightwiseness *n.* <u>evil</u>, right withheld, unfairness, unrighteousness, wickedness.

unrimed *adj.* unreckoned, untold.

unriming *adj.* beyond telling, endless, many, teeming.

unripe *adj.* 1) green, sour, underripe, 2) raw, <u>unfledged</u>, ungrown.

unroof *v.* 1) to take off the roof of a building, 2) (of the wind) to lift the roof off.

unroofed *adj.* roofless, open to the weather.

unruth *n.* coldness, hard-heartedness, heartlessness, ruthlessness, stony-heartedness.

unsaddle *v.* 1) to take the saddle off a horse, 2) to unhorse.

unsaid *adj.* unbreathed, understood, unspoken.

unsalted *adj.* (of butter and such) with no salt on.

unsawn *adj.* of timber that has been felled but not yet sawn into beams.

unsay *v.* to forswear, go back on one's word, withdraw.

unscathed[2] *adj.* unharmed, unmarked, unmarred, unwounded, whole.

unseam *v.* to undo the seams of.

unseamanlike *adj.* unsailorly, unseacraftly, unseamanly.

unseaworthy *adj.* (of a ship) rusting, leaking, unfit to go to sea.

unseeing *adj.* 1) blind, stock-blind, stone-blind, sightless, 2) short-sighted, wooden.

unseen *adj.* hidden, unbeheld, unbeknown, out of sight, out of eye-shot.

unseldom *adv.* many a time, often, oft-times, oftentimes, time and again.

unselfish *adj.* <u>free</u>, great-hearted, <u>kind</u>, mindful, self-forgetful, selfless, thoughtful.

unselfishly *adv.* <u>freely</u>, open-handedly, readily, willingly, unstintingly.

unselfishness *n.* great-heartedness, <u>kindness</u>, selflessness, thoughtfulness.

unsettle *v.* to <u>bewilder</u>, upset, shake, put one out of his stride, unsteady, <u>worry</u>.

unsettled *adj.* 1) shaky, unsteady, 2) (of the weather) sun and showers, windy, 3) churned up, on edge, restless, <u>shaken</u>, upset, 4) not cut and dried, still, open, 5) (of the reckoning) outstanding, owed, owing, 6) (of a land) empty, folkless, lonely, wild.

unsettling *adj.* upsetting, worrying, worrisome, weighing one down.

unsew *v.* to undo, unstitch, unthread.

unshackle *v.* to <u>free</u>, let go, undo, unfasten, unfetter, unlock, untie, unyoke.

unshackled *adj.* free, unbridled, unfettered, unhindered.

unshaded *adj.* without any shade or shelter.

unshaken *adj.* 1) <u>unyielding</u>, stalwart, 2) <u>abiding</u>, <u>settled</u>, <u>well-grounded</u>.

unshamed *adj.* not brought to shame, true, unsinning.

unshaped, unshapen *adj.* misshapen, shapeless, unhewn, unmade, unwrought.

unshapely *adj.* misshapen, unshapen, uncomely, unsightly, twisted.

unsharpness *n.* backwardness, oafishness, slowness, <u>unwisdom</u>, heedlessness.

unshaved, unshaven *adj.* bristly, hairy, rough, unshorn.

unsheathe *v.* 1) to draw a sword from its sheath, 2) to lay bare, throw open.

unsheathed *adj.* (of a sword blade) naked, threatening.

unsheltered *adj.* having no shelter from wind and weather.

unsheltering *adj.* giving no shelter from wind and weather.

unshielded *adj.* unwarded (against wind, weather or weapons).

unshifting *adj.* <u>abiding</u>, settled, <u>steadfast</u>, steady, unswerving, stead-hard.

unship *v.* (of a ship) 1) to unload, off-load, 2) to take out a mast or rudder.

unshod *adj.* 1) without shoes, barefoot, 2) (of a horse) having thrown a shoe.

unshoe *v.* 1) to take off a horse shoe, 2) (of the horse) to throw a shoe.

unshrinking *adj.* steady, stalwart, steely, tough, unblenching, <u>unyielding</u>.

unshroud *v.* 1) to lay bare, let in daylight, <u>make known</u>, 2) to take off a shroud.

unshrouded *adj.* laid bare, out in the open.

unshrouding *n.* forthtelling, making known, shadowing forth, unfolding.

unsifted *adj.* 1) unsieved, 2) not gone through, not looked into, undelved.

unsighted *adj.* blind, unseeing.

unsightly *adj.* misshapen, shapeless, unshapely, twisted, withered, worn.

unsinged *adj.* not burned, unseared.

unsinning *adj.* clean-living, God-fearing, upright, walking in God's way.

unsleeping *adj.* 1) awake, wakeful, wide-awake, sleepless, 2) aware, missing nothing, prick-eared, on the watch, watchful, 3) never resting, tireless, unresting.

unslumbering *adj.* 1) awake, unsleeping, 2) prick-eared, 3) unresting,

unsoftened *adj.* 1) not softened, 2) (of words) cutting, hard, not sparing, stinging.

unsold *adj.* not sold, left on one's hands, left on the shelf.

unsooth *n.* less than the truth, untruth, lie, downright lie, shameless lie, white lie.

unsought *adj.* not sought for, unasked, unbidden.

unsound *adj.* 1) strenghthless, unhealthy, wan, 2) not in one's right mind, 3) (of what one says or writes) not backed up, not well-grounded, shaky.

unsparing *adj.* 1) hard, heartless, heavy-handed, overbearing, ruthless, unbending, unforgiving, 2) free-handed, open-handed, sparing no outlay, unstinting.

unsparingly *adv.* free-handedly, heedlessly, unstintingly.

unspeaking *adj.* saying not a word, wordless, tongueless.

unsped *adj.* falling down, falling short, falling through, lost, misfired.

unspell *v.* to break a spell, end a spell, free one from a spell, undo a spell.

unspilled, unspilt *adj.* not spilled.

unspoken *adj.* not put into words, not spelt out, unbreathed, understood, unsaid.

unsteadfast *adj.* fickle, flighty, light-minded, restless, unsteady, wayward.

unsteadfastly *adv.* restlessly, unsteadily, waywardly.

unsteadfastness *n.* fickleness, flightiness, light-mindedness, unsteadiness.

unsteadful *adj.* 1) (*apostate*) fallen, trothless, 2) fitful, restless, steadless, unsteady.

unsteady *adj.* 1) shaky, 2) fitful, flighty, light-minded, steadless, two-minded.

unsteady *v.* to shake, throw one off his bearings, unsettle.

unsteadily *adv.* restlessly, unsteadfastly, waywardly.

unsteadiness *n.* giddiness, restlessness, unsteadfastness, trothlessness, waywardness.

unstick *v.* to come off, loosen.

unstiffen *v.* to loosen up.

unstill *adj.* flighty, fluttering, restless, shiftful, unsettled.

unstillness *n.* much ado, care, unrest, upset, weight on one's mind, worry.

unstinted *adj.* full, unsparing, unstinting.

unstinting *adj.* free, great-hearted, handsome, open-handed, unsparing, unstinted.

unstirred *adj.* cold, hard-bitten, hard-hearted, heartless, stony-hearted, unfeeling.

unstitch *v.* to undo, unknit, unpick, unsew, unthread.

unstring *v.* to loosen, slacken, unbind, undo.

unstrung *adj.* 1) loosened, slackened, undone, 2) mazed, not right in the head, wandering in one's mind, wildered in one's wits.

unstuck *adj.* brought to nothing, overthrown, undone.

unsummerlike *adj.* cool, on the cool side, rainy, wet.

unsung *adj.* unacknowledged, unknown, unnamed, nameless.

unsweet, unsweetened *adj.* sour, sharp, tart, bitter, biting, stinging.

unswept *adj.* dusty, filthy.

unswerving *adj.* 1) going neither to the right hand nor the left, straight as an arrow, 2) settled, steadfast, steady, true, true-hearted, unfaltering, unshaken, true to the end.

unswiven (*virgin*) *adj.* maidenly, unknown.

unswollen *adj.* not swollen or puffy.

untamed *adj.* wild, bold, fiery, hot-headed, hot-hearted.

untapped *adj.* not drawn upon.

untaught *adj.* badly brought up, unaware, unchidden, unknowing, unlearned.

unthanked *adj.* forgotten, unacknowledged, without thanks having been given.

unthankful *adj.* forgetful, heedless, unmindful.

unthankfulness *n.* cold thanks, thanklessness.

unthinking *adj.* careless, heedless, offhand, thoughtless, unmindful, unwitting.

unthinkingly *adv.* carelessly, heedlessly, offhandedly, thoughtlessly, unmindfully.

unthought *adj.* unthought of, not to be thought of, undreamt.

unthoughtful *adj.* thoughtless, off-hand, uncaring, unfeeling, unkind, unloving.

unthoughtfulness *n.* heedlessness, thoughtlessness, unmindfulness.

unthread *v.* to undo, unknit, unknot, unpick, unseam, unsew, unstitch.

untidy *adj.* awry, cluttered, scruffy, shabby, sloppy, tousled, unkempt, upside down.

untidily *adv.* anyhow, sloppily.

untidiness *n.* carelessness, clutter, sloppiness.

untie *v.* to free, loosen, open, unbind, unclasp, undo, unfasten, unknot, unloose.

until[2] 1) *prep.* till, to, unto, up to, up to the time of, 2) *conj.* up to the time that.

untilled *adj.* not dug over, undelved, unharrowed, unworked.

untimely *adj.* 1) before time, too soon for, 2) badly timed, mistimed, out of step.

untimely *adv.* at a bad time, too early, too soon.

untiring *adj.* dogged, tireless, steady, unfaltering, unresting, unsleeping, unwearied.

unto 1) *prep.* to, up to, up to the time of, 2) *conj.* until, up to the time that.

untold *adj.* 1) unreckoned, unrimed, ever so many/much, thick on the ground, coming thick and fast, alive with, 2) undreamed of, hidden, unknown.

untorn *adj.* not torn, unrent.

untoward *adj.* not right, untimely.

untowardly *adj.* froward, unbecoming.

untrodden *adj.* pathless, unpathed, unknown, wayless, wild.

untroth *n.* broken word, forswearing, unrightness, untruthfulness.

untrothful *adj.* fickle, forsworn, shifty, trothless, truthless, untrue, untruthful.

untrothfully *adv.* shamefully, trothlessly, unrightly, untruly.

untrue *adj.* 1) forsworn, trothless, truthless, two-hearted, two-tongued, 2) far from the truth, not right, wide of the mark/truth, 3) lying, misleading, sham.

untruly *adv.* shamefully, trothlessly, underhandedly, unfairly, unrightly.

untruth *n.* 1) less than the truth, lie, 2) truthlessness, untruthfulness.

untruthful *adj.* lying, shady, shifty, trothless, truthless, underhand, untrothful.

untruthfully *adv.* craftily, unsoothly, untruly.

untruthfulness *n.* forswearing, shiftiness, trothlessness, truthlessness, untruth.

untwine *v.* to undo by untwisting, to become untwisted.

untwist *v.* to straighten out, unknot, untwine, unwind.

unwakened *adj.* not woken, sleeping on, unstirring.

unwarded *adj.* unshielded, unwatched, wide open.

unware/s *adj.* 1) unwary, done unwarily, 2) unaware, knowing nothing, 3) unforeseen, unlooked for, 4) unknown (to one).

unware/s, unwarely *adv.* 1) startlingly, without warning, 2) carelessly, heedlessly, thoughtlessly, unheedingly, unwarily, 3) unknowingly, unthinkingly, unwittingly.

unwareness *n.* carelessness, heedlessness, rashness, recklessness, unwariness.

unwarily *adv.* carelessly, heedlessly, recklessly, thoughtlessly, warelessly.

unwariness *n.* carelessness, heedlessness, recklessness.

unwarned *adj.* given no warning.

unwarp *v.* to make straight, put straight, set straight, straighten out, unbend.

unwary *adj.* heedless, unheedful, unmindful, unthinking, unwatchful, wareless.

unwashed, unwashen *adj.* filthy, unclean,

unwatchful *adj.* careless, heedless, unheedful, wareless.

unwatered *adj.* 1) not soaked in water, 2) dry, waterless.

unwaxed *adj.* not smeared with wax.

unwayed *adj.* without ways or roads, pathless.

unwayward *adj.* steady, thoughtful, understanding, unwilful, wise.

unweal (*poverty*) *n.* hardship, hard going, lack, pennilessness, wretchedness.

unwealthy *adj.* badly off, hard up, needy, not well-off, penniless, short, weal-less.

unweaned *adj.* not yet weaned, still feeding at the breasts.

unweaponed *adj.* barehanded, bearing no weapons, weaponless.

unwearied *adj.* never tiring, tireless, unresting, unsleeping, untiring, unweary.

unweariness *n.* doggedness, steadiness, tirelessness.

unweary *adj.* tireless, untiring, unwearied.

unwearying *adj.* forbearing, never tiring, steadfast, steady, undying, unshifting.

unwearingly *adv.* selflessly, tirelessly, unswervingly.

unweave *v.* to undo, unpick, unthread, untwine.

unwedded *adj.* 1) not bound in wedlock, unwed, unwooed, wifeless, 2) maidenly.

unweighed *adj.* 1) not weighed in the weigh-scales, 2) not thought through.

unwelcome *adj.* bitter, dreadful, hateful, unbidden, unwinsome, unwished.

unwell *adj.* addled, ailing, sick, sickly, under the weather, unhealthy, unwhole.

unwemmed *adj.* 1) clean-handed, guiltless, matchless, sinless, 2) unmarred.

unwending *adj.* abiding, homefast, settled.

unwhole *adj.* ailing, sick, unwell.

unwholesome *adj.* loathsome, foul, fulsome, rank, stinking, unhealthy.

unwieldy *adj.* heavy, hefty, overweighted, top-heavy, unhandy, weighty.

unwilful *adj.* ready, steady, unselfish, unwayward, willing.

unwill *v.* 1) to will that which one was formerly against, 2) to take away someone else's will.

unwilled *adj.* unbidden, unchosen, unlooked for, unsought, unwished for.

unwilling *adj.* half-hearted, hindering, loath, misliking, not minded, unhelpful.

unwillingly *adv.* against one's will, half-heartedly, loathfully, unreadily.

unwillingness *n.* backwardness, slowness, unreadiness.

unwind *v.* 1) to unbind, undo, untwine, untwist, 2) to take a break, wind down.

unwinking *adj.* unblinking, steady.

unwinsome *adj.* 1) bitter, unwelcome, 2) frightful, uncomely, unlovely.

unwiped *adj.* not wiped down, unclean.

unwisdom *n.* heedlessness, recklessness, hot-headedness, dizzyness, rashness, carelessness, over-daring, playing with fire, lightmindedness, unwariness, wantonness, wildness.

unwise *adj.* headstrong, heedless, light-minded, rash, reckless, unwary, wild.

unwisely *adv.* heedlessly, redelessly, thoughtlessly, unwitfully.

unwishful *adj.* half-hearted, holding back, loath, unfain, unwilling.

unwist *adj.* 1) unknown to one, without it being known, 2) without knowledge (of something), 3) not known, uncanny.

unwit *v.* 1) to know not, be in the dark, 2) to make one witless in his/her doing.

unwitch *v.* to free from a witch's spell.

unwitful *adj.* clod-hopping, dim, slow, witless, wooden-headed.

unwitfulness *n.* empty-headedness, feather-headedness, heedlessness, unwisdom.

unwitting *adj.* 1) unmeant, unwilled, 2) unaware, unknowing, unseeing.

unwittingly *adv.* blindly, unawares, unknowingly.

unwittingness *n.* benightedness, blindness, darkness, unawareness, unknowingness.

unwitty *adj.* 1) slow-witted, unwitful, witless, 2) not having wittiness with words.

unwomanly *adj.* brazen, forward, headstrong, shameless, uncouth, unmaidenly.

unwooded *adj.* open, without trees.

unwooed *adj.* unasked, unloved.

unworked *adj.* 1) unhewn, not shaped, unwrought, 2) (of an ore field) not worked.

unworkmanlike *adj.* not well done/made, rough, rough-hewn, uncraftly.

unworldliness *n.* childlikeness, godliness, goodness, heavenly-mindedness.

unworldly *adj.* 1) childlike, green, open-hearted, right-hearted, unhardened, 2) godly, heavenly-minded, otherworldly.

unworried *adj.* cool, cool-headed, laid-back, steady, unshaken, unworrying.

unworth *n.* lack of true worth, unworthiness.

unworth *adj.* low, mean, underhanded, unworthy of.

unworthily *adv.* badly, foully, meanly, shamefully, trothlessly, unrightfully.

unworthiness *n.* emptiness, hollowness, shallowness, shamefulness.

unworthness, unworthship *n.* bad name, evil, shame.

unworthy *adj.* beggarly, beneath one, shabby, shameful, unknightly, unbecoming.

unwound *adj.* unbound, undone, untwined, untwisted.

unwounded *adj.* unbloodied, unharmed, unmarked, unmarred, unscathed, whole.

unwoven *adj.* undone, unpicked, unthreaded, untwined.

unwritten *adj.* 1) not down in black and white, 2) not spelt out, understood.

unwrought *adj.* uncut, unhewn, unshaped (by man), unworked.

unwyrd *n.* misfalling, elf-play.

unyielding *adj.* dogged, doughty, flinty, gritty, hard as nails/steel/stone, stalworth, standing fast, steadfast, steely, stern, stern-minded, strong-minded, strong-willed, tough, tough as steel, unbending, unshaken, unshrinking.

unyoke *v.* to free, set free, let out, unbind, unloose.

up *n.* a rise in the ground, a rise in life.

up *adj.* (of *trains*, wains and such) going up, running up.

up *v.* to lift up, put the helm (of a ship) up, stand up, to up and do.

up *adv.* 1) higher, uphill, upwards, 2) upon one's feet, 3) uprisen and weaponed (against the leaders of the land), 4) amiss, going on, 5) up before a deemster/*judge*.

up *prep.* towards the head of (a *river* and such), up wind, up inland, at the top of.

up against it *adj.* aground, at one's wits end, beset, in deep water, sore put.

up and coming *adj.* doing well, on the up and up, riding high, rising, stirring.

up and down[6] *adv.* backwards and forwards, here and there, in and out, to and fro.

ups and downs[6] *n.* ebb and flow, moods, rise and fall.

upbeat *adj.* 1) hopeful, looking on the bright side, 2) heartening, looking up.

upbraid *v.* to brand, chide, flay, give the rough edge of one's tongue, go for, have a go at, have one's head for, hold against, lay guilt, lay at one's door, name, pitch into, put in a bad light, rend, saddle with, show up, storm/thunder against, tear into, tell on, throw in one's teeth, throw the first stone, pick holes in, weigh into.

upbraiding *n.* chiding, hard words, talking-to, telling-off, word in one's ear.

upbringing *n.* bringing up, care, grounding, rearing, teaching.

upbuilding *adj.* broadening, growth, strengthening, unfolding.

upcoming *adj.* at hand, coming, forthcoming, in the offing, in the wind, nigh.

updraught *n.* upward draught of wind.

up-end *v.* to set up, stand something on its end.

upheave *v.* to heave up, stir, throw up.

upheaving *n.* clean sweep, overthrow, shake-up, storm, swing, unrest, uprising.

uphill *adj.* 1) climbing, rising, upward, 2) hard, steep, tiring, tough, wearing.

uphill, uphillward *adv.* upwards, up a slope.

uphold *v.* 1) to keep from falling, strengthen, underbear, 2) to back, give heart to one, help, side with, stand up for, 3) to back up, bear out, hold to.

upholder *n.* follower, backer, helper, friend, right-hand man, henchman.

upholster *v.* to fit settles and such with woven *stuff*.

upkeep *n.* 1) board and clothing, keep, 2) outlay, overheads.

upland *adj.* found or living on high ground, highland, moorland.

uplander *n.* highlander, hill-dweller.

uplands *n.* downs, heights, highlands, moorland, wolds.

uplift[2] *n.* bettering, new leaf, upswing.

up-lying *adj.* upland.

upmost *adj.* uppermost.

upon *prep.* on, on top of.

upon *adv.* thereupon, thereafter.

upper *n.* upper *part* of a shoe.

upper *adj.* 1) high, higher, top, topmost, 2) greater, outmatching.

upper hand *n.* overcoming, win, game and match.

upper house *n.* higher of the two houses of a folkmoot (*parliament*), House of Lords.

upper leather *n.* the leather of the upper of a shoe.

upper lip *n.* the upper of the lips of a man or *beast*.

upper works *n.* the upper *parts* of a laden ship.

uppermost *adj.* 1) upper, highest, upmost, 2) foremost, greatest, leading, main.

upping-stock, upping-stone *n.* stock or stone to help one climb on to a horse.

uppish *adj.* full of oneself, on one's high horse, overweening.

upright *n.* an upright shaft.

upright *adj.* clean, clean-handed, good, high-minded, holding to the truth, open, right-hearted, rightwise, straightforward, trothful, true, true-hearted, upstanding.

upright *adv.* in an upright way, uprightly.

upright *v.* to make upright, set up.

uprightly *adv.* forthrightly, openly, straightforwardly, trothfully, truly.

uprightness *n.* fairness, high-mindedness, openness, righteousness, strength of heart/mind/will, straightforwardness, true-heartedness, truthfulness.

uprise *n.* 1) rising from death, 2) sunrise, 3) a rise to high standing or wealth.

uprise *v.* 1) to rise from the dead, 2) (of the sun) to rise in the morning, 3) to rise to higher standing, 4) to rise from bed, rise to one's feet, stand up.

uprising *n.* 1) rising from death, 2) rising, outbreak, overthrow, stand, street fighting, tearing down, undoing, unmaking, uprooting.

uproar *n.* blast, bluster, outburst, storminess, wildness.

uproot[2] *v.* to pull out by the roots, pull down, tear out, sweep away, undo, unmake.

upset *n.* 1) let-down, overset, overthrow, setback, spill, upheaving, bolt from the blue, 2) much ado, to-do, shake-up, worry, 3) sickness, being unwell.

upset *adj.* churned up, harrowed, overwrought, shaken, sorrowful, unsettled.

upset *v.* 1) to knock over, overset, spill, 2) to overcome, overthrow, 3) to bewilder, sadden, shake, worry, wring, 4) to goad, madden, needle, nettle, put one's back up, put out, tread on one's toes.

upsetting *adj.* bewildering, harrowing, unsettling, worrisome, worrying, wringing.

upshot *n.* end, ending, outcome.

upside *n.* the upper side of something.

upside down[6] *adj.* 1) bottom up, 2) sloppy, untidy.

upside down[6] *adv.* bottom up, on its head.

upspring *v.* 1) to spring up, grow, 2) to come into being, 3) to leap upwards.

upspringing *adj.* beginning, growing, rising.

upstairs 1) *adv.* on a floor reached by stairs, to the upper floor, 2) *n.* the upstairs, the upper floor of a building, 3) *adj.* of that which is set upstairs.

upstanding *adj.* 1) standing upright, 2) good, true, upright.

upstart *n.* climber, go-getter, new rich, rising man, 'not one of us'.

upstream 1) *adv.* against the flow of a stream, 2) *adj.* set higher up a stream.

upstroke *n.* the upward stroke of a *pen*.

upward 1a) *adv.* to or towards that which is higher or further in, 1b) backward in time, 1c) upwards of, 2) *prep.* up, 3) *adj.* climbing, rising, uphill.

upwards 1) *adv.* upwards of, greater/more than, over, 2) *prep.* upward, up.

up-wind *adv.* against the wind.

urus *n.* *aurochs*, the great wild ox of old.

us *pron.* two or more folk, ourselves.

usward *adv.* towards us.

utmost *adj.* greatest, highest, matchless, unbounded, unbroken, whole.

utter *adj.* downright, outright, out-and-out, sheer, thorough, thorough-going.

utter gainsaying *n.* *antithesis*.

utterly *adv.* beyond, beyond telling/weighing, strongly, truly, indeed, above all.

uttermost *adj.* farthest off/out, greatest in reach, last in time.

vane *n.* 1) weather-vane, 2) an unsteady man or woman.

vat *n.* bin or tun in which drink (such as ale) is kept while it strengthens. Vats are also *used* in cheese-making, dyeing and *tanning*.

vixen *n.* 1) she-fox, 2) fishwife, quean, redhead, shrew, spitfire.

vixenish backbiting, fiery, prickly, sharp, sharp-tongued, shrewish, waspish.

vixenly bitingly, sharply, shrewishly, stingingly.

waddle *n.* waggle.

waddle *v.* to walk with short steps.

wade *v.* to ford/walk through water.

wader *n.* long-shanked bird (such as the redshank) that wades in shallow water.

wag *n.* shake, swing, wave.

wag *v.* to shake, swing, waggle, wave to and fro.

waggle *v.* to shake, wag, wave to and fro.

wain *n.* wagon, cart.

wainman *n.* driver of a wain.

wainway *n.* cart-road, high road, highway.

wainwright *n.* wain-builder.

waist *n.* 1) the narrow middle of the body, 2) that part of a *frock* which overlies the waist of the body, 3) (in seacraft) the middle stretch of the upper deck of a ship.

waist-cloth *n.* *loin*-cloth.

wake *n.* 1) time of wakefulness in the night, 2) time of watching by friends and kindred beside the body of one who has died.

wake *v.* 1) to keep watch while others sleep, 2) to wake up, bestir oneself, throw off heaviness or listlessness, 3) to awaken, to call up long buried thoughts.

wakeful *adj.* awake, watchful, watching, on the watch, all ears, all eyes.

waken *v.* 1) to awake from sleep, become lively, 2) to wake someone up, stir up,

wakening *n.* waking up, stirring.

waking *adj.* that is awake or keeps watch.

wale *n.* 1) mark, weal, wheal, 2) a 'ridge' in woven cloth, 3) (in seacraft) broader and thicker timbers of a ship's side, running from stem to stern.

walk *n.* 1) outing on foot, a wander, 2) footpath, pathway, way, path in the grounds of a great house, 3) way of walking, bearing, going, step, tread, 4) walk of life.

walk *v.* to go for a walk, go on foot, step, stride, tread, wander, go on shanks's mare.

walkabout *n.* walk taken by a 'somebody' (king, queen, or other worthy) to mingle with folk in the street.

walker *n.* one who goes on foot.

walking *n.* wayfaring on foot.

walking out *n.* (of a man and a woman) going a-wooing, going out with.

walking-stick *n.* stick or short staff wielded when out for a walk.

walk-out *n.* a downing of tools by workers, coming out on strike.

walk-over *n.* a quick, straightforward win (the losers not being up to the fight).

walkway *n.* path, pathway, footpath, footway, walk, way.

wall[4] *n.* stonewall, house wall, yard wall.

walled[4] *adj.* (of a yard, town and such) having a wall about it.

wallow *n.* wallowing in slime or filth (by swine).

wallow *v.* 1) to thresh about (in slime, water or such), 2) to give oneself up to, give way to, lose oneself in, yield to, 3) (of a ship) to heave and pitch in heavy seas.

wall-wright (*mason*) *n.* stonecutter, stone-wright.

walnut *n.* 1) the nut of the walnut tree, 2) walnut tree.

walnut-brown *n.* brown hue made from the sap of the green *husk* of the walnut, *used* as a brown 'dye' for the skin.

walnut-shell *n.* hard shell holding the seed of the walnut.

wan *adj.* grey, of a sickly/deathly hue, like death warmed up, sallow, washed out.

wander *v.* 1) to wander about, wander at will, 2) to fall away, go one's own way.

wanderer *n.* drop-out, loser, outsider, wayfarer, way-wender, 'hedge-bird'.

wandering *n.* wanderlust.

wandering *adj.* floating, homeless, on the road, rootless, kinless, wayfaring.

wandering away *n.* wandering away from the right path, falling away.

wanderlust *n.* restlessness, unsettledness, 'itchy feet'.

wane *v.* to dwindle, die down, lessen, shrink.

wan-health *n.* sickness.

wanhope *n.* hopelessness, forlorn hope, no hope, sorrow.

waning *n.* dwindling, dying down, ebb, falling off, going downhill, lessening.

waning *adj.* dwindling, dying, ebbing, shrinking.

wanly *adv.* wearily.

want[2] *n.* 1) dearth, lack, need, shortfall, 2) hand-to-mouth life, hardship, pennilessness, wretchedness, unweal, 3) craving, longing, wish, yearning.

want[2] *v.* 1) to be short of, be without, lack, miss, need, 2) to dream of, list, long for, 3) to crave, hunger/thirst for, set one's heart on, 4) to hold dear, love.

wanton *adj., n.* lewd, lustful, shameless, wild, wolfish.

wantonly *adv.* lewdly, lustfully, recklessly, shamelessly, wildly.

wantonness *n.* heedlessness, craving, running after, wildness, wolfishness.

war[3] *n.* blood-bath, bloodshed, fighting, weapon-heat.

war[3] **against** *v.* to fall upon, fight, put on a war footing.

war[3]**-craft** *n.* the business of shaping war, understanding of war.

ward *n.* 1) look-out, watch, 2) wardship of a child, 3) fatherless child in the care of a grown-up, 4) room in a sickhouse/*hospital*, 5) neighbourhood of a town under its own alderman.

ward *v.* 1) to keep an eye on, look after, look to, see to, shield, watch over, 2) to ward off, fight

off, keep off, keep at arm's length, keep in play, stave off, withstand.

wardman *n.* look-out, watch, watcher, watchman.

ward-room *n.* the meeting and eating room of the *officers* of a warship.

wardship *n.* 1) care and oversight (of a ward and his/her lands and goods), 2) the suchness of being a ward.

ware *n.* seaweed (at one time spread as *muck* on the fields).

ware/s *n.* goods, lines, stock.

ware *adj.* 1) aware, knowing well, 2) awake, careful, heedful, mindful, wary.

ware *v.* to beware, be on watch, take heed.

warehouse *n.* goods-house, stockroom.

warehouse *v.* to put/stow goods in a warehouse, stock up, build up one's stocks.

warehousing *n.* stowing goods in a warehouse, the outlay for the keeping of goods.

warehouseman *n.* worker or overseer in a warehouse, trader, wholesaler.

wareless *adj.* careless, headstrong, heedless, rash, reckless, unthinking, unwary.

warelike *adj.* awake, canny, careful, heedful, mindful, wary, watchful.

warelike-ness *n.* care, carefulness, heedfulness, watchfulness.

warely *adv.* cannily, carefully, heedfully, mindfully, warily, watchfully.

ware-ness *n.* foresight, forethought, heed, wariness.

waresmanship *n.* salesmanship, knowledge of selling.

ware-word *n.* word of warning, word in the ear, word to the wise.

warfare[3] *n.* making war, fighting.

warily *adv.* cannily, heedfully, mindfully, watchfully.

wariness *n.* forethought, foresight, forewit, heedfulness, watchfulness.

warlike[3] *adj.* bloodthirsty, fiery, ready/thirsting for a fight, war-loving.

warlock *n.* 1) the Fiend, 2) one who has handed his soul to the Fiend and been shown spell-making ways.

war[3]**-lord** *n.* 1) weapon-lord, 2) (*general*) field-leader, field-lord, 3) 'hawk'.

warm *adj.* 1) (of the weather) bright, mild, sunny, 2) (of a warm house) homely, sheltered, 3) (of winter clothing) thick, woolly, 4) friendly, great-hearted, hearty, 5) (of footmarks/a *trail*) strong, 6) (of following clues) hot, near to the truth, 7) burning, wroth, wrought up.

warm *adv.* heartily, warmly.

warm *v.* 1) to heat up, take the chill off, thaw, warm up, 2) to warm to, like.

warm-blooded *adj.* afire, aglow, burning, fiery, headstrong, quick-hearted, wild.

warm-hearted *adj.* friendly, kind, kindly, kind-hearted, loving.

warmish *adj.* fairly warm, somewhat warm.

warmly *adv.* 1) heartily, 2) heatedly, hotly.

warmth *n.* 1) homeliness, 2) friendliness, heartiness, 3) high words, wrath.

warmthless *adj.* cold, forbidding, grim, hard, unfriendly, unkind, withdrawn.

warm-up *n.* readying, work-out (before a show or a match).

warn *v.* 1) to forewarn, give fair warning, hint, 2) chide, talk to, tell off, threaten.

warner *n.* look-out, watchman.

warning *n.* 1) forboding, forewarning, gathering cloud, storm brewing, knell, writing on the wall, 2) chiding, talking-to, telling-off, upbraiding.

warning *adj.* of that which gives warning (such as 'a warning-shot'), threatening.

warp *n.* 1) (in weaving) the threads which are drawn lengthwise in the loom, most often twisted harder that the weft or woof threads, with which such are intwined to make the web, 2) rope tied at one end to a heavy stake and *used* in dragging a ship from one steading to another in a haven or a *river*.

warp *v.* 1) to throw, 2) to bend or twist something out of shape, unshape, 3) to become bent/twisted/uneven, 4) to bend or twist the right/truth.

warping *n.* 1) readying the warp for weaving, 2) dragging a ship from one steading to another in a haven or a *river*.

warship[3] *n.* fighting ship, long-ship, 'sea-mare'.

war[3]**-song** *n.* song to stir up men for the fight, or to make much of deeds wrought in the fight.

wart *n.* small outgrowth – dry and tough – on the skin.

warth *n.* 1) shore, strand, 2) meadow by a stream.

war[3]**-time** *n.* time of war.

wary *adj.* awake, canny, careful, heedful, mindful, watchful.

wash *n.* 1) bath, bathe, dip, shower, soak, 2) clean, clean-up, spring clean, 3) backwash, waves, 4) ebb and flow, rise and fall, swell, 5) film, layer, overlay.

wash *v.* 1) to bath, bathe, clean oneself up, dip, shower, soak, soap, 2) to clean, clean out, clean up, cleanse, spring-clean, wash down, 3) to break, flow, lap, 4) to sweep, take, 5) (of the onset of strong feelings) to overcome, stir, upset.

wash-bowl *n.* bowl for washing the hands.

wash-day *n.* day given over to doing the washing.

washed out *adj.* 1) of that which has lost hue in the wash, bleached, hueless, watery, 2) ashen, bloodless, drawn, wan, 3) drawn, fordone, foreworn, , weary, worn-out.

washerman *n.* man who works in a washhouse.

washerwoman *n.* woman who earns a living by washing filthy linen.

washhouse *n.* outbuilding given over to the washing of clothes.

washing *n.* wash, bath, bathing, cleansing, showering.

wash-leather *n.* soft leather made to look like *chamois* leather.

washout *n.* 1) the washing away by flood of some of a hillside, a roadway or such, 2) utter overthrow or loss.

wash-pool *n.* pool for washing sheep.

washroom (*lavatory*) *n.* bathroom.

wash-stand *n.* sideboard in a bedroom, with bowl and *pitcher* for washing oneself.

wash up *v.* to wash the bowls and other things after a meal.

washy *adj.* 1) (of food) sloppy, thin, watery, 2) (of hues) lacking body, wan.

wasp *n.* *insect* of black and yellow hue.

waspish *adj.* biting, cutting, shrewish, stinging, withering.

waspishly *adv.* bitingly, cuttingly, stingingly.

waspishness *n.* bitterness, sharpness, tartness.

wasp-waisted *adj.* having a slight waist (often through tight *lacing*).

waspy *adj.* 1) full of wasps, 2) wasp-like, biting, sharp, stinging.

watch *n.* 1) look-out, watchfulness, 2) time of keeping watch, dogwatch, morning watch, night watch, 3) watchman, night-watchman, body of watchmen, 4) sailor's turn (of four *hours*) helping with the working of the ship, 5) a wake beside the body of one who has died, 6) wristwatch, timekeeper.

watch *v.* 1) to look at, follow with the eyes, 2) to keep watch, look out for.

watch-dog *n.* 1) ward-dog, 2) a body having oversight – seeing that laws are kept.

watcher *n.* 1) one who watches by a sick bed, or by the dead, 2) look-out, wardman, watch, watchman.

watchful *adj.* awake, wakeful, on the watch, all eyes, on the look-out.

watch-glass *n.* sand-glass, *hour*-glass.

watchfulness *n.* heed, care, mindfulness, readiness, long-sightedness.

watchmaker *n.* one who earns a living by making and putting right watches.

watchman *n.* caretaker, gatekeeper, look-out, night-watchman, fire-watcher.

watchword *n.* key word/s (*password*).

water/s *n.* 1) drinking water, hard water, soft water, high/low water, rain water, running water, salt water, standing water, spring water, tap water, 2) depths, the sea.

water *v.* to drench, flood, soak, spray.

water-bearer *n.* one who bears water to the housefrom a spring or well.

water-bed *n.* 1) stone-layer (*stratum*) through which waters drips, 2) water-tight bedding (*mattress*) with water in it, making a bed for one who is sick.

water-beetle *n.* beetle that lives in the water of ponds and such.

water-boatman *n.* *bug* that walks on the 'skin' of the water of ponds and such.

water-borne *adj.* (of goods) borne by ship or barge, (of sickness) spread through the taking of foul water.

water-cress *n.* fen-cress.

water down[6] *v.* 1) to put water in, thin out, 2) to downplay, play down, soften.

water-drinker *n.* one who drinks water rather than wine or such, one who takes the healing waters at a *spa*.

water-drop *n.* drop of water, tear-drop.

water-elf (*nymph*) *n.* water maiden.

waterfall *n.* the fall of the water of a stream from a height over a stone ledge.

water-fastness *n.* water stock-hold (war-*camp*) shielded by waterways.

water-flood *n.* overflowing of water, body of water in flood.

waterfowl *n.* birds which live by the waters of meres and *rivers*.

water-furrow *n.* deep furrow dug so as to drain water from the ground and keep that ground dry.

water-gate *n.* 1) floodgate, 2) gate of a town or fastness, giving on to the waterside.

water-hole *n.* hole which holds water, pond, pool.

water-horse (*hippopotamus*) *n.* water-ox.

watering-can *n.* watering pot.

watering-house *n.* inn where a wayfarer may find water for himself and his horse.

water-leat *n.* drain, leat, overflow, runnel.

waterless *adj.* baked, dry, droughty, dusty, grassless, rainless, sere, withered.

waterlode (*aqueduct*) *n.* leat, runnel.

waterman *n.* man who works on or with boats (on *rivers* and inland waterways).

water-mark *n.* 1) mark left by water at high tide or after a flood, 2) mark set into a sheet of *paper* (so that it can be told from other *paper*).

water-meadow *n.* meadow alongside a stream and flooded from time to time.

water-mill[4] *n.* corn-mill whose works are driven by water.

water-mouse *n.* water *vole*.

water-nadder *n.* water snake.

water-pipe[4] *n.* pipe through which water is drawn.

water-quake *n.* earthquake under the sea.

watershed *n.* 1) upland ridge from one side of which water flows into one *river* network, while from the other side water flows into another network, 2) a time in the life of men and folkdoms in which minds must be made up and from which new outcomes flow.

watershoot *n.* 1) outflow of draining water from land, 2) *rapids*, white water.

waterside *n.* edge of the land by a stream or mere.

water-snake *n.* water nadder.

water-softener *n.* a set-up for softening hard water.

water-spring *n.* stead/*place* from which water rises from the ground.

waterway *n.* 1) water-runnel, 2) *canal* or stretch of *river* followed by goods-boats.

water-wheel *n.* water-driven wheel in a mill or such (which in turn drives the works).

water-witch *n.* witch said to live in water.

waterwork/s *n.* the building/s and works for bringing up water and sending it through pipes to a town.

watery *adj.* 1) drenching, marshy, wet, 2) thin, washed-out, watered-down.

wattle *n.* rods intwined with boughs of trees – to make hurdles, or walls for building.

wattle *v.* to bind rods and boughs together in wattle-work.

wave *n.* 1) ridge or swell of water running over the sea, breaker, 2) (of *invaders, immigrants*) flood, flow, stream, tide, 3) (of feeling) flood, shiver, stab, thrill, welling up, 4) wave of the hand, 5) outbreak, trend.

wave *v.* 1) (of waving in the wind) to flutter, stir, 2) (of a weapon or such) to shake, swing, wield, 3) (of the hair) to make wavy.

wavelength *n.* 1) the span from peak to peak or hollow to hollow of a wave of water, 2) *measure* of *sound*-waves *used* in *radio broadcasting*.

wave-like *adj.* like to a wave in shape and/or way of going.

wave-stream (*current*) *n.* sea-stream.

wavy *adj.* curly, woolly.

wax *n.* beeswax, earwax.

wax *v.* to grow, fill out, broaden, deepen, fatten, strengthen, thicken, widen, swell.

wax *v.* to smear on a layer of wax.

wax-cloth *n.* cloth smeared with wax to keep it from wet.

waxen *adj.* 1) made of wax, 2) ashen, bloodless, sallow, off-white, whitish, wan.

waxing *n.* growth, rise, broadening, lengthening, strengthening, widening.

wax-leather *n.* leather waxed or 'glazed' on the flesh side.

wax-light *n.* wax candle.

wax-maker *n.* worker-bee that makes wax.

waxwork *n.* likeness made in wax.

waxy *adj.* like wax in hue and/or suchness.

way *n.* 1) highway, lane, path, pathway, road, street, thoroughfare, 2) headway, 3) way of doing things, way of life, wont.

way *adv.* away, way-off.

waybread *n.* food taken with one when wayfaring.

wayfare *n.* wayfaring.

wayfare *v.* to fare on foot, make one's way, step out, wend one's way.

wayfarer *n.* one who fares (by road), forth-farer, wanderer, way-wender, wide-farer.

wayfaring *n.* wayfare, faring, going, outing, walking.

wayfaring *adj.* floating, homeless, on the road, rootless, wandering.

way-finder *n.* forerunner, pathfinder, way-leader.

wayfriend *n.* with-farer.

way in *n.* inway, way through, way to, doorway, gateway, opening, open door.

waylay *v.* to set a trap, fall upon, swoop upon, spring upon, spring from hiding.

way-leader *n.* forerunner, pathfinder, way-finder.

way-lorn *adj.* footsore, fordone, forworn, way-weary, way-worn, weary, worn out.

way-mark *n.* marker by a path or road (showing the way).

way meet *n.* cross-roads, road-meet.

way out *n.* door, doorway, gate, gateway, outgate, outway.

way-out *adj.* offbeam, outlandish, unheard of, weird.

way-reaving *n.* highway reaving, way-theft.

wayside *n. adj.* 1) side of a path or road, 2) of/by/growing by the way.

wayward *adj.* froward, headstrong, reckless, restless, self-willed, wild, wilful.

waywardly *adv.* frowardly, recklessly, wilfully.

waywardness *n.* pigheadedness, self-will, wildness, wilfulness.

way-weary *adj.* 1) foot-weary, forworn, weary, worn out, 2) life-weary, wretched.

way-wender *n.* wanderer, wide-farer.

way-worn *adj.* footsore, fordone, way-lorn, weary, worn out.

way-writing (*address*) *n.* writing on the *letter-sheath* (*envelope*) to lead the bearer.

we *pron.* speaker and one or more others.

weak[(2)] *adj.* 1) helpless, little, mightless, strengthless, unmighty, 2) feet of clay, weak-willed, giving, yielding.

weaken[(2)] *v.* 1) to lessen, shake, 2) to take the heart out of, throw a shadow over.

weak[(2)]**-headed** *adj.* 1) empty-headed, light-minded, 2) unsteady, unwitful.

weak[(2)]**-kneed** *adj.* helpless, mightless, rudderless, strengthless.

weakling[(2)] *n.* runaway, softling, softy.

weakly[(2)] *adj.* listless, sallow, seedy, sickly, unhealthy.

weakly[(2)] *adv.* lamely, limply.

weak[(2)]**-minded** *adj.* 1) addle-headed, goosish, half-witted, 2) flighty, hanging back, two-minded, unsettled.

weak[(2)]**-willed** *adj.* soft, two-minded, unsteadfast, wieldy.

weal *n.* blessedness, bliss, blitheness, frith, gladness, health and strength.

weal *n.* mark (of a *whip*), burn mark, old wound, wale, welt.

weald *n.* woods, woodland, weald-land, wild wood, wood-weald.

wealden *adj.* wild, woodland, woody.

weald-land *n.* weald, woodland, wild wood, wood-weald.

weal-less *adj.* needy, penniless, wretched.

wealsome *adj.* bringing/working weal (as of healing or winning words)

wealth *n.* 1) riches, acres, belongings, goods, heap, hoard, holdings, land, things, untold riches/wealth, weal, wealth-heap, wealth-hoard, wealthstock, well-being, welfare, wherewithal, fat of the land, more than enough, more than is needed, the needful, the ready, mathom, mathom-hoard, 2) (a lot of something other than *money*) fullness, great deal, heap, more than enough, richness.

wealthful *adj.* rich, wealthy, well-off.

wealth-heap *n.* wealth, wealth-hoard, wealthstock.

wealth-hoard *n.* holding, pool, wealth, wealthstock.

wealth-hold (*treasury*) *n.* strong room, mathom-hold.

wealth-holder, wealth-keeper (*treasurer*) *n.* bookholder, bookkeeper, steward.

wealthless *adj.* badly off, hard up, <u>needy</u>, penniless.

wealth-owning *adj.* doing well, rich, riding high, <u>wealthy</u>, well-off, well-to-do.

wealthstock *n.* wealth-hoard, holdings, the ready, <u>wealth</u>, wherewithal.

wealthy *adj.* wealthful, doing well, rich, riding high, rising, well-feathered, well-off, well-to-do, having the wherewithal, having it good, in clover, on the up and up, rich beyond one's wildest dreams.

weal-weaving *n.* 1) bringing blessing, working good, 2) folk-wealcraft/*governance*.

wean *v.* to get a young child or *beast used* to not having its mother's milk.

weanling *n.* young child or *beast* newly weaned.

weapon *n.* arrow, axe, bolt, bow, longbow, knife, shaft, spear, sword, shell, shot,

weaponed *adj.* weaponed to the hilt/teeth.

weaponed-kin *n.* menfolk of the kindred.

weapon-half, weapon-hand *n.* father's side of the kindred.

weapon-heat *n.* bloodshed, fighting, strife.

weapon-hoard, weapon-house (*arsenal, magazine*) *n.* stand of weapons.

weapon-less *adj.* unweaponed, helpless, mightless, unshielded.

weapon-lord *n.* fighter, fighting man, man of war, war-lord, weapon-wielder.

wear *n.* 1) clothes, things, 2) wear and tear.

wear *v.* 1) to be clothed in, have on, 2) to wear out, become threadbare, wear thin, 3) to wear well, bear up, hold up, last, stand up to wear, 4) (of time) to wear away.

wear down[6] *v.* 1) to outweary, 2) to weather, wither.

weariful *adj.* <u>dreary</u>, leaden, longsome, overlong, slow, tiresome, wearing.

wearily *adv.* drearily, listlessly.

weariness *n.* 1) aching all over, tiredness, overtiredness, 2) weariness of heart, down-heartedness, forlornness, heaviness, hopelessness, listlessness, wretchedness.

wearing *adj.* backbreaking, burdensome, crippling, draining, grinding, hard, hard-going, killing, tiring, tough, unrestful, uphill, wearisome, wearying.

wearisome *adj.* <u>dreary</u>, dry, endless, grey, heavy, weariful, wearing.

wearisomely *adv.* drearily, endlessly, heavily.

weary *adj.* all in, dead-beat, dead tired, dog-tired, dog-weary, done for, done in, drained, faltering, footsore, foot-weary, foot-worn, fordone,

foreworn, forworn, heavy-eyed, hollow-eyed, laid out, limb-weary, overcome, overdriven, overtired, overwearied, overwhelmed, overworked, ready for bed, ready to drop, swooning, tired out, washed out, way-lorn, way-weary, way-worn, worn out, at a low ebb, brought to one's knees, dead on one's feet, more dead than alive.

weary *v.* 1) to overwork, tire out, wear out, 2) to outweary, wear down.

wearying *adj.* draining, hard-going, killing, uphill.

weasand *n.* throat, windpipe.

weasel *n.* small meat-eating wild *beast*.

weather *n.* outlook, bad/foul/rough/settled/wet/windy weather.

weather *v.* 1) to bear up against, come through, pull through, ride out, rise above, weather the storm, <u>withstand</u>, 2) to harden, toughen.

weather-beaten *adj.* hardened, weathered, well-worn.

weather-bitten *adj.* gnawed/worn by the weather.

weatherboard *n.* 1) one of overlapping boards laid in rows (to shield a wall), 2) the windward side of a ship.

weather-bound *adj.* weather-fast, kept (by bad weather) from faring forth or sailing.

weather-driven *adj.* driven (backward/onward) by stormy weather.

weathered *adj.* hardened, weather-beaten, well-worn.

weather-eye *n.* to keep one's weather-eye open is to be on the look-out.

weather-fast *adj.* weather-bound.

weather-glass (*barometer*) *n.* weight-glass, weight-mete.

weathering *n.* the eating away by wind and rain of things that are out in all weathers.

weatherlore *n.* weather-learning, weather-foretelling.

weatherly *n.* of a ship that can sail nigh to the wind without falling away to leeward.

weatherman *n.* one who puts out (on the 'box' or wireless) the outlook for the weather over the next while.

weather-rope *n.* line, tow-line, tow-rope.

weather-ship *n.* ship that rides out at sea gathering weather-knowledge (to help with telling the likely outlook for the weather).

weather-side *n.* the side of a building, tree or such most open to the weather, the windward side of a ship.

weather-wisdom *n.* weather know-how, weatherlore, weather-wit.

weather-wise *adj.* of one who is shrewd in foretelling the outlook for the weather.

weave *n.* 1) woven cloth (such as broadcloth, homespun, worsted), 2) the warp and weft/woof of the cloth.

weave *v.* 1) to braid, twist, 2) to not give a straight answer, spin, 3) to work something in, 4) to weave one's way, wind in and out.

weaver *n.* workman or workwoman who weaves cloth.

web *n.* 1) cobweb, spider's web, gossamer, 2) (*conspiracy, plot*) frame-up, net, underhand dealing, web-weaving, wheels within wheels.

web-beam *n.* the beam/roller in a loom on which the web is wound as it is woven.

webbing *n.* wide *band* of woven *stuff* for the work of upholstering.

web-fingered *adj.* having folds of skin between the fingers.

web-foot *n.* 1) foot with webbed toes, 2) nickname for a fen-dweller.

webster *n.* woman who works as a weaver.

web-toed *adj.* web-footed.

web-weaving (*conspiracy, plot*) *n.* net, web, underhand dealing.

web-wright *n.* cloth-maker.

wed *v.* to plight one's troth as man and wife.

wedded *adj.* 1) bound in wedlock, 2) wedded to some line or way of doing things (and blind/deaf to other insights).

wedding *n.* plighting, tying the knot, church wedding, white wedding.

wedding-breakfast *n.* meal for the wedding guests.

wedding night *n.* bride-night, the first night together for the new husband and wife.

wedding song *n.* bride-song, song for the wedding at church or at the wedding meal.

wedge *n.* cleat, cut, finger, shred.

wedge *v.* to drive/hammer/knock in, fasten.

wedge-shaped *adj.* arrowhead-shaped.

wedlock *n.* wedding, living as man and wife, wifehood, wifeliness.

Wednesday (Woden's day) *n.* Midweek day, Fourth day.

weed *n.* plant seen as of little worth, yet taking up ground.

weed/s *n.* clothes, clothing, widow's weeds.

weed, weed out *v.* to root out, thin out.

weed-hook, weeding-hook *n.* hook for cutting away weeds.

weed-killer *n.* atter/*poison* put on the ground to kill weeds.

Weed-month *n.* *August.*

weedy *adj.* 1) full of weeds, overgrown with weeds, 2) fleshless, spare, spindly.

week *n.* span of seven days.

weekday *n.* a day of the week other than Sunday and Seventh Day/*Saturday.*

week-end *n.* holiday time at the end of the week's work.

week-long *adj.* going on for a week.

weekly *n.* weekly news*paper*, weekly write-up on business/gossip/other fields.

weekly *adj.* once a week.

weekly *adv.* by the week, every week, week by week, once in seven days.

week-night *n.* night in the week other than Sunday and Seventh Day/*Saturday.*

week-old *adj.* that which has lasted/lived for a week.

weel *n.* deep pool, deep stretch of a *river*-bed.

weel *n.* eel trap, willy.

ween *v.* to believe, bethink, deem, forween, reckon, think likely.

weep *n.* weeping, fit of weeping, a good weep.

weep *v.* 1) to burst into tears, shed tears, groan, moan, 2) (of a sore) to run.

weeping *n.* tears.

weeping *adj.* 1) tearful, wet-eyed, woebegone, 2) (of a sore) oozing, running.

weepingly *adv.* brokenly, sorrowfully, tearfully.

weeping-willow *n.* a kind of willow having long narrow boughs and leaves.

weepy *adj.* heart-broken, in tears, tearful, weeping, wet-eyed, woebegone.

weevil *n.* corn-worm.

weft *n.* (in weaving) the threads that go from side to side of a web at right *angles* to, and intwined with, the warp threads.

weigh *v.* 1) to heave up a ship's anchor before sailing, 2) to find the weight of something in the weigh-scales, 3) to weigh out goods for sale, 4) to think over, weigh up, 5) to have weight, outweigh, 6) to weigh one down, weigh upon one.

weigh-beam *n.* steelyard.

weigh-bridge *n.* a stand flush with the ground, on which livestock, wains and such are weighed.

weigh-scale/s[(2)] *n.* weighing bowl/s.

weight *n.* 1) burden, load, 2) goods weight, stock-weight, 3) good name, standing, worthship, 4) bear's share, bulk, main body, most.

weight *v.* 1) to hang weights on, overload, 2) to highlight unfairly, twist.

weightcraft *n.* the lore of rightly weighing and deeming.

weighted *adj.* leaning to one side, one-sided, unfair.

weight-glass (*barometer*) *n.* weather-glass, weight-mete.

weightiness *n.* heaviness, heft, mightiness, strength, thickness, weight.

weighting *n.* making good, making up for.

weightless *adj.* 1) light as a feather, 2) flimsy, lightweight, shaky.

weight-mete (*barometer*) *n.* weather-glass, weight-glass.

weighty *adj.* 1) great, heavy, hefty, unwieldy, 2) far-reaching, overriding, strong, telling, 3) foremost, leading, outstanding, 4) burdensome, worrying.

weir *n.* dam on a *river* (to hold back the water, then free it, thus steadying the flow).

weird *adj.* 1) bewildering, eerie, far-fetched, ghostly, nightmarish, uncanny, unearthly, 2) outlandish, out of the way, unwonted, unheard of, way-out, wayward, weird and wonderful.

weirdness *n.* uncanniness, unearthliness, waywardness.

weir-hatch *n.* the flood-gate of a weir.

welcome 1) *adj.* worthwhile, worth having, 2) *intj.* good to see you!

welcome *n.* 1) greeting, kind/warm welcome, open arms, 2) at home, gathering.

welcome *v.* to ask one in, be friendly, bid one come in, keep open house, throw open, warmly welcome, welcome with open arms.

welcoming *adj.* friendly, kind, open, warm.

weld *n.* binding, seam.

weld *v.* to soften by heat and then fasten together.

welding *n.* welding-work.

welfare *n.* 1) good, health, weal, wellbeing, 2) dole.

welkin *n.* 1) cloud, 2) the span of the heavens, 3) the sky above.

well *n.* 1) spring, stream, shaft, 2) springhead, wellhead, wellspring.

well *adj.* 1) hale, healthy, in good health, strong, 2) good, right.

well *adv.* 1) aright, deftly, 2) smoothly, 3) fully, thoroughly, 4) highly, markedly.

well *v.* to burst forth, flow out, stream out, well up.

welladay *intj.* lackaday! sadly! woe!

well-beam *n.* wooden beam over which the rope of the well-bucket runs.

well-behaved *adj.* good, well-bred, willing.

well-being *n.* blessedness, brightness, fullness, health and strength, weal, wholeness.

well-beloved *adj.* dearly loved, greatly loved, much loved.

well-born *adj.* great, highborn, lordly, top-drawer, worthful, worthy.

well-bred *adj.* fair spoken, knightly, ladylike, thoroughbred, well-spoken.

well-built *adj.* broad-shouldered, great-limbed, strong as an ox/horse, thickset.

well-chosen *adj.* (most often of words) carefully chosen.

wellcouth *adj.* household, oft-heard, well-known.

well-doing *n.* doing good/right.

well-done *adj.* 1) deftly or rightly done, 2) (of meat) thoroughly cooked.

well-drawn (*graphic*) *adj.* lifelike, striking, telling, true, true to life, truthful.

well-earned *adj.* fairly/rightly earned.

well-fed *adj.* 1) (of kine, sheep and such) healthy, sleek, 2) (of men) fat, fleshy.

well-fought *adj.* doughtily/gamely/fearlessly/steadily fought.

wellfully *adv.* freely, gladly, of one's own free will, readily, willingly.

well-grounded *adj.* cut and dried, dead-on, down to earth, first hand, holding water, homefast, in black and white, no other, right, rightly-grounded, settled, so, sound, straight, telling, truly-grounded, true, true to life, well-thought through, well-weighed.

well-grown *adj.* showing enough growth, nearly full-growth.

wellhead *n.* 1) the spot where a spring breaks out of the ground, head-spring of a stream, springhead, wellspring, 2) beginning/rise/start of anything.

well-heeled *adj.* rich, wealthy, well-off, well-to-do.

well-hole *n.* opening through a floor/s for a stairway.

well-house *n.* small building or room over a well.

well-kept *adj.* shipshape, straight, tidy, trim, uncluttered.

well-knit *adj.* bound together, like-minded, of one mind.

well-known *adj.* in all mouths, name-known, outstanding, talked of, widely-known.

well-lighted *adj.* bright, flooded with light, well-lit.

well-made *adj.* long-lasting, made to last, strong.

well-marked *adj.* for all to see, formarked, standing out, straightforward.

well-meaning *adj.* kind, kindly, helpful, well-wishing.

well-meant *adj.* kindly/rightly/truly meant (though perhaps not working out so).

well-near, well-nigh *adv.* all but, full-nigh, more or less, nearing, nearly, not far off.

well off *adj.* doing well, having it good, rich, riding high, wealthy, well-to-do.

well over *v.* 1) to overflow, burst with, 2) to have to overflowing.

well-pitched *adj.* (of *sound*) ringing, silver-tongued, true.

well-read *adj.* bookish, book-learned, bookwise, deep-read, thinking, widely read.

well-set *adj.* 1) rightly set, 2) (of a man) strongly built, (of a woman) well-knit.

well-shaped *adj.* becoming, goodly, lovely.

well-spoken *adj.* fair spoken, knightly, well-behaving, winning.

wellspring *n.* 1) springhead, wellhead, 2) depths one can always draw on.

well-thought-of *adj.* highly thought-of, looked up to.

well-timed *adj.* answering, right, timely.

well-to-do *adj.* doing well, having it good, rich, riding high, wealthy, well off.

well-trodden word (*truism*) *n.* open and shut truth, stock/tired/worn saying.

well-water *n.* water drawn from a well or spring.

well-willed *adj.* thinking kindly of and ready to help.

well-willing *adj.* ready to be kind or friendly.

well-wisher *n.* backer, friend.

well-witted *adj.* aware, deep, knowing. quick, sharp, shrewd, wise, witfast, witful.

well-worded *adj.* flowing, lively, meaningful, pithy, striking, telling, well-put.

well-worn *adj.* 1) shabby, threadbare, worn-out, 2) timeworn, tired.

well-worn saying (*cliché*) *n.* overworked words, worn-out saying, twice-told tale.

well-wrought *adj.* well made, well put together, well shaped.

welt *n.* mark, weal.

wen *n.* swelling, wart.

wen *n.* the stave/*letter* 'w' in the runes.

wench *n.* girl, maid, maiden, young woman.

wench *v.* to be wanton, sleep with anyone, whore, womanise.

wencher *n.* lady-killer, wolf, woman-hunter, womaniser.

wenching *n.* loosen/wild living, wantonness, whoring, womanising.

wend *v.* 1) (in seacraft) to turn a ship's bow or head to another *tack*, 2) to make one's way, step out, wander, wayfare, wend one's way.

weosand *n.* aurochs, bison.

werewolf *n.* one believed to make himself at times into a wolf.

wergild *n.* the worth set on a man (deemed by his standing in life) and given by the evil-doer and his kindred to offset his murder, wounding or other evil wrought.

west *adv.* in/towards the west, westwards.

west *n.* that length of the earth's rim which lies over against the east.

west *adj.* belonging to/lying towards/of the west, looking towards the west, blowing from the west.

west end *n.* west end of anything (such as a town).

westering *adj.* going towards the west, (of the wind) shifting to the west.

westerly *adj.* set towards the west, western, blowing from the west.

westerly *adv.* to the westward, from the west, on the west side.

westermost, westernmost *adj.* set farthest to the west.

western *adj.* coming from/living in/lying to the west, blowing from the west.

westerner *n.* dweller in the west.

westland *n.* western land or hundred.

westmost *adj.* most westerly.

west-right *adv.* dead/straight west.

west-side the side set/lying towards the west.

westward/s *adv.* to/towards the west.

westward *adj.* that which goes or looks westward.

westwardly *adv.* to/towards the west, from a western fourthing.

wet *n.* rainy/wet weather, drizzle, rain.

wet *adj.* 1) drizzly, rainy, 2) drenched, soaked, sodden, sopping wet, wringing wet.

wet *v.* to bedew, drench, rain hard, soak, steep.

wether *n.* *gelded* ram.

wetland *n.* fen, marsh, moss, slough.

wetness *n.* water, wet.

wey *n.* dry goods weight (for cheese, coal, corn, salt, wool and so on) being greater for one thing than for another.

whale *n.* great fish-like *creature* of the sea.

whalebone *n.* 1) *ivory* from the horse-whale/*walrus*, 2) horny *stuff* from the upper *jaw* of the whale.

whaler *n.* whale-hunter, ship *used* for whaling.

whaling *n* the business of hunting whales.

wharf *n.* berth, landing.

wharve *n.* the small fly-wheel of a spindle.

what 1) *pron.* of what worth? what is it? 2) *adj.* what kind of? how many/ much? 3) *adv.* for what end? in what way? how? 4) *intj.* what!

whatever 1) *interrog.* what?! 2) *pron.* anything at all which, anything that.

what-not *phr.* other things besides.

whatsoever 1) whatever, what, any, 2) whoever.

whatsomever whatever.

whaup (*curlew*) *n.* hwilpe.

wheal *n.* mark, wale, weal.

wheat *n.* the crop from which bread is made.

wheatear *n.* ear of wheat.

wheaten *adj.* of wheat meal, of the wheat crop.

wheatmeal *n.* meal of wheat.

wheel *n.* ring-shaped frame of wood, steel or such (either in one whole or with spokes), two such being fastened at either end of an ax-tree (about which these go *round*) to bear a wain along the road. Among other wheels are: driving-wheel, fly-wheel, ship's wheel, steering-wheel, water-wheel.

wheel *v.* 1) to wheel along, trundle, 2) to spin, 3) to reel, twist and turn.

wheel-back *n.* wooden seat with a back carved like to a wheel.

wheelbarrow *n.* barrow having a wheel at the fore-end and handles at the back.

wheeled *adj.* having a wheel or wheels.

wheel-house *n.* room on a ship where the ship's wheel is housed,

wheelsaddle (*bicycle*) *n.* two-wheeler, twywheel.

wheel-way *n.* road that will bear wains and such.

wheelwork (*machine*) *n.* tool.

wheelwright *n.* maker of wheels for wain-building, wain-builder.

whelk *n.* sea *creature*.

whelk *n.* pimple.

whelm *v.* 1) to turn a bowl or such upside down and set on top of something (so as to shield the latter), 2) to bury under earth or snow, to flood with water, drown.

whelp *n.* young hopeful, youngling, youngster, youth.

when 1) *adv.* at what time? 2) *conj.* at the time at which, whereupon, since.

whenas, when as *conj.* at the time at which, since, whereas.

whence 1) *adv.* from where? 2) *conj.* from or out of which, from where.

whencesoever *adv.* wherever from.

whenever *adv.* when, as often as, at any time when, at whatever time.

whensoever *adv.* whenever, at any time.

where 1) *adv.* whence? whither? in what? 2) *conj.* wherever, whereupon.

whereabout *interrog.* about where?

whereabouts 1) *adv.* about where? 2) *n.* where one is.

whereafter *adv.* after which.

whereas *conj.* inasmuch as.

whereat *adv.* at which.

whereaway *adv.* whither, in what way.

whereby *adv.* 1) beside/by/near what? 2) wherefore, upon which, whereupon.

wherefore 1) *adv.* for what? why? 2) *n.* 'the why and the wherefore'.

wherefrom *adv.* from which, whence.

wherein *adv.* 1) in what? 2) in which.

whereof *adv.* 1) of what? 2) from/out of which, whereby, wherefore, wherewith.

whereon *adv.* 1) on what? 2) on which.

wheresoever, wheresomever *adv.* wherever.

wherethrough *adv.* through which, whereby, wherewith, whence.

whereto *adv.* 1) to what? to what end? whither? 2) to which.

whereunder *adv.* under which.

whereupon *adv.* 1) upon what ground? 2) wherefore, upon which, about, as to.

wherever 1) *adv.* where? 2) *conj.* whithersoever.

wherewith *adv.* 1) with what? 2) through which, whereby, whereupon, along with.

wherewithal 1) *adv.* with what? 2) *n.* ready wealth, tools, ways and means.

wherewhither *adv.* wherever, which way.

whet *v.* 1) to hone, sharpen, put a sharp edge on, 2) to awaken, fire, quicken, stir.

whether 1) *pron. adj.* which(ever) of the two, 2) *conj.* whether or no, either, if.

whetstone *n.* shaped stone for giving an edge to cutting tools, grindstone, hone-stone, sharpener, knife-sharpener.

whey *n.* watery *part* of the milk left after the curds have been sundered and shaped into a 'clod'.

which *adj. pron.* what, that, that which, one which.

whichever *adj. pron.* any or either, that one who/which, whether one or another.

while *n.* span, spell, stint, tide, time.

while 1) *adv.* at a time/s, 2) *conj.* between whiles, for a time, whilst.

while *v.* to while away the time, mark time,

whilst *conj.* while, between whiles, for a time, for the time being.

whim *n.* sweet will, bee in one's breeches.

whimsical *adj.* fitful, flighty, giddy, light-minded, lively, merry, playful, wayward.

whimsy *n.* dreaminess, flightiness, giddiness, light-mindedness, playfulness.

whine *n.* 1) whine of an arrow in flight, 2) gripe, moan, whinge.

whine *v.* 1) (of an arrow in flight) to sing, whistle, 2) to bemoan, bleat, moan.

whinge *v.* to bemoan, bleat, moan, snivel, whine, not know when one is well off.

whisper *n.* 1) speaking under one's breath, 2) aside, gossip, hint, tale, word in the ear, 3) (of the wind) sigh, sighing, soughing, 4) breath, shadow.

whisper *v.* 1) to say/speak softly, 2) to spread tales, 3) to moan, sigh, sough.

whisperer *n.* ear-speaker, gossip, tale-teller.

whispering *n.* 1) speaking under one's breath, 2) gossiping, 3) sighing, soughing.

whistle *n.* 1) penny whistle, 2) piping, whistling.

whistle *v.* 1) to whistle (with narrowed lips) because one is in a light mood, 2) to blow, 3) (of the wind) to blast, blow hard, sigh, sing in the shrouds, sough.

whistler *n.* one who whistles or who blows a whistle.

whistling *n.* piping.

whistling *adj.* of that which whistles.

whit *n.* bit, least bit, crumb, drop, mite, shred, speck.

white *n.* white of an egg/the eye, white clothing, white man/woman, white hue.

white *adj.* 1) bright, light, silver, silvery, snowy, milk-white, snow-white, 2) ashen, bloodless, ghastly, grey, wan, waxen.

whitebeam *n.* tree.

whitebeard *n.* elder, old man, greybeard, hoary-head.

whitefish *n.* light-hued fish such as cod, *haddock*.

white-headed *adj.* 1) of birds and *beasts* having white on the head, 2) white-haired.

white heat *n.* 1) the heat at which *metals* give off white light, 2) strong feeling.

white horses *n.* breakers, foaming sea, overfall, sea-foam, spray, swell.

white-hot *adj.* heated so much as to give out white light.

white leek *n.* *onion.*

white lie *n.* lie seen as harmless (at least by the teller).

white lime *n.* lime mingled with water as a smearing for walls, whitewash.

white-livered *adj.* fearful, chicken-hearted, milk-livered, white as a sheet.

white meat *n.* light-hued flesh foods such as chicken.

whiten *v.* 1) to make white, whitewash, 2) to bleach, 3) to blench, go white, 4) to draw a rosy likeness of someone, 'whitewash'.

whitener *n.* something that whitens/bleaches.

whiteness *n.* the suchness of being white.

whitesmith *n.* worker in 'white iron', tinsmith.

whitethorn *n.* hawthorn.

white time *n.* winter, the cold time.

whitewash *n.* 1) white lime (for whitening walls), 2) let-out, outward show, shift.

whitewash *v.* 1) to smear a wall with whitewash, 2) to whitewash over misdeeds.

white water *n.* water with breakers, foaming water (as in a watershoot/*rapids*).

whither *adv.* 1) to where? 2) to/in which, whithersoever.

whithersoever *adv.* to whatever stead/*place*, whether to one stead/*place* or another.

whitherto *adv.* to what? whither?

whitherward *adv.* 1) towards what? whither? 2) towards which, whithersoever.

whitish *adj.* somewhat white, half-white.

Whitsun 1) *n.* Whitsuntide, 2) *adj.* of Whitsuntide/Whit Sunday.

Whitsunday ('white Sunday') *n.* the seventh Sunday after Easter kept by the Church as the day on which the Holy Ghost came upon the *Apostles* (see *Acts* 2). It was long marked by newly-*baptised* Christians wearing white.

Whitsuntide *n.* the time of Whit Sunday and the days following.

whittle *v.* to cut thin shavings from a stick or other bit of wood, to shape, shave.

who *pron.* who? (asking who one is, who is the doer, and such).

whoever *pron.* 1) whatever one, any who, 2) whomsoever.

whole *adj.* 1) well, hale and hearty, healthy, ruddy, strong, 2) full, uncut, onesome, 3) unscathed, unharmed.

whole *n.* 1) all, everything, 2) fullness, nothing lacking, wholeness, four fourths.

whole *adv.* fully, in one, thoroughly, truly, utterly, wholly.

whole-hearted *adj.* hearty, ready and willing, steadfast, true, true-hearted, warm.

whole-heartedness *n.* earnestness, one-mindedness, tirelessness.

whole-length *adj.* (of a *portrait*) the whole likeness of a man/woman.

whole meal *n.* meal made from the whole corn of wheat.

whole-minded *adj.* earnest, steady, thorough, unswerving.

wholeness *n.* 1) healthiness, well-being, 2) fullness, oneness, 3) becomingness.

wholesale *adv.* (of buying and selling) in bulk.

wholesale *adj.* 1) of dealing wholesale, 2) far-reaching, sweeping, thoroughgoing.

wholesaler *n.* buyer, seller, wholesale dealer.

wholesome *adj.* 1) bright, good, rightwise, 2) good for one, healthy.

wholesomeness *n.* cleanness, goodness, openness, rightwiseness.

wholly *adv.* altogether, fully, in full, from beginning to end, heart and soul, inside out, beam and bough, root and rind, indeed, strongly, thoroughly, to the hilt, truly, utterly, widely.

whom *pron.* who.

whomever *pron.* whoever.

whomsoever *pron.* whoever.

whore *n.* call girl, fallen woman, streetwalker, woman of the town.

whore *v.* to go a whoring, to play the whore, to make a whore of.

whorehouse *n.* brothel, brothel-house.

whoring *n.* going after whores, living a lustful/shameless/wanton life.

whose *pron.* who owns, of whom, of which.

whosesoever *pron.* of whomsoever.

whosoever, whosomever *pron.* whoever.

why 1) *adv.* wherefore? 2) because of which, 3) *n.* 'the why and the wherefore'.

whyever *adv.* why? (stronger than *plain* 'why?').

wick *n.* the twisted or woven *cotton* in a candle or other light, which draws up the *oil* so as to keep the *flame* burning.

wicked *adj.* black-hearted, evil, fiendish, sinful, ungodly, unrightwise, worthless.

be **wicked** *v.* to be sinful, fall into sin, sow one's wild oats.

wickedly *adv.* dreadfully, foully, shamefully, sinfully, wretchedly.

wickedness *n.* evil, foul play, sinfulness, ungodliness, unrightness.

wide *n.* (in stock-ball) ball sent down wide.

wide *adj.* 1) broad, far-reaching, outspread, sweeping, widespread, 2) full, roomy.

wide *adv.* 1) fully, right out, 2) nowhere near, off the mark.

wide-awake *adj.* bright, keen-minded, quick-thinking, sharp, witfast, witful.

wide-eyed *n.* bewildered, spellbound, speechless, struck dumb, thunderstruck.

wide-farer *n.* forth-farer, wanderer, wayfarer, way-wender.

widely *adv.* fully, greatly, markedly, thoroughly, utterly, wholly.

wide-mouthed *adj.* 1) (of man, a sea inlet) having a wide mouth, 2) loud-spoken, all-swallowing, greedy, quenchless, wolfish.

widen *v.* to broaden, greaten, open out/up, open wide.

wideness *n.* beam, breadth, broadness, span, spread, width.

widening *n.* broadening, growing, opening out, spreading, stretching.

wide-open *adj.* 1) outspread, 2) in the open, open to, unshielded, 3) not settled.

wide-sea *n.* the deep, fathomless/great deep, great sea, high sea/s, open sea.

widespread *adj.* broad, far-reaching, far-stretching, full-wide, land-wide, sweeping.

wide wielder *n.* high king, overlord.

wide-wielding *n.* far-wielding, overlordship.

widow *n.* woman whose husband has died.

widow *v.* to make a widow, to bereave (as in war).

widowed *adj.* made or become a widow, bereaved.

widower *n.* man whose wife has died.

widowhood *n.* the suchness of being a widow/widower, the time of widowhood.

width *n.* 1) beam, breadth, span, wideness, 2) reach, spread, sweep.

widthwise (*transversely*) *adv.* crosswise.

wield *v.* 1) to wield kingship/queenship, head, oversee, run, steer, 2) to have, hold, 3) to bring into play, handle, swing.

wielder *n.* holder/lord of the field, overcomer, overthrower, queller, winner.

wieldiness *n.* readiness, smoothness, straightforwardness.

wieldship *n.* kingship, lordship, overlordship, grip, hold, long arm, reach.

wieldy *adj.* 1) readily wielded or handled, 2) bidsome, willing, yielding.

wife *n.* helpmeet, better half, wedded wife, wife of one's bosom.

wife-child *n.* girl child, maid-child, maiden, wench.

wifedom *n.* wife-hood, wedded women.

wife-fast *adj.* wedded.

wife-half, wife-hand *n.* mother's side of the kindred.

wife-hood, wife-kin *n.* distaff side, womenfolk, womanhood, womankind.

wife-less *adj.* having no wife, unwed.

wife-like *adj.* having the way of a wife, womanly.

wifely *adj.* befitting a wife, womanly.

wight *n.* 1) being, elf, dark elf, light elf, 2) living being/soul, man.

wild *n.* emptiness, forsakenness, loneliness, wilderness, wildness.

wild *adj.* 1) bare, dreary, forsaken, gloomy, lonely, pathless, 2) untamed, hot-headed, 3) wanton, shameless.

wild boar *n.* wild swine.

wild deer *n.* *beast* of the wild.

wilderness *n.* wildness, dreariness, emptiness.

wild-fire *n.* a wild, blazing fire that is hard to hold back.

wild-fowl *n.* wild bird, game bird.

wild goose hunt (*chase*) *n.* a lot of work for nothing.

wild honey *n.* wood-honey.

wild horse *n.* horse not broken in by man

wilding *n.* apple-thorn (*crab* apple) tree, sour appletree, wild apple tree, wood-apple.

wildlife *n.* the *beasts* of the wild, plants and trees.

wildly *adv.* heatedly, madly, rashly, recklessly, stormily, wrathfully.

wildly out *adj.* far-fetched, offbeam, ungrounded, wide of the mark/truth.

wild man *n.* 1) a wayward, 'unhewn' man, 2) wild man of the woods, woodwose.

wildness *n.* 1) <u>heedlessness</u>, wantonness, 2) wilderness, dreariness, emptiness.

wild teasel *n.* wolf's comb.

wildwood *n.* woodland which grew up 'of itself' (that is, without man having anything to do with it) after the last Ice *Age*, and which has not known man's hand.

wilful *adj.* self-willed, headstrong, pig-headed, wayward, fickle, fretful, froward, <u>prickly</u>, restless, stiff-necked, unbending, unsteady, wanton, wayward.

wilfully *adv.* frowardly, waywardly.

wilfulness *n.* frowardness, pig-headedness, self-will, stiff neck, wildness.

will *n.* willing, free will, strength of will.

will *v.* 1) to bid, have one's way, 2) to be so minded, be willing, choose, wish, 3) to bequeath, hand on, leave, settle on.

willing *adj.* fain, forward, helpful, open, ready and willing, would-be.

be **willing** *v.* to be ready, have a great mind to, give a willing ear, lend an ear to, hearken, lean over backwards, not stand in the way, open the door to.

willingly *adv.* freely, gladly, readily, wellfully, with all one's heart.

willingness *n.* bent, good will, leaning, mind, readiness.

willow *n.* 1) windle-tree, withy, 2) willy/*basket*.

willowy *adj.* 1) shaded by willows, 2) springy, stretchy, 3) lissom, <u>lithe</u>, <u>lovely</u>.

willy *n.* windle/*basket*, fish-trap.

willy nilly *adv.* whether one likes it or not, whether or no, 'any old how'.

wilsome *adj.* bewitching, spell-binding, sweet, welcome, <u>winning</u>.

wilsomely *adv.* wellfully, willingly.

wilsomeness *n.* readiness, willingness.

wimple *n.* women's head-wear, neck-clothing.

win *n.* game and match, outright win, runaway win, overthrow, upper hand.

win *v.* 1) to come in first, come off best, win hands down, 2) to overcome, sweep the field, win the day, 3) to earn, 4) to steal one's heart, win the heart.

winch *n.* *gear* for drawing and lifting.

winch *v.* to draw/lift with a winch.

wind *n.* 1) blowiness, following wind, headwind, tailwind, 2) empty talk, idle talk.

wind *v.* 1) to bend, snake, twist and turn, 2) to reel, twine, wreathe.

wind-blown *adj.* blown about/along, blown upon by the wind

wind-bound *adj.* (of a sailing ship) kept in the haven by winds blowing against one.

wind-break *n.* shield of trees, hedge.

wind-driven *adj.* borne or driven onwards by the wind.

winded *adj.* blown, breathless, out of breath, short of breath.

winder *n.* the works for winding something up.

windfall *n.* find, godsend, unlooked for winnings.

wind-hole *n.* opening in stonework which lets the wind through.

windiness *n.* 1) blowiness, windy weather, 2) long-windedness, wordiness.

winding *n.* 1) snaking, twining, twisting, 2) going this way and that in thought or deed, 3) winding something in with a winch, winding up a clock, 4) bringing a meeting to an end, winding up a business.

winding *adj.* full of bends and twists (of a stairway, speech), twining, wandering.

winding-sheet *n.* grave-clothes, shroud.

windle *n.* 1) rush-box/*basket*, 2) corn-mete (about three half-sacks/*bushels*).

windless *adj.* mild, still, stilly.

windlestraw *n.* dry, thin and withered stalk of grass.

windmill[4] *n.* mill whose works are driven by the wind.

Wind-month (*November*) *n.* Blood-month.

window[2] *n.* eyethirl/eyethurl (eye-hole or window).

windpipe[4] *n.* weasand, throat.

wind-shaken *adj.* wind-struck.

wind-shield *n.* shield of glass before the driver of a car (to ward off the wind).

wind song *n.* the sighing/soughing/whispering of the wind.

wind-teller (*anemometer*) *n.* a *gauge* for reckoning the strength of the wind.

wind up *v.* 1) to draw up (with a winch or such), 2) to wind up a clock, 3) to bring a meeting to an end, to wind up a business.

windward (of a sailing ship) to windward, to the windward side, upwind.

wind-wheel *n.* wheel turned by the wind to drive the works of a windmill or such.

windy *adj.* 1) blowing, blowy, lively, rough, stormy, wild, 2) <u>long-winded</u>, wordy.

wine[4] *n.* *grape* drink.

winfast *adj.* blissful, sweet, wilsome.

win free *v.* to get free, find freedom, to free oneself, get away, get off, get out, to fly, flee, take to flight, to win one's freedom, to break away, break out, break through, to make off, to run, run away, run for one's life, to slip away, slip through, steal away, throw off the yoke, take to one's heels, be off, bolt.

winful *adj.* blithe, blithesome, gladsome, gleeful.

wink *n.* flicker of the eye (often as a meaningful hint), blink, flutter.

wink *v.* to blink, flutter, twinkle (of a light).

winless *adj.* forlorn, hopelorn, sorrowful, lorn, sick at heart, heart-sore, listless.

winlike *adj.* 1) blissful, sweet, welcome, wilsome, 2) lovely, winsome, winning.

winly *adj.* blissfully, blithely, blithefully, gladly, gleefully, laughingly.

winner *n.* leader of the field, match-winner, world-beater.

winning *adj.* 1) far ahead, first, leading, more than a match for, outmatching, 2) after one's heart, bewitching, comely, dear, fair, fetching, friendly, lovely, loveworthy, pretty, spell-binding, sweet, warm, wilsome, winsome.

winningly *adv.* bewitchingly, sweetly, warmly, winsomely.

winnow *v.* to throw threshed corn up into a draught so that the lighter chaff is blown away and the cornseed is left to be gathered up.

win over *v.* to bring over, smooth, soothe, speak fair, sweeten, talk into.

winpenny *n.* grasper, hoarder, holdfast.

winsome *adj.* 1) sweet, welcome, wilsome, 2) light, lissom, lithe, lovely, winning.

winsomely *adv.* bewitchingly, sweetly, warmly, winningly.

winsomeness *n.* becomingness, fair-speaking, loveliness, sweetness, winning ways.

winter *n.* the cold time, white time.

winter *v.* to overwinter, wintersleep/*hibernate*.

winter-beaten *adj.* beaten by winter storms.

winter-bitter *adj.* bitterly cold, freezing, raw, rime-cold, snow-cold, wintry.

winterbourne, winterburn *n.* stream (of chalk or limestone lands) that flows in winter but dries up in summer.

winter-cold *adj.* freezing, raw, rime-cold, wintry.

wintered *adj.* many-wintered, hoar, hoary, hoary-headed, old, old as the hills.

winter-fallow *adj.* land left fallow through the winter.

winter-feed *v.* to feed/keep livestock through the winter.

Winter-fulleth (*October*) *n.* Tenth-month.

winter-house *n.* house built to be lived in in winter.

winterling *n.* yearling.

winter-long *adj.* as long as winter, dreary, endless, longsome, wearisome.

winterly *adj.* of the winter-time, wintry.

winter-rime *n.* fullness/telling of years.

winter-tide, winter-time *n.* the time from Winter-fulleth (the month of the first full moon of winter) to the Lengthening-month (*March*).

wintry *adj.* biting, bitter, cold, freezing, frosty, icy, raw, rime-cold, snow-cold.

wipe *n.* clean, clean-up, sweep, wipe-down.

wipe *v.* to clean, clean up, dust, sweep, wipe down, wipe dry, wipe up.

wipe out *v.* to undo, unmake, bring to naught, do away with, overcome, tear up.

wiper *n.* wind-shield wiper.

wire *n.* 1) narrow thread of *metal*, 2) lead, line, 3) *telegram*, word.

wire *v.* 1) to fasten with wire, ring about with wire, 2) to send word, *telegraph*.

wired *adj.* fastened or strengthened with wire, ringed about with wire.

wireless *n. adj.* *radio*.

wirepuller *n.* string-puller, wheeler-dealer.

wirewrit *n.* *email*.

wirewrite *v.* to *email*.

wiry *adj.* lean, sinewy, spare, strong, thin, tough.

wisdom *n.* awareness, breadth/depth of mind, brightness, farsightedness, forethought, foresight, insight, know-how, long-headedness, lore, mind-strength, mother-wit, quickness, reach of mind, readiness, ready wit, ripe knowledge, ripe wisdom, sharpness, sharp wit, shrewdness, understanding, wit, worth-weighing.

wise *adj.* aware, bright, farsighted, foreknowing, foreseeing, foresighted, forethinking, high-thinking, insightful, deep, keen-minded, keen-thinking, keen-witted, long-headed, quick, ready, rede-fast, sharp, shrewd, thinking, understanding, well-witted, wide-awake, wise-fast, witfast, witful, wit-right.

to be **wise** *v.* to have one's wits about one, to show foresight, to fathom, grasp, ken, see through, to have a head on one's shoulders, to know what's what.

wise-fast *adj.* wise, wit-fast, witful, quick-witted, nimble-witted, sharp-witted.

wisehead *n.* thinker, deep-thinker, loreman.

wisely *adv.* carefully, redely, thoughtfully, forethoughtfully, witfully, with wisdom.

wise man *n.* learned man, man of learning, thinker, thinking man, wisehead.

wise woman *n.* learned woman, woman of learning, thinker, wisehead.

wish *n.* hope, longing, yearning.

wish, wish for *v.* to list, <u>long for</u>, set one's heart or mind on, yearn after/for.

wishful *adj.* dreaming, dreamy, listful, longing, wistful, yearnful.

wishy-washy *adj.* limping, milk-and-water, tame, thin, wan, watery.

wisp *n.* shred, straw, thread.

wispy *adj.* flimsy, gossamer, light, thin, wisplike.

wistful[7] *adj.* 1) careful, <u>heedful</u>, listful, mindful, 2) deep in thought, dreaming, dreamy, forlorn, longing, rueful, sad, <u>sorrowful</u>, thoughtful, wishful, yearnful.

wistfully[7] *adv.* 1) carefully, earnestly, heedfully, listfully, mindfully, 2) dreamily, forlornly, longingly, ruefully, sadly, sorrowfully.

wistfulness[7] *adj.* dreaminess, longing, thoughtfulness, yearning.

wit *n.* 1) <u>wisdom</u>, insight, shrewdness, 2) dryness, wittiness, ready wit, wry wit.

witch *n.* he- witch, seer, soothsayer, wise man.

witch *n.* hag, night-hag, wise woman.

witch, wych *n.* wych elm.

witchcraft *n.* working evil by unearthly help (namely, that of fiends out of hell), spell-making, spell-weaving, witching.

witchen *n.* 1) witchen elm, wych elm, 2) highland (*mountain*) ash.

witch hazel *n.* 1) wych elm, 2) hornbeam.

witch-hunt *n.* 1) hunting down those thought to be having dealings with the Fiend, 2) harrying/hounding/picking on the unliked.

witching *adj.* 1) spell-weaving, 2) bewitching, spellbinding.

witch knot *n.* twisted knot of hair thought to be made by witches.

wit-dom (*prophecy*) *n.* foreboding, foreknowledge, <u>foresight</u>, fore-speech, fore-wit.

wit-fast, witful *adj.* <u>wise</u>, thinking, deep, shrewd, farsighted.

with *prep.* alongside, near, towards.

withal 1) *adv.* as well, moreover, nevertheless, notwithstanding, 2) *prep.* with.

with child *adj.* great with child, heavy with child.

withdraw *v.* 1) to back out, draw back, leave, pull back, 2) to climb down, unsay, 3) to draw *money* from a *bank*, 4) to withdraw to another room or another neighbourhood, 6) to withdraw from the field of fighting, fall back, pull out.

withdrawn *adj.* inward-looking, indrawn, shrinking, standoffish, <u>unfriendly</u>.

withe *n.* tie made from something tough and bendy (such as willow rods).

wither *v.* to die away, dry up, dwindle, shrink, wilt, for-sear, for-shrink,

withered *adj.* 1) baked, dried up, waterless, 2) blighted, lither, shrunken, thin.

withering *adj.* 1) belittling, biting, blighting, cutting, harsh, shrewish, stinging, waspish, wounding, 2) (of shooting) deadly, death-dealing.

witheringly *adv.* bitingly, bitterly, cuttingly, shrewishly, waspishly.

withers *n.* (of the horse, ox) the stretch of the back between the shoulder blades.

with-farer *n.* wayfriend.

withhold *v.* 1) to hold on to, keep in one's own hands, 2) to <u>hide</u>, keep back.

within 1) *adv.* herein, indoors, inwardly, 2) *prep.* inside of, in/into the midst of.

within-doors *adv. phr.* indoors, in/into the house.

with-mete (to *compare*)*v.* to liken, draw out likenesses, match, set side by side.

with-meting (*comparison*) *n.* likening, matching, setting side by side.

without 1) *adv.* outside, 2a) *prep.* beyond, 2b) *prep.* lacking, needing, short of.

without-doors *adv. phr.* out of doors, outside the house, in the open.

with-sake *v.* to forsake, leave, throw over, withdraw.

withsay *v.* to witness for oneself, <u>gainsay</u>, stand up for oneself.

withset *v.* to set at naught, stand against, stand up to, <u>withstand</u>.

withsetting *n.* utter gainsaying/*antithesis*.

withstand *v.* to <u>abide</u>, bide, beard, dare, outdare, <u>fight</u> off, for-stand, gainstand, hold off, hold out against, hold one's own, match oneself with, not take it lying down, put up a fight, rise against, set against, set at naught, shake one's fist, show fight, stand against, stand one's ground, stand out, stand up for one's rights, stand up to, take one up on, throw away the sheath, throw in one's teeth, withset, wrestle with.

withwind *n.* bindweed.

withworker *n.* helper, henchman, right-hand man.

withy *n.* a willow tree, a bendy bough of the willow.

withy-bed *n.* clump of willows.

witless *adj.* addle-headed, bird-witted, dim-witted, dizzy, empty-headed, feather-headed, goosish, half-witted, <u>heedless</u>, idle-headed, <u>light-minded</u>, not bright, rede-less, shallow, shallow-brained, shallow-minded, short-sighted, slow, slow-witted, thick-witted, thimble-witted, unseeing, unthinking, unwise, unwitful, wooden-headed.

witling *n.* lackwit, half-wit, clod, addle-head, feather-head, idle-head, soft-head, wooden-head, know-nothing.

witness *n.* 1) saying what has happened/how it happened, 2) one who tells what he has seen and heard, ear-witness, eyewitness, onlooker.

witness *v.* 1) to behold, look on, mark, see, watch, 2) to bear witness, speak on oath, 3) to underwrite (set one's name to a law *paper*).

wit-right *adj.* <u>wise</u>, long-headed, wit-fast, witful, rede-fast, wise-fast.

wittily *adv.* cleverly, drily, merrily, wisely.

wittiness *n.* cleverness, dryness, liveliness, saltiness, wit, ready wit, wry wit.

witting *adj.* aware, done knowingly.

wittingly *adv.* knowing what one is doing, knowingly, with one's eyes open.

witty *adj.* clever, dry, lively, merry and wise, nimble-witted, quick, salty, sharp.

wive *v.* to take a wife, to wed.

wizen *v.* to dry up, wear away, wither.

wizened *adj.* dried up, grey, grey-haired/headed, hoary, shrunken, spare, spindle-shanked, stunted, thin, weazened, withered, worn, wrinkled, writhled.

woad *n.* 1) a plant, 2) the dye got from the woad.

woe *n.* grief, sorrow, sadness, sighing, tale of woe, burden, bitterness, blight, harm, heaviness, dreariness, wound, wretchedness, gloom, ordeal, evil plight, evil days, thorn in the flesh, sinking heart, weariness of heart, heart-ache, weight on one's mind.

woebegone *adj.* careworn, forlorn, <u>hopelorn</u>, heavy-hearted, wretched.

woeful *adj.* saddened, sore.

woefully *adv.* dreadfully, frightfully, unworthily.

woefulness *n.* sadness, soreness, sorrow.

wold *n.* down, hill, open upland, ridge.

wolf *n.* 1) hound-like *beast* of the northern wilds, 2) cut-throat, fiend, sharper, 3) lady-killer, woman-hunter, womaniser.

wolf *v.* to bolt, eat up, make short work of, put away, swallow up.

wolf-hearted *adj.* fiendish, grim, heartless, <u>ruthless</u>.

wolf-hound *n.* hound reared to hunt wolves.

wolfish *adj.* 1) bloodlusty, bloody, deadly, hateful, <u>ruthless</u>, wild, 2) fleshly, lewd, lustful, wanton, 3) all-swallowing, grasping, greedy, never full, quenchless.

wolfishness *n.* 1) bloodlust, bloodthirstiness, fiendishness, hatred, heartlessness, ruthlessness, 2) lewdness, lust, lustfulness, wantonness, 3) greed, greediness.

Wolf-month (*January*) *n.* After-yule.

wolf's comb *n.* wild teasel.

wolf's head *n.* 1) head of a wolf, 2) (in Old English law) a call for the hunting down of an outlaw.

woman *n.* frith-weaver, goodwife, wife, lady, maiden, wench.

woman child *n.* girl child, maid-child.

woman friend *n.* lady friend.

woman-hater *n.* misliker of women, woman-spurner.

womanhood *n.* wife-hood.

womanize *v.* to be wanton, keep a woman, lie with, sleep with, lust, whore.

womanizer *n.* lady-killer, wolf, woman-hunter.

womankind *n.* womenfolk, distaff side.

womanlike *adj.* kindly, motherly.

womanliness *n.* winsomeness, kindness, kindliness, motherliness.

womanly *adj.* 1) (of being) ladylike, maidenly, queenly, sweet, <u>winning</u>, 2) (of looks) bewitching, blooming, comely, fair, <u>lovely</u>, shapely, willowy, winsome.

womanly *adv.* wifely, in a womanly way, like a woman.

womb *n.* the 'seed-bed' or 'cradle' within a woman where the new life of a child has its beginning and early growth.

womenfolk *n.* womankind.

wonder *n.* eye-opener, nine-days' wonder.

wonder *v.* 1) to be overwhelmed, be struck, hold one's breath, not believe one's eyes, stand in amaze, stare in wonder, 2) to ask oneself, bethink, <u>think</u>.

wonder-craft *n.* wonder-work, *miracle*-working.

wonder-dealer *n.* wonder-worker.

wonder-deed *n.* wonderful deed.

wonder-filled *adj.* filled with wonder, wondering, wonder-struck, amazed.

wonderful *adj.* wonder-like, amazing, breathtaking, bright, great, good, out of this world, outstanding, overwhelming, startling, striking, too good to be true, unfathomful, unheard of, <u>weird</u>, weird and wonderful, wonder-working.

wonderfully *adv.* amazingly, bewilderingly, deeply, greatly, fearfully, highly, truly.

wondering *adj.* amazed, <u>bewildered</u>, breathless, dumb-struck, left without words, lost in wonder, open-mouthed, spell-bound, thunder-struck, wide-eyed, wordless.

wonderland *n.* a make-believe land of knights and maidens, of elves, outlandish *beasts*, of spell-binding and spell-weaving.

wonder-mathom *n.* a great and wonderful hoard (of bright gold and silver, rings, shining stones, weapons and such), wealth-heap, wealth-hoard.

wonder-smith *n.* wonder-wright, that is, a smith (in wonder tale) who makes things of great loveliness and wonder (in gold or silver, and with shining stones) and who shapes weapons that are 'alive' with dread deeds to be wrought.

wonder tale *n.* a tale of high deeds of old – of knights, maidens, elves, dread *beasts* and such – a high tale, knightly tale, tale of elder-days, tale of old.

wonder-wise *adj.* beyond fathoming, uncanny, weird, wonderful.

wonder-work (*miracle*) *n.* wonder-craft, wonder-deed.

wonder-worker *n.* worker of wonders (*miracles*).

wonder-wright *n.* wonder-smith.

wonder-wrought *adj.* wonderfully made.

woo *v.* to angle, be after, run after, fish, stalk.

wood, woods *n.* 1) brake, frith, grove, holt, holt-wood, wood-holt, hurst, shaw, thicket, thorn-wood, underwood. weald, weald-land, woodland, wood-weald, 2) bough-timber, cut/hewn wood, felled timber, 3) firewood, tinder.

wood-apple (*crab* apple) *n.* apple-thorn, sour appletree, wilding.

wood-ash *n.* ashes of burnt wood.

wood-bill *n.* axe.

woodbine, woodbind *n.* 1) honeysuckle, 2) other climbing plants, such as ivy.

wood-carving *n.* deft carving of household goods in wood.

woodcraft (*forestry*) *n.* 1) wealdcraft, woodmanship, 2) (*carpentry*) woodwork.

woodcraftsman (*carpenter, joiner*) *n.* woodwright, woodworker, tree-wright.

woodcut *n.* lay out (*design*) wrought in *relief* on a wood-*block* and stamped from thence on to *paper*.

woodcutter *n.* 1) one who fells trees, wood-hewer, 2) maker of woodcuts.

wooded *adj.* timbered, tree-clad, woody.

wood-elf (*dryad*) *n.* wood-maiden.

wooden *adj.* 1) made from wood, 2) hidebound, narrow-minded, small-minded, slow, 3) stiff, unforthcoming, unstirred, unwinking, without warmth.

wooden-head *n.* clod, half-wit, lackwit, witling, oaf.

wooden-headed *adj.* backward, clod-hopping, thick, thick-headed, unwitful, witless.

woodenly *adv.* coldly, stiffly.

woodenness *n.* narrow-mindedness, pig-headedness, small-mindedness, stiffness.

wood-fastness *n.* stock-hold (*camp*) deep in the woods.

wood-fowl *n.* woodland bird.

wood-girt *adj.* set about by woods.

wood-hewer *n.* woodcutter.

wood-holt *n.* grove, holt, holt-wood, shaw, thicket, underwood.

wood-honey *n.* wild honey.

woodiness *n.* 1) the suchness of being wooded/tree-grown, 2) wood-likeness.

woodland *n.* wooded land, woods, weald.

wood-leas *n.* opening in woodland, woodland meadow.

wood-louse *n.* *creature* found in old wood or under stones.

woodman *n.* hunter, wood-cutter.

wood-reek *n.* wood smoke.

wood-reeve *n.* woodward.

wood-rim *n.* edge/skirt of a wood.

woodside *n.* edge/side of a wood.

woodsman *n.* 1) woodward, 2) wood-hewer.

wood-smoother *n.* shaver (*plane*).

woodwall *n.* golden *oriole*.

woodward *n.* woodsman, wood-reeve.

woodwise knowledgable about woods and woodland ways

woodwork (*carpentry*) *n.* woodcraft.

woodworker *n.* woodcraftsman, woodwright, tree-wright.

woodwose, woodhouse *n.* wild man of the woods.

woodwright (*carpenter*) *n.* woodcraftsman, woodworker, tree-wright.

woody *adj.* 1) tree-grown, wooded, 2) wood-like.

wood-yard *n.* yard where felled timber is laid up and dried.

wooer *n.* lover, true love, young man.

woof *n.* the weft, thread for making the weft.

wooing *n.* love-making, love-play, love-song, tale of love.

wooing *adj.* bewitching, 'come hither', drawing, spellbinding.

wool *n.* fleece, hair, yarn.

wool-comb *n.* toothed tool for combing out and untwisting wool by hand.

wool-gathering *n.* 1) gathering bits of wool torn from sheep by thorns and such, 2) day-dreaming, lost in thought.

woollen 1) *adj.* made of wool, 2) *n.* woollen clothing, woolly.

woolliness *n.* fleeciness.

woolly *adj.* 1) fleecy, hairy, made of wool, woollen, 2) clouded, woolly-headed.

woolman *n.* dealer in wool.

wool-work *n.* working in wool, making woollen goods, needlework done with wool.

word *n.* 1) name, name-word, 2) saying, speech, wording, write-up, 3) byword, pithy saying, warning, 4) behest, bidding, 5) given/plighted word, 6) byspell, tidings, 7) Word of God (the *Bible*), Word made flesh (the man Jesus Christ).

word *v.* to find words for, highlight, make known, mean, put into words, put words together, speak, bespeak.

word-bearer *n.* errand-bearer, go-between, spokesman/spokeswoman, word-bringer.

wordbook (*dictionary, thesaurus*) *n.* wordhoard, wordstock.

word-building *n.* word-crafting/-framing/-making/-shaping, putting words, together.

word-chest[4] (*thesaurus*) *n.* wordbook, wordhoard, wordfinder/seeker, wordstock.

word-cluster *n.* 1) *clause*, 2) *phrase*, saying, wordset.

word-craft *n.* gift with words, love of words, song/tale/word-weaving.

word-craftsman *n.* songwright, wordcrafter, word-weaver, wordwright.

word-crafty *adj.* wordrich, word-wealthy, word-winsome.

word-fast *adj.* straightforward, trothworthy, true to one's word.

wordful *adj.* flowing, long-tongued, ready-worded, running on, smooth-spoken.

wordfully *adv.* readily, windily, wordily.

wordhoard (*dictionary, vocabulary*) *n.* wordriches, wordstock, word-wealth.

wordily *adv.* readily, windily, wordfully.

wordiness *n.* long-windedness, windiness.

wording (*terminology*) *n.* choosing of words, naming, word-spinning.

word-kinlore *n.* life-*story* of words, wordrootlore, word-shaping, word-tales.

wordless *adj.* 1) (*tacit*) understood, unspoken, 2) dumb, speechless, tongueless.

word-likeness *n.* drawing from life, speaking likeness, true likeness.

wordlore (*philology*) *n.* love of words, speechlore.

word-making *n.* word-building, word-crafting, word-framing, word-shaping.

word-match (*synonym*) *n.* kinword, likeword.

word-meeting (*debate*) *n.* talks, asking and answer, word-wielding.

word-play (*allusion*) *n.* aside, alighting, half-word, hint, sideways word.

wordrich[6] *adj.* word-crafty, word-wealthy, word-winsome.

wordriches[6] *n.* wordhoard, wordstock, word-wealth.

word-right *adj.* well-crafted, well-worded, word-winsome.

wordrootlore[2] *n.* life-*story* of words, word-kinlore, word-tales.

wordset (*phrase*) *n.* saying, word-cluster.

wordshaper (*poet*) *n.* songwright, wordcrafter, word-smith, wordwright.

word-shaping *n.* word-building/-crafting/-framing/-making/-weaving.

word-smith *n.* wordcraftsman, wordcrafter, wordshaper, wordwright.

word-sower *n.* one who sows thoughts, awakener, bestirrer, quickener.

word-spinner (*orator*) *n.* speaker, speech-maker, talker, word-smith, word-weaver.

word-spinning *n.* flowing tongue, speech-making, way with words.

wordstock (*vocabulary*) *n.* wordhoard, wordriches, word-wealth.

word-stretching (*hyperbole*) *n.* oversaying, overshooting, truth-stretching.

word-tale *n.* life-*story* of a word, word-kinlore, wordrootlore.

word-wealth (*vocabulary*) *n.* wordhoard, wordriches, wordstock.

word-weaver *n.* tale-weaver, writer.

word-weaving *n.* tale, telling, word-craft.

word-wielding (*debate*) *n.* talks, asking and answer, word-meeting.

word-wieldy *adj.* (of speech) 1) high-flown, long-worded, spellbinding, 2) meaningful, stirring, telling, well-put, well-worded.

word-winsome *adj.* 1) friendly, lively, 2) word-crafty, wordrich, word-wealthy.

word-wiseman (*sophist*) *n.* know-all, riddle-wright, word-weaver.

wordy *adj.* long-winded, speechful, windy, wordful.

work *n.* 1) business, calling, craft, line, livelihood, trade, 2) grind, hard work, sweat, 3) deed, doing/s, handiwork, 4) play, tale, written work, wrought-work.

work *v.* 1) to be up and doing, earn a living, 2) to sweat, work hard, 3) to go, run, 4) to come right in the end, work out, 5) to bring about, 6) to delve, till, 7) to drive, handle, 8) to knead, shape, 9) to work one's way, 10) to twitch, writhe.

workaday *adj.* day-to-day, earth-bound, everyday, homespun, rough and ready.

work at, work hard *v.* to bestir oneself, bury oneself in one's work, do one's best, do one's utmost, drudge, give oneself to, hammer away, grind away, have one's heart in one's work, have one's nose to the grindstone, keep at it, not let the grass grow under one's feet, put one's back into it, put one's heart and soul into it, put forth one's whole strength, wade through, work night and day, work one's fingers to the bone.

work-bench *n.* bench where a craftsman or wright works.

work-day *n.* working-day, week-day.

worker *n.* earner, hand, hired hand, hired man/woman, hireling, work-hand, worker, working man/woman, workman, craftsman, wright, right-hand man, breadwinner.

workfolk *n.* workers, working men/women, hands.

work-hand *n.* hand, worker, workman.

workhorse *n.* worker, hard worker, tireless worker.

workhouse *n.* house where the needy were boarded and set to work.

working *n.* work, workings, way of working, workmanship.

working *adj.* 1) in work, 2) going, running.

working-day *n.* work-day, week-day.

working-drawing *n.* drawing of a building/other work (for those who are putting it together).

working man *n.* breadwinner, hand, hired hand, worker, work-hand, workman.

working woman *n.* worker, work-hand, maid-of-all-work.

work-load *n.* burden, millstone, weight.

workman *n.* breadwinner, hand, hired hand, worker, work-hand, working man.

workmanlike *adj.* craftly, shipshape, well-done, well-made.

workmanship *n.* craftsmanship, handiwork.

work off *v.* to free oneself from, warm up (for a game), work off some weight.

work one's way into to find one's way in, win a way in.

work out *v.* to reckon up, rime, tell, take stock.

work-out *n.* warm-up.

works *n.* 1) wheelwork, 2) workshop, yard.

workshop[3] *n.* workroom, works, yard.

work-shy *adj.* idle, shiftless, slack, slothful.

work together *v.* to help each other, lay heads together, pull together, work as a team, stand shoulder to shoulder.

work up *v.* 1) to build up, 2) to climb, do well, go on well, rise in the world.

work-worth *n.* a reckoning of the money-worth of work done, a reckoning of monies coming in and going out.

world *n.* 1) earth, middle earth, 2) the world of men, mankind, everybody, everyone, all the world and his wife, 3) field, 4) good deal, great deal, wealth.

world-craft *n.* knowing/playing the world's game, shrewdness, worldly wisdom.

worldliness *n.* greed, worldly-mindedness.

worldling *n.* misbeliever, unbeliever, self-seeker, wanton.

worldly *adj.* 1) earth-bound, earthly, fleshly, in love with this world, 2) godless, grasping, high-living, self-seeking, worldly-minded, worldly-wise.

worldly *adv.* in a worldly way.

worldly-minded *adj.* earth-bound, fleshly, godless, self-seeking, worldly-wise.

worldly-speech *n.* worldly talk, light talk.

worldly wisdom *n.* knowingness, shrewdness, world-craft.

worldly-wise *adj.* canny, knowing, self-seeking, shrewd, worldly.

world-meed *n.* earthly/worldly winnings.

worldwide *adj.* far-reaching, far-stretching, widespread.

world-wise *adj.* learned, thoughtful, wise.

world-wit (*philosopher, scientist*) *n.* learner, thinker, seeker after truth.

worm *n.* earthworm.

worm *v.* 1) to hunt for worms, 2) to worm one's way in, 3) to worm out, find out.

worm-eaten *adj.* crumbling, moth-eaten, run-down, worn out, worse for wear.

wormling *n.* underhanded man or woman.

wormwood *n.* atter, bane, blight, curse, evil.

worn, worn out *adj.* 1) dog-eared, down at heel, moth-eaten, worm-eaten, rusty, seedy, shabby, threadbare, the worse for wear, 2) at a low ebb, careworn, drained, drawn, laid low, 3) dead tired, fordone, tired out, weary, way-worn.

worn-out saying (*cliché*) *n.* well-worn saying, overworked words.

worried *adj.* churned up, fearful, shaken, unsettled, upset.

worrier *n.* one who is given to worrying.

worrisome *adj.* worrying, harrowing, making one fearful of an outcome.

worry *n.* aching, gnawing ache/care, harrowing, sorrow, weight on one's mind.

worry *v.* 1) to be worried to death, be weighed down, be shaken/unsettled/upset, gnaw one's heart out, sigh, writhe, 2) to goad, harrow, harry, hound, needle, sting.

worrying *adj.* worrisome, harrowing, making one fearful of an outcome.

worse *adj.* less good, not so good, on the downward path, less well off.

worse *adv.* more badly/wickedly, more carelessly, less well.

worsen *v.* 1) to make the bad worse, make things worse, sour, 2) to go from bad to worse, go downhill, go to the bad, break down, crumble, fall away, rot, run down, rust, sicken, sink, slide, wane, wear out, wither.

worship *n.* blessing, holy fear, love, thanksgiving, worth-telling.

worship *v.* to bless/fear God, give thanks, lift up the heart, bow, kneel, wonder.

worshipper *n.* believer, church-goer, follower.

worshipful *adj.* 1) outstanding, well-thought-of, worthful, 2) high, high and mighty, lordly, kingly, queenly, 3) minded to worship.

worst *adj.* most bad/evil, hardest, least good.

worst *n.* one from among the most evil of men, behaviour that is most evil, that which is most to be dreaded, that which is of least worth, the harshest of reckonings.

worst *v.* to beat hollow, fell, outmatch, overcome, overwhelm, put to flight.

worst *adv.* in a way that is most bad/evil.

worsted *n.* woollen cloth made from well-twisted yarn spun of combed long-*staple* wool.

wort *n.* plant.

worth *n.* 1) dearness, reckoning, 2) good name, greatness, high name, standing, weight, weightiness, worthfulness, worthiness, worthship.

worth *n.* home paddock, homestead.

worth *adj.* 1) reckoned/weighed as, 2) all right, worth having, worthwhile.

worthful *adj.* 1) worth its weight in gold, dear, dearly bought, 2) best, bright, foremost, great, in all mouths, in the news, leading, matchless, on every tongue, outstanding, sung, talked of, kingly, knightly, lordly, ladylike, queenly, well-known, well spoken/ thought of, worthy.

worthily *adv* high-mindedly, trothfully, true-heartedly, uprightly, well, worthfully.

worthiness *n.* goodness, high standing, high worth, knightliness, troth, uprightness.

worthless *adj.* 1) beggarly, cheap, empty, nigh worthless, shabby, strawy, two a penny, 2) low, mean, shallow, shameful, shameless, unworthy, wretched, 3) draffish, good for nothing, hollow, meaningless, neither here nor there, no good, not worth a thought, not worth while, worn out.

worthlessness *n.* emptiness, hollowness, nothingness, shallowness, shamelessness.

worthly *adj.* worthful, worthwhile.

worth-saying *n.* wisdom in deeming worth, worth-reckoning, weighing up.

worthsome *adj.* dear, dearly bought, worthful.

worth-weighing *n.* breadth/depth of mind, mind-strength, understanding, wisdom.

worthwhile *adj.* good, outmatching, worth having, worthy.

worthy *adj.* great, high, highborn, high-souled, of high worth, high-wrought, matchless, the foremost, of mark, outstanding, true-hearted, upright, weighty, well-born, well-bred, thoroughbred, well-spoken, worshipful, worthful.

to be **worthy** *v.* to be found worthy, to befit, to have a right to.

would-be *adj.* hopeful, longing, wishful.

wound *n.* bruise, burn, cut, open wound, smart, sore, running sore, sting, swelling, weal, welt, black eye, bloody nose, broken bones/head/nose, thick ear.

wound *v.* 1) to bite, claw, cut, harm, hew, mar, rend, run through, stab, tear, 2) to cut to the heart/quick, draw tears, sting, upset.

wounded *adj.* 1) bitten, clawed, cut, marred, torn, 2) saddened, stung, upset.

woundedly *adv.* achingly, bitterly, chidingly.

wounding *adj.* biting, bitter, cutting, hard, keen, sharp, stinging, unkind, withering.

woundless *adj.* 1) unharmed, unmarred, unscathed, 2) heart-whole.

wound-up *adj.* edgy, on edge, keyed up, overwrought, restless.

woundwort *n.* a name for plants long *used* in the healing of wounds.

woven *adj.* 1) made by weaving, homespun, 2) wreathed, wrought.

wrack *n.* 1) (*vengeance*) reckoning, wrath-wreaking, 2) downfall, overthrow, undoing, 3) what is left after an overthrow, wreck.

wrath *n.* bitterness, hard feelings, high words, wrathfulness.

fill with **wrath** *v.* to madden, goad, make one's blood seethe, make one see red, put one's back up, stir the blood.

wrathful *adj.* bitter, black-browed, burning with wrath, glowering, heated, hot, hopping mad, mad/wild with wrath, nettled, seething, smarting, sore, speechless with wrath, stung, worked up, wroth, wrought up, black as thunder.

be **wrathful** *v.* to become mad/wild with wrath, bridle up, burn/quiver/seethe/shake with wrath, glower with wrath, grind one's teeth, look black, look like thunder.

wrathfully *adv.* bitterly, heatedly, in wrath.

wrathfulness *n.* wrath, bitterness, soreness, sourness.

wrath-wreaker (*avenger*) *n.* blood-reckoner.

wrath-wreaking (*vengeance*) *n.* reckoning, settling with, an eye for an eye.

wreakful (*vengeful*) *adj.* bitter, hoarding hatred, ruthless, unforgetting, wrathful.

wreak wrath *v.* to get even with, not take it lying down, settle with, strike back.

wreath *n.* ring.

wreathe *v.* to twine, weave, wind about.

wreathed *adj.* woven.

wreck[(2)] *n.* 1) broken bits, heap, shipwreck, 2) downfall, overthrow, undoing.

wreck[(2)] *v.* to overthrow, bring to naught, overcome, undo, unmake, tear to shreds.

wren *n.* small bird of woods and shaws.

wrench *n.* 1) pull, twist, 2) sundering.

wrench *v.* 1) to pull, tear, twist, wrest, 2) to draw out, pull out, 3) to grasp, grip.

wrest *v.* 1) to pull, twist, wrench, 2) to take, win.

wrestle *n.* wrestling, wrestling-match.

wrestle *v.* 1) to fight, match oneself with, 2) to strive against hardship/sorrow/woe.

wrestler *n.* strong man.

wrestling *n.* wrestling-match.

wretch, wretchman *n.* 1) outlaw, outsider, wanderer, 2) black sheep, good-for-nothing, good-for-nought, hound, idler, knave, ne'er-do-well, rough, swine.

wretched *adj.* careworn, forlorn, hopelorn, beaten, bowed, unmanned, woebegone.

wretchedly *adv.* badly, dreadfully, foully, shamefully, trothlessly, unrightfully.

wretchedness *n.* forlornness, gloom, loneliness, sadness, sorrow, woe.

wried *adj.* 1) twisted, writhed, 2) (*ironic*) wry, wrought awry.

wried-teaching (*heresy*) *n.* untrue teaching, misleading teaching, trothlessness.

wright *n.* doer, maker, worker, craftsman.

wring *n.* *flattener/press* for apple-ale/*cider* or cheese.

wring *n.* 1) the deed of twisting/wringing/writhing, 2) a clasp of the hand.

wring *v.* 1) to twist, wrench, wrest, 2) to wring out (water from washed clothes), 3) to wrest/wring goods from others (by threats of rough handling, or by twisting of the law), to bleed dry/white, fleece, milk, shear, 4) to clasp/shake the hand.

wringer *n.* 1) blood-sucker, 2) *machine* for wringing out clothes after washing.

wrinkle *n.* 1) furrow, line, 2) crinkle, crumple, fold.

wrinkle *v.* 1) to become wrinkled, 2) to make wrinkles, to crinkle, crumple, furrow.

wrinkled, wrinkly *adj.* 1) furrowed, time-worn, weather-beaten, withered, wizened, writhled, wrizzled, 2) crinkled, crinkly, crumpled.

wrist *n.* the link between hand and forearm.

wrist-bone *n.* any of the bones in the wrist.

wristwatch *n.* small watch on a thong about the wrist.

writ *n.* 1) a written work, 2) the say-so (in writing) of a law-hall/*court*.

write *v.* to write about, write fair, write up, bring to life, make one see, tell.

write down[(6)] *v.* 1) to put/set down in writing, set down in black and white, 2) (in bookkeeping) to write off yearly some of the book-worth of goods held.

write off *v.* (in bookkeeping) to take out the book-worth of any goods that have been lost or stolen, or have wholly broken down.

write-off *n.* crossing-out, tearing up, undoing, unmaking.

writer *n.* bookwright, playwright, wordsmith, word-spinner, word-weaver.

writership *n.* bookcraft, bookmanship, wordcraft.

write-up (*advertising*) *n.* getting out the word, spreading the word abroad, putting it about, putting it over, making much of.

writhe *v.* 1) to twist, thrash about, twitch, 2) to shiver with some sting or heartache.

writhen *adj.* knotted, misshapen, twined, twisted, warped.

writhled *adj.* furrowed, weather-beaten, withered, wizened, wrinkled, wrizzled.

writing/s *n.* 1) handwriting, longhand, 2) books, output, works.

writing-board *n.* writing-stand.

writing-book *n.* book of clean sheets of *paper* on which to write.

writing-feather, writing-reed (*pen*) *n.* reed-*pen*, reed-writ.

writing-stand *n.* writing-board.

writing-theft (*plagiarism*) *n.* 'borrowing', thought-theft.

wrizzled *adj.* crinkled, withered, wizened, wrinkled, writhled.

wrong[(2)] *n.* bane, evil, foul play, misdeed, misdoing, unfairness, unrightness.

wrong[(2)] *adj.* 1) evil, guilty, shady, sin-laden, unrightwise, 2) misleading, not right, off-beam, off the mark, out, wildly out, ungrounded, untrue, wide of the mark/truth.

go **wrong**[(2)] *v.* to miss the mark, misfire, mishandle, misread, misreckon, mistime, burn one's fingers, play into another's hands, put one's foot in it.

wrongdoing[(2)] *n.* <u>evil</u>, foul play, misdealing, misdoing, sin, sinning, wickedness.

wroth, wrothful *adj.* <u>wrathful</u>, hopping mad, mad/wild with wrath, wrought up.

wrought *adj.* crafted, hewn, made, shaped, woven.

wrought up *adj.* <u>wrathful</u>, burning, glowering, nettled, sore, stung.

wry *adj.* dry, sharp, twisted, wried, wrought awry.

wry *adv.* awry, sidewise.

wryly *adv.* drily, sharply.

wryness *n.* bitterness, sting.

wry speech (*irony*) *n.* riddle, truth a-wried, truth a-twisted, wry wit.

wych elm, witch elm *n.* kind of elm.

wynd *n.* narrow street, backway.

wyrd *n.* doom, end, foredoom, foredeeming, fore-shaping, fore-tokening, fore-wyrd, foreshadowing, foreweaving, foreworking, hidden hand, lot.

wyrdful *adj.* doomed, forboding, forechosen, foreshadowed, foreshapen, fore-willed, fore-woven, fore-written, fore-wrought, inwoven, inwrought, in the wind, overshadowing, willed, wyrd-written, wyrd-wrought.

wyrd-written, wyrd-wrought *adj.* doomed, fore-written, fore-wrought, wyrdful.

wyrm (worm) *n.* 1) nadder, snake, 2) (*dragon*), great fire-snake, gold-ward.

wyrm-hoard *n.* *dragon's* gold-hoard.

yammer *n.* 1) sorrowing, 2) gripe, moan, whinge.

yammer *v.* 1) to groan, sigh, <u>sorrow</u>, 2) to bemoan.

yard *n.* backyard, barnyard, haw.

yard *n.* 1) staff, stick, 2) spar hung from a mast and holding up a sail, 3) three feet, step, stride.

yard-arm *n.* either end of a ship's yard, or the yard as a whole.

yardland *n.* a fourth of a hide (and thus about 30 acres).

yardman *n.* head-worker in a yard (where goods such as timber are handled).

yardstick *n.* 1) meteyard, 2) bench-mark.

yare 1) *adj.* ready, quick, answering to the helm (of a ship), 2) *adv.* quickly.

yarely *adv.* readily, speedily.

yarn *n.* spun wool, flax, and such.

yarn-spinner *n.* fair-weather friend, shammer, snake in one's bosom.

yawn *n.* a great breath (with the mouth wide open).

yawn *v.* 1) to open the mouth wide and take in breath (through sleepiness or weariness), 2) to be/lie/stand wide open.

yawning *adj.* deep, wide, wide-open.

yea *adv.* aye, truly, yes.

yeanling *n.* young lamb or *kid*.

year *n.* twelve months

year-book *n.* year-reckoner, time-marker.

yearday (*anniversary*) *n.* great day, high day, birthday, yeartide.

yearhundred (*century*) *n.* one hundred years, hundredyear.

yearling *n.* year-old *beast*, youngling.

year-long *adj.* lasting for a year.

yearly *adj.* each year, every year, once a year.

yearly *adv.* by the year, every year, once a year.

yearn for *v.* to ache for, <u>long for</u>, list, hunger for, set one's heart on.

yearnful *adj.* burning, dying to, earnest, hungry, itching, keen, longing, thirsty.

yearnfully *adv.* earnestly, heartily, hungrily, keenly, longingly, thirstily.

yearning *n.* <u>longing</u>, aching, gnawing ache, heartache, craving, thirsting.

year-old 1) *adj.* a year old, 2) *n.* yearling, youngling.

year-reckoner (*calendar*) *n.* year-book, year-clock, time-marker, time-reckoner.

year-right *n.* right which comes up every year.

year-rime *n.* tally of years.

year's mind, year-mind *n.* thanksgiving for someone who has died (keeping the day of death year by year).

yeartide (*anniversary*) *n.* great day, high day, birthday, yearday.

year-words, year-writings (*annals*) *n.* the tale of the happenings in a folkdom, year by year.

yeast *n.* lightener, (*used* in making beer, making bread).

yeasty *adj.* full of yeast, like yeast.

yeld *adj.* 1) (of *beasts*) young-less, too young/too old to have young, 2) (of cows) not yielding milk.

yell *n.* scream, screech, shout.

yell *v.* to scream, screech, shout.

yellow *n.* the hue of gold or of leaves in the fall of the year.

yellow *adj.* 1) deep yellow, light yellow, fair-haired, fallow (reddish yellow), flaxen, gold, golden, straw-hued, 2) yellow through sickness, yellow with years.

yellow *v.* to become or make yellow.

yellowish, yellowy *adj.* somewhat yellow.

yelm *n.* bundle of straw ready for thatching.

yelp *n.* bark (of a dog).

yelp *v.* to give out a yelp, whine.

yelt *n.* young sow.

yeoman *n.* 1) household follower, 2) freeholder, householder, smallholder, stock-breeder/rearer, wool-grower.

yes *adv.* aye, truly, yea.

yes-man *n.* fairweather friend, hanger-on, toady.

yesterday 1) *adv.* on the day before today, 2) *n.* day before today.

yestereve, yester-even, yester-evening 1) *adv.* in the evening of the day before, 2) *n.* evening of the day before.

yester-morn, yester-morning 1) *adv.* in the morning of the day before, 2) *n.* morning of the day before.

yesternight 1) *adv.* last night, 2) *n.* the night but now gone.

yet *adv.* 1) even now, thus far, up to now, 2) right now, 3) besides, moreover.

yet *conj.* be that as it may, for all that, however, nevertheless, notwithstanding, still.

yew *n.* great evergreen tree.

yield *n.* output, earnings, throughput, work of one's hands, harvest, reaping.

yield *v.* 1) to back down, bend, bow before the storm, forgo, give in/into, give way, go/swim with the stream, have no fight left, have had enough, knuckle under, make way for, throw in one's hand, unsay, withdraw, 2) to hand over, make over, give over, lay down, 3) to give, bear, earn, afford, bring in, bring forth.

yielding *adj.* lither, mild, ready and willing, soft, springy, wieldy.

yieldingly *adv.* mildly, shamefastly, sheepishly, shrinkingly, shyly.

yoke *n.* 1) wooden beam set over the necks of oxen and fastened to the plough, 2) frame fitted to the neck and shoulders of someone bearing buckets (of milk, water or such) hanging from each end.

yoke *v.* to bring together, fasten, set, tie on.

yoked *adj.* fastened together, bound, tied together.

yoke team *n.* yoked oxen (and such).

yolk *n.* the yellow inside of an egg.

yon 1) *adj.* that, those (within sight, though not near), 2) *pron.* that or those (over there), 3) *adv.* 'hither and yon' (that is, 'hither and thither, this way and that').

yond 1) *adj.* the farther, the other, 2) *pron.* that one/thing, those ones/things, 3) *prep.* over, throughout, on/to the farther side of, beyond, 4) *adv.* yonder.

yonder 1) *adv.* over there (within sight, though not near), thither, 'hither and yonder' (that is, 'here and there, to and fro'), 2) *adj.* farther, 3) *pron.* yon.

yondmost *adj.* farthest, uttermost.

yonside *n. adv. prep.* the farther side, on the farther side, beyond.

yore *adv.* 1) a long time ago, of old, 2) before, formerly, 3) for a long time.

you *pron.* the one/s spoken to.

young *adj.* 1) fledgling, growing, in the springtime of life, ripening, youthful, 2) green, raw, unfledged.

young blood *n.* young folk with drive/fire/a new outlook.

young-eyed *adj.* having bright or lively eyes.

younger, youngest *adj.* of fewer winters/years.

young lady *n.* one in early womanhood, maid, maiden.

youngling *n.* 1) youth, beginner, 2) young of kine, sheep and such, yearling.

young man *n.* youth, lover.

young of the day *n.* daybreak, early morning, first light.

youngster *n.* whelp, youth.

young thing *n.* child or young woman.

young woman *n.* one in early womanhood, maiden, sweetheart, wench.

your *pron. adj.* of or belonging to you.

yours *pron.* that or those belonging to you.

yourself, yourselves *pron.* you as you are in your being.

youth *n.* 1) whelp, youngling, youngster, young man, 2) newness, youthfulness.

youthful *adj.* fledgling, growing, maidenly, ripening, young, young looking.

youthfulness *n.* newness, youngness.

Yule *n.* Christmas, *Feast* of the birth of Christ.

Yule-day *n.* Christmas Day, Christ's birthday.

Yule-even *n.* Christmas Eve, Mother-night.

Yule-month (*December*) *n.* Ere-yule, Midwintermonth.

yule-song *n.* Christmas song.

Yule-tide *n.* Christ-tide.

Anglo-Latin to English

abandon v. to drop, forsake, <u>leave</u>, ditch, throw aside/away/off/over, walk out on.

abashed adj. ashamed, shamefast.

abbreviate v. to make shorter, <u>lessen</u>, cut short, trim.

abdicate v. 1) to <u>yield</u> up, give up, hand over, or lay down, a) the wielding of leadership (such as kingship), b) one's field of work, c) one's rights, 2) to give up or shirk the tasks that one should rightly do.

abduct v. to make away with, run off with, steal away.

aberration n. 1) falling or wandering away, leaving the straight/right/narrow way, going one's own way, 2) a wandering of mind-wit.

abhor v. to hate, loathe, mislike, shrink from, not like the look of, shun, <u>spurn</u>.

abhorrent adj. <u>loathsome</u>, hateful.

ability n. breadth/depth of mind, reach of mind, cleverness, deftness, quickness, readiness, understanding, <u>wisdom</u>, know-how.

abject adj. 1) beaten, forlorn, <u>hopelorn</u>, <u>sorrowful</u>, 2) cringing, fawning, mean.

able adj. deft, good at, handy, ready.

to be *able v.* to have it in one.

ably adv. well, deftly, in a deft way.

abnormal adj. offbeam, outlandish, out of the way, unearthly, unheard of, <u>weird</u>.

abolish v. to bring to <u>naught</u>, do away with, put an end to, tear down, <u>undo</u>, <u>unmake</u>.

abolition n. making naught/nothing, making an end of, putting an end to, tearing down/up, undoing, wiping out.

abominable adj. <u>dreadful</u>, foul, <u>loathsome</u>, unwholesome.

abortion n. end, ending, undoing, unmaking.

abortive adj. bootless, brought to nought, ungrown, unwrought.

abound v. 1) to be many, bristle/burst with, <u>overflow</u>, swarm, teem, well over 2) to be rich or wealthy, to have to overflowing.

abounding adj. <u>overflowing</u>.

abrasive adj. biting, rough, shrewish, stinging, unfeeling, <u>unkind</u>, waspish, withering.

abridge v. to cut back, cut down, cut short, <u>lessen</u>, shorten.

abrogate v. to set aside, tear up, <u>undo</u>, <u>unmake</u>, withdraw.

abrupt adj. broken off, <u>sharp</u>.

abruptly adv. all at once, betimes, forthwith, quickly, sharply, <u>soon</u>, straightway.

abscond v. to be off, bolt, make off, run away, steal away, throw off the yoke.

absence n. 1) being away, being elsewhere, 2) time spent away.

absent adj. away, <u>far-away</u>, missing, not at home, nowhere to be seen, out.

absent-minded *adj.* <u>far-away</u>, forgetful, dreamy, head in the clouds, lost in thought.

absolute adj. 1) downright, outright, out-and-out, sheer, thorough, thorough-going, utter, 'dyed in the wool', 2) full, <u>greatest</u>, unbounded, unbroken, whole, 3) high-handed, overbearing, over-mighty, overweening, 4) cut and dried, black-and-white, known, settled, 5) widespread, worldwide.

absolutely adv. 1) <u>above all</u>, fully, thoroughly, to the hilt, 2) rightly, <u>truly</u>.

absorb v. 1) to soak up, swallow, 2) to fill/hold the mind, spellbind.

absorbed adj. <u>far-away</u>, gripped, spellbound.

abstain v. to <u>forbear</u>, do without, hold off, keep away, keep back.

abstract n. outline, pith, rundown, siftings, winnowings.

absurd adj. beyond belief, far-fetched, hard to swallow, hare-brained, mad, outlandish, utterly unlikely, wildly out.

abundance n. <u>wealth</u>, fullness, a great deal, a lot, more than enough, richness.

abundant adj. <u>overflowing</u>, full, coming thick and fast, swarming, teeming, <u>untold</u>.

abundantly adv. <u>freely</u>, fully, greatly, highly, markedly, richly, thoroughly, utterly.

abuse (by deeds) *n.* harm, mishandling, rough handling.

abuse (by words) *n.* <u>smearing</u>, backbiting, cursing, swearing, swear words.

abuse v. 1) to <u>smear</u>, blacken, curse, run down, speak evil of, swear at, 2) to <u>harm</u>, <u>mar</u>, rough up, twist, warp.

abusive adj. biting, cutting, shrewish, stinging, waspish.

abysmal adj. dreadful, woeful, worthless, wretched.

academic n. <u>thinker</u>, bookworm, man/woman of learning, thinking man/woman.

academic adj. 1) <u>learned</u>, highbrow, thinking, well-read, <u>wise</u>, 2) bookish, <u>far-away</u>, in cloud-land, islanded from daily life.

academy n. hall/house/seat of learning.

accelerate v. to quicken, gather speed, pick up speed, put on speed, <u>speed</u> up.

accept v. 1) to <u>acknowledge</u>, believe, do as asked, fall in with, go along with, say yes to, go/ swim with the stream/ tide, 2) to <u>abide</u>, go along with, put up with, 3) to take on, undertake, 4) to welcome.

acceptable adj. fair, <u>middling</u>, pretty good, worthy, worthwhile, worth having.

acceptance n. belief, the go-ahead, the green light, welcome.

access n. door, doorway, gate, gateway, inway, open door, opening, pathway, right of way, road, way in, way through, way to.

access v. to find one's way in, work one's way into.

accessibility n. 1) handiness, nearness, readiness, 2) friendliness.

accessible adj. 1) <u>handy</u>, 2) <u>friendly</u>, hearty, neighbourly, <u>open</u>.

accident n. befalling, misfalling.

accidental adj. not meant, <u>unforeseen</u>, unlooked for, misfallen, miswrought.

accidentally adv. unwittingly.

acclaim v. to speak highly/warmly/well of, <u>think highly of</u>.

accommodation n. 1) board, dwelling, home, housing, rooms, 2) deal, understanding.

accompany v. to go together, go with, go along with, walk with, be found with, be seen with, keep with, team up with, draw alongside, shadow, follow.

accomplish v. to <u>fulfil</u>, bring about.

accomplished adj. clever, deft, knowing, many-sided, quick, ready.

accordingly adv. hence, so, therefore, thus.

account n. 1) tale, telling, word-weaving, a witness to, answering for what one has done, 2) reckoning of the *money*-worth of work done, reckoning of *monies* in and out.

account v. to answer for, hold a thing to be such and such, reckon up.

accounts n. bookkeeping, reckoning.

accumulate v. to <u>build up</u>, <u>gather</u>, heap up, hoard, keep by one, put by.

accuracy n. <u>truth</u>, care for truth, rightness, thoroughness.

accurate adj. aright, dead-on, right, true, tuthful, straightstraight, thorough.

accurately adv. carefully, with care, heedfully, neither more nor less, on the dot, rightly, thoroughly, truly, to a hair, word for word.

accusation n. gainword, hard words, home-truth, <u>smearing</u>, <u>upbraiding</u>.

accuse v. to brand, lay at one's door, name, <u>smear</u>, <u>upbraid</u>.

accused adj. booked, branded, named.

accuser n. gainsayer, tell-tale, withstander.

accustomed adj. given to, hardened, at home in, wedded to, wont.

achieve v. to <u>fulfil</u>, come out on top, have the best of it, make one's mark, pull it off, reach one's goal, win one's spurs.

achievement n. breakthrough, good ending, good outcome, handiwork, outright win.

acid n. sourwater, burnwater, firewater.

acid adj. sour, sharp, tart, biting, bitter, burning, cutting, stinging, unsweetened.

acquaint oneself with to find out about, keep abreast of, <u>learn</u>.

acquiesce v. to bow to, fall in with, go along with, go/swim with the stream/tide, put up with, say yes to, <u>yield</u>.

acquire v. to come by, earn, fasten on, <u>gather</u>, lay hands upon, make one's own, net.

acquisition n. blessing, godsend, windfall.

acquit v. to find not guilty, say there is nothing to answer.

across 1) adv. from side to side, on the other side, 2) prep. beyond, on the other side of, over.

act n. 1) business, dealings, deed, doings, handiwork, stroke, step, work, workmanship, 2) playcraft, showmanship, 3) (of *parliament*) law.

act v. 1) to do, drive forward, handle, make, stand in for, wield, work, 2) to play a *part*, tread the boards, make a show of, put on, show off, 3) to hide the truth, keep something back, make as if, not give a straight answer, spin, weave.

action n. deed, doing, steps, work, working.

active adj. busy, hard-working, <u>lively</u>, quick, on one's toes, tireless, up-and-doing.

activity n. much ado, liveliness, quickness, readiness, sleeplessness, stir, tirelessness.

actor n. 1) player, leading man, playman, showman, star player, 2) fair-weather friend, shammer, snake in one's bosom, snake in the grass, yarn-spinner.

actress n. player, leading lady, playwoman, showwoman, star player.

actual adj. true, true to life, dead-on, down to earth, grounded, <u>well-grounded</u>, no other, of flesh and blood, right, so, straight.

actually adv. truly, in truth, indeed.

acute adj. <u>bright</u>, clever, keen-witted, nimble-witted, quick, quick-witted, ready, <u>sharp</u>, sharp-witted, shrewd.

adamant adj. flinty, gritty, hard, hard as iron/nails/steel/stone, hardened, stiff, stone-like, steely, stony, tough, unbending, <u>unyielding</u>.

adapt v. 1) to bring in step with, make right, 2) to do as others do, fall in with, go along with, go or swim with the stream.

adaptable adj. fitting in, quick to settle in, readily at home, yielding.

add v. 1) to reckon up, rime, take stock, tell, work out, 2) to fill out, heap on, lay up, put on, put together, stick on, strengthen, swell, 3) to speak or write further.

addition n. growth, rise, broadening, lengthening, strengthening, waxing, widening.

in *addition* to adv. along with, furthermore, likewise, more, moreover, too, to boot.

additional adj. further, greater, more, over and above.

addiction n. burning, craving, inward gnawing.

address n. set speech, talk.

address v. to speak, give a speech, give a talk, hold forth, talk to, take the floor.

adept adj. deft, good at, handy, ready.

adequate adj. enough, middling, meeting the need, all right, pretty good.

adjacent adj. beside, hard by, near, near at hand, nearby, neighbouring, nigh.

adjust v. to make right, put right, set right, straighten out.

adjustment n. 1) a making/putting/setting right, a shift, 2) falling in with, finding one's feet, settling in.

administer v. 1) to handle, look after, oversee, run, see to, steer, 2) to deal out, dole out, mete out, share.

administration n. 1) handling, overseeing, running, steering, 2) board, headship, leaders (of a body such as a business), leadership, steersmanship, 3) stewardship (of the wealth of one who has died), 4) dealing, handing/sorting out, sharing, bestowing.

administrative adj. overseeing, steering, stewarding.

admiration n. liking, looking up to.

admire v. to think highly of, think well of, look up to, wonder at, worship.

admirer n. follower, lover, worshipper.

admission n. 1) letting in, bringing in, indraught, inflow, 2) acknowledging, coming out with, making a clean breast of, owning, unburdening.

admit v. 1) to let in, bring in, open the door, show in, throw open, welcome, 2) to acknowledge, come out with, make a clean breast of, own, unburden.

adopt v. 1) to choose, settle on, take up, 2) to bring into one's kindred, bring up, foster, rear, take care of, take on.

adore v. to love, set one's heart on, think the world of, worship.

adroit adj. deft, good at, handy, ready.

adult n. grown-up, grown man, grown woman, grown to full years/riper years.

adultery n. guilty love.

advance n. 1) headway, ongoing, onwardness, 2) growth, rise, 3) loan.

advance v. 1) to go/step forward, make good ground, make headway, 2) to do well, go up in the world, make one's way, rise in the world, 3) to lend, loan.

advanced adj. ahead, ahead of the times, foremost, higher, leading.

advantage n. flying start, fair wind, following wind, tail wind, the edge, upper hand.

advantageous adj. better, good, greater, outmatching, worth having, worthwhile.

adventurous adj. bold, daring, fearless.

adverse adj. 1) hard, harmful, 2) bad, threatening, unhelpful, unhopeful, untimely, 3) biting, unfriendly, withering.

adversity n. hardship, hard going, bitterness, ordeal, weariness, wretchedness.

advertise v. to build up, highlight, make known, spread the word, write up.

advertising n. 1) write-up, 2) salesmanship, waresmanship, spreading the word.

advice n. input, word/s of wisdom, steer, warning, word of warning.

advise v. to forewarn, give warning, have one know, put it to one, steer.

advisory adj. warning.

aesthetic sense n. being alive to/aware of/stirred by/having a feeling for that which is lovely/becoming/goodly/well-shaped.

affair, affairs n. 1) business of life, dealings, doings, irons in the fire, undertakings, ups and downs of life, 2) love-making, love-play.

affect v. to bear upon, override, tell upon, work upon.

affected adj. overdone, put on, showing off, showy, smooth-tongued.

affection n. friendship, kindness, liking, warmth.

affectionate adj. friendly, kindly, warm, warm-hearted.

affirm v. to bear witness, highlight, mean what one says, set forth, swear on oath.

afflict v. 1) to cut, harm, prick, stab, tear, wound, 2) to harrow, sadden, sting, worry.

affluent adj. wealthy, rich, well-off, having the wherewithal, having it good.

afraid adj. 1) fearful, in a fright, 2) burdened, on edge, worried, 3) sorry, sad.

afternoon after-midday (until evening).

age n. 1) length of life or being, lifetime, oldness, 2) a <u>long time</u>, stream of time.

age v. to grow old, olden, go grey, ripen, mellow, wither, show one's years.

aged adj. old, timeworn, many-wintered.

agency n. 1) dealership, stewardship, handling business, undertaking, 2) 'bridge', hand, help, stepping-stone, way of doing.

agent n. dealer, go-between, middleman, steward.

aggravate v. 1) to <u>worsen</u>, make worse, 2) to <u>goad</u>, <u>madden</u>, nettle, upset.

aggressive adj. fiery, hot-hearted, ready for a fight, thirsting for a fight.

aggressor n. fire-eater, rough.

agile adj. <u>lithe</u>, <u>lively</u>, light-footed, light of heel, nimble, quick.

agitate v. to <u>goad</u>, harry, hound, shake, stir up, unsettle, upset, <u>worry</u>.

agony n. aching, <u>sorrow</u>, strickenness, tearing, wringing, writhing.

agree v. 1) to settle, settle with, be as one, be of one mind, fall in with, go along with, make a deal, see eye to eye, strike hands, team with, 2) to answer, belong together, match, meet, 3) to be good for, go with.

agreement n. deal, understanding, undertaking.

agriculture n. croplore, fieldlore, fieldcraft, earth-tilling.

aid n. backing, help, following wind.

aid v. to <u>help</u>, give a hand, hold out a hand to, lend a hand.

aim n. end, goal, mark.

aim v. to be minded, bid for, drive at, go after, go for, go all out for, have in mind, make for, mean to.

aimless adj. wandering, wayward, wind-driven.

air n. 1) sky, 2) breath, draught, wind, 3) bearing, look.

aircraft n. flying craft.

airport n. landing ground, runway, flight-*hub*.

alarm v. to frighten, give one a fright, fill with fear, startle, strike with fear.

alarming adj. chilling, <u>dreadful</u>, frightening, nightmarish, numbing, startling.

alert adj. <u>awake</u>, <u>heedful</u>, all ears, all eyes, on the watch, quick-witted, ready, <u>sharp</u>.

alienate v. to <u>sunder</u>, drive a wedge between, put one's back up, set against.

alienation n. bitterness, break-up, rending, setting against, sundering, unthreading.

allegation n. gainsaying, bearing witness against, <u>smearing</u>, speaking against.

allege v. to bear witness against, speak against, shame, <u>smear</u>.

all-*embracing* adj. thorough, thoroughgoing, with nothing left out/missing.

alliance n. friendship, brotherhood, coming together, understanding.

allied adj. alongside, bound together, standing shoulder to shoulder, teamed with.

allocate v. to deal out, earmark, give out, mete out, share out.

allotment n. cut, deal, lot, share, share-out.

allow v. 1) to be <u>willing</u>, give one's blessing, let, not stand in the way, say yes to, 2) to <u>acknowledge</u>, bow to, go along with, own.

allowance n. lot, meed, share, share-out, keep, upkeep.

allude v. to hint at, drop a hint, throw out a hint, breathe of, leave one to gather, let fall, mean more than one says, play with words, say by the way, speak aside.

alluring adj. bewitching, 'come hither', fetching, spell-binding, <u>winning</u>.

allusion n. aside, alighting, half-word, hint, sideways word, word-play.

ally n. <u>friend</u>, friend in need, backer, henchman, right-hand man.

ally v. to <u>team</u> up with, do a deal, stand shoulder to shoulder.

aloof adj. cold, frosty, standoffish, unforthcoming, unwelcoming, withdrawn.

alter v. to bring in new blood, shake up, shape anew, shift, tear/throw down, <u>undo</u>.

alteration n. shift, shake-up, swing, undoing, upset.

altered adj. other-shaped, shaken, shifted.

alternative n. another/other (of two), another of like worth/weight, stand-in.

alternative adj. another, other.

amalgamate v. to bind/grow/put/tie/weave together, team up with.

amateur n. 1) the lover/follower of a craft, game or work, who finds his/her meed (*reward*) in the doing thereof, and not in *payment*, 2) beginner, butter-fingers, clod-hopper, fish out of water, greenhorn, learner, self-taught man/woman, oaf.

amateur, amateurish adj. 1) *lay*, 2) badly done, half-baked, half-done.

ambassador n. spokesman/spokeswoman, word-bearer, word-bringer.

ambiguity n. deep word/saying, hard/knotted saying, riddle, two-edged saying.

ambiguous adj. backhanded, dark, deep, <u>knotted</u>, two-edged, two-sided.

ambition n. dream, goal, seeking.

ambitious adj. bent upon, go-ahead, grasping, keen, seeking, set upon, up-and-coming, would-be.

ambush v. to lie in wait, set a trap, waylay, <u>fall upon</u>, swoop upon, take unawares.

amendment n. righting, making/putting/setting right, shaping or writing anew, straightening, undoing and doing again, word-crafting.

amount n. batch, great deal, heap, lot, spoonful, thimbleful, weight.

ample adj. <u>overflowing</u>, ever so many, ever so much, full, rich, teeming, untold.

amusement n. 1) gladdening, laughter, mirth, 2) game, play.

amusing adj. laughter-making, lively, merry, playful, rich, witty.

analyse v. to <u>delve</u> into, seek out, sift through, rake through, root through.

analysis n. breakdown, delving, going-over, going through, <u>sifting</u>, winnowing.

ancestor n. forebear, forefather, forerunner.

ancient adj. <u>old</u>, old as time, olden, <u>timeworn</u>.

anger n. bitterness, hard feelings, high words, soreness, wrath, wrathfulness.

anger v. to quicken/stir one's wrath, <u>madden</u>, make one's blood seethe, sting, upset.

angle n. 1) bend, elbow, hook, horn, 2) mind, outlook, stand, way of looking at things, way of thinking.

angry adj. <u>wrathful</u>, wroth, burning, heated, hopping mad, seething.

anguish n. bitterness, broken-heartedness, heartache, <u>sorrow</u>, wretchedness.

animal n. deer, wild deer, living being, living thing.

animated adj. aglow, glowing, afire, alive, <u>lively</u>, on fire, quickened, sparkling.

animosity n. <u>hatred</u>, loathing, misliking, spurning.

annihilate v. to bring to <u>naught</u>, do away with, lay in the dust, <u>overcome</u>, quench, root up, stamp out, tear down, <u>undo</u>, <u>unmake</u>, wipe out.

anniversary n. great day, high day, yearday, yeartide.

announce v. to give out, <u>make known</u>, make news of, <u>speak</u> out, spread abroad, tell the world.

announcement n. making known, spreading abroad, telling forth, word, write-up.

annoy v. to <u>goad</u>, harry, hound, <u>madden</u>, needle, put out, tease, unsettle, upset.

annoying adj. maddening, teasing, tiresome, wearisome.

annual adj. yearly.

antagonise v. to drive a wedge between, make foes, stir hatred or loathing, sunder.

antagonism n. bitterness, <u>hatred</u>, loathing, misliking, shunning, spurning.

anticipate v. 1) to <u>foresee</u>, 2) to be beforehand, be ready for, forestall.

anticipation n. <u>foresight</u>, forethought, looking forward, readiness for.

antipathy n. coldness, <u>hatred</u>, loathing.

anxiety n. burden, care, gnawing care, weight on one's mind, worry.

anxious adj. 1) dreading, in dread, <u>fearful</u>, harrowed, over-heedful, over-wrought, worried, 2) harrowing, worrisome, worrying, 3) earnestly or strongly wishing, longing/yearning to see something done.

apart adv. aside, to one side, asunder, sundered, a little way off, alone.

apologize v. to say sorry, ask for forgiveness.

appalled adj. aghast, <u>shaken</u>, struck dumb, thunderstruck.

appalling adj. <u>dreadful</u>, frightening, frightful, ghastly, grim, harrowing, nightmarish.

apparatus n. tools, set up, works.

apparent adj. outward, on the outside.

apparently adv. as far as one can tell, at first sight, belike, outwardly, to the eye.

appeal n. 1) asking, beseeching, bidding, 2) draw, pull.

appeal v. to ask earnestly, beseech, beset, crave, make bold to ask, seek, sigh for.

appear v. 1) to look as if, look like, look so, look to be, have/wear the look of, 2) to come to light, arise, become known, be seen, come forth/forward, come into sight, come out, stand out/forth.

appearance n. 1) bearing, cut, look/s, look of things, shape, 2) arising, becoming, shadowing forth, showing, sight, unfolding.

application n. 1) bid, asking, seeking, 2) bearing, insight, meaning, reading (as in taking what is written in a book and showing its bearing on life), 3) doggedness, hard work, <u>steadfastness</u>, tirelessness, whole-heartedness.

apply v. 1) to ask, beseech, bid for, put in for, seek, 2) to bring into play, bring to bear, 3) to lay on, put on, smear on, spread on, work in.

appoint v. to choose, hire, mark out, name, pick, pick out, put forward, put in one's hands, set, settle, swear one in.

appointment n. 1) choosing, naming, 2) livelihood, walk of life, work, 3) meeting, undertaking.

appreciate v. 1) to <u>think highly of</u>, think much of, think well of, know the worth of, 2) to be aware of, be alive to, grasp, <u>know</u>, know well, <u>understand</u>,   3) to be thankful, give thanks ,<u>acknowledge</u>,   4) to go up, grow (in dearness), climb, swell, wax.

appreciation n.   1) liking,   2) awareness, insight, knowledge, mindfulness, understanding,   3) thanks, hearty thanks, thankfulness,   4) growth, rise,   5) weighing the worth of a written work.

apprehension n.   cold feet, dread, fear, misgiving, <u>worry</u>.

approach n.   1) coming, coming towards, drawing near, nearing, onset,   2) way of doing things, way through, way to, path, pathway,   3) bid, feeler, offer.

approach v.   1) to bear down on, come on, creep up on, make towards, near, draw near,   2) to make an offer, speak to, talk to.

approaching adj.   full-nigh, more or less, nearly, not far off, roughly, well-nigh.

appropriate adj.   answering to, aright, bearing upon, becoming, belonging, cut out for, in keeping, right, straight.

approval n.   backing, blessing, the go-ahead, the green light, liking, welcome.

approve v.   to <u>acknowledge</u>, be <u>willing</u>, bless, give leave, give one's blessing, give the go-ahead/green light, go along with, <u>settle</u> on.

approved adj.   acknowledged, <u>settled</u>.

approximate adj.   near, near enough, rough.

April n.   Easter-month.

aptitude n.   bent, deftness, leaning, quickness, readiness.

arbitrary adj.   1) <u>wilful</u>, a law to oneself,   2) <u>overbearing</u>, high-handed.

arc n.   bend, bow.

archery n.   bowmanship.

architect n.   1) house-builder, house-crafter, house-wright, over-builder, over-draftsman,   2) driver, leader, maker, shaper.

ardent adj.   afire, burning, hot-blooded, red-hot, strong, warm.

ardour n.   <u>longing</u>, fire, hunger, thirst, warmth, yearning.

arduous adj.   back-breaking, hard, tiring, tough, wearing, wearying.

area n.   ground-breadth, ground-width, land-breadth, land-width, length and breadth.

argue v.   1) to <u>gainsay</u>, speak against, speak out, speak up, to fall out, fight,   2) to hold, put forth/forward, talk through, thrash out.

argument n.   1) words, high words, stormy words, fight, bone to pick,   2) talking over, talking through, thrashing out, weighing the fors and againsts.

arid adj.   1) dry, droughty, dusty, grassless, rainless, sere, waterless, withered,   2) (of some learning) drearisome, dreary, heavy, overlong, wearisome, dry as dust.

arm v.   to give out weapons to.

arms n.   weapons.

army n.   1) fighting body,   2) drove, sea of, swarm, throng, wealth of, world of.

around prep.   1) about, on all sides, on every side of,   2) about, in the neighbourhood of, nearby, not far off.

around adv.   everywhere, here and there, to and fro.

arouse v.   to awaken, <u>hearten</u>, spark, stir up, breathe new life into, quicken, spur.

arrange v.   to <u>ready</u>, make ready, <u>settle</u>, lay out, put into shape, set out, straighten out.

arrangement n.   1) draft, framework, lay-out,   2) deal, understanding, undertaking,   3) (of *music*) song-crafting.

array v.   to lay out, set out.

arrest n.   binding, holding, keeping, taking, taking hold, warding.

arrest v.   1) to hold, lay by the heels, lay hands on, pick up,   2) to <u>stop</u>, end, hinder,   3) to grip or hold the mind, spellbind.

arresting adj.   amazing, eye-opening, gripping, striking, telling.

arrival n.   coming, reaching.

arrive v.   to be on the doorstep, come to, draw near, reach, fetch up at.

arrogant adj.   headstrong, high-handed, high and mighty, overweening, pig-headed.

arsenal n.   weaponhoard.

art n.   1) craftwork, weave-work,   2) craft, craftsmanship, deftness.

artery n.   1) life-blood leat,   2) highway, key road, through road, through way.

artful adj.   <u>crafty</u>.

article n.   1) thing, tool, ware,   2) leader, write-up,   3) (in *treaty* or *charter*) heading, rider.

artist n.   craftsman, craftswoman, dreamer.

artistic adj.   craftly, clever-handed, <u>deft</u>, rich in thought/deed, insightful.

artistry n.   craft, craftsmanship, deftness, mindsight.

ascend v.   to climb, go up.

ascertain v.   to find out, <u>learn</u>.

aspect n.   bearing, look, outlook.

aspire v.   to <u>long for</u>, list, set one's heart/mind on, wish for, yearn for.

assault v.   to <u>fall upon</u>, lay into, set upon, storm, strike at.

assemble v.   1) to gather, foregather, bring together, come together, draw together, gather together, meet, hold a meeting, 2) to build up, put together, set together.

assembly n. 1) body, cluster, gathering, house, meeting, throng, 2) building up, putting together, setting up, 3) law-body, house of law-making, steering body.

assent v. to acknowledge, fall in with, go along with, say yes to, settle on, yield.

assertive adj. bold, dreadless, fearless, forthright, forward, strong-minded.

assess v. to eye up, reckon up, weigh, weigh up, work out.

assessment n. reckoning, reading, weighing up.

asset n. something in hand, wealth.

assign v. to deal out, earmark, make over, put in one's hands, settle on, share out.

assist v. to help, help out, lend a hand.

assistant n. backer, friend, helper.

associate v. 1) to belong, go hand in hand, to go/pull/put/work together, put one's name down, team up with, 2) to be friends, befriend, be seen with, hold together, mingle, stick together, 3) to bind, think of together, tie, yoke.

association n. 1) body, cluster, forgathering, gathering, set, 2) brotherhood, coming together, friendship, sharing, togetherness.

assuage v. to allay, deaden, lessen, lighten, quench, slake, smooth over, soften, soothe, still, take the sting out of, unburden.

assume v. 1) to believe, dare say, take as read, take something as so, think likely, 2) to put one's hand to, to take on, take up, take upon oneself, undertake, 3) to put on, wear, make a show of, show off, 4) to take, take for oneself, take over, wrest.

assumption n. 1) belief, 2) taking on, taking up, 3) taking, takeover, wresting.

assurance n. 1) plight, plighted word, undertaking, 2) brazenness, overstepping, 3) (in *insurance*) underwriting.

assure v. 1) to bring over, hearten, soothe, win over, 2) to clinch, settle, 3) to plight one's word, swear to, take oath, underwrite.

astonish v. to amaze, bewilder, make speechless, smite dumb, startle.

astonishing adj. bewildering, breathtaking, startling, striking.

astounding adj. amazing, bewildering, beyond belief, overwhelming.

astronomy n. starcraft, starlore, star-watching.

astute adj. bright, clever, insightful, keen-witted, quick, sharp, shrewd.

atmosphere n. 1) the draughts and wind-streams infolding and shielding a heavenly body, hence 'draught-shield', 2) background, feel, feeling, infolding, mood, setting.

atom n. 1) that which may not be put in sunder/put in two, 2) bit, crumb, dot, drop, mite, mote, seed, shred, speck, whit.

atomic adj. not to be sundered/put in two.

attach v. 1) to fasten, stick/tie on, 2) to lay at the door of, put down to, set down to.

attached adj. 1) doting, liking, loving, smitten, sweet on, 2) betrothed, chosen, spoken for.

attack n. 1) onset, 2) smearing, backbiting, blackening, 3) sickness, sick-bed, outbreak, stroke.

attack v. 1) to fall upon, bear down on, beset, set upon, storm, strike at, 2) to smear, blacken, run down, 3) to lay on a bed of sickness, strike down with sickness.

attain v. 1) to gather, get hold of, get in one's hand, come by, earn, fulfil, grasp, land, make one's own, net, reap, win, 2) to fetch up at, get there, reach one's goal.

attempt n. bid, deed, having a go, step, undertaking.

attempt v. to bid, do something about, go for, seek, undertake.

attend v. 1) to be at, be here, be there, come to, go to, look in on, 2) to heed, 3) to be found with, follow after, follow in the wake of, flutter about one, go with, keep with, shadow, walk with.

attention n. 1) heed, heedfulness, thought, 2) care, looking after, thoughtfulness, 3) awareness, knowledge of, mindfulness of, understanding of.

attentive adj. 1) all ears, all eyes, awake, careful, heedful, 2) listful, mindful.

attic n. roof-room.

attitude n. 1) belief, feeling, mind, mood, outlook, stand, thinking, thought, way of thinking, way of thought, what one thinks, 2) bearing, look, look in one's eyes, way.

attract v. 1) to draw, pull, 2) to bewitch, take someone's eye, win over.

attractive adj. bewitching, comely, fetching, lovely, winning, winsome.

audacious adj. bold, daring, daring-hearted, dreadless, fearless, hot-blooded.

audible adj. loud enough, within earshot.

audience n. 1) onlookers, playgoers, following, gathering, house, throng, 2) hearing, meeting, talk.

augment v. to build up, heap on, lay on, strengthen, forstrengthen, swell.

august adj. foremost, great, kingly, queenly, lordly, high and mighty, highborn, well-born, matchless, weighty, worthful.

August n. Weed-month.

aunt n. father's sister, mother's sister, near kinswoman, wife to one's father's brother, wife to one's mother's brother.

austerity n. carefulness, forholding, giving up, hardness, holding back, withholding, spareness, starkness.

authentic adj. true, true as steel, true-bred, true to life, first hand, well-grounded.

author n. 1) bookwright, playwright, wordsmith, writer, 2) doer, framer, maker.

author v. 1) to write, write about, write fair, bring to life, set down, tell, 2) to bring about, be/ lie at the bottom of, draw out, make, set afoot, shape, sow, spark off.

authorise v. to let, give the green light for, give one's blessing, open the door/way.

authoritarian adj. overbearing, above oneself, high-handed, hard on, self-willed.

authoritative adj. 1) more than a match for, overbearing, overweening, strong-willed, 2) first-hand, key, learned, weighty, well-grounded.

authority n. 1) headship, leadership, lordship, arm of the law, 2) eye witness, one in the know, wise man, 3) blessing, freedom, free hand, go-ahead, green light, leave, right, say-so, writ.

automatic adj. 1) blind, unthinking, unwilled, 2) self-starting, self-doing.

automatically 1) blindly, unthinkingly, without thinking, willy-nilly, 2) of itself.

autumn n. leaf-fall, harvest, harvest-tide, harvest time, fall, fall of the leaf/year.

availability n. 1) handiness, nearness, readiness, 2) friendliness.

available adj. 1) at hand, handy, on hand, ready to hand, before one's eyes, within reach, 2) up for sale, under the hammer.

avaricious adj. grasping, greedy, griping, mean, mean-minded, selfish.

avenge v. to settle the reckoning, wreak wrath.

avenue n. 1) drive, path, pathway, road, walk, way, 2) a way forward, opening, path ahead.

average adj. 1) fair, middling, middle-of-the-road, not bad, 2) mid, middle, middlemost, midmost, mid-way, half way.

averse adj. loath, dragging heels, half-hearted, shrinking back, unminded, unwilling.

avoid v. to shun, shrink from, sidestep, spurn.

avoirdupois n. stock-weight, goods weight.

await v. to abide, bide.

award n. 1) meed, 2) (in law) deeming, finding.

award v. 1) to acknowledge, bestow, give, hand out, thank, 2) (in law) to deem, find for, settle.

awe n. dread, fear, wonder.

awesome adj. amazing, dreadful, fearful, fearsome, frightening, overwhelming, striking, wonderful.

awe-struck adj. amazed, fearful, frightened, wonder-struck.

awful adj. 1) bad, dreadful, foul, frightful, ghastly, harrowing, loathsome, sickening, stinking, 2) sick, unhealthy, unsightly, unwell, under the weather.

awkward adj. clod-hopping, heavy-footed, slow, stiff, uncouth, unhandy, unwieldy.

axiomatic adj. of that which goes without saying.

axis n. ax-tree, pintle, shaft, spindle, swivel.

baby n. bairn, little child, little one, newborn child, suckling.

backtrack v. to draw back, go back, back out, withdraw.

badger v. to goad, harry, harrow, hound, worry.

bad-*tempered adj.* bearish, churlish, fiery, prickly, unfriendly, vixenish, like a bear with a sore head.

baffle v. 1) to bewilder, throw one out, 2) to hinder, bring to a stand, overcome.

bag n. holdall, overnighter, wallet.

balance n. 1) coolness, steadiness, wholeness, 2) fairness, rightness, 3) (in book-keeping) reckoning, left-over.

balance v. 1) to steady, hold steady, keep steady, 2) to even up, match, make up for, offset, set off, set against, 3) to weigh, set side by side, 4) (in book-keeping) to reckon, reckon up, get the books right/straight, settle, write up the books, work out.

balanced adj. 1) fair, fair-minded, even-handed, even-minded, open-minded, right-minded, unswerving, unwarped, upright, 2) (of food eaten) healthy, 3) cool, steady.

band n. body, knot, drove, gathering, herd, set, team, throng.

band n. binding.

band n. length (of cloth or such), tie.

bankrupt adj. beggared, brought to nothing, beyond meeting one's owings, overwhelmed with owings, 'broke', 'in the red'.

baptism n. 1) cleansing (that is, a going down into water, or sprinkling of water, likened to: a) cleansing from sin, b) the death of the old life of sin), 2) given meanings: beginning, opening, start.

barbaric *adj.* bloodlusty, bloody, hellish, loutish, <u>ruthless</u>, wild, wolfish.

bargain *n.* 1) giveaway, good buy, good deal, 2) deal, understanding, undertaking.

bargain *v.* to <u>deal</u>, undertake, beat down, sell.

barometer *n.* weather-glass.

barrel *n.* tun, fourthing (*firkin*).

barren *adj.* 1) cold, <u>dreary</u>, empty, forsaken, hard, lonely, pathless, stony, wild, 2) childless.

base *n.* 1) bed, bottom, floor, foot, groundwork, rest, stand, 2) underneath, underside, 3) abode, home, home ground, stamping ground.

base *v.* to build, ground, rest, root, set.

baseless *adj.* groundless, mistaken, untrue.

basement *n.* lower ground floor, under-floor, underground room.

bashful *adj.* blushful, mild, mousy, shamefast, sheepish, shy.

basic *adj.* deep-rooted, going to the root, inwrought, key, main, underlying.

basically *adv.* at bottom, at heart, firstly, mainly, mostly, only.

basis *n.* bed, flooring, footing, ground, groundwork, root, way.

basket *n.* rush-box, windle.

bat *n.* rearmouse/reremouse.

battle *n.* blood-bath, <u>bloodshed</u>, fighting, head-to-head, set-to, stand.

battle *v.* 1) to <u>fight</u>, , fight it out, make a stand, give hard knocks, lock horns, pitch into, 2) to do one's utmost, give it one's all, go to all lengths, hammer at, put forth one's whole strength, put one's back/heart and soul into it, work, wrestle.

bay *n.* bight, cove, inlet, roadstead, arm of the sea.

beautiful *adj.* <u>lovely</u>, comely, fair, pretty, shapely, winsome.

beauty *n.* comeliness, loveliness, winsomeness.

because *adv.* on the grounds of, for, for that.

beef *n.* meat, red meat, cowflesh, cow, cowmeat, kinemeat.

beguile *v.* 1) to <u>bewitch</u>, bind, spellbind, lay under a spell, weave a spell about, weave a web, bewilder, play upon, 2) to hoodwink, <u>mislead</u>, take in.

behaviour *n.* bearing, doings, walk, way of doing things, ways, way of life.

bellicose, belligerent *adj.* <u>bold</u>, fiery, hot-hearted, ready/thirsting for a fight.

belt *n.* girdle.

beneficial *adj.* good for, healthy, heaven-sent, helpful, wholesome, worth-while.

benefit *n.* blessing, godsend, good, help, great help, windfall, worth.

benefit *v.* 1) to be good for, bless, come in handy, do good to, forward, help, stand one in good stead, work, 2) to do well out of, make hay with, make the most of.

berserk *adj.* mad (with wrath), hot-blooded, hot-hearted, afire, wild.

besiege *v.* to begird, beset, cut off, ring about, hedge in, shut in.

bet *v.* to gamble, make a book, have a flutter.

betray *v.* 1) to break one's word, forswear, let down, stab in the back, work against, 2) to give away, let drop, tell on.

bias *n.* blindness, blind side, mind made up, set mind, narrow mindedness, one-sidedness, pig-headedness, unfairness, warped mind.

bibliography *n.* book-list, reading list.

bicycle *n.* two-wheeler, wheelsaddle.

big *adj.* <u>great</u>, broad, broad-shouldered, heavy, <u>strong</u>, thick, weighty.

bigger *adj.* <u>greater</u>, more, further, higher, over and above.

biggest *adj.* <u>greatest</u>, most, highest, matchless, unbounded, unbroken, utmost, whole.

bigoted *adj.* narrow-minded, small-minded, twisted, unfair, warped.

bill *n.* 1) draft law, 2) reckoning.

binoculars *n.* field-glasses.

biodegradeable *adj.* made to rot down.

biography *n.* life, lifetale, life-writing.

biology *n.* lifelore.

bizarre *adj.* <u>weird</u> and wonderful, outlandish, uncanny.

blame *n.* chiding, hard words, home-truth, upbraiding.

blame *v.* to bring home to, <u>chide</u>, lay at the door of, put down to, set down to, think the worst of, <u>upbraid</u>, throw the first stone.

blameless *adj.* clean-handed, guiltless, free from guilt, not guilty, unguilty, <u>upright</u>.

blameworthy *adj.* guilty, shabby, shameful, too bad, unbecoming, unworthy.

blank *adj.* 1) clean, empty, not filled in, not written on, unmarked, white, 2) lifeless, slow, unsmitten, unforthcoming, wooden, 3) at sea, <u>bewildered</u>, clueless, floored, lost, stuck, 4) downright, outright, out and out, thorough, utter.

blanket *n.* bedspread.

blanket *v.* to cloud, hide, mask, overlay, spread over, swathe.

blanket *adj.* broad, full, sweeping, thorough, wholesale, wide.

bleak *adj.* bare, cold, dreadful, dreary, forlorn, forsaken, godforsaken, gloomy, lonely, pathless, stark, wild, 'bereft'.

blend *n.* brew, mingling.

blend *v.* 1) to brew, make up, mingle, pound together, put together, shake/stir together, 2) to go well together, go with, match.

block *n.* 1) building, flats, 2) wooden-*block*, 3) batch, lot, 4) hindering, hurdle.

block *v.* to hinder, stop.

blonde *adj.* fair, fair-haired, flaxen, flaxen-haired, golden-haired.

bloom *v.* to grow, do well, fare well, ripen, rise, sprout, strengthen, swell, wax.

blooming *adj.* blossoming, bursting with health, glowing, hale, healthful, healthy.

blow *n.* 1) dint, knock, stroke, 2) misfalling, bolt from the blue, death-knell, hammering, overthrow, setback, thunderbolt, thunderclap, undoing, upset, shipwreck.

blunder *v.* to make a mistake, misread, play into another's hands, put one's foot in it.

blunt *adj.* 1) edgeless, unsharpened, unwhetted, 2) bald, bare, downright, forthright, making no bones, outspoken, rough-tongued, short, uncouth, unfeeling, withering.

boast *v.* to crow, put oneself forward, show off.

boastful *adj.* crowing, full of oneself, showing off, swollen-headed, uppish, windy, wise in one's own eyes.

boil *v.* 1) to be hot, seethe, spit, steam, 2) to be wrathful, become heated, fly off the handle, go off the deep end, storm.

bombshell *n.* bolt from the blue, thunderclap.

bond *n.* link, foreward, matching, of one mind, setting at one, understanding.

bond *v.* 1) to bind, hold together, put together, stick, weld, 2) to draw together in friendship, get to know one another, get on well together.

bondholder *n.* backer, lender (on the strength of a *bond*).

boom *n.* (of business) growth, upswing.

boom *v.* to do well, grow, rise, strengthen, swell.

boring *adj.* drearisome, dreary, heavy, overlong, tiresome, wearing, wearisome.

boss *n.* foreman, hard driver, head, headman, high-up, leader, overseer, owner.

bother *n.* ado, much ado, to-do, stir, unrest, upset, worry.

bother *v.* to gnaw at, harrow, harry, hound, needle, sting, unsettle, upset, worry.

bound *v.* to fly, hurdle, leap, leap-frog, spring forward.

boy *n.* whelp, young hopeful, youngling, youngster, youth.

boycott *v.* to cold-shoulder, cut, black, shut out, spurn.

branch *n.* 1) bough, limb, shoot, offshoot, spur, 2) arm.

brave *adj.* bold, daring, daring-hearted, doughty, fearless, stern, steadfast, steely.

brawny *adj.* broad-shouldered, great-limbed, heavy, mighty, strong, thickset.

breach *n.* break, cleft, crack, hole, opening.

breach *v.* 1) to break, go against, rend, 2) to break through, burst through, sunder.

breeze *n.* wind, light wind, breath of wind.

breezy *adj.* 1) blowing, blowy, windy, 2) blithe, carefree, giddy, light-hearted, light-minded, lively, playful, sparkling, sunny.

bribe *n.* 'backhander', 'sweetener'.

brief *adj.* 1) fleeting, quick, short, short-lived, 2) not long in the telling, pithy, short and sweet, sparing of words.

briefly *adv.* 1) fleetingly, for a time, for the time being, quickly, sparely, here today and gone tomorrow, 2) in a few words, in a nutshell, in outline.

brilliant *adj.* 1) ablaze, bright, gleaming, sparkling, 2) bright, keen-minded, quick-witted, sharp-witted, 3) great, good, outstanding, wonderful.

brisk *adj.* 1) astir, lively, nimble, quick, speedy, up-and-doing, 2) biting, fresh, keen, sharp, 3) busy, going hammer and tongs.

browse *v.* 1) to chew, crop, eat, feed, graze, 2) to dip into, leaf/look/thumb through.

brush *n.* 1) besom, broom, sweeper, 2) clean, dust, sweep, 3) meeting, fight, set-to.

brush *v.* 1) to clean, sweep, wash, 2) to play with, stroke.

brusque *adj.* bearish, offhand, rough, sharp-edged, short, sparing of words, uncouth.

brutal *adj.* cold-blooded, heartless, ruthless, stony-hearted.

brutality *n.* bloodlust, bloodthirstiness, fiendishness, heartlessness, ruthlessness.

budget *n.* spending frame/draft.

bunch *n.* 1) batch, cluster, handful, heap, sheaf, 2) crowd, gathering, knot, swarm.

bureaucracy *n.* 'reevedom', that is, the unbending ways of 'reeve-lings' (bound as they are to little laws and *paperwork*).

bureaucratic *adj.* high-handed, hindering, overbearing, unbending.

burglary *n.* break-in, housebreaking, theft, thieving.

burgle v. to housebreak, make off with, steal from, thieve.

bursar n. book-keeper, steward.

bus n. many-seater, for-all.

butcher n. 1) meat seller, meat trader, 2) cut-throat, killer, man of blood, slayer, wholesale murderer.

bypass n. ringroad, throughway.

bypass v. to cold-shoulder, have nothing to do with, hold off, keep away, let alone, not go near, take the other way, give one the go-by.

cabin n. 1) cot, cote, shed, 2) berth, room (on shipboard).

cabinet n. 1) cupboard, 2) board, inner team.

café n. eating-house.

calculate v. 1) to reckon up, take stock, work out, 2) to bethink, think likely, deem, reckon on, think through, weigh.

calculated adj. framed, in a fair way to, leading to, put-up, ready-made, weighed, willed, working towards.

calculating adj. canny, crafty, hard-headed, knowing, not straightforward, shady, sharp, shrewd, too clever by half, watchful.

calendar n. year-book, year-clock, year-reckoner, time-marker, time-reckoner.

callous adj. hard as nails/steel/stone, stiff, stony-hearted, unbending, unyielding.

calm adj. 1) cool, cool-headed, steady, unshaken, unworrying, 2) mild, smooth, at a stand/standstill, still, stilly, unstirring, windless.

calm v. to allay (fears), set one's mind at rest, soothe, smooth, steady, still.

campaign n. drive, fighting, onset.

campaign v. 1) to take the field, 2) to bestir oneself, do one's utmost, drive through, hammer at, put out one's whole strength.

campus n. seat of learning.

canal n. 2) waterway.

cancel v. 1) to axe, ditch, drop, end, have done with, put an end to, undo, unmake, 2) to cross out, strike out, tear up.

cancer n. 1) growth, 2) blight, evil, sickness.

candidate n. hopeful, runner, seeker, sitter (in an *examination*).

candour n. boldness, forthrightness, openness, outspokenness, straightforwardness.

cap v. 1) to hedge in, hold down, keep a tight hold on, put a drag on, stop, 2) to clinch, fulfil, reach a new high, rise to a new peak, 3) to beat, better, outdo, outmatch, outshine, top, overtop, put in the shade.

capability n. deftness, handcleverness, long-headedness, quickness, readiness, sharpness, wisdom.

capable adj. bright, clever, deft, insightful, knowing, ready, sharp, wise, witful.

capacity n. 1) deftness, readiness, strength, wisdom, 2) breadth, depth, length, width, greatness, fullness, room, headroom, 3) field, line.

cape n. overhood, riding hood.

cape n. foreland, headland, sea-ness.

capital n. hoard, holdings, the ready, wealth, wealth-stock, wherewithal.

capitalism n. buying and selling, free ownership.

capricious adj. bewildering, fickle, flighty, froward, giddy, light-minded, restless, shiftful, self-willed, unsettled, unstead, wayward, wilful.

captivating adj. bewitching, fetching, holding, spellbinding, winning.

capture v. 1) to bind, fasten on, grasp, grip, hold fast, lay hands on, lay hold of, 2) to reach to the heart of a thing, narrow down, put in a nutshell, 3) to bewitch, spellbind, fill/hold the mind.

car n. four wheels, wain.

card n. stiff reed-sheet/drawing-sheet/writing-sheet.

career n. life's work, livelihood, path, walk of life.

carnage n. blood-bath, bloodshed, slaying, wholesale killing/murder.

carriageway n. high-road, highway, main road, road, roadway.

carry v. to bear, bring, fetch, hold, pick up, shoulder, take, uphold.

case n. 1) befalling, happening, 2) business on hand, plight, setting, suchness, 3) (in law) gainsayong to answer, talking through, thrashing out, weighing the fors and againsts, 4) plight of a sick man/woman.

case n. box, chest, holdall, holder, sheath.

cash n. ready wealth, wealth in the hand, the needful, silver, wherewithal.

cash v. to draw ready *money* (from a *bank*).

cast n. 1) throw, 2) reckoning, 3) players, showfolk, stars, 4) likeness, set, shape, 5) bearing, bent, kind, look, stamp.

cast v. 1) to heave, pitch, throw, 2) to reckon, tell, 3) to choose, name, pick, 4) to make, set, shape, work up, 5) to bestow, give out, shed, spread.

castigate v. to blast, chide, go for, lay into, tear into, upbraid, weigh into.

casual adj. careless, cool, heedless, laid-back, offhand, unthinking.

catastrophe n. doom, downfall, end, fall, meltdown, overthrow, stroke, undoing, unmaking, wreck.

catch n. 1) clasp, clip, fastener, grip, hasp, hook, hook and eye, 2) down side, drawback, hurdle, 3) pickings, takings, winnings.

catch v. 1) to bind, clutch, fasten on, get hold of, get in one's hands, grasp, hold fast, lay hands on, lay hold of, make one's own, overtake, pick up, hook, net, land, take, trap, win, 2) (of setting off by *ferry* or such like) to board, get on, make, 3) (of something said) to follow, grasp, hear, make out, take in, understand, 4) to bewitch, fill/hold the mind, grip, spellbind, 5) (of a feeling or mood) to bring out, find the words for, get to the heart of, put into words, 6) (of sickness) to become sick, fall sick, break out with, go down with.

category n. head, heading, suchness.

catholic adj. 1) worldwide, 2) broad, broad-minded, wide.

cause n. 1) beginning, ground, root, spring, mainspring, the why and wherefore, 2) father, hidden hand, maker, 3) end, goal, seeking.

cause v. to begin, draw out, lead to, open up, spark off, be at the bottom/root of.

caution n. 1) care, carefulness, foresight, forethought, heed, heedfulness, wariness, watchfulness, 2) warning, word, word in one's ear, word to the wise.

caution v. to warn, forewarn, give fair warning, threaten.

cautious adj. awake, canny, careful, heedful, mindful, wary, watchful.

cavalry n. horse, horsemen, horse-fighters, horse-lords, light horse.

cease v. to bow out, break off, drop, end, have done with, leave off, stop.

ceiling n. 1) underlayer (of the floor above), 2) the farthest reach, upper mark.

celebrate v. 1) to hallow (bread and wine at Holy *Communion*), 2) to acknowledge, bless, bring to the fore, give thanks for, make much of, speak well of, 3) to have a good time, kill the fatted calf, make a stir, make merry, make much ado.

cell n. 1) lock-up, small room, 2) inner team, ring.

cellar n. underground room, hold, stockroom.

censure n. black mark, chiding, thumbs down, upbraiding.

central adj. 1) inner, inside, main, mid, middle, midmost, inland, midland, in between, 2)

deep down, deep-rooted, going to the root, innermost, inward, key, main, overriding, telling, weighty.

centre n. 1) heart, inside, kernel, middle, mid-way, 2) backbone, heartland, marrow, pith, soul.

century n. 1) hundred years, hundredyear, yearhundred, 2) (in stockball/*cricket*) hundred runs.

certain adj. cut and dried, settled, well-grounded.

certainly adv. come what may/will, indeed, no two ways about it, truly, rain or shine, sink or swim, couthly, forsooth.

certainty n. finding, foreknowledge, full belief, last word, truth, sworn truth.

cessation n. breaking off, ending, winding up.

chain n. 1) fetter, shackle, irons, 2) run, string, one thing after another, 3) a *measure* of length, being sixty-six feet or four poles.

chair n. bench, seat, settle, stool.

chairman n. head, leader, steersman.

challenge n. dare, threat.

challenge v. to dare, gainsay, match oneself with, stand up to, withstand.

chamber n. 1) bower, bedroom, room, sleeping room, den, 2) hall, meeting hall.

champion n. 1) backer, befriender, friend in need, helper, henchman, right-hand man, spokesman, upholder, 2) match-winner, winner, nonesuch, overcomer, the best.

champion v. to back, fight for, speak up for, stand by, stand up for, take up the cudgels for, uphold.

chance n. hap, hidden hand, lot, wyrd.

chance adj. startling, unforeseen, unlooked for, wyrdful.

chandler n. candle-maker, candle-seller.

change n. break, shake-up, shift, swing, undoing, upset.

change v. to bring in new blood, make right, make unlike, shape anew, shift, undo.

changeable, changeful adj. shifting, fickle, flighty, restless, wayward.

changeless adj. abiding, holding, lasting, settled, standing fast, steadfast, timeless.

channel n. 1) path, stepping-stone, way, 2) narrows, sound, stretch of water, tideway, waterway, 3) ditch, drain, leat, overflow, runnel.

chaos n. free-for-all, hell let loose, madhouse, rough house, storm, to-do, upheaving.

chaotic adj. awry, all anyhow, bedraggled, cluttered, sloppy, tousled, untidy, upside down, windswept.

chapel n. house of worship, meeting-house.

chapter n. 1) (in a book) fore-marking, heading, 2) (in the unfolding tale of a folkdom) spell, step, time, 3) (at a *cathedral* or other great church) leadership gathering/meeting.

character n. 1) bent, bent of mind, breed, hue, ilk, kind, leaning, make, make-up, mark, 2) misfit, one-off, outsider, 3) name, fair name, goodness, uprightness, known worth, truthfulness, worth, worship, 4) grit, manliness, steadfastness.

characterise v. to bring to life, draw, make a likeness, make one see, mark, show, write about, brand, stamp.

characteristic n. hall-mark, mark, streak, suchness, the way one is, wont.

characteristic adj. deep-rooted, inborn, inward, inwoven, inwrought, settled, tell-tale.

charge n. 1) burden, load, weight, 2) hire, outlay, owings, worth, 3) undertaking, 4) gainsaying, speaking against, 5) drive, onset, run-in, strike, swoop.

charge v. 1) to fill, lade, load, top up, 2) to ask for, set, 3) to bid, lay upon, put in one's hands, put to, swear one in, 4) to hold one guilty, lay guilt at one's door, 5) to bear down on, beset, fall upon, go for, lay into, ride down, set upon, storm, strike at.

charm n. 1) spell, 2) birth-stone, 3) loveliness, sweetness, winning ways, winsomeness.

charm v. to bewitch, fill with longing, steal one's heart, sweep off one's feet.

charming adj. bewitching, spell-binding, winning.

chart n. map, seaway-finder, sealore, shore-outline.

charter n. deed, land-book.

chase v. 1) to be hard on the heels of, follow, go after, harry, hunt, ride down, run down, stalk, tail, 2) to be mad about, run after, set one's heart/mind on, woo, go a-wooing, 3) to drive away, hound, put to flight, send away.

chatter v. to gossip, run on, talk away thoughtlessly.

cheat n. good-for-nothing, knave, ne'er-do-well, sharper, shammer, twister, wolf.

cheat v. to break one's word, do out of, fleece, hoodwink, mislead, rook, steal.

check v. 1) to bridle, hinder, put a spoke in someone's wheel, stop, 2) to forhold, hold back, 3) to delve into, look at, look into, look over, sift through, work over.

cheerful, cheery adj. beaming, blithe, bright, glad, hopeful, light-hearted, lively.

chief adj. best, first, greatest, key, leading, main, outstanding, overriding, uppermost.

chiefly adv. above all, firstly, mainly, mostly, in the main, on the whole.

chivalrous adj. fair-spoken, high-minded, knightly, upright, well-bred.

choice n. 1) choosing, picking and choosing, leaning, liking, mind, naming, wish, 2) freedom of choosing.

chronic adj. 1) baleful, beyond hope, holding no hope, deadly, deathly, deep-rooted, lasting, long-lasting, unyielding, 2) hardened, hidebound, hopeless, dyed in the wool, set in one's ways, settled, 3) as bad as can be, dreadful, wretched.

chronicle n. book of high deeds, book of years, time-book, time-tale.

chronicle v. to put in writing, set down in black and white, write down.

chronology n. tell-craft, time-craft, timelore.

cigarette n. smoke.

cinema n. filmhouse.

circle n. 1) hoop, ring, ring-shape, trendle, 2) cluster, knot, set, 3) field, world.

circle v. to gird/go about, beset, hem in, lap, ring, wheel about, wind one's way.

circuit n. lap, long way about.

circular adj. ringed, ringlike, ring-shaped, ring-wise.

circumspect adj. canny, careful, heedful, mindful, thorough, wary, watchful.

circumstance n. background, the lie of the land, the look of things, the times, set-up, standing, footing.

cite v. 1) (of the doom-hall/*court*) to bid, call, send for, 2) to name the writer from whom one has drawn.

citizen n. freeman, town-dweller, townsman, townswoman.

city n. great town, burh, borough.

civil adj. 1) home, land-wide, 2) fair-spoken, friendly, knightly, ladylike, neighbourly, well-bred, well-spoken.

claim n. 1) call, right, birthright, 2) putting forth, speaking out, taking one's stand, witness, 3) beat, ground, holding, lot, pitch.

claim v. 1) to stand up for/uphold one's rights, go to law, have the law on one, 2) to say outright, set forth, speak out, swear on oath.

clarity n. broad daylight, forthrightness, openness, straightforwardness.

clash v. to fall out with, fight, gainsay, lock horns, lay into, speak out.

class *n.* 1) set (within a folkdom), 2) learning-set, 3) kind, set.

classic *adj.* 1) stock, true to kind, well-known, well-worn, 2) <u>great</u>, matchless, outstanding, rich, wholly <u>worthy</u>, <u>worthful</u>, 3) <u>abiding</u>, deathless, lasting, undying.

classical *adj.* acknowledged, longstanding, olden.

classification *n.* matching, naming.

clear *adj.* 1) bright, fair, set fair, light, shining, cloudless, unclouded, undimmed, 2) glassy, see-through, sheer, 3) readily grasped/understood, 4) (of *sound*) ringing, silver-tongued, true, well-pitched, 5) guiltless, sinless, 6) open, free, unhindered.

clear *v.* 1) (of the weather) to brighten, lighten, 2) to find not guilty, find there is nothing to answer, set free, 3) to straighten, straighten out, tidy up, 4) to drain out, empty, free, open, unclot, 5) to leap over, spring over, leave the ground, overtop, 6) to settle one's owings.

clear-cut *adj.* black-and-white, cut and dried, for all to see, marked, well-marked, <u>settled</u>, straightforward, striking, wide-open.

clear-headed *adj.* quick-thinking, ready-witted, <u>sharp</u>, shrewd, wide-awake.

clearly *adv.* markedly, needless to say, openly, rightly, ringingly, truly.

clear-sighted *adj.* <u>awake</u>, far-sighted, insightful, keen-minded, quick-sighted, <u>sharp</u>.

clerk *n.* book-keeper.

client *n.* buyer, hanger-on.

climate *n.* 1) weather, 2) background, feel, feeling, mood, setting.

climax *n.* end, fullness, height, highlight, highwater mark, peak, upshot, top.

clinical *adj.* cold, cool, frosty, hard, icy, unstirred, without warmth.

cliché *n.* overworked word/s, well-worn saying, worn-out saying.

close *v.* 1) to shut, shut up, fasten, lock, stop up, 2) to be over, end, come to an end, go out of business, put an end to, shut down, <u>stop</u>, wind up.

close *adj.* 1) narrow, shut in, 2) (of the weather) sweltering, warm, 3) unforthcoming, not open, saying little, sparing with words, 4) <u>mean</u>, stingy, hard-fisted, 5) handy, <u>hard by</u>, neighbouring, next to, nigh, not far, in the wind, in the offing, 6) <u>friendly</u>, loving, shoulder to shoulder, 7) careful, keen, sharp, thorough, 8) even, evenly matched, much like, akin, neck and neck, with nothing between.

closely *adv.* keenly, thoroughly, narrowly, hard on the heels.

clumsy *adj.* clod-hopping, heavy, heavy-footed, loutish, oafish, rough, slow, stiff, unhandy, unready, unwieldy, all thumbs.

coach *n.* 1) many-seater, 2) handler, teacher.

coach *v.* to bring on, foster, lick into shape, open the eyes/mind, ready, teach.

coarse *adj.* 1) (of cloth) hairy, homespun, rough, 2) earthy, rough-edged, rough-hewn, <u>uncouth</u>, unwomanly, 3) foul-mouthed, foul-spoken, lewd, loutish, <u>shameless</u>.

coast *n.* seaboard, sea-rim, shore, seaside, strand.

coat *n.* 1) wind-breaker, 2) fleece, hair, hide, rind, wool, 3) layer, overlay, whitewash.

coating *n.* dusting, film, glaze, layer, overlaying, sheet, smearing.

code (of law) *n.* law-right.

coerce *v.* to bear hard on, bend, browbeat, drive, <u>hold down</u>, make, <u>overcome</u>, throw one's weight about, twist one's arm, wring from.

coherent *adj.* meaningful, readily grasped/understood, straightforward, well-written.

coincidence *n.* coming together, meeting.

collaborate *v.* to help one another, lay heads together, pull together, stand shoulder to shoulder, team up, work as a team, work together, work with.

collapse *n.* 1) breakdown, fall, downfall, break-up, 2) blackout, fit.

collapse *v.* 1) to fall, <u>fall down</u>, fall in, give out, give way, 2) to break down, come to nothing, fall by the wayside, fall through, fold, go out of business, go under, be wound up, sink, 3) to black out, drop, swoon.

colleague *n.* brother, <u>friend</u>, helper, henchman, right-hand man.

collect *v.* 1) to come by, fetch, <u>gather</u>, heap up, hoard, pick up, 2) to meet, cluster, come together, forgather.

collection *n.* hoard, heap, heaping up, set, stock.

collective *adj.* clustered, gathered, shared.

college *n.* hall/house/seat of learning.

colloquial *adj.* everyday, homely.

colour *n.* 1) hue, shade, 2) blush, flush, glow, 3) life, liveliness.

colourful *adj.* bright, bright-hued, many-hued, lively, rich.

colourless *adj.* ashen, dreary, hueless, sickly, wan, washed out.

column n. 1) shaft, upright, 2) body (of fighting men), line.

combat n. bloodshed, <u>fight</u>, hand-to-hand fighting, stand-up fight.

combat v. to <u>fight</u>, stand against, stand up to, <u>withstand</u>.

combination n. 1) mingling, 2) making one, gathering, team.

combine v. 1) to bind, mingle, pound together, put together, shake/stir together, 2) to get together, link up, make one, team up.

comedy n. light-hearted play/work.

comfort n. 1) heartening, strengthening, 2) every good thing, well-being.

comfort v. to allay (fears), gladden, <u>hearten</u>, lighten, put/set the mind at rest, <u>soothe</u>, strengthen, take from one's shoulders, unburden, warm.

comfortable adj. 1) homely, restful, warm, 2) well-off, well-to-do.

command v. to bid, lay down the law, say so, say it must be done, tell.

commander n. head, leader.

commence v. to <u>begin</u>, go ahead, lead off, open, start, start off/up.

commend v. to <u>acknowledge</u>, make much of, speak highly/warmly of, speak well of.

comment n. byword, pithy saying, ready speech, say, spoken word, talk, write-up.

comment v. to be spokesman, deal with, deem, go into, handle, put a meaning on, say something about, speak about, talk about, throw light on, understand by, unfold, write about, write up.

commercial adj. business, trade, trading, sales.

commission n. 1) writ, 2) board, body, team, 3) cut, earnings, income.

commissioner n. reeve.

commit v. 1) to do the deed, have a hand in, put through, 2) to give, hand over, make over, put in the hands of, 3) to put in hold.

commitment n. owing, undertaking, word, plighted word.

committed adj. earnest, plighted, <u>steadfast</u>, tied, true, whole-hearted.

committee n. board, body, team.

commodity n. goods, stock, wares.

common adj. 1) all in the day's work, daily, everyday, homespun, workaday, foreseen, <u>middling</u>, nothing wonderful, oft, oft-coming, oft-times, run-of-the-mill, stock, widespread, wonted, 2) for everybody, shared, 3) churlish, loutish, cheap, rough, <u>shameless</u>, <u>uncouth</u>, <u>worthless</u>, 4) broad, sweeping.

commonly adv. oft, often, oft-times, often-times, many a time and oft, not seldom.

common sense n. mother wit, wit, understanding, <u>wisdom</u>.

communicate v. to bring word, give out, leave word, <u>make known</u>, put it about, ring up, send word, speak, spread the word, talk, write.

communication n. hearsay, news, talk, telling, tidings, word, writing.

community n. 1) body, folk, townsfolk, 2) neighbourhood, ward, 3) brotherhood, crowd, set.

companion n. friend, best/bosom/dear/fast/good/near/warm friend, brother, helper, helpmeet, henchman, other self, sharer.

company n. 1) body, forgathering, gathering, set, team, throng, 2) business, business house, house.

comparable adj. a match for, as good as, akin, alike, like, much like, no better, no worse, cut from the like cloth.

compare v. to liken, draw out likenesses, match, set side by side, bring near.

comparison n. likeness, likening, matching, setting side by side.

compass n. 1) north-finder, pathfinder, wayfinder, 2) field, reach, stretch.

compassion n. <u>kindness</u>, loving-kindness, ruth, softness, warmth.

compassionate adj. great-hearted, <u>kind</u>, loving, ruthful, soft-hearted, warm-hearted.

compatible adj. in keeping, in step, like-minded, of one mind.

compel v. to bend, browbeat, drive, <u>hold down</u>, make, twist one's arm, wring from.

compelling adj. 1) not to be gainsaid, overwhelming, strong, telling, weighty, 2) binding, overriding, strong-arm.

compete v. 1) to be in the running, <u>fight</u>, match oneself, stand, take on, wrestle.

competent adj. <u>bright</u>, <u>deft</u>, clever, knowing, many-sided, ready, <u>sharp</u>.

competition n. fight, one-upmanship.

competitive adj. cut-throat, keeping abreast, ruthless, self-seeking, worldly.

complain v. to bellyache, bleat, moan, whine, whinge, be sorry for oneself, have a chip on one's shoulder, not know when one is well off.

complement n. 1) fullness, match, other half, twin, 2) body, hands, men.

complete v. to build up, clinch, do thoroughly, end, fill up, follow through, fulfil, make whole, see through, settle.

complete adj. 1) out-and-out, outright, thoroughgoing, utter, 2) all, full, full-length, nothing left out/missing, unbroken, uncut, whole, 3) done, ended, fulfilled.

completely adv. down to the ground, every inch, fully, in full, heart and soul, inside out, beam and bough, root and rind, thoroughly, utterly, wholly, widely, 'hook, line and sinker'.

complex adj. 1) manifold, 2) knotted, mazy, mingled, thorny, winding.

complicated adj. deep, knotted, knotty, mingled, thorny, winding.

compliment n. fair word, good word, pretty speech.

compliment v. to speak fair, speak highly/warmly of, make much of.

component n. bit.

compose v. to draw/dream up, frame, put together, shape, write, write songs.

composed adj. cool, even-minded, steady, unshaken, unworried.

composer n. song-writer.

composition n. 1) make-up, set-up, weave, 2) crafting, framing, making, putting together, setting-up, shaping, 3) drawing, output, work, word-building, writing.

comprehend v. to fathom, grasp, know, make out, see, see it all, understand.

comprehensive adj. broad, full, lengthy, nothing left out/missing, sweeping, thorough, thoroughgoing, widespread.

compromise n. give and take, middle ground, middle of the road, middle way, mid-stream.

compromise v. 1) to bridge over, bring together, do a deal, give and take, hold out one's hand, live and let live, make the best of it, meet half-way, speak fair, 2) to drag through the mire, give one a bad name, pull asunder, run down, smear.

compulsory adj. binding, needful, overriding, not to be gainsaid.

compute v. to mete, reckon, reckon up, tell, tell off, work out.

computer n. main-reckoner.

conceal v. to bury, hide, shroud.

conceited adj. full of oneself, looking down on one, nose-wise, overbearing, showing off, swollen-headed, too clever by half, wise in one's own eyes.

conceive v. 1) to become with child, bring to life, quicken, 2) to dream up, see in the mind's eye, take into one's head, think up, 3) to believe, grasp, think, ween.

concentrate v. 1) to bethink, bring one's mind to bear, heed, give one's mind to, put one's mind to, think, 2) to cluster, come together, forgather, gather, throng.

concentrated adj. 1) rich, strong, thickened, 2) all-out, hard.

concentration n. 1) deep thought, hard thinking, carefulness, mindfulness, one-mindedness, tirelessness, 2) cluster, drawing together, narrowing down, thickening.

concept n. awareness, insight, thought, understanding.

conception n. 1) becoming with child, quickening, 2) insight, thought, understanding, 3) lay-out, weave.

concern n. 1) bane, burden, care, headache, weight on one's mind, worry, 2) business, doings, house, undertaking, work.

concern v. to gnaw at, harrow, harry, hound, prick, sting, unsettle, upset, worry.

concerned adj. burdened, weighed down, fearful, harrowed, restless, shaken.

concert n. show, making song-craft together.

concise adj. pithy, short, shortened, put in a nutshell, in a few well-chosen words, sparing of words.

conclude v. 1) to deem, find, reckon, work out, 2) to be over, end, bring to an end/ come to an end, make an end of, put an end to, put a stop to, stop, wind up, 3) to bring about, clinch, settle.

conclusion n. 1) end, ending, outcome, upshot, 2) finding, insight, reckoning.

conclusive adj. clean-cut, clinching, cutting through, overriding, settled.

concrete adj. 1) clean-cut, strong, thorough-going, weighty, well-grounded, 2) bodily, earthy, hard as stone.

condemn v. 1) to chide, cold-shoulder, cut dead, harden one's heart, have nothing to do with, shun, spurn, upbraid, 2) to doom, find one guilty, have one's head for.

condescend v. 1) to come down to, go more than half-way, go to meet, have time for, put oneself out, stoop down, unbend, 2) to speak as to a child, talk down to.

condition n. 1) a must, rider, strings, 2) plight, setting, walk of life, 3) shape, suchness, trim, 4) fettle, health, well-being.

conditioned adj. brainwashed, mistaught.

conduct n. 1) handling, running, way of doing things, 2) bearing, ways, way of life.

conduct v. 1) to handle, oversee, run, undertake, 2) to send through, spread, 3) to lead, steer.

conductor n. driver, leader.

conference n.   gathering, meeting, putting heads together, talks.

confess v.   1) to <u>acknowledge</u> one's guilt, make a clean breast of, own, say one is sorry, unbosom, unburden,   2) to bear witness (to one's beliefs), take one's stand.

confidence n.   1) belief, full belief, hope and belief, strong feeling,   2) boldness, high hopes, self-belief, strong hope,   3) a word aside, making some business known to a friend, sharing, telling.

confident adj.   <u>bold</u>, ever-hoping, hopeful, in high hopes, self-believing, unshaken.

confidential adj.   hidden, whispered, 'between ourselves', 'not to go any further'.

confirm v.   1) to bear out, bring one's witnesses, <u>find out</u>,   2) to clinch, settle, <u>strengthen</u>.

confirmed adj.   hardened, settled, dyed in the wool.

conflict n.   <u>fight</u>, misunderstanding, set-to, bad blood.

conflict v.   to fall out, <u>fight</u>, <u>gainsay</u>, have words, set oneself against, stand against.

confluence n.   water-meet.

confront v.   to <u>gainsay</u>, lock horns, meet head-on, pitch into, set at naught, stand up to, take one up on, <u>withstand</u>.

confuse v.   to beriddle, <u>bewilder</u>, addle, cloud, darken, put one off his stroke, throw one off his bearings.

confused adj.   awry, addled, all anyhow, <u>bewildered</u>, forstraught, giddy, <u>untidy</u>.

confusion n.   clutter, free for all, madhouse, to-do, untidiness, upheaving.

congratulate v.   to bless, make much of, speak well of, speak warmly of.

congregation n.   brethren, forgathering, flock, gathering, meeting.

congress n.   gathering, body, house, meeting, moot.

connect v.   to bridge, earth, fasten, hook up with, put/rope/string together, thread together, tie up with, yoke together.

connected adj.   akin, kindred, earthed, matched.

connection n.   earthing, fastening, kinship, link, tie-in, tie-up.

conquer v.   to <u>overcome</u>, overwhelm, beat, outmatch, put to flight, worst.

conscience n.   inner warning, inward word, inwitness, knowing good from evil, guilt, shame.

conscientious adj.   careful, earnest, high-minded, thorough, <u>upright</u>.

conscious adj.   <u>awake</u>, wide-awake, aware, on the stretch, alive to, knowing.

consciousness n.   1) awareness, knowledge, mindfulness, understanding,   2) awakeness.

consecutive adj.   following, one after the other, running.

consent n.   blessing, leave, the go-ahead, the green light.

consequence n.   1) backwash, end, fall-out, follow-on, outcome, upshot,   2) greatness, standing, weight, weightiness, worth, worthship.

consequently adv.   all along of, and so, because of, it follows that, thereby.

conservative adj.   careful, die-hard, hidebound, middle-of-the-road, wary.

consider v.   1) to believe, bethink, <u>think</u>, deem, hold to be, look on as, look upon, see, set down for, ween,   2) to chew over, work over, eye up, think about, weigh,   3) to bear in mind, reckon with.

considerable adj.   goodly, <u>great</u>, marked, much, weighty.

considerably adv.   greatly, markedly, much.

consideration n.   1) brooding, <u>thought</u>, deep thought, inmost thoughts, thinking through,   2) fair-speaking, friendliness, kindness, rising above oneself, selflessness, thoughtfulness, unselfishness,   3) weight, weightiness,   4) sweetener, token, worth.

considering prep.   bearing in mind, keeping in mind, in the light of, reckoning.

consist of v.   to be made up of, have, hold.

consistent adj.   1) as good as one's word, even, right, settled, steady, true,   2) all of a kind, in keeping,   3) <u>well-grounded</u>, well-put, well-thought through, well-weighed.

consistently adv.   rightly, steadfastly, steadily, truly.

consisting adj.   having, holding, made up of.

console v.   to hearten, lighten, put/set the mind at rest, <u>soothe</u>, take the load off someone's mind/from someone's shoulders, wipe away the tears.

consolidate v.   1) to build up, <u>strengthen</u>, stiffen, thicken, toughen,   2) to lay/put together, make one, yoke.

conspicuous adj.   for all to see, foremost, in high light, in the limelight, in the open, leading, outstanding, standing out, striking, unhidden, well-marked, well-seen.

conspiracy n.   stealth-work, web, web-weaving, underhand dealing.

constant adj.   <u>steadfast</u>, <u>true-hearted</u>, earnest, <u>abiding</u>, unshaken, <u>unyielding</u>.

constantly *adv.* all the time, at all times, day after day, day and night, for ever and a day, on and on, one after another, till doomsday, unendingly, without a break.

constitute *v.* 1) to be, 2) to frame, make, make up, 3) to name, put together, set up.

constitution *n.* 1) body of law, laws, framework of the body *politic*, 2) body, build, frame, make-up.

constitutional *adj.* good in law, lawful, within the law.

constrain *v.* to bind, bridle, hem in, hold back, hold down, twist one's arm.

construct *v.* to build, frame, make, put together, put up, set up, shape.

construction *n.* 1) building, shape, work, workings, 2) light, meaning, reading.

consult *v.* to ask, lay/put heads together, talk to, pick one's brains.

consumer *n.* buyer.

contact *n.* 1) coming together, meeting, tie-up, 2) go-between, link man.

contact *v.* to call, get hold of, ring up, send word, speak to, write to.

contain *v.* 1) to have, hold, 2) to cut off, hedge in, hem in, hold back, hold in.

contemplate *v.* to bethink, brood over, have in mind, think about/of/on/over/upon.

contempt *n.* looking down on, spurning, weighing lightly someone's worth.

content *adj.* blessed, blithe, fulfilled, unworried, with nothing left to wish for.

contentment *n.* blessedness, bliss, blitheness, gladness, happiness, weal, well-being.

contest *n.* fight, match, run-off.

contest *v.* to fight, lock horns, match oneself, play against, stand against, take on.

context *n.* 1) background, framework, lay of the land, 2) times.

continental *adj.* mainland.

continually *adv.* all the time, endlessly, time and again, time after time.

continue *v.* 1) to abide, go on, keep going, stick to, pick up where one left off, 2) to hold good, last, live on, run on, stand.

continuity *n.* coming straight after, following on, flow, steady flow, long run, never-endingness, overlap, one thing after another, timelessness, unbroken run.

continuous *adj.* endless, ever-flowing, flowing, ever-running, long-lasting, never-ending, not stopping, ongoing, overlapping, timeless, unbroken.

continuously *adv.* all the time, everlastingly, steadfastly, steadily.

contract *n.* deal, plighted word, understanding, foreward.

contradict *v.* 1) to gainsay, answer back, give the lie to, say no, withsay, 2) to go/stand against, set at naught, take one up on.

contrary *adj.* 1) against, anything but, far asunder, far from it, off-setting, on the other side, unlike, untoward, 2) fretful, hindering, unwilling, wayward, wilful.

contrast *n.* otherness, unlikeness.

contribute *v.* to bear/lend a hand, bestow, give, help, open one's hand, open the door to, share.

contribution *n.* 1) input, sharing in, 2) hand-out.

control *n.* 1) grip, hold, leadership, long arm, mightiness, over-mightiness, oversight, running, steering, 2) fetter, shackle, 3) coolness, steadiness, strength of mind/will.

control *v.* 1) to do as one will, handle, have it all one's own way, have the upper hand, hold down/under, lay down the law, lead, lord it over, oversee, steer, hold in the hollow of one's hand, lead by the nose, throw one's weight about, 2) to bridle, hinder, hold back, shackle, steady, tame, throw cold water on.

controversy *n.* gainsaying, words, high words, stormy words, strong words.

convenience *n.* good, help, handiness, nearness, readiness.

convenient *adj.* 1) good for, handy, heaven-sent, helpful, not hard, wieldy, 2) at hand, nearby, ready, within reach, 3) timely, well-timed.

convention *n.* 1) done thing, 2) deal, understanding, undertaking, 3) gathering, meeting, talks, moot.

conventional *adj.* 1) dyed in the wool, hidebound, wonted, 2) by the book, meet and right, starchy, stiff, unbending, 3) run-of-the-mill, set, stock, trodden, well-worn.

conversation *n.* gossip, talk, small talk, word and answer.

conversion *n.* 1) making other, winning, 2) doing up, bettering, making into, uplift.

convert *v.* 1) to bring to the Lord, bring over, win over, bring to one's side, make one believe, shape anew, wean from, 2) to become (a new man/woman), win free or break away (from one's old life), come to belief, leave the old life behind, see the light, think better of, 3) to better, brighten, do up, make better, make into, make over.

conviction *n.* 1) belief, steadfastness, doggedness, one-mindedness, steadiness, strength of mind, 2) doom, doom-saying, finding one guilty, reckoning.

convince v. to bring home to, bring over, make one believe, talk into, win over.

convincing adj. belief-worthy, telling, winning belief, likely, straightforward, well-grounded, winning over.

co-operate v. to go hand in hand, lay heads together, pull together, work together, work as a team, team up, feather the shaft.

co-operation n. give and take, goodwill, helpfulness, helping hand, readiness, team work, understanding, willingness, willing help, working together.

co-operative adj. brotherly, helpful, of one mind, thoughtful, willing.

cope v. to abide, deal with, handle, hold one's own, see to, work through.

copse n. grove, holt, holt-wood, wood-holt, shaw, thicket, underwood.

copy n. borrowing, cribbing, likeness, shadow, sham.

copy v. to behave like, make oneself like, borrow, crib, follow, shadow, take a leaf out of someone's book.

cordial adj. earnest, friendly, hearty, warm, warm-hearted, heartfelt, welcoming, well-wishing, wholehearted.

core n. heart, kernel, marrow, pith.

corner n. 1) bend, 2) hideaway, hide-out, burrow, den, hole, hollow, lair, 3) backyard, neighbourhood, neck of the woods.

corporate adj. embodied, shared.

corporation n. 1) body, business house, 2) town-moot.

corpus n. body of work, writings, written works, gathered works, whole works.

correct adj. 1) meet and right, right-minded, ladylike, upright, well-bred, well-spoken, stiff, straightforward, upstanding, 2) aright, right, dead-on, straight, true, true to life, truthful, shipshape.

correct v. 1) to put right, set right, righten, straighten out, 2) to book, chide, give one a black mark/talking to, tell off, upbraid.

correspondence n. 1) fair/near likeness, nearness, kinship, match, 2) tidings, writing, writing to and fro.

corresponding adj. answering, matching, twinning.

corrupt adj. 1) crafty, lying, misdealing, shady, shifty, slippery, twisted, warped, 2) evil, fallen, foul, godless, loathsome, shameless, unclean, unhallowed, unholy.

corruption n. badness, blight, evil, foul play, misdeed, misdoing, shamefulness, unrightness, wickedness.

cost, costs n. 1) dearness, outgoings, outlay, overheads, worth, 2) harm, loss.

cost v. to be worth, come to, set one back.

costly adj. 1) dear, pretty penny, steep, stiff, worthful, worthly, 2) dearly bought, showy, richly-wrought, worth its weight in gold, 3) blighting, dreadful, harmful.

cottage n. cot, cote, dwelling, homestead, steading.

council n. board, body, gathering, house, meeting.

count v. 1) to go over, reckon up, take stock, tell, mete, 2) to be somebody/ something, tell, weigh, 3) to deem, look upon, think of, 4) to come within, fall under, reckon among.

counter v. 1) to fight/go/work against, hinder, keep in play, stave off, ward off, withstand, 2) to answer, come back, strike back.

countless adj. endless, ever so many/much, swarming, teeming, unrimed, untold.

country n. 1) land, kingdom, homeland, fatherland, motherland, folk-body, 2) folk, 3) back of beyond, middle of nowhere, outdoors, outlands.

county n. shire.

couple n. 1) two, twosome, twain, 2) husband and wife.

courage n. boldness, daring, fearlessness, fire, heart, steadfastness.

courageous adj. bold, daring, daring-hearted, doughty, dreadless, fearless, stalworth, steadfast, steely, unshrinking.

course n. 1) line, path, road, way, 2) way forward, way of doing things, 3) (of *events*) flow, set, stream, tide, unfolding, 4) (*education*) path of learning, 5) running field/ground, horse-running field/ground, 6) span, sweep, time.

court n. 1) yard, 2) pitch, playing field/ground, 3) kingly hall, 4) (of law) doom-hall, the bench.

courteous adj. fair-spoken, knightly, old-world, well-bred, well-spoken, winning.

courtesy n. fair-speaking, good breeding, knightliness, winsomeness.

cousin n. near kinsman, kinswoman.

cover n. 1) shield, wind-break, woods, 2) (*insurance*) set-off, 3) lid, sheath, top, 4) bedclothes, bedding, sheets, 5) binding (for a book), boards, cloth, 6) let-out, shift, red herring.

cover v. 1) to shield, watch over, 2) (*insurance*) to make good, make up for, offset, 3) to clothe, put the lid on, roof in, 4) to bestride, spread, spread out, overspread, straddle, 5) to bind (a book), overlay, overspread, 6) to becloud, bedarken, hide, hood, shade, shroud, 7) to smear on, 8) to flood, overrun, wash over, 9) to deal with, tell of, write about, write up, 10) to *pay* for, be enough for.

coverage n. nothing left out, putting it about/over, spreading the word abroad.

covering n. clothing, layer, overlap, overlay, top.

covert adj. dark, deep, hidden, hooded, shrouded, stealthy, underhand.

coward n. chicken, runaway, softling.

cowardly adj. bowed, broken, fearful, fear-ridden, frozen/numbed with fear, shrinking with fear, quaking, unmanned, worsted.

crash n. 1) wreck, 2) loud *sound* of a knock or fall, clatter, din, 3) (in business) fall, downfall, folding.

crash v. 1) to hit, run into, 2) to clatter, 3) (of a business) to fold, go under.

crawl v. 1) to creep, drag/pull oneself along, drag one's feet/steps, fall behind, feel one's way, go on all fours, go on hands and knees, go slowly, inch, slither, take one's time, 2) to bow and scrape, bow one's neck to the yoke, cringe, fawn, show no fight, stoop to anything, throw oneself at the feet of, toady, worm one's way.

crazy adj. daft, mad, mazed, off one's head, wildered in one's wits.

cream n. 1) milk-*oil*, milk-ream, 2) salve, eye-salve, 3) best, chosen few, pick, salt of the earth, top drawer.

create v. to bring into being, build, craft, make, shape.

creation n. 1) life, all living things, world, living world, 2) brainchild, handiwork, 3) beginning, ground-work, laying down, making, shaping.

creative adj. rich in thought, lively, sharp, insightful, witful.

creature n. 1) being, soul, living soul, living being, 2) follower, hanger-on, henchman.

credible adj. winning/worthy of belief, likely, straightforward, well-grounded.

credit n. 1) good name, standing, uprightness, worth, worthiness, 2) good reckoning.

crew n. 1) hands, seamen, ship-folk, 2) men, team, 3) crowd, herd, lot, set, swarm.

cricket n. bat-and-ball, stockball.

crime n. evil, foul play, misdeed.

criminal n. cut-throat, evil-doer, fiend, knave, lawbreaker, rough, tough, twister.

criminal adj. black-hearted, evil, fiendish, given up to evil, hardened, hateful, lawless, loathful, shady, outside the law, unlawful, warped, wicked.

crisis n. day of reckoning, doomsday, dread day, gathering cloud, key time, meltdown, plight, storm, threat, thing of life and death, time to meet the truth.

criterion n. bench-mark, meteyard, yardstick.

critic n. 1) leader-writer, thinker, worth-weigher, 2) backbiter, shrew.

critical adj. 1) key, now or never, timely, weighty, 2) biting, bitter, chiding, cutting, sharp, sharp-edged, smearing, stinging, strongly-worded, waspish, withering.

criticism n. 1) deeming, setting side by side, sifting, weighing, worth-weighing, 2) backbiting, blackening, home-truth, smearing.

crooked adj. 1) bent, bowed, knock-kneed, misshapen, out of shape, twisted, warped, 2) twisting, wandering, winding, 3) awry, leaning, to one side, uneven, 4) crafty, lying, misdealing, shady, shifty, slippery, two-tongued, underhand, untruthful.

crown n. 1) wreath, 2) end, fullness, height, highlight, peak, 3) head, top.

crucial adj. far-reaching, going to the root, key, overriding, timely, weighty.

cruel adj. cold, cold-blooded, grim, heartless, stony-hearted, ruthless, wolfish.

cry n. 1) whine, 2) call, roar, scream, screech, shout, yell.

cry v. 1) to shed tears, snivel, weep, whine, whinge, 2) to beseech, call out, roar, scream, screech, shout, sing out, yell.

cryptic adj. knotted, dark, deep, hidden, shadowy, shrouded.

culmination n. end, fullness, height, highlight, highwater mark, peak, top.

culpable adj. evil, guilty, red-handed, sinful, unbecoming, unworthy, wicked.

cultivate v. 1) to delve, ditch, leave fallow, plough, work, seed, sow, set, dung, rake, till, water, weed, bring on, grow, gather in, harvest, pick, reap, thresh, winnow, sift, grass over, cut a swathe, mow, scythe, 2) to foster (a friendship, way of thinking, or such), seek to grow a friendship, befriend, forward, further, run after, seek out.

cultural adj. 1) folk, 2) broadening, enlightening, enriching, mind-opening.

culture n. good breeding, lore, way of life.

cumbersome *adj.* heavy, hefty, top-heavy, unhandy, unwieldy.

cunning *n.* 1) craftiness, foxiness, knowingness, shrewdness, stealth, 2) cleverness, craft, deftness, handcleverness, handiness, quickness.

cunning *adj.* crafty, knowing, shady, sharp, shrewd, slippery, stealthy, underhand.

cure *n.* answer, healing, help.

cure *v.* 1) to bind up, heal, help, make better, make well, 2) to break of, make good, put right, 3) to dry, salt, smoke.

curiosity *n.* 1) seeking mind, itch/thirst for knowledge, mind thirst, wishing to know, 2) nosiness, sight-seeing, 3) fish out of water, sight, wonder, nine days' wonder.

curious *adj.* 1) all ears, hungering for news, nosy, seeking, 2) weird, wonderful.

current *adj.* adoing, in keeping with the times, in the news, in the wind, latest, on foot, ongoing, today's, of today, with the times.

currently *adv.* at this time, even now, now, now-a-days, today.

curriculum *n.* set bookwork, set learning.

curt *adj.* cutting, keen, offhand, rough, sharp, short, sparing of words, tart, uncouth.

curve *n.* bend, horse-shoe.

curve *v.* to bend, bow, snake, twist, wind.

custom *n.* 1) folkway, lore, unwritten law, way, wont, done thing, the old way, 2) business, trade.

customer *n.* buyer.

cycle *n.* summer and winter, twice-told tale, wheel of life.

cynical *adj.* belittling, biting, cold, cutting, looking for the worst, outspoken, sharp, stinging, waspish, withering, worldly-wise.

damage *n.* harm, loss, mark, tear, undoing.

damage *v.* 1) to break, harm, mar, mark, overwork, shake, tear, twist, undo, warp, wear out, worsen, 2) to blacken, give a dog a bad name, smear, tell/weigh against.

damn *v.* to beshrew, call down on, curse, storm against.

damp *adj.* clammy, dewy, drizzly, sodden, wet.

dance *n.* reel, quickstep, light-stepping, lithe-step.

dance *v.* to tread lightly and lithely and with meted (*measured*) steps (within hall or in the open) – gliding and weaving in time to *music*.

danger *n.* deathtrap, gathering cloud, leap in the dark, storm brewing, threat.

dangerous *adj.* baleful, deadly, harmful, threatening.

data *n.* knowledge to go on, held/kept/stowed knowledge, knowledge stock.

date *n.* 1) day, time, year, 2) meeting.

date *v.* 1) to settle the time of, 2) to go out with, walk out with, 3) to become old-fangled/outworn.

dated *adj.* behind the times, old-fangled, old world, timeworn.

daunting *adj.* dreadful, fearful, fearsome, frightening, numbing, threatening, unmanning.

dazzling ablaze, alight, blinding, bright, gleaming, shining, sparkling.

debacle *n.* let-down, meltdown, misfire, overthrow, wash-out.

debatable *adj.* bewildering, knotty, left open, moot.

debate *n.* talks, asking and answer, word-meeting, word-wielding.

debate *v.* to talk over/about/through, to thrash out, weigh the fors and againsts, to wield words.

debt *n.* borrowing, burden, overdraft, owings, something owed, dead-weight, fetter, load on one's back, millstone, shackle.

decade *n.* ten years, tenyear.

decay *n.* crumbling, going bad, wear and tear, away-fall.

deceit *n.* craftiness, foxiness, lying, sharp-dealing, untruth, untruthfulness.

deceitful *adj.* crafty, hollow, lying, sham, shameless, slippery, underhand.

deceive *v.* to hide the truth, hoodwink, mislead, make game of, shroud, spin, take in.

December *n.* Ere-Yule, Yule-month, Midwintermonth.

decent *adj.* 1) all right, fair, good enough, middling, pretty good, up to the mark, 2) becoming, befitting, clean, ladylike, tidy, 3) good, rightwise, right-hearted, 4) friendly, helpful, kind, neighbourly.

deceptive *adj.* 1) hollow, lying, misleading, shifting, truthless, untrue, wide of the truth, 2) crafty, slippery, underhand.

decide *v.* to choose, settle, make a deal, make up one's mind, strike hands.

decision *n.* 1) finding, outcome, upshot, 2) drive, steadiness, strength of mind/will.

decisive *adj.* cutting through, overriding, putting one's foot down, striking while the iron is hot.

declaration *n.* word, saying, speech, making known, putting/telling forth, spreading abroad.

declare *v.* to give out, hold forth, put about, say out, speak, set forth, bear witness, go as far as, lay down.

decline n. drop, dwindling, falling off, lessening, shrinking, waning, worsening.

decline v. 1) to drop, dwindle, ebb, fall away, go downhill, lessen, wane, wither, worsen, 2) to forgo, say no, spurn.

decrease n. cutback, dwindling, ebb, fall, falling off, lessening, loss, shrinking.

decrease v. 1) to cut back/down/ hort, make less, narrow down, thin out, trim, weed out, whittle away, 2) to ebb, ebb away, grow less, become less, lessen, die down, die away, drain away, drop, dry up, dwindle, fall, shrink, sink, tail off, wane.

dedicated adj. caring, earnest, loving, self-forgetful, selfless, steadfast, trothful, true, whole-hearted.

dedication n. steadfastness, steadiness, strength of heart, one-mindedness.

defeat n. beating, downfall, fall, graveyard, hiding, loss, overthrow, thrashing.

defeat v. to overcome, overwhelm, beat, fell, outmatch, put to flight, worst.

defence n. fight, holding, shielding, stand, ward, withstanding.

defend v. 1) to fight back, fight off, hold back, hold out against, keep, keep at arm's length, keep off, stand against, withstand, shield, fight to the death/end, ward off, 2) to speak up for, stand by, stand up for, take up the cudgels for, uphold.

defendant n. answerer, witness for oneself.

defensive adj. 1) holding, keeping, shielding, watchful, withstanding, 2) prickly, unforthcoming, wary.

defiant adj. 1) bold, daring, doughty, fearless, 2) all edges, a law to oneself, downright, forthright, outspoken, prickly, self-willed, stiff, wilful.

deficient adj. 1) lacking, missing, short of, running short, starved of, unfilled, unworthy, 2) backward, slow, out of one's depth, witless.

define v. 1) to mark out, outline, 2) to give the meaning of, name, put a meaning on, unfold, 3) to set.

defined adj. cut and dried, marked, well-worn.

definite adj. black-and-white, cut and dried, for all to see, known, settled, striking, marked, formarked, well-marked.

definitely adv. come what may/will, indeed, no two ways about it, truly, rain or shine, sink or swim, couthly, forsooth.

definition n. 1) unfolding, 2) sharpness.

definitive adj. clinching, overriding, settled.

defraud v. to break troth, do out of, fleece, steal, thieve.

defy v. 1) to dare, outdare, fight off, not take it lying down, set at naught, stand against, stand up to, take one up on, throw away the sheath, withstand, 2) to answer back, go one's own way, have a will of one's own, not listen, not do as one is told, outstare, say no, own no law, will otherwise, 3) to be beyond, leave speechless.

degenerate adj. evil, fallen, godless, lewd, loathsome, lustful, shameless, twisted, wanton, warped, wicked, wild, blind/deaf/dead to.

degree n. 1) mark, pitch, reach, shade, standing, step, 2) written deed.

dejected adj. forlorn, hopelorn, hopeless, sorrowful, down at heart, wretched.

delay n. dragging out, hold-up, idling, putting off, setback, spinning out.

delay v. to be long about it, bide one's time, drag one's feet/heels, put off, stand/sit about, while away the time, take one's time, let the grass grow under one's feet, sit on one's hands.

delayed adj. after time, behind time, behindhand, belated, held up, hindered, late.

delegate v. to lay upon, put in one's hands.

delete v. to black out, cut out, strike out, wipe out.

deliberately adv. 1) knowingly, of one's own free will, out of one's own head, wilfully, with one's eyes open, wittingly, 2) carefully, heedfully, slowly, thoughtfully, warily.

delicate adj. 1) becoming, elf-fair, elf-like, light, 2) brittle, flimsy, 3) sickly, unhealthy, 4) choosy, picksome.

delight n. bliss, blissfulness, blitheness, gladness, glee, list, thrill.

delight v. to gladden, do one's heart good, bless, fill with wonder, thrill, take one's breath away, bewitch.

delightful adj. bewitching, endearing, winning, winsome.

deliver v. 1) to atone for, free, set free, let out, throw a life-line to, unbind, unburden, unlock, unloose, unshackle, 2) to bear, bring to birth, bring forth, bring into the world, give birth, 3) to give up to, give over, hand over, hand to, make over, yield up, 4) to deal a stroke/dint.

delivery n. 1) freeing, setting free, 2) birth, birth-throes, child-bed, childbirth, lying-in, 3) hand-over, making-over, yielding up, 4) speaking, way of speaking, speech-making.

delusion n. daydream, dream world, make-believe, wild dream, wishful thinking,

demand n. bidding, call, need.

demand v. to ask for, bid for, make bold to ask, call for, seek, stand up for/uphold one's rights.

demanding *adj.* 1) draining, hard, tiring, tough, uphill, <u>wearing</u>, 2) tiresome, wearisome.

democracy *n.* folk-will.

democratic *adj.* on a like footing.

demolish *v.* to make an end of, pull down, tear down, throw down, <u>unmake</u>.

demonise *v.* to blacken, give one a bad name, put in a bad light, <u>smear</u>.

demonstrate *v.* 1) to bear out, set out, show, throw light on, unfold, 2) to call out, come out, down tools, make a stand, rise up, set at naught, show fight, stand against, stand up to, take up the cudgels, walk out.

demonstration *n.* 1) show, showing, unfolding, 2) sit-in, taking to the streets, uprising.

density *n.* 1) crowdedness, thickness, 2) body, weight.

dentist *n.* gum-smith, gum-wright, tooth-drawer, tooth-smith, tooth-wright.

deny *v.* 1) to <u>gainsay</u>, answer back, say no, 2) to go/stand against, set at naught.

depart *v.* 1) to be off, be on one's way, fare forth, go, go away, go off, leave, leave the nest, set foot in the stirrup, set forth, set out, start out, strike out, withdraw, 2) to swerve, swing away, go aside.

department *n.* 1) arm, 2) borough, shire, township, ward, 3) business, care, field.

departure *n.* 1) flight, forthfaring, going, going away, leaving, pulling out, setting off/out, starting out, 2) falling away, going one's own way, leaving the straight/right way, shift, swing, upset, wandering away.

depend *v.* 1) to hang upon, rest on, 2) to build upon, lean on, reckon on.

dependent *adj.* beholden, bounden, helpless, needy, penniless, unfree.

deplorable *adj.* 1) <u>dreadful</u>, grim, harrowing, woeful, wretched, 2) not bear thinking about, not to be thought of, not good enough, shameful, too bad, utterly bad.

depose *v.* to unseat, unsaddle, strike off.

depressed *adj.* forlorn, <u>hopelorn</u>, 'down', heavy-hearted, wretched, <u>sorrowful</u>.

depression *n.* forlornness, gloominess, heart-sickness, hopelessness, <u>sorrow</u>, black mood, weariness of heart.

deprivation *n.* dearth, <u>hardship</u>, neediness, wretchedness.

deputy *n.* righthandman, spokesman, spokeswoman, steadsman, steward, stand-in.

deride *v.* to belittle, laugh at, look down on, put down, set at naught, <u>spurn</u>.

derive *v.* to draw, gather, lay at the door of, put down to, say how something has happened, set down to.

descend *v.* 1) to go down, come down, dip down, drop down, drop, go underground, 2) to get down, get off, alight, light, land, 3) to dive, nose-dive, swoop, 4) to fall, fall down, fall off, fall to the ground, miss one's footing, 5) to go downhill, go under, lose height, reach the depths, sink to the bottom.

describe *v.* to bring to life, draw, make a likeness, make one see, mark out, set out, set forth, outline, put in words, show, tell, write about.

description *n.* 1) drawing from life, outline, likeness, speaking likeness, striking likeness, thumbnail likeness, true likeness, word-likeness, 2) brand, breed, hue, ilk, kind, make.

desert *n.* wild, wilderness, drear lands, drylands, forsaken lands, lone-lands.

desert *v.* to forsake, ditch, <u>leave</u> high and dry, walk out on.

deserve *v.* to be <u>worthy</u>, to befit, behove, earn, be one's right, be fair to one.

design *n.* 1) draft, drawing, lay-out, outline, shape, 2) dream, end, goal, wish.

design *v.* 1) to do one's homework/spadework, draft, draw, draw up, frame, lay out, mark out, outline, put into shape, set out, think out/through/up, 2) to mean.

desirable *adj.* 1) helpful, worthwhile, worth having, 2) after one's heart, all that is wished for, looked-for, sought-after, 3) bewitching, fair, fetching, pretty, <u>winning</u>.

desire *n.* 1) <u>longing</u>, dreaming, wish, yearning, 2) craving, lust.

desire *v.* 1) to wish for, dream of, list, <u>long for</u>, set one's heart/mind on, yearn after/for, 2) to crave, hunger/thirst/itch for, 3) to ask, beseech, make bold to ask.

desk *n.* writing-board, writing-stand, reading-stand.

despair *n.* forlorn hope, forlornness, hopelessness, no hope, no way out, <u>sorrow</u>, bitterness, heaviness, wretchedness.

despair *v.* to be <u>hopelorn</u>, to <u>sorrow</u>, be broken, lose heart.

desperate *adj.* <u>hopelorn</u>, hopeless, forlorn, wretched, 2) aching, itching, longing, yearning, 3) earnest (as in 'earnest wish'), deep, great, 4) last ditch, rash, reckless, stopping at nothing, headstrong, daring, wild, <u>heedless</u>.

desperately *adv.* madly, utterly, truly (as in 'truly sad').

despise v. to be too high for, hate, hold beneath one, look down on, spurn.

despite prep. against the tide/stream/wind, in the teeth of, notwithstanding, though, although.

destiny n. doom, foreshadowing, foreworking, hidden hand, lot, wyrd.

destroy v. 1) to break down, pull down, root out, undo, unmake, uproot, break up, bring to naught, bring to nothing, 2) to overwhelm, overthrow, 3) to do away with, kill, put an end to, put down, slay.

destruction n. end, downfall, fall, overthrow, tearing down, undoing, unmaking, uprooting, wiping out.

destructive adj. deadly, harmful, overwhelming, tearing, uprooting, worsting.

detail n. whit, every whit, every last word, every whit and word, bit, dot, stop.

detailed adj. full, lengthy, thorough, thoroughgoing, with nothing left out/missing.

detective n. hound, bloodhound.

deter v. to head off, put off, shake, threaten, throw cold water on, steer one away from, talk out of.

detergent n. cleaner, cleanser, lye, quicklime, soap.

deteriorate v. to worsen, wither, crumble, rot, run down, rust, wear out.

determination n. backbone, doggedness, grit, steadfastness, steeliness, tirelessness.

determine v. 1) to work out, will, make up one's mind, choose, settle, 2) to know one's own mind, put one's foot down, steel oneself.

determining n. making up one's mind, overriding, settling.

detrimental adj. bad, baneful, bringing to naught, dreadful, harmful, undoing.

devastation n. overthrow, tearing down, uprooting, wiping out, bringing to naught.

develop v. 1) to grow, blossom, build up, ripen, spread, spring up, strengthen, unfold, do well, 2) to follow from, follow on, arise, spring from, come about, come from, come of, come out of, grow from, 3) to begin, make, put together, set up, start.

developing adj. blossoming, growing, ripening, spreading, swelling.

development n. broadening, growth, headway, rise, spreading, strengthening, unfolding, upbuilding, widening.

deviate v. to go out of one's way, leave the right/straight way, sheer off, steer away from, step aside, swerve, swing, wander, wheel about.

device n. blind, game, little game, shift, makeshift, dust in the eyes.

devious adj. crafty, foxy, misdealing, shifty, slippery, two-tongued, underhand.

devolution n. hand-over, giving others a freer hand, sharing/spreading leadership.

devoted adj. caring, earnest, loving, self-forgetful, selfless, steadfast, true.

diabolical adj. fiendish, hellish, mad, nightmarish, wicked, wild.

dialect n. folkspeech, home speech.

diameter n. beam, breadth, broadness, span, spread, wideness, width.

dictionary n. wordbook, wordhoard, word-stock.

diet n. 1) fare, food, 2) fast.

diet v. to eat sparingly, fast, forbear, know when one has had enough, lose weight, watch one's weight, thin.

difference n. 1) otherness, unlikeness, no match, 2) (in rimecraft) left over, what is left, 3) misunderstanding, set-to.

different adj. another, other, otherwise, out of the way, outlandish, owing nothing to, weird and wonderful, unheard of, unalike, unlike, anything but, far from, far above.

difficult adj. 1) burdensome, hard, steep, tiresome, tiring, tough, uphill, wearing, wearisome, 2) knotty, thorny, 3) bearish, choosy, churlish, crabbed, moody, pigheaded, short, unbending, uncouth, unknightly, unyielding.

difficulty n. hardship, hard going, the hard way, rough ground, hindering, hurdle.

diffusion n. spreading.

dignity n. bearing, becomingness, breeding, highness, knightliness, lordliness, kingliness, queenliness, self-worth.

dilemma n. cleft stick, headache, hole, knot, maze, riddle, teaser.

diligent adj. careful, earnest, hardworking, steady, thorough, tireless, whole-hearted.

dimension/s n. 1) look, outline, shape, 2) height and depth, length and breadth, thickness.

dine v. to eat, fall to, keep hall, sit down to eat, set to, take a meal.

dinner n. meal, evening meal, heavy meal, main meal, spread.

diplomatic adj. careful, insightful, smooth spoken, thoughtful, understanding, wise.

direct v. to lead, lead on, lead through, show the way, steer.

direct adj. 1) straight, dead straight, straight as an arrow, 2) downright, forthright, open, outspoken, straightforward, true, truthful.

direction n. bearing, path, road, set, trend, way.

directly adv. 1) by the shortest way, as the crow flies, in a beeline, straight, unswervingly, 2) at once, forthwith, right away, quickly, soon, as soon as may be, straightaway, speedily, 3) forthrightly, openly, straightforwardly, truthfully.

director n. head, headman, leader, overseer.

disagree v. to gainsay, say no, shake one's head, speak out/up.

disappear v. 1) to be gone, be lost to sight, bury oneself, dwindle to nothing, go, leave, wear away, 2) to bolt, fly away, go missing, hide away, lie low, lie out of sight, make off, melt away, melt into the mist, run away, withdraw, cut and run.

disappoint v. to belie one's hopes, come to naught, fall short, go awry, let down, overthrow one's hopes, put one out, sicken, stick in the throat, upset.

disapprove v. to have nothing to do with, look down one's nose at, not hold with, not think much of, think little of, raise an eyebrow, spurn, upbraid.

disarm v. 1) to lay down one's weapons, to take away the weapons of others, 2) to allay, give a soft answer, meet halfway, smooth over, soften, soothe, sweeten, take the sting out of, win over.

disaster n. downfall, end, fall, meltdown, overthrow, stroke, undoing, unmaking.

discerning adj. awake, bright, insightful, keen-witted, quick-thinking, shrewd.

discharge n. 1) firing, shooting, 2) fulfilling, 3) meeting, settling, 4) lay-off, 5) forgiveness, freeing, let-off, setting free, unbinding, 6) bleeding, leaking, oozing, running sore, sweating, weeping.

discharge v. 1) to fire, let off, set off, shoot, 2) to do thoroughly, follow through, fulfil, see through, 3) (of owings) to meet, settle, settle the reckoning, 4) to axe, drop, fire, lay off, 5) to free, set free, let go, let off, 6) to drain, empty, give off, leak, ooze, 7) (of a ship) to off-load, unload.

discipline n. 1) field of learning/teaching, 2) forgoing, giving up, selflessness, steadiness, strength of mind/will, 3) readying, strong hand, 4) beating.

discipline v. 1) to break in, drive, knock into shape, ready, 2) to bring to book.

disclosure n. hearsay, leak, lid taken off, making known, telling, spreading abroad.

discomfort n. 1) ache, head-ache, prick, smarting, soreness, sting, 2) bitterness, hardship, roughness.

disconcerting adj. bewildering, unsettling, upsetting, worrying.

discontented adj. bitter, fretful, put out, unfulfilled.

discontinue v. to stop, break off, end, have done with, leave off, wind up.

discourage v. 1) to get one down, take the heart out of, throw cold water over, throw a shadow over, 2) to fill with fear/dread, frighten, overcome, shake, unman.

discover v. to become aware, bring to light, find out, come upon, learn, open up, pitch upon, unearth.

discovery n. breakthrough, daylight, eye-opener, find, finding, insight, leap, step forward, unfolding.

discriminate v. 1) to comb, delve into, have insight, know what's what, rake/sift through, winnow, 2) to be unfair, lean to one side, withhold rights.

discriminating adj. canny, insightful, keen-minded, sharp, shrewd, witfast, witful.

discrimination n. 1) awareness, breadth/depth of mind, canniness, insight, long-headedness, sharpness, shrewdness, understanding, wisdom, 2) unfairness, leaning (to one side), withholding the right.

discuss v. to go into, talk about, talk over, talk through, thrash out.

discussion n. talks, asking and answer, talking through.

disease n. 1) addle, blight, sickness, upset, 2) curse, evil, running sore.

disgrace n. shame, evil, bad name, unworthness, unworthship.

disgruntled adj. bitter, crabbed, put out, sore, sour.

disgusting adj. dreadful, foul, frightful, hateful, sickening, stinking, loathsome.

dishearten v. to take hope away, take the heart out of, throw gloom over, throw cold water over, throw a shadow over.

dishonest adj. crafty, lying, misdealing, shady, shifty, two-tongued, untruthful.

disillusioned adj. bitter, borne down, downhearted, forlorn, hopelorn, let down, listless, lorn, overborne, saddened, sadder and wiser, shaken, sore.

disingenuous adj. crafty, not open, shifty, truthless, underhanded, unstraightforward,

disinterested adj. high-minded, knightly, self-forgetful, thoughtful, unselfish.

dislike v. to hate, loathe, mislike, have no liking for, have no time for, not abide, not stand, not care for, not like the look of, shrink from, shun, spurn.

dismay n. 1) fear, fright, dread, 2) bitterness, come-down, let-down, setback, upset.

disobedient adj. off-handed, pigheaded, self-willed, unbidden, untamed, wild, wilful.

disobey v. to give a deaf ear to, go one's own way, not do as one is told, not hearken, not heed/listento , play up, say no to, stand out, throw off the yoke.

disorganised adj. awry, all anyhow, untidy, upside down.

displace v. to cut out, draw out, pull out, put out, root out, send away, send flying, send out, shift, shove, shunt, sweep away, throw out, unsaddle, uproot.

displacement n. driving out, shift, throwing out, uprooting.

display n. 1) show, showing, 2) brazenness, shamelessness, idle show, showiness.

display v. to lay bare, make known, make a show of, put on a show, set out, show off.

disposal n. offloading, throwing away.

disproportionate adj. overdone, over much, too much, uneven, weighted.

dispute n. falling-out, fight, misunderstanding, bone to pick.

dispute v. to gainsay, answer back, fall out, speak out, speak up.

disreputable adj. evil, hardened, loathsome, mean, shabby, shady, shameful, shameless, unbecoming, unbridled, unworthy, wanton, wicked, wild, worthless.

disrespect n. churlishness, off-handedness, roughness, shortness, uncouthness.

dissatisfied adj. bitter, crabbed, fed up, fretful, unfulfilled.

dissident n. gainsayer, heckler, withstander.

dissociate v. to break away, have nothing to do with, stand against, spurn, withdraw.

dissuade v. to head off, hold one back, keep back, put off, quench, set against, shake, steer one away from, talk out of, warn, throw cold water on, wean away from.

distance n. 1) farness, length, span, spread, stretch, sweep, width, 2) coldness, coolness, frostiness, stiffness, standoffishness, unfriendliness.

distant adj. 1) far, faraway, far off, farther, 2) cold, forbidding, frosty, standoffish, unforthcoming, unfriendly, unwelcoming.

distinct adj. 1) like no other, marked, 2) black-and-white, for all to see, in high light, outstanding, shining, striking, unclouded, unhidden, well-marked, sharp, 3) heard, out loud, well-spoken.

distinction n. 1) marking out, 2) greatness, standing, worthship, 3) mark, name.

distinctive adj. marked, other, like no other, one on its own, outstanding.

distinguished adj. foremost, great, in the news, leading, not like, not as others are, outstanding, starring, talked of, well-known.

distraught adj. bestraught, forstraught, floored, shaken, unsettled.

distress n. aching, bitterness, broken-heartedness, hardship, heartache, heart-sickness, soreness, sorrow, weariness, woe, wretchedness.

distribute v. 1) to deal out, fordeal, dole out, give out, hand out, mete out, share out, 2) to spread, strew.

distribution n. handling, sharing out, spread, spreading.

district n. neighbourhood, neck of the woods, hundred, ward.

distrust v. to find hard to believe, misbelieve, have fears/misgivings, hold back, think twice, be wary of.

disturb v. to goad, harrow, harry, put out, unsettle, upset, worry.

disturbance n. ado, much ado, to-do, bane, burden, care, harrowing, heartache, unrest, unstillness, upset, weight on one's mind, worry.

disturbing adj. harrowing, unsettling, upsetting, weighing down, worrisome, worrying.

dither v. to beat about, be at a stand, be in two minds, hedge, play for time.

diverse adj. manifold, manykind, many-sided, other, sundry, unalike, unlike.

diversity n. many-sidedness, otherness, sundriness, unlikeness.

divide v. 1) to sunder, put asunder, come between, drive a wedge between, stand between, set against, unknot, untie, 2) to deal out, share, go halves, weigh out.

divine v. 1) to foresee, foreknow, foretell, forewarn, forween, see through, understand, be on to something, 2) to read one's hand, read the stars, read the tokens, soothsay.

division n. 1) sundering, cutting up, rending, sharing, 2) break, setting against, misunderstanding, soreness, sourness, 3) hundred, shire, arm (as in 'an arm of *government*').

divisive adj. souring, sundering, unsettling, unthreading, upsetting.

divorce n. sundering, putting away, broken word, forsaking, leaving, oath forsworn, unthreading.

divorce v. to break, put away, put asunder, forsunder, forswear, unthread, untie the knot, unweave.

doctor n. 1) healer, houseman, 2) learned man/woman, thinker.

doctrine n. belief, teaching, what one holds, lore.

document n. working *paper*, written witness, written work

dogmatic adj. forthright, hard-mouthed, small-minded, stiff, wilful.

domestic adj. home, home-keeping, home-loving, homely, household, housely, housewifely.

dominate v. 1) to bear hard on, do as one will, have the upper hand over, hold down, hold under, hold in the hollow of one's hand, keep under one's thumb, overcome, override, 2) to dwarf, overlook, overtop, stand over.

double adj. twice, twicefold, twofold, two-edged, two-sided, matching, twin.

doubt n. cold feet, fear, hedging, looking twice, misgiving, not knowing one's own mind, two-mindedness.

doubtful adj. 1) knotty, left open, moot, two-minded, 2) crafty, shady, shifty, slippery, two-tongued, underhand, unworthy.

dozen n. twelve.

draconian adj. hard, stern, strong, tough.

dragon n. 1) great fire-snake, great wyrm (worm), gold-ward, 2) fishwife, redhead, she-wolf, shrew, spitfire, vixen, witch.

drama n. 1) play, playcraft, show, 2) business/thing of life and death, day of reckoning, storm.

drastic adj. hard, searing, stern, strong, tough, unsparing.

dress n. clothes, clothing, shift.

dress v. to clothe, don one's clothes, get into, get one's clothes on, ready.

dressing n. 1) dip, 2) cloth-swathing.

drill n. 1) bit, 2) hardening, making ready, warm-up, work-out.

drill v. 1) to sink in, 2) to break in, drive, get into shape, hammer, harden, put through the mill, ready, take in hand, teach.

drug n. 1) healing draught, 2) draught that numbs.

due adj. 1) looked for, 2) becoming, bounden, right, rightful, well-earned, 3) outstanding, owed, owing, unsettled.

dumbfounded adj. struck dumb, amazed, bewildered, floored, knocked back, overcome, shaken, speechless, thunderstruck.

duplicity n. empty talk/words, hollowness, honeyed words, shiftiness, two-talking.

during adv. through, throughout, throughout the time of.

duty n. behoof, least one can do, right thing, troth, undertaking, what is up to one, what ought to be done, what is owing, word.

dynamic adj. driving, full-blooded, go-ahead, keen, lively, tireless, up-and-doing.

eager adj. alive, awake, hungry, thirsty, itching, keen, lively, on one's toes, quick, ready, up-and-doing, yearning.

ease n. having no cares/worries, rest, restfulness, all the time in the world, putting one's feet up, well-being.

ease v. 1) to lighten, unburden, take off one's shoulders, 2) to lessen, die down, dwindle, smoothe, soften, soothe.

easier adj. lighter, readier, smoother.

easily adv. far and away, readily, smoothly, straightforwardly, 'with one's eyes shut'.

easy adj. leaf-light, light, no sooner said than done, not hard, ready, soft, straightforward, 'all in a day's work'.

eccentric adj. off-beam, one and only, outlandish, out of step, wayward, weird.

ecology n. earthhome-lore.

economic adj. 1) business, trade, 2) towardly, wieldy, worthwhile.

economical adj. 1) marked down, not dear, 2) canny, careful, earnest, forgoing, mindful, minding the pence, spare, sparing, steady, watching the pennies.

economy n. 1) wealth-making framework, 2) care, carefulness, good housekeeping, good stewardship, sparingness.

ecstatic adj. beside oneself, afire, all-a-quiver, dizzy, giddy, gleeful, laughing, lively, sparkling, thrilled.

ecumenical adj. whole-churchly, worldwide, of the whole Christian world.

edition n. set, bound set.

editor n. reader, writer, leader-writer.

editorial n. leader, write-up.

educate v. to bring light to bear, open the mind, rear, teach.

educated adj. learned, book-learned, book-wise, taught, well-taught, deeply read, well-read, widely read.

education n. learning, teaching, upbringing.

educational adj. life-learning, light-bringing, mind-growing.

effect n. fall-out, follow-on, hangover, outcome, upshot, backwash.

effective adj. deft, good at, handy, quick, ready, telling, well up in.

effectively adv. 1) as good as, in all but name, in truth, 2) cleverly, deftly, readily, well.

effectiveness n. cleverness, handcleverness, deftness, quickness, readiness.

efficiency n. craftlikeness, going like clock-work, handcleverness, readiness.

efficient adj. clever, deft, good at, handy, many-sided, nimble, quick, ready.

effort n. hard work, one-mindedness, steadiness, tirelessness, whole-heartedness.

elaborate adj. 1) deep, highly wrought, knotted, winding, 2) showy.

elated adj. all-a-quiver, beaming, beside oneself, dizzy, flushed, giddy, heart-full, in seventh heaven, merry, on a high, sparkling, thrilled.

elect v. to back, choose, come down for, pick out, settle on.

election n. 1) choosing, picking, poll, show of hands, 2) (in Christian godlore) God's choosing of his own.

electric, electrical adj. 1) drive-giving, 2) fiery, heady, live, lively, stirring, thrilling.

element n. 1) that of which all earthly bodies are made (long held to be earth, fire, *air*, water), 2) bit, little bit, hint, slight hint, 3) set.

elementary adj. 1) everyday, homely, homespun, not hard, straightforward, unwrought, 2) backward, childish, raw, shallow.

eligible adj. 1) cut out for, fit, right, worthy, 2) free (to wed), worth thinking of.

eliminate v. to bring to naught, do away with, kill, put an end to, put down, slay, undo, unmake.

eloquent adj. 1) high-flown, high-flying, silver-tongued, spellbinding, stirring, word-wieldy, 2) meaningful, telling, well-put, well-worded.

elucidate v. to bring to light, draw forth, highlight, lay bare, lay open, open, open up, put a meaning on, set forth, shed/throw light upon, teach, unfold.

embarrassed adj. ashamed, forshamed, shamefast, shown up, withered.

embryonic adj. beginning, early, fledgling, unhewn, unshapen, unwrought.

emerge v. to arise, become known, break through/out, come forth/forward/out, come to light, stand forth.

emergency n. business of life and death, deep/hot water, meltdown, plight, storm, time to meet the truth.

emigrant n. incomer, newcomer, outsider, settler, homeless wanderer.

emission n. giving off/out, leak, outflow.

emotion n. feeling, strong/warm feeling, soft-heartedness, soul.

emotional adj. 1) feeling, heart-rending, heart-warming, stirring, thrilling, warm-hearted, 2) fiery, flighty, giddy, highly-strung, unsteady, up and down.

emphasis n. mark, say-so, weight.

emphasise v. to bring to the fore, draw out, drive home, dwell on, highlight, make one see/understand.

emphatic adj. downright, forthright, marked, outright, stark, striking, telling.

empire n. kingdom, great kingdom, high-kingdom, over-kingdom.

empirical adj. first-hand, straightforward, true to life, well-grounded.

employ v. 1) to hire, take on, 2) to bring to bear, bring into play, give to.

employee n. hand, hired hand, work-hand, worker, working man/woman, workman.

employer n. head, headman, foreman, hirer, leader, overseer, owner.

employment n. 1) hire, hiring, taking on, 2) business, business on hand, calling, line, livelihood, trade, work, daily work, life-work, walk of life, daily bread.

emulate v. to ape, behave like, follow the footsteps of, make oneself like, shadow, take after, take a leaf out of someone's book.

enable v. to forward, further, give a free hand, give someone the means/right, help on, let, make an opening/path for, open the door to, open/smooth the way, say yes to.

enchant v. to bewitch, fill with longing, spellbind, steal one's heart.

enclose v. 1) to beset, begird, gird about, ring about, hedge, lock in, shut in, 2) to put in, send with.

encounter n. 1) happening, meeting, 2) fight, onset, run-in, set to.

encounter v. 1) to come upon, light upon, meet, run into, 2) to go through, live through, undergo, 3) to fight, meet head on, pitch into.

encourage v. to hearten, put heart into, quicken, spur, stir up, strengthen, whet.

encouraging adj. heartening, stirring, strengthening.

endeavour v. to do one's best, do something about, give it one's all, have a go, pull hard, seek.

endorse v. 1) to back, give one's blessing, throw one's weight behind, uphold, 2) to put one's hand to, underwrite, witness.

endure v. to abide, keep on, outlast, stand fast, stand one's ground.

enemy n. foe, bitter foe, foeman, no friend, outsider.

energy n. drive, fire, go, hammering away, hard work, life, strength, warmth.

enforce v. to bend, bind, bring about, browbeat, drive, lead by the nose, make, override, put one's foot down, twist one's arm, wring from.

enforcement n. binding, browbeating, driving, fulfilling, overriding.

engage v. 1) to underwrite, 2) to betroth, bind, give/plight one's word, 3) to bewitch, busy, draw, fill/hold the mind, fill/take up one's time, grip, tie up, win, 4) to set forward, set going, 5) to book, do/clinch a deal, hire, take on, 6) to go in for, set about, take up, undertake, 7) to come to grips, fall on, fight with, meet, pitch into.

engagement n. 1) betrothal, plight, plighted word, troth, 2) meeting, undertaking, 3) set-to.

engine n. works.

engineer n. 1) craftsman, framer, maker, wright, 2) driver, handler, minder, worker.

engineer v. 1) to build, draft, frame, put together, set up, shape, think up, work out, 2) to bring about, hatch, set afoot, weave.

engineering n. craftsmanship, workmanship.

enhance v. to better, brighten up, heighten, strengthen, swell.

enigma n. dark/hard saying, deep or hidden word, knot, maze, riddle, teaser, web.

enigmatic adj. knotted, dark, shadowy, shrouded, thorny, unfathomed, beyond one, bewildering, over one's head, riddle-wrought.

enjoy v. 1) to be keen on, like, like well, love, wallow in, 2) to be blessed with, do what one likes with, have, hold, own.

enjoyment n. blessedness, bliss, full life, gladness, merry-making, well-being.

enmity n. bitter/hard feelings, coldness, hatred, loathing, soreness, unfriendliness.

enormous adj. great, far-stretching, high, roomy, tall, full-wide, broad-shouldered, great-limbed, heavy, hefty, strong, thickset.

enquire v. to ask, delve into, go into, look into.

ensure v. to settle.

enter v. 1) to go in/into, come into, drop in, set foot in, step in, walk in, darken the door, 2) to begin, go in for, set about, set out on, start, take up, begin/start work at, 3) to set down, put in writing, put down, write down, write up, take down, book.

enterprise n. 1) business, business on hand, undertaking, 2) boldness, daring, drive, liveliness, readiness, seeking.

entertain v. 1) to awake/stir laughter, make one laugh, make merry with, be witty, play with, take one out of oneself, tell a good tale, 2) to befriend, have to a meal, keep open house, make welcome, put up, 3) to bear/keep in mind, bethink, give thought to, hold, look on as, look upon, think about/over, weigh.

entertainment n. 1) gladdening, laughter, mirth, 2) game, play.

enthrall v. 1) to bewitch, draw, grip, lead on, hold spellbound, take someone's eye, 2) to awaken, bestir, fire up, madden, stir/warm the blood, thrill.

enthusiasm n. drive, earnestness, headiness, keenness, liveliness, sparkle, warmth.

enthusiastic adj. afire, all aglow, earnest, hearty, keen, lively, whole-hearted.

entire adj. downright, outright, out-and-out, sheer, thorough, thorough-going, utter.

entirely adv. all, fully, down to the ground, thoroughly, utterly, wholly.

entitle v. 1) to give the right to, 2) to call, name.

entrance n. door, doorway, gate, gateway, ingoing, inway, open door, opening, threshold, way in.

entrance v. to bewitch, draw, lead on, spellbind, take someone's eye, win.

entreaty n. asking, begging, beseeching, bidding, craving.

entry n. 1) door, gate, ingoing, inway, open door, opening, threshold, way in, 2) coming in, incoming, inflow.

envelope n. holder, sheath, sleeve.

envious adj. fretful, mean-minded, green-eyed, hungry, thirsty, restless, selfish.

environment n. 1) background, 'home', setting, 2) neighbourhood.

environmental adj. green.

envy n. misliking (of one who has greater gifts than oneself), craving, hunger, thirst, bitterness, restlessness, selfishness.

epidemic n. bane, growth, outbreak, spread, wave.

epidemic *adj.* far-reaching, far-stretching, full-wide, sweeping, widespread, wholesale.

epigram *n.* pithy saying, play upon words, witty saying.

episode *n.* 1) business, 2) bit, lot, share, length, 3) spell, step, time, while.

epitomise *v.* to body forth, bring out, highlight, put in a nutshell, set in outline.

equal *n.* brother, match, twin.

equal *adj.* 1) even, alike, like, evenly-matched, matched, matching, neither more nor less, no better no worse, all one, on a like footing, 2) even-handed, fair, right.

equality *n.* 1) evenhood, evenness, likeness, meetness, 2) even-handedness, fairness, rightness.

equally *adv.* evenly, likewise, as good as.

equation *n.* likeness, match.

equipment *n.* outfit, stock, tools, wherewithal.

equipped *adj.* all ready, fitted out, stocked up.

equivalent *n.* match, twin, offset, set-off.

equivalent *adj.* alike, of a kind, even, of like worth, worth-even, like for like, word-for-word.

era *n.* time span, timestretch, stretch of time, stream of time, time beginning with a key happening. (Thus 'the Christian era' is the time, told in years *Anno Domini*, beginning with the birth of Christ.)

erosion *n.* crumbling, eating away, gnawing away, grinding down, wearing, wearing away/down.

erratic *adj.* fitful, light-minded, shifting, uneven, unsteady, wayward.

error *n.* loose thinking, misreckoning, mistake, misunderstanding, oversight.

escape *v.* to fly, make off, run away, win free.

especially *adv.* above all, above all things, beyond telling, the more so, utterly.

essential *adj.* deep-rooted, inwoven, inwrought, key, main, needed, needful, not to be overlooked/spared.

essentially *adv.* at bottom, at heart, at root, in the main.

establish *v.* 1) to begin, build, set on its feet, set up, start, 2) to bear out, find out, make out, show, 3) to ground, root, put down roots, settle, strike root.

establishment *n.* 1) making, setting up, 2) business, house, trading house, setup, 3) building, house.

estate *n.* 1) acres, broad acres, grounds, holdings, lands, 2) belongings, goods, wealth, 3) footing, lot, standing, walk of life.

estimate *n.* reckoning, weighing up, worth-reckoning, worth-saying.

estimate *v.* to eye up, reckon, reckon up, take stock, weigh up, ween, work out.

estuary *n.* inlet, mouth, roadstead, tidefleet, fleet.

eternal *adj.* abiding, deathless, lasting, everlasting, unending.

eternity *n.* 1) afterlife, life everlasting, heaven, the hereafter, the next world, 2) endless time, endlessness, timelessness, time without end, everlastingness, never-endingness.

ethical *adj.* fair, fitting, good, high-minded, right, right-hearted, rightwise, true, upright, upstanding, worthy.

ethics *n.* goodness, high-mindedness, rightwiseness, uprightness.

euphemism *n.* eyewash, fair-wording, honey-speech, smooth-lip, softened wording.

euphemistic *adj.* soothing but soothless, soothing more than sooth, honey-lipped, smooth-lipped, soft-lipped.

evaluation *n.* reckoning, reading, weighing up, worth-reckoning, worth-saying.

evasive *adj.* deep, misdealing, misleading, shifty, slippery, two-edged, two-hearted, two-tongued, underhand, unstraightforward, winding.

event *n.* 1) business, happening, milestone, 2) games, meeting, show.

eventually *adv.* after all, all in good time, as things/times go, as the world goes, hereafter, in the end, in the fullness of time, in the long run, in time, later, not yet, some day, some time, sooner or later.

evidence *n.* 1) grounds, hearsay, hint, 2) marks, fingermarks, footmarks, tokens, 3) witness, word.

evident *adj.* before one's eyes, cut and dried, under one's nose, for all to see, in broad daylight, in the open, open and shut, right in the foreground, wide-open, written all over one.

evidently *adv.* as far as one can tell, at first sight, as like as not, belike, in all likelihood, most likely, no two ways about it, openly, outwardly, to the eye.

exact *adj.* aright, dead-on, lifelike, right, settled, straightforward, thorough, thorough-going, true, truthfast, word for word.

exacting *adj.* hard, tough, unbending, unsparing, unyielding.

exactly *adv.* carefully, mindfully, neither more nor less, rightly, thoroughly, truly, truthfully, to a hair, word for word.

exaggerate v. to deal in wonders, greaten, heighten, make overmuch of, make too much of, overdo, overdraw, overplay, <u>overreckon</u>, oversell, stretch the truth, draw the long bow, outstep the truth.

examination n. 1) (in law) hearing, 2) asking, delving, looking into, sifting, weighing, worth-weighing, 3) going-over, look-over, once-over.

examine v. to <u>delve</u> into, go deep into, go over, go/root/sift through, <u>seek</u> out.

example n. 1) *part* for whole, 2) framework, light (for the path), pathfinder, 3) teaching, warning.

excel v. to be good at, earn/make a name, go beyond, <u>outdo</u>, outplay, shine, stand high, stand well with, take the lead.

excellent adj. good, goodly, <u>great</u>, matchless, outstanding, rich, <u>worthful</u>, <u>worthy</u>.

except conj. aside from, but for, let alone, other than, outside of, short of.

exception n. one-off, wonder.

excess n. overflow, over-fulness, overload, overspill, overweight.

excessive adj. far-going, flooding, going too far, more than one looked for, <u>overflowing</u>, overfull, overlong, overmuch, too many, too much of a good thing.

exchange n. 1) talk, word and answer, 2) business deal, dealing, buying and selling, trade.

excitable adj. highly-strung, hot-headed, like tinder, <u>lively</u>, on edge, edgy, quick-hearted, restless, out for the thrills, thrill-loving, thrill-seeking, unsteady.

excited adj. a-quiver, flushed, all of a flutter, overwrought, restless, thrilled, worked up.

excitement n. headiness, heat, stirring up, thrill, working up.

exciting adj. gripping, heady, heart-stirring, heart-swelling, heart-thrilling, thrilling, sparkling, stirring, soul-stirring, striking.

exclusive adj. 1) hidebound, narrow, 2) better, hand-picked, only one of its kind, wholly worthy, wonderful.

exclusively adv. alone, fully, only, wholly.

excuse n. let-out, grounds, shift, whitewash, why and wherefore.

excuse v. 1) to bear with, forgive, not be hard upon, overlook, soften, whitewash, wink at, 2) to free, let off, let out.

executive n. head, key man/woman, leading player, overseer, steersman.

exercise n. doings, work-out.

exercise v. 1) to bring to bear, do the work of, handle, make play with, stand in for, wield, work, 2) to ready oneself, warm up, work out, 3) to burden, harrow, <u>worry</u>.

exhausted adj. dog-tired, overworked, tired out, <u>weary</u>, worn, fordone.

exhaustive adj. full, lengthy, thoroughgoing, with nothing left out/missing.

exhibit v. 1) to put on show, set before one's eyes, set out, show, show off, 2) to bear the marks of/stamp of, bespeak, betoken.

exhibition n. show, showing.

exist v. 1) to be, draw breath, have life and breath, live, walk the earth, 2) to eke out a living, get by, keep alive, make ends meet, keep one's head above water.

existence n. 1) being, givenness, suchness, thatness, life, 2) way of life.

existing adj. 1) alive, living, under the sun, 2) given, here-and-now, standing.

exit n. 1) way out, door, doorway, gate, gateway, outgate, 2) farewell, going away, going out, out-going, goodbye, leave-taking, starting out, setting out.

expand v. 1) to <u>build up</u>, greaten, grow, make great strides, swell, wax, widen, 2) to open, open out, outspread, spread, spread out, stretch, stretch out, unfold.

expanding adj. broadening, growing, opening out, spreading, strengthening, stretching, swelling, waxing, widening.

expansion n. build-up, growth, spread, stretching, swelling, unfolding, widening.

expect v. to hope for, be ready for, foresee, keep an eye out for, look out for, see it coming, think likely, watch out for, ween.

expectation n. <u>foresight</u>, belief, hope, likelihood, reckoning, looking forward, well-grounded hope.

expel v. 1) to drive away, drive out, outlaw, shut the door on, <u>spurn</u>, throw out, 2) to pitch, send flying/headlong, sweep before one.

expenditure n. buying, outgoings, outlay, overheads.

expense n. dearness, outgoings, outlay, overheads, worth, high worth.

expensive adj. dear, dearly bought, pretty penny, steep, stiff.

experience n. 1) arising, becoming, happening, outcome, shadowing forth, showing, upshot, 2) breadth/depth/reach of mind, knowledge, know-how, lifemanship, ripe knowledge/wisdom, understanding.

experience v. to come up against, feel, go through, have, know, live through, meet with, run into, undergo.

experienced adj. hardened, knowing, heedful, watchful, ripened, weathered, worldly, worldly-wise, well up in.

experiment n. reckoning/weighing the fors and againsts, work-out, dry run.

experiment v. to bend one's mind to, delve into, feel one's way, follow up, give one's mind to, go into, look into, seek for knowledge/truth, fathom, sift, thresh out, winnow, work through.

experimental adj. ground-breaking, new-fangled, new-fledged, new-fleshed, unknown.

expert n. leading light, shining light, one in the know, wiseman.

explain v. to give an answer, open up, put into words, set forth, set out, teach, throw light on, unfold.

explanation n. answer, ground, light, meaning, the why and wherefore.

explicit adj. 1) down in writing, meaningful, straightforward, 2) bold, daring, downright, forthright, open, outspoken, shameless.

exploration n. combing, delving, hunt, hunting, rooting, seeking, sifting, seeing the world.

explore v. to comb, delve into, feel one's way, follow up, find out about, go deep into, hunt for, look for, look into, open up, seek, wish to know, work over.

exposed adj. 1) bare, open to, wide-open, unshielded, 2) shamed, shown up.

exposure n. 1) baring, laying open, showing, 2) frostbite.

expound v. to bring/draw forth, bring to life/light, bring out, draw out, hold forth, open up, put a meaning on, set forth, shed/throw light upon, teach, unfold.

express adj. 1) outright, thorough, true, truthfast, utterly alike, 2) fast, flying, quick, speedy, swift, as the wind, quick as lightning/thought.

express v. to bring out, find words for, make known, mean, put, put into words, put words together, say, set forth, speak, bespeak, highlight, tell, unfold, word.

expression n. 1) look, meaning, shaping, showing, token, unfolding, 2) saying, speech, word, wording.

expressive adj. well-worded, lively, telling, flowing, meaningful, outspoken, pithy, quick, ready, striking, strong, strongly worded.

exquisite adj. 1) bewitching, bright, comely, elf-fair, lovely, queenly, shapely, willowy,

winning, 2) biting, bitter-sweet, harrowing, keen, sharp, 3) high-wrought, matchless, outstanding, rich.

extend v. to broaden, greaten, lengthen, widen, build up, let out, make longer, draw out, spin out, stretch out, stretch, run on, bestride, straddle, go as far as, reach, span, spread, spread out.

extension n. 1) broadening, growth, growing out, spreading, outspreading, swelling, unfolding, waxing, widening, 2) arm.

extensive adj. far-reaching, full-wide, great, lengthy, overflowing, thorough, thoroughgoing, widespread.

extent n. breadth, height, length, width, reach, span, spread, sweep.

external adj. outer, outermost, outside, outward.

extortion n. foul play, grasping, theft by means of threats.

extra adj. 1) further, more, new, other, 2) above one's needs, over and above, leftover, needless, unneeded, on one's hands, spare.

extraordinary adj. 1) unheard of, unwonted, weird, out of this world, 2) amazing, beyond belief, earth-shaking, outstanding, stirring, striking, wonderful.

extremely adv. greatly, highly, markedly, overly, utterly.

fabric n. 1) cloth, warp and woof, weave, web, 2) frame, framework, stonework.

face n. side, foreside, outerside, likeness, look.

face v. 1) to look onto, overlook, look out on, give onto, 2) to meet with, deal with, come up against, meet head-on.

facilitate v. to forward, further, help on, let, make an opening/path for, open the way for, put one in the way of, smooth the path/way of, speed.

facility n. 1) readiness, smoothness, straightforwardness, wieldiness, 2) craft, deftness, quickness, readiness.

fact n. finding, last word, truth, gospel truth, naked truth, sworn truth, not a dream, outcome, upshot, thatness.

factor n. that which goes to bring about some deed or happening.

factory n. mill, works, workshop.

fail v. 1) to fall by the wayside, fall down, fall short, give out, ground, lose, miss, run aground, 2) to break one's word, forsake, leave high and dry, let down, 3) to break down, cut out, die, give up, stop, stop working, 4) (of a business) to fold, go out of business, go under, be wound up, sink, 5) to die away, dim, dwindle, sicken, wane.

failure *n.* 1) falling short, overthrow, loss, washout, 2) breakdown, breaking-off, cutting out, let-down, shut-down, 3) also-ran, has-been, lame-duck, loser, write-off.

faint *adj.* 1) dim, half-heard, half-seen, soft, tongueless, 2) slight, 3) half-hearted, lukewarm, unsteadfast, 4) dizzy, dog-weary, done for, fordone, giddy, light-headed, more dead than alive, tired out, wan, washed out, way-worn.

fairy *n.* elf, black/dark elf, down (*mountain*) elf, light elf, sea-elf, wood elf.

faith *n.* belief, troth, straightforwardness, uprightness.

faithful *adj.* 1) steadfast, true-hearted, 2) lifelike, true, truthful, word for word, 3) believing, godly, holding to the truth, heavenly-minded, otherworldly, unworldly.

faithless *adj.* fickle, truthless, untrue, untruthful, unbelieving, untrothful, worldly.

false *adj.* 1) hollow, misleading, mistaken, 2) misdealing, slippery, truthless, underhand, untrue, untruthful, 3) shallow, sham, 4) lying, smooth-spoken, smooth-tongued, two-hearted, two-tongued.

familiar *adj.* 1) everyday, well-beaten/trodden/worn, home, household, oft-heard, oft-seen, stock, well-known, wonted, 2) dear, friendly, near, open, 3) bold, brazen, forward, free, overfree.

family *n.* 1) house, household, kin, kindred, kinsfolk, folk, next of kin, kith and kin, kinsman, kinswoman, kinsmen, one's nearest and dearest, one's own flesh and blood, stock, 2) forebears, forefathers, blood, line, 3) brood, children, little ones, offspring, young, aftercomers, afterkin, 4) kind, network.

famous *adj.* great, high, name-known, well-known, widely-known, in all mouths, in the news, on every tongue, starring.

fanatical *adj.* bent, blind, burning, deaf, hard-headed, hard-mouthed, headstrong, hidebound, hot-headed, hot-hearted, leathery, mad, narrow-minded, one-sided, stiff-necked, twisted, unbending, unyielding, warped, wild, wilful.

fantastic *adj.* amazing, new-fangled, outlandish, out of this world, unearthly, unwonted, weird, wonderful.

farm, farm-stead *n.* steading, holding, smallholding, croft, fields, meadland.

farm *v.* to till/work the land, delve, grow crops, breed stock, herd cows/sheep.

farmer *n.* acreman, crofter, earth-tiller, smallholder, grazier, herdsman, stock-breeder/rearer, wool-grower.

fascinating *adj.* bewitching, fetching, thrilling, winning.

fashion *n.* cut, last word, latest thing, look, new look, trend, way.

fashionable *adj.* clothes-aware, smart, trendsetting, in the swim.

fate *n.* doom, end, foreshadowing, hidden hand, lot, wyrd.

fault *n.* 1) falling short, feet of clay, misdoing, 2) breakdown, breaking-off, shut-down, 3) makeshift, mistake, 4) chine, chink, cleft, cut, break, furrow, rent.

favour *n.* forbearingness, friendliness, goodwill, kindness, light hand, mildness.

favour *v.* to back, bring forward, bring on, care for, choose, forward, further, go for, have a heart/kindness for, help, like best/better, make much of, pull strings for, side with, think well of.

favourable *adj.* 1) looking good/hopeful, fair, heaven-sent, timely, towardly, 2) friendly, helpful, kind, kindly, understanding, welcoming.

favourite *n.* beloved, darling/dearling, dear, first love, near friend, apple of one's eye.

favourite *adj.* best-loved, dearest, most-liked.

feature *n.* 1) cut, mark, hall-mark, trade-mark, stamp, 2) leader, writing, write-up, 3) crowd puller, draw, highlight.

February *n.* Cole-month, Kale-month, Sol-month, 'Fill-ditch'.

fell (*mountain*) *n.* height, highland, hill, ridge, moorland ridge, peak, upland, wild-land.

female *n.* lady, maiden, wench, wife, woman.

female *adj.* she-, womanish, woman's.

feminine *adj.* 1) (of being) ladylike, maidenly, queenly, sweet, winning, womanly, 2) (of looks) bewitching, comely, fair, heavenly, lovely, willowy, winsome.

ferment *n.* ado, stir, storm, to-do, unrest, upheaving, uproar.

ferry *v.* to bear folk/goods/wains over a *river*, or from one haven to another, to run between havens.

festival *n.* field day, great day, highday, holiday, holy day.

fiasco *n.* breakdown, let-down, misfire, overthrow, undoing, unmaking, wash-out, wild goose hunt.

fibre *n.* cloth, thread, wisp.

fiction *n.* 1) tale, light reading, 2) lying, untruth, wishful thinking.

fierce adj. afire, bloodthirsty, burning, fiery, hot-blooded, hot-headed, quick-hearted, untamed, wild.

figurative adj. forlikening.

figure n. 1) build, cut, frame, 2) likeness, outline, shadow, shape, 3) leader, somebody, worthy, 4) drawing, framework, 5) (*character, symbol*) marker, staff, token, 6) (*sum*) end-rime, rime-tally, tale, tellship, worth, 7) forlikening, given-meaning (*metaphor*), word-play.

file n. 1) binder, folder, 2) working *papers*, 3) (of a body of men) line, row, string.

final adj. 1) end, last, latest, 2) over and done with, played out, settled.

finally adv. 1) at last, at the last, at long last, lastly, at length, after a long time, in the end, endly, in the fullness of time, in the long run, to the bitter end, when all is said and done, 2) for all time, for ever, for good, no two ways about it, once and for all.

finance n. 1) backing, holding, lending, wherewithal, 2) business.

finance v. to back, float, lend, underwrite.

financial adj. business.

financing n. underwriting.

fine adj. 1) good, goodly, <u>great</u>, matchless, outstanding, wonderful, worthwhile, sterling, upright, <u>worthful</u>, <u>worthy</u>, 2) good-looking, handsome, <u>lovely</u>, pretty, striking, 3) high-stepping, lordly, overweening, standoffish, uppish, 4) rich, sparkling, 5) filmy, gossamer, light, sheer, slight, thin, thread-like, wispy, 6) honed, keen-edged, sharp, 7) clever, keen-minded, quick, <u>sharp</u>, 8) dead-on, right, true, straight, thorough, 9) (of *reasoning*) narrow, 10) (of the weather) bright, cloudless, dry, fair, set fair, sunny, 11) (of health) hale, healthy, hearty, in good health, well.

finish v. to break off, end, leave off, play out, see through, settle, <u>stop</u>.

firm adj. settled, <u>steadfast</u>, steady, <u>abiding</u>, steely, <u>strong</u>, unshaken, <u>unyielding</u>.

firmly adv. doughtily, earnestly, manfully, steadfastly, steadily, strongly.

fix v. 1) to bind, fasten, make fast, root, stick, tie, 2) to choose, name, set, settle, 3) to put back together, put right, see to, set right.

flame n. 1) brightness, fire, fire-light, glow, light, spark, 2) fire, keenness, warmth.

flash n. 1) (of light) beam, blaze, flicker, gleam, shaft, spark, sparkle, streak, 2) burst, outburst, outbreak, show.

flash v. 1) to beam, blaze, flicker, gleam, glisten, light up, sparkle, 2) to fly, shoot by, speed by, sweep by, tear along, 3) to show quickly.

flat adj. 1) even, flush, trodden, unbroken, 2) laid down, low-lying, lying/stretched at full length, spread out, 3) (of such as a box) shallow, not deep, 4) (of such as a *fee*) set, settled, 5) blown out, empty, 6) downhearted, drained, tired out, <u>weary</u>, foreworn, worn out, 7) mild, milk-and-water, tame, thin, watery, wishy-washy, 8) off-key, off-pitch, 9) <u>dreary</u>, dry, grey, heavy, leaden, lifeless, limping, 10) glassy, smooth, still, 11) (of a 'no') downright, outright, out-and-out, straight.

flat n. haugh, marsh, marshland, salt-marsh, wash.

flatter v. 1) to <u>bewitch</u>, fawn on, lay it on thick, make much of, not spare one's blushes, overdo it, smooth, soothe, toady to, 2) to become, do something for, set off.

flexible adj. 1) lissom, lithe, springy, stretchy, willowy, bendsome, 2) open, quick, ready to take another look, ready to think again, ready-witted, shrewd, 3) <u>two-minded</u>, wieldy, yielding.

flourish v. to blossom, <u>do well</u>, grow, make great strides, ripen, rise, spread, strengthen, swell, wax, <u>overflow</u>.

flourishing adj. blossoming, doing well, going strong, growing, riding high, rising, spreading, up and coming, on the up and up.

flower n. 1) blossom, 2) best, chosen few, heart, height, nonesuch, peak, pick.

flower v. to be out, blossom, burst forth, open, put forth, unfold, 2) to <u>do well</u>, fare well, greaten, grow, spread.

fluent adj. flowing, ready, ready-worded, running on, smooth, smooth-spoken.

fluid n. sap, water.

fluid adj. 1) flowing, melted, running, runny, streaming, watery, 2) floating, shapeless, <u>shifting</u>, unshapen.

flux n. 1) flow, flowing, inflow, outflow, 2) restlessness, unrest, stir.

focus n. 1) hearthstead, 2) heart, kernel.

focused adj. <u>earnest</u>, mindful, steady, thorough, tireless, unshaken, unswerving.

fog n. dimness, greyness, mist.

foggy adj. dim, grey, misty, shadowy, thick.

foil n. thin leaf (of silver, tin or such).

foil v. to forestall, hamstring, <u>hinder</u>, outwit, set at naught, <u>stop</u>, <u>withstand</u>.

fool n. addle-head, clod, half-wit, know-nothing, <u>witling</u>, wooden-head.

fool v. to get the better of, have one on, hoodwink, make game of, <u>mislead</u>, outwit, pull the wool over one's eyes, string one along, take in.

foolhardy adj. headstrong, <u>heedless</u>, rash, reckless.

foolish adj. <u>witless</u>, unwise, unwitful, dim-witted, half-witted, slow-witted, addle-headed, empty-headed, soft-headed.

force n. 1) might, strength, life-strength, weight, 2) arm-twisting, browbeating, overriding, 3) drive, fire, 4) weaponed body, 5) (in a business) hands, workfolk, work-team, 6) (of words) bearing, meaning.

force v. to bear hard on, bend, bring about, browbeat, drive into, <u>hold down</u>, overbear, override, shape.

forceful adj. 1) bold, driving, fiery, full-blooded, <u>lively</u>, lusty, strong, 2) (of words) pithy, strongly-worded, telling.

foreign adj. outborn, otherlandish, outlandish, oversea-ish, outland.

foreigner n. otherlander, outlander, outsider, incomer, newcomer.

forest n. wood, woods, woodland, weald, weald-land, holt.

form n. 1) build, cut, frame, framework, kind, likeness, look, look of things, set, shape, stamp, way, 2) (in a school) set, stream, year, 3) done thing, wont, 4) fettle, health, trim, 5) sheet (of *paper*, to be filled in), 6) bench.

form v. 1) to bring about, build, draw up, frame, make, make into, make up, shape, put into shape, put together, set up, stamp, think up, 2) to come into being, grow, rise, settle, take shape, 3) to bring up, rear, shape, teach.

formal adj. by the book, set, starched, starchy, stickling, stiff, unbending.

formation n. building, framing, making, setting up, shaping, starting, set.

formula n. 1) way (for doing something), 2) wording, word-set.

fortunate adj. 1) blessed, bright, heaven-sent, 2) doing well, rich, rising, <u>wealthy</u>, well-off, 3) helpful, timely

fortunately adv. beyond one's dreams.

fortune n. 1) hidden hand, lot, <u>wyrd</u>, 2) <u>wealth</u>, riches, wherewithal.

found v. to begin, bring into being, build, lay the groundwork, set going, set on its feet, settle, set up, start.

foundation n. 1) beginning, bottom, footing, grounding, groundsel/ground-sill, groundstone, groundwork, staddle, 2) ground, heart, key, root, mainstay, 3) setting up, starting.

fraction n. 1) bit, little bit, mite, shred, whit, 2) cut, share.

frank adj. 1) <u>bold</u>, downright, <u>forthright</u>, free, heart-to-heart, <u>open</u>, outspoken, 2) out-and-out, thoroughgoing, utter, whole-hearted.

frantic adj. at one's wits' end, beside oneself, <u>bewildered</u>, forstraught, harrowed, hot-headed, mad, horn-mad, overwrought, <u>shaken</u>, stormy, unsteady, wild.

freight n. goods, lading, load, ware.

frequency n. harping, oftenness, run, steadiness.

frequent v. to be found at, go often to, hang about.

frequent adj. daily, everyday, oft, oft-coming, oft-times, thick-coming, wonted.

frequently adv. again and again, at all times, day after day, often, many times, many a time, much, night and day, not seldom, over and over again, oft, ofttimes, oftentimes, oft-readily.

fresh adj. 1) new, brand-new, new-fangled, new-fleshed, new-made, forward-looking, go-ahead, from nowhere, ground-breaking, 2) further, more, other, 3) 'green', raw, unfledged, young, youthful, 4) bold, brazen, forward, gamesome, free, overfree, light-hearted, 5) (of foods) undried, unsalted, not smoked, 6) (of water) not salt or bitter, 7) clean, cleanly, good, shining, 8) bright, dewy, fair, glowing, healthy, 9) clean-handed, wholesome, 10) (of the wind) blowy, cold, cool, keen, lively, sharp, strong.

friction n. 1) fretting, grazing, wearing away, 2) bad blood, bad feeling, hard feelings, no love lost.

front n. 1) fore, head, lead, start, top, 2) foreside, outer side, 3) foreground, 4) (at the seaside) strand-walk, 5) field (of war), firing line, first line, forward line, 6) bearing, look, show, 7) blind, mask, show.

front adj. first, foremost, forward, head, headmost, lead, leading, topmost.

frontier n. gateway, threshold, back of beyond, mark-lands, outer edge, outlands.

fruit n. 1) crop, growth, harvest, output, yield, 2) brain-child, handiwork, outcome, outgrowth, work of one's hands.

frustrate v. 1) to <u>madden</u>, make one's blood seethe, 2) to forestall, hamstring, <u>hinder</u>, <u>stop</u>.

fuel n. 1) coal, wood, firewood, tinder, 2) food, 3) goad, prick, spark, spur.

fun n. good time, mirth, play, playfulness, horseplay.

function n. 1) business, field, line, 2) gathering, do, merrymaking, night out.

function v. 1) to be in business, go, run, work, 2) to behave, do the work of, stand in for.

functional adj. going, in play, ready, up and doing/running, working, hard-wearing.

fund n. hoard, holding, stock, wealth-hoard, wealth-stock.

fund v. to back, float, lend, underwrite.

fundamental adj. deep down, deep-rooted, going to the root, innermost, inward, inwoven, inwrought, key, main, underlying, weighty.

funeral n. burying, laying to rest.

funny adj. 1) laughter-making, lively, merry, playful, rich, witty, 2) mazed, not right in the head, outlandish, out of the way, uncanny, weird and wonderful, wildered in one's wits, 3) dizzy, giddy, light-headed, not well, sick, under the weather.

furious adj. 1) wrathful, 2) burning, hot-blooded, hot-hearted, mad, maddened, quick-hearted, wild, 3) headlong, heedless, over-bold, over-daring, rash, reckless.

furnish v. 1) to bestow, give out, hand out, 2) to fit out, make ready, stock.

furniture n. goods, household goods, house fittings, belongings, things.

future n. aftertime, aftertide, forthcoming-time, hereafter, hither days, coming days, what lies ahead, outlook.

future adj. about to be, ahead, coming, forthcoming, in the offing, in the wind, later, nearing, near in time, nigh, overhanging, to be, to come, yet to come.

gain v. 1) to get in one's hand, clutch, grip, fasten on, gather, hook, land, net, win 2) to win ground, reach one's goal, get there, fetch up at, make headway, make land.

gallery n. 1) upstairs seating or walkway (in a church or playhouse), 'the gods', 2) those in the playhouse *gallery* (playgoers, listeners, onlookers), 3) room or building for works of craftsmanship, 4) boring, cutting, shaft, underground way.

garage n. 1) lock-up, outhouse, wain-house, 2) roadside fill-up.

garden n. grounds, yard, greenyard.

gasp v. to fight for breath, heave, lose one's wind, puff.

gay adj. 1) blithe, bright, carefree, gamesome, gleeful, light-hearted, light-minded, lightsome, lively, playful, sparkling, sunny, 2) bright-hued, lively, rich, showy.

gaze v. to be all eyes, follow with the eyes, drink in, look at/on, open one's eyes wide, stand and stare, stare at, stare hard, watch, stand in amaze, stare in wonder.

general n. field-leader, field-lord.

general adj. broad, over-all, set, stock, widespread.

generally adv. all in all, in the long run, mainly, overall.

generate v. to beget, bring about, bring to life, give rise to, make, quicken.

generation n. 1) akin-in-time folk (that is, the young/younger folk, the middle-yeared folk, the old/older folk), 2) lifespan, lifetime, days, time.

generosity n. goodness, great-heartedness, kindness, open-handedness, open-heartedness, selflessness, unselfishness.

generous adj. free, open-handed, great-hearted, unsparing, unstinting.

genius n. 1) other self, 2) bent, leaning, 3) brain/s, cleverness, insight, quickness, sharpness, wit, 4) brainbox, great mind, highbrow, one in a thousand, thinker, wonder child, lore-smith.

gentle adj. 1) forbearing, kind, kind-hearted, kindly, lamb-like, loving, mild, ruthful, soft, soft-hearted, sweet, warm-hearted, 2) light, lithe-like, slight, soothing.

gentleman n. man of his word, fair player, true man, 'true knight', man about town.

gentlewoman n. lady.

gently adv. lightly, mildly, softly, soothingly, sweetly, whisperingly, yieldingly.

genuine adj. 1) true, true to life, true as steel, true-bred, 2) heartfelt, hearty, earnest, whole-hearted, mean what one says, 3) steady, straight, straightforward, open.

gesture n. 1) beck, by-play, clenched fist, clenching/gritting one's teeth, look in one's eyes, stamp of the foot, tearing one's hair, wagging one's forefinger, wave, wink, wringing one's hands, 2) mark/token (of goodwill).

giant n. ent, oak of a man.

gigantic adj. great, broad-shouldered, entish, great-limbed, heavy, high, mighty, strong, thick, thickset.

gingerly adv. carefully, heedfully, mindfully, warily, watchfully, watching one's step.

gist n. burden, heart, kernel, marrow, meaning, pith, long and the short of it.

glance n. look, quick look.

glance v. 1) to glimpse, look, 2) to dip into, leaf through, run/thumb through.

glimmer *n.* dim/soft light, flickering, glowing, shimmering.

glint *n.* flicker/play of light, <u>gleam</u>, shimmer, shine, sparkle, twinkle.

gloat *v.* to crow over, <u>shame</u>.

glory *n.* brightness, high name, high standing, weightiness, <u>worth</u>, worthfulness, worthiness, worthship, undying name, deathlessness.

gorgeous *adj.* 1) ablaze, aglow, bright, bright-hued, gleaming, glowing, rich, showy, 2) good-looking, great, handsome, <u>lovely</u>, matchless, outstanding, wonderful.

govern *v.* 1) to handle, lead, lay down the law, make laws, oversee, wield, 2) to bridle, get the better of, tame.

government *n.* folk-body, leadership.

grace *n.* 1) becomingness, flow, readiness, smoothness, 2) forbearingness, <u>kindness</u>, light hand, mildness, 3) (in Christian teaching) God's unlooked-for kindness towards sinners, 4) thanks, thanksgiving.

graceful *adj.* becoming, comely, elf-fair, flowing, lithe, <u>lovely</u>, ready, smooth, willowy.

gracious *adj.* 1) <u>friendly</u>, kindly, knightly, open, warm, winsome, <u>winning</u>, 2) kind, loving, warm-hearted, 3) becoming, fair, flowing, handsome.

grade *n.* 1) brand, hue, kind, make, pitch, 2) mark, 3) footing, rung, standing, step, stream.

grade *v.* to brand, mete, reckon, sift out, weigh.

gradually *adv.* bit by bit, drop by drop, creepingly, evenly, little by little, slowly, steadily, step by step.

graduate *n.* scholar.

graduate *v.* 1) to get through, 2) to <u>do well</u>, get ahead, get on, go forward, rise, 3) to mark off.

grain *n.* 1) grist, kernel, seed, 2) barley, corn, oats, rye, wheat, 3) bit, chip, crumb, mite, mote, shred, speck, whit, 4) growth lines (of wood), thread, weave.

grand *adj.* amazing, breathtaking, great, high, high and mighty, outstanding, stirring, striking, <u>wonderful</u>, <u>worthy</u>.

grant *n.* bequest, hand-out, share-out.

grant *v.* 1) to bequeath, bestow, give, give away, hand out, hand over, make over, settle on, 2) to <u>acknowledge</u>, give way, go half-way to meet, meet one's wishes, do as asked, own, say yes, yield.

graphic *adj.* bold, lively, sharp, striking, telling, well-drawn, well-worded.

grateful *adj.* beholden, thankful.

gratitude *n.* thankfulness, thanks, hearty thanks, thanksgiving.

grave *adj.* 1) grim, cold, cool, forbidding, gloomy, stern, stiff, thoughtful, unlaughing, unsmiling, 2) deep, <u>earnest</u>, great, life-and-death, weighty.

grief *n.* <u>sorrow</u>, heart-break, heart-sickness, sadness, <u>woe</u>, wretchedness.

grievance *n.* axe to grind, chip on the shoulder, gripe, moan, whinge.

group (*club, society*) *n.* brood, cluster, set, team.

grudge *n.* bitterness, hard feelings, hate, <u>hatred</u>, misliking

grudging *adj.* 1) backward, dragging heels, half-hearted, holding back, <u>loath</u>, slow, unforthcoming, unminded, unready, unwilling, <u>two-minded</u>, 2) churlish, grasping, hard-fisted, hoarding, <u>mean</u>, selfish, shabby, sparing, stingy, tight-fisted, unfriendly.

grumble *v.* to bellyache, bleat, croak, groan, moan, bemoan, whine, whinge, be sorry for oneself, have a chip on one's shoulder, not know when one is well off.

guard *n.* look-out, watch, watchman,

guard *v.* to keep an eye on, keep watch, keep one's eye on, look after, look to, see to, shield, watch over, watch out for.

guess *n.* 1) feeling, shaft of insight, shot in the dark, 2) belief, thought.

guess *v.* 1) to fathom, <u>foresee</u>, work out, 2) to believe, dare say, forween, ween, moot, put forward, reckon, think.

guidance *n.* input, leading, steer, teaching, word of warning, word/s of wisdom.

guide *n.* 1) forerunner, pathfinder, wayfinder, way-leader, 2) friend, redesman, steersman, teacher, 3) framework, key, list, listing, marker, waymark, 4) leading star, light (for the path), teaching.

guide *v.* 1) to lead along the way, shepherd, show the way, 2) to bring light to bear, help, open/shape the mind, rear, sow the seeds, steer, teach, 3) to mark out.

gullible *adj.* over-ready to believe, readily taken in, born yesterday, childish, green.

guy *n.* man, wight.

habit *n.* leaning, steadiness, the old way, way, wont.

hamper *v.* to hamstring, <u>hinder</u>, make it hard for, put a drag on.

hardy *adj.* doughty, manly, stalwart, <u>steadfast</u>, steely, <u>strong</u>, tough, unshrinking.

harmony *n.* 1) friendship, goodwill, like-mindedness, thinking alike, understanding, good understanding, 2) song, harp-song, 3) evenness, fitness, wholeness.

haste *n.* 1) quickness, speed, swiftness, 2) heedlessness, rashness, recklessness, unwariness.

hastily *adv.* 1) quickly, swiftly, 2) rashly, recklessly.

hasty *adj.* headlong, heedless, hot-headed, rough and ready, running, shoving.

haunt *v.* 1) to fill/hold the mind, not let one forget/sleep, weigh on, 2) to bewitch, fill with fear, frighten, hang over, harrow, hound, 3) to abide, be wont, live.

havoc *n.* free for all, hell let loose, madhouse, rough house, storm, to-do, upheaving.

hazardous *adj.* baleful, harmful, threatening.

hectic *adj.* all a-doing, all anyhow, hard at it, much coming and going, on the go, up to one's eyes, wild.

heritage *n.* bequest, birthright, folk-wealth.

hero *n.* 1) deed-doer, fighting man, great man, man of mark, worthy, 2) (at the play) leading man, leading light, star.

heroic *adj.* bold, daring-hearted, doughty, dreadless, fearless, knightly, manful.

heroine *n.* fighter, high lady, 2) (at the play) leading lady, leading light, queen of hearts, star.

hesitant *adj.* 1) two-minded, at a loss, bestraught, forstraught, brought to a stand, 2) loath, backward, dragging heels, half-hearted, hanging back, unminded.

hesitate *v.* to back away, beat about, be at a stand, be in two minds, blow hot and cold, falter, hang back, hedge, hold back, play for time.

hijack *v.* to steal, take over.

historian *n.* time-writer.

historic *adj.* 1) old, olden, old-world, time-worn, 2) deathless, great, named.

historical *adj.* early, olden, time-wise, true, well-grounded.

history *n.* tales of the years, time-writing.

honest *adj.* aright, right, upright, open, straightforward, thorough, true, truthful.

honour *n.* good name, good standing, high standing, greatness, weight, weightiness, worth, worthiness, worship.

honour *v.* to speak well of, think highly of, think everything of, look up to.

horde *n.* crowd, drove, swarm, throng.

horizon *n.* 1) earth-hem, earth-rim, sea-rim, farthest reach, field of sight, outer/outside edge, the uttermost, 2) ken, stretch.

horrible *adj.* dreadful, foul, frightful, hateful, hellish, loathsome.

horrific *adj.* dreadful, frightful, ghastly, harrowing, hellish, nightmarish.

hospice *n.* care-house, home for the dying.

hospital *n.* sickhouse.

host *n.* 1) fighting body, 2) drove, sea of, swarm, throng, wealth of, world of.

host *n.* 1) innkeeper, landlord, 2) (of a *radio* or *TV* show) lead.

hostile *adj.* bitter, cold, fiend-like, hate-filled, hating, prickly, unfriendly, unkind.

hostilities *n.* bloodshed, fighting, strife, war, warfare.

hotel *n.* inn, rest house, bed and breakfast.

hour *n.* tide, spell, watch.

huge *adj.* breathtaking, great, great-limbed, heavy, meaty, mighty, overweight, overwhelming, unwieldy, weighty, widespread.

human, human being *n.* man, woman, everyman, everywoman, flesh and blood, living being, soul.

human *adj.* 1) earth-born, earth-bound, fleshly, manlike, mannish, 2) feet of clay, mightless, shaky, unsteady, yielding, 3) good, helpful, kind, kindly, kind-hearted, ruthful, warm-hearted.

humanity *n.* 1) man, mankind, womankind, flesh, the world, 2) manship, mannishness, 3) brotherliness, goodwill, kindliness, kindness, kind-heartedness, loving-kindness, mildness, ruth, softness, understanding, unselfishness, warm-heartedness.

humble *adj.* lowly, mouselike, mousy, shy, shamefast.

humour *n.* 1) laughter-making, mirth, play, 2) bent, frame of mind, mood, whim, 3) dryness, wit, wittiness, ready wit, wry wit.

humour *v.* to make much of, smooth, soothe, take one out of oneself.

hurried *adj.* heedless, quick, short, speedy, swift.

hurry *n.* 1) quickness, speed, headlong speed, lightning speed, utmost speed, swiftness, 2) ado, flutter, much ado, stir, to-do.

hurry *v.* 1) to bolt, fly, have no time to lose/spare, lose no time, run like a hare/the wind, shoot, speed, tear along, 2) to drive forward, goad, quicken, speed up.

hurt *v.* 1) to bite, cut, harm, prick, stab, sting, tear, wind, wound, 2) to cut to the quick, harrow, sadden, upset, worry, wring.

hypocritical *adj.* empty, hollow, lying, mealy-mouthed, put on, slippery, smooth, smooth spoken, smooth-tongued, soothing, two-tongued.

icon *n.* 1) likeness, 2) darling, star.

idea n. belief, brainchild, brainwave, insight, thought, understanding.

identical adj. alike, like, match, matching, of that ilk, twin.

identification n. 1) hand, markings, name, naming, watchword, 2) likening.

identify v. 1) to brand, earmark, make out, mark out, name, pick out, put a mark on, put one's finger on, 2) to make up one's mind on, settle on, work out, 3) to make as one, liken.

identity n. 1) name, 2) inner self, oneself, self, selfhood.

ideally adv. at best, if it may be, rightfully.

ideology n. beliefs, framework of beliefs.

idiomatic adj. homespun, homely, everyday, workaday.

ignorant adj. backward, benighted, clueless, unlearned, unthinking, loreless.

ignore v. 1) to give no heed, have no time for, have nothing to do with, keep at arm's length, not listen, set at naught, spurn, think nothing of, 2) to be blind to, shut the eyes to, stop one's ears, look the other way, overlook, wink at.

ill adj. 1) bad, shameful, unworthy, woeful, 2) ailing, bedridden, laid up, sick, under the weather, unwell.

ill-fated adj. doomed, stricken, undone, untimely, wretched.

illness n. addle, sickness, upset, waning health.

illogical adj. far-fetched, groundless, hard to swallow, hare-brained, meaningless, outlandish, ungrounded, utterly unlikely, wildly out.

ill-treatment n. foul play, harm, mishandling, rough handling, wrong, wrongdoing.

illusion n. daydream, misbelief, outward show, sham.

illustrate v. 1) to draw forth, highlight, mark out, set forth, show, 2) to bring home, bring out, shed/throw light on.

illustration n. 1) drawing, line-drawing, likeness, shadowing forth, showing, 2) teaching, warning.

image n. 1) look, looks, bearing, 2) drawing, likeness, outline, shadow, sheen.

imaginary adj. dreamed-up, dream-like, made-up, make-believe, shadowy, not of this world.

imagination n. inmost thoughts, insight, mindsight, mind's eye, thought-life.

imaginative adj. insightful, lively, rich in thought.

imagine v. to bring to life, see in one's mind/mind's eye, dream, see into, think of.

imitation n. borrowing, likeness, shadow.

immaterial adj. 1) bodiless, ghostly, shadowy, otherworldly, unearthly, 2) flimsy, leaf-light, light, lightweight, lean, mouselike, slight, thin, wispy.

immediate adj. forthwith, near, nearest, next, on hand, quick.

immediately adv. at once, forthwith, now, right now, right away, speedily, straight away, on the nail, there and then, at first hand, nearly.

immense adj. great, far-reaching, far-stretching, full-wide, widespread, overflowing.

immigrant n. incomer, newcomer, outsider, settler, wanderer, inwanderer.

immoral adj. evil, godless, lewd, lustful, misdealing, shameless, shifty, worldly.

immortal adj. 1) deathless, abiding, everlasting, endless, timeless, undying, unending, 2) bright, great, high-named, matchless, shining, worthful.

impact n. 1) backwash, fall-out, outcome, upshot, 2) knock, stroke.

impartial adj. even-handed, fair, fair-minded, open-minded, rightwise, upright.

impatience n. craving, edginess, heedlessness, hunger, thirst, keenness, longing, rashness, restlessness, shortness, wilfulness, yearning.

impatient adj. 1) edgy, fiery, headstrong, heedless, prickly, rash, reckless, self-willed, wilful, 2) athirst, earnest, hot, hungry, keen, longing, restless, yearning.

imperfect adj. half-done, half-grown, lacking, makeshift, middling, not good enough, twisted, underdone, uneven, unhewn, unripe, unthorough, warped.

impersonal adj. cold, cool, businesslike, forbidding, frosty, hard, standoffish, stiff, unfeeling, unforthcoming, unfriendly, unwelcoming, without warmth, at arm's length.

implement v. to bring about, do, fulfil, follow up, follow through, put through, see through, set going, stretch forth one's hand, be as good as one's word.

implicate v. to lay at one's door, name, smear, upbraid, blacken, brand, chide.

implication n. half-spoken word, hint, meaning, wheels within wheels.

imply v. 1) to bear the marks of, bear the stamp of, bespeak, betoken, mean, stand for, tell its own tale, follow as night follows day, 2) to hint at, give one to understand, leave one to gather, let fall, say by the way.

importance n. greatness, standing, weight, weightiness, worth, worthship.

important *adj.* 1) earth-shaking, far-reaching, going to the root, overriding, telling, weighty, 2) foremost, head, leading, outstanding.

impose *v.* 1) to lay down/upon, put, set, 2) to bear hard on, bind over, bring to book, come down on, deal hardly with, saddle with, settle with, 3) (*impose* on) to hoodwink, make game of, mislead, take in.

imposing *adj.* amazing, great, breathtaking, high, high and mighty, outstanding, stirring, striking, wonderful, worthy.

impossible *adj.* hopeless, knotty, thorny, uphill, undreamt, unheard of, unthought of.

impress *v.* to amaze, bewilder, fill with wonder, overcome, overwhelm, startle, stir.

impressed *adj.* amazed, filled with wonder, floored, overcome, speechless, stirred.

impression *n.* 1) mark, outline, stamp, 2) awareness, feeling, something half-called to mind, thought, belief, 3) takeoff.

impressive *adj.* amazing, great, stirring, striking, wonderful, worthy.

improbable *adj.* beyond belief, far-fetched, hard to believe, too good to be true, unheard of, unlikely, weird, wild.

impromptu *adj.* makeshift, quick as thought, rough and ready, straight out, unbidden.

improve *v.* 1) to get better, grow better, look up, pick up, 2) to better oneself, come on, get on, make headway, make one's way, make strides, leave behind, never look back, rise above, rise in the world, 3) to better, brighten, do up, forward, hone, make better/over, make the most of, open up, shape anew, strengthen, tidy up.

improvement *n.* bettering, new leaf, next step, upswing.

impulse *n.* 1) drive, overdrive, mainspring, spring, sparkle, 2) craving, feeling, itch, longing, need, whim, wish, yearning, 3) carelessness, heedlessness, rashness, recklessness, thoughtlessness, wildness.

inability *n.* helplessness, mightlessness.

inaccurate *adj.* careless, half-done, misleading, misread, mistaken, off-hand, out, wildly out, unthorough, wide of the mark/truth.

inadequate *adj.* good for nothing, lacking, leaf-light, narrow, not enough, not good enough, not much, sparing, thin, unbusinesslike.

incalculable *adj.* far-reaching, far-stretching, great, overflowing, untold.

incentive *n.* hope, meed, spur.

incident *n.* 1) uproar, 2) business, happening.

incidentally *adv.* by the bye, by the way.

incite *v.* to awaken, drive, goad, hound, play upon, prick, put up to, quicken, set against, set by the ears, set going, set on, spark off, spur, start, stir up.

incline *v.* 1) to bow, yield to, 2) to be minded, be drawn towards, lean towards.

include *v.* to bring/come within, come/fall under, find room for, have, reckon among.

inclusive *adj.* all-in, all-together, broad, full, having, holding, overall, sweeping.

incompatible *adj.* badly-matched, mismatched, unfriendly, unlike, at sixes and sevens.

incomplete *adj.* bitty, half-baked, half-done, half-grown, left hanging, makeshift, marred, rough-hewn, short, thin, unready, unthorough.

incomprehensible *adj.* beyond one's grasp, hard, hidden, meaningless, not to be fathomed/grasped/understood, shadowy, wandering.

inconceivable *adj.* beyond belief, far-fetched, hard to believe, not to be thought of, undreamed of, unheard of, unthought of, wonderful.

inconclusive *adj.* flimsy, open, unsettled, woolly.

incorrect *adj.* misleading, mistaken, not right, untrue, wide of the mark, wildly out.

increase *n.* build-up, growth, rise, spreading, strengthening, swelling, upbuilding, waxing.

increase *v.* to build up, grow, swell, wax.

increasingly *adv.* all the more, more and more, more so, up and up.

incredible *adj.* 1) beyond belief, far-fetched, hard to believe, too good to be true, unheard of, unlikely, unworthy of belief, 2) amazing, breathtaking, out of this world, overwhelming, wonderful.

incredulous *adj.* misbelieving, unready to believe, unbelieving.

indecisive *adj.* two-minded, at a loss, at one's wits' end, bestraught, forstraught, bewildered, hanging back, pulled this way and that, unsettled.

indefinite *adj.* 1) broad, unsettled, untold, 2) half-seen, shadowy, unknown.

independent *adj.* 1) free, free as the wind, free-born, free-minded, free-souled, free-speaking, free to choose, law to oneself, unbound, self-willed, 2) even-handed, fair, fair-minded, open-minded, straight.

index *n.* 1) key, list, listing, yardstick, 2) clue, hint, mark, token.

indicate *v.* to bear the marks/stamp of, bespeak, betoken, give one to understand, hint, make known, mark, mark out, show, show the way, spell, stand for, witness.

indication n. clew/clue, footfall, forewarning, warning, hint, mark, showing.

indifferent adj. cold, listless, soulless, thoughtless, uncaring, unmindful.

indirect adj. 1) wandering, winding, 2) not straightforward, slippery, underhand, 3) long drawn out, wordy, 4) unforeseen, unlooked for, unwitting.

indiscriminate adj. all anyhow, careless, sweeping, upside down, wholesale.

individual n. being, everyman, everywoman, self, inner self, one, soul, living soul, somebody, someone.

individual adj. like no other, lone, marked, own, owing nothing to.

industrial adj. business.

industry n. 1) hard work, steadiness, tirelessness, doggedness, 2) business, undertaking, work.

ineffective adj. broken down, clueless, good for nothing, helpless, hopeless.

inefficient adj. clueless, hopeless, rudderless, sloppy, unhandy.

inequality n. unevenness, unfairness.

inevitable adj. bound to be, bound to happen, brewing, cut and dried, doomed to be, fore-woven, hanging over one, no other way, not to be gainsaid, settled.

inevitably adv. come what will, no two ways about it, willy-nilly, by the strong arm.

inexcusable adj. beyond belief, dreadful, shabby, shameful, too bad, unbecoming, unworthy.

inexperienced adj. clueless, green, knowing no better, new, raw, unfledged.

inexplicable adj. almost/nigh unheard of, beyond one, far-fetched, knotted, new-fangled, outlandish, thorny, uncanny, unearthly, unwonted, weird, wonderful.

inference n. deeming, reading, reckoning, understanding, weighing up.

inferior adj. cheap, lesser, lightweight, under-weight, little, bad, makeshift, mean, middling, unworthy, worse, wretched.

infiltrate v. to creep in, find one's way in, go through, leak into, make inroads into, seep, sink in, soak into/through, spread through, work/worm one's way in.

infinite adj. bottomless, endless, everlasting, never-ending, unending, unfathomful, untold, without end, a thousand and one.

inflammatory adj. fiery, hot-blooded, hot-headed, red-hot, seething, stormy.

inflation n. becoming dear, going up, growth, rise, swelling.

inflexible adj. 1) dogged, set, 2) hard and fast, set in one's ways, steely, stiff-backed, stiff-necked, unbending, unforgiving, unyielding, dyed in the wool, 3) hard, hardened, stiff, tough.

inflict v. to be heavy-handed, burden, deal out, drive, lord it, mete out, ride roughshod, stamp on, tread underfoot, wreak.

influence n. hold, leadership, mightiness, over-mightiness, spell, standing, weight.

influence v. to bend, drive, have a hold on, have the ear of, lead, lord it over, make oneself felt, play upon, pull strings, put up to, steer, stir, weigh in, work upon.

influential adj. leading, listened to, strong, telling, weighty.

inform v. 1) to fill one in, give away, give one to understand, lay bare, let in the daylight, let one know, make known, make a clean breast of, send word to, tell, unfold, 2) to spread right through.

information n. hearsay, news, tidings, witness, word, knowledge, learning, lore.

information technology n. the holding and handling of knowledge through means of main reckoners (*computers*), main reckoner know-how.

inherent adj. belonging, deep-rooted, inborn, inbred, inbuilt, inward, inwoven, inwrought, one's own, underlying.

initial adj. beginning, early, earliest, first, maiden, opening.

initiative n. 1) lead, start, upper hand, 2) boldness, daring, drive, free-hand, leadership, 3) deal.

injure v. 1) to break, bruise, cripple, cut, harm, lame, rough up, tear, wound, 2) to cut to the quick, harrow, mar, befoul, smear, twist, warp.

injury n. 1) cut, harm, rough handling, sore, wound, 2) misdeed, misdoing, right withheld, unfairness, unrightness.

injustice n. evil-doing, foul play, misdeed, misdoing, misreckoning, narrow-mindedness, one-sidedness, right withheld, unfairness, unrightness, unfairness.

innocence n. 1) childlikeness, harmlessness, maidenhood, openness, unworldliness, 2) clean hands, goodness, rightwiseness, sinlessness, uprightness, wholesomeness, 3) backwardness, greenness, unawareness.

innocent adj. childlike, clean, clean-handed, guiltless, harmless, lamb-like, open, sinless, *unfallen, unguilty, unhardened, unworldly,* upright.

innovative *adj.* 1) lively, quick, sharp-witted, witful, 2) ground-breaking, new.

inquiry *n.* delving, combing, hunting, rooting, sifting.

insect *n.* ant, emmet, earwig, flea, louse, midge, mite, moth, nit, weevil.

insensitive *adj.* blind/deaf/dead to, cool, hard-bitten, hardened, rough, tough, uncaring, uncouth, unfeeling, unkind, wooden.

insincere *adj.* crafty, empty, hollow, not straightforward, smooth-tongued.

insist *v.* 1) to know one's own mind, lay down the law, make a stand, not take no for an answer, put one's foot down, stand one's ground, 2) to make bold to ask, stand up for/uphold one's rights, 3) to be in earnest, dwell on, hold, say again and again, stand to, swear.

insoluble *adj.* bewildering, hard-wrought, knotted, too hard, unfathomful.

inspection *n.* look, look-over, once-over, looking into, weighing, worth-weighing.

inspiration *n.* 1) brainwave, insight, mindsight, spur, earnestness, feeling, headiness, 2) putting heart into, stirring up, 3) (of the Holy Ghost stirring men to write) leading, stirring, inblowing, inbreathing, onblowing, on-breathing.

inspire *v.* 1) to awaken, fire, give rise to, put life into, spark, spur, stir, warm the heart, 2) to hearten, put heart into, make a man of.

inspiring *adj.* gripping, heady, heartening, heart-stirring, heart-swelling, soul-stirring, stirring, thrilling.

install *v.* to lay, put in, set up, settle.

instance *n.* 1) framework, 2) behest, bidding, say-so.

instant *n.* 1) breath, 'prick' in time, twinkling of an eye, 2) time.

institute *n.* body, hall/house/seat of learning, school.

institution *n.* 1) body, hall/house/seat of learning, school, 2) law, way, wont, 3) beginning, birth, bringing in, opening, setting up, 4) home, care home, lock-house/*prison*, sickhouse/*hospital*.

instruction *n.* 1) behest, bidding, saying, say-so, word, writ, 2) grounding, teaching, upbringing.

instrument *n.* 1) bridge, hand, help, key, makeshift, stepping-stone, tool, watchword, weapon, 2) go-between, handmaid, hanger-on, helper, henchman, middleman, midwife, right-hand man, tool, yes-man, 3) deed.

insult *v.* to smear, blacken, curse, run down, speak evil of, speak foully of, swear at.

insurance *n.* foresight, underwriting.

insure *v.* to hedge, underwrite.

insurrection *n.* breakaway, outbreak, overthrow, rising, uprising, street fighting.

integral *adj.* 1) needed, 2) full, whole.

integrate *v.* to bring together, knit, make whole.

integration *n.* bringing/growing together, oneness.

integrity *n.* even-handedness, fairness, open-heartedness, righteousness, steadfastness, truth, uprightness.

intellect *n.* 1) mind-wit, insight, quickness, sharpness, shrewdness, wisdom, 2) brain, seat of thought.

intelligence *n.* insight, understanding, wit, quickness, sharpness, wisdom.

intelligent *adj.* awake, bright, insightful, keen-minded, sharp, wise, thinking.

intend *v.* to foresee, frame, have in mind, make up one's mind, look for, mean to, reckon to, set one's heart/mind on, will.

intended *adj.* meant, willed.

intense *adj.* 1) great, heartfelt, heightened, deep, deep-hued, bright-hued, rich-hued, glowing, stark, strong, warm, 2) afire, aglow, burning, earnest, hot-blooded, keen.

intensive *adj.* all-out, full, greater than ever, in-depth, thorough, thoroughgoing.

intention *n.* by-end, end, goal, heart/mind set on something, mind, will, wish.

interactive *adj.* two-way.

intercede *v.* to befriend, help, put oneself between, speak up for, stand by, stand up for, step in, take the side of, take up the cudgels for.

intercept *v.* to come between, cut/head off, hook, net, stand in the way, stop, waylay.

interest *n.* 1) footing, holding, right/share in something, 2) care, heed, mindfulness, 3) game, play, itch/thirst for knowledge, 4) growth, pound of flesh.

interested *adj.* 1) drawn, gripped, keen, stirred, struck, 2) having a right or share in something (such as a business deal).

interesting *adj.* gripping, spellbinding, stirring, striking.

interface *v.* link.

interfere *v.* to come between, have a finger in every bowl, hinder, not mind one's own business, stick one's nose in, put/shove one's oar in, unsettle, work against.

interference n. busybodying, hindering, putting one's oar in, stirring unrest, unsettling.

interior adj. 1) deep down, hidden, inner, inside, inward, 2) highland, midland.

intermediary n. go-between, link, middleman, mid-speaker, spokesman, spokeswoman, thirdsman, word-bearer.

intermediate adj. grey, halfway, in-between, mid, middle, middlemost, middling, midmost, midway.

internal adj. home, indoor, in-house, inland, inner, innermost, inside, inward, inwoven, inwrought.

international adj. world, worldwide.

internet n. net, web, world wide web.

interpretation n. insight, light, meaning, reading, understanding, unfolding.

interruption n. break, broken thread, hold-up, stand, stop, untimeliness.

interval n. 1) span, spell, stretch, time, while, 2) break, breather, breathing time, rest.

intervene v. 1) to hinder, step in, work against, 2) to come between, lie between, stand between, 3) to be a go-between, bridge over, put oneself between, 4) to break in upon, put/shove one's oar in, 5) to arise, befall, happen.

intervention n. coming between, forestalling, help.

interview n. asking about, delving, meeting, talk.

intimate n. bosom friend, best/dear/fast/good/near/warm friend, other self.

intimate adj. 1) dear, friendly, loving, matched, near, nearest and dearest, together, warm, 2) (of one's knowledge) deep, first-hand, full, in-depth, thorough.

intimidating bodeful, deadly, dreadful, harmful, hanging over, threatful.

intolerable adj. beyond bearing, loathsome, more than flesh and blood can stand, not to be borne, not to be put up with, utterly bad.

intolerant adj. blind, hard, narrow, narrow-minded, overbearing, ruthless, small-minded, one-sided, unyielding.

intrinsic adj. belonging, deep down, deep-rooted, inborn, inbred, inbuilt, inward, inwoven, inwrought, underlying.

introduce v. 1) to begin, break the ice, bring into being, lead into, set up, start, 2) to bring in, lead off, open, 3) to put into, work in, 4)

to make (two) known to each other, 5) to outline, begin to teach.

introduction n. beginning, foretale, forespeech, foreword, groundwork, lead-in, opening, outline, start.

intruder n. house-breaker, picklock.

invade v. to beset, drive against, fall upon, fight, make an onset, make inroads, overrun, storm, strike at, take the field, take the fight to the foe.

invaluable adj. of high worth, worth its weight in gold, not to be had for love or gold, forworthy.

invariable adj. dreary, grey, set, settled, smooth, steady, stock, unbroken.

invariably adv. again and again, always, 'day in, day out,' ever, every time, smoothly, time and again, time after time.

invasion n. breakthrough, drive, inroad, onset, strike, swoop.

invention n. 1) brainchild, brainwave, finding, setting up, 2) lie, downright lie, tall tale, untruth, 3) brain-work, head-work, insight, mindsight, sharpness.

inventory n. stock book, stock-list, listing.

invest v. 1) to clothe, fill, steep, 2) to put into the hands of, swear one in, 3) to begird, beset, gird about, ring about, hedge in, hem in, keep in, lock in, shut in, 4) to back, lay out, put in, sink in.

investigate v. to delve, seek, burrow, comb, go through, root through, look into.

investigation n. sifting, asking, delving, rooting, going through/into/over.

investment n. backing, buying shares, holding, lending, outlay.

invitation n. asking, bidding, fair words, open door, welcome.

invite v. to ask, ask one in, ask one over, beseech, welcome.

involve v. 1) to call for, give rise to, mean, open the door to, put in the way to, 2) to bespeak, draw in, 3) to brand, lay at one's door, link, name.

involvement n. 1) doings, hand, irons in the fire, 2) deep feeling, sharing in, understanding, 3) guilt.

irksome adj. burdensome, tiresome, untimely, unwelcome, wearing, wearisome.

ironic, ironical adj. 1) bitter, dry, sharp, stinging, two-edged, wried, wry, wrought awry, 2) (*paradoxical*) unfathomful, riddled, uncanny, weird and wayward.

irony n. 1) bitterness, sting, 2) riddle, truth a-wried, truth a-twisted.

irrational adj. brainless, empty-headed, feather-headed, mindless, unsteady, unseeing, unthinking, unwise, wild, <u>witless</u>.

irregular adj. 1) fickle, flighty, shaky, <u>shifting</u>, unsteady, 2) awry, broken, misshapen, not straight, not true, rough, twisted, twisting, uneven, unshapely, warped, 3) back-door, not right, shady, unlawful.

irrelevant adj. beside/wide of the mark, empty, lightweight, <u>long-winded</u>, meaningless, neither here nor there, off-beam, out-of-the-way, unmeaning.

irresistible adj. 1) <u>great</u>, overmighty, overriding, overwhelming, <u>strong</u>, not to be gainsaid, telling, weighty, 2) after one's heart, bewitching, to one's mind.

irresponsible adj. careless, empty-headed, feather-brained, flighty, giddy, hare-brained, headstrong, <u>heedless</u>, <u>light-minded</u>, rash, reckless, self-willed, shiftless, thoughtless, unsteady, wayward, wild, <u>wilful</u>.

isolated adj. alone, lonely, <u>forlorn</u>, friendless, islanded, by oneself, out on a limb.

issue n. 1) outflow, outgoing, 2) children, offspring, seed, young, one's flesh and blood, aftercomers, <u>afterkin</u>, 3) end, outcome, upshot, 4) business on hand, 5) sending out, 6) one of a weekly or monthly *paper*.

issue v. 1) to arise, rise, come forth, come out, flow, overflow, spring, stem, well up, 2) to give forth, give out, put out, send forth, spread, 3) to give, yield.

isthmus n. land-bridge, neck/tongue of land.

item n. 1) bit, thing, something, 2) write-up.

jacket n. 1) wind-breaker, 2) folder, housing, sheath, shell, 3) dust-shield (for a book).

jail, gaol n. den, hold, lock-house, lockup, man-hold, ward-house.

January n. After-yule, Wolf-month.

jargon n. insider-speech, *ink*horn speech.

jealous adj. bitter, mean-minded, restless, green-eyed.

jeopardy n. death-trap, pitfall, quicksands, shoal, thin ice, threat.

jersey n. pullover, sweater, woolly.

jet n. 1) burst, flood, flow, outflow, spring, stream, 2) flying craft.

job n. 1) business, craft, field, livelihood, work, 2) shift, spell of work, stint, stretch, undertaking, work, work in hand, uphill work.

join v. 1) to bind, <u>fasten</u>, hook on, link together, make one, put together, stick on, tie on, yoke, 2) to make a match, make one flesh, wed, 3) to become one of, be in on, come aboard, put

one's name down, team up with, 4) to meet, meet up.

joiner n. woodcraftsman, woodworker, woodwright.

joint adj. shared.

joke n. 1) laugh, whimsy, 2) empty words, half-truth, make-believe, shadow, sham.

joke v. to chaff, play the wit, tease.

journal n. daybook, daily, monthly, weekly.

journey n. drive, faring, flight, outing, walking, wayfaring.

journey v. to fare, fly, go, make one's way, set off/out, step out, take to the road, walk, wayfare, wend.

joy n. bliss, blissfulness, blitheness, blessedness, gladness, list.

joyful adj. <u>blithe</u>, blithesome, gladsome, gleeful, winful.

jubilant adj. beside oneself, cock-a-hoop, crowing, flushed, glad, gleeful, laughing, on a high, shouting, thrilled.

judge n. bencher, deemster, doomster, one laying down the law.

judge v. to deem, find for/against, find guilty/not guilty, reckon, see straight, <u>settle</u>, mete out, weigh.

judgement n. 1) finding, reckoning, weighing up, 2) <u>wisdom</u>, awareness, belief, insight, long-headedness, shrewdness, understanding.

July n. After-litha, Meadow-month.

jump n. 1) hop, leap, spring, springy step, 2) gate, hurdle, 3) rise, upswing, 4) shake, start, twitch.

jump v. 1) to hop, leap, leap-frog, spring, 2) to hop over, hurdle, leap over, sail over, spring over, 3) to climb, rise, 4) to quake, shake, start, twitch.

June n. Ere-litha, Fore-litha, Midsummer-month, Sere('dry')-month.

June July n. Litha.

jungle n. 1) deep woodland, weald, the wild, wilderness, 2) maze, web.

junior n. 1) follower, newcomer, underling, whelp, youngling, youngster, youth, 2) first-year man.

junior adj. lesser, young, younger, youngest, youthful.

jurisdiction n. 1) say, 2) field, free hand, <u>lordship</u>, right.

just adv. 1) lately, only now, 2) but, nothing but, only, no more than, 3) at most, barely, hardly, 4) altogether, truly.

just adj. 1) even-handed, fair, fair-minded, good, <u>right</u>, righteous, right-minded, <u>rightwise</u>, true, upright, unswerving, 2) rightful, meet and right.

justice *n.* fairness, fair play, folk-right, right, rightfulness, rightness, truth.

justification *n.* 1) grounds, right, rightness, sooth, 2) (in *Christian* Godlore) rightening.

justified *adj.* 1) fair, right, rightwise, 2) put right, rightened, freed (from the grip of sin), bought back (by *Christ's* blood).

justify *v.* 1) to bear out, put right, uphold, 2) to deem guiltless, make good, righten, set right, set to rights.

kid *n.* young goat, goatling.

kidnap *v.* to make away with, run off with, steal away.

kindle *v.* 1) to light, fire, set fire to, start a fire, strike a light, 2) to awaken, bestir, bring to life, liven up, quicken, sharpen, thrill.

label *n.* 1) marker, sticker, 2) brand, brand name, mark, trademark, trade name, 3) name, by-name.

label *v.* 1) to mark, stamp, 2) to brand, call, name.

laborious *adj.* backbreaking, burdensome, grinding, hard, tiring, tough, uphill, wearing, wearisome.

labour *n.* 1) hard work, heavy work, uphill work, warm work, spadework, grindstone, striving, 2) bitterness of child-bearing.

laconic *adj.* of few words, pithy, put in a nutshell, saying little, short, sparing of words, unforthcoming.

lake *n.* inland sea, land-locked water, mere, pool.

lamentable *adj.* 1) harrowing, sorrowful, 2) hopeless, sorry, woeful, worthless, wretched.

landscape *n.* landship, backcloth, background, outlook, setting.

language *n.* speech, folk speech, ready speech, tongue, mother tongue, spoken word, wording.

lapse *v.* 1) to backslide, fall away, follow a bypath, go downhill, leave the straight way, sink, slide, 2) (in law) to end, go by, run out.

large *adj.* great, far-reaching, roomy, tall, full-wide, wide, widespread.

largely *adv.* greatly, mainly, markedly, mostly, richly, strongly, widely.

larger *adj.* greater, more, further, higher, over and above.

largest *adj.* greatest, most, highest, matchless, utmost, whole.

lass *n.* girl, maid, maiden, wench, young woman.

launch *v.* 1) to begin, open, set going, set on foot, start, 2) to fire, send off, shoot, throw,

3) to get under way, lead off, put to sea, set afloat, set sail.

lavish *adj.* endless, ever so much, full, great, overflowing, rich, swarming, teeming, untold, free-handed, open-handed, unsparing, unstinting.

lay *n.* song, song-dream.

lazy *adj.* good-for-nothing, idle, shiftless, slack, slothful, slow, workshy.

lazybones *n.* good-for-nothing, foot-dragger, heel-dragger, idler, layabout, slacker, slow-bones, slow-foot.

league *n.* 1) coming together, understanding, 2) three miles.

lecture *n.* 1) reading, speech, set speech, talk, 2) chiding, home-truth, talking-to, telling-off, upbraiding.

leg *n.* shank, limb, lower limb, nether limb.

legal *adj.* lawful, good in law, within the law, made law, law-giving, law-heeding, binding, rightful, in the right.

legend *n.* 1) wonder tale, tale of elder-days, tale of old, 2) dream, dream-tale, folk-tale, make-believe, 3) great name, high name, star.

legislation *n.* laws, body of law, written law, law-giving, law-making.

legislative *adj.* law-binding, law-giving, law-making.

legislator *n.* law-giver, law-maker, helmsman, steersman.

legislature *n.* house of law-making, law-body, steering body.

legitimate *adj.* lawful, good in law, within the law, fair, right, rightful, meet and right.

lesson *n.* meaning, reading, teaching, warning, word to the wise.

letter *n.* line, written tidings, written word, written answer, errand.

level *adj.* of like height, even, smooth.

level *v.* 1) to even out, even up, smooth, 2) to break down, bring down, cut down, hew down, knock down, lay in the dust, make an end of, overthrow, pull down, tear down, throw down, 3) to make ready to fire, set one's sights on.

liability *n.* 1) drag, drawback, millstone, 2) burden, guilt, 3) bent, leaning, likelihood, likeliness, trend.

liable *adj.* answering for, beholden, bound, bounden, guilty, laid open.

liberal *adj.* 1) free-handed, free-hearted, open-handed, open-hearted, handsome, lordly, overflowing, unsparing, unstinting, 2) enough and to spare, more than enough, 3) broad-minded, free-minded, free-thinking, open-minded.

liberalise v. to <u>free</u>, lighten, unburden, unfetter, unshackle.

liberty n. freedom, free-hand, free play, free speech, unfettering, unshackling, opening, room.

library n. bookhoard, book-house, hall/house of books, reading room, reading house.

license v. to give leave, let, open the door, swear one in.

lieutenant n. henchman, righthandman, spokesman, stand-in.

limit n. end, farthest reach, outside edge, threshold, utmost, uttermost, deadline.

limit v. to bridle, fetter, hem in, <u>hinder</u>, hold back, hold down, keep in, stop the flow.

limitation n. 1) fetter, forholding, 2) drawback, lameness, shortcoming.

limited adj. bridled, cut off, fettered, hamstrung, hedged in, hindered, kept down, little, narrow, shackled, shut off, small.

linear adj. 1) lineways, linewise, straight, 2) forefatherly, in a line (father to son).

linguistics n. speech-craft, speechlore, word-craft.

liquid n. sap, water.

liquid adj. flowing, melted, running, runny, thawed, watery, water-like, wet.

liquidity n. ready goods/wealth, wealth in hand.

liquor n. strong drink, ale, beer, home-brew, mead.

literal adj. 1) word for word, stave-fast, 2) bald, bare, everyday, homely, homespun, stark, workaday.

literally adv. truly, word for word, stave for stave, even as written.

literature n. writing, writings, written word, written works, book-craft, booklore.

lobby n. 1) hall, hallway, fore-room, 2) set (that seeks deeds from leaders).

local adj. near, nearby, neighbouring.

location n. setting, when and where, whereabouts, stead, stow.

lodge n. 1) dwelling, homestead, steading, 2) brotherhood.

lodge v. 1) to house, put up, 2) to bide at, board, dwell in, live in, put up at, settle at, 3) to lay, put, set, stow.

logical adj. meaningful, thought through, <u>well-grounded</u>, holding water.

long-*term* adj. <u>abiding</u>, deep-rooted, lifelong, livelong, longlived, longstanding.

loophole n. 1) arrow-slit, 2) backdoor, let-out, shift, way out.

lottery n. 1) draw, gambling, throw, 2) hap, mayhap, hidden hand, lot, <u>wyrd</u>.

loyalty n. <u>steadfastness</u>, strength of heart, troth, true-heartedness, <u>uprightness</u>, doughtiness, knightliness.

luck n. 1) break, windfall, 2) lot, stars.

lucky adj. 1) blessed, 2) unforeseen, unlooked for, timely.

lumber n. clutter, throw-outs.

lunch, luncheon n. light meal, midday meal.

lurch v. to heel/lean over, nose-dive, pitch, reel, see-saw, swerve, thresh about, tilt, topple, wallow, weave.

luxurious adj. full, having it good, rich, unsparing, sparing no outlay, throwing wealth about.

luxury n. <u>wealth</u>, fullness, a great deal, every good thing, more than enough, fat of the land, too much, untold riches, well-being.

machine n. 1) tool, wheelwork, 2) setup, ring.

magazine n. 1) weaponhoard, weaponhouse, 2) weekly, monthly.

magic n. 1) witchcraft, spell-making, spellweaving, works of wonder, 2) deftness, quickness, readiness, 3) greatness, stardom.

magisterial adj. keen-minded, <u>learned</u>, strong-willed, weighty, well up in.

magnetic adj. bewitching, spell-binding, <u>winning</u>.

magnificent adj. great, high and mighty, highborn, well-born, of mark, weighty, kingly, queenly, lordly, <u>worthy</u>, <u>worthful</u>.

magnifying glass n. hand-glass, reading-glass.

magnitude n. 1) greatness, mark, standing, weight, worth, worthship, 2) breadth, depth, height, length, mightiness, strength, thickness, weight, width.

maintain v. 1) to follow through, keep going, keep on, keep it up, see it through, 2) to <u>bear witness</u>, believe in, deem, hold one's ground, hold to be true, look upon as, stand by what one says, speak out, 3) to keep from falling, make lasting, stand behind, stand by, strengthen, uphold, 4) to care for, clothe, feed, find, keep, look after, put up.

major adj. 1) <u>great</u>, far-reaching, far-stretching, key, sweeping, telling, weighty, widespread, 2) better, elder, greater, head, higher, lead, leading, main, outstanding.

majority n. 1) all but a few, almost all, most, nearly all, the bear's share, 2) full years, grown-upness, manhood, womanhood.

male n. man, he-kind, spear-kin.

malicious adj. baleful, biting, bitter, cutting, <u>deadly</u>, hateful, hate-filled, stinging, tearing, withering, evil-minded, shrewish, wolfish.

manage *v.* 1) to be head of, handle, head, lead, look after, oversee, pull strings, run, see to, steer, wield, 2) to fare, get along, get by, get on, get through, have a way with, make do, make out, see to, shift.

management *n.* 1) care, handling, housekeeping, leadership, oversight, running, steering, steersmanship, stewardship, 2) board.

manager *n.* head, one's man of business, overseer, steward, reeve, landreeve.

maniac *n.* madman, madwoman, crack-brain.

manifest *adj.* for all to see, in the foreground, in the limelight, in the open, wide-open, showing, shown, straightforward, striking, well-known, well-marked, well-seen, written all over one.

manifestation *n.* making known, mark, shadowing forth, showing, token, unfolding, likeness, speaking likeness, striking likeness, whole truth.

manipulate *v.* 1) to have a way with, make a tool of, pull strings, steer, twist about one's little finger, 2) to bring into play, handle, make the most of, run, twist, wield, work, 3) to be up to something, play upon, spin, weave, work upon.

manner *n.* 1) way, way of doing things, wont, 2) bearing, behaviour, way of life, 3) brand, breed, kind, make.

manœuvre *n.* 1) headway, sternway, 2) foul play, gamesmanship, shift, sharp-dealing, underhand dealing, web, web-weaving, 3) deed, step, stroke.

mantle *n.* 1) hood, 2) shade.

manufacturer *n.* builder, businessman, maker.

manufacturing *n.* building, making, shaping, output, work, craftsmanship, workmanship.

manuscript *n.* first written draft, handwritten work, written work, writing.

map *n.* *chart*, earth-likeness, land-likeness, land-outline.

marble *n.* shining stone.

March *n.* Lengthening-month, Loud-month, Rough-month.

march *v.* 1) to stamp, step, stride out, tread, 2) to go to war, take the field, 3) to take to the streets.

marginal *adj.* 1) on the edge, 2) small, slight.

marine *adj.* seafaring, seagoing, seamanlike, salty.

market *n.* 1) business, buying and selling, dealing, trade, 2) call, need.

market *v.* to buy, sell, trade.

marketing *n.* business, buying and selling, dealing, tradesmanship.

marriage *n.* 1) wedding, wedlock, match, life together, living as man and wife, one flesh, wifedom, wifehood, wifeliness, 2) team, tie-up.

married *adj.* wed, wedded, made man and wife, matched, one, wife-fast.

marry *v.* 1) to wed, become man and wife, be made one, bestow one's hand, make a match, make one flesh, take to wife, plight one's troth, knit, yoke, 2) to bind, link up, make one, team up.

marshal *n.* 1) high lord of war, field-lord, 2) high reeve.

marshal *v.* 1) to draw up, gather, 2) to lead, shepherd, steer.

marvel *n.* eye-opener, nonesuch, wonder.

marvellous *adj.* amazing, great, matchless, outstanding, wonderful, worthful.

mason *n.* stonecutter, stoneworker, stone-wright, wall-wright.

mass *n.* 1) batch, heap, load, lot, mish-mash, 2) almost/nearly all, the bear's share, 3) body, crowd, drove, herd, swarm, throng, 4) clod, greatness, heft, weight.

massacre *n.* blood-bath, blood-letting, bloodshed, wholesale killing.

massive *adj.* great, far-reaching, far-stretching, high, mighty, strong, weighty.

master *n.* head, leader, lord, overlord, overseer, owner, reeve, helmsman, steersman.

mastery *n.* 1) cleverness, deftness, grasp, grip, handcleverness, know-how, knowledge, understanding, 2) hold, overlordship, ownership, upper hand.

mate *n.* 1) friend, helper, 2) helpmeet, husband, wife, 3) match, twin.

mate *v.* 1) to lie with, live with, sleep with, wed, breed, 2) to match, yoke.

material *n.* 1) body, flesh and blood, 2) cloth, weave, 3) (*matter* for a book or *paper*) food for thought, gatherings, gossip, news).

mathematical *adj.* aright, dead-on, careful, right, thorough, true.

mathematics *n.* rimecraft.

matter *n.* 1) business, thing, 2) body, flesh and blood, 3) burden, pith, 4) standing, weight, weightiness, 5) upset, worry.

matter *v.* to mean something, tell, weigh, cut any ice.

mature *adj.* 1) fledged, full-fledged, full-blown, full-grown, fully ripe, ripe, ripened, manly, womanly, weathered, 2) deep, farsighted, grown-up, understanding, wise.

mature v. to grow, ripen, rise in the world.

maturity n. 1) full growth, fullness, manhood, womanhood, ripeness, riper years, eldership, 2) wisdom, ripe knowledge/wisdom, breadth or depth of mind, farsightedness, long-headedness, mind-strength, reach of mind, wit.

maximum n. adj. 1) fullness, greatness, utmost height, one's fill, 2) best ever, most.

May n. Three-milkings, Thry-milchmonth.

mayhem n. 1) crippling, laming, marring, wounding, 2) madhouse, storm, upheaving, uproar.

mayor n. elderman, reeve, town-reeve, town-head.

means n. 1) answer, handiness, help, know-how, make-do, makeshift, opening, stepping-stone, tools, way, 2) fullness, income, riches, wealth, wherewithal.

meanwhile adv. between whiles, while, whilst.

measure n. 1) reckoning, taking stock, weighing, cut, deal, share, share-out, 2) ready reckoner, reckoning-board, yardstick.

measure v. to mark off, mete, reckon up, take readings, take the length and breath of, take stock of, weigh up, work out, fathom, heave the lead.

measured adj. 1) marked out, read, reckoned up, weighed, 2) cool, even, heedful, steady, well-thought-out.

measurement n. reckoning, breadth, depth, height, length, thickness, weight, width, spoonful, thimbleful.

mechanical adj. 1) self-driving, self-working, 2) blind, unfeeling, unthinking, unwitting.

mechanism n. tool, workings, works.

meddle v. to come between, have a finger in every bowl, hinder, not mind one's own business, stick one's nose in, put/shove one's oar in, unsettle, work against.

media n. newshounds, newsmakers, newsmen, newsmongers, gossipmongers.

mediate v. to be a go-between, bring together, heal, settle, step in.

medicine n. 1) healing craft, 2) healing-draught.

meditate v. to bethink, brood upon, chew over, give thought to, think about, think over, think upon, weigh, sleep on it.

medium n. 1) middle, middle ground, middle path, middle way, 2) background, setting, 3) way, 4) seer, soothsayer, spokesman/spokeswoman of the dead.

medium adj. fair, middle, middling, midway.

medley n. 1) blend, heap, mingling, mish-mash, witches' brew, 2) dream-song.

meek adj. lamb-like, mild, mouselike, shamefast, shrinking, shy, tongueless, withdrawn.

melody n. song, harp-song.

member n. 1) limb, forelimb, hinderlimb, arm, forearm, shank, 2) one of a set/team.

membership n. 1) belonging, togetherness, 2) body, gathering.

memorable adj. deathless, earth-shaking, mark-worthy, outstanding, stirring, striking, timeless, undying, unforgotten.

memorial n. after-mark, marker stone.

memory n. mind, mind-hoard, mind-stock.

mend v. 1) to make good, put/set right, settle, sew, stitch, straighten out, 2) to get better, get well, pull through.

mental adj. mindly, thinking.

mention n. naming, word.

mention v. to acknowledge, bring up, hint at, make known, name, put in a word or two, speak about/of, tell of.

mentor n. friend, leader, teacher, thinker, wise man.

merchant n. businessman, businesswoman, man/woman of business, buyer, seller, dealer, middleman, salesman, saleswoman, trader, wholesaler.

mercury n. quicksilver.

mercy n. forgivingness, kindness, mildness, mildheartness, ruth, understanding.

to show *mercy* v. to forbear, forgive, let off, overlook, spare.

mere adj. 1) bare, shadowy, stark, no more than, nothing more than, 2) lightweight.

merely adv. only, but, barely, lightly.

meretricious adj. 1) begilt, brassy, gilded, made-up, overdone, picked out, shameless, showy, whorish, 2) hollow, make-believe, put-on, sham.

merger n. coming together, making one, mingling.

merit n. goodness, strength, uprightness, worth, worthiness.

merit v. to be worthy of, earn, have a right to.

mermaid n. sea-elf, sea-maid.

mesmerise v. to bewitch, spellbind, hold spellbound, bewilder, grip, play upon.

mess n. 1) share-out of food, helping, 2) wardroom, 3) clutter, mish-mash, untidiness, 4) deep water, hot water, hole, plight.

message n. word, tidings, byspell, errand.

metal n. brass, gold, iron, lead, silver, tin.

metaphor n. forlikening, given-meaning.

meteorology n. weatherlore.

method *n.* 1) way of doing things, 2) evenness, steadiness, tidiness.

methodical *adj.* businesslike, dogged, settled, steadfast, steady, tidy, unswerving.

meticulous *adj.* heedful, right, straight, true, thorough, with nothing left out/missing.

metropolitan *adj.* built-up, towny.

microcosm *n.* world in a nutshell, outline.

microscope *n.* small glass.

migrant *n.* incomer, newcomer, otherlander, outsider, wanderer.

militant *adj.* daring, fighting, ready for a fight, reckless, sword in hand.

military *n.* fighting body.

military *adj.* fighting, weaponed.

million *n.* a thousand thousands.

mimic *v.* to chaff, laugh at, make game of, make merry with, play with, put on, show up, take off, wield one's wit against.

minimal *adj.* least, little, littlest, not many/much, smallest.

minimise *v.* 1) to lessen, make less/smaller, narrow down, shorten, shrink, take away, whittle down, 2) to make light/little of, mark down, play down, set at naught.

minimum *n.* drop in the sea, next to nothing, pennyweight, thimbleful, whit, shadow of a shade.

minimum *adj.* hardly any, least, little, slightest, smallest.

minister *n.* 1) leader, reeve, sheriff, steward, spokesman, 2) (in a church) elder, leader, shepherd.

ministry *n.* 1) help, helpfulness, helping hand, willing help, 2) leadership, stewardship.

minority *n.* 1) handful, the few, too few, one or two, two or three, 2) the mightless, the overlooked, the strengthless, the unheeded, 3) wardship, leading strings.

minute *n.* little while, 'prick' in time, breath, short span/time, smoke in the wind, stroke, twinkling of an eye.

minx *n.* hussy, quean, vixen, wanton.

miracle *n.* wonder, wonder-work, wonder-craft.

mire *n.* marsh, marshland, fen, fenland, moor, moorland, moss, slough.

mirror *n.* glass, looking-glass.

mirror *v.* to bespeak, be like, give back, shine back, throw back, match, shadow.

misapprehension *n.* misunderstanding, misreading, mistake.

misappropriate *v.* to bear away, fleece, make away with, make off with, mishandle, reave, steal, pull strings, thieve, twist.

miscalculate *v.* to make a mistake, misdeem, misfire, misread, misreckon, miss the mark, mistime, play into another's hands, put one's foot in it, under-reckon.

miscarry *v.* 1) to come to the birth over-early so that the child is still-born, 2) to come to naught/nothing, do no good, fall down, fall through, go awry, misfire.

miscellaneous *adj.* manifold, mingled, sundry.

mischievous *adj.* 1) bad, baleful, evil, good-for-nothing, harmful, idle, misleading, shady, shrewish, 2) badly behaved, naughty, playful, wayward.

misconception *n.* misreckoning, mistaken belief, misunderstanding.

miserable *adj.* forlorn, hopelorn, broken-hearted, heart-sick, sorrowful, wretched.

misery *n.* forlornness, hopelessness, loneliness, sadness, sorrow, woe, wretchedness.

misinterpret *v.* to misread, misunderstand, read into.

misjudge *v.* to misunderstand, overplay one's hand, overreach oneself, think too little of, under-weigh.

mismanage *v.* to come unstuck, fall down, go wide of the mark, let slip through one's fingers, make sad work of, mar, misfire, mishandle, overwork.

misogyny *n.* hatred/misliking of women, having no time for women, having nothing to do with women, loathing/shunning/spurning women, setting woman at naught, thinking the worse of women.

misrepresent *v.* to belie, lie about, misteach, overdraw, twist, read/write into, warp.

missile *n.* arrow, bolt, shaft, shell, shot, spear, weapon.

mission *n.* 1) undertaking, work, life-work, 2) business, goal, 3) go-betweens, spokesmen/spokeswomen.

mix *v.* to brew, make up, mingle, pound together, put together, shake/stir together.

mixture *n.* mingling, brew, witches' brew.

mobile ('*phone*) *n.* handset.

mobile *adj.* flighty, restless, shifting, wandering, wayward.

mock *v.* to belittle, chaff, laugh at, laugh in one's sleeve, make game of, play with, put down, smirk at, tease, wield one's wit against.

mode *n.* 1) way, way of doing things, weave, wont, 2) cut, last word, latest thing, look, new look, trend.

model *n.* 1) drawing, lay-out, likeness, outline, 2) leading light, man of mark, nonesuch, worthy, 3) sitter (for a *picture*).

moderate *adj.* fair, half-way, in between, middle-of-the-road, middling, mild, neither one nor the other, so-so, steady.

moderate *v.* to cut back, lessen, lighten, make less, trim.

modern *adj.* latest, latter-day, new, newfangled, up with the times.

modest *adj.* maidenly, mild, shamefast, shrinking, shy.

module *n.* 1) likeness, outline, 2) bit (of some craft), 3) learning-step (in a path of learning).

molest *v.* to befoul, harm, mar, mishandle, rough up, twist, warp.

moment *n.* breath, heart-beat, 'prick' in time, little while, this while, short span, smoke in the wind, stroke, twinkling of an eye.

(in a) **moment** *adv.* all at once, at a stroke, at one swoop, in the same breath, in the twinkling of an eye, like a shot, no sooner said than done, now, overnight, readily.

momentous *adj.* breathtaking, earth-shaking, far-reaching, going to the root, key, newsworthy, now or never, on the anvil, overriding, stirring, telling, weighty.

money *n.* wealth, riches, gold, silver, wherewithal, the needful.

monopoly *n.* ring, owning all.

monotonous *adj.* dreary, dry, endless, longsome, overlong, wearing, wearisome.

monument *n.* 1) gravestone, headstone, marker, 2) token, witness.

morale *n.* grit, heart, good heart, hope and belief, high hopes, strong hope, self-belief, steadfastness, steel, steeliness, stiff upper lip, strength of heart/mind/will.

morality *n.* cleanness, earnestness, fair play, godliness, godly fear, goodness, righteousness, rightwiseness, rightness, sinlessness, uprightness, truth.

moratorium *n.* freeze, standstill.

mortal *adj.* death-bound, time-bound, doomed, earth-born, fleeting, flesh and blood, flickering, short-lived.

mortgage *n.* borrowings, owings.

motel *n.* road house, inn, bed and breakfast.

motion *n.* 1) coming, going, headway, flow, gliding, sliding, restlessness, unrest, rising, sinking, shift, run, running, walking, 2) draft, rough draft, feeler (put forward at a meeting).

motivate *v.* to awaken, drive, fire up, lead, play upon, put up to, quicken, shame into doing, spur, stir, work upon, work on the feelings.

motive *n.* ground, mainspring, spring, spur, why and wherefore.

motorway *n.* fast road, freeway, highway, mainway, throughway.

mould *n.* frame, shape, shell, stamp.

mount, mountain *n.* 1) height, high land, horn, peak, ridge, 2) backing, frame, setting, stand, 3) horse, steed.

mount *v.* 1) to clamber up, climb up, go upwards, make one's way up, 2) to frame, set off, 3) to bestride, climb onto, get up on, straddle, 4) to climb up on, get on to, step aboard, 5) to build up, gather, grow, swell, 6) to begin/make/set on foot an onset, make a strike, 7) to set, set up, 8) to put on.

move *n.* 1) bid, coming, deed, doing, going, opening, play, rise, stirring, work, working, 2) game, shift, step.

move *v.* 1) to bestir oneself, be up and doing, bring into play, come, go, come and go, drag, draw, drive, handle, pull, quicken, rise, sink, run, send, set on foot, set going, shift, shove, spur on, start up, step, stir, sweep along, wield, work, 2) to awaken, draw tears, fire up, set on fire, quicken/stir/warm the heart, stir the feelings, 3) to moot, put forward a draft/rough draft (to a meeting), put to.

movement *n.* 1) ado, coming, going, doing, working, breakthrough, drive, flow, headway, gliding, sliding, rising, sinking, running, shift, steps, stirring, 2) one 'dream' or song (*movement*) in a work of dreamcraft/song-craft (*music*), 3) body, brotherhood, following, gathering, set, side, team.

mud *n.* clay, filth, ooze, slime.

multiple *adj.* manifold, many, many-headed, many more, ever so many, much, not a few, overflowing, sundry, thousand and one, untold.

multiply *v.* 1) to build up, flood, spread, swarm, teem, throng, widen, 2) to blossom, breed, bring forth, hatch, shoot up, sprout, yield.

multitude *n.* crowd, drove, flood, great deal, heap, herd, lot, muchness, stream, swarm, throng, wainload, sea of, wealth of, world of, the world and his wife.

mundane *adj.* 1) day-to-day, everyday, workaday, 2) earthly, fleshly, worldly.

municipal *adj.* borough, town.

muscle *n.* 1) thew, 2) might, right arm, strength, 3) pull, weight.

music *n.* dreamcraft, dream-song, song-craft, cradle-song, singing, song, love-song, undersong, burden, setting, work.

musician *n.* dreamer, harper, horn-player, player, singer, song-smith, songster, songstress, songwright, song-writer.

mutual *adj.* shared, two-way.

mysterious *adj.* <u>knotted</u>, hard to fathom/understand, dark, deep, hidden, shadowy, shrouded, unknown.

mystery *n.* brain-twister, maze, riddle, teaser, hidden depths, the unknown.

myth *n.* 1) old-tale, folk tale, dream-tale, shadow, 2) make-believe, old wives' tale, tall tale.

naïve *adj.* childish, goosish, green, <u>open</u>, raw, readily taken in, born yesterday, <u>unfledged</u>, unlearned, untaught, unwary, unworldly, <u>witless</u>.

narrative *n.* book, tale, word-craft, word-weaving.

nasty *adj.* bad, <u>dreadful</u>, evil, filthy, foul, <u>loathsome</u>, sickening, unwholesome.

nation *n.* folkdom, kingdom.

national *adj.* land-wide, widespread.

nationalism *n.* father-/motherland love, homeland-love, love of one's birth-land.

native *n.* folklander, hearthlander, homelander, homeling, inlander.

native *adj.* homeborn, settled.

natural *adj.* 1) inborn, inbred, in the blood, 2) everyday, stock, wonted, 3) friendly, <u>open</u>, open-hearted, straightforward, unbidden, warm, 4) homely, homespun, true to life, unmingled, wholesome.

nature *n.* 1) earth, world, wild life, landship (*landscape*), 2) bent of mind, breed, hue, ilk, kind, leaning, make, make-up, outlook.

navigate *v.* to find one's way, handle (a ship), hold the helm, sail, steer, make a landfall, make for, see how the land lies, take one's bearings, work a ship, head for.

navy *n.* fleet.

neat *adj.* 1) bright, clean, 2) (of strong drink) hard, heady, straight, strong, unmingled, 3) shipshape, smart, straight, tidy, trim, uncluttered, well-kept, 4) (of looks) elf-fair, lithe, willowy, winsome, 5) (of wording) pithy, put in a nutshell, in a few well-chosen words, 6) <u>deft</u>, handy, nimble, quick.

necessarily *adv.* all along of, because of, willy-nilly.

necessary *adj.* needed, needful, needwise, bound to be, binding, overriding.

necessity *n.* must, need, needfulness.

negative *adj.* dead against, hindering, unwilling, withholding.

neglect *v.* to leave hanging/undone, let slide, not follow through, slack, <u>daydream</u>.

negligence *n.* carelessness, flightiness, forgetfulness, <u>heedlessness</u>, slackness, sloppiness, thoughtlessness.

negligent *adj.* careless, forgetful, head in the clouds, <u>heedless</u>, reckless, slack, thoughtless, unheeding, unmindful, unthinking.

negotiation *n.* dealing, wheeling and dealing, talks.

nerve *n.* 1) coolness, daring, fearlessness, grit, <u>steadfastness</u>, 2) boldness, brazenness, forwardness, shamelessness, uppishness.

nervous *adj.* churned up, cringing, <u>fearful</u>, forstraught, highly-strung, on edge, quaking, restless, rudderless, <u>shaken</u>, shaky, shrinking, treading warily, wary, unmanned, unsettled.

neutral *adj.* even-handed, fair, middle-of-the-road, keeping to the middle, half and half, half-way, in between, lukewarm, neither one nor the other, neithersome.

newspaper *n.* broadsheet, news-sheet, morning/evening news.

nice *adj.* 1) careful, choosy, well-bred, 2) dead-on, narrow, right, true, straight, thorough, 3) (of food) toothsome, 4) (of the weather) bright, cloudless, dry, fair, sunny, 5) (of looks) lovely, pretty, soft, 6) <u>friendly</u>, good, goodly, helpful, kind.

noble, nobleman *n.* earl, elder, elderman, lord, lady, knight, 'ætheling'.

noble *adj.* <u>worthy</u>, highborn, of high worth, kingly, queenly, lordly, ladylike, of mark, well-born.

noise *n.* clatter, din, <u>loudness</u>, roar, uproar, stamping.

noisy *adj.* clattering, deafening, dinning, ear-rending, loud, ringing, thundering.

nonplussed <u>bewildered</u>, all at sea, at a loss, in two minds.

nonsense *n.* childishness, empty/idle talk, meaninglessness, outlandishness.

noon *n.* full-time of the day, mid-daytide, middle day.

norm *n.* benchmark, yardstick, run of the mill, standing-kind.

normal *adj.* 1) all in the day's work, everyday, nothing wonderful, stock, wonted, 2) in one's right mind, not wandering, witfast, wit-right.

normally *adv.* in the main, mostly, most often, on the whole, overall, wontedly.

notable *adj.* earth-shaking, in the foreground/limelight, newsworthy, marked, outstanding, stirring, striking, top-flight, well-known.

note *n.* 1) key (of a *piano*), 2) bird song, 3) hint, mark, token, 4) outline, 5) name, talk of the town.

note *v.* 1) to bear in mind, be aware, give heed to, 2) to put down in black and white, put in writing, set down, write down, 3) to mark, see.

noteworthy *adj.* amazing, foremost, leading, marked, outstanding, starring, striking, to the fore, unwonted, <u>wonderful</u>.

notice *n.* 1) foretoken, warning, word, 2) news, write-up, 3) heed, 4) forewarning of work-ending.

notice *v.* to become aware of, <u>heed</u>, mark, see, sit up and listen, wake up to.

notion *n.* 1) belief, insight, thought, 2) whim, wish.

novel *n.* tale, work.

novel *adj.* ground-breaking, new, new-made, unheard-of, upstart.

November *n.* Wind-month, Blood-month.

nuanced *adj.* careful, carefully weighed/worded, thoughtful.

nude *adj.* bare, naked, stripped, unclothed, shorn, unclad, in the raw, naked as the day one was born, without a stitch on.

nuisance *n.* 1) <u>evil</u>, goad, pin-prick, sting, upset, 2) busybody, <u>evil-doer</u>, gossip, ne'er-do-well, stirrer, undoer.

number *n.* reckoning, end-rime, rime-tally, rime-tell, tale.

numerous *adj.* ever so many, lots, manifold, many, not a few, overflowing, thick on the ground, untold, a thousand and one.

nurse *n.* carer, caregiver.

obedient *adj.* law-abiding, well-behaved, wieldy, willing, yielding.

obesity *n.* fatness, fleshiness, heaviness.

obey *v.* to bow to, give in, give up, listen to, <u>yield</u> to.

obfuscate *v.* to becloud, cloud, darken, hide, leave no wiser.

object *n.* 1) body, thing, 2) end, goal, the why and wherefore, wish.

objective *n.* end, by-end, goal, mark, hope, <u>longing</u>, wish, yearning.

objective *adj.* 1) <u>right</u>, <u>true</u>, true to life, <u>well-grounded</u>, down to earth, 2) even-handed, fair, fair-minded, middle-of-the-road, open-minded, thoughtful, unswerving.

obligation *n.* burden, oath, owings, plighted word, undertaking.

obliged *adj.* 1) bound, bounden, fain, willing, 2) beholden, behoven, thankful.

oblivious *adj.* blind to, deaf to, careless, forgetful, <u>heedless</u>, taken up, unaware, unhearing, unseeing, unheeding, unmindful.

observation *n.* 1) awareness, heed, look, look-over, <u>sifting</u>, watching, weighing, 2) byword, deeming, feedback, finding, input, insight,

ready speech, say, spoken word, thought, understanding, word, write-up.

observe *v.* 1) to become aware, be all ears/eyes, deem, say, see, mark, <u>heed</u>, put a meaning on, say something about, speak about, talk about, throw light on, understand by, watch, write about, write up, 2) to abide by, hold to one's word.

observer *n.* beholder, bystander, look-out, looker-on, onlooker, speaker, spokesman, watcher, watchdog, witness, eyewitness, gossip writer, newshound.

obsession *n.* blind belief, one-mindedness, unwisdom, bee in one's breeches,

obstinate *adj.* pig-headed, stiff-necked, unbending, <u>wilful</u>.

obtain *v.* to <u>gather</u>, come by, fasten on, make one's own.

obvious *adj.* open, straightforward, unclouded, unhidden, well-known, well-marked, cut and dried, open-and-shut, for all to see, right before one's eyes, right under one's nose, written all over one.

obviously *adv.* markedly, needless to say.

occasion *n.* 1) time, marked time, high time, right time, 2) gathering, happening, 3) opening, 4) ground/s, the why and wherefore.

occasional *adj.* almost unheard of, few and far between, uneven, unsteady.

occasionally *adv.* from time to time, sometimes, <u>fitfully</u>, off and on, once in a while.

occupation *n.* 1) business on hand, craft, daily work, livelihood, walk of life, 2) take-over, overrunning, 3) holding.

occupied *adj.* 1) full, taken, 2) lived-in, settled, 3) busy, hard at it, hard at work, working, tied up.

occur *v.* 1) to arise, be, become, befall, betide, come about, follow, spring up, start up, come off, crop up, fall out, 2) to be found, be met with, fill, run through, spread through, show itself.

occurrence *n.* arising, outcome, showing.

ocean *n.* 1) the deep, fathomless deep, great deep, great sea, high seas, great waters, open sea, the sea, the waves, wide sea, 2) great deal, a heap/load/lot.

October *n.* Winter-fulleth (month of the first full moon of winter), Tenth-month.

odd *adj.* 1) bewildering, far-fetched, hard to swallow, nigh beyond belief, outlandish, out of the way, uncanny, unheard of, <u>weird</u>, 2) mazed, not right in the head, wandering, wildered in one's wits, 3) left over, over, lone, uneven.

offence n. 1) guilt, misdeed, misdoing, overstepping, sin, 2) bad/hard/wounded feelings, bitterness, soreness, wrath, 3) harm.

offensive n. breakthrough, drive, inroad, onset, over-running, strike, swoop.

offensive adj. 1) biting, cutting, <u>uncouth</u>, 2) bad, foul, fulsome, <u>loathsome</u>, rank, sickening, stinking, unwholesome.

office n. 1) business house, workroom, 2) business, work, field, field of work.

officer n. lord, reeve, sheriff, right-holder.

official n. reeve, reeveman, town reeve, right-hand man, sheriff, shire-man, steward, right-holder.

official adj. binding, straight from the horse's mouth, <u>well-grounded</u>.

oil n. 1) *oil* 2) salve.

okay adj. intj. n. 1) all right, fair, good, <u>middling</u>, well, 2) all right, right, fair enough, well and good, yes, 3) blessing, go-ahead, green light, say-so.

omission n. 1) leaving out, shortcoming, good left undone, 2) carelessness, falling short, forgetfulness, oversight, slackness, slip.

onerous adj. burdensome, hard, heavy, tough, <u>wearing</u>, weighty.

onus n. burden, load, weight, worry.

opaque adj. 1) bedimmed, clouded, cloudy, darkened, dim, filmy, 2) full of long words, <u>knotted</u>, unfathomful.

opera n. singing work, dream-play, dream-setting.

operate v. 1) to bring to bear, drive, further, handle, oversee, run, see to, wield, work, 2) to be in business, be in play, play upon, deal, pull strings, 3) to cut open, put right/straighten out/work on someone's inside, put someone under the knife, 4) to fight, take the fight to the foe.

operation n. 1) running, working, working setup, 2) business, doing, handling, undertaking, 3) working, 4) (*surgery*) cutwork, handwork, 5) fighting.

operational adj. going, in play, live, ready, running, up and doing/running, working.

operator n. 1) craftsman, dealer, driver, handler, player, worker, 2) string-puller, wheeler-dealer, wirepuller.

opinion n. belief, mind made up, stand, thought, way of thinking/thought.

opportunistic adj. self-seeking, sharp and shifty, worldly.

opportunity n. opening, room, freedom, free hand, free field, stepping-stone.

oppose v. to <u>fight</u>, <u>withstand</u>, set at naught, stand against, stand up to.

opposite adj. anything but, other, over against, telling against, unlike.

opposition n. 1) going against, hindering, stand, unhelpfulness, unwillingness, <u>uprising</u>, walk-out, withholding, dragging one's heels, headwind, 2) the other side.

optimal adj. <u>best</u>, foremost, highest, peak, <u>worthful</u>.

optimistic adj. <u>bright</u>, carefree, hopeful, in good heart, <u>lively</u>, forward-looking, sunny, looking on the bright side.

optimum adj. best, first, foremost, highest, leading, outstanding, peak, <u>worthful</u>.

option n. free choosing.

opt out v. to back out, drop out, leave, pull out, withdraw.

oral adj. aloud, out loud, spoken, unwritten.

orange adj. brass-hue, gold-hue, old gold, yellow-red.

order n. 1) smoothness, steadiness, tidiness, 2) kind-name, 3) bidding, behest, say-so, word, writ.

order v. 1) to put into shape, <u>ready</u>, set out, sift out, 2) to bid, lay down, say so, tell.

orderly adj. 1) careful, steady, well-behaved, 2) businesslike, shipshape, smooth, straight, thorough, tidy, trim, well-kept.

ordinary adj. everyday, homespun, all in a day's work, stock, workaday.

organic adj. 1) live, living, 2) blossoming, growing, 3) inwoven, inwrought, key, underlying, 4) whole, 5) (of food growing) unmingled, wholesome.

organisation n. 1) body, cluster, gathering, ring, 2) drafting, fitting out/up, groundwork, handling, oversight, running, setting up, steering, working out.

organise v. 1) to draw up, draft, frame, lay out, mark out, put together, <u>ready</u>, run, see to, set up, shape, put into shape, put to rights, settle, straighten out, take care of, think through, 2) to write out.

origin n. beginning, cradle, dawn, root, starting, wellspring, womb.

original adj. 1) early, earliest, first, opening, starting, 2) from nowhere, ground-breaking, new, newfangled, new-made, owing nothing to, unheard of.

originally adv. at first, first, firstly, at the start, at the outset, in the beginning, to begin with.

ostensible adj. outward, on the outside, meeting the eyes.

oust v. to put out, root out, throw out, topple, unsaddle, throw out on one's ear.

outdated, out-of-date, outmoded adj. behind the times, of other times, old-fangled, timeworn, has-been.

outstrip v. to beat, leave behind/standing, outdo, outgo, outmatch, outrun, outstride.

overpower v. to overcome, beat, bring down, fell, outmatch, outplay, overthrow, overwhelm, throw down, worst.

overture n. 1) foreglimpse, forelook, foreshowing, foretale, opening, unfolding, 2) feeler, hand of friendship, reaching out.

pace n. 1) step, footstep, stride, tread, yard, 2) liveliness, quickness, speed, fair speed, swiftness.

pacific adj. friendly, mild.

pack n. 1) bundle, burden, load, 2) crowd, drove, flock, herd, lot, set.

pack v. 1) to bundle, load, stow, tie up, 2) to crowd, fill, flock into, throng.

package n. 1) box, 2) bundle, lot, set, swathe.

page n. 1) leaf (of a book), sheet, side, 2) (of an *episode*/time in *history*) day, spell, time, time-tale, while-time.

pain n. ache, bitterness, heartache, smart, sore, soreness, sorrow, sting.

painful adj. 1) aching, biting, bitter, burning, raw, searing, sharp, shooting, smarting, sore, stinging, tearing, 2) cutting, gnawing, harrowing, saddening, stabbing, upsetting, wounding, wringing, 3) backbreaking, hard, rough, tough, uphill, wearing.

paint n. dye, madder, hue-wash, whitewash, water-hues, woad, make-up.

paint v. 1) to brighten, do over, do up, put on, smarten, whitewash, 2) to do in water-hues/in black and white, draw, make a likeness, pick out, 3) (with words) to bring to life, make one see, put into words, set forth, show, tell in a lively way.

painter n. hue craftsman/craftswoman.

painting n. drawing, line-drawing, likeness, still life, lifecraft, huecraft, water-hue.

pair n. 1) match, set, matched set, two of a kind, 2) twain, twosome.

palace n. king's hall, king's house, great house.

pale adj. 1) light, light-hued, soft, soft-hued, 2) ashen, ashen-hued, ashy, bleached, bloodless, ghastly, like a ghost, hueless, sallow, wan, washed-out, watery, waxen, whitish, like death warmed up.

palfrey n. 1) saddle-horse for daily riding, riding-horse, 2) small horse for ladies.

palliative adj. lessening, softening, soothing.

pandemic n. quelm, sickness.

pandemonium n. din, free for all, madhouse, much ado, to-do, shouting, storm, upheaving, uproar, wildness.

panel n. 1) body, team, 2) board, sheet.

panic n. dread, fear, fright, affright, cold feet.

panic v. to be filled with fear, frightened to death, take fright, shake/shrink with fear, shiver, quake, feel one's blood run cold, feel one's hair stand on end.

panorama n. eyeful, landship, outlook.

paper n. 1) reed-sheet, drawing-sheet, writing-sheet, 2) broadsheet, daily, news-sheet, 3) working *paper*, written work.

parable n. byspell, teaching-tale, likening, life-tale, tale with a meaning.

parade n. 1) show, street show, field day, gathering, 2) shopping street.

parade v. to show, show off, make a show of, stamp, step, stride out, tread.

paradox n. hard saying, knotty saying, riddle, one truth against another, unmatched meanings.

paradoxical adj. riddled, weird and wayward.

parallel adj. 1) akin, like, matching, 2) abreast, alongside, side by side.

paramilitary n. fighter, hired fighter, dog of war.

paramount adj. first, foremost, greatest, leading, main, nonesuch, overriding.

pardon v. to forbear, forgive and forget, spare, whitewash, write off what is owed.

parent n. father, mother, foster-father, foster-mother, begetter, the old man, head of the kindred, forbear, forefather.

parliament n. folkmoot, gathering, speech-house, steering body.

part n. 1) bit, cut, deal, limb, lot, share, fourth, half, length, wedge, 2) neighbourhood, neck of the woods, 3) limb, 4) (in playcraft) lead, lines, words, 5) business, hand, say, work.

part v. to break away, break up, come between, go one's own way, sunder, unbind.

partially adv. by halves, halfly, halfway, not wholly, somewhat.

participate v. to be in on, be one of, come in for a share, feel with, have a hand in, share in, share and share alike.

participation n. sharing in, taking a hand in.

particle n. bit, crumb, mite, mote, shred, speck, whit.

particular adj. 1) cut and dried, known, marked, named, right, settled, shown, true, 2) all edges, choosy, prickly, stiff, unbending, 3) careful, mindful, <u>sharp</u>, thorough, thoroughgoing, with nothing left out/missing.

particularly *adv.* 1) <u>above all</u>, above all things, the more so, 2) <u>greatly</u>, highly, mainly, markedly, outstandingly, much, strongly, utterly.

partisan *n.* 1) backer, follower, <u>friend</u>, good friend, henchman, leftist, rightist, right-hand man, stalwart, upholder, well-wisher, 2) freedom fighter, underground fighter.

partisan *adj.* one-sided, narrow, narrow-minded, small-minded.

partly *adv.* a bit, a little, half, in a small way, not fully, not wholly, somewhat.

partner *n.* 1) <u>friend</u>, fast friend, henchman, right-hand man, sharer, 2) folk (that is, *common*) law husband/wife.

part-time *adj.* half-time, less than full-time.

party *n.* 1) at home, gathering, get-together, merrymaking, mirthmaking, gathering, 2) body, brotherhood, following, set, side, team.

pass *v.* 1) to go, go over, make one's way, leap-frog, leap over, overgo, wend, 2) to beat, go beyond, go one better, leave behind, <u>outdo</u>, overstep, overtop, pull ahead, 3) to deal out, give, hand down, hand on, hand over, let someone have, make over, 4) (in some games) to head, send, throw, 5) to be bequeathed, be left, have willed to, have come to, 6) to befall, fall out, 7) (of time) to flow, go by, glide away, run, wear on, 8) (of time) to fill, while away, 9) to blow over, die, dwindle, ebb, end, go, have had its day, melt away, wane, wear away, 10) (of a *test, examination*), to get through, come off well, do well, do enough, do what is needed, 11) to give/make a new law (through *parliament*), to back/fall in with the new law, give it one's blessing, 12) to empty one's inside, go to stool, make water, let out.

passage *n.* 1) hallway, inway, way in, way through, 2) gateway, narrow lane/street, back street, by-street, side street, path, pathway, way, wynd, 3) (from a book) bit, cutting, reading, 4) flow, shift, 5) inlet, mouth, opening, throughput, 6) faring, wayfaring, going, 7) crossing, overgoing.

passenger *n.* 1) farer, rider, 2) dead-weight, drag, idler.

passion *n.* 1) burning wish, strong wish, craving, hunger, thirst, 2) wrath, bitterness, hard feelings, heat, high words.

password *n.* key word, leave-word, watchword.

past *n.* 1) days gone by, foretime, former times, heretofore time, long-ago days, bygone days, old days, olden times, days/times of yore, 2) background, life.

pat *n.* stroke.

pat *v.* to play with, stroke.

patchy *adj.* bitty, fickle, <u>fitful</u>, flighty, makeshift, uneven, <u>shifting</u>, unsteady, half and half, few and far between.

patent *n.* right, trademark.

pathetic *adj.* 1) bitter, harrowing, heartbreaking, heart-rending, heart-wringing, sad, upsetting, 2) heart-lorn, <u>lacking</u>, listless, mean, shallow, <u>sorry</u>, woeful, <u>worthless</u>.

pathology *n.* sick-lore.

patience *n.* 1) forgiveness, kindness, sweetness, 2) doughtiness, heart-strength, <u>steadfastness</u>, steadiness.

patient *n.* sick one.

patient *adj.* <u>abiding</u>, dogged, forbearing, forgiving, mild, <u>steadfast</u>, understanding.

patrol *n.* watch, watchman, night-watch.

patrol *v.* to keep an eye on, keep watch, sweep.

pattern *n.* 1) benchmark, draft, framework, drawing, lay-out, outline, teaching, 2) leading light, man of mark, nonesuch, worthy.

pause *n.* break, breather, breathing time, let-up, rest, standstill, stop.

pause *v.* to bide one's time, break, hang fire, lie fallow, play for time, rest, rest on one's oars, stand by, stop for a while, stop for breath, stop to think, think twice.

pay *n.* earnings, income, meed, takings.

pay *v.* 1) to lay out, meet, settle, settle the reckoning, 2) to be worth while, bring in, bring grist to the mill, come right in the end, do good, earn, stand one in good stead, yield, 3) to bestow, give, hand out.

payment *n.* outgoings, outlay, reckoning, settling.

peace *n.* 1) weal, well-being, wholeness, friendship, frith, fighting forsworn, understanding, hand of friendship, sword-sheathing, 2) rest, restfulness, stillness, sweet dreams/sleep.

peaceful *adj.* 1) <u>friendly</u>, mild, 2) restful, soothing, still, unstirring.

peculiar *adj.* 1) other, outlandish, out of the way, uncanny, unearthly, unlike, unwonted, <u>weird</u>, 2) mazed, not right in the head, wildered in one's wits.

pedestrian *n.* walker, footfarer, footgoer, sidewalker.

peer *v.* to look narrowly, look out, look over.

penalty *n.* 1) doom, reckoning, 2) drawback.

pending *adj.* held over, on hold, on ice, frozen, on the back burner, put off, set aside.

penetrate v. 1) to bore, get into, get in through, go through, make inroads, prick, stab, 2) to fathom, get to the bottom of, grasp, understand, work out.

penetrating adj. insightful, keen-minded, sharp, sharp-witted, wise, thinking, understanding, witfast, witful.

peninsula n. byland, foreland, half-island, headland, head, horn, seagirt land, spit.

pensive adj. dreaming, dreamy, deep in thought, heedful, insightful, listful, lost in thought, mindful, thinking, thoughtful, wise, wistful.

people n. 1) folk, mankind, men and women, 2) the crowd, the herd, 3) folkdom, 4) kin, kindred, kinsfolk, kinsman, kinswoman, kith and kin, household, nearest and dearest, one's own flesh and blood.

per annum a year, year by year, yearly.

perceive v. to become aware of, find out, know, understand.

per cent (so much) in a hundred.

percentage (so many) out of a hundred, by hundredths.

perception n. awareness, insight, long-headedness, quickness, sharpness, shrewdness, understanding, wisdom, wit.

perceptive adj. awake, bright, insightful, keen-minded, sharp, sharp-witted, wise, thinking, understanding, witfast, witful.

perfect adj. 1) full, matchless, smooth, unbroken, unmarred, whole, with nothing missing, wholly worthy, 2) clean-handed, wholly good, guiltless, free from guilt, not guilty, in the right, sinless.

perfection n. worth, full worth, high worth, fullness, guiltlessness, height of goodness, last word, nothing like, wholeness.

perfectly adv. fully, matchlessly, thoroughly, truly, utterly, wholly.

perform v. 1) to bring about, clinch, do, follow through, pull off, shape, 2) to play, put on, tread the boards, 3) to behave, drive, go, handle, run, work, 4) to fulfil.

performance n. 1) doing, making, shaping, handiwork, work, workmanship, output, through-put, 2) playcraft, playing, show, 3) running, working.

perhaps adv. maybe, it may be, if so be, for all one knows.

period n. 1) length of time, run, shift, span, spell, stint, stretch, time, 2) days, years, time, stretch of time, stream of time, time span, timestretch.

permanent adj. abiding, deep-rooted, holding, long-lasting, outlasting, settled.

permission n. blessing, freedom, go-ahead, green light, leave.

permit n. free hand, leave, right, writ.

permit v. to be willing, give leave, give one's blessing, let, not stand in the way, open the door, say yes to.

perpetuate v. to keep alive, keep going, keep on foot, keep up, uphold.

perplexed adj. bewildered, forstraught, at a loss, at one's wits' end, lost.

persecution n. evil, harm, harrying, heavy hand.

persevering adj. dogged, earnest, lasting, steadfast, steady, strong-minded, tireless, undying, unshrinking, unyielding.

person n. being, everyman, everywoman, one, soul, living soul, self, inner self, somebody, someone.

personal adj. 1) own, in one's hand, unshared, 2) live, in the flesh, 3) inward, inwoven, inwrought, 4) forward, off-hand, 5) bodily, fleshly, 6) first-hand.

personality n. 1) bent, bent of mind, breed, ilk, kind, make, make-up, mark, 2) name, household name, leading name, a somebody, a worthy, 'star'.

personally adv. 1) in one's thinking, for oneself, 2) alone, by oneself, in one's own right, on one's own, in the flesh, 3) at bottom, in the main.

perspective n. 1) outlook, way of looking, 2) line of sight.

persuade v. to bring over, make one believe, put over, settle, talk into, win over.

persuasive adj. likely, telling, straightforward, well-grounded, weighty, winning.

pertinent adj. answering to, bearing upon, becoming, belonging, in keeping, meaningful, meet, right, timely.

pervert v. to befoul, foul, beslime, mar, mislead, teach wickedness, twist, warp.

pessimistic adj. downhearted, forboding, heavy-hearted, hopeless, hopelorn, listless, sad, wretched.

petitioner n. asker, seeker.

phase n. lap, run, span, spell, step, stretch, time.

phenomenon n. 1) arising, becoming, shadowing forth, showing, upshot, 2) eye-opener, nonesuch, wonder.

phenomenonal adj. 1) almost/nigh unheard of, dreamlike, outward, showing itself, shown, unearthly, <u>weird</u>, 2) amazing, striking, unheard of, <u>wonderful</u>.

philosophical adj. 1) <u>learned</u>, thoughtful, wise, 2) cool, even, <u>steadfast</u>, steady, unshaken, unworried, unworrying.

philosophy n. 1) awareness, knowledge, thought, understanding, <u>wisdom</u>, 2) beliefs, outlook, thinking.

'phone n. see *'telephone'.*

'phone v. see *'telephone'.*

photograph n. shot, film-shot, slide, still, lightshot, likeness.

phrase n. saying, word-cluster, wordset.

physical adj. 1) bodily, earthly, fleshly, of flesh and blood, 2) done by hand, 3) earthy, fleshly, lewd, lustful, thrill-seeking, worldly.

physically adv. in body, in flesh.

piano n. keyboard.

picture n. 1) drawing, black and white drawing, line-drawing, likeness, still life, water-hue, woodcut, 2) film, 3) setting.

piece n. 1) bit, cut, length, mouthful, shard, sliver, shred, wedge, 2) spread, stretch, 3) handiwork, short play, show, work.

pierce v. to cut through, hole, honeycomb, knock holes in, prick, riddle, run through, spear, spit, stab, stave in, stick into, wound.

piercing adj. 1) (of *sound*) high-pitched, loud, sharp, 2) keen, keen-sighted, searing, <u>sharp</u>, shrewd, 3) shooting, stabbing, 4) (of wind or weather) biting, bitter, chill, cutting, freezing, raw, wintry.

pilot n. 1) flyer, flight-man, 2) helmsman, steersman.

pink adj. flushed, light red, reddish.

pioneer n. 1) leader, pathfinder, 2) newcomer, settler.

pioneer v. to break new ground, dare, go first, lay the groundwork for, lead the way, make a path for, open the door to, open up, set going, show the way, start.

pip, pippin n. kernel, (hard) seed, stone.

pity v. to feel for/with, feel sorry for, <u>sorrow</u>, bleed for, weep for, yearn over.

place n. 1) neighbourhood, pitch, setting, stead, steading, stow, when and where, whereabouts, 2) abode, dwelling, <u>home</u>, homeground, <u>house</u>, room, stamping ground, backyard, fireside, 3) footing, ground, standing, 4) work, 'berth', 5) one's business/care/right/work.

place v. 1) to lay/put/set down, lay out, set out, settle, stand, stow, 2) to put.

placing n. 'berth', pitch, setting.

plagiarism n. 'borrowing', lifting, sham-work, stealing, theft, thieving, thought-theft, writing-theft.

plain n. grassland, uplands.

plain adj. bald, bare, everyday, homely, homespun, stark, workaday.

plain-speaking, plain-spoken adj. bald, downright, <u>forthright</u>, outright, outspoken.

plan n. draft, drawing, lay-out, readying, weave.

plan v. to draw up, draft, find a way, frame, lay out, mark out, put into shape, <u>ready</u>, think through, think up.

plane n. drawing-knife, shaver, spokeshave, wood-smoother.

planet n. heavenly body, world.

planning n. drafting, forethought, groundwork, setting up, working out.

plaster n. 1) cloth-swathing, 2) a mingling of lime, sand and hair spread on to a bare wall.

plaster v. 1) to bind up, 2) to do over, overlay, smear, besmear, spread.

plastic adj. bendsome, soft, stretchy, yielding.

plate n. 1) *dish*, 2) sheet.

plausible adj. likely, telling, <u>well-grounded</u>, winning over.

pleasant adj. blissful, sweet, welcome, wilsome, winsome, <u>winning</u>.

please v. to <u>bewitch</u>, bless, gladden, leave nothing more to wish for.

please be kind enough to, kindly.

pleased adj. blessed, glad, thankful.

pleasure n. blessedness, bliss, gladdening, gladness, mirth, thrill.

plenty n. <u>wealth</u>, fullness, a great deal, a lot, more than enough, riches, rich harvest.

plot n. 1) ground, land, lea, mead, meadow, 2) (in playcraft) heart, pith, thread, play outline, 3) shift, underhand dealing, understanding, web, web-weaving, frame-up.

plot v. 1) to be up to something, lay heads together, play a deep game, play the fox, shift, spin/weave a web, work against, 2) to draft, draw, frame, mark, outline.

plunge v. to bathe, dip, dive, fall, fall in, go down, go under, reach the depths, sink.

plural adj. manifold, many, many-sided, more than one, upwards of.

plus prep. and, besides, with.

pocket n. 1) *pocket*, 2) wherewithal, 3) (as in *'pocket* of *resistance'*) cluster, island.

poem n. song, song-dream.

poet n. songwright, wordwright, wordcraftsman, wordcrafter, wordshaper.

poetic adj. dreamy, wordcrafty.

point *n.* 1) burden, ground, heart, marrow, meaning, pith, 2) end, goal, 3) side, 4) time, right time, 5) pitch, setting, 6) sharp end, spur, peak, top, 7) mark, 8) bill, foreland, headland, ness, spit.

point *v.* to bespeak, betoken, earmark, hint, mark out, set one's sights, show.

pointed *adj.* 1) edged, sharp, spear-like, 2) sharp, stinging, telling, waspish.

pointing *n.* 1) (in written *Semitic*) putting in *vowel* marks, 2) filling up the seams in *brickwork* with mingled lime, sand and water (*mortar*), infilling.

poise *n.* 1) bearing, becomingness, breeding, coolness, queenliness, steadiness, winsomeness, 2) evenness, even-weight.

poison *n.* bane, blight, curse, hemlock, wormwood.

polarise *v.* to drive asunder, drive a wedge between, set against.

police *n.* arm of the law.

policy *n.* line, steps.

polished *adj.* 1) bright, glassy, gleaming, shining, slippery, smooth, 2) fair-spoken, well-bred, 3) matchless, outstanding, shining, worthful.

polite *adj.* fair-spoken, knightly, ladylike, well-behaved, well-bred, well-spoken.

politician *n.* lawmaker, old hand.

politics *n.* line, give-and-take, horse-dealing.

pollution *n.* 1) badness, blight, breakdown, break-up, fouling, 2) evil, foul play, shamefulness, ungodliness, unrightness, wickedness.

pompous *adj.* 1) full of oneself, high and mighty, on one's high horse, overbearing, overweening, showy, stiff, swollen-headed, unbending, wise in one's own eyes, 2) (of speech) high-flown, long-worded, overblown, windy, wordy.

ponder *v.* to bethink oneself, brood upon, chew over, give thought to, think, think about, think over, think upon, weigh, sleep on it.

poor *adj.* 1) badly off, hard up, needy, not blest with this world's goods, not making ends meet, not well-off, penniless, short, unwealthy, weal-less, 2) wretched, 3) broken, mean, worthless.

popular *adj.* 1) liked, well-liked, well thought of, made much of, sought-after, 2) broad, stock, sweeping, widespread, 3) for everybody, for the man in the street, straightforward, 'middlebrow'.

population *n.* folk, landfolk, townsfolk.

porch *n.* doorway, hall inway.

portable *adj.* handy, light, lightweight.

portion *n.* 1) bit, share, 2) (of food) cut, helping, sliver, wedge, 3) lot, share, wyrd.

portray *v.* to bring to life, draw, make a likeness, make one see, mark out, set out, set forth, put in words, show, tell, write about.

pose *n.* bearing, look.

position *n.* 1) bearings, when and where, whereabouts, 2) footing, standing, suchness, weight, worthship, 3) livelihood, opening, walk of life, work, 4) belief, mind, outlook, stand, way of thinking.

positive *adj.* 1) forward-looking, hopeful, 2) helpful, worthwhile, 3) (of giving an answer) good, heartening, understanding, welcome, 4) set, settled, unshaken.

possess *v.* 1) to have, have to one's name, hold, own, be the owner of, 2) to be blessed with, be stirred/awakened, 3) to bewitch, drive mad, madden, put under a spell, take someone over.

possessed *adj.* beside oneself, bewitched, cursed, fiendsick, horn-mad, maddened, under a spell, wild.

possession/s *n.* 1) grasp, hand, hold, holding, ownership, bird in the hand, 2) belongings, goods, things, wealth.

possessive *adj.* clinging, grasping, greedy, griping, hard-fisted, hoard-hungry, mean, selfish, self-seeking.

possibility *n.* likelihood, what may/might be, field, opening, stepping-stone.

possible *adj.* likely, not too hard, open, still open, towardly, wieldy.

possibly *adv.* 1) maybe, it may be, if so be, for all one knows. 2) at all, in any way.

post *n.* tidings.

post *n.* livelihood, opening, work, berth.

post mortem *n.* 1) sifting, delving, going over or looking into what has gone on (seeking the root of death), 2) going over a game or match afterwards (to see what went right/did not go right), combing, rooting, threshing out, weighing.

postpone *v.* to hold over, hold up, lay over, leave hanging, leave undone, not follow through/up, play for time, put back, put off, put off to tomorrow, spin out, withhold, put on ice, put on the back burner.

postulate *v.* to dare say, lay down, put forward, think.

potential *n.* quickness, readiness, sharpness, understanding.

pour *v.* 1) to let flow, spill, 2) to flow, overflow, run, spew, stream, 3) (of rain) to come down in sheets, rain hard/heavily, teem, 4) to crowd, flood, stream, swarm, throng.

poverty n. beggarliness, bitterness, hand-to-mouth life, hardship, hard going, lack, last shift, need, neediness, pennilessness, unweal, wretchedness.

powder n. dust.

powder v. 1) to strew, 2) to grind, mill, pound.

power n. 1) cleverness, deftness, 2) lordship, headship, leadership, 3) greatness, lustihood, lustiness, main-strength, might, mightiness, right arm, strength, weight.

powerful adj. 1) more than a match for, overbearing, overweening, strong-willed, 2) broad-shouldered, great-limbed, lusty, mighty, stalworth, strong.

practical adj. down to earth, handy, helpful, rough and ready, shrewd, up and doing, workaday.

practically adv. 1) all but, almost, nearly, well-nigh, 2) wisely.

practice n. 1) bearing, walk, way, wont, working, 2) business, work, 3) going-over, groundwork, work-out (to get ready for a match or a race).

practise v. 1) to do one's homework, get into shape, go over, go through, harden oneself, keep one's hand in, make oneself ready, play oneself in, run through, warm up, work at, work out, 2) to follow, live up to.

pragmatic adj. broad-minded, businesslike, down to earth, everyday, workaday, hard-headed, rough and ready, straight.

praise v. to speak warmly/well of, bless, make much of, hold up.

prayer n. bidding, asking, begging, beseeching.

precarious adj. crumbling, on the edge, shaky, slippery, strengthless, unsettled, unsteady, hanging by a thread.

precaution n. care, foresight, forethought, wariness.

preceding adj. above, aforesaid, earlier, foregoing, former.

precious adj. 1) dear, dearly bought, worthful, 2) beloved, loved, darling, dear, dearest, worth its weight in gold, 3) brassy, long-worded, loud, overdone, over-loaded, put on, rich, shallow, 4) out-and-out, 'great'.

precipitate adj. headstrong, heedless, rash, reckless, redeless, self-willed, wilful.

precise adj. 1) aright, right, careful, clean-cut, cut and dried, dead-on, straight, true, 2) starchy, stiff, unbending.

precisely adv. 1) by the book, on the dot, 2) altogether, indeed, truly, yes, 3) neither more nor less, to a hair, word for word.

precision n. care for truth, downrightness, sharpness, true likeness, truth-speaking, truth-telling.

predecessor n. 1) forerunner, pathfinder, 2) forebear, forefather.

predicament n. cleft stick, deep/hot water, headache, hole, knot, riddle, slippery slope, teaser.

predict v. to forebode, foresay, foresee, foreshadow, foretell, forewarn.

predominant adj. great, mighty, overcoming, winning, world-beating.

pre-empt v. to forestall, get in first, strike first.

prefer v. 1) to care more for, come down/out for, have rather, like better/best, list, long for, wish for, 2) to bring forward, put forward, bring on, foster, further, help.

preferred adj. better liked, chosen, sought after, wished for.

prejudice n. blindness, blind side, set mind, narrow mindedness, one-sidedness, right withheld, unfairness, warped mind.

preliminary n. beginning, foreword, groundwork, opening, start.

preliminary adj. first, opening.

premier adj. first, foremost, head, highest, leading, main, top.

preparation n. forethought, groundwork, homework, readying, spadework.

prepare v. to ready, be beforehand, foresee, forestall, lay the groundwork.

presence n. 1) being, being there, givenness, nowness, thatness, whereness, 2) nearness, neighbourhood, 3) bearing, 4) ghost, shade, shadow.

present n. the here and now, the now-time.

present adj. at hand, before one's eyes, here, nearby, ready.

present v. 1) to bestow, give, hand out, 2) to put before one, put forward, set before one's eyes, set out, 3) to bring out, put on, show, 4) to make known.

presentation n. 1) bestowing, giving, 2) show, speech, talk, 3) layout, look.

presently adv. 1) now, nowadays, these days, today, 2) anon, before long, erelong, by and by, in a little while, shortly, soon.

preserve v. 1) to hold fast, make fast, keep from falling, keep from harm, shield, stand by, steady, strengthen, uphold, watch and ward, 2) to salt, smoke, sun-dry.

president n. head of the board.

the ***press*** *n.* the news world, news business.

press *v.* 1) to bear down, lean on, ram down, 2) to elbow, shoulder, shove, wedge, 3) to iron, smooth, 4) to grind, mash, mill, pound, tread, 5) to wring, 6) to clasp, fold in one's arms, 7) to beset, drive, 8) to cluster, crowd, flock, forgather, gather, swarm, throng, 9) to ask for, beg, beseech, 10) to dwell on, put to, say outright, speak out, spur on, work upon.

pressing *adj.* 1) beseeching, besetting, bold, dogged, driving, earnest, forward, steady, tireless, unshaken, unshrinking, 2) now or never, with no time to lose, overriding, stopping for nothing.

pressure *n.* 1) heaviness, weight, 2) drive, 3) bitterness, burden, hardship, hard going, load, ordeal.

prestige *n.* footing, greatness, kingliness, lordliness, standing, weight, weightiness, worship, worth, worthship.

presumably *adv.* as likely as not, belike, likely, most likely, in all likelihood.

presume *v.* 1) to take something as so, take as read, take into one's head, think likely, dare say, believe, 2) to take upon oneself, make free with, forget oneself, ride rough-shod over, lord it over.

presumptuous *adj.* high-handed, high and mighty, over-mighty, brazen, headstrong, overweening, wilful.

pretend *v.* to hide the truth, say less than the truth, keep something back, make-believe, make out, not give a straight answer.

prevail over *v.* to bear hard on, hold down, hold in the hollow of one's hand, keep under one's thumb, overcome, override, win the upper hand.

prevent *v.* to bring to a stand, forbid, forestall, head off, hinder, put a stop to, put the lid on, quell, shut down, stave off, stop, ward off.

prevention *n.* binding over, forestalling, hindering, shutting off.

previous *adj.* 1) earlier, earliest, erstwhile, first, former, last, one-time, sometime, timely, 2) aforesaid, foregoing.

previously *adv.* aforetime, already, at one time, a while ago, back then, before, before now, before this, beforehand, earlier, ere now, ere this, formerly, heretofore, hitherto, in days/years gone by, once, until now.

price *n.* cheapness, dearness, hire, outlay, what something will fetch, worth.

pride *n.* 1) highness, high mightiness, swelled head, uppishness, 2) gladness (at seeing something good or worthy).

primarily *adv.* 1) above all, firstly, in the main, mainly, mostly, on the whole, 2) at first, at/from the start, in the beginning.

primary *adj.* 1) best, first, greatest, highest, leading, main, top, 2) going to the root, inwoven, inwrought, underlying, 3) foremost, key, main.

prime *adj.* 1) foremost, head, key, leading, main, overriding, 2) best, highest, matchless, 3) underlying, 4) stock.

primitive *adj.* backward, slow-growing, stunted, uncouth, ungrown, untaught.

prince *n.* ætheling, king's son, lord.

princess *n.* king's daughter, lady, high-born lady.

principal *adj.* first, foremost, greatest, key, leading, main, overriding, strongest.

principle *n.* 1) high-mindedness, knightliness, uprightness, 2) belief, mind, stand, leading/main thought, 3) ground, truth, spring, mainspring, well-spring.

print *v.* 1) to mark, stamp, 2) to make a book, run off.

prior *adj.* aforesaid, before, earlier, earliest, elder, eldest, erstwhile, first, first-born, first in the field, fore, foregoing, former, given, one-time.

prior *adv.* afore, aforetime, already, beforehand, before now, before then, earlier, ere, ere now, ere then, erewhile, on the eve of, theretofore, until now, whilom, yet.

priority *n.* coming first, the thing, first thing, great thing.

prison *n.* den, hold, lockhouse, lockup, ward-house.

private *adj.* 1) hidden, innermost, inside, 2) not overlooked, one's own.

prize *n.* meed, pickings, share-out, winnings, windfall.

probability *n.* likelihood, likeliness, likely belief, reckoning, well-grounded hope.

probable *adj.* likely, most likely, brewing, coming, in a fair way, near at hand, nearing, nigh, well-grounded, worthy of belief, in the wind.

probably *adv.* belike, likely, as likely as not, most likely, maybe, in all likelihood, to the best of one's knowledge and belief.

problem *n.* 1) hurdle, hindering, hard-going, 2) knot, hard saying, headache, maze.

procedure *n.* forward way, steps, way of doing things.

proceed *v.* to begin, get going, get under way, go ahead, go forth, go on, make a start, make for, set off.

process n. business, growth, making, shaping, steps, way of doing things, working.

processing n. bringing out, making, shaping, working.

procurement n. buy, earning, picking up, winning.

prodigious adj. 1) great, great-limbed, heavy, meaty, mighty, weighty, 2) amazing, breathtaking, overwhelming, startling, striking, wonderful.

produce n. crop, growth, harvest, mowing, output, reaping, yield.

produce v. 1) to bear, beget, breed, bring forth, bring into the world, bring up, give birth to, grow, hatch, rear, yield, 2) to build, carve, churn out, frame, make, put together, set up, shape, weave, 3) to bring about, give rise to, lead to, set off, set afoot, 4) to bring forward, bring to light, come up with, put forward, set forth, 5) (of a play or show) to bring off, bring out, do, put on, show.

product n. goods, handiwork, hardware, output, work, work of one's hands, yield.

production n. building, making, output, shaping, craftsmanship, workmanship, breeding, growing.

productive adj. alive with, heavy with, overflowing, rich, teeming, worthwhile.

profession n. 1) acknowledged belief, bearing witness, given word, undertaking, 2) business, craft, life-work, livelihood, walk of life.

professional adj. 1) craftly, book-wise, learned, businesslike, 2) full-time.

profit n. 1) earnings, meed, share-out, takings, winnings, windfall, yield, 2) good, help, worth, worthwhileness.

profit v. 1) to do well, earn, gather, get in one's hand, make a good thing of, make the most of, reap, 2) to be good for, bless, forward, help, stand one in good stead.

profound adj. deep, farsighted, thinking, understanding, witfast, witful, wise.

profusion n. fullness, a great deal, a lot, more than enough, an overflow, richness, wealth.

programme n. 1) draft, foredraft, steps, undertaking, ways, 2) show.

progress n. doing well, making good ground/great strides/headway, onwardness.

progressive adj. 1) abreast of the times, bold, forward-looking, go-ahead, up-and-doing, 2) growing, ongoing, worsening (of sickness).

prohibit v. to ban, forbid, hinder, outlaw, say no, stop, warn off.

project n. work in hand, homework, undertaking.

prolific adj. alive/heavy with, swarming, teeming, ever so many/so much, coming thick and fast, thick on the ground.

prolonged adj. drawn-out, ever-running, lengthened, lengthy, livelong, long, long-drawn, longlasting, strung out, too long.

prominent adj. bold, foremost, in the foreground, to the fore, in the limelight, leading, top, main, marked, outstanding, standing out, striking, well-known, well-marked, well-thought-of.

promiscuous adj. 1) all anyhow, meaningless, mingled, tousled, windswept, 2) fast, lewd, lustful, shameless, unbridled, wanton, wild.

promise n. 1) plighted word, troth-word, betrothal, oath, undertaking, 2) something one has bound oneself to give, 3) that which bodes well, and makes one look for good to come.

promise v. to give/plight one's word or troth, answer for, bind oneself, mean what one says, take oath, undertake, underwrite.

promising adj. bright, hopeful, in a fair way, likely, rising, sharp, up-and-coming.

promontory n. head, headland, foreland, ness, spur, tongue of land.

promote v. to back, bring on, bring forward, foster, further, help.

promotion n. 1) bettering, rise, 2) backing, helping forward, 3) hard sell.

prompt adj. early, in good time, timely, on time, quick, ready, speedy, swift.

promptly adv. at once, quickly, readily, speedily, swiftly, on time, on the dot, on the nail, at the drop of a hat, no sooner said than done.

proof n. findings, grounds, marks, showing, last word, truth, unfolding.

propaganda n. brainwashing.

proper adj. 1) belonging, right, rightful, meet and right, becoming, shipshape, 2) high-minded, ladylike, rightwise, well-bred, well-spoken, worthy.

properly adv. aright, rightly, by right, in one's own right, becomingly, fairly, good, in keeping with, true, well.

property n. 1) belongings, goods, hoard, holdings, land, acres, riches, stock, things, wealth, 2) mark, hallmark.

prophetic adj. foreshadowing, forewarning, insightful.

proportion n. 1) share, fourthing, half, 2) becomingness, evenness, fitness, shapeliness, wholeness.

proposal n. bid, draft, feeler, offer.

propose *v.* 1) to make an offer, come up with, moot, put forth, 2) to have in mind, 3) to name, put forward, put up, 4) to ask a woman for her hand in wedlock.

prosaic *adj.* clod-hopping, dry, earth-bound, everyday, leaden, tame, wearisome, workaday.

prospect *n.* 1) beam/gleam of hope, likelihood, likeliness, looking forward, thought, 2) outlook, landship (*landscape*), seaship (*seascape*), setting, sight.

prospective *adj.* 1) about to be, to come, nearing, nigh, soon-to-be, upcoming, 2) coming, forthcoming, hoped for, likely, looked-for.

prosperity *n.* blessings, fat of the land, good times, the good life, high tide, riches, weal, wealth, welfare, well-being.

prosperous *adj.* doing well, rich, riding high, rising, wealth-owning, wealthy, well-off, well-to-do, in clover.

protect *v.* to care for, foster, keep, look after, shield, stand by, stand up for, take up the cudgels for, ward, watch over.

protection *n.* care, shielding, ward, watch.

protest *n.* gainsaying, gripe, rising, go-slow, sit-in, walk-out.

protest *v.* to gainsay, have one's say, say no to, set oneself against, speak against, stand up to, take up the cudgels, withstand, come out on strike, down tools, walk out.

protester *n.* gainsayer, heckler, withstander.

proud *adj.* 1) high and mighty, high-handed, looking down on one, overbearing, overweening, rank, showy, strutting, 2) glad (at seeing something done well), bursting with gladness, a foot taller, heart-high, thrilled.

prove *v.* to bear out, bring home to, make one believe, put over, settle, show.

proverb *n.* by-saying, byword, byspell, folksaying, pithy saying, stock saying.

proverbial *adj.* 1) pithy, wise, witty, 2) acknowledged, household, stock, understood, well-known.

provide *v.* 1) to be ready for, get ready, put in readiness, put together, lay in, stock up, 2) to clothe, feed, find, give, hand out, keep, lend, man, put up.

provision *n.* 1) keep, wherewithal, 2) readying, settling, 3) a must, rider, strings, understanding, undertaking.

provisional *adj.* for the time being, makeshift, short-lived.

provocative *adj.* 1) goading, greatly daring, reckless, warlike, 2) naughty, shameless, unbridled, wanton.

provoke *v.* 1) to bring about, call forth, 2) to fill with wrath, goad, madden, make one's blood seethe, make one see red, nettle, stir up.

prudent *adj.* 1) canny, farsighted, mindful, shrewd, wary, wise, 2) careful, sparing, telling the pence.

psychological *adj.* all in the mind, inner.

'pub', public house *n.* alehouse, beer-house, inn, neighbour house (*local*), roadhouse, taproom, watering hole.

public *n.* folk, man in the street.

public *adj.* 1) (*civic*) home, land-wide, 2) shared, widespread, 3) free to all, not hidden, open, 4) acknowledged, known, well-known, leading.

publication *n.* 1) word, write-up, making known, spreading abroad, telling forth, 2) book, work.

publicity *n.* getting out the word, spreading the word abroad, putting it about, putting it over, making much of.

publicly *adv.* for all to see, in the limelight, in the open, openly.

publish *v.* to make known, bring out, speak out, spread abroad, tell the world.

pulsate *v.* to beat, hammer, heave, pound, quiver.

pump *n.* 1) water-drawer, that is, a tool for drawing up water from below (from the hold of a ship or from under ground), 2) tool for putting wind into a *tyre*.

pump *v.* 1) to drain, draw off, empty (water from the hold of a ship), 2) to draw water from a well, 3) to put wind into a *tyre*.

puncture *v.* 1) to cut, prick, slit, 2) to go down, 3) to bedwarf, bring down to earth, take the wind out of one's sails.

pundit *n.* great mind, leading light, one in the know.

punish *v.* to bear hard on, beat, bind over, bring to book, come down on, deal hardly with, get even with, have one's head for, settle with, stamp on, thrash.

punishment *n.* beating, doom, day of reckoning, reckoning, rough handling.

pupil *n.* beginner, learner, schoolchild, schoolgirl.

purchase *n.* 1) buy, buying, buying up, good buy, 2) edge, footing, grasp, grip, hold, foothold, toehold.

purchase *v.* to buy, buy back, buy outright, buy up, come by, get hold of, get in one's hand, make one's own, pick up.

pure *adj.* 1) childlike, clean, clean-handed, good, guiltless, lamb-like, rightwise, sinless, upright, 2) bright, shining, unmingled, whole, wholesome, 3) downright, outright, out-and-out, sheer, thorough, thorough-going, utter.

purely adv. alone, at most, no more than, nothing but, only, wholly.

purge v. 1) to clean out, cleanse, wash, 2) to cut down, mow down, put to the sword, wipe out, 3) to axe, do away with, empty, strip, sweep away, weed out.

purpose n. 1) end, goal, mind, will, the why and wherefore, 2) steadfastness, one-mindedness, mind made up, strength of mind/will, 3) good, outcome, worth.

pursuant to under, because of, in line with.

pursue v. to go after, follow, harry, hunt, look for, ride down, run down, run after, seek, send after, send for, shadow, stalk, tail.

push v. 1) to drive, elbow, hound, manhandle, quicken, set going, shove, shoulder, spur on, stir, work upon, 2) to go ahead, go forward, go on, make inroads, overrun.

puzzled adj. bewildered, brought to a stand, forstraught, at sea, at a loss, goalless, going nowhere, in the dark, in two minds.

puzzling adj. knotted, dark, deep, thorny, unfathomed, unfathomful.

quagmire n. fen, marsh, quicksand, slough.

quail v. to be chilled with fear, be frightened, blench, cringe, falter, fear, give way, go white as a sheet, have cold feet, quake, quiver, shake, shiver, shrink back.

quaint adj. old-fangled, old-world.

qualified adj. 1) careful, wary, 2) deft, knowing, ready, up to the mark, well up in.

qualify v. 1) to learn (a craft), learn the ropes, read up, 2) to ready, make ready, put in readiness, teach, 3) to lessen, lighten, play down, soften, take the edge off, take the sting out.

quality n. 1) name, fair name, good name, high name, worth, known worth, standing, weight, worship, 2) mark, streak, suchness, way (the way one is), wont.

quandary n. cleft stick, headache, maze, riddle, teaser, two minds.

quantity n. 1) batch, heap, load, lot, manyness, 2) greatness, depth, height, weight.

quarrel n. fight, misunderstanding, high words, stormy words.

quarrel v. to fall out, fight, gainsay, have words, have a bone to pick with.

quarter n. 1) fourth, fourthling, farthing, fourthing, 2) neighbourhood, ward, 3) forgivingness, kindness, mildness, mildheartness, ruth.

quarters n. boarding house, rooms, berth.

quash v. to bring to naught, fordo, undo, unmake.

queer adj. 1) eerie, ghostly, outlandish, uncanny, unearthly, unwonted, weird, 2) dizzy, giddy, light-headed, not well, sick, taken bad, under the weather.

query v. 1) to ask, delve, go into thoroughly, hunt for answers, seek, 2) to stand up to, take one up on, dare, set at naught, throw in one's teeth.

question n. 1) asking, delving, looking into, sifting, 2) business on hand, heart of the business, headache, knot, riddle.

question v. to ask, delve, go into thoroughly, hunt for answers, seek, sift.

questioning n. asking about, delving, looking into, rooting, seeking, sifting.

questionnaire n. asking-list, asking-sheet.

quid pro quo n. like for like, offset.

quiet adj. restful, smooth, soft, still, stilly, whispered, 2) home-keeping, mild, shy, tongueless.

quietly adv. mildly, softly, under one's breath.

quit v. 1) to drop, end, go away from, go out of, leave, stand down, step down from, stop, withdraw from, yield, 2) to forsake, give in/up, let one down, pull out of, throw in one's hand, throw up the game.

quite adv. 1) fairly, pretty well, rather, somewhat, well enough, 2) ever so much, never so much, fully, thoroughly, wholly, wonderfully.

quote v. 1) to take from another work, take the words of another speaker, tell again, 2) to give word for word, name, 3) to name/set the worth of, set the dearness of.

race n. blood, breed, folk-stock, house, kin, kindred, offspring, stock.

racial adj. folk, inborn, inbred, kin-born.

radiant adj. alight, bright, gleaming, shining, aglow, glowing, in the glow of heightened/quickened/stirred feelings.

radical adj. 1) downright, far-reaching, going to the root, out-and-out, sweeping, thorough, thoroughgoing, earth-shaking, world-shaking, 2) leftist, rightist.

radical n. bitter-ender, die-hard, last-ditcher, leftist, rightist, fighter, shaker, stirrer.

radio n. wireless.

rage v. to be wrathful, become heated/mad/wild, be sore/upset, bridle up, burn/glower/quiver/seethe/shake with wrath, fly off the handle, look like thunder.

railway n. line, network.

raise v. 1) to set upright, up-end, 2) to help someone rise from the ground, 3) to heighten, put up, 4) to make better, uplift, 5) to stir up, gather a fighting body, 6) to build, put up, 7) to bring about, start, 8) (of children) to bring up, rear, 9) (of crops, *beasts*) to breed, grow, keep, rear, 10) (of speaking) to heighten one's *voice*, make louder, shout, 11) to bring up, moot, speak about, 12) to bring someone forward, bring on, 13) to end the hemming in of a stronghold by making the onsetters withdraw, or by the onsetters choosing to withdraw.

rampant adj. headlong, out of hand, quick-hearted, rising up, spreading like wildfire, unbridled, wanton, widespread, wild.

rapid adj. fast, flying, quick, speedy, swift.

rapidly adv. like an arrow/lightning/a shot, quickly, speedily, swiftly, hotfoot.

rare adj. 1) hard to come by, not to be had, of unnamed worth, wonderful, 2) almost unheard of, few and far between, not like, outstanding, out of the way, seldom-seen.

rarely adv. almost never, hardly ever, little, once in a while, only now and then, seldom.

rate v. to deem, reckon, weigh.

rate v. to beshrew, curse, go for, thunder against, upbraid.

rational adj. 1) long-headed, right-minded, in one's right mind, understanding, wise, thinking, 2) holding water, strongly-grounded, well-grounded, well-thought-out.

ray n. 1) beam, gleam, shaft, 2) hint, spark.

reaction n. 1) answer, feedback, outcome, upshot, 2) answering back, bloody nose, swing-back.

reactionary n. bitter-ender, die-hard, far-righter, last-ditcher.

real adj. 1) true, true to life, true-bred, one and only, 2) bodily, down to earth, earthy, fleshly, of flesh and blood.

realisation n. awareness, insight, knowledge, mindfulness, reckoning, understanding.

realise v. 1) to be aware of, come to know, grasp, see the light, understand, 2) to bring about/off, fulfil, see through, 3) to bring in, draw upon, earn, go for, make, net, sell for, sell up.

realism n. 1) downrightness, openness, sharpness, starkness, knowing what can/cannot be done, 2) drawing from life, speaking likeness, true likeness, truthfulness, truth-speaking, truth-telling, 'warts and all'.

realistic adj. 1) black and white, businesslike, down to earth, earth-bound, everyday,

workaday, hard-headed, open, stark, straight, 2) lifelike, sharp, true, true to life, truthful, truth-telling, well-drawn, well-grounded.

reality n. home-truth, pithiness, rightness, thatness, truth, stern truth, no dream.

really adv. indeed, truly, truthfully, word for word.

rear n. back, back end, heel, tail end.

rear adj. after, hind, hinder, hindermost.

reason n. 1) ground, spring, why and wherefore, 2) awareness, brains, brainwork, head-work, insight, mind-strength, thinking out, understanding, wisdom, wits.

reason v. to bend the mind, give one's mind to, give thought to, set the mind to, pull one's wits together, think hard, think on, think through, think out, make out, work out.

reasonable adj. 1) long-headed, thinking, understanding, wise, 2) in one's right mind, right-minded, right in the head, not wandering, 'all there', 3) fair, right, well-grounded, well-thought-out, 4) good enough, so-so, steady, 5) not dear, cheap.

reasonably adv. fairly, on the whole.

rebel v. to come out against, rise up, run wild, stir up dust, take to the streets, throw off the yoke.

rebuke v. to chide, give one a black mark/talking to, put right/straight, upbraid.

rebuttal n. gainsaying, knock-down answer, thorough answer, truth made fast.

recall v. 1) to set aside, take back, undo, unmake, unsay, withdraw, 2) to bring to mind, know again, hark back, bethink, think back upon, not forget.

receive v. 1) to be given, have from, take on, take up, come in for, come into, reap, 2) to welcome, bid one welcome, make welcome, welcome with open arms, 3) to acknowledge, believe, go along with.

recent adj. new, brand-new, new-fangled, new-fleshed, new-made, late, latter-day, overnight.

recently adv. lately, latterly, of late, newly, not long ago, a short time ago, only yesterday, the other day.

reception n. 1) bringing in, taking in, 2) greeting, open arms, welcome, 3) at home, gathering, get-together, 4) (of picking up *sound*) hearing, loudness, softness.

recognise v. 1) to acknowledge, be aware of, believe, light upon, own, see the truth, 2) to come to understand, ken, know, make out, mark, pick out, put one's finger on, see it all, sight, 3) to fall in with, hold out one's hand, open the door, say yes, welcome.

recognition *n.* awareness, insight, knowledge, mindfulness, understanding.

recollect *v.* to bethink, <u>bring to mind</u>, hark back.

recommend *v.* to back, lend one's name, put forward, put in a good word for, put up, speak well of.

recommendation *n.* 1) input, 2) blessing, good word.

reconcile *v.* 1) to bring back together, heal, win back/over (to friendship), 2) to put to rights, settle.

reconsider *v.* to look again at, take another look at, think again, think better of, think over, think twice.

record *n.* 1) day-book, name-book, writing, 2) deed, witness, 3) best time, fastest time, 4) background.

record *v.* to put down, put in a book, put in words, set down in black and white, set forth, take down, tell, write down, write about.

recover *v.* 1) to feel oneself again, get better, get back on one's feet, get well, make ground, pull through, 2) (of the *economy*, trading) to make a come-back, pick up, 3) to free, get one out of, 4) to find again, get back, make good, make up lee-way, win back.

recovery *n.* 1) come-back, pulling through, 2) upswing, uptrend, 3) freeing, 4) finding again, getting back.

recreation *n.* break, breather, game, holiday, outing, play.

recruit *v.* 1) to build up one's strength, harden, stiffen, toughen, 2) to call up, draft, gather, hire, take on.

rector *n.* church leader, man of God, man of the church, shepherd (of God's flock).

redeem *v.* to atone for, buy back, <u>free</u>, free from guilt, set free, win back.

redress *n.* giving back, making good, putting right, upholding folk-right.

reduce *v.* to bring down, cut back/down/short, <u>lessen</u>, <u>lighten</u>, shorten.

reduction *n.* cut, cut-back, cutting, <u>lessening</u>, shortening, shrinking.

redundant *adj.* 1) laid off, out of work, 2) no longer needed, not needed, one too many, unneeded, 3) <u>long-winded</u>, overlong, wordy.

refer to *v.* 1) to bring up, hint at, speak of, 2) to bear upon, bespeak, speak of, have to do with, mean, stand for, tell of, 3) to look up, seek out (in a book).

reference *n.* 1) aside, hidden meaning, 2) handing over, 3) good word.

reflect *v.* 1) to bear out, bespeak, give back, shine back, show, throw back, 2) to ask oneself, bethink, <u>think</u>, think about, think over, wonder.

reflection *n.* 1) likeness, outline, 2) backshine, sheen, sending back, throwing back, 3) look of things, shadowing forth, shape, show, showing, 4) bad light, home-truth, shame, 5) brooding, deep/hard thought, inmost thoughts, thinking through, <u>thought</u>.

reform *n.* bettering, building, shaping anew, putting/setting right, straightening out.

reform *v.* 1) to better, bring in new blood, build/shape anew, make better, put right, set to rights, straighten, 2) to go straight, turn over a new leaf.

refrain from *v.* to <u>forbear</u>, hold back, hold off, keep oneself from, <u>stop</u>, withdraw.

refresh *v.* to bring in new blood, breathe new life into, gladden, hearten, liven up, quicken, put new life into.

refrigerator *n.* cold-chest, cooler, freezer, deep-freeze, ice-chest.

refund *v.* to give back, make good.

refuse *v.* 1) to <u>say no to</u>, give a deaf ear to, not hear of, harden one's heart, cold-shoulder, <u>spurn</u>, 2) to drive away, do without, go without.

regard *v.* 1) to behold, eye, look at, look upon, see, watch, 2) to deem, hold, hold dear, know/see the worth of, look up to, make much of, <u>think highly of</u>, think well of.

regardless *adj.* careless, <u>heedless</u>, reckless, thoughtless, unhearing, unheeding, unmindful, unreckoning, unthinking, unthorough.

regardless of *adv.* anyway, nevertheless, nonetheless, notwithstanding, come what may, for all that, rain or shine.

regime *n.* leadership, inner ring, set up.

regiment *n.* body of men.

region *n.* neighbourhood, hundred, shire.

register *n.* day-book, name-book,

register *v.* 1) to book, put in writing, put down, set down, take down, write down, write up, 2) to mark, read, show, tell.

registration *n.* booking.

regret *v.* to bemoan, forthink, rue, sigh for, <u>sorrow</u>, wring one's hands.

regular *adj.* 1) even, even-sided, matched, rightly/truly shaped, rightly wrought, smooth, straight, true, 2) daily, everyday, oft-coming, set, settled, steady, well-beaten/trodden/worn, time after time, wonted.

regularly *adv.* again and again, all the time, at all times, always, 'day in, day out', every time, ever, oft, often, over and over, time and again, time after time.

regulation n. handling, law-making, settled law, written law.

rehabilitation n. making good, making like new, new look, putting back, righting.

reinforce v. 1) to back up, bring up to strength, come to the help of, stand up for, steel, strengthen, 2) to build up, harden, hold up, make good, steady, stiffen, toughen, underset, 3) to deepen, foster, greaten, heighten.

reject v. to spurn, ban, cold-shoulder, drive away, drive out, hunt out, send away/back, set at naught, shun, throw out, warn off.

rejected adj. ditched, dropped, forsaken, thrown aside/away/off/over.

rejoice v. to be blithe/glad/gleeful/light-hearted, to clap one's hands, give thanks, laugh, let oneself go, make merry, throw cares aside.

relate v. to have one know, let one know, say what has happened/how it happened, set forth, talk, tell.

relation n. 1) bearing, kinship, link, tie-in, 2) kin, kinsman, kinswoman.

relationship n. 1) kinship, 2) love-making, love-play, 3) link, network, tie-up.

relative adj. answering to, bearing upon, sharing.

relax v. to rest, lighten, slacken, soothe, unburden.

release n. freedom, freeing, setting free, leaving hold of, unbinding.

release v. 1) to free, set free, let go, let off, let out, unbind, unburden, undo, unfasten, unfetter, unlock, unshackle, untie, 2) to bring out, give out, make known, put out, send forth, send out.

relevant adj. answering to, bearing upon, belonging, in keeping, meaningful, meet, right, timely.

reliable adj. lasting, steadfast, steady, true-hearted, truthful, unswerving, upright, as good as one's word.

relief n. 1) break, break in the clouds, let-up, load off one's mind, rest, 2) help, helping hand, timely help, 3) stand-by, stand-in, steadman.

relieved adj. glad, thankful.

religion n. belief, fear of God, teaching, worship.

religious adj. 1) believing, earnest, God-fearing, godly, heavenly-minded, holy, righteous, unworldly, 2) careful, high-minded, mindful, law-abiding, thorough, thoroughgoing, unswerving.

reluctant adj. backward, dragging heels, half-hearted, holding back, loath, shunning, slow, unforthcoming, unminded, unready, unwilling, two-minded, unfain, wary.

rely on v. 1) to fall back on, ground oneself on, lean on, reckon on, 2) to believe, rest in the belief, hold for true, swear by, take one at his word.

remain v. to abide, be left, bide at, dwell, live on, outlive, not stir, outlast, rest, settle, still be.

remainder n. leavings, tail end, what is left.

remark n. saying, thought, word.

remark v. 1) to mark, see, 2) to bear witness, give out, say out/outright, speak out, talk about.

remarkable adj. amazing, bewildering, startling, striking, weird, wonderful.

remedy n. 1) help, answer, healing, 2) makeshift, two strings to one's bow, ways and means, way out, wherewithal.

remember v. to bring to mind, know again, hark back, bethink, not forget.

remind v. to bring back to mind, call back to mind, make one think of, not let one forget, put in one's head, put one in mind, say in one's ear.

remonstrate v. to make a stand, speak/stand against, stand up to, withstand.

remote adj. 1) far, faraway, far-off, furthermost, lonely, outlying, out-of-the-way, at the world's end, on the edge of the world, in the middle of nowhere, 2) cold, forbidding, frosty, standoffish, unforthcoming, unwelcoming, withdrawn, 3) beside the mark, empty, far-fetched, meaningless, neither here nor there, 4) outside, small, unlikely.

removal n. 1) cutting out, drawing out, shifting, stamping out, stripping, taking away/off/out, tearing out, uprooting, wiping out, 2) end, ending, sending away, striking off, throwing out, clean sweep, 3) going away, leaving, pulling out.

remove v. 1) to gang, go away, leave home/neighbourhood, shift, take off, wend, withdraw, 2) to do away with, kill, murder, 3) to see the back of, show one the door, throw out, unsaddle, 4) to climb out of, pull off, shed, 5) to clean off, root up, strike out, take out, tear out, wash off, wipe off, 6) to cut off, hack off, lop off, make room, take away.

renaissance n. awakening, new dawn, new life.

render v. 1) to leave, make (as in '*render* of little worth'), 2) to give/hand back, make good, 3) to bring to life, draw, play (*music*), shapen, 4) to put into other speech, 5) to give up, hand over, yield, 6) (of stonework and such) to do over, overlay, spread (with *plaster*).

renew v. 1) to begin again, breathe new life into, start again, 2) to top up, 3) to do up, make better, tidy up.

rent v. 1) to hire, 2) to let.

reorganisation n. new lay-out, shake-up, spring-clean.

repair v. 1) to make good, put/set right, set to rights, righten, settle, sew, stitch, straighten out, 2) to betake oneself to, go, head for, leave for, set off for.

repeal v. to undo or unmake (a law or such), withdraw, do away with, set aside, tear up, bring to naught.

repeat v. to do again, say again, do after, say after, drive home, follow, go over, say over, highlight, spin out.

repent v. to be ashamed, be sorry about, sorrow, beat one's breast, rue, wish undone.

repercussion n. fall-out, follow-on, outcome, upshot.

replace v. 1) to fill/step into someone's shoes, follow, stand in for, stand in the stead of, take over from, take the stead of, 2) to drop, root out, throw out, unsaddle, strike off, 3) to put back, sheathe.

replacement n. fill-in, stand-in.

reply v. 1) to answer, say in answer, acknowledge, come back to, write back, 2) to have an answer, cut the ground from under, stop the mouth.

report n. 1) news, tale, tidings, word, write-up, 2) gossip, hearsay, talk, 3) blast, roar, shot, 4) good name, standing, weight, worth.

report v. 1) to bring/send word on, put into words, set out, set forth, speak of, tell, write to, write about, write up, 2) to blow the whistle on, put about, tell on, tell tales of, 3) to come, show up.

reporter n. gossip-writer, newshound, newsman, wordsmith, writer.

represent v. 1) to bear witness, say outright, set forth, speak out, 2) to draw, make a likeness, mark out, set out, shadow forth, show, stand for, 3) to answer for, do the work of, speak for, speak on behalf of, stand in for, stand in the stead of.

representation n. 1) likeness, showing, unfolding, 2) doing the work of, standing in for, forspeaking, steadsmanship.

representative n. 1) spokesman, spokeswoman, steadsman, steward, stand-in, 2) salesman.

reprisal n. reckoning, settling with, striking back, an eye for an eye, wrath-wreaking.

reproach n. 1) home-truth, telling-off, the rough edge of one's tongue, upbraiding, 2) byword, shame, unworthiness.

repudiate v. 1) to cut off, ditch, forsake, spurn, throw over, walk out on, wash one's hands of, 2) to gainsay, not acknowledge, give the lie to, 3) to back out, call back, go back on, set aside, take back, tear up, undo, unmake, unsay, withdraw.

reputation, repute n. name, fair name, good name, high name, known worth, standing, weight, worth, worship.

request n. asking, begging, beseeching, bid, bidding, longing, seeking, wish.

request v. to ask for, beg, beseech, bid for, make bold to ask, put in for, seek.

require v. to beseech, bid for, crave, have need of, need, stand in need of, make bold to ask, seek, wish.

requirement n. craving, must, need.

rescue v. to come to the help of, set free, throw a life-line to.

research n. book work, combing, delving, groundwork, head work, hunting, learning, lore, mind work, reading, rooting, seeking, sifting, working *paper*.

resemble v. to bear a likeness to, be like, have the look of, look like, put one in mind of, take after.

resent v. to be bitter/wrathful about, have hard feelings about, leave one's sting behind.

reserve n. 1) hoard, holding, stock, 2) coolness, few words, shyness, 3) misgiving, 4) fall-back, stand-by, twelfth man.

reserve v. 1) to heap up, hoard, hold over, keep in hand, lay by, lay up, put away, put by, put aside, stow away, 2) to bespeak, book, keep for oneself, 3) to keep for another, set aside, 4) to keep back, lay over, put off, withhold.

reserved adj. not speaking/talking, not to be drawn, saying little, sparing of words, unforthcoming, withdrawn.

reside v. to abide, bide, dwell, live, put up at, settle.

residence n. house, dwelling-house, dwelling, home, homestead.

residential adj. built-up.

resign v. to break off, end, give up, leave, stand down, step down, stop, yield up.

resilient adj. 1) springy, 2) doughty, steadfast, strong, tough.

resist v. to fight, withstand, stand against, stand up to, set at naught, ward off.

resistance *n.* going against, hindering, stand, unhelpfulness, unwillingness, uprising, withholding, dragging one's heels, headwind.

resolute *adj.* doughty, earnest, stalwart, steadfast, steely, stern-/strong-minded, unyielding.

resolve *n.* steadfastness, doggedness.

resolve *v.* to settle on a thing, steel oneself, give oneself to, give up everything for, go for, go to all lengths, know/make up one's mind, set one's heart on.

resource *n.* 1) hoard, pool, 2) help, 3) shift, makeshift, way out.

resourceful *adj.* canny, clever, craftful, craftly, deft, keen-thinking, nimble-witted, quick, quick-witted, ready-witted, sharp, sharp-witted, witfast, witful.

respect *n.* 1) dread, fear, wonder, 2) fair name, good name/standing, high name, standing, weight, worth, worship.

respect *v.* to think highly of/well of, look up to, make much of, think everything of.

respectable *adj.* 1) good, goodly, law-abiding, truthful, upright, worthful, worthy, 2) cleanly, shipshape, tidy.

respective *adj.* own.

respectively *adv.* each to each, one by one.

respite *n.* break, breather, breathing time, let-off, let-up, playtime, rest, time off.

respond *v.* 1) to acknowledge, answer, write back, 2) to have an answer, cut the ground from under, give the lie to, stop the mouth.

response *n.* answer, comeback, feedback.

responsibility *n.* 1) business, care, undertaking, 2) burden, guilt, 3) leadership, steersmanship, 4) trothworthiness.

responsible *adj.* 1) at the bottom of, behind, guilty, 2) at the helm, 3) beholden, bound, bounden, owing, 4) true, true-hearted.

restaurant *n.* eating-house, mealhouse.

restore *v.* to bring back, give back, hand back, heal, make good, make like new, make up for, make whole, put back, put/set right, yield up.

restriction *n.* ban, forholding, lock-out.

result *n.* end, handiwork, outcome, outworking, upshot.

result *v.* to arise, flow from, follow, spring, stem.

resume *v.* to begin again, come back to, go on with, pick up where one left off, take up again.

retail *v.* 1) to deal, do business, sell, trade, 2) to put about, speak of, spread abroad, talk of, tell over again.

retain *v.* 1) to cling to, grasp, grip, hang on to, hold, hold fast to, hold on to, hold up, hold steady, keep steady, make fast, 2) to have and hold, hoard, hold back, keep, keep back, keep in one's own hands, keep for oneself, put by, stow away, withhold, have by the throat, 3) to bear/hold/keep in mind, bring to mind, keep (alive) in one's thoughts, keep in mind, learn, learn by heart, not forget.

retaliate *v.* to get even with, get one's own back, give as good as one got, not take it lying down, settle with, strike back.

retire *v.* 1) to give up work, lay down one's work, leave, hand over to another, make way for another, stop working, stand aside, stand down, 2) to go to bed, go to one's room (to sleep), betake oneself, 3) to back out, draw back, fall back, give ground, give up, give way, pull back, pull out, throw in one's hand, withdraw, yield.

retirement *n.* 1) giving up work, stopping work, 2) loneliness, withdrawing (from the world).

retract *v.* to back down, eat one's words, take back, give in, unsay, withdraw, tear up, undo, yield.

retreat *v.* 1) to back away, back off, draw back, fall back, give ground, go back, leave, pull back, shrink away, withdraw, 2) to back down, climb down, eat one's words, 3) to ebb, fall, flow out, go down.

return *n.* 1) coming back, going back, homecoming, homeward way, landfall, landing, 2) bringing back, giving back, 3) earnings, income, meed, takings, yield.

return *v.* 1) to come back, go back, come again to, come/go home, come back to where one started, 2) to give back, put back, send back, take back.

reveal *v.* to find out, lay bare, let in daylight, make known, show, speak out, unearth.

revenge oneself *v.* to get even with, get one's own back, give as good as one got, not take it lying down, settle with, strike back, wreak wrath.

revenue *n.* income, takings, yield.

reverse *v.* 1) to go backwards, back up, back-water, go back to the beginning, undo, unmake, wheel about, withdraw, 2) to shift, upend, 3) (in law) to overthrow, overset, set aside, tear up, upset, undo.

review *n.* a drawing out of the key goals and findings of a work, pith, rundown, siftings, winnowings.

revise *v.* to go over again (so as to make better), look again, make right, read again, shape anew, work anew.

revival *n.* 1) awakening, coming back to life, quickening, 2) comeback, picking up, upswing.

revolution *n.* 1) breaking up, break with the old ways, overthrow, uprising, tearing down, unmaking, uprooting, 2) break, clean sweep, shake-up, shift, sea-shift, swing, upheaving, upset, 3) spin, wheel, full wheel.

revolutionary *n.* fighter, fire-brand, fire-eater, thunderer.

revolutionary *adj.* 1) overthrowing, upheaving, uprooting, 2) new, ground-breaking, thoroughgoing, world-shaking.

revulsion *n.* hatred, loathing, shrinking from.

rhythm *n.* 1) beat, flow, song-flow, smoothness, swing, time, timing, 2) (in *nature*) coming and going, ebb and flow, waxing and waning.

rid *v.* to bring to naught, free, make/set free, root out, send out, shake off, smoke out, throw out, unburden, undo, unmake, uproot.

ridiculous *adj.* beyond belief, far-fetched, hard to swallow, hare-brained, mad, outlandish, utterly unlikely, wildly out.

rifle *v.* to reave, sift through, steal, clean out.

rigid *adj.* 1) hard, stiff, 2) pig-headed, set, stern, stiff-necked, unbending, unyielding, wilful.

rigorous *adj.* careful, thorough.

risk *n.* leap in the dark.

ritual *n.* set way (of doing things).

rival *v.* 1) to fight against, match oneself with, stand against, take on, 2) to come up to, match, be a match for.

river *n.* 1) bourne, burn, stream, waterway, 2) flood, flow, wave.

riveting *n.* spell-binding, thrilling.

rob *v.* to bear away/off, beggar, hold up, drive off, make away with, make off with, reave, fleece, steal, thieve, waylay.

robbery *n.* hold-up, raiding, reaving, stealing, theft, thieving.

robust *adj.* stalwart, strong, thickset, tough, hale, hearty, healthy, well.

rock *n.* 1) cliff, outcrop, pebble, stone, 2) mainstay.

role *n.* 1) business, craft, field, livelihood, walk of life, work, life-work, 2) *part* in a play.

roll *v.* 1) to reel, spin, wheel, run on wheels, 2) (of a ship) to heave and pitch in heavy seas, heel over, lean over, thresh about, wallow, 3) to make into a bundle, 4) to spread out (with a *rolling*-pin), 5) (of *drums* and such) to roar, thunder, 6) to bind, fold, swathe, twist, wind, 7) to set something going by making it turn over and over, trundle, 8) (of tears) to flow, run, stream.

romantic *adj.* 1) loving, loverlike, love-lorn, 2) dreamy, starry-eyed, head in the clouds, 3) high-flown, lively, made-up, wild.

rotten adj. bad, crumbling, foul, loathsome, mildewed, moth-eaten, rotting, stinking.

round *prep.* all about, all through, from beginning to end of, on all sides of, throughout.

round *adj.* 1) bead-shaped, ring-shaped, beadlike, ringlike, bowed, 2) full, unbroken, whole, 3) bosomy, fleshy, full-fleshed, overweight, well-fed.

round *adv.* all about, all over, from beginning to end, from all sides, on all sides, on each side, in the neighbourhood, throughout.

rouse *v.* to awaken, fire, hearten, quicken, stir up.

route *n.* 1) path, road, way, way to, way through, 2) beat, run.

routine *n.* 1) daily path, way, wont, 2) deadness, dreariness, grind, lifelessness, treadmill.

routine *adj.* 1) everyday, wonted, workaday, 2) mind-numbing, run-of-the-mill, tiresome.

royal *adj.* kingly, queenly.

rude *adj.* churlish, clod-hopping, loud, loutish, oafish, rough, uncouth.

ruin *v.* to undo, bring to naught, break down, overwhelm, put an end to.

rule *n.* 1) overlordship, 2) law, settled law, way.

rule *v.* 1) to have the upper hand over, head, lay down the law, lead, override, oversee, steer, wield, 2) (in law) to deem, find for/against, find guilty/not guilty, lay down, reckon, settle, mete out.

ruling *n.* finding, reckoning.

rumour *n.* gossip, hearsay, news, talk, idle talk, talk of the town, tidings, whisper, word of mouth.

rural *adj.* out-of-town.

rush *n.* 1) quickness, speed, headlong speed, reckless speed, run, swiftness, no loss of time, 2) breakthrough, drive, inroad, onset, 3) flood, flow, streaming.

rush *v.* 1) to fly, ride hard, run like mad/the wind, speed, spur on, step out, sweep along, tear along, 2) to make an onset, storm, take by storm, 3) to flood, flow, run, shoot, stream, well up.

rustle *v.* to sough, whisper.

sacrifice *n.* 1) offering, sin-offering, 2) forswearing, giving up, loss.

sacrifice v. 1) to offer up, 2) to do without, forgo, give up, let go, lose, say goodbye to, yield up.

safe adj. 1) all right, free from harm, out of harm's way, spared, unharmed, 2) shielded, well-grounded, 3) mind-numbing, tame, tiresome, wearisome, 4) harmless, wholesome, 5) canny, careful, heedful, mindful, wary, watchful.

safeguard v. to care for, hide away, infold, keep, keep an eye/sharp eye on, keep from falling, keep from harm, look after, look to, mind, see to, shade, shelter, shepherd, shield, stand by, stand up for, take care of, watch over, uphold.

safety n. well-being, storm blown over, wide berth.

salary n. earnings, income.

saline adj. salty.

salvation n. atoning, buying back, cleansing, forgiveness, freeing, making like new, making whole, putting right, setting free, unbinding, unshackling.

same adj. alike, much like, all one, of one kind, of that ilk, twin.

sanctions n. trade ban, stop on trade, lock-out.

sane adj. in one's right mind, not wandering, sharp, wise, witfast, wit-right.

sarcastic adj. belittling, biting, cutting, sharp, stinging, shrewish, waspish, withering.

satisfaction n. 1) full life, gladness, well-being, all that could be wished for, 2) atoning, settling.

satisfactory adj. all right, fair, enough, good enough, middling, up to the mark, pretty good, worthy, worthwhile, worth having.

satisfy v. 1) to be enough, fill up, go down well, quench one's thirst, 2) to bring over, make one believe, put over, talk into, win over, 3) to answer, fulfil, match up to, meet the need.

Saturday n. Seventh Day, Weekend-day, Lord's Day Eve.

sauce, sauciness n. answering back, backtalk, boldness, brazenness, forwardness, lip, shamelessness, uppishness.

savage adj. biting, cutting, rough, stinging, waspish, wild, withering, wolfish.

save v. 1) to free, set free, keep alive, throw a life-line to, unbind, unshackle, 2) to be sparing, heap up, hoard, hold, keep, keep back, keep in hand, lay by, lay in, lay up, put aside, put away, put by, fill up, stow away.

savings n. heap, hoard, holding, stock, wealth.

scale n. 1) breadth, spread, 2) ladder, standing, step, 3) (in *mapmaking*) drawing-to-life *size*, miles to the inch.

scandal n. backbiting, gossip, smearing.

scar n. mark, burn mark, mark, old wound, weal, welt.

scarce adj. 1) dried up, far short, hard to come by, hard to get, not to be had, short, 2) almost unheard of, few and far between.

scarcely adv. barely, hardly, hardly at all, lightly, as little as may be, ever so little.

scare v. to fill with fear/dread, frighten out of one's wits, affrighten, shake, startle.

scared adj. fearful, frightened to death, frozen with fear, overcome, shaken, startled.

scatter v. 1) to bestrew, strew, send all ways, shower, sow, spread, thin out, throw about, 2) to bolt, fly, go each his own way, melt into the mist, run away, cut and run, 3) to beat, fell, outmatch, overcome, overwhelm, put to flight, send flying, send/sweep to the four winds, sweep away, worst.

scene n. 1) field, whereabouts, 2) *part* of a play, 3) back-cloth, backdrop, background, set, setting, 4) landship/*landscape*, outlook, 5) outburst, stormy meeting, to-do, upset.

sceptical adj. looking for the worst, outspoken, misbelieving, unbelieving, worldly-wise.

schedule n. foredraft, outline.

scheme n. 1) shift, makeshift, make-do, 2) blind, little game, dust thrown in the eyes.

scholar n. bookworm, learner, seeker, learned man/woman, man/woman of learning, thinker, thinking man/woman.

scholarship n. book-learning, book-lore, learning, lore, reading.

science n. body/field of knowledge, lore, lore-craft, world-wisdom.

scientific adj. thorough, thought-through, well-grounded.

scientist n. learner, seeker after truth, thinker, world-wit.

scope n. 1) play, free play, full play, field, free field, free hand, freedom, leeway, opening, room, elbow-room, sea-room, 2) outlook, reach, span.

scorn n. coldness, loathing, looking down on, misliking, spurning, weighing lightly someone's worth.

scornful adj. belittling, biting, cutting, looking down on one, off-handed, running down, stinging, withering.

scrap v. to break up, ditch, drop, shed, throw away/out, write off.

scrape v. 1) to bite into, claw, cut into, rough-hew, 2) to grind, screech, 3) to graze, 4) to clean.

scratch v. 1) to claw, cut, graze, mark, wound, 2) to strike out, 3) to write badly.

screw v. 1) to fasten, twist, wind, work in, 2) to crumple.

script n. 1) book, lines, playbook, words, 2) hand, handwriting, writing, longhand, *pencraft*, pot-hooks and hangers.

scrupulous adj. careful, mindful, straight, true, thorough, thoroughgoing, upright, watchful, with nothing left out/missing.

search n. burrowing, combing, delving, hunt, rooting, seeking, <u>sifting</u>.

search v. to comb, <u>delve</u> into, <u>find out</u> about, go deep into, hunt for, <u>learn</u>, look for, look into, root through, <u>seek</u>, thresh out, unearth.

season n. time, stream of time, time of year, span, spell, while, spring-time, summer-time, leaf-fall, winter-time.

second adj. 1) other, following, further, next, 2) back-up, spare, twin.

secondary adj. lesser, lightweight, makeshift, mean, <u>middling</u>, unworthy.

secret adj. hidden, <u>knotted</u>, buried, shrouded, stealthy.

secretary n. 1) right-hand, 2) meeting-writer (one who writes down what was talked about and settled at a meeting).

secretive adj. canny, dark, deep, hard to fathom, unfathomed, hooded, not open, not to be drawn, stealthy, tight-lipped, unforthcoming, wary, withdrawn.

section n. 1) head, heading, length, limb, share, 2) hundred, neighbourhood, ward, 3) arm.

sector n. 1) arm, 2) neighbourhood.

secure adj. 1) fast, fastened, knotted, locked, set, shut, steady, wedged, 2) out of harm's way, shielded.

secure v. 1) to bind, bolt, <u>fasten</u>, make fast, lock, lock up, shut, stick, tie up, 2) to keep, shield, strengthen, 'earth', 3) to come by, get hold of, pick up, win, 4) to answer for, underwrite.

security n. 1) shield, well-being, storm blown over, wide berth, 2) backing, underwriting.

seductive adj. bewitchful, binding, 'come hither', fetching, spell-weaving, taking, witching.

seem v. to have the look of, look as if, look like, look to be, look so.

seize v. to clutch, fasten on, get hold of, get in one's hands, grip, lay hands on, lay hold of, pick up, hook, net, land, take.

select v. to choose, make up one's mind, mark out, pick out, settle upon, sift through.

selection n. 1) choosing, naming, pick, picking and choosing, 2) gathered writings (*anthology*), not the whole.

self-*important adj.* full of oneself, high and mighty, on one's high horse, <u>overbearing</u>, overweening, stiff, swollen-headed, unbending, wise in one's own eyes.

senior adj. elder, older.

sensational adj. amazing, bewildering, beyond belief, breathtaking, heady, out of this world, overwhelming, startling, thrilling.

sense n. 1) feeling, stirred feeling, true feeling, warm feeling, hearing, sight, smell, 2) awareness, insight, quickness, understanding, <u>wisdom</u>, 3) bearing, flow, line of thought, meaning.

senseless adj. <u>heedless</u>, <u>light-minded</u>, meaningless, mindless, silly, unwise, <u>wilful</u>.

sensible adj. aware, <u>bright</u>, keen-witted, shrewd, thinking, <u>wise</u>, understanding, wit-right.

sensitive adj. 1) alive to, aware, feeling, kind, kindly, thoughtful, understanding, 2) highly strung, over-strung, readily upset, raw, sore, 3) (as in 'a *sensitive issue*') thorny, 4) (as in 'a *sensitive instrument*') aright, dead-on, keen, sharp, straight, true, thorough, well-pitched.

sensitivity n. 1) feeling, insight, thoughtfulness, timing, understanding, 2) prickliness.

sensuous adj. bewitching, spell-weaving, sweet, taking.

sentiment n. feeling, lovesickness, softness, thought, way of thinking.

separate adj. asunder, <u>sundered</u>, broken away, cut off, islanded, alone, lonely.

separate v. 1) to <u>sunder</u>, come between, drive a wedge between, set against, cut off, 2) to break away, break up, go one's own way.

separation n. break, break-up, sundering, rending, setting against, unthreading.

September n. Harvest-month, Holy-month, Barley-month.

series n. 1) row, run, set, string, thread, 2) 'soap'.

serious adj. dark, <u>earnest</u>, forbidding, grim, stern, thoughtful, unlaughing, unlively.

seriously adv. 1) indeed, in earnest, on oath, upon one's word, truly, truthfully, 2) earnestly, in good earnest, manfully, thoughtfully, 3) badly, sorely.

servant n. follower, hand, helper, hired man/woman, hireling, maid-of-all-work, maid, man, underling, <u>worker</u>.

serve *v.* 1) to be under, to follow, see to, work for, 2) to answer, fulfil, match up to, meet the need.

service *n.* 1) good deed, helpfulness, helping hand, willing help, worship, 2) yoke.

session *n.* 1) hearing, meeting, sitting, 2) spell, stretch, time.

several *adj.* a few, a handful of, manifold, more than one, not alone, some, sundry, upwards of.

severe *adj.* 1) baneful, woeful, 2) biting, burning, cutting, harrowing, searing, sharp, unsparing, 3) flinty, forbidding, grim, hard, stern, stony-hearted, tough, unbending, 4) (of the winter) bitter, cold, freezing, rough, wild.

sewage *n.* ditch-water, filth, swill.

sex *n.* 1) he-kind/she-kind, manhood/womanhood, spear-kin/spindle-kin, 2) going to bed with, lying with/sleeping with someone, lovemaking.

sexual *adj.* fleshly, hot-blooded, 'come hither'.

shatter *v.* to break down, bring to naught, overcome, overwhelm, tear down/up, throw down, unmake, wipe out.

shirk *v.* to back away, be loath, fight shy of, get out of, idle away, let one down, set at naught, shrink from, shun, sidestep.

shock *n.* 1) eye-opener, quake, upset, thunderbolt, thunderclap, the unforeseen, 2) breakdown, fit, stroke, 3) fright, affright, start.

shock *v.* to amaze, frighten, numb, shake, shake up, take aback, unsettle, upset.

shudder *v.* 1) to shake or shiver with cold, 2) to shake or shiver with fear, quake, dread, 3) to be sickened at, bristle, loathe, shrink from, shun.

sign *n.* 1) beacon, mark, marker, token, 2) forth-showing, unfolding, 3) clue, hint, giveaway, 4) board, landmark, waymark.

sign *v.* 1) to beckon, wave, 2) to put/set one's hand to, underwrite, write one's name.

signal *n.* 1) beacon, beacon-fire, beam, warning light, 2) go-ahead, green light.

signature *n.* hand, underwriting.

significance *n.* 1) greatness, standing, weight, weightiness, worth, worthship, 2) meaning, pith.

significant *adj.* 1) marked, showing, striking, weighty, well-grounded, 2) knowing, meaning, meaningful, telling.

silence *n.* dumbness, stillness, speechlessness.

silent *adj.* a-dumb, soft, still, stilly, speechless, tongueless, wordless, unspeaking, unspoken, still as the grave, tongue-tied.

similar *adj.* akin to, alike, like, much like, matching, something like, such like, twin.

similarly *adv.* also, as, as if, as it were, in a way, like, likewise, so to speak.

simile *n.* likening, setting side by side.

simple *adj.* 1) bare, forthright, straightforward, 2) lone, onefold, fewfold, 3) light, no sooner said than done, not hard, short, 4) childlike, everyday, homely, home-made, homespun, open-hearted, uncluttered, unworldly, 5) nothing but, nothing less/more than, sheer, 6) childish, green, raw, readily taken in, shallow, witless.

simply *adv.* 1) freely, openly, with an open heart, readily, straightforwardly, 2) alone, only, no more than, 3) starkly, 4) altogether, utterly, wholly.

simultaneously *adv.* all together, along with, together with, therewith, in the one breath.

sincere *adj.* earnest, forthcoming, heartfelt, hearty, not lying, open, true-hearted, warm, whole-hearted.

single *adj.* 1) lone, one, onefold, only, only one, one and only, 2) known (*particular*), 3) unbroken, unshared, straight, 4) free, unwed, wifeless.

single-minded *adj.* one-minded, steadfast, stern-minded, strong-minded, earnest, gritty, iron-willed, steely, unbending, unshaken, unshrinking, unyielding.

sinister *adj.* baleful, bodeful, deadly, dreadful, evil, forbidding, harmful, hanging over, threatening, threatful.

site *n.* 1) ground, pitch, 2) setting, when and where, whereabouts.

situation *n.* 1) hole, plight, 2) lie of the land, look of things, 3) setting, set-up, whereabouts, 4) field, livelihood, walk of life, work, world.

size *n.* greatness, length, width.

skilful *adj.* clever, deft, keen-minded, knowing, quick, ready, sharp, well up in.

skill *n.* craft, deftness, knowledge, wisdom.

skilled *adj.* good at, handy, nimble, quick, ready.

slander *v.* to smear, backbite, blacken, curse, run down, speak evil of, speak foully of, swear at.

slang *n.* by-talk, street-talk, under-talk.

slave *n.* 1) thrall, hewer of wood and drawer of water, 2) drudge, handmaid, maid-of-all-work.

slump *n.* dive, drop, dwindling, fall, falling off, hard times, bad times, lessening, meltdown, shrinking, trough.

sly *adj.* crafty, foxy, knowing, shady, sharp, shifty, slippery, underhand.

smile *n.* beaming look, blithe look, glad/warm look, laughing eyes, twinkling eyes.

smile v. to beam, laugh with, welcome.

snap v. 1) to bite at, 2) to speak sharply, fly off the handle at, 3) to break, give way, 4) to get a shot of, shoot.

sober adj. 1) 'dry', water-drinking, 2) canny, careful, cool, earnest, <u>heedful</u>, steady, stern, thoughtful, unlaughing, wary, 3) bald, bare, dark, forbidding, sad, stark.

sociable adj. <u>friendly</u>, neighbourly, outgoing, warm.

society n. 1) mankind, folk, the world, 2) body, togetherness, 3) brotherhood, 4) right set, smart set, top drawer.

soil n. 1) clay, dust, earth, ground, loam, 2) land, homeland.

soldier n. fighter, fighting man, man of blood.

solecism n. missaying, mis-spelling, miswording, miswriting, slip of the tongue.

solely adv. alone, no more than, nothing but, only.

solemn adj. 1) <u>earnest</u>, heavy, stiff, thoughtful, unlaughing, weighty, 2) hallowed, holy, worshipful.

solicitor n. lawyer, man of law.

solid adj. 1) frozen, hard, heavy, meaty, set, weighty, 2) <u>strong</u>, well-built, 3) <u>upright</u>, upstanding, worthy, 4) good, 5) outright, thorough-going.

solitary adj. alone, lonely, lonesome, by oneself, <u>forlorn</u>, forsaken, friendless.

solstice n. midsummertide, midwintertide, summer's height, winter's depth.

solution n. answer, key, light, unfolding.

solve v. to answer, find the key to, find the meaning, get to the bottom of, make out, unfold, unriddle, work out.

sophisticated adj. 1) all-knowing, in the know, choosy, worldly, worldly-wise, 2) cleverly/deftly wrought, craftly.

sordid adj. <u>dreadful</u>, foul, frightful, <u>loathsome</u>, mean, shameful, unwholesome, <u>worthless</u>.

sort n. brand, breed, hue, ilk, kind, make, stamp, strain.

sound n. 1) clatter, din, <u>loudness</u>, pitch, bellow, blast, knocking, roar, uproar, scream, screech, 2) sighing, soughing, whispering, wind song, 3) earshot, hearing.

sound v. 1) to be loud, bellow, blast, clatter, deafen, give tongue, go off, hammer, ring, ring in the ear, roar, scream, screech, set off, thunder, toll, wind the horn, 2) to sough, sigh, whisper.

source n. 1) beginning, head-spring, springhead, wellhead, wellspring, stem, 2) (of

spoken or written words) grounding, groundwork, root, witness.

sovereign n. king, queen, high king, overlord.

sovereignty n. kingship, <u>lordship</u>, overlordship, grip, hold, long arm, reach.

space n. breadth, field, length and breadth, room, span, spread, stretch, sweep, open moorland, upland, wild, wilderness.

special adj. far above, first in the field, foremost, marked, other, otherwise, out of the way, owing nothing to, unalike, unlike.

specialist n. highbrow, leading light, shining light, man/woman of learning, one in the know, wiseman.

species n. breed, kind.

specific adj. cut and dried, known, marked, named, right, settled, shown, true.

specifically adv. in a nutshell, namely, that is to say.

spectacular adj. breathtaking, marked, shining, striking.

speculative adj. 1) in cloud-land, only in the mind, only on the drawing board, dreamy, daydreaming, far-minded, 2) over-bold, over-daring, reckless, wild.

sphere n. 1) bead, drop, 2) business, field, setting, walk of life, world.

spinney n. thorn-wood, brake, frith, grove, holt, holt-wood, hurst, wood-holt, shaw, thicket, underwood.

spirit/s n. 1) soul, inmost soul, breath, inner self, innermost being, life, mind, heart of hearts, 2) ghost, shade, shadow, soul of one dead, 3) backbone, doggedness, drive, gameness, <u>steadfastness</u>, steeliness, will, 4) earnestness, fire, liveliness, sparkle, warmth, 5) heart, lifeblood, soul, 6) meaning, pith, 7) feel, feeling, mood, 8) strong water.

spirited adj. alive, awake, gamesome, keen, <u>lively</u>, on the go, quick, sparkling.

spite n. bitterness, fiendishness, hardness, hatred, heartlessness, ruthlessness.

splendid adj. ablaze, aglow, <u>bright</u>, gleaming, goodly, great, high, matchless, outstanding, rich, shining, wonderful, <u>worthful</u>.

spoil v. 1) to bend, blacken, blight, harm, mar, mark, smear, soil, twist, <u>undo</u>, upset, warp, wreck, 2) to be all over one, kill with kindness, let one get away with, make much of, smother, 3) to go bad, go off, rot.

sponsor n. backer, oath-helper.

sponsor v. to back, lend one's name to, put up.

spontaneous adj. childlike, from the heart, homely, home-made, open-handed, open-hearted, rough and ready, straight out, unbidden.

sport, sports *n.* games, field games.

spurious *adj.* hollow, misleading, make-believe, shallow, sham, truthless, untrue.

squander *v.* to be careless, run through, 'blow' everything.

stability *n.* 1) steadfastness, steadiness, stiffening, evenness, 2) long innings, long run, long standing.

stable *adj.* 1) abiding, deep-rooted, lasting, longstanding, steadfast, strong, well-grounded, 2) cool, steady.

stadium *n.* ground, pitch, playing field/ground, ring, 'bowl'.

stage *n.* 1) lap, milestone, step, stop, stopover, 2) boards, stand, 3) field, ground.

stagnant *adj.* rank, standing, still, stinking, unwholesome.

stagnate *v.* 1) to become foul, stop flowing, 2) to be at a standstill, do nothing, go nowhere, go to seed, idle, lie fallow, not lift a finger, not stir a step, rot, rust, slacken, slumber, stand by, fold/sit on one's hands, let the grass grow under one's feet, rest on one's oars.

stain *n.* 1) mark, finger mark, smear, streak, 2) shame, smear, 3) dye.

stain *v.* 1) to foul, mark, 2) to blacken, put to shame, smear, 3) to dye.

stale *adj.* dry, hard, old, still, withered, worn.

stance *n.* 1) outlook, stand, way of thinking, 2) bearing.

standard *n.* 1) benchmark, yardstick, 2) belief, high thought, 3) fane (*flag*).

standard *adj.* everyday, set, stock.

state *n.* 1) kingdom, land, homeland, folkdom, 2) shape, suchness, 3) frame of mind, mood, 4) setting, walk of life, 5) smartness, stiffness.

state *v.* to bear witness, give one to understand, make known, put, say, set forth, tell.

statement *n.* word, set word, saying, speech, putting forth, telling forth, witness, write-up, hand-out.

station *n.* 1) pull-up, stop (on a *railway*), 2) wavelength, 3) lot, standing, walk of life, worthship.

stationary *adj.* at a standstill, stock-still, stopped, laid up.

status *n.* 1) lot, walk of life, 2) footing, standing, weight, weightiness, worship, worth, worthship, 3) how the land lies, lay of the land, look of things.

staunch *adj.* doughty, stalwart, stalworth, steadfast, trothfast, true, true-hearted, unyielding, upright.

stay *v.* 1) to abide, bide, dwell, put up at, settle, stand, sleep at, stop, 2) to bring to a stand/standstill, hold over, lay over, put a stop to, put off, stop.

stifling *adj.* 1) heavy-handed, overbearing, overwhelming, 2) (of the weather) clammy, heavy, hot, steamy, sticky, sweaty, sweltering, sweltry.

stimulate *v.* to awaken, hearten, quicken, stir the blood, stir up.

stipulation *n.* a must, rider, strings.

stomach *n.* belly, inner man, inside/s, maw, midriff.

stomach *v.* to abide, forbear, put up with, stand, swallow.

storage *n.* hoarding, holding, stowing.

store *n.* 1) shop, outlet, 2) heap, hoard, holding, stock, wealth, 3) barn, byre, hold, stockroom, strong-room, warehouse.

store *v.* to heap up, hoard, hold, keep, lay by, lay in, put aside, put away, put by, fill up, stock up, build up one's stocks, stow, stow away.

store (of words) *n.* wordhoard, wordstock, word-wealth, word-web.

story *n.* 1) tale, old wives' tale, tall tale, yarn, 2) gossip, news, tidings.

strain *n.* 1) burden, weariness, weight of care, worry, 2) bitterness, restlessness, 3) pull, wrench, 4) song.

strain *v.* 1) to bear hard on, go to all lengths, go too far, not know when to stop, overburden, overdo, overwork, stretch, wear out, weary, 2) (of the truth) to bend, stretch, twist, warp, 3) to cripple, lame, pull, tear, twist, wrench, 4) to bend over backwards, break one's back/neck, give one's all, go all out for, sweat blood, 5) to riddle, sift.

strait *n.* narrows, sound, stretch of water, tideway, waterway.

strange *adj.* beyond fathoming, fathomless, outlandish, uncanny, uncouth, unknown, weird, wonderful.

stranger *n.* farcomer, farfarer, newcomer, newfarer, outlander, outsider.

stranglehold *n.* clutches, grasp, grip, iron grip, handhold, hold, tight hold.

strategic *adj.* 1) framed, worked out, 2) key.

strategy *n.* line, steps.

stress *n.* 1) burden, hardship, hard going, weariness, weight of care, worry, 2) weight, 3) beat.

stress *v.* to bring to the fore, drive home, dwell on, give weight to, highlight, lay the finger on, make much of, make one see/understand.

strict *adj.* 1) cold, forbidding, grim, hard, heartless, hidebound, stern, stern-minded, stiff, strong-willed, tough, unbending, unsparing, unyielding, 2) rightly believing, right-minded, upright, upstanding.

strictly *adv.* heavy-handedly, narrowly, sharply, sternly.

structural *adj.* framing, holding.

structure *n.* 1) build, framework, layout, make, make-up, set-up, shape, workings, 2) building.

struggle *n.* fight, running fight, grind, hard going, hardship, hard work, stiff work, uphill work, nightmare, ordeal.

struggle *v.* to fight, stand against, get to grips with, make a shift to, sweat blood, withset, withstand, work, wrestle.

student *n.* bookworm, learner, seeker, thinker, thinking man/woman.

studio *n.* den, workroom, workshop.

study *n.* 1) book work, head work, mind work, learning, lore, reading, seeking, thinking through, grind, weighing the fors and againsts, 2) working *paper*, 3) den, bookroom, workroom, 4) drawing, black and white drawing, line-drawing, outline, likeness.

study *v.* to bend one's mind to, delve into, give one's mind to, go into, learn, read up, seek for truth, thirst after knowledge, bury oneself in one's books.

stuff *n.* 1) belongings, things, 2) goods, stock, things for sale, wares, 3) marrow, pith, cloth, weave, warp and weft/woof, 4) chaff, draff, dross, sweepings.

stumble *n.* fall, topple.

stumble *v.* to fall, falter, grope, miss one's footing, reel, topple.

stunning *adj.* 1) amazing, benumbing, bewildering, breathtaking, startling, striking, mind-blowing, 2) bewitching, heavenly, lovely, wonderful, out of this world, outstanding, overwhelming.

stupendous *adj.* amazing, breathtaking, great, startling, striking, wonderful.

stupid *adj.* addle-headed, dim-witted, empty-headed, half-witted, slow-witted, thick, unwise, unwitful, witless.

style *n.* 1) way of speaking/writing, feeling for words, wording, 2) way of doing things, way of life, 3) becomingness, flow, readiness, smartness, smoothness, 4) cut, last word, latest thing, look, new look, trend, way.

subject *n.* 1) business, gossip, news, pith, what it is about, 2) (of *study*) field, 3) sitter, 4)

(*citizen*) freeman, townsman, townswoman, 5) follower, tool, underdog, underling.

subject *v.* 1) to lay open, put through, 2) to bind, hold down, keep down/under, lay one's yoke upon, overmatch, override, put down, quell, tread down.

subjective *adj.* dreamy, inward-looking, inwrought, not of this world.

sublime *adj.* 1) far-stretching, great, high, on high, stirring, wonderful, 2) outright, thorough, thoroughgoing, utter.

submarine *n.* deep-sea craft, underwater craft.

submarine *adj.* deep-sea, undersea, underwater.

submit *v.* 1) to yield to, bow to, give in, give up, 2) to send, give.

subsequent *adj.* after, following, later, next

substance *n.* 1) being, body, 2) meaningfulness, weight, worthship, 3) burden, heart, kernel, marrow, meaning, pith, the great thing, main thing, 4) truth, light of truth, 5) riches, wealth, wherewithal.

substantial *adj.* 1) goodly, worthwhile, 2) great, hefty, meaty, strong, well-built, 3) meaningful, thorough, thorough-going, true, weighty, well-grounded.

substantially *adv.* 1) greatly, markedly, 2) mainly, in the main, more or less.

substitute *n.* stand-by, stand-in, another of like kind/worth/weight, steadman.

substitute *v.* to make do with, make a shift with, stand in for, step into the shoes of.

subtle *adj.* 1) hair-shredding, narrow, thin-spun, 2) crafty, foxy, knowing, ready, sharp, shrewd, over-clever, too clever by half.

suburban *adj.* 1) edge of town, out-of-town, 2) dreary, narrow, small-town.

subversive *adj.* lawless, self-willed, unbridled, underground, wayward, wild, wilful.

succeed *v.* 1) to do well, make one's mark, rise in the world, speed well, 2) to come after, come into, follow, step into someone's shoes, take over from.

success *n.* 1) breakthrough, overcoming, upper hand, win, outright win, game and match, 2) good speed, riches, weal, wealth, 3) best seller, sell-out, match-winner, winner, world-beater.

successful *adj.* 1) leading, match-winning, on the up and up, up and coming, winning, world-beating, 2) doing well, well-off, well-to-do.

successfully *adv.* well, swimmingly, beyond one's wildest dreams.

succession *n.* 1) flow, run, string, one thing after another, 2) coming to/into, taking over.

succinct *adj.* pithy, short, shortened, put in a nutshell, in a few well-chosen words.

succour *n.* backing, help, helping hand, strengthening, uplift.

succour *v.* to bear a hand, befriend, come to the help of, hold out a hand to, stand by, strengthen, take up the cudgels for, uphold.

succumb *v.* 1) to bow before the storm, bow one's neck to the yoke, give in/way, show no fight, wilt, yield, 2) to be at the end of one's strength, breathe one's last, die from/of, fall sick with, give up the ghost, go down with, go downhill, go under.

sudden *adj.* forthwith, over-early, quick, quick as lightning/thought, sharp, startling, straight out, swift, unbidden, unforeseen, unlooked for, without warning.

suddenly *adv.* all at once, at a stroke, at one swoop, like a shot, overnight, quickly, readily, sharply, shortly, here today and gone tomorrow, at the drop of a hat, in the twinkling of an eye, like a thief in the night, no sooner said than done.

sue *v.* 1) to go to law, have the law on one, 2) to ask for the hand of, beg hard, beseech, go down on one's knees, sigh at the feet of, woo, go a-wooing.

suffer *v.* 1) to know bitterness/hardship, mourn, sigh for, sorrow, weep over, 2) to abide, bear with, put up with, stand, swallow.

suffering *n.* hardship, sickness, burden, hard life, heart-ache, sorrow, wound, weight on one's mind, woe, wretchedness.

sufficient *adj.* enough, good enough, all right, fair, middling, up to the mark.

sufficiently *adv.* as one would wish, rightly, well.

suggest *v.* 1) to bring to mind, make one think of, put one in mind of, 2) to awaken, put up to, quicken, set going, stir up, 3) to hint at, lead one to believe, shadow forth, show, 4) to moot, put forth, put forward, put to.

suggestion *n.* 1) breath, hint, play, shade, shadow, whisper, 2) draft, first draft.

suggestive *adj.* 1) half-spoken, hinting, meaningful, showing, teasing, tell-tale, 2) shameful, twisted, unclean, unwholesome.

suit *n.* 1) going to law, taking one to law, 2) asking, love-making, love-play, love-song, tale of love, wooing, 3) clothing, outfit.

suit *v.* to answer, become, belong, go with, match up to, meet the need, show one off.

suitable *adj.* 1) answering, becoming, fitting, right, timely, well-timed, 2) cut out for, in keeping with.

suitcase *n.* holdall, overnight box.

suite *n.* 1) rooms, set of rooms, flat, 2) followers, following, hangers-on, henchmen, household.

sum *n.* 1) hoard, wherewithal, 2) reckonings, 3) fullness, whole, beginning and end, be all and end all, length and breadth.

summary, summing-up *n.* a drawing out of the key goals and findings of a work, pith, rundown, shortening, siftings, winnowings.

summit *n.* 1) height, utmost height, head, highwater mark, peak, top, 2) high gathering, high meeting, talks.

superb *adj.* good, goodly, great, high, rich, wonderful, worthful, worthy.

superficial *adj.* 1) childish, empty, empty-headed, light-minded, lightweight, shallow-minded, 2) careless, heedless, half-done, hardly begun, left hanging, makeshift, off-hand, thoughtless, unmindful, unthorough, 3) hollow, light, shadowy, shallow, thin.

superfluous *adj.* above/beyond one's needs, needless, unneeded, on one's hands, over, left over, over and above, spare, to spare.

superior *adj.* 1) better, cut above, foremost, greater, greatest, higher, highest, marked, matchless, outmatching, outstanding, 2) lordly, on one's high horse.

supermarket *n.* shopping haven.

supervision *n.* care, handling, oversight, running, stewardship.

supper *n.* bite, even-meat, evening fare/meal, full meal, light meal, main meal.

supplement *n.* 1) broadening, strengthening, waxing, 2) pull-out.

supplement *v.* to build up, eke out, fill out, strengthen, top up.

supply *n.* goods, heap, hoard, holding, load, something in hand, stock, two of everything.

supply *v.* to build up, come up with, find, fulfil, give, make good, meet, stock.

support *n.* backing, backup, friendship, help, stay, willing help, upholding.

support *v.* 1) to back up, help, side with, speak up for, stand behind, stand by, stand up for, take up the cudgels for, underwrite, uphold, 2) to clothe, feed, find, give, help out, keep, put up.

suppose *v.* to believe, dare say, dream up, moot, put forth/forward, take into one's head, take something as so, think likely.

suppress *v.* to bring to naught, hold down, put an end to, put down, undo, unmake.

supreme *adj.* best, first, foremost, greatest, highest, topmost, uppermost, leading, main, matchless, nonesuch, on top, outstanding, overriding, world-beating.

sure *adj.* known, settled, true, right, unshaken, well-grounded.

surely *adv.* 1) come what may/will, indeed, no two ways about it, truly, rain or shine, sink or swim, couthly, forsooth, 2) doggedly, steadfastly, steadily, unfalteringly, unswervingly.

surface *n.* rind, shell, outside, outer side, outwardness, outer layer, outward look, rim, edge, overlay.

surmise *v.* to dare say, dream up, moot, put forth/forward, take it into one's head, take something as so, think likely.

surpass *v.* to better, leave behind, leave standing, outdo, outmatch, outshine, overtake, overtop, put in the shade.

surpassing *adj.* best, first, foremost, far better, goodly, great, greatest, matchless, nonesuch, outstanding, wonderful, worthful.

surplus *n.* over-fulness, more than enough, more than is needed, overflow, overspill, richness.

surplus *adj.* left over, over and above, spare.

surprise *n.* 1) afterclap, start, the unforeseen, the unlooked-for, thunderclap, 2) eye-opener, wonder.

surprising *adj.* amazing, bewildering, breathtaking, startling, striking, unlooked-for.

surrender *n.* forgoing, giving up, handing over, yielding.

surrender *v.* to yield, give in, give up, have no fight left, throw in one's hand.

surround *v.* to begird, beset, cut off, gird about, ring about, hedge in, hem in, keep in, lock in, shut in.

surroundings *n.* background, neighbourhoood, setting.

survey *n.* looking over, reckoning, sighting, taking stock.

survey *v.* to look over, make out, mark off, mete, over sweep, pick out, reckon up, eye up, sight, take readings, take the length and breadth of, take stock of, weigh up the worth of, work out.

survival *n.* holding on to life, keeping alive, life span.

survive *v.* 1) to be spared, get away, hold on/out, live through, pull through, stand fast, keep body and soul together, keep one's footing/ground, keep one's head above water, live to fight another day, weather the storm, 2) to abide, last, outlast, live longer than, live on after, outlive.

suspect *n.* one under a cloud/shadow, one who may be guilty.

suspect *v.* 1) to believe, feel, think likely, 2) to find hard to believe, misbelieve, have fears/misgivings, hold back, not go all the way, shrink, shy at, think twice, be in two minds, be wary of, wonder about.

suspect *adj.* left open, not straightforward, shady, shifty, slippery, smooth, too clever by half, underhand.

suspend *v.* to break off, hold off, leave off, stand, stop, down tools.

suspicion *n.* misgiving, half-belief, misbelief, unbelief, wariness.

sustain *v.* 1) to follow up, follow through, keep on foot, keep on, keep it up, see it through, 2) to give/lend a hand, give heart to one, help, keep alive, keep from falling, stand behind, stand by, strengthen, uphold, 3) to abide, bear up, feel, go on, keep going, undergo, withstand.

symbol *n.* likeness, mark, marker, shadow, token.

symbolic *adj.* shadowy, token.

sympathetic *adj.* 1) feeling, kind, kindly, ruthful, soft-hearted, understanding, warm-hearted, 2) friendly, like-minded.

sympathy *n.* deep feeling, ruth, soft heart, softness, thoughtfulness, understanding, warmth.

symptomatic *adj.* boding, hinting, tell-tale, telling, warning.

synonymous *adj.* akin, alike, bound up with.

system *n.* network, setup, set way, web.

systematic *adj.* businesslike, set, settled, straight, thorough, thought-through, well-grounded.

table *n.* 1) board, stand, 2) lay-out, list, 3) fare, food, spread.

tactful *adj.* careful, insightful, thoughtful, understanding, wise, witful.

tactics *n.* answer, dealings, shift, steps, ways, craft, gamesmanship, wit.

talent *n.* bent, brain, brightness, deftness, wit, mother wit, wisdom.

tangible *adj.* earthy, fleshly, of flesh and blood, weighty.

tangled *adj.* 1) knotted, knotty, thick, tousled, twisted, 2) dark, deep, hard to fathom/grasp/understand, riddle-wrought, thorny, wordy.

target *n.* goal, mark.

task *n.* business, undertaking, work, hard work, uphill work.

taste v. 1) to smack of, 2) to sip, 3) to come up against, feel, have knowledge of, know, meet with, undergo, 4) to make out, pick out.

tawny adj. brown, nutbrown, brownish, light-brown, yellowish brown, brown as a berry, dark, sunburnt.

tax n. 1) toll, 2) burden, drain, load, weight.

technical adj. 1) craftily, 2) (of wording) insider.

technique n. 1) steps, way, 2) craft, craftsmanship, deftness, handcleverness, know-how, quickness.

technology n. know-how, way of doing things.

tedious adj. dreary, dry, endless, grey, heavy, leaden, longsome, overlong, slow, tiresome, weariful, wearing, wearisome.

telegraph v. to send, wire.

telephone n. ringer, speaker, farspeaker.

telephone v. to call, call up, ring, ring up, give someone a call/ring, make a call.

telescope n. long-glass.

television n. 'the box', farseer.

temperature n. coldness, coolness, heat.

temple n. house of worship.

temporarily adv. fleetingly, for a little/short while, for a time/short time, for the time being, here today and gone tomorrow.

temporary adj. 1) fleeting, makeshift, short-lived, short and sweet, 2) caretaker, fill-in, stand-in.

temptation n. draw, honeyed words, spell, witching.

tempting adj. bewitching, misleading, mouth-watering, teasing.

tenacious adj. dogged, doughty, game, gritty, iron-willed, lasting, steadfast, steady, strong-willed, tireless, tough, true, unshrinking, unyielding.

tend v. to have the care/oversight of, feed, keep, see to (a herd or flock), to care for, take care of, look after, watch over (the sick).

tend v. to stretch towards, be drawn towards, lean towards, make's one's way towards, be likely to, be minded.

tendency n. bent of mind, leaning, readiness, set, trend.

tender adj. 1) caring, kind, kind-hearted, kindly, loving, mild, ruthful, soft, soft-hearted, soothing, sweet, warm, warm-hearted, 2) green, new, unripe, young, youthful, 3) aching, bruised, raw, smarting, sore.

tense adj. 1) afire, alive, awake, heedful, keyed up, never-resting, never-sleeping, restless, sleepless, treading warily, wary,

watchful, 2) edgy, on edge, fearful, overwrought, worried, wound up.

tension n. 1) edginess, gnawing care, restlessness, weight of care, weight on one's mind, worry, 2) bitter/hard feelings, hatred, misliking, 3) stiffness, stretching.

tentative adj. backward, faltering, groping, halting, limping, unsettled, wary.

tenuous adj. flimsy, shadowy, shaky, thin, thread-like, wispy.

term/s n. 1) span, spell, time, while, 2) a stretch of time in the law or school year, three months, four months, sitting, 3) set day, time of childbirth, 4) rider, strings, 5) footing/standing between two folk, 6) name, word, way of speaking.

term v. to name.

termination n. 1) ending, making an end of, putting an end to, tearing down/up, undoing, unmaking, uprooting, wiping out, 2) the deed whereby the growth of a child in the womb is stopped (so that it is still-born), end, ending.

terminology n. naming, wording.

terrain n. going, ground, land, landshape.

terrible adj. dreadful, fiendish, frightful, ghastly, harrowing, hellish, loathsome, nightmarish.

territory n. acres, beat, ground, land, pitch.

terror n. dread, fright, affright, cold feet, misgiving, shrinking.

test n. 1) work-out, ordeal, uphill work, hard row, 2) hearing, 3) yardstick.

test v. 1) to stretch, 2) to delve into, sift, take a look at.

testament n. 1) last wishes, will, witness, 2) the foreward/undertaking between God and man, the Old and New Writings (of the *Bible*).

testimony n. witness, word, sworn word.

text n. 1) wording, words, 2) book, written work, 3) line.

textile n. cloth, weave.

theatre n. 1) playhouse, show hall/house, 2) field, setting, 3) (in *surgery*) body-stitching room.

theme n. thread.

theology n. godlearning, godlore.

theoretical adj. bookish, in cloud land, islanded from daily life, only in the mind, only on the drawing board.

theory n. belief, brainwave, insight, thinking, what one thinks, understanding.

thermal adj. (of winter clothing) thick, warm.

thesaurus n. wordbook, wordfinder, wordseeker, wordstock, word-chest.

thrifty adj. canny, careful, earnest, forgoing, heedful, mindful, minding the pence, spare, sparing, steady, watching the pennies.

thrive v. to gather, grow, blossom, make strides, ripen, rise, spread, strengthen, wax.

thrust v. 1) to bear upon, drive, elbow one's way, shoulder, shove, tell upon, 2) to cut through, have at, run through, stab, stick, strike at, strike hard, strike home.

ticket n. 1) token, 2) marker.

tiny adj. little, thimbleful.

tissue n. 1) cloth, weave, 2) (of lies and such) network, web, 3) the 'weave' of a living body/plant, 4) cleaning cloth, wipe.

title n. 1) heading, name, 2) 'handle' to one's name, knighthood, 3) ground of right, freehold, ownership, 4) book, work, 5) (in games) shield, spurs, wreath.

toast v. to drink to, drink a health to, hold one's glass to.

toil v. to work at, work hard, hammer away, keep at it, put one's back into it.

tolerate v. to abide, forbear, bear with, go along with, put up with, swallow, stand.

toleration n. forbearingness, light hand, mildness, open-mindedness.

tone n. 1) (of speech) pitch, strength, way of speaking, 2) feeling, mood, 3) health, strength, 4) (of *painting*) hue, shade, softness, warmth.

torch v. to burn, set fire to, set on fire, set alight, set light to.

tornado n. howling storm, wild storm, storm-wind, wild wind, windstorm.

tortuous adj. awry, bent, mazy, misleading, twining, twisted, twisting, twisty, unstraightforward, winding.

torture v. 1) to harm, tear, wound, 2) to cut to the quick, gnaw at, harrow, harry, hound, worry, wring.

toss v. 1) to shake, stir, 2) to thrash about, twitch, writhe, 3) to heave, pitch, spin (*a coin*), throw, throw back, 4) (of a boat) to heave, heel over, pitch, thresh about, wallow.

total n. answer, fullness, whole.

totally adv. all, altogether, down to the ground, fully, thoroughly, utterly, wholly.

touch n. 1) feeling, handling, stroke, 2) bit, drop, hint, speck, 3) awareness, understanding, 4) craft, deftness, grip, 5) hand.

touch v. 1) to feel, handle, hold, finger, thumb, lay a finger/hand on, run the hand over, play about with, stroke, 2) to get through to, make one think, stir.

touching adj. harrowing, heartbreaking, heart-rending, melting, sad, stirring, woeful.

touchy adj. bristly, prickly, sharp-edged.

tour n. 1) holiday, outing, 2) shift, spell, stint, stretch.

tournament n. match, meeting, run-off.

toxic adj. baneful, blighting, deadly, death-bringing, harmful, withering.

trace n. 1) bit, drop, hint, mark, shadow, token, all that is left, hardly anything, next to nothing, 2) footmark, footstep.

trace v. 1) to find, follow, hunt down, seek out, unearth, 2) to draft, draw, mark out, outline.

track n. 1) beaten path, bridle path, footpath, path, pathway, ride, road, walk, way, 2) line, 3) running way.

track v. 1) to follow, follow after, shadow, dog, tail, sit on one's tail, 2) to bring to light, find, go after, hunt down, look for, run to earth/ground, seek out, shadow, stalk, tail.

tradition n. 1) lore, folklore, teaching, 2) the old way, unwritten law, word of mouth.

traditional adj. acknowledged, deep-rooted, longstanding, old, old-fangled, old as the hills, unwritten.

traffic n. coming and going, shipping.

trafficking n. business, buying and selling, dealing, handling.

tragedy n. 1) play, work, 2) bad ending, death-knell, doom, downfall, hard stroke, undoing, unmaking.

tragic adj. dreadful, harrowing, heartbreaking, heart-rending, sorrowful, wretched.

trail n. 1) beaten path, footpath, path, pathway, road, way, 2) line, stream, string, 3) footsteps, mark, path.

trail v. 1) to dog, follow, go after, hound, hunt, run to ground, shadow, stalk, tail, sit on one's tail, 2) to drag along, draw, pull, tow, 3) to come after, drop/fall behind, follow, limp along, wander, 4) to hang down, hang over, overhang, sprawl over, spread over.

train n. 1) tail (of a *robe*), 2) followers, following, hangers-on, henchmen, household, 3) (of happenings) set, string, 4) wainway (*railway*) *train*.

train v. 1) to break in, make ready, put through the mill, ready, rear, take on, take in hand, tame, teach, 2) to be taught, get into shape, learn, warm up, work out, 3) to bring to bear, sight.

training n. body building, breaking-in, getting into shape, grounding, groundwork, hardening, learning, readying, spadework, strengthening, taming, teaching, toughening, warming up, working out.

trample v. 1) to run over, stamp down, tread, walk over, 2) to lord it over, put down, ride roughshod over, stamp on, tread underfoot.

transaction n. 1) business, deal, deed, doings, trade, undertaking, 2) clinching, handling, settling, thrashing out.

transcend v. to go above, go beyond, leave behind, leave in the shade, outdo, outgo, outmatch, outshine, overfare, overgo, overstep, overtop, rise above.

transfer n. handover, selling off, shift.

transfer v. to give into the hands of, hand down, hand over, hand to, leave it to, make over, put into the hands of, shift.

transform v. to bring in new blood, do up, hew into shape, make better, make into, make something of, make/shape anew, pitch anew, put right, set right, straighten out, work anew, forshape.

transformation n. makeover, new leaf.

transition n. overgoing, shift, shifting.

transitional adj. 1) restless, shifting, unsettled, 2) caretaker, fill-in, make-do, makeshift.

transparent adj. 1) glassy, see-through, sheer, thin, through-shining, through-showing, 2) forthright, open, straight, straightforward.

transport n. 1) shipping, wheels, 2) bliss, heaven, wonder, 3) fit (of wrath).

transport v. 1) to bear, bring, fetch, run, send, shift, ship, take, take away, 2) to fill with wonder, gladden, spellbind, take one's breath away, thrill, bewitch.

traumatic adj. dreadful, frightful, ghastly, harrowing, startling, upsetting.

travel v. to fare, fly, go, make one's way, set off/out, step out, take to the road, walk, wayfare, wend.

treacherous adj. crafty, forsworn, not straightforward, shifty, slippery, smooth, smooth-tongued, two-tongued, trothless.

treasury n. strong room, wealth-hold.

treat v. 1) to behave towards, look upon, 2) to bind up, care for, heal, help, make better, put right, set, 3) to buy, give, lay on, shower upon, stand, 4) (of learning) to deal with, go into, handle, set out, write about, write up, 5) to do/strike a deal, settle, talk, hold talks.

treatment n. 1) dealings with, handling, way of doing things, 2) care, after-care, healing.

treaty n. deal, truce, understanding, foreward.

tremble v. to flutter, quake, quiver, shake, shiver, writhe, be frightened to death, fear for one's life, quake/shake in one's shoes.

trembling adj. heaving, quaking, quivering, shaking, shivering.

tremendous adj. 1) fearsome, great, 2) amazing, startling, wonderful, 3) deafening, roaring, thundering.

trial n. 1) delving, dry run, reckoning, sifting, weighing, 2) hearing, doom-reckoning, meed-weighing, 3) evil, hardship, hard times, load, ordeal, sorrow, thorn in the flesh, woe, worry, 4) bane, weight about one's neck, wormwood.

tribunal n. bench, board, hearing, borough-moot/-mote, folkmoot, wardmote.

tributary n. bourne, brook, feeder, side-stream.

tribute n. 1) good word, high word, thanks, thanksgiving, 2) toll.

trip n. 1) day out, drive, outing, run, 2) fall, misstep, topple.

trip v. 1) to go, hop, spring, tread lightly/nimbly, walk, 2) to fall, fall over, lose one's footing, miss one's footing, misstep, topple.

trite adj. lifeless, set, stock, threadbare, tired, well-beaten/trodden/worn.

triumph n. outright win, runaway win, upper hand, walkover, game and match.

triumph v. 1) to beat hollow, be more than a match for, come out on top, outmatch, outplay, overcome, overmatch, overwhelm, sweep aside, win, 2) to bring down, put down, take down, crow over, shame, show off.

trivial adj. childish, empty, everyday, lightweight, little, meaningless, unmeaning, shallow, small, worthless, not worth a thought.

troop, troops n. 1) body, crowd, drove, flock, herd, swarm, team, throng, 2) men, fighting men.

trouble n. 1) ado, much ado, to-do, bane, care, stir, unrest, upset, worry, 2) aching, hardship, heartache, sorrow, woe, worry, 3) sickness, upset, 4) work, hard work, grind, hard going, uphill work, 5) breakdown, breaking-off, shut-down.

troubled adj. burdened, care-worn, fearful, in fear, fluttering, harrowed, restless, shaken, unsettled, worried.

truant v. to be off, bolt, make off, run away, slip away, steal away, take to one's heels, throw off the yoke.

truck n. business, dealings, trade.

truck n. pick-up, goods-wain.

truism n. emptiness, open and shut truth, threadbare/tired/worn saying, stock saying, unmeaningness, well-trodden word.

trust n. 1) belief, hope, 2) care, safekeeping.

trust *v.* 1) to believe, believe in, lean on, swear by, take as gospel, think likely, 2) to give into the hands of, hand over, leave it to, make over, put into the hands of, 3) to hope, hope and believe, think likely.

trustee *n.* keeper, steward, wealth-holder, wealth-keeper.

try *n.* bid, deed, go, step, undertaking.

try *v.* 1) to bestir oneself, give it one's all, keep at it, seek after, do one's best/utmost, 2) to find out what something is like, give something a go, sip, 3) (in law) to hold a hearing, delve into, fathom, get to the bottom of, go into, sift, take a look at, thresh out, winnow.

tsunami *n.* ground-swell, sea-wave.

tube *n.* pipe.

turmoil *n.* fight, free for all, madhouse, restlessness, stir, storm, to-do, upheaving.

type *n.* 1) (in Christian teaching) fore-likeness, foretoken (a man, thing, or happening in the Old *Testament* which foreshadows one such in the New *Testament*), 2) breed, ilk, kind, stamp, strain.

typhoon *n.* howling storm, wild storm, storm-wind, wild wind, windstorm.

typical *adj.* everyday, foreseen, in keeping, known, well-known, run-of-the-mill, set, settled, stock, true to kind, well-beaten/trodden/worn, nothing wonderful.

tyranny *n.* burden, heavy hand.

ugly *adj.* foul, frightful, grim, loathsome, misshapen, misbegotten, uncomely, unhandsome, unlovely, unwinsome.

ultimate *adj.* 1) end, furthest, last, 2) inwrought, root, underlying, 3) best, worst, greatest, highest, topmost, utmost.

ultimately *adv.* 1) after all, at last, at length, at long last, in fulness of time, in the end, in the long run, some day, sooner or later, 2) at heart, deep down.

ultimatum *n.* last word, threat.

unable *adj.* cannot, no good at, not up to, unhandy.

unacceptable *adj.* beyond bearing, more than flesh and blood can stand, not on, not to be borne, not to be put up with, too bad, unwelcome.

unambiguous *adj.* bald, downright, forthright, outspoken, straightforward.

unanimous *adj.* at one, like-minded, one-minded, of like mind, of one mind.

unassuming *adj.* mild, shy, overshy, unknown, unsung, yielding.

unavailing *adj.* bootless, falling short, going nowhere, hopeless, idle.

unavoidable *adj.* bound to be, not to be gainsaid, overriding, overwhelming, settled.

unbelievable *adj.* 1) beyond belief, hard to believe, far-fetched, outlandish, 2) amazing, breathtaking, overwhelming, startling, too good to be true, wonderful.

unbiased *adj.* fair, fair-minded, even-handed, even-minded, open-minded, right-minded, upright, unswerving, unwarped.

uncertain *adj.* two-minded, not knowing one's own mind, at a loss, bestraught, forstraught, brought to a stand, pulled this way and that, slow, unsettled.

unclear *adj.* 1) half-seen, knotty, left open, moot, unsettled, 2) misty.

uncommon *adj.* 1) almost unheard of, few and far between, thin on the ground, 2) marked, outstanding, worth looking at.

uncompromising *adj.* pigheaded, set in one's ways, stiff, unbending, unyielding.

unconscious *adj.* 1) fast asleep, blacked out, knocked out, benumbed, out, out cold, dead to the world, 2) blind to, unaware, unknowing, unseeing, wooden, 3) unthinking, unwitting, 4) (*subconscious*) inner, nether.

uncover *v.* to become aware of, bring to light, find out, lay bare, learn, make known, understand.

undaunted *adj.* doughty, fearless, gritty, stalwart, steadfast, steady, steely, true-hearted, unshrinking, unyielding.

undeniable *adj.* cut and dried, in black and white, known, no getting away from it, open and shut, right, settled, true, unshaken, well-grounded.

undercurrent *n.* 1) underflow, underswell, undertow, tideway, 2) feeling, hint, trend.

undermine *v.* 1) to burrow, delve, hollow out, 2) to cripple, gnaw at the roots, hinder, lame, play a deep game, spin/weave a web, tell/weigh against, threaten, under-delve, work against.

undoubtedly *adv.* come what may/will, indeed, no two ways about it, truly, rain or shine, sink or swim, couthly, forsooth.

uneasy *adj.* churned up, edgy, on edge, fearful, flighty, forstraught, restless, shaken, shaky, shifting, unsettled, upset, wary, worried, like a fish out of water.

unemployment *n.* hard times, idleness, more men/women than work, worklessness.

unenviable *adj.* thankless, unwelcome, unwished for.

unequivocal *adj.* bald, black-and-white, cut and dried, downright, <u>forthright</u>, no two ways about it, stark, straight, straightforward.

unexpected *adj.* <u>unforeseen</u>, unlooked for, startling.

unfamiliar *adj.* beyond one's ken, little known, unknown, unbeknown, new-fangled, out-of-the-way, seldom seen, unwonted, weird.

unflinching *adj.* unshrinking, <u>unyielding</u>, steely, iron-willed, doughty, fearless.

unfortunate *adj.* blighted, doomed, stricken, undone, untimely, untoward, wretched.

unfortunately *adv.* sadly, sad to say.

ungrateful *adj.* forgetful, heedless, unmindful, unthankful.

uniform *adj.* 1) even, matching, of one kind, smooth, steady, tidy, unbroken, 2) alike, like, <u>dreary</u>, dry, grey.

unimportant *adj.* harmless, lightweight, little, mean, mouselike, small, not worth a thought.

uninhibited *adj.* unbridled, wild, headstrong, hot-headed, <u>shameless</u>.

unintelligible *adj.* dark, hidden, <u>knotted</u>, meaningless, not to be understood, unfathomful.

unintentional *adj.* makeshift, misfallen, miswrought, not meant, <u>unforeseen</u>, unlooked for, unthinking, unwitting.

uninteresting *adj.* <u>dreary</u>, dry, grey, heavy, leaden, mind-numbing, tiresome, wearisome, dry as dust.

union *n.* 1) oneness, understanding, 2) wedlock, yoke.

unique *adj.* only, one and only, one-off, only one of its kind, onefold, matchless, unmatched.

unit *n.* 1) fullness, oneness, whole, wholeness, 2) team, 3) one, 4) bit, deal, share.

united *adj.* bound together, like-minded, one, one-hearted, one-minded, of one mind, well-knit, yoked together.

unity *n.* one-mindedness, oneness, wholeness, holding together, meeting of minds, understanding.

universal *adj.* all-holding, for all, far-stretching, widespread, worldwide, whole, wholesale.

university *n.* hall of learning, house of learning, lorehall.

unjust *adj.* <u>evil</u>, one-sided, unfair, unright, unrightwise, warped.

unlimited *adj.* endless, without end, full, unstinted, untold, unfettered, unhindered, unshackled, without strings.

unlucky *adj.* doomed, stricken, undone, wretched, untimely, untoward.

unnatural *adj.* 1) eerie, <u>weird</u>, nightmarish, uncanny, unearthly, 2) unkind, unloving.

unnecessary *adj.* above/beyond one's needs, needless, not needed, unneeded, left on one's hands, over and above.

unpalatable *adj.* 1) bitter, foul, hard, leathery, overdone, underdone, raw, stinking, tough, unsweetened, 2) <u>dreadful</u>, hateful, nightmarish, sickening, threatening, too bad, unbidden, unwinsome, unwished.

unprecedented *adj.* 1) ground-breaking, new, one and only, unbeheld, <u>unforeseen</u>, unheard of, unlooked for, unmatched, 2) amazing, outstanding, startling, <u>wonderful</u>.

unpredictable *adj.* 1) <u>light-minded</u>, <u>wilful</u>, fickle, unsteady, wayward, 2) <u>unforeseen</u>, unlooked for, startling, without warning.

unprejudiced *adj.* even-handed, fair, fair-minded, straight, rightwise.

unprincipled *adj.* <u>crafty</u>, misdealing, <u>sharp</u>, slippery, stealthy, underhanded.

unproductive *adj.* dry, empty, good for nothing, idle, stony, unblest, <u>worthless</u>.

unqualified *adj.* raw, unfitted, untaught, unworthy.

unrealistic *adj.* 1) blind, hopeless, mad, short-sighted, starry-eyed, ungrounded, wild, 2) unlifelike, untrue to life, wooden.

unreliable *adj.* fickle, flighty, hot-headed, <u>light-minded</u>, restless, <u>shifting</u>, unsettled, unsteadfast, unsteady, wayward.

unrestrained *adj.* headstrong, hot-headed, out of hand, quick-hearted, <u>shameless</u>, unbridled, wanton, wild, spreading like wildfire.

unruly *adj.* a law to oneself, headstrong, reckless, unbridled, wayward, wild, <u>wilful</u>.

unsafe *adj.* crumbling, on the edge, shaky, slippery, top-heavy, unsteady, built on sand, hanging by a thread.

unsatisfactory *adj.* <u>lacking</u>, makeshift, not good enough, short.

unscrupulous *adj.* <u>crafty</u>, misdealing, <u>ruthless</u>, <u>shameless</u>, sharp, slippery, stealthy, underhanded.

unsuccessful *adj.* 1) empty-handed, falling down, falling short, falling through, losing, misfired, out of one's depth, wide of the mark, 2) badly off, in utmost need, not doing well, not well off, on the wane, unblest, unbusinesslike.

unsuitable *adj.* not right, out of keeping, out of step, unbecoming, unmeet, untimely.

unsure *adj.* at a loss, brought to a stand, forstraught, <u>two-minded</u>, unsettled.

unused *adj.* 1) new to, not up to, not ready for, unhandy, all thumbs, ham-fisted, 2) new, 3) idle, in hand, left, left over, spare, ungathered, unhandled, unworked.

unusual *adj.* almost/nigh unheard of, far-fetched, new-fangled, outlandish, out-of-the-way, unearthly, unwonted, <u>weird</u>, <u>wonderful</u>.

urban *adj.* built-up, town, towny.

urge *v.* 1) to <u>speak</u> out, say outright, stir, dwell on, 2) to drive, hound, play upon, prick, quicken, elbow, shoulder, shove, spur on, work upon.

urgent *adj.* driving, now or never, with no time to lose, overriding, stopping for nothing.

use *n.* 1) handling, running, 2) wear, wear and tear, 3) end, need, 4) good, goodness, handiness, weight, weightiness, worth.

use *v.* 1) to bring into play, bring to bear, do with, drive, get the best out of, handle, make hay with, make the most of, wield, work, 2) to burn up, get through, go through, run through, swallow up, wear out, 3) to make a tool of, milk, overwork, play with, play off against.

used *adj.* dog-eared, not new, well-thumbed, well-trodden, well-worn, worn.

useful *adj.* handy, good for, helpful, of help, in play, ready, up and doing, working.

useless *adj.* broken down, draffish, good for nothing, hopeless, idle, loss-making, no good, not working, not worth while, unhandy, unneeded, worn out, <u>worthless</u>.

usual *adj.* daily, everyday, foreseen, known, well-known, set, <u>settled</u>, stock, well-beaten/trodden/worn, widespread, wonted, all in the day's work, nothing wonderful.

usually *adv.* all in all, 'day in, day out', mainly, in the main, mostly, most often, on the whole, overall, over and over, time and again, wontedly.

utility *n.* good, handiness, help, great help, helpfulness, helping hand, willing help, readiness, worth.

utopia *n.* better life, better world, dream world, dream, far-hope, wishful thinking.

utopian *adj.* dreamy, other-worldly, starry-eyed.

vacancy *n.* opening, berth.

vacation *n.* break, holiday, leave, rest, time off.

vacillating *adj.* forstraught, shifty, <u>two-minded</u>, unsettled, wayward.

vacuum *n.* bareness, emptiness, nothingness.

vague *adj.* dim, dreamy, daydreaming, <u>far-away</u>, forgetful, head in the clouds, lost in thought, in a world of one's own, with one's mind on other things, unmindful.

vain *adj.* 1) full of oneself, too clever by half, overweening, showing off, showy, swollen-headed, wise in one's own eyes, 2) beside the mark, empty, good for nothing, idle, <u>hollow</u>, lightweight, meaningless, <u>worthless</u>.

valiant *adj.* <u>bold</u>, doughty, fearless, daring, daring-hearted, stern, steely, <u>unyielding</u>.

valid *adj.* aright, good, lawful, telling, <u>true</u>, weighty, <u>well-grounded</u>.

valley *n.* coomb, dale, dean/dene, dell, hollow, slade.

valuable *adj.* dear, dearly bought, worth its weight in gold, <u>worthful</u>.

value *n.* worth, reckoning, what a thing will fetch, dearness.

value *v.* 1) to <u>think highly of</u>, think well of, hold dear, see the worth of, 2) to weigh the worth of, weigh up, reckon.

van *n.* goods-wain.

vanish *v.* 1) to be gone, be lost to sight, fly away, hide from the light, leave, lie low, lie out of sight, make off, melt away, melt into the mist, slip away, steal away, wear away, withdraw, 2) to die out, dwindle, end.

variable *adj.* fickle, <u>fitful</u>, flighty, giddy, restless, <u>shifting</u>, uneven, unsettled, unsteady, wayward.

varied *adj.* manifold, many-sided, sundry, unalike.

variation *n.* otherness, shift, swing, unlikeness.

variety *n.* 1) many-sidedness, sundriness, 2) brand, breed, hue, ilk, kind, make, stamp, strain.

various *adj.* manifold, many, manykind, many-sided, sundry.

vary *v.* to blow hot and cold, ebb and flow, go up and down, rise and fall, see-saw, <u>shift</u>, be shifty, swing, wax and wane, writhe.

varying *adj.* fitful, flickering, restless, <u>shifting</u>, unsettled, unsteady, wayward.

vast *adj.* <u>great</u>, far-stretching, roomy, full-wide, <u>overflowing</u>, widespread.

vehement *adj.* afire, blazing, <u>bold</u>, burning, earnest, <u>lively</u>, outspoken, strong, strongly-worded, thundering, warm, making no bones.

vehicle *n.* dray, pick-up, wain.

vein *n.* 1) blood-leat, 2) bent, frame of mind, mood, stamp, way, 3) hint, streak, thread.

velocity *n.* liveliness, quickness, <u>speed</u>, headlong speed, utmost speed, swiftness.

veneer *n.* 1) thin layer of wood, 2) mask, shallowness, show.

vengeance *n.* getting even, reckoning, settling with, striking back, wrath-wreaking, an eye for an eye.

vent v. to be open about, come out with, speak out, unbosom oneself, unburden one's heart.

venture n. 1) bid, go, shot, throw, 2) business, trade, undertaking.

verbal adj. spoken, unwritten, word-of-mouth, wordy, free-speaking.

verbatim adv. word for word, truly.

verdict n. finding, reckoning, weighing up, doom-saying.

verify v. to back up, bear out, clinch, delve into, get to the bottom of, learn, seek out the truth, find out the truth, settle, strengthen.

versatile adj. deft, good at, handy, helpful, many-sided, nimble, quick, ready, ready for anything, readily at home.

verse n. 1) song-craft, 2) stave.

version n. 1) brand, kind, 2) (of a *translation/rendering*), reading, 3) tale/understanding (of things done).

verve n. drive, life, liveliness, sparkle.

very adj. right, true, nothing more than.

very adv. deeply, ever so, fully, greatly, highly, more than ever, truly, utterly, wholly, wonderfully.

veteran n. elder, old hand, old-timer, man of the world,

veto v. to ban, forbid, put a stop to, give the thumbs down to.

via prep. by way of, by, through, with the help of.

viable adj. not over-hard, towardly, wieldy.

vibrant adj. 1) ringing, 2) alive, astir, go-ahead, keen, lively, sparkling, up-and-doing, 3) bold, bright, glowing, rich-hued.

vice n. besetting sin, evil, godlessness, shamelessness, sinfulness, wantonness, wickedness.

vicious adj. baleful, biting, bitter, evil, lewd, loathsome, lustful, cutting, shrewish, stinging, waspish.

victim n. 1) loser, shorn lamb, wretch, 2) one readily taken in, softling.

victor n. leader of the field, made man, overcomer, winner, match-winner, world-beater.

victory n. beating, overcoming, quelling, upper hand, walkover, well-fought field, win, outright win, game and match.

view n. 1) eyeful, eyeshot, sight, 2) outlook, landship (*landscape*), seaship (*seascape*), setting, 3) belief, deeming, feeling, insight, outlook, reckoning, stand, thinking, way of thinking, thought, understanding.

view v. 1) to behold, eye, follow with the eyes, have in sight, look at, look before one, look over, look up/down, see, see with one's own eyes, sight-see, stare at, sweep, watch, witness, 2) to deem, look on, reckon, take stock of, think about, think of, ween, weigh.

vigorous adj. astir, bold, go-ahead, hearty, keen, lively, lusty, mainfast, quick, sparkling, tireless, up-and-doing.

vilify v. to blacken, run down, smear, speak foully of.

village n. ham, small town, thorp, wick.

vindication n. righting, right/truth upheld.

violation n. 1) lawbreaking, wrongdoing, 2) befouling, maidhood-theft.

violence n. 1) bloodshed, fighting, rough handling, strong-arm work, 2) bloody-handedness, might, strength.

violent adj. bloodthirsty, bloody, heavy-handed, hot-blooded, lawless, a law to oneself, quick-hearted, reckless, threatening, unbridled, wild.

virgin n. maid, maiden.

virgin adj. 1) maidenly, unswiven, 2) new, unknown, untrodden.

virtually adv. almost, as good as, in the main, nearly, more or less.

virtue n. 1) goodness, high-mindedness, knightliness, manliness, rightwiseness, sinlessness, troth, uprightness, worth, worthiness, 2) mark, strength, 3) maidenhead, maidenhood.

virulent adj. baleful, bitter, deadly, harmful, withering.

visible adj. before one's eyes, under one's nose, for all to see, in broad daylight, in the open, right in the foreground, striking, well-marked, well-seen, written all over one.

vision n. 1) eyesight, sight, seeing, 2) beyond-seeing, far-seeing, 3) daydream, hopes, 4) awareness, farsightedness, foresight, insight, shrewdness, 5) brighteyes, dream, eyeful, fair one, sight.

visit n. break, coming, dropping in, stop, stopover.

visit v. to drop in on, go to see, look in on, look someone up, stop by.

visitor n. dropper-in, newcomer, sightseer.

visual adj. seeing.

vital adj. key, main, needed, needful, not to be spared.

vivid adj. 1) life-like, lively, true to life, sharp, strong, stirring, telling, 2) ablaze, alight, bright, glistening, glowing, shimmering, shining, 3) fiery, lively, sparkling.

vocabulary n. wordhoard, wordstock, word-wealth, word-web.

vocal *adj.* 1) aloud, out loud, read aloud, said, spoken, sung, 2) <u>forthright</u>, free-speaking, outspoken, loud.

vociferous *adj.* besetting, bold, deafening, dinning, driving, ear-rending, <u>forthright</u>, forward, full-throated, loud, lusty, many-tongued, shouting.

voice *n.* 1), ready speech, tongue, 2) words, 3) feeling, will, wish, 4) input, say, 5) spokesman, spokeswoman.

volatile *adj.* fickle, flighty, giddy, hot-headed, <u>shifting</u>, unsettled, up and down.

volume *n.* 1) book, written work, one of a set of books, 2) (in *physics*) body, <u>greatness</u>, 3) (in *acoustics*) loudness, softness.

voluntary *adj.* unasked, unbidden, unsought.

volunteer *n.* ready worker, willing worker.

vote *n.* choosing, show of hands.

vote *v.* to back, choose, come down for, pick out.

vulnerable *adj.* feet of clay, helpless, kinless, naked, unshepherded, unshielded, open to, wide open, weaponless.

wagon *n.* wain, haywain.

warren *n.* 1) burrow, den, earth, set, 2) maze of buildings/rooms, back-street housing, crowded housing.

waste *n.* 1) high living, wild living, 2) chaff, draff, dross, leavings, sweepings, throw-outs, dead wood, spilt milk, utter loss, 3)

emptiness, heath, wild, unsown wild, wilderness.

waste *v.* 1) to be careless, drain, eat up, mishandle, run down, run through, spill, throw away, throw before swine, unhoard, 2) to dwindle, <u>lessen</u>, shrink, wear out, wither away.

waver *v.* to beat about, be all at sea, be at a stand, be in two minds, blow hot and cold, draw back, falter, hang back, hedge, hold back, lose the thread, play for time.

whirl *v.* to reel, spin, twist, wheel.

whisky *n.* malt-barley drink, firewater.

wile *n.* craft, net, outwitting, sharp-dealing, shift, stealth, underhand dealing, web.

willpower *n.* <u>steadfastness</u>, steeliness, strength of heart/mind/will.

wily *adj.* <u>crafty</u>, fox-like, knowing, shady, sharp, shrewd, stealthy, underhand.

wing/s *n.* 1) feathering, flight feathers, 2) side (of a house), 3) arm, set.

wrap *v.* to bind, bundle up, fold, overlay, shroud, swathe, wind.

zealous *adj.* afire, alight, burning, dying to, earnest, forward, itching, keen, quick, ready and willing, restless, sleepless, tireless.

zero *n.* naught, nought, nothing, nothing at all, nothingness, none.

First Steps in Old English
An easy to follow language course for the beginner
Stephen Pollington

A complete and easy to use Old English language course that contains all the exercises and texts needed to learn Old English. This course has been designed to be of help to a wide range of students, from those who are teaching themselves at home, to undergraduates who are learning Old English as part of their English degree course. The author has adopted a step-by-step approach that enables students of differing abilities to advance at their own pace. The course includes practice and translation exercises, a glossary of the words used in the course, and many Old English texts, including the *Battle of Brunanburh* and *Battle of Maldon*.

£16-95   272 pages

Old English Poems, Prose & Lessons   2 CDs
read by Stephen Pollington

These CDs contain lessons and texts from *First Steps in Old English*.

Tracks include: 1. Deor. 2. Beowulf – The Funeral of Scyld Scefing. 3. Engla Tocyme (The Arrival of the English). 4. Ines Domas. Two Extracts from the Laws of King Ine.
5. Deniga Hergung (The Danes' Harrying) Anglo-Saxon Chronicle Entry AD997.
6. Durham 7. The Ordeal (Be ðon ðe ordales weddigaþ) 8. Wið Dweorh (Against a Dwarf)
9. Wið Wennum (Against Wens) 10. Wið Wæterælfadle (Against Waterelf Sickness)
11. The Nine Herbs Charm 12. Lǽcedomas (Leechdoms) 13. Beowulf's Greeting
14. The Battle of Brunanburh 15. A Guide to Pronunciation.
And more than 30 other lessons and extracts of Old English verse and prose.

£15   2 CDs - Free Old English transcript from www.asbooks.co.uk.

Wordcraft: Concise English/Old English Dictionary and Thesaurus
Stephen Pollington

This book provides Old English equivalents to the commoner modern words in both dictionary and thesaurus formats. The Thesaurus presents vocabulary relevant to a wide range of individual topics in alphabetical lists, thus making it easily accessible to those with specific areas of interest. Each thematic listing is encoded for cross-reference from the Dictionary. The two sections will be of invaluable assistance to students of the language, as well as to those with either a general or a specific interest in the Anglo-Saxon period.

£9.95   256 pages

An Introduction to the Old English Language and its Literature
Stephen Pollington

The purpose of this general introduction to Old English is not to deal with the teaching of Old English but to dispel some misconceptions about the language and to give an outline of its structure and its literature. Some basic knowledge of these is essential to an understanding of the early period of English history and the present form of the language.

£5.95   48 pages

The Rebirth of England and English: The Vision of William Barnes
Fr. Andrew Phillips

English history is patterned with spirits so bright that they broke through convention and saw another England. Such was the case of the Dorset poet, William Barnes (1801–86), priest, poet, teacher, self-taught polymath, linguist extraordinary and that rare thing – a man of vision. In this work the author looks at that vision, a vision at once of Religion, Nature, Art, Marriage, Society, Economics, Politics and Language. He writes: 'In search of authentic English roots and values, our post-industrial society may well have much to learn from Barnes'.

£6.95 160 pages

Monasteriales Indicia
The Anglo-Saxon Monastic Sign Language
Edited with notes and translation by Debby Banham

The *Monasteriales Indicia* is one of very few texts which let us see how evryday life was lived in monasteries in the early Middle Ages. Written in Old English and preserved in a manuscript of the mid-eleventh century, it consists of 127 signs used by Anglo-Saxon monks during the times when the Benedictine Rule forbade them to speak. These indicate the foods the monks ate, the clothes they wore, and the books they used in church and chapter, as well as the tools they used in their daily life, and persons they might meet both in the monastery and outside. The text is printed here with a parallel translation. The introduction gives a summary of the background, both historical and textual, as well as a brief look at the later evidence for monastic sign language in England.

£5.95 96 pages

The Battle of Maldon: Text and Translation
Translated and edited by Bill Griffiths

The Battle of Maldon was fought between the men of Essex and the Vikings in AD 991. The action was captured in an Anglo-Saxon poem whose vividness and heroic spirit has fascinated readers and scholars for generations. *The Battle of Maldon* includes the source text; edited text; parallel literal translation; verse translation; a review of 103 books and articles.

This edition has a helpful guide to Old English verse.

£5.95 96 pages

Beowulf: Text and Translation
Translated by John Porter

The verse in which the story unfolds is, by common consent, the finest writing surviving in Old English, a text that all students of the language and many general readers will want to tackle in the original form. To aid understanding of the Old English, a literal word-by-word translation is printed opposite the edited text and provides a practical key to this Anglo-Saxon masterpiece.

£6.95 192 pages

Anglo-Saxon Runes

John. M. Kemble

Kemble's essay *On Anglo-Saxon Runes* first appeared in the journal *Archaeologia* for 1840; it draws on the work of Wilhelm Grimm, but breaks new ground for Anglo-Saxon studies in his survey of the Ruthwell Cross and the Cynewulf poems. It is an expression both of his own indomitable spirit and of the fascination and mystery of the Runes themselves, making one of the most attractive introductions to the topic. For this edition new notes have been supplied, which include translations of Latin and Old English material quoted in the text, to make this key work in the study of runes more accessible to the general reader.

£5.95   80 pages

Looking for the Lost Gods of England

Kathleen Herbert

Kathleen Herbert sifts through the royal genealogies, charms, verse and other sources to find clues to the names and attributes of the Gods and Goddesses of the early English. The earliest account of English heathen practices reveals that they worshipped the Earth Mother and called her Nerthus. The tales, beliefs and traditions of that time are still with us in, for example, Sand able to stir our minds and imaginations.

£5.95   64 pages

Rudiments of Runelore

Stephen Pollington

This book provides both a comprehensive introduction for those coming to the subject for the first time, and a handy and inexpensive reference work for those with some knowledge of the subject. The *Abecedarium Nordmannicum* and the English, Norwegian and Icelandic rune poems are included in their original and translated form. Also included is work on the three Brandon runic inscriptions and the Norfolk 'Tiw' runes.

£5.95   88 pages

Anglo-Saxon FAQs

Stephen Pollington

125 questions and answers on a wide range of topics.

Are there any Anglo-Saxon jokes? Who was the Venerable Bede? Did the women wear make-up? What musical instruments did they have? How was food preserved? Did they have shops? Did their ships have sails? Why was Ethelred called 'Unready'? Did they have clocks? Did they celebrate Christmas? What are runes? What weapons and tactics did they use? Were there female warriors? What was the Synod of Whitby?

£9.95   128pages

Tastes of Anglo-Saxon England

Mary Savelli

These easy to follow recipes will enable you to enjoy a mix of ingredients and flavours that were widely known in Anglo-Saxon England but are rarely experienced today. In addition to the 46 recipes, there is background information about households and cooking techniques.

£5.95   80 pages

Anglo-Saxon Attitudes – A short introduction to Anglo-Saxonism
J.A. Hilton

This is not a book about the Anglo-Saxons, but a book about books about Anglo-Saxons. It describes the academic discipline of Anglo-Saxonism; the methods of study used; the underlying assumptions; and the uses to which it has been put.

Methods and motives have changed over time but right from the start there have been constant themes: English patriotism and English freedom.

£5.95 hardback 64 pages

The Origins of the Anglo-Saxons
Donald Henson

This book has three great strengths.

First, it pulls together and summarises the whole range of evidence bearing on the subject, offering an up-to-date assessment: the book is, in other words, a highly efficient introduction to the subject. Second – perhaps reflecting Henson's position as a leading practitioner of public archaeology (he is currently Education and Outreach Co-ordinator for the Council for British Archaeology) – the book is refreshingly jargon free and accessible. Third, Henson is not afraid to offer strong, controversial interpretations. The Origins of the Anglo-Saxons can therefore be strongly recommended to those who want a detailed road-map of the evidence and debates for the migration period.

Current Archaeology

£18.95 296 pages

The Elder Gods – The Otherworld of Early England
Stephen Pollington

The purpose of the work is to bring together a range of evidence for pre-Christian beliefs and attitudes to the Otherworld drawn from archaeology, linguistics, literary studies and comparative mythology. The rich and varied English tradition influenced the worldview of the later mediaeval and Norse societies. Aspects of this tradition are with us still in the 21st century.

£35 70 illustrations 528 pages

A Departed Music – Readings in Old English Poetry
Walter Nash

The *readings* of this book take the form of passages of translation from some Old English poems. The author paraphrases their content and discusses their place and significance in the history of poetic art in Old English society and culture.

The author's knowledge, enthusiasm and love of his subject help make this an excellent introduction to the subject for students and the general reader.

£9.95 hardback 240 pages

Organisations

Þa Engliscan Gesiðas (The English Companions)

Þa Engliscan Gesiðas is a historical and cultural society exclusively devoted to Anglo-Saxon history. The Fellowship publishes a quarterly journal, *Wiðowinde,* and has a website with regularly updated information and discussions. Local groups arrange their own meetings and attend lectures, exhibitions and events. Members are able to share their interest with like-minded people and learn more about the origins and growth of English culture, including language, literature, archaeology, anthropology, architecture, art, religion, mythology, folklore and material culture.

For further details see www.tha-engliscan-gesithas.org.uk or write to: Membership Secretary, The English Companions, PO Box 62790, London, SW12 2BH, England, UK

Regia Anglorum

Regia Anglorum is an active group of enthusiasts who attempt to portray as accurately as possible the life and times of the people who lived in the British Isles around a thousand years ago. We investigate a wide range of crafts and have a Living History Exhibit that frequently erects some thirty tented period structures.

Our site at Wychurst has a large Anglo-Saxon hall – defended manor house - which has been reconstructed using the best available evidence. Members can learn weapon skills with accurate copies of weapons of the period. We own and operate six full scale vessels ranging from a 6 metre Faering to a 15 metre ocean-going trader!

We have a thriving membership and 40 branches in the British Isles and United States - so there might be one near you. We especially welcome families with children.

www.regia.org   *General information* eolder@regia.org   *Membership* join@regia.org

The Sutton Hoo Society

Our aims and objectives focus on promoting research and education relating to the Anglo Saxon Royal cemetery at Sutton Hoo, Suffolk in the UK. The Society publishes a newsletter SAXON twice a year, which keeps members up to date with society activities, carries resumes of lectures and visits, and reports progress on research and publication associated with the site. If you would like to join the Society please see website: www.suttonhoo.org

Wuffing Education

Wuffing Education provides those interested in the history, archaeology, literature and culture of the Anglo-Saxons with the chance to meet experts and fellow enthusiasts for a whole day of in-depth seminars and discussions. Day Schools take place at the historic Tranmer House overlooking the burial mounds of Sutton Hoo in Suffolk.

For details of programme of events contact:-
Wuffing Education, 4 Hilly Fields, Woodbridge, Suffolk IP12 4DX
email education@wuffings.co.uk website www.wuffings.co.uk
Tel. 01394 383908 or 01728 688749

Places to visit

Bede's World at Jarrow

Bede's world tells the remarkable story of the life and times of the Venerable Bede, 673–735 AD. Visitors can explore the origins of early medieval Northumbria and Bede's life and achievements through his own writings and the excavations of the monasteries at Jarrow and other sites.

Location – 10 miles from Newcastle upon Tyne, off the A19 near the southern entrance to the River Tyne tunnel. Bus services 526 & 527

Bede's World, Church Bank, Jarrow, Tyne and Wear, NE32 3DY

Tel. 0191 489 2106; Fax: 0191 428 2361; website: www.bedesworld.co.uk

Sutton Hoo near Woodbridge, Suffolk

Sutton Hoo is a group of low burial mounds overlooking the River Deben in south-east Suffolk. Excavations in 1939 brought to light the richest burial ever discovered in Britain – an Anglo-Saxon ship containing a magnificent treasure which has become one of the principal attractions of the British Museum. The mound from which the treasure was dug is thought to be the grave of Rædwald, an early English king who died in 624/5 AD.

This National Trust site has an excellent visitor centre, which includes a reconstruction of the burial chamber and its grave goods. Some original objects as well as replicas of the treasure are on display.

2 miles east of Woodbridge on B1083   Tel. 01394 389700

West Stow Anglo-Saxon Village

An early Anglo-Saxon Settlement reconstructed on the site where it was excavated consisting of timber and thatch hall, houses and workshop. There is also a museum containing objects found during the excavation of the site. Open all year 10am (except Christmas) Last entrance summer 4pm; winter 3-30pm. Special provision for school parties. A teachers' resource pack is available. Costumed events are held on some weekends, especially Easter Sunday and August Bank Holiday Monday. Craft courses are organised.

For further details see www.weststow.org or contact:

The Visitor Centre, West Stow Country Park, Icklingham Road, West Stow,
Bury St Edmunds, Suffolk IP28 6HG   Tel. 01284 728718